Afro-Caribbean Religions

Kelly Hawes

Afro-Caribbean Religions

An Introduction to Their Historical,
Cultural, and Sacred Traditions

Nathaniel Samuel Murrell

Temple University Press
Philadelphia

Temple University Press
Philadelphia PA 19122
www.temple.edu/tempress

♾ The paper used in this publication meets the requirements of the American National
Standard for Information Sciences—Permanence of Paper for Printed Library Materials,
ANSI Z39.48-1992

Library of Congress Cataloging-in-Publication Data

Murrell, Nathaniel Samuel.
    Afro-Caribbean religions : an introduction to their historical, cultural, and sacred traditions /
Nathaniel Samuel Murrell.
        p. cm.
    Includes bibliographical references and index.
    ISBN 978-1-4399-0040-6 (cloth : alk. paper) — ISBN 978-1-4399-0041-3 (pbk. : alk.
paper) 1. Afro-Caribbean cults. I. Title.
    BL2565.M87 2009
    299.6'89729—dc22   2009012263

112210-P

Contents

Acknowledgments

This book was written on a shoestring-budget advance against royalties
from Temple University Press. Contrary to my experience with my first
book, *Chanting Down Babylon*, my travel, research, and resource materials for this project were not substantially covered by funding agencies and
institutions. As a result, the book was in development for more than nine years,
during which time I became indebted to many people, especially friends and
students at the University of North Carolina at Wilmington (UNCW), who
encouraged and helped me along the way.

Two of my friends—Ann Burgh, of Wilmington, North Carolina, and Professor William David Spencer, of Gordon-Conwell Theological Seminary—
read chapters of the manuscript's early drafts and offered invaluable sugges-
tions for clarification. I am grateful to UNCW for offering me a one-semester
research reassignment to bring the final phase of the manuscript to comple-
tion. I am indebted to my cartographer, Shane Baptista, at the Center for Teaching Excellence (UNCW) for designing the book's map images. I am also much
obliged to artist Kelly Hawes, of Wilmington, who drew all of the non-map
illustrations for the book.

Some students who assisted me in the early phase of the project disap-
peared from my computer database before I could secure their names in new
computer files. I am greatly indebted to William Freedman and Keith Wise, of
Wilmington; Charles Frame, of Washington, North Carolina; and Rebecca
Hein, of Cedena Cove, Orlando, Florida, for their support when I reached the
midpoint of the project. My research and resource assistants, Christopher
Ripley, Brittany N. Andrews, and Renee Lynn Farrar, and Renee's husband,
Gary Allen Farrar, were my lifeline in the final phase of the research. They
worked with me during long evening hours and on weekends to help me meet
manuscript deadlines. Renee read, edited, and corrected all sixteen chapters of

the book in a mere four days. Gary, Chris, and Brittany provided a wide range of technical research and technology support.

My wife, musician Joy Murrell, assisted me with the ethnographic research on Cuban Santeria and Jamaican cultural traditions. I am grateful for her understanding and for that of Ethan and Lanielle, especially when my writing continued late into the night and kept me away from their soccer and basketball games.

Special thanks go to the participants in the "blind review" process, who read the manuscript with a most helpful critical eye. Both an unidentified reviewer and Professor Terry Rey offered sentient and perceptive critiques, which greatly enhanced the quality of the book.

Introduction

Religion is one of the most important elements of Caribbean culture that links Afro-Caribbean people to their African past. Scattered over the three-thousand-mile-long rainbow-shaped archipelago and nestled near the American mainland bordering the beautiful Caribbean Sea are living spiritual memories and traditions of the African diaspora. A family of religions (big and small, long-standing and recently arrived, defunct and vigorous, ancestral and spiritual) and their peoples dot the unique Caribbean map. J. Lorand Matory puts it succinctly: "The Atlantic perimeter hosts a range of groups profoundly influenced by western African conceptions of personhood and of the divine. Their religions include Candomble, Umbanda, Xango, and Batique in Brazil, as well as Vodou in Haiti and 'Santeria,' or Ocha, and Palo Mayombe in Cuba."[1] These diverse religious traditions share several commonalities: They show strong African connections and harbor African cultural memory; they are religions of the people, by and for the people; they are nontraditional and creole faiths shaped by cultures; they are an integral part of the Caribbean colonial legacy; and they continue to generate international interest and inspire a huge body of literature worthy of academic study.

The robust African religious traditions in the region have muted the voice of academic skeptics who have questioned the ability to prove for certain that African religions survived oppressive conditions of colonialism in the Americas. "A persistent white view had been that Africa had little particular culture to begin with, and that the slaves had lost touch with that as well."[2] The provocative Frazier-Herskovits debate, which has raged since the early 1940s, about how much of African religion and culture survived among African Americans epitomizes the ripening of the controversy that is almost a century old. Most scholars who have participated in the debate agree that the Caribbean is a clear exception to the "defunct religions" thesis, providing undeniable evidence of the vitality of African religions and cultures[3] in peoples' lives. Well documented[4] is the fact that, during colonialism and slavery, Africans brought to the Americas preserved cultures that represented many ethnic groups and affiliations. The numerical strength of some of these groups quite naturally exerted greater influence on African cultures in the diaspora than others. Originating mainly from West Central Africa, these groups owe their existence in the region to the interaction among several historical, economic, and political forces that have influenced and shaped Caribbean peoples.

A renewed interest in Afro-Caribbean religions helps form part of a wider cultural and academic phenomenon. The last half century ignited a global explosion of religious-cultural exchange and movements that continue to wrest attention from diverse academic disciplines, fields, and institutions. As part of this global phenomenon, a plethora of new religious groups has emerged, tiny sects have mushroomed into larger movements, religious traditions are being invented and reinvented, and various aspects of faiths are being borrowed and reconfigured into new ones.[5] Indeed, cultural trends have brought the study of nontraditional and marginal religions and cultures of the Americas to Main Street. The rise of the Ogun sect in the United States as a new movement, for example, parallels the Orisha phenomenon in the Caribbean region and interest in the Yoruba religion in general. The popular Ifa divination system—common among the Yoruba, Fon Ewe (Dahomey), Ebo, Igbo, and other peoples of West Africa—is not only alive in Cuba, Brazil, and Trinidad,[6] it is an academic and cultural pursuit both inside and outside the region.

Reason, Scope, and Method

Since the 1930s, scholars in different fields of the humanities have published important works providing a rich study of the Afro-Caribbean religious culture. So why another book? The modern interest in the Caribbean, the wealth of literary works that Caribbean studies generate, the fact that in the last few decades Afro-Caribbean culture has been and continues to be popularized in film, the media, pop music, and other areas of the arts, make this book as exciting as it can be valuable. I seek to complement the ethnographic studies of well-known researchers of the different religions.[7] My interest in writing this monograph is both personal and academic. I am a child of the Caribbean seeking new ways to tell the story of my creole peoples and their religious cultures in the region. Born five generations removed (over one hundred years) from my Nigerian Yoruba ancestry, my umbilical chord was cut in Grenada where my great, great grandfather landed as an indentured worker in the late 1840s (Grandpa was born in 1884). My study of Caribbean history and politics at the University of the West Indies, St. Augustine, Trinidad, stimulated my interest in this field. I made frequent visits to Haiti, Puerto Rico, and the eastern Caribbean states, and I studied, worked, and got married in Jamaica after college. Academic pursuits have given me a distaste for accepted popular portraits of African peoples' cultures, one that encouraged me to echo another voice on Caribbean religions.

This book also originated from a practical concern: providing a classroom-friendly book that introduces students to all the African-derived religions of the Caribbean under one cover. I have taught Caribbean religions since 1990 but, up to when I began research on this book in 2000, no one book treated all of the religions. Apart from Simpson's *Black Religions in the New World* (1978), most books on this subject offer a study of aspects of one or a few Caribbean religions. For example, in 1980 Brian Gates edited *Afro-Caribbean Religions*, which offers only a few topical essays. Guyanese historian Dale Bisnauth's *A History of Religions in the Caribbean* (1989) provides a survey of Hinduism, Islam, and Roman Catholic Christianity in the region, with only a cursory chapter on "Africanism" in the Caribbean. Many books (too numerous to mention here) focus on one religion[8] and several recent monographs treat some Afro-Caribbean religions[9] in ways I found invaluable to this study. My book is an extension of the vision of these works, with a trajectory treating all Afro-Caribbean religions under one cover.

Historically, Afro-Caribbean religions were treated as backward pagan practices on the margins of Caribbean society, more appropriate for study in African folk culture than in the history of religions. I contend, however, that African cultural and religious expressions among Caribbean peoples must be treated as a field of study sui generis—after its unique kind, and with its own set of categories. Caribbean studies runs amok if they assume, however tacitly, that these religions should not be studied on their own terms.[10] As a *religionsgeschichte* (history of religions), my book is largely descriptive; it investigates African-based religions within their historical, social, cultural, and political settings. I hold the view that Afro-Caribbean religions developed from known African Traditional Religions (ATRs) to their present creole form, but I do not advocate the theory that the religions evolved from animism to their modern state.[11] I am not committed to a functional analysis of religion, as are trained social scientists. Where I parallel Melville Herskovits, Roger Bastide, George Simpson, Rene Rebeiro, and others, I do so to show how the cogwheels of the African religions meshed so that they could survive and flourish in a colonial Caribbean context. As an insider to the culture, I study Afro-Caribbean religions with empathy for our peoples' myths, rituals, and traditions. At the same time, the focus and content of this book are not Afrocentric in methodology; I do not attempt to analyze the data through African lenses or with a predetermined African point of view. While this book is, of necessity, critical of the European legacy in the Caribbean and its attempted destruction of African spirituality, the idea that African peoples and cultures are primary, superior, or more important than other ethnic groups in the study of religions and cultures does not orient my thinking.

I also do not promise an exhaustive study that offers everything one wants know about Caribbean religions and cultures. The label "Afro-Caribbean" imposes ethnographic restrictions on the scope of the book, which is not defined exclusively by regional geography. The Caribbean Sea washes many shores not always regarded as part of the archipelago—for example, Brazil, Guyana, Surinam, Venezuela, Panama, and Belize. Also, Caribbean history, economics, culture, and religion have been tied to countries on the mainland of South and Central America almost as strongly as the region is linked by soccer and cricket. Mainland Guyana and Suriname function as Caribbean islands[12] but, because of linguistic and cultural ties to Europe, Martinique and Guadeloupe—located in the center of the island chain—have had more communication, commerce, and cultural exchange with France than with their Caribbean neighbors. Brazil, on the other hand, lies outside of the archipelago, but since the 1500s has had stronger economic, religious, and cultural ties to the rest of the Caribbean islands than the two French Islands.

My less-than-logical juggling act that includes Brazil in this study is based partly on the fact that it has the largest African population in the world outside of Africa, and also because of its strategic ties to the Caribbean historically, culturally, and economically. As religion historian Rachel Harding says, "In the *engenhos* of the Brazilian northeast captaincies, a model of sugar production and plantation agriculture was established and perfected that by the mid seventeenth century would be adopted throughout the colonial island economies of the Caribbean, at great human cost to Africa and great financial reward to Europe."[13] Many Africans were rerouted and distributed to the Caribbean after their initial "breaking in" in Brazil. Others were smuggled in through Bahia after 1807, when Britain began policing the Caribbean to stop the African trade in human cargo. In modern times, Caribbean peoples continue to forge strong cultural bonds with Brazil. Trinidad's Carnival inspired groups that emerged from the Candomble houses in the early 1970s; and Afro-Jamaican culture has such a noticeable presence in Brazil through Rastafari and reggae music that Pelourinho and Bahia are referred to colloquially as "the second Jamaica."[14] More important is the fact that African creole religions have a uniquely strong presence in Brazil; African religions in the region of Bahia are much stronger than in many Caribbean islands.

Creole Phenomena

The vast majority of Caribbean peoples are hyphenated; our forebears are foreigners and their identity is the product of their prolonged encounter with other cultures. In the Caribbean, this involved an interfacing of Africans, Europeans, East Indians, Chinese,[15] Middle Easterners, and native peoples. We are creole because we are the product of "a process of 'this and that *too*' in the creation of new forms through creative recombination of the old."[16] Our hyphenated religions are Afro-Caribbean because after they exited their homeland Africa, they too became creole; like a baby severed from its mother's placenta and fed new foods in its new environs, the religions outgrew their exit point and "could not go home again." In colonial times, European pedigree and power separated the white rulers from the black slaves, but today our peoples are separated by geography, language, economics, politics, and religion; ours is a stratified society of the small, ruling, educated class and the less-educated poor masses, with shades of gray in between. Haitians seized their independence from France, in a bloodbath, at the end of the 1700s, but in British territories the granting of universal adult suffrage came about 150 years later, allowing the people to vote, own property, and seek upward mobility. As a result, a growing black, educated, middle class labeled "Afro-Saxon," whose education or training has elevated them in society, gives leadership to fledgling former British colonies and acts as a buffer between the haves and the have nots, thus lessening the possibility for Haitian-type revolts by the suffering and disenchanted poor masses.

Occasionally, as in the case of Fidel Castro's Cuban Revolution of 1959 and the Grenada Revolution of 1979 (that my late contemporary and countryman Maurice Bishop led), corruption in the Caribbean drives the masses or the proletariat to lead violent overthrows of greedy and decrepit dictators, some of whom acted as pawns of the U.S. government while stashing away millions of the poor's taxpayers dollars in their personal accounts in foreign banks. Extremely high unemployment and lack of advancement opportunities for the young, aspiring, educated class contribute to a large northern migration tradition and what is called the Caribbean brain drain, which I represent. As a result of this migration phenomenon, Afro-Caribbean religions and cultures have enriched the cultures of the United States, Canada, and Europe. In return, we Caribbean-Americans provide a steady and vital stream of financial support to our extended families and, thereby, help keep some fragile Caribbean economies from total collapse.

Outside of the Caribbean, ideas and stereotypes of the region, our people, and their religion run amok. When Europeans began writing about our ancestors in the 1700s, most of their works reflected anti-African bias, ignorance of the nature and meaning of African beliefs and practices, and intolerance of non-Christian and creole-Christian ways of being religious. For this reason, Joseph Murphy cautions readers who evaluate European accounts of Afro-Caribbean religions not to forget that these religions were not only a source of disruption among the workers of European masters; "they were also a direct threat to these white authorities"[17] who delighted in portraying them in the worst possible light. The Caribbean is still seen as merely an economically impoverished place where tourists spend foreign currency, snorkel, get great sun tans on magnificent beaches, pose for photos with dreadlocks, smoke ganja, and drink local brew. This comes at a time when many have abandoned churlish labels of the Caribbean as a doormat for America's "Manifest Destiny" and a helpless "third-world country" (singular) of third-class peasants seeking U.S. handouts. Paradoxically, international pharmaceuticals, hotel chains, banks, oil companies, and other multinational corporations derive huge profits from tax shelters in the Caribbean, while depressing wages and contributing to our underdevelopment and impoverishment by not reinvesting part of their wealth in the region. Venezuela and Trinidad and Tobago supply 15 to 17 percent of U.S. oil. At the same time, Caribbean countries are strapped by outrageously high-interest-bearing IMF (International Monetary Fund) loans that support a cycle of dependency, poverty, and political corruption that threaten the stability of the region.

Most people in the Caribbean region regard themselves as Christians, Muslims, Hindus, or Buddhists; this is so even in Haiti, where Vodou is the religion of many, and Cuba, where Santeria is most popular. Until more recent times, elite creole sons and daughters of the colonists were taught to despise the African heritage that the mass of peasant folks have kept alive and made the core of their culture. Since the 1960s, however, Afro-Caribbean peoples have prided themselves in their African origin.[18] Some practice their "despised religion" in secret, while others celebrate it publicly and parade it as a folk tradition during cultural festivals. Like their ancestral ATRs, Afro-Caribbean religions are oral; they are written in the hearts and minds of the people who passed them down to new generations. Unlike ATRs, which some African scholars characterize as singular,[19] Afro-Caribbean religions are pluralistic and share varied historical experiences. These religions did not all survive with the same vigor in the Americas. Some germinated and spread while others faded in memory and became extinct. Some early arrivals survived, others arrived late and disappeared. Some survived in physical isolation, others thrived in symbiosis with larger groups and Christianity. The persistent traditions spread and continued to thrive, after the conditions that bore them disappeared.[20] These are seen in the dominant creole religions, as well as in those showing greater adaptations and change, as in religions in Jamaica, Grenada, St. Lucia, and among the Black Caribs in Belize.

The migration features of enslaved Africans influenced the spread and survival of their cultural traditions in the Americas. "Where the volume and duration of the slave trade were heavy and protracted, African-based ethnomedicine and religion not only survived, but in some cases came to predominate."[21] One, however, should not overlocalize the peculiar phenomenon of these traditions, or limit them to one country on the basis of the Atlantic slave trade. Cross-cultural defusion occurred across various countries and island states and among ethnic groups as a result of the intercolonial slave trade and the movement of slaves from one colony to another and from plantation to plantation. The spread of these cultures and religions in the Caribbean followed no systematic patterns, and their preservation is neither uniform throughout the region nor influenced by any one tragedy. In the cases of Vodou, Santeria, and Candomble, Africans continued practicing old traditions they knew home on the continent and augmented them with new ones.[22] Practitioners of newer religions, like Orisha in Trinidad and Rastafari in Jamaica, became wary of what they saw as contradictions and double standards in established colonial religions and moved away from traditional Christianity to a faith experience that blended physical and spiritual needs with African cultural traditions or West African Islam; these were often labeled "extra-church traditions."[23] Caribbean peoples did not lose faith in God—although many rejected colonial European understanding of that God's view of human relations with reference to Africans.

Religions of Africa adopted distinctly Caribbean features, as they blend African, European, and other cultures. In the context of their colonial experience, they syncretize elements of ATRs, Christianity, Amerindian religions, and to a lesser extent Islam and Hinduism. They produced tertium quids, different kinds of religious expressions that met the social, psychological, and spiritual needs not satisfied in established religions. Africans modified, reshaped, and adapted ideas of the sacred, ritual tendencies, liturgical practices, lyrics and musical style, drum and dance, and religious myths and symbols, which they took mainly from African religions and Catholicism, to form elements of religious traditions of their own carving. From ATRs, practitioners took names of important divinities and their peculiar characteristics, sacred paraphernalia, "musical and dance patterns, possession by spirits, initiation rites of seclusion and indoctrination, death rituals, proper types of offerings to divinities and spirits, magical charms, methods of divination, and concern for the goodwill of the ancestors."[24] The nature of the modification and adaptations were determined by whether Africans were influenced by the Roman Catholic Christian tradition—as in the case of Vodou, Santeria, and Candomble—or Protestant faiths and ethics, as in the case of religions in Jamaica, in the process of forming their new religious heritage.

Some religious practitioners are uncomfortable with the category of "creole" religions, because it implies a less pristine form of African religion. Several theories related to the creolization of religion among enslaved Africans are proffered: (1) that the adoption of Catholic saints' names and characteristic features in Santeria, Candomble, Vodou, and Orisha was an intentional strategic mechanism on the part of early Afro-Caribbean peoples to dupe their white oppressors into believing they were being Christians; (2) that the integration of Catholic hagiography into African religions was really a conversion strategy, on the part of the Church, to win converts; (3) that the phenomenon was a natural symbiosis of ATRs with Catholicism because of the church's theology; and (4) that Africans' familiarity with Christianity, on the continent of Africa, made it easy and natural for them to synthesize their religions with Catholic hagiography. Of course, African divinities are not the same as Catholic saints, and the fit between them is odd. As Robert Voeks shows, even if Catholicism and ATRs exhibit a shared vision related to spiritual actors, they nonetheless show cosmological distinctions among their respective divinities and their abode. Voeks states, for example, that "the Yoruba and their New World descendants have retained much of their original view of the spiritual universe and the hereafter, and it has little in common with the Christian concepts of heaven and hell. . . . The Candomble cosmos is characterized by a simple opposition [between] the realm of the spirits."[25] So why did they comingle?

It is instructive that African religious entities were in symbiosis with Roman Catholic Christianity in Cuba, Saint Domingue, Brazil, and Trinidad, but not in smaller Roman Catholic Martinique and Guadeloupe. Others—which mixed with Protestant Belize, Jamaica, Barbados, Grenada, Dominica, St. Lucia, St. Vincent, or the Protestant-Hindu-Muslim Guyana—were not dominant in the larger islands.[26] Neither the eastern Caribbean islands nor Jamaica preserved Vodou, Santeria, or Candomble. While under French Catholic control, Vodou survived in Saint-Domingue and helped the country become independent Haiti. The strong French presence among Trinidadian planters from Saint Domingue and their slaves, between 1783 and 1807, brought African-Haitian religion into the larger entity of Columbus's "Trinity," but the religious elements resurfaced as Orisha/Shango, not Vodou. Cuba and Puerto Rico remained under Spanish Catholic control until the Spanish-Cuban-American War in 1898. Jamaica and the other English-speaking territories, however, retained African traditions from Fanti-Ashanti, Kongo, and Fon, and made them creole with Protestantism, for reasons that are not transparent.

Although Brazil and, to a much lesser extent, Cuba and Saint Domingue have a much larger land mass than the British territories in the Caribbean region, size is clearly not an important factor in the religious fusion in these countries. For example, Vodou did not have a significant presence in the United States before the Haitian Revolution and the 1803 Louisiana Purchase, which doubled the size of the country and brought large numbers of French Catholics into the Union. On the other hand, French Catholic Martinique and Guadeloupe retained elements of African culture,[27] but not in the form of Vodou. So the dominance of French and Spanish cultures in the region also cannot take full credit for the preponderance of Vodou and Santeria in French and Spanish-speaking Caribbean countries.

Could the fact that some African religions survived in Spanish territories and not in British ones be because British policy did not aim at, or encourage, assimilation of foreigners and their cultures in the Caribbean as did the Spanish? The British upheld this policy in Yorubaland and, as H. Hoetink contends, the "Church of England," both at home and overseas, preached that the descendants or posterity of Abraham keep to themselves and not unite the races. The "Spanish Catholic concept of the all-embracing faith, which includes racial assimilation," made Catholicism more appealing to Africans and thus allowed them to practice their ATRs, which blended with Roman Catholic hagiography.[28] While this theory of the embrace of the Catholic faith may have been true of Candomble, in Bahia, and Santeria, in Cuba, it certainly was not the case with Haitian Vodou. French Catholics viciously persecuted and, for over a hundred years, attempted in vain to stamp out Vodou in Haiti. Later in the mid-1900s, the Church adopted the policy toward Vodou devotees that "if you can't beat them, join them," in an attempt to incorporate them into itself.

Among other things, these observations suggest that diverse African religious traditions in the Caribbean are parts of a complex reality influenced, to some degree, by the preponderance of Kongo and Yoruba adherents in historically Catholic-dominated countries. But the variables in this peculiarity are many: the country of origin of the enslaved and free African immigrants, migration features of slavery itself, the retention ability of the African slaves themselves, their contact with others who knew ATRs, the official policies of the state church and slave masters on African religions, the presence of Protestantism in a country, and the specific character of the local Catholic hagiology where the slaves lived and worked. For example, Bahians transformed the Orisha Ogun, the "Yoruba orixa of the river," into the goddess of the sea who guides the fate of fishermen in Brazil. Oxumare, one of the important orixas in Brazil, who alternates between male and female, is a Benin-Yoruba deity. As Voeks notes, leading ethnic groups in Bahia reconstituted their native beliefs and practices in a religious framework aided by the Yoruba. "The Yoruba provided the central structural text within which various ethnic and cultural messages could be retained. Candomble is represented by a variety of religious types, each founded with a unique set of cultural elements, and each following its own individual trajectory."[29] Notwithstanding many variables affecting African religions in the Caribbean, Catholic hagiography, or the mediator system of sainthood, and the strong mystical elements in the church's rituals have had a great attraction for people of African origin and their religions.

Content of the Book

As an introductory study of these creole religions and their interaction with the dominant culture in the region, this book has three foci: (1) the African connection to Caribbean religions, (2) the nature and ethos of the religions, and (3) the social and cultural context in which the religions survived. Most of the chapters are four-dimensional, covering the historical cultural background, the religious cosmology and beliefs, the organizational structure and professional leadership, and the ritual practices or performance. For pedagogical reasons, some religions are presented in two chapters, each one providing sufficient reading for a single class period in a Caribbean religions course. The two chapters that constitute Part I, "African Connections: Historical Roots of Afro-Caribbean Religions," link the African continent to the diaspora and provide a backdrop to the history, culture, and traditions of its derived religions. The diversity of issues included in the lengthy chapter discussions separates this work from most introductions to the religions and cultures of the African diaspora, which have been criticized for their perfunctory treatment of Africa. As the chapter discussions illustrate, the link between African religions and the social and political life of the peoples of Africa is essential to this book.

Part II, "Vodou: Haitian Religion," provides a natural sequence to the African background, with a discussion of Vodou, one of the oldest and most resilient African religions in the Caribbean. This introductory-level study of Vodou as a complex, living, African-based religion explores its triumph over adversity and rise to prominence; its many creole characteristics; its religious hierarchy; its basic belief system; and its social, cultural, and religious ethos in Haiti. Chapter 3 looks at the inseparable relationship between Haiti's history and politics and a cultural and religious heritage that is shrouded in mystery and marked by tragedy, stereotypes, and misconceptions. Chapter 4 explores Vodou mythologies, cultus, and leadership; the Vodou belief system; and the performance of Vodou rites and rituals. Following the formula set out in Part II, Part III focuses on the historical, cultural, and religious heritage of Africans in colonial Cuba and their struggle for survival, freedom, and identity in the face of oppression and prejudice. Chapters 5 and 6 showcase the life-giving force of the Lucumi/Santeria belief system (or mythologies) and cultus: the religion's divinations, ceremonies, rites and rituals, and popular festive celebrations. Chapter 7 provides a short introduction to the less well-known and less well-researched Regla de Palo Monte (Palo Monte).

Part IV, "Creole Religions of the Southern Caribbean," is included as a special feature of the book. Chapter 8, "Dancing to Orixas' Axe in Candomble," is devoted to the history of Brazil's most African religion, Candomble (its nations and their struggles, its religious myths, its practitioners, its ceremonies, and its pharmacopeia). The chapter includes an analysis of various phenomena associated with the religion, in order to underscore essential features and highlight areas that show New World adaptation or creolization. Chapter 9, "Umbanda and Its Antecedents," navigates through the diverse creole religious traditions of Brazil, some of which may barely qualify for categorization as Afro-Caribbean but all of which have a very popular multiethnic following and African connection. Chapter 10, "Orisha Powers: Creole Religion in T&T," looks at characteristics that are shared with the creole religions of Brazil. Although its following is smaller than that of Candomble, Yoruba Orisha/Shango rivals Candomble in its cross-fertilization and strong borrowing from other traditions in the Trinidad culture.

Part V, "Jamaica's Creole Religions: Culture of Resistance and Rhythms," devotes its discussion to the African religions of Jamaica. Like all other Caribbean religions that have their roots in Africa, Obeah (see Chapter 11) emerged from an oppressive colonial environment and exists as a resistance and survival movement. It finds its *Sitz im Leben* in early plantation life and Africans' struggle for freedom and dignity in the colonial Caribbean region. The Myal, Kumina, Poco, Convince, and Revival Zion religions, now largely overshadowed by the Rastafari chant, are a vital part of Jamaica's religious cultural past (see Chapters 12 and 13). Rastafari, one of the latest religious cultures to appear on the Caribbean scene (see Chapter 14), did not originate in Africa. However, the movement's cultural ethos, belief system, ritual and other practices, and reggae cultural revolution constitute the Caribbean's most vocal Afrocentric movement and one of the strongest cultural appeals to modern intergenerational pop culture fans internationally. Rastafari thus forms part of a logical bravado finale to the study of African creole religions in the Caribbean.

PART I

African Connections

Historical Roots of Afro-Caribbean Religions

I

Yoruba, Fon-Ewe, Ashanti, and Kongo Cultural History

KEY TOPICS

The Yoruba People • Akan and Fanti-Ashanti •
Fon-Ewe (Dahomey) • Kongo Culture and Religion •
Religion in West Africa • Orisa Divinities-a-Thousand

Appreciation of Afro-Caribbean religious and cultural ties to central West Africa is grounded in an understanding of the various peoples' religions and cultures in their original settings. In the second half of the twentieth century, scores of books and other scholarly works have devoted much attention to the study of peoples of the African diaspora. Two of the many stimuli for this academic interest are the facts that (1) Africa has been, and still is, the society of origin for numerous peoples and their cultural and religious traditions in the Americas since the 1500s and (2) a strong desire exists among people in the diaspora to reconnect with their ancestral roots. Candomble, Vodou, Santeria, Orisha, Palo Mayombe, and other creole religions in the Americas can scarcely be appreciated without some understanding of their African moorings. Conceptions of the sacred linguistic expressions, practices, and cultural norms among those religions require a good grasp or appreciation of their historical, social, cultural, and political backgrounds in West and Central Africa. Such knowledge is essential not only for understanding the complexity and uniqueness of life in African cultures as well as the religions of the Caribbean that have been derived from them but also for correcting long-standing stereotypic perceptions of the nature of those African cultures. Here I survey briefly, as samples, just a few of these cultural historical traditions.

West African Origins

As Robert Collins, an American historian on West Africa, notes, "Beyond the clusters of states' societies, huddled on the headland of West Africa, a series of forest kingdoms, whose sophisticated political and social organization enabled them to exert widespread cultural and economic influence, existed from the Ivory Coast to Cameroon."[1] Among these forest kingdoms are the Yoruba, Fon-Ewe (formerly Dahomey), Fanti-Ashanti, and Kongo (West Central Africa) of West Africa, who had, over centuries, developed advanced civilizations ready to expose their culture to the Western world. These peoples' early contact with Muslim Berbers and Sudanic nations to the northwest; their encounter with European traders, missionaries, and explorers on the coast; the coming of the Atlantic slave trade; and the dynamic changes within West African political and social institutions precipitated drastic historical developments within Yoruba, Kongo, Ashanti, and Fon states. The changes put the states in a position of power and prominence on the West African coast, but they led to Islamic and European exploitation of Africa's natural and human resources, the destruction of its social systems, and the exporting of African peoples and their cultures to foreign lands.

The Yoruba People

The Yoruba remain one of the largest ethnic and religious groups in the southern region of West Africa (north of the equator). Noel King says that from west to east, they "inhabit the rain forest and lagoon country of West Africa from Benin (Dahomey) to the beginning of the creeks of the Niger Delta; south to north, from the sea up into the Savannah grasslands."[2] It is commonly held that Yoruba people migrated into Western Sudan from the Upper Nile in the early first century B.C.E. This origin is debated,[3] but the people have lived for well over a thousand years in the western part of the present-day Republic of Nigeria, Ghana, Togo, and Benin (Dahomey), from which many were taken by brute force to the Americas during the Atlantic slave trade. The Yoruba developed a complex society consisting of independent city-states united into a single civilization with a common language and religious traditions. The society was well known for its fortified cities with large populations and for smaller villages in rural regions, all steeped in religion; in fact, the Yoruba make up the most dominant group in West African traditional religions (ATRs). The number of Yoruba people in ATRs is conjectural—some estimates run the gamut from five million to thirty million.[4] Yoruba-speaking peoples constitute the second-largest language group in Nigeria. They comprise about twenty-five distinct ethnic subgroups but share special cultural, religious, and historical affinities[5] and are part of a family of languages (including Ewe, Ga, Akan, Igbo, and Kru) that traverse the southern part of West Africa. According to African specialist John Pemberton, the evolution of regional dialects distinguishing "Yoruba subgroups and the process of urbanization, which developed into a social system unique among the sub-Saharan African peoples," occurred during the first millennium C.E.[6]

Beginning as large clans around 1350 C.E., the Yoruba Oyo states evolved into a powerful force through the military feats of legendary leaders and chiefs like Ajaka, Sango, Abipa, and Oduduwa. According to Collins, Oyo rose to prominence during the 1600s and subdued Yorubaland to the rule of Alafin of Oyo. The Yoruba maintained stable governments with the help of their sacred traditions, myths, and distinguished councils, which offered checks and balances to royal rule. The Oyo Mesi Council of Notables (elders) chose the king and installed him at Ile-Ife as the spiritual, ancestral, and political head of all the Yoruba. The Ogboni Secret Council, consisting of one thousand renowned, politically astute, and morally upright older men and headed by the *Oluwo*, or chief priest, represented the people's will and advised the king on major policy issues and other types of decisions.[7] Since the late 1700s, internal disputes over power related to trading, the size of the kingdom, slavery, attacks from Muslims, economic decline, leadership weakness, civil wars, and secession by Egba and Dahomey led to the downfall of the Oyo empire;[8] it was invaded by the Fon-Dahomey people, whose slave-raiding campaigns became a significant supply line for the Atlantic slave trade. Finally, the British attacked Lagos with heavy artillery in 1851 and annexed it as a colony ten years later. This ended four hundred years of the Oyo empire[9] and began one hundred years of British occupation. When Nigerians gained their independence in 1960, the Yoruba played a key role in the new government.

Large urban towns like Ile-Ife and Oyo functioned as both religious and political centers of Yoruba culture. Early in its history, the city of Ile-Ife emerged as the chief center of the Yoruba. The ruler of Ile-Ife and head of the Yoruba people was the *ooni*, from whom kings, or *obas*, of the nation-states derived their power. Yoruba myths make the *ooni* a direct descendant of Oduduwa, an African divinity and founder of Ile-Ife (Ife). Oduduwa is one of the divinities that Olodumare, the self-existent and supreme God, sent to earth to guide human destiny. The *oonis* still trace their ancestry to Oddudua. In addition to this religious legitimization of political power, sacred myth now shrouds the ancient history of the Yoruba. A Muslim-influenced legend says, "Oduduwa arrived from Mecca and founded a settlement at Ile-Ife, which became the cradle of the future Yoruba kingdoms and empire. In due course, his sons and grandchildren left the Yoruba cradle and founded . . . the seven original states of the Yoruba," at which time "Ile-Ife was the cradle of the creation of the world."[10] At best, the legend suggests that a leader named Oduduwa founded the Yoruba people, who deified him and made his city, Ile-Ife, the center of their universe.

Ile-Ife is thus home to any number of divinities and is the axis mundi of Yorubaland. Ile-Ife is associated with the deity Orunmila and his brand of divination wisdom. Both Yoruba myth and oral history, which regard Oduduwa (Odua) as the founder and first great king of Yoruba, claim that the world was created at Ile-Ife, all kings are descended from Ife's first king, and the city is the seat of the throne of Oduduwa. In regard to the evolution of the myth, Pemberton says that it is true that the social and political model of a city ruled by a paramount chief or king was well established in Ile-Ife and was present among other Yoruba groups but that Oduduwa's followers created the myth and tradition that enhanced the role of the king in the society. Later, leaders who sought to establish the legitimacy of their political or spiritual base were expected to trace their descent to Oduduwa. Such persons, called the sons of Oduduwa, distinguished themselves from others by wearing beaded crowns (*adenla*) as the symbol of their power and sacred authority.[11] Thus, as Thomas Lawson shows, the Yoruba system claims two spheres of reality. It claims the city of Ile-Ife as its foundation and the center of all religious power, and it is manifested in sacred places and through diviners, priests, family heads, and other actors. The deity Orisa-nla performed the first act of creation at Ile-Ife, so all Yoruba sacred places and sources of power derive their authenticity from there. Hence, each urban center traces its origins to Ile-Ife; a paramount chief of Ile-Ife confirms a new chief's status. It is not without significance that in Cuban Santeria, those at the highest level of the priesthood (including priestesses), especially the babalawo, claim to receive special power from Ile-Ife.[12]

Akan and Fanti-Ashanti

Occupying regions of southern Ghana, the large eastern section of Ivory Coast, and much of Togo is a cluster of peoples known as the Akan; this is also a fairly large linguistic group of ethnic peoples speaking different dialects that are all referred to as Twi. The more than five million Akan nation members constitute several groups of people in twelve independent kingdoms, among whom are the Ashanti (also Asante), whose city, Kumasi, is the most well known of the Akan capitals.[13] The Ashanti controlled most of the forested and agricultural land in northern Ghana and were among the most powerful of the Akan peoples. The chief occupation of the forest-dwelling Akan is farming, with timber, oil palms, cocoa, and minerals being important export industries that have brought the Akans a higher standard of living than exists in many other parts of Ghana. The proud, industrious, and self-supporting Ashanti now live in a large enclave in the heart of southern Ghana, just over 180 miles from the Atlantic coast. They have a relatively long history as an established kingdom whose region of influence reaches the coast. In their prime, they fought the British successfully a number of times during the Victorian era.[14]

The Akan kingdom was founded in the late 1400s, but its people first occupied the savanna of northwestern Ghana and the eastern part of the Ivory Coast, later migrating to the forested regions of the southeast around the beginning of the first millennium. Many Akans intermarried with the forest region's earlier inhabitants, who spoke a similar dialect known as Guan. Over time, the Akan established several kingdoms based on clan systems. Bono-Tetchiman became their first powerful kingdom, one founded by the Aduana clan in the 1400s. In its more recent history, the nation experienced very turbulent times. In addition to internal rivalry among ethnic groups, clans, and kingdoms, the Akan had to defend themselves against warring neighbors, conquerors, Muslim intruders, slave-trading hunters, and European invaders. Their long struggle against colonialism is the subject of much study inside and outside Africa. As anthropologist K. Hart says, "Nowhere in Africa, perhaps in the world, has a pre-colonial policy been more thoroughly researched than the kingdom of the Asante."[15]

The Denkyiras kingdom that had occupied the modern district of Manso Nkwanta and the surrounding regions as far south as Jukwa dominated the Ashanti. Various neighboring powers exploited their lack of cohesion in political life and forced them into a vassal relationship in which they were required to pay taxes and homage to their conquerors. In the 1700s, the rise of resourceful rulers to power united the people and developed an extensive system of forest agriculture as well as trading. The Oyoko clan united several existing states under Kumasi, forming the basis of the modern Ashanti and enabling them to maintain control over trading and politics until British control in the 1800s. A national tale has it that the chief architect of the Ashanti political development was a young prince named Osei Tutu,[16] an intelligent subordinate in the court of the superior Denkyira chief. Tutu is said to have escaped from paying tribute to Denkyira and met and befriended an equally intelligent priest, Okomfo Anokye of the chiefdom of Akwamu. Prince Osei Tutu became chief of Kwaman, the political center of the Ashanti nation, and with the help of Anokye welded Ashanti into a strong kingdom. After Tutu became the first king of Ashanti—with the priest as his trusted adviser, seer, and designer—he remodeled and centralized political power, with Kumasi as the capital of the new kingdom.

Tutu not only refused to pay taxes and other tribute to Denkyira but also defeated him and freed the Ashanti. After seizing their independence, the Ashanti discovered that the real strength of Denkyira was held by the European traders in slaves, arms, and ammunition along the Gold Coast. Under Tutu, King Opoku Ware, and others in that line of succession, the Ashanti remained a formidable force against both neighboring kingdoms and European incursion.[17] But Britain solidified its grip on the region after the Berlin Conference. Later, in September 1901, by an "Order in Council," the British arbitrarily carved out the boundaries of the Akan's roughly 105,900 square miles in their infamous Fante National Constitution. The constitution limited the Ghanaians on where they could settle and farm and required that they obtain permission from European settlers if they wanted to reside in a new village. The constitution recognized the importance of the clan and family structure in Akan society and the fact that each "original inhabitant" is a member of a clan, the relationship being traced through the mother's lineage. Patrilines and noncorporate groups called *ntoro* run across multilingual lines and social structure among the Ashanti. Both male and female ancestry is important to the Akan, who believe that the blood of individuals comes from their matrilineal clans, their personalities come from their patrilineal lines, and their souls come from God. Between father and child a spiritual bond exists, the vigor and strength of which comes from the *sunsum*, or spirit, of the father, which protects a child from danger, including attacks by malevolent spirits.[18]

According to Ghanaian-born William Abraham, the interrelation of several lineages in the community brings a formality to the larger society and "creates the foundation of the community personality" that is at the heart of the Akan idea of the State: "The State is almost personified, and takes precedence over every individual."[19] The *Ohin* is head of the state, chief magistrate, military leader, first in the country's councils, and chief executive officer. Once invested with the symbolic Golden Stool, the *Ohin*, or king, should not be "destooled" flippantly. In accordance with the customary law, the authority that called the king to the stool is the only one that can call for his destoolment and must show due cause. According to Ghanian scholar J. Caseley Hayford, the king "must have had full opportunity of showing cause why he should not be destooled. . . . The proper tribunal, in accordance with the law, must try the King, and the law is jealous of the procedure on such occasions."[20] The great King Pempeh II reigned from the symbolic golden stool, said to contain the spirits of all of the Ashantis. The priest Anokye is said to have promulgated the myth of the Golden Stool designed to promote loyalty and unity. This stool was made of a metal that the Ashanti are said to regard as most precious and sacred. It became the official emblem of the new kingdom as well as the symbol of its authority.

Fon-Ewe (Dahomey)

The roughly three million Fon-Ewe peoples live in Benin (formerly Dahomey), Togo, and eastern Ghana and share linguistic and cultural traditions with the Yoruba. The Fon-Ewe's ancestors are said to have migrated across the Niger River and inhabited Yorubaland, finally breaking away and settling in what is now the Republic of Benin. There they built the capital city and kingdom, Abomey, in central Benin, and the city-kingdom of Allada; this is the root word from which the Haitian Vodou Rada spirits get their name. Different groups of Fon, Ajar, and other nation peoples were united to form the Kingdom of Dahomey, which evolved in ways similar to that of Yorubaland. Dahomey fought a long series of battles with neighboring tribes and kingdoms under many brave princes,[21] who established treaties with the Yoruba of Oyo. The monarchs eventually secured the independence of Dahomey from Oyo and, under Agaja Trudo (1708 to 1740) and his successors, had a monopoly in the Atlantic slave trade. The Yoruba Fon-Dahomey War furnished hundreds of thousands of prisoners for the slave market while Dahomean embassies secured from Lisbon a monopoly on the trade to Bahia.[22] As shown in the next section, the slave trade was a colossal disaster for the region.

The Ewe of Togo and Ghana were at the outpost of the Fon empire and so shared similar history and population shifts from Oyo in Nigeria, an experience that is still commemorated at annual festivals. In preslavery Benin, they also shared certain cultural and religious traditions. For example, they claimed many deities in common, such as Mauw, the distant creator in the sky, and Torgbi-nyigbla, who heads the nature gods of war and thunder. The northern inland Ewe, however, have local clans that lack centralized political authority, while coastal groups have traditionally had fragile or weak kingship, "dispersed clans, and ancestral shrines that are of central importance in the religious life of the community. Each Ewe lineage keeps a carved wooden stool, which is the locus of the cult of the lineage deity. During communal ritual performance this stool is the place to which ancestral spirits may temporarily be summoned."[23] These spirits form an essential part of the African and Afro-Caribbean cosmology.

Modern Dahomeans are organized into scattered patrilineal clans in which the oldest living man is regarded as being between the world of the living and the world of the dead. The human founder of a clan is deified and worshiped as an ancestor who is personified as Dambada Hwedo, which is the name of a popular deity who survived in Haitian Vodou. The Dahomey historic exposure to Europeans and their lucrative trade brought economic strength and military hardware needed to fortify their armies—but at a huge price. The massive export of human cargo, the ravages of war on the population, displacement of escapees, destruction of the African habitats and the environment during captures, and foreign values and ways or cultures spelled destruction to the Dahomey kingdom, its institutions, its peoples, and much of its cultural heritage. The traditional complex Dahomey hierarchal political organization of kingship and chieftaincies (chiefdoms) disappeared, leaving only a shadow kingdom, one that lost name and stature to European colonialism and slavery.

It is far easier to catalogue general European-African slave-shipping statistics than to tell precisely which slaves were the trophies and casualties of national and tribal wars. Sample estimates in the reliable study of David Eltis and others show that from 1595 to 1640 slave disembarkation in Spanish America alone was about 268,200. Portuguese vessels disembarked 187,700 slaves to Spanish colonies from 1601 to 1640 and 173,700 to Brazil between 1600 and 1650. From 1650 to 1700, estimates show more than 325,000 Brazilian arrivals.[24] These numbers may be increased by 25 to 30 percent for losses to Middle Passage mortality and various casualties of capture by enemy ships and so forth. From 1662 to 1713, British, Dutch, Portuguese, French, and other European ships embarked a staggering 413,990 victims from the Bight of Benin and 109,252 from the Bight of Biafra. These numbers increase to 847,921 when captives from Senegal-Gambia, Gold Coast, West Central Africa, and South-East Africa are included for the same short period.[25] Eltis reports that, after 1713, estimates show that "vessels from ports in the British Americas carried off 280,000 slaves,"[26] but that from 1647 to 1807 "British slavers carried five slaves across the Atlantic for every four in Portuguese vessels."[27] As much as a 5-to-10-percent margin of error could perhaps be countenanced for these numbers, given the many variables controlling slave trade statistics. West Africa's

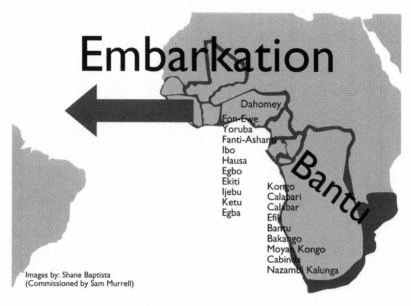

Embarkation. (Image by Shane Baptista.)

total loss in human capital to the Atlantic slaver trade (see the section that follows) was catastrophic, and the impact of the arrivals on the cultures of the Americas was indelible.

Central African Origin

The peoples from the Central African regions originated from several different nation-tribes, principalities, chieftaincies, cultures, and traditions and had many things in common: they were among the Bantu-speaking peoples with many other languages and dialects; they were colonized by Europeans, whose culture and languages were imposed on them; huge numbers of their peoples were taken by brute force from their homelands in Central and southern Africa to the Americas; they were largely agricultural societies; they brought with them memories of their people's history, culture, religious traditions (for example, Kongo and Mayombe), languages, and knowledge of various occupations and skills; and when they could, they used their religion, culture, and knowledge to survive in an unforgiving environment. A review of multiple cultural traditions of the region essential to a work on ATRs is beyond the scope of this book. The fact that space limitations force me to restrict my discussion to the Kongo's historical and cultural-religious traditions does not imply that these were the only Central African peoples of consequence to the study of Afro-Caribbean religions. The Congolese are chosen because they serve as a good example of the cultural traditions of the region and because of the Kongo's dominance in Afro-Caribbean religious heritage.

Kongo Culture

The diverse cultures of the modern Kikongo-speaking peoples of western and Lower Zaire, the Democratic Republic of the Congo (Central Africa), and Angola (Niger-Congo) have their roots in the ancient Kongo kingdom. If Kongo represents the broader region, political structures, and peoples of the Kongo Kingdom, the Kongo or Bakongo (plural) peoples belong to the region in Central West Africa once conquered, divided, and ruled by France (Moyen Kongo), Portugal (Cabinda), Belgium (Belgian Congo, now western or Lower Zaire), and Britain (northwestern Angola). The larger Kongo constituencies were drawn into several kingdoms and large chieftaincies, such as the Loango, Kakongo, and Ngoyo kingdoms, which were coastal; the Vungu, with its many chieftains, which was inland on the north bank of the Kongo River; and the Nsundi and Kongo, located on the south bank. Anthropologist John Janzen states that "in all of these, polities, shrines, and insignia of authority represented the complementarity of power"[28] among the early Congo or Kongo peoples.

Like the Oyo empire, the Kongo Kingdom was founded sometime in the fourteenth century C.E. and covered a sizable region. Although the Bakongo made major conquests and incorporated many new territories in the sixteenth century, by the time Portuguese navigators reached Kongo's Atlantic shores in 1483, the country had encompassed much of the territory that it would occupy in its heyday. African scholar Simon Bockie, born in a Banza-Lele village in Lower Zaire, claims, "The Kingdom of Kongo, flourishing impressively when Europeans first reached Africa, was historically one of the great pre-modern African civilizations. The present-day Bakongo, although in the midst of rapid social change, still derive their character and their way of life from the enduring traditions of their ancestors"[29] and their history. Since agriculture was their chief occupation, during this historical period the Kongo people lived mainly by cattle grazing, hunting, fishing, and small-scale farming of various food crops. Later, sculpting, carpentry, tanning, weaving, and trading in the well-known Kongo markets, especially along the coast, were important commercial skills. These gradually became vital to Kongo economy and brought Kongo's peoples into direct contact with European merchants, traders, and missionaries.[30]

This contact created wealth in the Kongo but set in motion a chain of events that would haunt Kongo history for almost five hundred years. Portugal established diplomacy, trade, and missionary relations with Kongo chiefs that radically changed Kongo life. In time, a bitter succession struggle that ensued between Kongo prince Mpanzu, a follower of ATRs, and the foreign Christian prince Afonso in 1510 saw the early establishment of Roman Catholicism as a state religion. Catholic schools became standard for the Kongo, and the Europeanization of its culture began with a centralized government patterned after and supported by Portuguese colonial powers. After Afonso's departure in the mid-1400s, "the kingdom began to disintegrate and, although usually supported by Portuguese militia and Catholic missionaries, it became increasingly subject to extended succession feuds between contending houses and lineages,"[31] one supporting the Dutch occupation and its Calvinism, the other supporting Roman Catholicism. As Anne Hilton puts it:

> Christianity was intimately associated with the Kongo kingship and was based on Catholic forms of worship. To change the forms [to suit the Dutch] would be to undermine the kingship as well as the Catholic faith. Catholicism was also a *sine qua non* of the relationship with Portugal and Rome and the Portuguese had not been exterminated from Angola.[32]

Concomitantly, the Atlantic slave trade began having an adverse impact on the kingdom, while the internal political and religious struggles took their awful toll.

John Thornton claims that two sectors influenced precolonized Kongo society (the towns developed one set of beliefs, while rural villages had another), both centered on the ideas of economic integration and political sovereignty. "Those who lived off the surplus of the village economy justified this privilege by their talents and service—the *kitomi's* special prerogatives were justified by his ability to mediate the unseen natural forces of the spirit world, and while the *nkuluntus's* claims are less clear, he too provided leadership in some aspects of community life."[33] The towns were different; while "the king might provide some spiritual direction to the town sector, and find his position justified within that sector, in his relation with the country as a whole his rule was justified simply by the right of conquest."[34] By the 1600s, dire inequalities were widespread throughout the Kongo. "Village rulers stood in unequal relation to the villagers, and the entire town sector was likewise set above the villages. Within the town as well there were inequalities between the slave and the noble. These inequalities were justified by the right of conquest and by the *itomi's* sacralizing of the rulers,"[35] a privileged few.

Social anthropologist-historian Wyatt MacGaffey, an authority on the Kongo, divides Kongo history up to independence into three periods: (1) the period of the ancient kingdom, the 1200s to the 1660s; (2) the era of the Atlantic slave trade to European occupation, the 1660s to the 1880s; and (3) the period of the colonial "divide and rule," the 1880s to the 1960s.[36] During the early period, the Kongo became accustomed to slavery on a small scale. Domestic slaves consisted of prisoners of war from tribal wars, "emblems" of peace between nations, humans as "merciful sacrifice," and persons in some form of indebtedness. External slave trading was started by the Portuguese to Europe and to Muslim trader-countries and was then extended to the Americas when the trade was systematized into large commercial volumes. The second period was dominated by heavy slave trafficking to the Americas that involved Kongo leaders and foreign traders and that resulted in increased internal wars and massive depopulation of the region. The Kongo established new patterns of long-distance trading between the coast and the Congo Basin and placed a new premium on the copper and slave trades, which they linked with a migration movement of the Bakongo from Angola to the north. Between the 1700s and 1800s, Bakongo controlled the important transfer of goods from the coast to inland Mpumbu, where the wealthy Teke warehouse men and brokers operated slave and other trading depots at certain navigable points. Other centers like Kisangani, Maninga, and Kimpese of the present-day Democratic Republic of the Congo were large markets for "slaves, ivory, rubber, oil, pigs, sheep, goats, and fowl."[37] They also traded tropical fruits and vegetables needed to feed plantation chattels in the Americas. On the coast, several small states controlled a similar exchange of European merchandise for African goods, especially human cargo, with the Dutch, the Portuguese, and other Europeans hawking the Atlantic slave trade.

Massive numbers of Congolese, Angolans, and other peoples from West Central and, to a lesser extent, South-East Africa were brought to Brazil, Cuba, Haiti, and other Caribbean states during Atlantic slavery. For example, from 1600 to 1640 and between 1701 and 1810, Portuguese vessels alone departed the Angolan ports of Luanda and Benguela with at least 959,300 and 874,800 victims, respectively, bound for the Americas.[38] A slightly lower number may be an appropriate estimate for the period between 1641 and 1700 (when heavy trading shifted north for a while) and about one-third that number before 1600. When the number of post-1810 victims is added to the number of departures on ships other than Portuguese, the results are dumbfounding. According to Eltis, except for 1676 to 1725, "West Central Africa sent more slaves to the Americas than any other region . . . between 1519 and 1867. . . . For a century at the beginning and a quarter century at the end of the trade, West Central Africa dispatched more slaves than all other regions combined, and between 1800 and 1850 it came close to doing the same."[39]

The region's exact total human loss to slavery may never be known. Conservative estimates of slave departures to the Americas from West, Central, and southern African depots vary by hundreds of thousands among well-known historians of the Atlantic slave trade: 11,200,000 (Philip Curtin, 1969), 11,863,000 (Paul Lovejoy, 1989), 12,689,000 (Joseph Inikori, 1982), and 12,789,000 (Per Hernaes).[40] Statistics from undocumented contraband slaves, disguised slavers, smuggled human cargo, and creative bookkeeping suggest that these numbers are much higher. Kongo slave trade was lucrative and contributed handsomely to the coffers of greedy chiefs, war lords, and middlemen. Also, and more important, the trade furnished massive numbers of Africans shipped to the Americas over more than three hundred years; as much as 40 percent of those went to

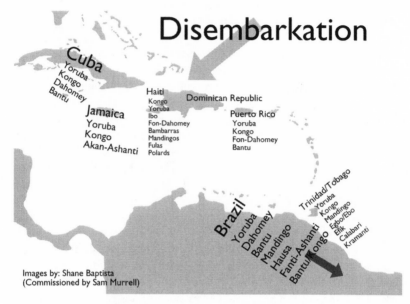

Disembarkation

Cuba
Yoruba
Kongo
Dahomey
Bantu

Jamaica
Yoruba
Kongo
Akan-Ashanti

Haiti
Kongo
Yoruba
Ibo
Fon-Dahomey
Bambarras
Mandingos
Fulas
Polards

Dominican Republic

Puerto Rico
Yoruba
Kongo
Fon-Dahomey
Bantu

Brazil
Yoruba
Dahomey
Bantu
Mandingo
Hausa
Fanti-Ashanti
Bantu-Kongo

Trinidad/Tobago
Yoruba
Kongo
Mandingo
Egbo/Ebo
Efik
Calabari
Kramanti

Images by: Shane Baptista
(Commissioned by Sam Murrell)

Disembarkation. (Image by Shane Baptista.)

Brazil and a large number to Cuba, Haiti, and the French Windward Islands. Africa's loss to slavery was felt most greatly in the Kongo. The slave trade reduced Kongo's population by more than half—a reduction that did not improve before the 1930s. So devastating to the region was the colonial trade's dislocation that, for its duration, the Kongo showed negative population growth in spite of a high birthrate.[41]

In the late nineteenth century, European forces from the coast penetrated Kongo's interior and consolidated colonial conquest and power. The need to intervene in a rival faction among several leaders tied to European economic and political interests in 1859 gave the Portuguese a long-sought opportunity to occupy Mbanza Kongo and control succession to the throne. During European occupation, British Protestant missionaries established stations in the Kongo interior. By the 1880s, Europeans were entrenched, and the Kongo peoples who were lucky enough to survive the slave trade lost complete control of their destiny: "All of the region's historical kingdoms gradually lost their control over tax levying, trade, and orderly"[42] government. In 1885, those Europeans declared their occupied territory the "Congo Free State," which, within a few years, owned Kongo lands and channeled all of its male labor into industrial enterprises through government labor taxation policy. These stupendous events had a disastrous impact on Kongo life and culture. European conquest of Kongo meant that the country's government, education, trade, and native social and cultural narratives that would influence future chapters of Kongo history were taken over by foreigners and replaced by white-oriented counterparts.[43]

In spite of the disastrous impact of Europe's colonization and slavery on Kongo society, traditional cultural and religious bonds survived colonialism and persist into the present. Within Kongo society, family-unit ties are very strong. The people live in *libatas*, very small villages of about thirty to forty houses, and *ke-belo*, or hamlets. These houses are divided into lineages, or *futa*, in which members hold rights to certain property and goods. While individuals retain close matrilineal relations, ties with their fathers' kin provide religious and social stability and guarantee their freedom within the community. Everyone assumes certain specific roles and responsibilities according to his or her gender and age. Most of Kongo's subsistence farming duties of planting and harvesting, gardening, and domestic work are left to women. In many ways, Kongo kinship ties form a social nexus in which an individual finds social security.[44] The leader of a clan is often a local chief who not only defends the community but carries mystical powers in a society where the sacred is found in the profane and where ritual practices are not separated from everyday life. Economic resources and social status can play an important role in choosing who leads the community and its ritual activities. In some cases, Kongo tradition requires the man who wishes to gain power to consult with the ancestors and solicit their help.[45]

Religious Cosmologies

Among the many theological perspectives in African life and thought, belief in the one supreme deity is primary. The supreme God is not seen as all-powerful to the Fon-Ewe people, to whom no single deity is omnipotent, but to the Yoruba, Olodumare certainly has that power. So too does the Kongo deity Nazambi Kalunga. To the Akan, Onyankopon (Nyankupon), the greatest of all beings, is invisible, lives in the heavens, and makes the winds his messengers. As Michelle Gilbert contends, the Akan regard their Supreme Being as "omniscient and omnipotent, the creator of the world, and the giver of rain and sunshine. Born on Saturday, Both he and Asase Yaa, the Thursday-born Goddess of the Earth, are formally appealed to in all prayers, although in general, it is the ancestors and deities who mediate between god and man."[46] In Africans' idea of the world, divine entities control the cosmos in what Bolaji Idowu calls a "diffused monotheism,"[47] a theism in which a single omnipotent creator, along with hundreds of lower gods, rules over the universe. As the Supreme Being at the apex of this divine cosmic hierarchy, Olodumare, Nana Buluku, Nazambi Kalunga, or Onyankopon is owner of the skies, source of all existence, and originating power behind the world of spirits and human life.[48] The name Olodumare is a combination of *olo*, *odu*, and *mare*. *Olo odu* means "owner of *odu*," the principle that underlies the operation of the universe, and *mare* is "light" or "rainbow."

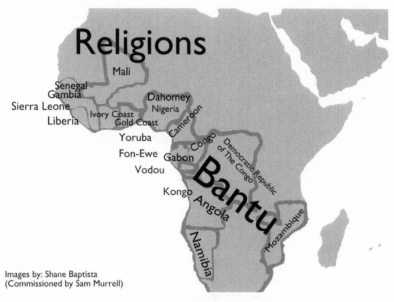

Images by: Shane Baptista
(Commissioned by Sam Murrell)

Religions (Africa). (Image by Shane Baptista.)

As Creator and sovereign ruler, God is the repository of the destinies of all creatures, visible and invisible.

God in Africa is no different from the benevolent, compassionate, and merciful Judeo-Christian God who created the world and sovereignly controls it, but Africans' view of God is not monolithic. To some Africans, God is an all-pervading reality and an active participant in human affairs. The divine, who may be male or female, is accessible to all, irrespective of race, tribe, gender, or religion,[49] and is approached directly through sacrifices, worship, and prayers or indirectly via intermediaries. As Evans Zuesse notes, "There is often a direct cult devoted to him, which may be personal . . . or communal."[50] In some Ashanti homes, one can find a six-foot pole set in a corner, on which is placed a small receptacle containing eggs for periodic sacrifice to Onyankopon. Some African scholars, however, say that Africans rarely approach the Supreme Being directly; God does not micromanage African life and is not the center of gravity in African spirituality. God receives no direct worship from devotees, and no shrines are dedicated in his or her honor. He or she "has no cult, images, temples, or priesthood";[51] showers no blessings on anyone; and, although he or she approves everyone's destiny at birth, is uninvolved in daily life. Worship in ATRs is usually made to lesser deities to whom many propitiatory sacrifices and oblations are directed. In some religions like Kongo's, however, the role of lower intermediary spirits above ancestors is less pronounced than it is in West Africa.

Echoes of Kongo Religion

Kongo traditional religion consisted largely of oral traditions and therefore did not lend itself readily to outside study. For a long time, the only available sources on Kongo religious rituals, rites, and beliefs came from foreign Christian missionary narratives and stories, many of which were unorganized and not free of misunderstanding and bias. (Some missionaries believed the long-held myth that Kongo and other African peoples had no religious cosmology or religion, art, or culture.) Precolonial Kongo was a diverse region with many peoples, customs, traditions, and beliefs. No one body of beliefs was accepted by all of Kongo societies, and life was not compartmentalized into secular and sacred as it is in the West today. As in other ATRs, spirituality was associated with people's everyday struggle for good health, food, and economic or political survival. Rulers occupied both secular and sacred roles with what Thornton calls "actions for the public (or social) sphere and actions for the private sphere, although the borders between them were not clearly defined";[52] the sacred lived with the secular. Here I review only a few echoes of Kongo religion pertinent to Afro-Caribbean religions.

According to Thornton, in one region of the Kongo, a kitomi (singular) was largely a public figure but the *nganga* was seen as a private one. The former kept rather closely to his public role, but the averred private nganga also filled public roles regularly. "In addition to helping private persons overcome hardship or obtain luck, nganga regularly sought to bring rain, cure epidemics, and engage in other functions on behalf of society at large."[53] The nganga rendered services to clients in return for an in-kind or monetary fee. Such services included curing illness, divining the future, warding off the evil eye, supplying good-luck charms for various endeavors, and preventing tragedies, accidents, and other types of misfortunes. Much like practitioners in Kongo-influenced Caribbean religions (Obeah, Myal, Kumina, Palo Myombe or Palo Monte), the *"Nganga* could . . . work on both sides of what Kongo society considered ethical, and the very fact that they worked on behalf of private clients made much of what they did suspect" when dealing with evil; even the Catholic priests were seen as a type of nganga who often dealt in evil.[54]

The kitomi filled several important public roles: mediator between nature and human society; protector of social customs and institutions; legitimizer of kingship, provincial rulership, and political order; and preserver of the balance between nature and society. As a result, Christian missionaries sometimes likened the kitomi (singular) to a bishop or patriarch as well as to an earth god. The itomi were seen as playing such a central role in agriculture—as the source of rainfall, fertility, and good harvest—at crop-reaping time that "they received the first fruits, and it was held that eating the first fruits without giving them to the kitomi would kill the consumer."[55] In fact, "so delicate was the balance between the itomi and the forces of nature that it was considered unwise to let them die a natural death, as this might upset nature. As a result, moribund itomi were ritually strangled by their successors";[56] this bears some similarity to how a chief may be "put to sleep" in another culture because his sacred office shields him from some types of suffering and death or because he is a sacrificial offering (victim) in settling tribal scores.

Patterned after divine kingship insignia, the investiture of a chief was a sacred event marked by what MacGaffey calls "a series of rituals that included the consecration of charms and the healing of individual afflictions. All the rites of this series likewise had political and economic function. . . . Men also purchased charms to help them in their enterprise, especially hunting, trade, and war."[57] In Manianga, the chief of a kanda embodies ancestral power and is chosen on the basis of several ancestral values. According to Bockie, the chief "must be a representative senior of his group; be intelligent and wise; understand the ancestors' wishes from their invisible realm; have leadership skills; be free from harmful kindoki ('witchcraft') and discrimination based on lineage descent; and be a strong representative and good public speaker in major events such as marriage, death, and land disputes."[58] If the chief has children, works hard, feeds the hungry who are unemployed and receive no welfare assistance, has good relations with the people, and defends the village, he enjoys great prestige and the ancestors are said to work their powers through him. He has religious and judicial authority and is "supreme arbiter in all matters affecting the well-being and solidarity of the whole group."[59] Some of these values and traditions survived in creole form in some parts of the Caribbean through Kongo religious influence.

Various Kongo regions showed a sense of unity in different aspects of life, and religious beliefs and practices were derived from pervasive social realities and vicissitudes of the country's checkered history. The Kikang-speaking peoples experienced a range of different cults, movements, and beliefs. Among these was the common belief in the Supreme Being Nzambi Kalunga, or Nzambi Mpungu Tulendo, who was thought to be all powerful. Congolese do not show strong beliefs in a pantheon of divinities or universal spirits, as their northwestern neighbors do. According to Janzen, "Nzambi Kalunga is the creator and the ultimate source of power," and ancestral spirits "mediate between humanity and the supreme being," not as gods but as family agents. These exist concomitantly with the reality of evil, disorder, and injustice as resulting from "such base human motives as greed, envy, or maliciousness."[60] As Bockie notes, the ancestral spirit's blessings were sought for the community's well-being, fertile soil and good crops, and individual or family success. "An inexplicable misfortune or epidemic is enough to make people speculate that the cause is the breaking of the covenant between human and spiritual beings: either all members have acted contrary to the ancestors' expectations and orders or at least one of them has done so."[61]

In Bakongo cosmology, humans are part of the continuous cycle of life and the ancestral spirits who encircle the community with their protection are an integral part of that process. As Robert Thompson understands it, the indestructible soul lives on after death (a mere transition in the process of change) in the land of the dead or departed ancestors. This cycle (mimicking Hindu reincarnation) is symbolized by the constant rising and setting of the sun and the drum of life from birth and death. In a special cross called the *yowa*—resembling the Christian cross but having very different theological signification—the Bakongo signify the "compelling vision of the circular motion of human souls about the circumference of its intersecting lines. The Kongo cross refers to the everlasting community of all righteous men and women."[62] Dianne Stewart observes that the Kongo cross does not signify the death of Christ or any divinity. "The Yowa cross counteracts death by mediating extended life, connection, and metaphysical continuity across the invisible-invisible worlds domains."[63] MacGaffey agrees that the cosmic *yowa* cross signification is reenacted in Cuba by ritual experts "in a circle divided into four equal segments" and a cross inscribed in it. The four points carry the labels *nsulu* or sky, *kumangong* or land of the dead, *ntoto* or earth, and *kalunga* or ocean.[64] The crude but fascinating cosmographic piece of art is a powerful echo of Kongo religious thought not only in Cuban Palo Mayombe but also in Jamaican Kumina and Obeah.[65]

Religion in West Africa

The traditional West African cosmos envisions a universe of interactions among many divinities, spirits, ancestors, humans, animals, and cosmic life, as well as evil forces, but everything is not divine. John Mbiti says that many ideas about God and the world evolved in African thought over millennia. They are expressed in sacred stories, legends, myths, proverbs, symbols, rituals, and sayings of the sages. When these ideas converge, a picture emerges of a complex understanding of the cosmos.[66] It shows an underlying search for an ordered universe in the *Orun*, the abode of the gods and ancestors. There are the *Aiye*, who make up the world of humans and animals, and the *amoraiye*, children of the world who perform sorcery and witchcraft. Anthropologist Marla Berns holds that this ordered universe is achieved when individuals realize their roles in three conceptual zones of interaction: the realm of humans, the realm of the ancestors, and the realm of the spirits. Each realm is distinct, but all three are interdependent; they are connected by the idea of reincarnation, which originated in the Yoruba creation myth. The relationships among the three realms are based on the basic attributes that each shares. "Both the spirits and the ancestors have the capacity to influence man's well-being and can interfere, either constructively or destructively with his civilized, orderly world."[67] Because of the interaction in the three realms of existence, the sacred is intertwined with the profane; in Africa, religion is societal, society is religious, and rituals maintain the happy marriage.

DIVINE RULER-CREATION MYTHS

Although God is the central character in myths narrating the creation of the world, he is a hidden or distant controller of the universe, a form of deus obsconditus, who governs the world through intermediary *orisa*, or lesser deities. A Fon-Ewe myth says the creator gave birth to twin gods named Mawu and Lisa, called locally Mawu-Lisa; "the first, female, was given command of the night, and the second, male, was associated with the day."[68] An Akan myth has it that God once lived close to the earth, but after a woman who wanted better food disobeyed him, God withdrew to heaven and broke his direct link with humans. Zuesse says, "Some Yoruba legends have a pair of gods, Orishala (Obatala or Orisa-nla) and his wife Odudwa, as supreme creating deities, either independently of almighty Olorun or preceding him. One legend has Olorun creating the world and then leaving Obatala and Odudua to finish up the details."[69] Substantial variations exist on ideas of the deities from region to region and city to city as a result of the oral nature of these myths of origin. A deity can be female in one region or village and male in another, or a single deity in a neighboring region may embody the characteristics of two or three deities.[70]

The Akan people distinguish the greater personal deity *obosom* from the smaller nonpersonalized spirits *asuman* or *suman*, not to be confused with *asaman* or ancestors. They also classify sacred objects such as charms, amulets, and talisman as *suman*, which are sometimes called fetishes.[71] Along with the *asuman* exist the *mmoatia*, the little folk, the fairies and the witches who live in forested areas; this is similar to the Irish belief in the existence of elves and other beings. In Fon-Ewe cosmology, the forces of nature are represented in public gods: Sagbata, a deity who watches over the earth's fields and waters and punishes offending humans with disease, and Sogvo or Xevioso, the god of water, who fertilizes the earth but whose thunderbolt strikes like an ax. Under this supreme god are the divinities (*vodou*), each having different tasks. Through the pantheon, the Great One is incarnate in the world as the force "*ashe*, the blood of cosmic life and the power of Olodumare toward life, strength, and righteousness. Ashe is like a divine current that finds many conductors of greater or lesser receptivity",[72] it is experienced in the world via the *orisa* (orisha). This same *ashe* empowers the *orixas* and *iyalorixas* in Brazilian Candomble, the *lwa* and *oungan* in Vodou, and the *oricha* and babalawo in Santeria.

ORISA DIVINITIES-A-THOUSAND

An old Yoruba myth tells of 1,700 divinities conspiring against Olodumare and insisting that he abdicate his power and authority to them so that they could govern the world. Another tells of 401 servant spirits of God (in a sacred vodun or pantheon) that constitute the complex body of deities called orisa (orisha). These "divinities-a-thousand," like the 330 million gods of India, are emanations from the Supreme (Brahma or God) and personifications, attributes, and forces of the Almighty in a diffused monotheism made accessible to humans through ritual. Wande Abimbola of Ile-Ife, Nigeria, says that in Ifa texts not one but two pantheons exist with the supernatural powers that compete for control of the universe. These are "four hundred supernatural powers of the right, and the *ajogun* . . . two hundred supernatural powers of the left. The orishas are by their very nature benevolent to human beings while the *ajogun* are malevolent."[73] In mythopoetic literary traditions of the Yoruba religion, Ifa controlled these two opposing forces in the universe that governed all aspects of people's lives. Ifa is a cosmological system of divination that is affected by, and often controls, the actions of the orishas and the destiny of individuals through professional ritual. It is also a literary tradition common among the Yoruba, Fon-Ewe, Igbo, Edo, and Ijo.[74]

According to legend, some orishas were created by Olodumare and others are human beings elevated to divinity upon death because they led heroic lives. Shango, founding king of Oyo, because of his exceptional military life, became an orisha upon his death. The orishas represent an important source of spiritual power that can be tapped ritually for good or ill; each is associated with realities that can directly affect the basic order of the African cosmos: "The positive response of the divinities to the problems and needs of the communities they serve is indicative of their reality and potency, as intermediaries between God"[75] and humans. The orishas are not infinite. Myth claims that they "came into the world at its beginning, at the holy city Ile-Ife, where they established such Yoruba arts and science as farming, hunting, smithing, and divination. Eventually, through their immense power and influence, they 'passed through the earth' and became divine patrons of Yoruba" people.[76]

The orishas are neither omnipresent nor omnipotent; they have to be summoned through rites and rituals. They have their own sphere of operation in the world—each charged with responsibility before leaving the *orun*, heaven. The recognition of their powers, potency, and authority also varies considerably from one city to another and from region to region. Shango, for example, the patron deity of the kings of Oyo, has important shrines in cities that were traditionally part of the old Oyo empire (circa 1600 to 1790). However, in communities to the south and east, Shango's role and worship diminishes significantly. In other parts of Yorubaland, it is Osun, Oko, Erinle, Obatala, or Agemo whose festivals and shrines dominate the cultus and life of the people. Each village adopts a principal orisha such as Shango, the orisha of Oyo, who is accorded the most ritual attention by the priesthood and at public shrines. Other orishas are relegated to individual and family veneration. Multiple objects—persons, sacred apparel, sacred objects, shrines, sacred places, and Yoruba art—represent each of the 401 orisha entities. Visual and auditory symbols, animals, physical peculiarities, illness, metal like iron and steel, tools, ceremonial swords, elements of nature, favorite foods, and different cultic paraphernalia also represent the orishas. Many local divinities of rivers, trees, hills, and other elements of nature exist. "There are gods of smallpox, whose worshipers try to protect the people

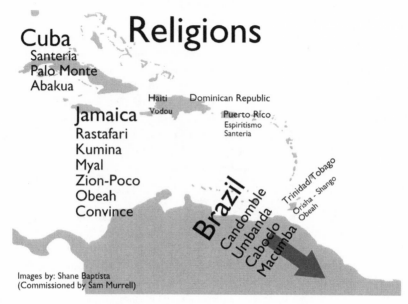

Religions (Caribbean). (Image by Shane Baptista.)

from this disease; gods of hunting, farming and other activities; and gods who showed people how to perform rituals such as the Gelede society dances."[77] In West African culture, one's fate is often tied to one's orisha, who is directly involved in an individual's life.

The orisha of a devotee is often revealed through a medium during divination, spirit possession, or some other ritualized festive activity directed by the local babalawo or priest. Behind each significant Yoruba activity exists an orisha whose power and authority authenticates it and whose mystique makes it mysterious and profound.[78] The actions of the spiritual forces are predictable only through ritual; the forces are capricious and pose an ever-present threat of chaos and disorder that can send the Yoruba world order into a tailspin—or into a sphere of dynamic flux. Although hundreds of orishas exist, relatively few received extensive ritual attention; a still smaller number are popular throughout Central West Africa. The respected ones have their own cult worshipers, priests, priestesses, and shrines in Yoruba and Fon cities. The following orishas are the most popular in Yoruba religion and art and became dominant in Afro-Caribbean religions.

Male Orishas: Shango. The invulnerable god of thunder, lightning, and destruction, Shango (Sango) might hold a position as the most feared in the orisha pantheon, both in African Yoruba and Cuban Santeria. He symbolizes a lingering authority of the once powerful fourth king and royal state of Oyo, which Shango's father, Oduduwa's grandson, founded. The Yoruba believe Shango creates thunder and lightning by casting down "thunderstones" from heaven to the earth. Anyone who offends Shango is struck with lightning speed. When lightning struck, followed by peals of thunder, ancient Shango priests went scrambling around in search of thunderstones or the "throne stone," which had special powers. These stones were found enshrined in temples to the gods. Believers say Shango can ward off terrible tornadoes that strike West Africa. In addition to the terrifying forces of nature that announce his presence, the four major Nigerian rivers (chief of which is the River Niger) are Shango's wives. He also imparts beauty to women with whom he sleeps, does as he pleases, and is very unpredictable. Shango has more shrines than any other orisha and his priests and devotees carry his symbols of wooden staff emblems, names, and red and white colors. Ritual objects, sculptures, figurines, and other paraphernalia in his temples dominate his ceremonies. Devotees offer special dishes, do possession dances, and sing praises to Shango. Priests perform special rituals to him and, in return, Shango provides protection and good luck.[79]

Orisa-nla. Also called Obatala in African and Santeria Yoruba, Orisa-nla is a male deity who has a multiplicity of functions in African mythology. He is Olodumare's son or deputy and partakes of the creator God's essence and work. A Yoruba myth says that Orisa-nla assisted Olodumare in hurriedly creating the first sixteen humans on earth, who were less than perfect and passed on their imperfection to the human race. Orisa-nla therefore is represented by the physically challenged, impaired, hunchbacked (even the hunchback of Notre Dame), deformed, and poor. He is patient, kind, playful; he is a lover and defender of children and the god of success and failure, poverty and wealth. He is said to take money from the pockets of the rich to feed the poor and his children. Orisa-nla's devotees dislike palm oil and dogs but love to wear the color white. His shrines carry his signs, and his priests, who wear his white colors and symbols, offer sacrifices in his name. Orisa-nla also has special gourmet foods and drinks (among which are large snails and cooked vegetables) that devotees must present to him before securing his aid. Ignoring these requirements could bring a bad fate from this "old man with the strength of youth."[80]

Ogun. Ogun is considered among the most worshiped and important national deities in Nigeria. His influence is so widespread that seven Oguns exist, among whom are Ogun of blacksmiths, Ogun of hunters, Ogun of warriors, and Ogun Onire.[81] He has a large number of devotees and many household shrines and temples. The identity and reality of Ogun, however, is shrouded in myth and paradox, which makes him one of the most puzzling orisha. He is the enraged orisha who committed suicide when his dreams were shattered, yet he lives. He is the god of warfare, iron technology, and kingship who helped build the Yoruba empire. Two scholars noted that as a Yoruba empire builder, "the

Ogun concept encapsulated the progression from hunting to agriculture and the mastery of metallurgy, to urbanization and, ultimately . . . to the development of empire."[82] Ogun is one of the original gods of the heavens and one of the highest spirits, who cleared the path to earth for other deities. He was the first king of Ifa but became an ancestor and deity. Sandra Barnes says that the modern Ogun presents two different images: one is a terrifying violent warrior, armed with frightening charms and destructive medicines, and another is society's macho man, "a leader known for his sexual prowess, who nurtures, protects, and relentlessly pursues truth, equality, and justice. . . . This African figure fits the destroyer/creator archetype. However, to assign him a neat label is itself an injustice, for behind the label lies a complex and varied set of notions"[83] of a paradoxical deity.

Ogun stands for justice and fair deals in matters involving the law. His devotees swear in Yoruba law courts to "tell the truth and nothing but the truth so help me God" while kissing Ogun's sacred steel machete. Anyone who annuls a legal contract made in his name or fails to fulfill an obligation to him could receive his swift revenge, for his wrath is dreaded. In addition to recognizing Ogun by the ax made of iron, steel, or metal that represents him, the Yoruba recognize him by his "title staff," a wooden stick on which is carved a figure of him. Functionally, the brass staff (*iwana*) and the sword (*ada*) "transcend their practical form," for "they identify the authority of titled members of the Ogun cult. The figure on the staff represents an important cult leader, wearing the regalia and weapons appropriate to his high office."[84] The title staff also signifies the jurisdiction of the senior blacksmith, and the elaborate ceremonial sword embodies his power. Nigerians keep Ogun's cult alive in their annual community-wide festival called Odun Ogun, in which chief participants represent three distinct aspect of Ile-Ife society: kingship, chiefdom, and occupations.[85]

Orunmila. Celebrated internationally almost as much as Shango or Ogun is the god of knowledge and wisdom, Orunmila, who is seen as the epitome of Ifa divination and the orisha of all babalawo priests. In a Yoruba creation myth, Orunmila helped Olodumare fix human destiny, knowledge of which he kept a secret. As John Pemberton contends, "In *orisha* worship it is the wisdom of Orunmila, the *orisha* of Ifa divination, and the work of Eshu, the bearer of sacrifices, that stand for the meaningfulness of experience and the possibility of effective action. The vast corpus of Ifa poetry, organized into 256 collections called *odu* (also known as *orisha*) is a repository of Yoruba cultural values."[86] Abimbola labels the 256 collections "chapters," each of which has about 800 poems, making a grand total of 204,800 Ifa poems. The African babalawo, priest of Ifa and Cuban Santeria (renamed *babalorisha* and *babalosha*), "father of ancient wisdom," has the wisdom of Ifa to perform rites of divination. Ifa literature also says that Orunmlila mediates between two supernatural powers and, through sacrifices offered by the priest, shoots death with his arrow. Since every ritual action requires a sacrifice to open the gate or path to particular orisha, the wisdom of

Orunmila and Eshu are crucial in divining the right sacrifice, foods, and prayers appropriate for each orisha's worship. Africans call this ritual procedure "profiling of the orisha" or "finding the right *iwa*," loosely translated as "character," "quality," or "match."[87]

Esu or Eshu. Eshu, also called Elegba, the god of fate, commonly mistaken for the devil, is an ambiguous messenger trickster deity who carries out Olodumare's wishes by rewarding and punishing devotees. This is a complex orisha who is a prankster, a sower of discord, and a busybody. He characterizes Olorun's might and is said to have taught the secrets of wisdom to Orunmila. Esu has within him yin and yang, good and evil forces, right and wrong, love and anger, joy and sorrow, reverence and irreverence and is able to meditate between earth and heaven. His contrary qualities "make it possible for him to assume the key role of mediator between the many levels of power conceived of in Yoruba thought, particularly between the worlds of divine and human power."[88] Esu can resolve all conflicts in the Yoruba world with Ifa divination, through sacrifice and rituals. As the deity who takes the people's offerings to Olorun, Esu is the divine middleman; one must first appease him through sacrifice before one can gain access to the other deities. No ritual activity involving the spirits can be done without sacrifice, and Esu must have his share. He has no shrines named in his honor and no special priests or devotees, but wherever there is a worship or ritual, Esu is present;[89] he is the orisha of crossroads, opportunities, decisions, and indecision.

Female Orishas: Oshun. Oshun (Osun), the wisdom of rivers, goddess of water, sensuality, and affection, is the mother deity of the Yoruba. She is regarded as the cooling ashe (force) of the orisha and a complement to the hot-tempered power of Ogun. As patron of the river that bears her name, she cleanses the head as clean water purifies the body and is the cooling water of the divine. Oshun is the deity of fertility and medicine who makes her barren devotees conceive; pregnancy and a bountiful harvest are signs that she is actively at work in her children (devotees). Oshun's avatars claim that she succeeds where doctors fail and heals where modern medicine is ineffectual; she cures her children with cooling waters and feeds barren women with fertile honey. In Santeria, Oshun is associated with the Virgin Mary because of her grace, elegance, and gentleness. In Cuba and Cuban neighborhoods in the United States, Oshun is La Caridad del Cobre, Cuba's patron saint, and the Virgin Mother of Charity.[90] Since the November 1999 debacle of Elian Gonzalez's sea rescue, Oshun has become a cultural icon for religious unity among her children in the Cuban diaspora, as well as an object of artistic, festive, religious expression. Through a female medium, Oshun makes her exciting appearance at the sacred ritual, whirling and dancing to drums and rhythms in grace and gentleness, and addresses her devotees as children who wear her favorite color yellow and feast on her choice foods—white hen, goat, sheep, and juicy fruits.

Yemaja. Queen-mother of the fishes of the deep, "mother of weeping breast," the other female deity, Yemaja (Iemaja, Yemaya, Yemoja, Yemowo), is the orisha of maternal love (the other goddess of the sea) and one of Shango's wives. The Yoruba name *Yeyeomo eja* signifies "the Mother whose children are the fish [and who] is domiciled in Abeokuta. She is represented as a beautiful matron with prominent breasts."[91] Yemaya is associated with the Cuban Catholic saint Lady of Regla and with Iejama of the orixas in Brazil. In Cuba, Yemoja is worshiped as a very popular female deity whose initiates do special dances reflecting the turbulence and peacefulness of the ocean. As the mother of the orixas and owner of the seas in Candomble, she dresses in blue and white to represent the waves and has a silver crown with clear beads dangling from her forehead. She hugs a silver sword tightly to her breast with one hand, and in the other she delicately turns her mirrored fan. In a modern community or family shrine operated by devotees, ritual specialists eat Yemoja's favorite foods (duck, turtle, and goat), carry her emblem (a fan shell),[92] wear her special colors, sing her songs, and do her special dances.

The African deities, brought into the colonial Caribbean largely through slavery, became permanent features of religion in the region and stamped their imprimaturs on all aspects of religious life, as seen in the lives of religious functionaries and in institutions, mythology, and practices. Little of consequence happens in Afro-Caribbean religions without the involvement of the divine, the divinities, and the ancestors.

2

African Cultus and Functionaries

KEY TOPICS

Ancestral Phenomenon • Ritual Performance •
Women, Medium, and Power • African Divination •
Magic and Medicine • Cultural Significance

An important avenue of communication in the African sacred cosmos is the cult of the ancestors, "living-dead" spirits of forebears with whom the living maintain filial relations. All African traditional religions (ATRs) follow the way of the ancestors.[1] They are the closest link humans have to the world of the spirits; they speak both human and divine languages. Ancestral beliefs hold that human life continues beyond death, the dead can communicate with the living, and the living-dead can influence human affairs for good or ill. In some communities, ancestors function as deities; they are the object of worship and take the place of intermediary divinities. Ancestors of Western Africa, especially among the Yoruba, are grouped into two classes: (1) family ancestors whose center of action is the home and (2) deified ancestors whose sphere of operation encompasses the community and who serve the village as well as the family. In many regions, shrines are dedicated to the ancestors and sacred paraphernalia symbolize the presence of these living-dead, who form sources of power with which myth and ritual are associated. Not all the living-dead become ancestors; this category is reserved for persons who reach adulthood, die a natural death, have the gift of longevity as a sign of moral character, and have conscientious descendants who are committed to honoring their elders as ancestors and carrying on their traditions.[2]

Ancestral Phenomenon

Tradition shows that ancestors are ubiquitous, that they have left evidence of their presence everywhere, and that they are found in the chronologies of forebears who are invoked at each family ceremony that celebrates their presence.

A female deity of fertility.
(Illustration by Kelly Hawes.)

They are also among the bearded crowns with which faces of Yoruba kings are veiled, and remind couriers that they are standing in the company of the sacred. Ancestral cults in several regions of Kongo show a close association with leaders and chiefs and are an important part of cooperative Kongo society. Family ancestors of the Kongo called the *Nkuyu* are below the unpredictable *simbi*, who are associated with water and can bring good and bad fortune. Further removed from the human species are *inquices*, who are often equated with the orishas; *inquices* have, at some point, lived on earth but have been elevated as ancestors.[3] Wyatt MacGaffey tells of three related ancestral cults he observed among the BaMpangu of eastern Kongo. The first involves ordinary headmen of the clan who performed a routine function at a cemetery. In the second, a slightly more complex cult exists in which priests function as "patrifilial children" of the clan and where a "smith" (priest type) officiates on important occasions. In this ancestral cult, the main figure is *mfumu mpu*, a chief or clan head whose relics would ultimately find their way in with those of the ancestors (*lukobi lu bakulu*). One who lived an honest life and followed the customs of the forefathers becomes *nkulu*, one step below the *mfumu mpu*. Finally, the smith, the one who conse-crates the chiefs with the blessing of the ancestors, leads the third cult. In this group, one must be initiated into the cult of the *simbi* spirits. Kongo priests per-form most rituals, but in certain circumstances, chiefs make ritual offerings to the ancestors without the help of the priest and without opening the "ancestral basket of relics" left to them.[4]

Ancestors are also present at a personal family level, in one's moral character and physical characteristics. Among the Yoruba, the family is a corporate entity that includes the living, the unborn, and the ancestors—spirits that constantly circulate between earth and heaven or *ori*, the realm of a person's ancestral guide or personal orisha. The living share "heads" or *oris* with the ancestors and are considered their living manifestations. Often this belief is enshrined in the names of children—for example, *Babatunde* ("father returns") and *Yetunde* ("mother returns").[5] MacGaffey's summation of the ancestral cults in Kongo may be true of West, Central, and Southern Africa: the ancestral cult represents "cor-porate cults of the dead. In them the ancestors are presented as capricious fig-ures who, like living elders, must be kept sweet by obeisance, obedience, and gifts lest they turn nasty."[6] The faithful invoke their power to counteract forces that threaten the equilibrium of the community: sickness, infertility, high infant mortality, epidemics, natural disasters, or evil spirits. Ancestors know the actions and deeds of the living and may punish individuals with illness or bad luck for wrongdoing. Africans appease the wrath of the ancestors by offering proper pro-pitiatory sacrifices. They place offerings on ancestors' graves to gain their favor and ward off misfortune that befalls them as a result of disrespect for moral and ethical conventions. The cult preserves ancient African traditions and contrib-utes to community solidarity and cultural consciousness. The death, burial, and later deification of an elder as ancestor constitute an occasion for much celebra-tion, empathy, and intrareligious fraternizing;[7] they encourage local commerce as celebrants sell, purchase, and barter merchandise in local open markets. Ances-tral veneration offers to African societies a mantra for social and moral values. Imbedded in the collective social consciousness and traditions are moral codes, conventions, and accepted customs upheld and honored in reverence for the ancestors.

Ancestral myth plays an important role in Kongo death rituals, especially during the three days of mourning for a deceased person. On the night of the first day of mourning, men sing songs and beat drums through the night while women continue to wail in typical ancient Hebrew and African style. At mid-night, a spokesperson designated by the family addresses the deceased by name and urges him or her to be brave on the long journey to join the *bakulu*, or ancestors. The Akan's national *Odwira* festival in praise of the ancestors, at which the mythic Blackened Stool is honored annually in Kumasi, Wenchi, Akwamufie, Kibi, and Akropong-Akwapim, promotes national cultural iden-tity.[8] This annual celebration is held in September to honor departed Akan Kings and also to ritually purify the nation so that it will not defile the gods. A royal procession held in honor of the honored Stool was designed to apprise the ancestral spirits of the houses of Kumasi about the important business to be taken care of.[9] The Great Stool, which I had the privilege of seeing in Kumasi in 1993, is blackened with sacrificial blood and other emblems because, as Gilbert says, it acts as a shrine that temporarily houses the ancestral spirits of some matrilineal clans who summon them. The Akan believe their ancestors (*asaman* or *asamanfo*) live together somewhere beyond the mountains or across the river[10] and need to be petitioned through rituals.

Among the Yoruba, the presence and relevance of ancestors to the community is ritualized in the annual *egungun* appearance at the celebration of the yam harvest. During the *Odun Egungun,* the annual festival dedicated to the return of the patrilineal ancestors, carnival-type masks made of layers of dark-color fabric are worn in gleeful celebration. Egungun wear various types of masks and charms because they believe that anyone who wears the family *egungun* attire (ago') is also endowed with spiritual powers of the ancestors he or she represents. The *egungun* may adjudicate difficult cases and call into question or pass judgment on the behavior of members of the community.[11] The ancestral spirits, represented by these dancers, make their awesome and sometimes frightful appearance to reaffirm the values of traditions on which the community operates and by which it is linked to its past. The masked performance takes on a commercial tone during tourist shows at annual festivals for the orisha Ogun. The forces of the spirits and ancestors are often demonstrated in art for admiration as well as in commerce and trading.[12]

Ritual Performance

From the point of view of ATRs, social conflicts and moral misdeeds can cause physical and spiritual misfortune; therefore rituals aimed at restoring social, spiritual, and physical health are a necessity. Benjamin Ray says that since human life passes through several critical stages, "one of the important tasks of traditional religion is to move people successfully through the major stages of life. . . . Each phase has its duties, and rites of passage make sure people know their responsibilities. In this way, people's lives are given shape and pattern."[13] Some human acts involving propitiation seek to establish better relations between the gods and the human world. Others are modes of social celebration[14] or attempts at dealing with national and personal crises. John Janzen observes that, up to the seventeenth century, some Kongo rites and rituals pertaining to crises, localized near rivers and streams, were performed at certain times of the year that correlated with intensified natural disasters. Janzen believes that large demographic shifts from one area to another and from the countryside to urban centers in what is now Nigeria, Benin, Kongo (in Kinshasa, Luanda, and Barzzaville) and elsewhere caused certain religious practices to gravitate toward the cities. Although some initiatory and curing rites in existence in the Kongo since the 1700s have been abandoned, practices related to many aspects of life continue to be held sacred. Some religious practices center around female and male fertility rites. These provide "the legitimacy of authority roles at lineage and clan levels, presiding over rites of passage—naming, puberty, marriage, bride price payment—and death, restoring ancestral ties where lineages have been segmented or where, in urban settings, lineage fragments seek to return to their roots."[15] The proper performance of these African rites and rituals communicate meanings that have great religious significance[16] for African communities.

Priest and Priestess

Life's uncertainties, personal and communal tragedies, the desire to understand and deal with life's miseries, and the longing for good fortune have, throughout the evolution of human societies, sustained the need for priests, prophets, diviners, mediums, sorcerers, magicians, and healers or medicine men. Frequently in Africa, the priest embodies most of these roles and the family head, the clan head, the chief, and the king assume priestly functions. Ray notes that since the thirteenth century, kingship became a dominant part of the African religious system and rulers attained control of historical territorial cults on a national level.[17] When the king functions as a religious head, he officiates at annual rites and major ceremonies. Mensah Sarbah says that in Fanti districts, officiating priests at the Nansam ("ancestors'") shrine in Mankesim are ascribed such broad powers and great influence that the view is held that the high priest, or *braffo*, ought to be the sovereign ruler of Fanti Ashanti. The Yoruba household, on the other hand, has a family shrine headed by the *olorie ebi*, the priest of the family clan, who assumes ritual power for communicating with the objects of devotion and the ancestors. The *olorie ebi* must be present at important household events: the birth of a baby, the sending away of a daughter in marriage, and the funeral of a family member. He may even perform family rites.[18]

The professional priests, connected mainly to the orisha cultus, are called *aworos* and *olorisha*. They are servants of the divinities honored in temples, shrines, and sacred groves of the ancestral spirits. As bridges to the divine, priests act as a conduit of the sacred into the profane. To facilitate communication between humans and the divine, priests practice a range of life-cycle rites and rituals: weddings, funerals, the coronation of a king, and initiation into adulthood, a secret society, or the priesthood all begin and end with rituals. Some traumatic rites like circumcision can take several weeks and involve entire families and the community. A primary responsibility of the priest, however, is to divine the mind of the orisha and mediate between people and the spirits.[19] They enhance the harmonious working of society, procure healing and psychological support for people in distress, and ward off the "evil eye."

In ATRs, some priests inherit the office and believe they are predestined from birth to serve and follow a divinity, or, as in Yoruba, claim they have received a call or a vision from Ile-Ife. Most, however, are appointed in a public ceremony even when they occupy the office through family lineage. To become a senior priest involves a long period of training. R. S. Rattray saw three stages in the training period for Ashanti priests, each of which lasts for one year. The trainee must claim to have had a call from a divinity or an ancestor before embarking on the priestly training and must undergo an intense initiation and education in sacred traditions—sacred dances, divination knowledge, prayer songs, herbal healing, and ritual performance—under an experienced priest. Trainee priests must observe rules and conventions that govern their morality and calling. Young priests must keep strict taboos with regard to marriage and temporary chastity, food and alcohol, sacred apparel, and mixing with the common people. After the training is completed, the initiate is regarded as married to the spirit first and can marry in real life or return to a wife or husband to begin the sacred practice.[20] The death of a local priest, the need for a priest in one's village, and personal skills in forming a new shrine are often a new priest's greatest job-creation assets. A Yoruba babalawo claims his commission to the priesthood from Orunmila, who enables him to divine circumstances, events, tragedies, or good will that will befall an individual or community. Since priests divine successful harvests and crop failure, impending disaster from natural phenomena, invasion by another tribe, and personal misfortune, a babalawo is consulted on many different matters. He uses sixteen sacred palm nuts or the *apele* chain to divine "the *odu* whose verses he will chant in addressing problems of the supplicant and determining the sacrifices that must be made";[21] this art is preserved intact in Cuban Santeria.

Women, "Mediumism," and Power

In African societies, women are seen often as both villain and victor; they are regarded not only as conveniences but as purveyors of evil and misfortune and "polluters of the sacred."[22] A large number of Central and West African myths blame women for human misfortunes like the origin of sickness and death. Many also see women as responsible for human separation from God. An Ashanti myth says God once lived closer to humans, but a woman was constantly knocking God's feet with the top end of her pestle while pounding cassava to make *fu-fu*, a staple dish, and forced God to move to higher ground. Another woman attempted to reach God by having her children build a tower of mortars, but it collapsed and left a huge gap between God and humans. As a result, God can no longer be approached directly. According to a Bambuti Pygmy myth, the first humans obeyed the one rule God gave them, "eat of all the trees of the garden except from one tree," until a pregnant woman was overcome by food pangs and prevailed on her husband to bring her the forbidden fruit. The moon saw the man pick the fruit and reported it to God. Once humans ate the fruit, God made them experience sickness and death.[23] A Burundi and Rowanda myth says God told his people to stay indoors while he hunted death to destroy it. A woman disobeyed God and went to work in her field and, while there, had pity on death and allowed it to seek protection from God in her mouth. When God came with his hunting dogs chasing after death, he found it hidden in the woman's mouth and told her and all of her offspring to keep death forever. A Dinka myth states that death and separation from God occurred when a woman, who was being reprimanded for disobeying God, hit him in the eye with a pole, causing God to withdraw from humans. Another myth from the Nuer claims that humans lost their heavenly status because a young woman met a boy foraging for food on earth and requested to stay with him. The couple cut the rope on which they had descended to earth to forage and, as a result, made humans earthbound and mortal.[24]

African women are also seen as mysteriously powerful and dangerous. Cattle-ranchers' folklore from southern Africa views women as having mysterious powers that are dangerous to a herd of cattle, causing herders to excuse women from most pastoral activities and confining them to field labor. Several African origin myths link the creation of human beings directly to God through a woman. God created the woman directly and she in turn became the main instrument of all human life. The Akposso of Togo say that after creating woman as the first human being, Uwolowu (God) bore her the first child, from whom came man. Nigerian Ibibio people believe the deity Obumo, the son of the mother-deity Eka-Abassi, gave birth to human beings through a woman. Another myth has women inventing the world's first fire and providing food for humans for the first time.[25] As John S. Mbiti observes, Africans, known for their love of proverbs and wise sayings, praise women as virtuous, wise, and invaluable to society: "To beget a woman is to beget a man!" "A wife is bought with elephant tusks!" "The safety of a pregnant woman is off-spring." Two popular Ghanian proverbs say "The wisdom of an old woman is worth a thousand young men" and "A woman is a flower in a garden, her husband is the fence around it,"[26] and the family her fruits.

In Ashanti culture, the powerful role of wise women was recognized early in the nation's history. The popular idiom "consult the old woman" makes the woman the final authority in important decision making in the community. The woman is the custodian and repository of knowledge in the community. She is regarded as a reputable connoisseur whose verdict may not be widely challenged in her area of specialty. J. W. Tufuo and C. E. Donkor state that however inferior an Ashanti woman may appear, "she is the final arbiter of what is good or bad for the whole community. Wars have been started because a Queen Mother said the war should be fought. . . . A whole village has been sold into slavery because the wife of a chief had led him to enter into an unholy alliance with her people. Tyrants whom the people could not remove have fallen easy prey to the wiles of a woman."[27] Women's role in ATRs is paradoxical, diverse, and often equal to that of men.

In many parts of Central and West Africa, there are female deities, ancestors, priests, herbalists, healers, workers of witchcraft, mediums, and sorcerers. Most mediums in spirit possession and divination trances are women. Women serve as seers to whom are attributed natural and spiritual powers that allow them to have foresight into events. In Akan society, Queen Mother and king maker is the most powerful woman in the royal court. Among the Yoruba, a respected woman, the *ia agan*, is the only person allowed to be in physical contact with the *engungun* that perform at annual festivals. As a female devotee, she supervises and dresses the male *engungun*, whose face women should not see, according to popular folklore. Women almost always provide the music and dance at African ceremonies. Most African Vodou experts who provide leadership and who perform rites and ritual dances among the Tegetege, Anagogogoo, and Nesufoowea dancers of Savalou, Benin, are women. Yoruba and Fon women prepare corpses for burial and carry them in ritual dance processions while men trail behind the cortege. Through these many roles in society, African women "become autonomous persons, no longer recipients of 'reflected glory.'"[28]

Anthropologist Paula Girshick Ben-Amos, who studied Benin culture extensively, says that in the Edo Olokun cult throughout Benin City, Nigeria, women play critically important roles. Edo women establish shrines in Olokun's (God) honor, wherein young women are trained to be spiritual leaders in direct communication with the deity. After they complete the process of initiation in the cult and become priestesses, the women get immediate access to Olokun, the major source of their new power and, from then on, speak as a direct proxy of God. They gain power and prestige through the performance of healing, divination, singing, and ritual dances and through the wearing of the liturgical garb of Olokun's shrine. Over time, the women acquire substantial financial resources that they usually invest in real estate in the City of Benin; they buy or invest in apartments that attract tenants whom a landlady-priestess is able to influence. With this new financial autonomy and high social status, the priestess is not only patroness to her clients, she is also a political power broker in her community and a chief to the devotees of the cult in her town. She settles local disputes, gives advice, and influences a whole network of charitable redistributions of resources to the needy.[29]

Throughout Africa, women control secret societies responsible for performing various types of rites dealing with womanhood. In Sierra Leone and Liberia, for example, male and female secret societies compete for dominance and prestige. The mysterious societies Sande Bundu (among Gola women) and the Wara Wara (among the Bafoda Limba of northern Sierra Leone) seemed designed primarily to give women control over their bodies and sexuality in a masculine world. Among the Gola women, Warren L. d'Azevedo sees the Sande association as a prime example of a widespread West African women's organization that acts as a vehicle for women's influence in political life and in the maturation of young women, as well as for female power in religion. The elusive Kinu and other mysterious rites, revealed only to women in a code of secrecy, are believed to give Gola women power over their sexuality; secret societies are sources of pride and spiritual and political power to women.[30]

In traumatic, highly controversial, and often fatal ritual female genital mutilations (FGMs)—practiced in most African countries but also done secretly in Europe, Asia, Australia, and the Americas[31]—women naturally dominate this rite of passage. A Demographic Health Survey of the World Health Organization showed that in some cases, 43 to 97 percent of women in the Central African Republic, Cote d'Ivoire, Egypt, Mali, Somalia, and the Sudan are circumcised. Ritual women control and perform the African rite on minors and occasionally on grown women, but outside of Africa, it is women who lead the fight against the practice.[32] Surprisingly, although different types of FGM (e.g., Sunna, clitoridectomy, and infibulation) have deadly side effects, in most countries women outnumber men among the most avid defenders of the practice, mostly because of concerns related to economic empowerment[33] and ancestral religion.

The role of women in ATRs is influenced, in part, by Africans' views of God; in many parts of Africa, God is still seen as male, but in other regions God is female. The Ndebele and Shona peoples of Zimbabwe recognize God as Father, Mother, and Son. The Nuba (Nubia) people of the Sudan speak of God as the Great Mother. South-West African Ovabo people say "God is mother of the people." Among the Yoruba, several orishas are female. Oduduwa, the male deity, was originally a strong and powerful female divinity and progenitor of the Yoruba people. "The priesthood of Orisa-Oko is open to both male and female, but actually has more priestesses than priests. His priestesses form a secret society of their own, and no man dare injure or offend any of them."[34] Many Ashantis regard the earth as a female deity second only to God, while the Igbo call the earth God's daughter, who helps their crops and protects people. Mbiti states that "the Zulu are reported to have the so-called 'Queen of Heaven' who is said to be of great beauty. Rainbows, mist and rain are emanations of her glory, and she is surrounded by light. She is a virgin, and taught women how to make beer, among other useful arts"[35] and crafts.

Notwithstanding the oppression and harsh social, political, and economic realities women face in Africa,[36] they are not always the helpless sheep being led to the slaughter that the West often makes them out to be. Women serve as professional leaders of their country, organizations, societies, and religions; they perform religious rites and rituals, administer healing medicine, do divination, and counsel. This tradition of women's leadership in African religion and culture has significantly influenced women's dominance in Afro-Caribbean religions.

African Divination

Because religion governs every aspect of African life, most crises have religious dimensions that require appropriate responses involving divination, sorcery, magic, or even witchcraft. As Janzen notes, after Kongo peoples lost control over their own destiny to Portuguese domination in the eighteenth and nineteenth centuries, and chiefs and kings lost their legitimacy through the decline of the central states, new "insignia" and symbols of power proliferated to augment lo-cal authority. The impact of colonialism, war, and epidemics on fertility and the acute population decline encouraged midwives in certain western regions of Kongo to organize cults such as Pfemba, which specialize in fertility and birthing medicines and magic.[37] Diviner-consultants called *upons* are at the heart of the health-care system of the Batammaliba or Gar-speaking peoples in the Atacora mountains of Tambera, northern Togo, and Benin. These diviners connect communities, individuals, and families with sources of power to se-cure answers to their troubling medical and social problems. They diagnose causes of psychological, spiritual, and social problems and prescribe means of resolution. In the course of his field research in Togo and Benin, it became clear to Rudolph Blair that diviner-consultants serve as important "pastoral guides" who redefine, reexplain, and reinterpret the core cultural dimensions of their society. "These consultants must be understood not only as spiritual guides for troubled individuals but also as interpreters and annunciators of the community's main cultural values"[38] and mores.

African divination is a channel of human-divine communication and one of the primary ways of bringing order out of crisis and chaos. It is often the only institutional means by which most West Africans articulate their theory of knowledge of the world and the spirits. The idea that humans can know the real causes of all effects pervades African culture, but ordinary or mundane ways of seeking this knowledge are inadequate for revealing deep secrets. As a result, specialists employ divination to ensure that all pertinent information is considered before one takes an action. Because most diviners are also herbal-ists and medicine men, the diagnostics and methods of treatment they employ are also invaluable to the study of traditional healing systems.[39] Although divi-nation does not deal solely with the manifestations of religious beliefs, a sacred cosmology forms its kernel. According to Janzen, "Divination and diagnosis al-ways accompany rituals, either independent of the healing role or as a part of the specialized techniques and paraphernalia of a particular cult."[40] The divi-natory system of the Yoruba and Fon ascribes divination to Orunmila, a divin-ity also known as Ifa, the source of wisdom. A Yoruba legend traces divination back to the mythic city of Ile-Ife, the birthplace of many orishas and great lead-ers. Another legend common among the Atuot of the Sudan and the Lobi of Burkina Faso has it that improper human behavior disrupted the originally harmonious world, and therefore God punished humans with ignorance, sick-ness, and death,[41] which then required divinatory works to set right.

Evans Zuesse identifies several basic forms of divination in the modern world, among which three general types are not uncommon in Africa and the Caribbean: (1) In intuitive divination, the diviner spontaneously knows a situa-tion or the future. (2) In possession divination, spiritual beings communicate with humans through intermediary agents. This may involve a range of divina-tory practices—divination by arbitrary movements of heavenly bodies; divination by fire, water, and the throwing of objects; or divination by observation of the flight of birds. Divination by body twitching or pain, by "judicial ordeal," by dreams and glossolalia, and by "full mediumism or oracle trance" are crucial to possession divination. (3) In wisdom divination, which involves divination by body forms and mathematical correspondence or numerology, the diviner decodes impersonal patterns of reality. This type of divination claims to be a science. According to Zuesse,

> Much of science itself has evolved from forms of divination and may be said to continue certain aspects of it. Astronomy, for example, is deeply indebted to ancient Near Eastern and Hellenistic astrological researches; mathematics and physics were advanced by Indian, Pythagorian, and Arabic divinatory cosmological speculations. . . . Yet it would be incorrect to label divination a mere infantile science or pseudoscientific magic, for modern science and traditional divination are concerned with essentially distinct goals.[42]

A sophisticated system of divination known as *bokomo*, probably originating from the Yoruba and controlled by the professionals, allows individuals to know their decreed destiny, which can be altered only by special divine oracle. African diviners are not charismatic charlatans who use clever manipulative esoteric knowledge to coerce a people already driven by anxiety and distress, as some might claim. Diviners take their work seriously because clients will hold them responsible if they divine recklessly. If a diagnosis is untrue or fails, the diviner is regarded as being only a human or having lost spiritual power, is called a deceiver, and loses his or her credibility in the community. Several methods are used during a consultation to judge the efficacy of the advice, and most communities have a system for certifying the veracity of a divination. In some cases, family advisers in Togo and Benin go to different consultants to get confirmation on the consultation-advice they received; they check it against advice given by other consultants from one village to another. When one advice contradicts that received from others, it is considered suspicious.[43]

Would-be diviners undergo long and intense periods of training; Yoruba diviners train for a minimum of ten years in various branches of knowledge in Ifa divination.[44] A trainee first serves in informal ways as an apprentice under the watchful supervision of an experienced diviner who has already established a reputation in the community for knowing how the *jao* (the "powers") work and is be able to deal effectively with them. To mark an apprentice's understanding of the *jao*, his teacher performs a ritual during which a goat is sacrificed to the powers. Without this sacrificial rite, the initiate will not gain the ability to discern or see things like a *jok*. Only after the initiate comes to understand the "ways of powers" is he or she able to perform rituals of divination and exorcism. As specialists, diviner-consultants are expected to be "supergeneralists"—that is, to know a range of issues pertinent to their consultations. In the course of their training, they draw expertise from situations of illnesses, and their prescribed treatments come from a wealth of knowledge related to physiology, medicine, psychology, and social, political, historical, and cultural factors.[45]

Magic and Medicine

Magic

Imagine living in a remote village on the northern reaches of Ghana two hundred miles from the nearest medical center in Kumasi. Your four-year-old falls gravely ill at midnight and you have no transportation for the four-hour drive into the Asante capital. Your only recourse may well be homemade herbal medicine or the local medicine man and priest. Magic and medicine or healing play such important roles in ATRs and are so intertwined that distinguishing between them and isolating them from religion itself are almost impossible. Although in much of the Western world magic is equated with superstition and sleight of hand for public entertainment, in many societies it forms an integral part of religion and human behavior. Magic, as a means of affecting human fate at the hands of the gods by controlling "natural and cosmological orders,"[46] is as old as religion itself, and its use in Africa and primal world cultures is still current. All peoples have magic—magic is manifold: so-called black magic, white or natural magic, and magic for the exorcism and the evocation of spirits. Some of these attempt to manipulate that which the gods control, without making proper supplication for intervention by the deity. In this sense, magic depends more on art and practice than on divine aid. That is, the efficacy of magic is based on the correct performance of a special ritual technique, one in which the language, order of the ritual, and reasons for the actions involved do not have to be understood or believed by the client.[47]

Magic is an art form and a spiritual law in which certain actions or words done in a certain way will result in a known effect. Scholars have found three basic principles that govern the ways in which the art works in ATRs: the principles of similarity, contiguity, and unusualness. (1) Similarity is based on the notion that "like produces like"; that is, a similarity exists between the performance of an act and the result expected and desired. (2) Contiguity centers around the idea that once things are in contact with one another, they can continue to interact, even if the contact is broken. Magic of this type is done by processing an object that belongs to or once was in contact with the person at whom the spell is directed; such objects include a favorite material possession, a personal effect, or even the earth in which a footprint is embedded. (3) The principle of unusualness involves a combination of unrelated actions and words in order to make a protective spell or to ward off evil. According to these three principles of magic, naming something, or knowing the true name of an object, creature, or spirit, allows one to control it.[48]

Africans have magic to deal with many problems in life. Wande Abimbola says that among these types of magic are *madarikan* magic that protects people from their enemies; *ajeppo* magic that enables someone to vomit ingested poison; and *ajera* magic that renders the poison harmless. "Then we have *ogun awon agba* magic that neutralizes the effect of the witch; *awure* magic that effects good luck; *ataja* magic that helps sales; *iferan* magic that makes everyone love one another; and *awijare* magic that enables one to win a case."[49] As Bolaji Idowu notes, magic makes no moral demands and can function automatically and inexorably with any operator, once he performs it correctly. Since the performance of magic does not concern itself with particular moral values, it is practiced as both good and bad magic, the latter being used for evil purposes. Destructive magic, sometimes called black magic, is defined as that which works against society or merely for the self-interest of the practitioner or client. This magic is performed mostly without social approval and is deemed illegitimate, although it may occasionally work for the good of the community.[50]

Well known throughout the African world are two types of destructive magicians: sorcerers and witches, entities defined as living outside a society's norms. Their magic may not always be undesirable, but they are seen as antisocial, nonconformist, strange, mystical, and scary. This mystical scariness and nonconformity enhance the magic power of African witches and sorcerers. Sorcerers are usually perceived as being male, whereas witches are regarded as female, stereotypes that are not uniquely African. Sorcerers intentionally use destructive magic for their own purposes or against others. Their work may take the form of casting an illness on someone, the cause of which is determined through magic-science or the efforts of a medicine man who advises the ill on how to placate the sorcerer. Often, when death results from the sorcerer's work, the sorcerer is punished by exile or death.[51] A distinction should be made between the learned art of witchcraft and popular notions of witches and sorcerers like Cruella DeVille, Harry Potter, and Sabrina the teenage witch, all to some extent figments of Hollywood's imagination. Like the Haitian *lugbawoo* ("vampire"), witches of our time are created by society on the basis of some flawed perception. Other witches are self-made, especially among those who follow the occult.

As is true of their Caribbean counterpart, most Africans feel a level of discomfort with the knowledge that there is destructive magic and witchcraft in their community. To them, anyone who turns to these art forms to rectify grievances is out of sync with the rest of society. According to Janzen, these are agents of power "responsible for inaugurating positions of authority and healers who treat mental or bodily illness: They use esoteric codes relating the visible realm of plants and substances and apply them to the invisible realm of emotions, society, and the beyond."[52] Among the Fon-Ewe, various kinds of magical charms (*gbo*), allegedly given by the divinities Legba and Sagbata, are the most popular sorcerer's divinatory corrective means in the community.

A wide assortment of items from plants, animals, and personal effects feature among the paraphernalia of witchcraft and sorcery[53] and are part of traditional medicine (TM).

Traditional Medicine

TM is a way of life for millions of people around the world who have no health providers. The Ghanaian physician Kofi Appiah-Kubi reported that most of the 750 million Africans have poor or no health care; more than 100 million have no access to even good drinking water. Statistics on epidemics and starvation are staggering; in some places, the infant mortality rate is as higher as 80 percent, and life expectancy is much shorter than in Western countries.[54] Families with life-threatening health problems, especially in remote rural areas, turn to the local medicine men or traditional healers (herbalists, priests, diviners, and magicians) for help. So the use of TM in Africa is very existential and practical, a matter of life and death. Protective medicine is an important complement to preventive medicine and health improvement. Janzen observes that medicine cult networks in West Africa also "arose to buttress regional market and alliance structures and to protect those who were involved in the trade from the envy of their subordinates. Lemba, the great medicine of markets and government," and "Nkita, an ancient medicine of lineage fragments," used TM "to restore authority and ties to ancestors."[55] Kongo prophetess Kimpa Vita (Dona Beatrice) rose to national prominence during the long succession crisis in the eighteenth century, and after being accused by the misguided Capuchin missionary Bernardo da Gallo, tragically was executed on heresy charges for reviving African traditional religious health practices.[56]

Africans see no problems in complementing medical science with the application of magic and TM. It is just another way, and too often the only way, of helping people secure healing—a view of pharmacology that persists in Afro-Caribbean religions. In recent times, several African governments have had to collaborate with traditional healers to address the acute need of bringing medical provisions to people in remote villages. Among the most successful of these collaborations has been a project by the government of Ghana in Tetchemon, Buno, in which traditional healers are educated on how to better use their craft in conjunction with modern medicine to solve a national medical crisis. This successful project has benefited modern medicine and traditional healing and is now being replicated in other African countries. Of a healing ceremony in Botswana and Namibia, for example, Benjamin Ray says, "The healer, in trance, goes to the gods or ancestors responsible for the arrow of illness and intercedes on behalf of the victim. The healer lays hands on the ill people gathered at the dance and if the intercession is successful, they get well. If it is not, the illness persists or gets worse."[57] A local woman Kung healer in Botswana gave this explanation of trance healing:

It is in trance that the healing power works. . . . You touch people, laying on hands, carrying those you touch. When you finish, other people
hold you and blow around your head and your face. . . . My father had
the power to cure people with trance medicine, with gemsbok-
song trance medicine. Certain animals—gemsbok, eland, and giraffe—
have trance songs named after them, songs long ago given by God.
These songs were given to us to sing and to work with. That work is
very important and a good work; it is part of how we live."[58]

The function of traditional healers is threefold: counselor, healer, and
herbalist. The medicine men (*eloogun*) are specialists who, because of their
training, experience, spiritual gifts, and knowledge of herbal plants and other
healing "media," prescribe and treat illnesses and diseases and attempt to remedy other personal tragedies. Medicine men must cure, alleviate, and prevent
diseases as well as restore and preserve health. These healers also divine the
causes of ailments and even death. They are concerned with misfortune caused
by the ill will or ill action of one person against another, usually through witchcraft, sorcery, or Obeah. They provide aid to infertile women, take preventive
measures to ward off the evil eye, and right wrongs caused by mystical evil
powers. Medicine specialists treat deadly snake and insect bites with special
herbs. Their medicines can also harm or kill and warn of impending danger. In
Africa, many illnesses are blamed not on malignancy or disease but on an evil
magic. If such sickness is fatal, an individual or an agent, rather than a disease,
is blamed for the death. Traditional healers have a wide range of healing paraphernalia: herbal plants or "sacred leaves of grass," special roots and barks of
trees, kola nuts, fruits, powders, bones, seeds, roots, minerals, and liquids. These
healing medicines are used to treat disease or illness and involve "medicaments"
as well as prophylactic measures.[59]

Traditional healers do not view their work in isolation from everyday life
and take great pains preparing a "potion" for a case. As Appiah-Kubi says, when
completed, their medicine is infused with supernatural powers: "The person
who is to wear a ring or an amulet, or he who is to apply a black powder into the
incised portion of his body, or use a soap to bathe," does so with incantations
that "imbue the medicinal preparation with power. . . . Because of the powers
inherent in these medicinal preparations, anyone who uses them has to observe certain taboos"[60] related to health, cleanliness, sex, and foods. TM is
used also to prevent things from happening, or to bring certain events into being. Medicine designed to bring good luck, aid one in a quest, or offer protection from natural disaster takes the form of charms in which the medicine resides. The nature of these charms and the means by which they are produced
follow the principles of magic and are performed through specific rituals.

As is true of diviners, not everyone can become a medicine man; Africans
say the profession must be inherited from a relative, received via a "call" from
an orisha or ancestor, or be a specially endowed gift. No set rules govern this

call; it comes to the young, single, and restless as well as to the mature, settled, and wise "elder." But the "called" must be morally upright, trustworthy, and amiable and must devote much time to their clients. Their knowledge of an illness and the medicine's power to cure it are said to come from God. Since the medicine man or woman often embodies the offices of priest, medical healer, magician, herbalist, diviner, and medium, he or she becomes a very important and powerful figure in the community. This traditional doctor or healer "claims to have supernatural powers and considers himself as the agent of the divine healer who works through him. Unlike the traditional priest who is more or less confined to the parameters of the shrine, the medicine man is mobile and works in odd places at odd times. Many diseases related to psychological and other mental disorders that cannot be treated in modern African hospitals are said to be cured with herbal medicine in homes of the African traditional healers.[61]

Cultural Significance

Colonialism, the slave trade, massive demographic dislocation, foreign religions—especially Christianity and Islam—and the cultural modernism of the twentieth century have had a significant impact on the decline in traditional religions in Africa.[62] Mbiti shows that in 1900, ATRs were practiced by 58 percent of the population, by far the largest percentage on the continent; Islam claimed 32 percent; and Christianity came a distant third with 9.2 percent, while other faiths had less than 1 percent. In 1972, the number of Muslim and Christian converts were equal. By 1984 Christians numbered 234 million (45 percent), Muslims 211 million (41 percent), followers of ATRs 63 million (12 percent), and other religions 7 million followers (2 percent). A 1994 survey classified 70 million Africans as followers of traditional religions.[63] Although African peoples often claim dual religious allegiance for cultural, political, and other reasons, the biggest loser in this statistics is obvious. Abimbola estimates that the Yoruba religion lost approximately 40 percent of its followers during the latter half of the twentieth century but could still claim about 60 percent of Nigeria's population.[64] These religions and cultures, however, continue to affect African thought and life at home and abroad. African traditional religious practices have been retained even among persons who embrace Islam and Christianity, and they continue to play an important role in African cultural festivals. More than 40 percent of Christians and 35 percent of all Muslims in Nigeria attend the festivals honoring the local orisha. Yoruba medicine and magic still influence modern society, where even Muslims, Christians, and other peoples seek out local bush doctors and herbalists for cures for ailments and chronic problems;[65] in so doing, they contribute to the preservation of African cultural traditions.

The West African Ogun—who appeals to people across lines of nationality, ethnicity, and class—is another popular cultural icon in Western culture. Some Ogun symbols are international and appear in Hollywood, the media, on bumper stickers of taxicabs in Africa and the United States, in highway safety signs, on clothing, and in technology. Afro-Caribbean and American peoples use modern technology to perfect their Shango, Ogun, Vodou, and Candomble art. Yoruba motor vehicle drivers often carry a metal charm representing Ogun to guard against accidents and bring good luck. Approximately seventy million people worldwide either participate in, or are familiar with, myth and ritual performance associated with Ogun.[66] The fact that in 1974, "drivers of the Ibadan University Motor Transport system performed a sacrifice to Ogun in the presence of the Vice-Chancellor and a dozen or so of the other high officials of the university"[67] shows that education, politics, and culture recognize the power of this African religion. Ogun is more than a mythic orisha of iron and steel; he is a living cult with vast appeal in Africa and the West.

This chapter makes it clear that Yoruba, Kongo, Ashanti, and Fon-Ewe (Dahomey) religions and cultural traditions are the soul of Afro-Caribbean religions. Enslaved Africans who were removed to the New World took much of their religion with them. They brought Yoruba's Ifa divination system to many parts of the Americas, especially Cuba, where a strong community of Ifa priests thrived for centuries before they spread to other Caribbean and American communities as a result of the Cuban revolution. Today, the Ifa system of divination is very active in the Americas,[68] although in a creole form. This creolization of African religion is evident in the synchronizing of Catholicism and Vodou in Haiti, Macumba and Umbanda in Brazil, and Santeria in Cuba. In addition to the universal appeal of West Africa's Ogun cult, Yoruba drums, mask dancers, and other art—especially seen in the body marks of identity, well-being, and beautification—continue to influence the practice of Afro-Caribbean religions.

PART II

Vodou

Haitian Religion

3

Vodou and the Haitians' Struggle

What do Jean-Bertrand Aristide's picture on icons and religious altars, chromolithography of Catholic saints, ritual flags and crosses, pictures of a python, spirits riding horses, and a battery of ritual drums have in common? They are vehicles of Vodou, the religion that, up until the early twentieth century, claimed the majority of Haitians as adherents. Versions of an incredulous and comical, but popular, folklore claim that Haitians were "100 percent Catholics and 90 percent vodouisants,"[1] or 15 percent Protestants, "95 percent Catholic and 150 percent Voodoo."[2] None of the cynical hyperboles could have ever been true of Haiti in the past, and Christianity has become the religion of choice for most Haitians in the twenty-first century. The myth, however, points to Vodou's prevalence in the history of Haiti and the dominance of Christianity in the land of Dambala (Danbala).[3] Historically, the country has clung to the traditions of two worlds: the world of Western Roman Catholic religiosity (and more recently Protestant Christianity) and the world of African traditional religion (ATR), amalgamating several different traditions into one religion called Vodou.

Vodou has been as tenacious and indomitable as its warrior deity *Ogun* and the spirit of the Haitian people; it remains the most publicized and notoriously stereotyped of Afro-Caribbean religions. This notoriety results from Vodou's status as the most despised religion in the Americas; it is vilified for its alleged cabal of evil practices. Just mention the word "Vodou" and the American mind conjures up any number of sensational images: deadly "black" or evil magic, the sticking of poisonous pins in dolls, satanic rituals, gross sacrifices of humans, zombies, hex-casting witchcraft, demonic spells, infamous human-preying zombies, blood-sucking vampires, and African cannibalism. In the United States,

Veve of Legba, guardian of crossroads and intersections.
(Illustration by Kelly Hawes.)

the terms *Voodoo economics* and *Voodoo politics* represent a sinister or phony political program and fiscal irresponsibility. Will the real Vodou be allowed to stand up in the United States?

Meanings of Vodou

This religious phenomenon inherited many designations: *vodou, vodu, voudou, vodoun, voodoo,* and *hoodoo,* among others, some of which are preferences for linguistic equivalences but others of which say more about users' perceptions of Vodou than about the religion. Non-Haitians often use the words *voodoo, hoodoo,* and *vodun* as pejorative equivalents of sorcery, magic spells, witchcraft, and other features of what arguably is a less sociable side of African religions. Therefore a traditional view is that Vodou is "an African form of [magic] and witchcraft mixed with New World elements, complete with the ruling mother goddess, a pantheon of lesser deities, a psychic ritual and a manipulative world-view."[4] Until recently, *voodoo* was an accepted spelling of the word, but Haitians and modern scholars acknowledge *Vodou* as the historically correct term for the religion; it is preferable because it is seen as phonetically more correct than many of the other terms used for the religion. Vodou is African derived and represents several different African religious traditions. The French savant Mederic Louis Elie Moreau de St.-Mery, who lived in Saint Domingue between 1780 and 1790 and is credited with calling the religion Vaudoux, believed it owes its origin to "the serpent cult" of Dahomey and the kingdom of Arada on the slave coast.[5] In Togo and the Fon-Dahomey language from which the word *Vodou* originated, it means many things: serving the spirits, sacred objects, a set of divinities, and "an invisible force, terrible and mysterious."[6] A vodou is a pantheon of deities as well as the spirituality and rites developed around, and devoted to, those spirits. *Vodou* also refers to one of the ritual dance styles, or rhythmic patterns and movements, that bring the community in sync with the spirits in a progressive and mutual relationship of experience and fullness.

Some attempts to understand the close relationship between the divine and the physical world in Vodou have labeled the religion "animistic." However, although symbols and objects may represent its pantheon of gods, Vodou does not make those objects gods or see a spirit in every gourd tree. Additionally, Vodou is neither a mere belief in ghosts and zombies, as critics have suggested, nor a route of escape from the misery of life in Haiti to the world of fantasy and mythic beings. One will also do a great disservice to Vodou by viewing its intellectual core through the theological lenses of Christian dogmas and by attempting to explain the relationships that exist among the divinities in the Vodou pantheon with the same rational reasoning used to debate Christian dogma on God. Vodou has a historical substance and function; its historic emergence in Haiti is concomitant with the Haitian revolution and is a symbol of the Haitian struggle,[7] but it is a living spirituality with multiple purposes. As Karen Brown puts it, Vodou is "an African-based, Catholic-influenced religion that serves three, not always clearly distinguished, categories of spiritual beings: *lemo, lemiste,* and *lemarasa* (respectively, 'the dead,' 'the mysteries,' and 'the sacred twins')."[8] I will add only the word *Caribbean* to Brown's apt description.

Vodou in the Caribbean has features distinct from ATRs. As Joan Dayan says, Vodou preserves a core of beliefs in the "ritual enactment of Haiti's colonial past"; the people reconstructed and preserved their own traditions that were "ignored, denigrated, or exorcized by the standard 'drum and trumpet' histories of empire,"[9] but that are kept alive in their dance of life. The religious ethos of this dance is partly a struggle for life and liberty, Haitian cultural identity, and African belief in God and spiritual forces to battle human suffering and misery where unemployment can reach heights of 80 percent and the poor masses are like the wretched of the earth. In the painful conditions of life in Haiti, Vodou enables its followers to deal with historical and contemporary realities of Haitian society by relating the sacred and the profane to their difficult dance of life. In their religious dance, devotees serve the lwa ("divine spirits") through rites and rituals for healing, spiritual guidance, and survival. Vodou encompasses a variety of complex religions "with complicated rituals and symbols that have developed for thousands of years."[10] The rituals and practice of Vodou throughout Haiti show such variations that one might even speak of the Vodou religions. This divine-human system of relationship is "spiritually wired" in a belief system that is orchestrated in ceremonies and in practices that represent various forms of Vodou called *nantions* ("nations"), which existed in colonial Haiti[11] but originated in West and Central Africa.

The aim of Vodou is not to cause hexes, inflict pain on helpless victims, and propagate evil in the world, as portrayed in horror movies and the media, but to counteract evil actions and forces with ashe, or spiritual power. Haiti has many *wangas* and *gardes*, objects that could channel invisible forces in aggressive ways; some Haitians believe spirits may even be the source of this aggression. However, Vodou is concerned with developing relationships with the spirits through a system of beliefs and practices that seek to give meaning to life. As Leslie Desmangles explains, "It uplifts the spirits of the downtrodden who experience life's misfortunes, instills in its devotees a need for solace and self-examination, and relates the profane world of humans to that of incommensurable mythological divine entities called *lwas* who govern the cosmos."[12] This religious phenomenon developed in the plantation culture of French colonialism in Saint-Domingue, formerly Spanish Santo Domingo, and remains a powerful religious force in Haiti today.

Vodou is sheltered in the mountainous 10,724-square-mile western third of Saint Domingue, the northern shores of which battle the forbidding Atlantic Ocean as if to keep it out of the more peaceful Caribbean Sea. At the same time, the island's windward peninsula lengthens its jaw westward as if poised like a great fish to swallow its much larger neighbor, Cuba. The Haitian people have "swallowed" much tribulation, not from Cuba, but from their own Haitian leaders, European nations, and the Americans. Once the Pearl of the Antilles— one of the richest countries in the world per capita, a showcase of French culture in the 1700s, and every superpower's dream—Saint Domingue became Haiti, the first self-determined country of creole peoples but the poorest sovereignty in the West and, for about two hundred years, an erstwhile demonized enemy of Europe and the United States.[13]

Haiti's fall from riches to rags was not caused by Vodou's "evil black magic," as is alleged. Vodou has also been in the United States since the days of slavery, but it did not impoverish the creole peoples of the Gulf states and New York; if nothing else, it enriched New Orleans' creole culture. Haiti's poverty is the result of its battle against slavery, its history of suffering as an independent nation, its isolation from the economic community by superpowers, and its self-destruction. It is part of a history of corruption and the abuse of political power by its affluent creole minority population, fiscal and agricultural irresponsibility, and mistreatment of natural resources, especially as seen in Haiti's careless deforestation. The bad press that Vodou and Haiti received from the West, the political alienation they experienced from the U.S. government, and the crippling stereotypes they sustained in popular cultural discourse are gigantic hurdles in the Haitian people's marathon for dignity, economic development, and preservation of their creole culture.

Vodou and Freedom's Fight

The Haitian struggle began as early as the residents' first arrival in Hispaniola from different parts of West Africa (Fulas, Polards, Bambarras, Mandingos, Fon-Dahomey, Ibo, Kongo, Yoruba, and other African nations). The Spanish were convinced that Africans were a better alternative to the rapidly disappearing natives enslaved on *encomiendas*, a precursor to the slave plantation, and made trading in African slavery legal. Spain did not develop large-scale plantations on the island, so the number of arrivals remained relatively small until the western third of Santo Domingo was ceded to France at the Treaty of Ryswick in 1697. During the next century, France made its new colony, Saint-Domingue, one of the world's most profitable sugar producers and a supplier of the lion's share of France's gross national product. Eric Williams and others report that Saint-Domingue's "exports in 1788 amounted to 31,350 tons of clayed sugar, 41,607 tons of brown sugar, 2,806 tons of cotton, 30,425 tons of coffee, [and] 415 tons of indigo," valued at 193 million livres, or eight million pounds, at the time. The colony operated 800 sugar, 3,000 coffee, 800 cotton, and 2,950 indigo plantations. Half of Europe got its tropical goods from Saint-Domingue. To maintain this thriving plantation economy, French planters imported between 865,000 and 1,300,000 Africans as slaves.[14]

Resistance to Colonialism

In colonial Saint Domingue, planters sought to maximize profits and minimize the possibility of slave revolts by resorting to a rigid system of control to ensure slave compliance. This included the constant use of capital punishment under harsh working conditions, poor nutrition and shelter, and sixteen- to eighteen-hour workdays. The harsh realities of slavery reduced slave survival to only about seven years on the plantation, and abridged the average life span of a slave to thirty years. Although the French brought well over nine hundred thousand Africans to the colony in their one-hundred-year rule, at the beginning of the Haitian Revolution fewer than five hundred thousand Africans were in Saint Domingue, an estimated two-thirds of whom were African-born.[15] Not only were family, communal, and linguistic bonds broken by the act of enslavement, but once slaves were in the colony, concerted efforts were made to rid them of any vestige of their African heritage and to remake them into compliant cogs in the wheel of the colonial machinery. For almost two hundred years, French Catholics attempted to teach slaves "Christian civilization" and to stamp out Vodou's "paganism." Vodou meetings were banned, and violations were severely punished under both state and canon laws, which collaborated to rid Haiti of alleged pagan practices. The Catholic Church required planters to provide Christian education as stipulated under the *Code Noir* (Black Code) of 1685, allegedly designed for the protection of slaves' rights. The code demanded that all slaves be baptized, receive instruction in the Catholic faith, attend Sunday Mass and confession, and renounce the practice of outlawed Vodou.

The constant fear of slave revolts resulted in subsequent regulations in 1758 and 1777 to impose limitations on the movements of slaves, ban drumming and dancing, and proscribe their assembly. Slaves were prohibited from meeting without a Catholic priest in attendance and from gathering near their master's home or in remote places.[16] Infractions were met with harsh and often deadly penal measures, which forced the practice of African religion underground until the 1790s. The clandestine operations made it difficult to tell exactly when Vodou began in Haiti; reports of secret meetings with "dances, funeral practices, and even trance possession among enslaved and freed Africans indicate that they preserved ancient traditions in the face of enormous obstacles."[17] Evidence of this are found mainly in scattered eighteenth-century colonial reports, ordinance codes, a few unsympathetic and biased personal musings, and in monographs on the Haitian revolution. George Eaton Simpson states that between 1780 and 1790, when slave importation to Hispaniola was increasing, Vodou emerged "with a gradual ascendancy of Fon ideas. Finding the rites useful for their cause, revolutionary leaders in the last decades of the eighteenth century and the early years of the nineteenth century brought about a . . . synthesis"[18] of African religious ideas in Haitian creole culture. Given the importation of the Congolese as slaves into the colony, however, Kongo religious ideas would have already been part of the emergent faith.

In the repressive plantation society, Africans nurtured the desire for both physical and cultural freedom. They employed whatever means were available to preserve and perpetuate their sense of self. Ignoring the interdiction and condemnation of their religious practices, they sneaked into the bushes during the night to perform their Vodou rituals and dances in small gatherings. These gatherings not only preserved African religious traditions and cultural identity, they also served to establish a communal bond among oppressed peoples with diverse backgrounds. Coerced into Christianity through forced conversion in segregated parishes, the slaves learned the art of pursuing their African religious practices in the penumbra of French Catholicism. Of course, the real conversion was not that of Africans to Christianity but that of elements of Catholicism to buttress African spiritual reality[19] and resist oppression; some slaves also had contacts with the Catholic heritage back in the Kongo, even before the Atlantic slave trade began in the 1500s.

Resistance communities created a pan-Haitian creole identity among the ʲous ethnic groups represented on the slave population. The need to present a ˆ ʲnt in their common cause led to the sharing of knowledge and the forg- ʲmmon culture. Incorporating the myths, rituals, and practices of various ethnic groups, slaves invented a culture around Vodou and a creole language as their most efficient means of communication. This creole culture and language came to reflect the spirit of resistance in the Haitian revolution and the harshness of the circumstances in which it was forged. Vodou still bears this element of outrage in the fiery *petwo* (*petro*) spirits of the lwa (divinities) who emerged in the crucible of the Haitian struggle for freedom. With its West and Central African spirituality existing side by side with French Catholicism, Vodou became the axis mundi of the black community in Haiti.

Vodou in the Revolution

The Maroon-Vodou collaboration was pivotal at the outbreak of the Haitian Revolution, and Vodou became "the symbol of Haitian autonomy and nationalism as the only black republic in the Americas"[20] in 1803. Boukman Dutty, a founder of the revolution, was a Maroon leader and Vodou priest, or *papaloi*, with an imposing physical stature. He was also known as Zamba. On August 22, 1791, he and an elderly priestess, described as an aged African woman with gruesome eyes and "briskly hair," almost as forbidding as her counterpart, presided at a *petro* (type of spirit) ceremony in a heavily wooded reserve called Bois-Caiman, which served as a catalyst for the revolution. Boukman used the warlike petro spirit of Vodou to organize, plan, and give the signal that began the revolt, which became bigger than his Maroon slave uprising itself. Legend has it that the elder priestess, possessed by Africa's *Ezili Kawoulo*, lwa of lightening and thunder, sacrificed a pig and presented the blood to all those assembled while Boukman enjoined them to pledge to resist slavery to the death.[21] Historian Carolyn Fick relates that Boukman was "a *commandeur*" and a coach on the Celement plantation, one of the first plantations consumed in the flames of the revolt. Although the social and cultural components of the Vodou ceremony held at Bois-Caiman are not very clear, "African religious elements characteristic of Saint-Domingue voodoo in a broader composite sense, especially the petro rites, certainly predominate: the sacrificial pig, the drinking of its blood, the militaristic atmosphere and call to arms, the vow of secrecy, and the invocations of the gods."[22] There, the spirit of resistance that Vodou embodied gushed forth in waves of violent rage, which produced the most successful slave rebellion led by blacks in the history of human civilization.

In spite of Vodou's pivotal contribution to the revolution, the religion suffered repression from the political leadership that emerged from the liberation struggle. The suppression was motivated by a morbid fear, among Haitian leaders, of the insurgent potential of an angry Vodou mob.[23] The political elite that arose from the revolution knew too well the danger and power of slave discontent as well as the potent force of Vodou ritual. Furthermore, the diffusive nature of Vodou made it difficult, if not impossible, for the new leaders to control it by institutional means. The political and social elite also were concerned about the negative image the outside world had of Haiti—an image due partly to the perceptions of Vodou as primitive and satanic and partly because of the black revolution itself. After Haitians wrested their freedom in "a ritual of blood" that shocked the world, Europeans and Americans judged the presence of the first black republic in the Americas as a political pariah rather than as the rise of a sovereign republic.

Until the late 1900s, this sentiment generated an anti-Haitian culture and "black scare" that besmirched Afro-Haitian traditions for years to come. The anti-Vodou culture became so pervasive that it transformed into loathing; many of Haiti's presidents between 1807 and 1942, although black or mulatto, worked in league with the Catholic Church either to stamp out "evil" African Vodou culture in Haiti or to trivialize it as folklore and "politicize the religion through co-option of its leaders."[24] On the other hand, despite the collapse of the Haitian Catholic Church in the wake of the revolution and the Vatican's continued refusal to acknowledge Haiti as an independent country, Haitian presidents embraced Catholicism as the national religion and sought to suppress Vodou in order to gain for Haiti international recognition and respect from the Vatican. It is noted that although Toussaint L'Overture's Constitution of 1801 granted freedom of conscience and worship to Haitians, it declared Roman Catholicism the only national religion.

Much to the chagrin of Jean-Jacques Dessalines and Jean-Pierre Boyer, two of Haiti's earliest leaders, their unpopular policies indirectly contributed to the entrenchment of Vodou in the rural areas. Seeking to revive Haiti's export economy, Dessalines—the merciless, vengeful, calculating, and deadly despot who ambushed and slaughtered Haitian whites when they emerged from hiding to accept his fake clemency—imposed a nationwide militarized agricultural program on the country. Former slaves were forced to work on the plantation under mulatto overseers and strict supervision from the government. Although they were, theoretically, free wage earners, the working conditions of the ex-slaves constituted slavery by a different name. To escape forced labor, pitiful wages, and appalling conditions, many blacks fled to the mountains and rural areas, where they engaged in subsistence farming and became ancestors of the emergent peasantry[25] and the preservers of Vodou. Alezandre Pétion later dismantled militarized agriculture, Dessalines' land grants to soldiers, and the renting of plots to the landless for subsistence farming.

In 1825, President Boyer agreed to pay France 150 million francs over a period of five years in return for France's recognition of Haiti's independence. His 1826 Code Rural also returned to mulattoes the land that belonged to them before the revolution. But Boyer's thirst for French recognition curried favor with mulattoes and the elite as he sought to pay his French obligation on the backs of the poor. His rural code again reduced poor Haitians to the status of slaves who were relegated to subsistence on marginal lands. Dayan argues that in Boyer's monarchy sustained by blood, "a small fraction of Haiti's population could live off the majority, collecting fees—with the help of their lackeys, the rural *chief de section*—for produce, for the sale, travel, and butchering of animals, and even for cutting of trees."[26] One result of this regimented state is that among the emerging peasantry in the rural areas, Vodou was relatively free to thrive and rivet itself in the psyche and lives of the people. President Boyer paid little attention to Vodou in the early years of his rule, but the penal code he enacted in 1835 named Vodou among the superstitions that were illegal.[27] Devotees who ignored the proscriptions against certain activities were either tortured or executed.

As Haitian as U.S. Apple Pie

Haitian leaders forgot that Vodou was as Haitian as apple pie is American—too Haitian and deeply entrenched in the culture and psyche of the nation to be silenced through military might. To root out Vodou, the government would have had to destroy the people and, by extension, obliterate itself. Furthermore, the revolution had wreaked havoc on the Catholic Church and left a religious void in the country. Several priests were killed, and many others fled to safety. Church properties sustained severe damage from the revolt's mayhem and vandalism. Uneducated and morally bankrupt Haitians were elevated to the priesthood with no training. Catholic traditions were compromised and the influence of the Church fell to an all-time low.[28] In descriptions of the 1845 struggle between the Church and Vodou, scholars tell of how confused social and religious life in Haiti become after 1804. Dayan writes, "African and European materials converged: bags with fetishes, human bones, and snakes were employed in Catholic rituals, while vodou practitioners, called 'freres,' carried out priestly functions and recited Catholic liturgy. The guyons, called 'loup-garous' . . . and reputed to be cannibals, were thought to carry human flesh in their *macoutes* (sacks)."[29] Vodou became the damned and dreaded religion corrupting Catholic Christianity.

Rodman makes the point that Dessalines' Constitution of 1805 drove a wedge between Church and state and made marriage a strictly civil contract. For the next fifty-five years, an open schism caused the Vatican to refuse to allow any of its priests to enter Haiti. As a consequence, although Catholicism persisted in the country, it was confused with folk religion. During the reign of president Faustin Soulouque (1847 to 1860), Vodou enjoyed a period of reprieve from repression and "rites of the heretical Church were scarcely distinguishable from the African ones."[30] In this atmosphere, Vodou thrived among the Haitian populace, although the elite—as well as most Africans—professed to be Catholics. Soulouque, a Vodou devotee, publicly encouraged the practice of the religion. Moreover, he provided a climate in which members of Haiti's elite could openly show their affinity to Vodou as part of black culture. The unfortunate overthrow of Soulouque, in 1860, marked the return of the campaign to suppress Vodou.

The new president, Fabre Nicolas Geffrard, and the Vatican resolved the conflicts between the state and the Church in the 1860 Concordat, thus opening the way for the Church's renewed influence in the life of the nation. One of their first objectives, however, was to stamp out Vodou, the "last vestiges of barbarism and slavery, superstition and its scandalous practices."[31] In tandem, the Church and the state carried out repeated campaigns in 1864, 1896, and 1912 that were aimed at rooting out Vodou from the society. During the U.S. occupations of Haiti (1915 to 1934 and 1940 to 1941), Vodou was again the object of repressive measures. In response to the *corvée*—the forced labor system employed by the U.S. marines in their program to build infrastructure—the peasants rose up in revolt, inspired by the country's spirit of resistance. The Marines blamed the rebellion on Vodou, whose leader, Charlemagne Péralte, wore the symbols of Ogun, the warrior lwa. The Marines' campaigns against the uprising were really a crusade against the practices of Vodou. In the aftermath of the U.S. occupation, the Haitian social, religious, and political elite collaborated in yet another effort to dislodge Vodou from Haitian peasant life. Again, Vodou was criminalized as a bunch of evil superstitions and its practices prohibited under penal threat.[32]

In 1941, as a last-ditch effort to destroy Vodou and its alleged demonic manifestations for good, president Elie Lescot's government and Catholic clergy waged an all-out "demon-hunt" war against Vodou, intent on saving the souls of Vodou devotees from eternal damnation. As Haitian writer Gerard Ferere notes, Church and state prepared to celebrate their religious victory in a huge bonfire, destroying irreplaceable folklore treasures such as vast pyramids of drums and painted utensils of many descriptions, including necklaces, talismans, and other Vodou paraphernalia. The anti-Vodou campaigns included the confiscation and destruction of Vodou objects, especially drums; the razing of Vodou temples; the felling of supposedly sacred Mapou trees; and the interrogation and imprisonment of Vodou devotees. The following year, getting wind of a political backlash for destroying the religion of its populous support, the government was forced to discontinue its futile crusade of terror. Haitian activist Jacques Roumain advocated tolerance of Vodou during the last three years of Lescot's presidency, until Dumarsais Estime, who succeeded Lescot, began a Vodou truce in 1946 that lasted for almost thirty years.[33]

President Estime belonged to the *noirist* indigenous movement, which saw the repression and deprecation of Vodou as part of an imperialist agenda to suppress blacks' spirit of resistance. *Noirists* advocated a reappraisal of Vodou as an authentic cultural tradition of the masses that should be preserved as the basis of Haitian nationalism. Since these *noirist* ideas helped fuel the development of strong cultural and national sentiments among Haitian intellectuals and the middle class, Vodou was released from political imprisonment and celebrated as the culture of the Haitian people. However, Vodou was "folklorized" with staged ceremonies, chants, and dances to entertain tourists and the urban elite. As a result, it was not given its rightful place as a living, viable religion in Haiti.

Duvalier's Vodou

François Duvalier, one of the founders of Haitian ethnology and an intellectual of the *noirist* movement, had a nauseating association with Vodou. He apparently was a *servitor* ("devotee") of the lwa, or an *'oungan* ("priest"); popular opinion considered his role a *bokor*, a priest who also engages in sorcery. Duvalier (Papa Doc) encouraged his rumored possession of spiritual powers by donning the red robe associated with sorcerers of Petwo spirit traditions and by assuming the personality of Baron Samedi, a feared lwa of the dead; Papa Doc's symbolic characteristically black outfit and dark glasses incarnated the lwa. Although an advocate of Haitian nationalism and black culture, he was interested only in co-opting and controlling Vodou, as he did also the army and the Catholic Church. He portrayed himself as the embodiment of Vodou powers to instill fear in the peasant class. He enlisted numerous Vodou priests in a secret police organization called the *Tonton Macoutes* (*Makout*), which used terror to eliminate the smallest inkling of opposition to his regime.[34] The despot's use of these henchmen as armed civilian militia to keep the Haitian army in check and to stave off a possible coup of his government was cowardly. Through his private lynch mob, he deceptively used Vodou to play on the Haitian people's deepest loyalties related to family relations, property, and ancestral heritage.

Among Papa Doc's *Makouts* were heads of large clans, local leaders, regular police officers, and well-known Vodou priests. The joining of forces between oungan and *Tonton Makout* to terrorize people was an absurdity and a sinister nightmare of the lowest order. Karen Brown said it best: "The stories of corruption, intimidation, and violence that surround the Makout make heavy irony of their identification with Kouzen Zaka, a gentle spirit whose power resides . . . in herbal knowledge. . . . These priest-soldiers . . . ran the gamut from assassins for hire to local leaders who used the added power of the Makout network to promote" their self-interests.[35] The downfall of Duvalier's regime and the exile of his son and heir, Jean Claude, in 1986, were followed by a backlash of terror against Vodou in general and its priests in particular. A *dechoukaj* (uprooting) ensued to rid Haiti of all persons believed to be in complicity with the horrors of the dictatorship of the Duvaliers. Because of the exploitation and co-option of Vodou in the regime, mobs were encouraged to murder Vodou priests and destroy their temples, sacred implements, and symbols.[36] But Vodou survived the *dechoukaj* of the mob and resurfaced to gain recognition as a special feature of Haitian culture, because its gods are immortal.

Some Church leaders openly condemned the violence perpetrated against Vodou devotees in the wake of the Duvalier regime's demise, and both progressive culturalists and Vodou priests formed organizations such as Zantray and Bòde Nasyonal to promote Vodou culture and defend it against assault.[37] Furthermore, freedom of religion was enshrined in the new Haitian constitution of 1987. Jean-Bertrand Aristide, elected president in 1990, supported this freedom of religion, allowing Vodou avatars to practice without political and religious reprisal. Aristide also enacted legislation in 2003 that once more made Vodou a legitimate and official religion of Haiti. As a result, a picture of Aristide appears among the icons surrounding Vodou altars; he may thus be destined to be lwa *genteel*. Vodou has traveled the long road through waves of repression, campaigns of terror, and ideological assaults, but for the moment it is celebrated for its contribution to Haitian culture, particularly in music and the visual arts, none of which is able to help the religion completely erase its sinister public representations.

A Sinister Heritage

Since the late 1700s, a large body of literature on Vodou[38] has developed, some of which reflects anti-Haitian culture. In 1797, an influential French traveler described Vodou as a most horrible mysterious cult, a weapon of terror and torment, and a religion that dupes devotees or robs them of their senses. In the nineteenth century, a view of Vodou as cannibalistic was taken to new heights when a story was fabricated that a girl named Claircine mysteriously disappeared in Port-au-Prince on December 27, 1863, because her wicked kidnappers sacrificed and ate her in a Vodou ceremony and were later prosecuted and shot for the heinous crime.[39] No evidence of this disappearance, prosecution, and shooting was found, yet the myth persists. By the 1880s, Haiti was regarded as a place of satanic rituals and was "the most ridiculous caricature of civilization in the world."[40] Sensational books like *Haiti or the Black Republic* (1884) by Spencer St. John and *The White King of La Gonave* by Faustin Wirkus blamed the backwardness of the country on sorcery, cannibalism, and human and animal sacrifices of Vodou. William Seabrook's *Magic Island* (1929) and Philippe Thoby-Marcelin and Pierre Marcelin's *The Beast of the Haitian Hills* (1946) exacerbated the negative view of Vodou: their reports of living-dead walking the streets in a dazed stupor were a source of much hype and stereotype on Vodou.[41]

Scholars[42] have documented the history of epithets heaped on Haiti in order to prove that Vodou is a deviant and devilish religion of a barbarous people from the "dark continent." During the U.S. occupation of Haiti (1915 to 1934), the demonizing of Vodou reached an all-time high. Haiti as the dark side and "heady substratum of Africa," a land of zombies, phantoms, blood-sucking vampires, sorcerers, walking headless corpses, cannibals, werewolves, and the burning of witches, colored U.S. news tabloids' sensational columns.[43] The movie *Ferris Beuller's Day Off*, with Ben Stein, and the popular James Bond film *Live and Let Die* exaggerated the "evil" of Vodou. *The Serpent and the Rainbow* turned Wade Davis's objective portrayal of the religion into a stereotypic depiction of evil and sorcery, as does the more recent film *The Believers*. To satisfy public fancy, pictures show "witches and sorcerers who, filled with hatred, attempt to inflict diseases or even death on unsuspecting victims by making wax wooden representations of them."[44]

In Hollywood and in tourist gift shops in Haiti, baby dolls are still stuck with long pins to demonstrate the spooky magic of Vodou. The simpleminded think this commercial creation originated in Haiti, but as Rene Benjamin explains, "One has only to read the history of France to know that the figurine, made of wood or wax, that was stabbed with a pin in order to kill the King or another person, was in use even before the discovery of Haiti. In fact, although this was current practice in Europe since the 13th century, its popularization in the Court of France was the work of Signor Costino Ruggieri of Florence, a protegé of Catherine de Medeci."[45] Haitian-born scholar Alfred Metraux contends that France's contribution to this magic-sorcery mythology is substantial: "A great many beliefs and practices in Haitian magic originated from Normandy, Berry, Picardy or ancient Limousin."[46] Sensational novels, as well as biased traveler's accounts, joined the media in painting a most sinister picture of Vodou. The U.S. government's effort to demonize Vodou has been unrelenting. During his fight for the presidency in 1980, George Bush, Sr. labeled Ronald Reagan's proposed policies "Voodoo economics" in his speech at Wheaton College in 1980, and at the capture and illegal trial of Panamanian President Manuel Noriega, whose only crimes against humanity was allegedly practicing "deadly Vodou."

Creolization of Vodou

Haitian Vodou is neither pure African nor American; it is creole, a recreation and blending of ATRs with Christianity and native Caribbean religions. Haitian Africologist Patrick Bellegarde-Smith states that "Vodou is a heteroclite compendium of many African cults 'rendered' in a Haitian historical and sociological context. It appears perhaps as the most creolized of African-centered systems in the Americas. Its liturgical language is Haitian (Creole), not Fon, Ewe, Yoruba, or Lingala. Cut off from the source of 'fresh' Africans . . . Vodou has become the least 'pure' of the new religions, neither Nago [nor] Kongo, yet African in its essence."[47] Even if Vodou may neither be the least pure nor the least African religion in the Caribbean, it is surely creole. Creolization, described as "the process of furnishing a home with imported objects arranged according to the peculiar tastes and needs of the new owner,"[48] germinated in the oppressive conditions of slavery and the need for Africans to adapt to their new French-Colonial environment. When they landed in Saint-Domingue, their lives had already changed and so too would their culture; before long, they would make Creole their linguistic heritage. Their prayers and rituals preserve fragments of West African languages, but the Creole language, with its

French-based vocabulary, became their primary means of communication and the language of their religion.[49] Therefore the birthing of Haitian culture among the slaves is the first stage in the creole-making process in Vodou.

Another important stage in the creole evolution is the fusion of the belief systems of the African ethnic groups brought to Haiti. Vodou, said to be a religion in process with a voracious appetite for swallowing other religious traditions in its path,[50] merged diverse religious and cultural elements. People from different ethnic backgrounds, languages, and customs all thrown together in the crucible of the plantation were able to forge a common identity and piece together their religion using various elements from African traditions. For example, Fon/Dahomey, Lemba, Kongo, and other African peoples combined their beliefs and practices with those of European Catholic folk myths about the saints, thus forming Haitian Vodou. In that cultural mix, religious elements from Fon-Dahomey and Kongo peoples became prominent in Vodou. The strength of Kongo influence was predicated on their numerical dominance and on their penchant for escaping and forming Maroon communities. Fon-Dahomean strength resulted from the highly developed religious system the people brought with them, the number of ritual experts among them, and their well-known tendency to exercise power over others.[51]

CARIBBEAN VODOU

Creolization was facilitated by the fact that the religious systems were open to cultural borrowing—a process already at work in Africa in the Dahomean adoption of Yoruba deities like Ifa and Fa. As Karen Brown explains, "It was a matter of habit. The African cultures from which the slaves were drawn had traditionally been open to the religious system they encountered through trade and war and had routinely borrowed from them."[52] Thus, slaves possessed the disposition for mutual facilitation. Various ethnic groups also shared a similar substratum or religious orientation and cultural outlook. Vodou's cultural tapestry includes Taino, Masonic, and other elements encountered in Haitian culture. The presence of Taino and Roman Catholic practices in Vodou shows that the creole process extends far beyond the fusion of elements from diverse African cultures. Although the Taino population was virtually decimated within a hundred years of the arrival of the Spanish and did not survive colonialism as a distinct ethnic group, whispers of their culture survives in the world of Vodou. For example, aspects of *Bawon Samd*—the powerful spirit of the family of lwa named Gedes, who rule over death and the cemetery—is traced to the Tainos' cult of the dead. Azaka or Papa Zaka, the beloved lwa of agriculture, emerged only in Haiti, and his name has been traced to several Taino farming words.[53] *Vèvés*, the sacred symbolic drawings representing the lwa and inviting them to appear in the *peristil* or sanctuary, may have been influenced as much by a Taino practice as by a West African one. It was once held that even the ritual symbolism of the priest's power as held in the *ason*, or sacred African-derived rattle, shows Taino influence.[54]

Vodou has several sects called *nanchons*, a few of which are indigenous to Haiti. Each of these sects carries the name of its most dominant pantheon.[55] Haitians infused their own heroes with spiritual powers peculiar to Haiti. As Dayan explains, "The lwa most often invoked by today's Vodou practitioners do not go back to Africa; rather, they were responses to the institution of slavery, to its peculiar brand of sensuous domination. A historical streak in these spirits, entirely this side of metaphysics, reconstitutes the shadowy and powerful magical gods of Africa as everyday responses to the white master's arbitrary power."[56]

In Vodou, Dessalines is referred to as both *lwa kreyol,* or "creole god," and *Ogou Desalin*, the god of war and revolution. Although he was assassinated and dismembered by his own people, the spirit of his ruthlessness lives potently in Vodou creole mythology. Other creole folklore heroes of the revolution are immortalized and given mythic standing in Vodou. Dayan records a story of Dedee Bazile, from Cap Francais, in northern Haiti, who marched with Dessalines and more than 25,000 troops in an assault on General Rochambeau's army that forced his surrender. At great risk, Bazile brought supplies to the many columns of troops and invigorated their spirits. Her indomitable spirit and actions, motivated by revenge for the rape she suffered at age eighteen from a white man, still lives on. As a result of Bazile's courage and daring, upon the death of Dessalines in 1806 she emerged under the heroic name of Defilee and "became the embodiment" of the Haitian victorious struggle. This is a distinctly creole political feature of Vodou.[57]

CATHOLIC VODOU

Creole Catholic elements in Vodou are visible in many forms, but their precise relationship is much debated. At issue is the question of whether Vodou syncretized African and Catholic elements to create a new religious phenomenon, or whether it is a totally African religion that uses Catholicism only as a means to distract its detractors. Syncretism implies the blending of different religious elements into an undifferentiated religion. Scholars who question whether that form of blending actually occurred claim that Africans used Catholicism only as a facade behind which they continued venerating their African spirits and ancestors;[58] the Catholic face of Vodou is just a veil that provided some measure of protection for its followers during periods of repression. Brown offers another interpretation she calls imitation and mimicry. Eighteenth-century slaves "incorporated mimicry of their masters into their traditional worship as a way of appropriating the masters' power. . . . On a broader canvas, this way of getting to know the powers that be by imitating them is a pervasive and general characteristic of all the African-based religions in the New World."[59] Desmangles argues that the relationship was a "symbiosis," the spatial juxtaposing and blending of the religious traditions from Africa and America that coexist without replacing one another.[60] The geographical proximity of Catholic churches to an ounfo ("temple") facilitated the spatial juxtaposition of Vodou and Catholic

Christianity. The Vodou *peristil* and the *pe*, at the center of the ounfo, also parallel the Catholic altar, as do symbols, crucifixes, lithographs of saints, missals, and other sacred objects.

Of the extensive Catholic influence on Vodou, the most readily observable falls into three categories: the Vodou pantheon, iconography, and liturgy.[61] A lwa has many manifestations and is often a collective entity for a family of spirits. Therefore incorporating Catholic saints into families of lwa, according to their traditional responsibilities, was an easy task. Closely tied to the saints-lwa synchronicity are the pervasive Catholic icons, especially chromolithographs. Vodou's sacred spaces are decorated with figures of Catholic saints among the numerous sacred objects. On the altar of Ezili Freda, a picture of the Virgin is displayed prominently, and on the altar of Ezili Dantò, the fiery, protective lwa of maternity, the Black Madonna and Child are similarly exhibited. Other sacred symbols of Catholicism, such as crucifixes and candles, occupy Vodou's visual topography; Catholic motifs, like colors and objects closely associated with saints, frequently appear on the sequined Vodou flags. Within Vodou ceremonies, elements of Catholic liturgy are evident in the lighting of candles, the use of holy water, the singing of hymns, and the presence of Latin words in the ritual language. Probably most significant is the ritual known as *Dyò*, with which all major ceremonies begin. Presided over by the *pretsavann*, an untrained Catholic (bush) priest whose role in the ritual is perfunctory, this series of incantations addresses "'Grand Père Eternal,' or God. It continues with the Lord's Prayer, the Hail Mary, and the Apostles' Creed, and goes on with an acknowledgment of all known male and female Christian saints."[62] As Karen Brown observes, the *pretsavann* emerged after the revolution when the Vatican refused to fill parishes in the new black republic. He gives Catholic prayers in French and Latin and sprinkles holy water on food, as well as on the tomb of the deceased[63]—a distinctly Haitian creole phenomenon.

In Vodou, African and Christian cultures are juxtaposed in the blending of two religious calendars. Enslaved Africans performed their ceremonies on major Catholic feast days: the ritual of purification in the Christmas cycle up to the Epiphany, and the Feast of all Saints, which falls on November 1, as a time to honor the spirits of departed ancestors. Elements of Catholicism in Vodou liturgy begin with the ritual calendar, which the adherents of Vodou follow in honoring the various lwa. The feast days of the saints double as *manje* lwa, the feast days of Vodou spirits. On Ash Wednesday, rites are observed in the service of the lwa, and during Holy Week, images of the lwa are sometimes covered in a manner similar to the covering of Catholic statues. This facilitates the symbiosis by identity in which, on the basis of similarities between Catholic and African myths and symbols, the spirits are identified with the gods of Vodou. Ezili, who finds her origins in the African goddess, carries the same name in Benin and Oshun (in Nigeria) as the creole Virgin Mary. Damballah, the python god in Benin, is Vodou's Saint Patrick; his mythic character is influenced by the Catholic myth of St. Patrick of Ireland triumphing over snakes.

Legba, the guardian spirit of destiny and the keeper of gates to the nether-world, doubles as creole Saint Peter. Bondye is both God and Christ, the fe-male spirit Oshun is Saint Mary, the *morassa* (spirit of the dead twins) are twin saints Cosmas and Damian, and Obatala is Saint Anne.[64]

SECRET VODOU SOCIETY

Another important influence on creole Vodou is Freemasonry, the world's larg-est secret society, whose strongest following is in North America and Britain. It traces its history to medieval Masonic guilds and the Grand Lodge organized in London in 1714. Freemasons hold to some Judeo-Christian beliefs but seek spiritual and psychological fulfillment "through a complex system of degrees correlated to a symbolic spiritual initiation advancing from darkness to full con-sciousness."[65] Africans appropriated the Masonic leadership title, "*Gran Mèt*" or "Grand Master," to refer to the Supreme Being, Bondye. Vodou priests have also appropriated the Masonic handshakes and secret passwords as a form of ritual greeting. This is not surprising, since many priests are also members of the brotherhood. Masonic symbols, such as the skull and crossbones and an all-seeing or universal eye, appear regularly in the iconography of Vodou. The most dramatic appropriation of Masonic symbols is the black outfit and top hat asso-ciated with Bawon Samdi, the persona of the lwa of cemeteries. Bawon Samdi and other lwa (Ogouè, for example) even occupy places of prominence in the Masonic brotherhood.[66]

Vodou thus has a multifaceted character and a fluidity that pervades its belief system and practices, together resulting in both heterodoxy and hetero-praxy. Beliefs and ritual styles differ from one region to another and from ounfo to ounfo ("church"). Vodou spirits are also adaptable to new situations; a spirit may manifest itself one way in one region and a different way in another. Variations in cultic practices and different kinds of spirits are also observed among families.[67] Dayan says that in spite of an apparent "capriciousness of spirits and terminologies, something incontrovertible remains: the heritage of Guinea maintained in Haiti by serving the gods. Those who live are reclaimed by the ancestors who do not die . . . and by the gods who cajole, demand, and sometimes oppress the mere mortals, the *chretiens-vivants* who forget their an-cestral origins."[68] Important to the Vodou reality are several beliefs: the exis-tence of a hierarchy of mystical spiritual beings who relate to natural, social, and human phenomena; the concept of *Ginen* as a link to Africa; and the role of *konesans* (second sight) in negotiating a cosmos in which an array of super-natural forces are immanent in the magical workings of the world.[69] The struc-ture, function, dynamic relationship, and cultus of this divine-human cosmol-ogy form the content of the next chapter; what follows represents the living elements of the Vodou cultus that keeps the religion alive and vibrant.

4

Serving the Lwa

KEY TOPICS

Hierarchy of the Lwa • Rada and Petwo Lwa •
Female Lwa • Lwa of the Peasantry • Macho Male Lwa •
Veves of the Mysteries • Lougawou, Zombies, and "Monsters" •
Leadership, Rites, and Rituals

Vodou mirrors the classic African concept of a structured cosmos in which exists a hierarchy of spiritual beings (the supreme high god Bondye or Grand Mèt, a host of spiritual powers, the spirits of ancestors, and evil forces), human, animals, and the inanimate world.[1] Bondye governs and orders the universe so that it has cosmic balance and order. He is rarely approached directly, is far removed from the vagaries and day-to-day affairs of human life, and manifests himself through spiritual powers or mysteries. Called saints (*sint*), mysteries (les *misté*) invisibles (*envizib*), and more popularly *loa* or *lwa*, the spiritual entities are not regarded as individual gods but as active agents whom Bondye has placed in charge of the workings of specific aspects of the world. There are primary agents and secondary ones, good lwa and malevolent ones. Although there could be hundreds of lwa (according to legend there are either 401 or 1,701 lwa), only a few receive widespread recognition and ritual attention; many of those have currency mainly within the confines of the families and communities that serve them. Individual devotees worship specific mysteries based on ancestral tradition, personal temperament, spiritual need, and their situation in life;[2] the ancestors join these powers as recipients of significant ritual attention from the individual as well as from the family and community.

In colonial times, Vodou adepts grouped the lwa into seventeen families representing nations (*nanchons*); each of which historically had its own ethnic and religious connections to Africa. These *nanchons* were organized and identified as Wangol, Mondon, Rada, Petro, Ginen, Dhomey, Kongo, Djouba, Ibo, Gede, Nago, and other names derived from the various West African ethnicities that made up the black population in Haiti.[3] Originally, every ethnic group among the slaves worshiped its own deity, but they often stood for the same principles throughout West Africa. As scholars note, practically every group had a spirit representing the feminine principle, power, herbs, rivers and lakes, war and weaponry, and so forth. In time, groups amalgamated in a loose confederation to fight the common enemy, slavery, and employed a range of rituals to this end. After centuries of ethnic religious interchange, the *nanchons* lost their ethnic significance. The cultic activities and traditions of the *nanchons* were brought together "as a single constellation of rites maintained by individual congregations"[4] and directed to their lwa, under a priest ('oungan) or priestess (*mam'bo/manbo*). As Milo Rigaud states: "The gods of Voodoo . . . reach the place where the houn'gan or mam'bo summons them by leaving the atmospheric abode assigned them by the occult spirit referred to as the 'source higher than ourselves.'"[5] The fusing of some rites, practices, and divine powers also probably occurred during colonial plantation slavery.

The Gods of Haiti

The pantheon of lwa, focused on human problems and natural phenomena, are the objects of their devotees' affection. Scholars group these lwa, especially in urban centers, into one of two categories of spirits: *Rada* and *Petwo*. Some scholars see Kongo as a third category of lwa, but others consider Kongo lwa a part of the Petwo tradition. Kongo lwa, identified in names like Kongo Zando, Kongo-Savann, and Rwa Wangol, are of Bantu origin and known collectively as *lwa-gad*. They originated from the region encompassing the Congo Basin and Angola, are reputed to provide devotees protection from harm, and various charms like *paketas, wangas, and gardes* are associated with them. Many of the lwa, ritual implements, and much of Vodou's cosmology have their origin in the Dahomey-Fon religious system. Most Rada lwa, or "cool spirits," are Fon-Dahomey, whereas those of the Petwo, "hot" or "fiery," variety are from Kongo and Angola. Rada lwa, often referred to as a *lwa-Ginen*, reference things that have their origin in Africa; the term *Rada* comes from the city of Allada (Dahomey) and was creolized in Haiti to *Arada*, then shortened to *Rada*.[6]

Rada lwa are known by their special duties: Legba, guardian of entrances and crossroads; Marasa, the twin spirits representative of childhood; Loko, the patron of 'oungan and *manbo* and the spirit of healing; "Ayizan, guardian of the marketplace; Dambala, source of energy and life; Ayida, the female aspect of Dambala; Agwe, master of the sea; Lasiren, mistress of the sea and music; Ezili Freda Daome, spirit of love and femininity; and Agaou, deity of thunder."[7] Unlike the Rada lwa, the Petwo are hot because they are aggressive and vengeful and appear violent in nature; they reflect the black rage of the slaves against brutality and oppression. Joan Dayan states that some Petwo gods "bear the names of revolt, the traces of torture and revenge, like Brise' Pimba, Baron Ravage, Ti-Jean-Dantor or Mater Salvatoris, Ezili-je-wouj (. . . with red eyes), and Jean Zombie."[8] Petwo rituals and ceremonies can therefore take on violent characteristics and the possessing Petwo spirits can display an array of aggressive behaviors. Made into a lwa, Dessalines is said to reflect the most angry Petwo spirit, who manifests himself during warlike liturgical song and dance.

Karen McCarthy Brown notes that the two categories of lwa express contrasting views of the world and relations, and likens them to insiders and outsiders. Rada spirits reflect the disposition of family and other insiders, but the Petwo spirits articulate the ethos of foreigners and outsiders. The insiders are benevolent, intimate, sociable, trustworthy spirits that protect devotees on a daily basis, whereas Petwo spirits are said to be malevolent. The symbols and powers of Petwo lwa are associated with the left side of things (left foot and left hand) and with upward direction. Their devotees however, are required to be adroit, keep promises made to Petwo lwa, and render services with care. Rules must not be broken or bent in one's dealing with Petwo lwa, or consequences may be grave. The Petwo possess great herbal knowledge and healing powers. Rada lwa are gentle, good-natured, and concerned mainly with promoting the well-being of their servitors. Most Vodou initiates receive a Rada lwa and become its wife (*ounsi*) or husband (*ounsis*).[9]

One is cautioned not to hold the distinction between Rada and Petwo too rigidly. A number of Petwo lwa might in fact be aspects, emanations, and counterparts of Rada lwa. In their Petwo guise, they take on aggressive qualities. Ezili Freda, the sweet Rada lwa of romance and sensuality, becomes Ezili or je-wouj, an ill-tempered and dangerous lwa, in Petwo tradition. Good Danto spirits of Ezili exist, as well as evil ones; she is kind and gentle, but aggressive and fierce. On the other hand, although they are associated with benevolence, Rada lwa may cause affliction on persons who anger or neglect them, whereas Petwo lwa are extremely protective of their servitors. According to Leslie Desmangles, "Gede in his Rada persona does not usually inflict illness upon a devotee, but in his Petro persona as Gede-Zarenyen who, as the name indicates, crawls and stings like a spider, he does."[10] Dayan notes further that "Even the best of gods, those of the *Rada (Arada)* rite from Alladah or Dahomey, can sometimes do evil, while a tough deity like Marinette-Bois-Cheche (Marinette-Dry-Bones) of the Petwo rite, known for her bloody behavior and preference for pimento, gunpowder, and gasoline, can be calmed if served properly."[11] These lwa show a multiplicity of personalities that can reflect Rada, Petwo, or Kongo traits.

The origin of the Petwo lwa is debated. Some scholars trace this group of spirits back to Africa and others to Don Pedro, a creole-Spanish slave priest. Others believe Petwo originated among the Maroons and Tainos of Saint-Domingue and are therefore indigenous to Haiti. Ezili Danto and Jean Pedro are among their most well-known deities; so is the Gede lwa, the spirit of death. Bosu Trois, Simbi d'leau, Mait Gran Bois, and Mait Calfour are also among the Petwo spirits. If the Petwo lwa are Haitian creole, their music and rites are African; they emerged from the crucibles of the Haitian experience and thus are considered the most creole of the lwa. These lwa might be larger than life but they are not other than life. Their virtues are not an inherent characteristic trait but an ascribed dynamic mythological state of existence; they operate in responsive relationships that require constant attention and care. This care is demonstrated in the gifts they receive in the form of food, money, respect, worship, and other intangibles in return for protection and guidance.[12] Lwa have their likes and dislikes—special gourmet tastes that require pandering on various occasions, specially designated worship days and times, distinct colors that their devotees wear, dances and movements, songs and prayers, and special symbols to be displayed in rites and rituals. The most well-known lwa, male and female, are Ezili, Azaka, Legba, Gede, Dambala, and Ogou.

Female Lwa

The female spirits that belong to the Ezili family are many in number and personality, including Danto, Freda, Daome, je-wouj, and Marinet, among others. Ezili Danto, lwa of womanhood and eroticism, is Creole and has no precedent in Dahomey. She has many personae said to embody the collective historical memory of women in the Haitian past. Devotees believe that this protective mother fought bravely for her Haitian children during the revolution. Ti-Jean Danto, another persona of Ezili Danto and associated with the trickery of a female prankster, has many heterosexual lovers, including Ogou, who sired one of her children. Ezili Freda is a flirtatious female who clothes herself in the romance of her lovers; she loves jewelry and fine clothes and seems to get her identity from the men in her life. This Black Venus of Haiti typifies a lovingly passionate side of African human sensuality.[13]

Ezili je-Rouge is the opposite of Freda; she exemplifies female anger or rage. Grann Ezili takes on the personae of an elderly woman and Ezili Lasyrenn, the mermaid-like creature, connects Afro-Caribbean women's sense of power to the spirit of rivers, lakes, seas, and the African homeland. Brown argues that "Lasyrenn, Ezili Danto, and Ezili Freda are each conflated with manifestations of the Virgin Mary: Nuestra Senora de la Caridad del Cobre, Maer Salvatoris, and Maria Dolorosa."[14] Ezili is one of the most powerful but arbitrary of lwa. She reflects the existential angst of Haitian life in her extremely contradictory personality. Dayan says Ezili is "a spirit of love who forbids love, a woman who is the most beloved yet feels herself the most betrayed. She can be generous and loving, or implacable and cruel. . . . As spirit of vengeance, she is fiercely jealous and sometimes punishes wayward devotees with death, impotence, or frigidity if they dare drink or have sex on those days devoted to her."[15] As a friend of priestesses, Ezili is also caretaker of the ounfo, the place of worship.

Lwa of Peasants

In the more than two hundred years since the revolution, harsh economic realities have forced Haitians to focus their energy on domestic problems and the struggle for survival. As a result, Vodou's mythology shows the strong social emphasis acquired during colonialism, one that has a close tie to subsistence on the land. As scholars observe, in rural Haiti human and natural disasters such as drought, political turmoil, and poverty have forced large numbers of people into urban centers, away from the land and the extended families that sustained a simple lifestyle and gave them a sense of identity. Mythic spirit characters are made to deal with these tragedies. Azaka, affectionately called cousin Zaka and papa Zaka, lwa of the peasants, reminds urban Haitians of their lost societal bond and simpler lifestyle in the midst of "urban tendencies toward elaboration of ritual and the creation of religious hierarchies."[16] Zaka adorns himself in the characteristic peasant outfit: blue pants and shirt, straw hat, red handkerchief around the neck, and a small straw bag hanging from the shoulders. Azaka is an uneducated peasant associated with John the Baptist because of his humility.

Legba, the androgynous patron of the cosmos, is the umbilical chord that links Bondye with human beings. He is the guard of all crossroads, directs the destiny of everyone, protects the home, and aids in making tough decisions. As the spirit that opens and guards opportunity, gates, and doors, Legba makes a way for the poor and clears paths between the human and spirit worlds, so he is usually the first spirit invoked in a Vodou ceremony. Legba is the lwa of most rural practitioners, wears farming attire, smokes a pipe, and walks with a cane and a peasant tow bag. Legba appears as many creole characters—Papa Legba, Atibon Legba, Legba-zinchan, Legba-signangon, Legba-katarula, and Mèt Kalfou—and competes with Dambala for the title of chief lwa.[17] Legba is also a prankster whom outsiders mistakenly call Satan, although he doubles as the personae of Saint Peter and Saint Anthony. Occasionally, because of his strength and in spite of his lofty status, even the mighty spirit Dambala is seen as a friend of the peasants who inhabit and work the hostile and arid land.

Gede, lwa known affectionately among the peasants as Papa Gede, is master of Ginen and Petwo's *Baron Sanmdy,* or power. Gede represents a family of spirits from the constellation of lwa families. He lives in the cemetery and is naturally associated with disease and the dead, but he fills multiple roles and has many manifestations and personae: Bawon Samdi, Bawon Simityè, and Bawon Lakwa.[18] To some initiates, he is the link between life and death and is acknowledged at the end of every ceremony. To beggars and panhandlers he represents charity, but to women he is an enabler of sexual prowess and fertility. As a prankster, Gede could be a source of laughter and joviality as well as humor in bad taste. He eats with his bare fingers and throws food around like a helpless infant. Gede breaks social conventions; he can be impolite and ill-mannered, and delights in saying the corniest things. Unexpectedly, he can be chauvinistic and predatory, appearing to an outsider to sexually harass women[19] with his "generous greeting." In plain view, using a ritual gesture, Gede also fills his pocket with goods pilfered from people's market booths while venders are expected to look the other way. Like the African griot and Trinidadian calypso singer, Gede can criticize the rich and powerful in society with caustic satire without being punished by politicians or sued for character assassination. He claims healing as his main activity, can be compassionate and caring, and has an interest in family; therefore, Saint Gerard is one of his creole doubles.

Macho Male Lwa

Dambala (danballah, danbala), python spirit of supreme mysteries, sign and court-of-arms for Vodou enthusiasts doubling as St. Patrick, is one of the oldest and most complex of the lwa. He assisted Bondye in the creation of the world and, as the persistent life force and source of energy, helps to sustain it. The aged noble father Dambala Wedo, source of all motion in life, giver of rainbows and floods, is the most powerful spirit of the Vodou pantheon. Newell Booth writes, "So strong is his influence in Haiti, the sign of the serpent can even be seen in the architecture of the land. . . . Haiti could easily be called the land of Dambala."[20] Because of his Dahomean ancestry and association with Vodou in preindependent Haiti, he acts as a uniting force of past, present, and future Haitian reality. He writhes on the ground in simulation of a serpent's movement. His coiling, snakelike actions are symbolic of his encircling power around Haitian communities; via the rainbow, he allegedly encircles and unites land and ocean and brings life-giving water to the barren hills of Haiti. He is accommodated symbolically in a temple pool, a pond, or in a river basin, where his devotees worship him in ritual glee while jumping from the river banks, dancing, singing, and beating drums until he makes his dramatic appearance through possession. Dambala is also said to be pure and clean, and often avoids the sick. Although he lives with his wife, Ayida Wedo, Our Lady of the Immaculate Conception, he loves Erzili. Dambala's presence is recognized in the hissing snakelike sound made by his servitors, with whom he communicates. The machete Ogou carries is symbolic of Dambala's power,[21] as well as the fighting power of the Haitian spirit.

Ogou, the aggressive Petro lwa of war and weapons of iron and steel, is not short in creole personae: Agaou, Ogou Balanjo, Ogou Batala, Ogou Yansan, Ogou-badagri, and Ogou-ferraille, among others. In Haiti's historical mythology, Ogou symbolizes the military might of the nation; his images often appear on flags and lithographs, and brave soldiers are said to have the spirit of Ogou, who teaches them how to fight. The Sword of La Place and Ogou's dagger and machete are not only symbols of the deity's fierceness and dread, but carry mystical power. They symbolically kill the sacrificial victim, cut through great mysteries, and reveal spiritual secrets. As a negotiator par excellence, Ogou mediates in crises among peoples and between opposing forces, as represented in the lwa. He is capable of complex emotions; he shows feelings of rage and empathy and is known for his generosity. Because of his great herbal knowledge and healing powers, his advice is sought in most pharmacopeial rituals.[22]

Ogou's creole personae find several doubles in Haitian Catholicism. As Ogou Ferraille, he is St. James the Great, who rides a white horse and fights the heathen; he is honored on July 25, the feast day of James the Elder. As Ogou Balanjo, he is Saint Joseph[23] and also St. Jacques, who appeared to halt the Muslims' advance in Europe and was adopted into the family of Ogoué, the lwa of war, justice, and technology. This integrative impulse of Vodou mythology has led to a fusion of personalities of lwa with counterparts in Catholic hagiography, thus creating creole doubles for the lwa in a system of parallels between these spirits and Catholic saints.

Veves of the Mysteries

The lwa are recognized not only by their special idiosyncrasies, but each has a visual representative drawing called a *vever* (veve), a powerful cosmic symbol, one that brings to perfection all other images and representations of the spirits to focus the energy of lwa mysteries. The intricate drawing is made on the floor around the *poto-mitan* (*poteau-mitan*) at the beginning of a Vodou service to court the presence and honor of a specific lwa. The *poto-mitan*, the center post of the ounfo located in the *peristil* around which the ceremony revolves, symbolizes the middle doorway to the spirit world. The *peristil* is a partly enclosed and often roofed courtyard where priests and priestesses perform their rituals and treat ailments. The *poto-mitan* is the symbolic nexus of sky, earth, and the spirit world and connects Haiti to Africa; it has its roots in Ginen, home of the lwa, and therefore acts symbolically as the conduit through which the lwa enter the *peristil* from Africa to take possession of devotees. While *poto-mitan* is the unique representative link between Haiti and[24] Africa, the veve reveals the presence of the deity in a visual form, has an emblematic as well as a magical character, and is used only by a spiritually authorized person, the 'oungan or mam'bo.

By tracing the veve, the 'oungan forces a lwa to respond and appear at the ceremony. The priest consecrates the veve to the lwa by placing on it small heaps of grilled maize and other dried foods that are sprinkled with rum, kola, and a drink made of maize starch or flour.[25] The orderly placement of each veve around the *poto-mitan* indicates also how the liturgy is to proceed. The priest makes a liquid libation around the veve and places on it the consecrated animal slaughtered as food for the lwa. Each libation is made three times while the 'oungan shakes the *ason* (a rattle) over the drawing, humming or mumbling ritual words. The veve becomes "the first point of reception for these gifts, the pictorial face through which the lwa may eat. Once fed through the veve gateway in the earth, the lwa are energized to come up and mount their horse."[26] These food sacrifices therefore access spiritual power.

Veves of the spirits have become international representations of Vodou "works." As Anthony Pinn shows, Legba is depicted symbolically in a very intricate veve, containing a rectangle with two horizontal lines that five vertical lines dissect. The outside of this rectangle depicts a machete on the left side and a sickle on the right. Another sickle is placed on top and an arch is placed over a box below the rectangle covered with different symbols. Legba's veve shows two worlds, represented in crossed horizontal lines, on one side of which is drawn a staff. Dambala's veve comprises two pythons on either side of his favorite goblet, a Masonic emblem over which are drawn two eggs. Three circles on a special horizontal line connect Marassa's veve. Ogou has several symbols, but his characteristic marks, the menacing machete and gun of the hunter, are prominent in his veve. The veve of Erzili, an enlarged heart, depicts her sensuality and capacity for lovemaking.[27] In contrast to Erzili's love for men, Zaka's veve shows his love for women. In addition to the ason and the veves representing the ethos of the lwa, Vodou uses many other symbols. There are the amulets and talismans that, like fetishes and charms, are supposed to ward off evil spirits and influences. The tree of good and evil is represented in a specially notched pole called the *joukoujou*. Just as symbolically powerful as the weapons of the lwa are the visually colorful ritual flags usually carried by two women devotees or priests. They show the magical importance of the spirits' acceptance of the ceremonial offerings dedicated to them.[28] These symbols and signs are windows to Vodou's mythology.

Lougawou and Zombie

LOUGAWOU

The mythological world of Vodou is inhabited by a variety of unsavory spiritual entities like werewolves, vampires, and zombies, most of which are manipulable by sorcery or gray magic. *Bakas*, malevolent spirits whom sorcerers deploy to harm or protect someone, can be dangerous to one's health, according to myth; they are said to make grave demands, such as the life of a family member. The existence of human sacrifice in Vodou, however, is folkloric speculation that has not been documented. The werewolf, or *lougawou*, are shape-shifting creatures that allegedly attack people, especially babies and young children, so that their physical condition deteriorates rapidly. Folklore distinguishes between vampires (as lougawou) and werewolves and claims that the former can change themselves into animals and inanimate objects, shed their skin, suck blood, and terrify those who walk late at night.[29] This lougawou legend is common in Caribbean mythology and is not a distinctly Haitian phenomenon. As the myth goes, lougawou are humans of questionable character accused of becoming vampires at night, entering locked doors and assaulting victims while they sleep unless the family obtains a ritual potion to protect their home. The folklore reveals other myths and tales of persons, often bearded whites, and evil beings who sneaked up on folks, kidnapped their children, and sold the souls of their victims to the devil for the purpose of launching ships. These tales are a remnant of the dangerous memories of the slave colonial past of Africans on the continent and in the diaspora. In perceptions of Haiti, the myth is inverted. The "evil voodooist" becomes the lougawou, a stereotype of the Haitian religion specially favored among Vodou critics, the media, and Hollywood.

ZOMBIE

The zombie is another example of mythic manipulation in the Vodou spirit world, involving the rising and enslaving of the living dead. This Haitian folk-loric myth is portrayed in popular culture as a malevolent, flesh-eating vampire, a scary skeletal Frankenstein-like monster. This disembodied ghostlike phantom who darts out from behind trees and dark alleys and strikes terror in the hearts of unsuspecting victims is a controversy of mythic proportion. People who regard zombies as a reality vouchsafe their existence. Alfred Metraux contends that in the 1950s "all Haitians, whatever their social status, have trembled in their youth at stories of *zombi* and werewolves and learnt to dread the power of sorcerers and evil spirits. Most of them . . . react against such fancies but some give in to them and consult a Voodoo priest in secret."[30] Haitians and American missionaries tell fables of witnessing incidences in Haitian villages where people were "slain," buried, resurrected, enslaved, drugged, reburied and finally returned to life when a *bokor,* or wicked priest, dies. From his interesting study of this myth, published in *The Serpent and the Rainbow,* Wade Davis suggests that the zombie phenomenon in Vodou is brought about by administering the potent hallucinogenic datura plant and puffer fish substances to individuals, which cause psychotic behavior that leaves them in a stupefied or catatonic state, to be revived later. Belief in this phenomenon has been widespread within and outside of Haiti.

The zombification of Vodou in Hollywood is responsible for propagating much of the zombie myth. In the first zombie film, *White Zombie* (1932), and later in *Ferris Bueller's Day Off* (1986), Vodou is portrayed with demonic rage and stupor. After the Americans left Haiti in 1934, the demonizing of Vodou accelerated in grotesque zombie movies: *The King and the Zombie* (1941), *I Walked with a Zombie* (1943), *Zombies of Mora Tau* (1957), *Voodoo Woman* (1957), *Orgy of the Dead* (1965), *The Plagues of the Zombie* (1966), and *Revenge of the Zombie* (1981). The zombie myth contains misogynist notions; most zombies are either female or associated with women.[31] A different view of this phenomenon is that the belief in zombies, like belief in the lougawou, is an echo of a Taino belief in ghosts. There is also the view that the zombie myth evolved from the sight of the emaciated bodies of starving Haitians who roamed the countryside almost as ghosts; this zombie is supposedly a human void of affect, will, or sensitivity. One tradition holds that the dead person's body is revived by a *bokor* and used for malevolent purposes. This is done by magically seizing the victim's *ti bòn-anj,* collective faculty, and personality, "leaving behind an empty vessel subject to the commands of the *bokor*"[32] and his fancies.

Exactly where the zombie myth originated is not clear but, like the lougawou, it has a long historical connection to Africa, slavery, and Vodou. Melville

Herskovits notes that in Dahomean folktales, zombies are beings "whose death was not real but resulted from the machinations of sorcerers who made them appear as dead, and then, when buried, removed them from their grave and sold them into servitude in some far-away land."[33] In Haiti, the zombie myth is creolized with grotesque characteristics; the zombie is a lwa or an ancestor most mean-spirited and demonic, or a child of the revolution. In 1804, Jean (last name unknown), a bloodthirsty mulatto from Port-au-Prince, was Dessalines' chief butcher in the merciless slaughtering of whites and earned many ugly descriptors for his heartless acts—one of which is Zombie. As a result, Zombie became not only Jean's familial name but a most interesting prototype of Vodou folklore. Once the name Zombie was attached to Jean the butcher, it revealed the effects of a different dispensation in Haitian mythology. As Dayan crafts it, the names, gods, and heroes that were originally "from an oppressive colonial past remained in order to infuse ordinary citizens and devotees with a stubborn sense of independence and survival. The un-dead zombie, recalled in the name of Jean Zombie, thus became a terrible composite power: slave turned rebel, ancestor turned lwa, an incongruous, demonic spirit."[34] What is a real zombie? Dayan thinks it may be the sublimated reign of terror orchestrated by the Haitian leaders, a past that is too gruesome to relive so it is projected onto a defamed, maligned, and phantom-like apparition. The real zombie is not in the malevolent image but in the threat it poses to historical memory.[35] It is so grotesque that it strikes terror in the heart of anyone who dares to believe in "zombified" Vodou.

Accessing Ginen-Potomitan

Ginen, or Guinea, was one of the many nations under which African religions in Haiti first operated. After the nation idea became less significant in Vodou, Ginen became a spirit and a mythological place in Africa and the netherworld. Finally, Ginen represented the original home of the Rada lwa and their current abode in the underside of the world. It conjures an entirely mythic Africa in the present, "the sacred world of Haiti's past that is present in the dances oriented to the *poto-mitan*" in the Vodou ounfo.[36] Vodouisants believe that during the final stage of spirit possession, when the lwa mounts its horse, the medium has no recollection of the experience because the person's "good big spirit" migrates across the sea back to Ginen, the original homeland of Haiti and her Dahomey children. The spirit, people, and country are tied in a mythological web to Ginen, which lies over the great waters and is revisited as a memory of crossing waters in Vodou liturgy. The priest petitions Agwe, the lwa of the ocean, to carry the lwa to the ceremony in his sailboat. Then the great tree Loko, which has its roots in the waters underneath the earth, pulls the lwa up from the netherworld via the *poto-mitan* strategically placed in the center of the *peristil*. Africa is made a central source of harmony, moral action, and authority through faithfulness to the traditions of Ginen that exist in the Vodou ceremony. Ginen lends authenticity to the practice of Vodou at various levels: as Murphy holds, "The community orients itself toward Africa through the architecture of the *peristil*, centering on the great tree of the *poto-mitan* which links the visible trunk and branches of Haiti with the roots in the invisible earth of Ginen,"[37] the life of the other world or African heaven.

Leadership and Cultus

Vodou has developed its own creole *Gemeinschaft* and character. No religious hierarchy or centralized leadership overseeing all vodouisants exists. The fraternities maintain a network of communication among themselves, especially through the personal relations of the leaders, but it is all spontaneous, casual, and decentralized. Each ounfo is its own authority, and its ritual specialist communicates directly with its deities. Yet, Vodou fraternities are not disorganized, chaotic, or void of leadership. The ounfo has a simple two-tier organizational structure—the religious leaders and the other members of the community—but within each cultus exists a spiritual gradation of relationships based on the degree of one's participation, initiation, experience, and importance in ritual function. Each Vodou community is organized around an autonomous atypical temple, the ounfo or *lakou*, which is Kongo for "sacred place." The *lakou* comprises a small number of residences and people that form the communal social unit or extended Vodou family, especially in rural Haiti. As in Africa, it often has its own cemetery for burying its deceased members on land that is owned jointly and that should not be sold. Modern labor migration and urbanization have scattered Haitian families so that the *sosiete* forms the more common Vodou unit in the city.[38] In most urban centers, the ounfo comprises a family of initiates instead of blood kin, who serve the same family of lwa. The physical facility of the ounfo, which Rigaud says closely resembles Moses' design of the Hebrew Ark of the Covenant and the Tabernacle in the wilderness, could have a single room or several chambers in larger ones. In larger ounfos, each chamber has its own *pe* ("altar") and is reserved for adoring a single lwa. In small temples, the spirits are worshiped in a single holy place that has many altars consecrated to specific deities.[39]

'Oungan and Mambo

A Vodou ounfo is operated and often owned by the priest or priestess who, because of their knowledge and experience, have the most direct contact with the spirits. The 'oungan (male) or mam'bo (female) is the sole authority figure in each ounfo. They combine the offices of religious and administrative leader of the small charitable fraternity, ritual expert, diviner or magician, herbal therapist, and confidential counselor. These leaders do not attend institutions of religion, but are trained in the practical knowledge of Vodou "works" under a senior priest-practitioner. They acquire intimate knowledge of diverse characteristics and idiosyncrasies of various lwa; the intricacies of signs and symbols in the ceremonies and rituals; and appropriate songs, prayers, incantations, dances, and drumbeats through which lwa are approached and worshiped.[40] Priests must learn the names, attributes, and special idiosyncrasies of the gods and are able to perform rites appropriate to the ceremonies honoring each spirit. After a long and tedious training, they are given the ason ("rattle") "as healer, adviser, and teacher,"[41] characteristics of their profession. As J. Lorand Matory says, "Candomble priests command the technology to purify bodies, houses, and other vessels of unwanted influences and to insert, or secure the presence of, the divinities in the bodies and altars of their devotees."[42] This is true of all African-Caribbean priesthood.

To become an 'oungan or mam'bo, initiates undergo the rite of *haussement,* called the "lifting" because those being initiated are lifted three times in an armchair as they take the oath to respect the lwa. The candidates first undergo ritual cleansing and seclusion in the ounfo for nine days. After the initial period of confinement, they take an oath of allegiance to the lwa and pledge to uphold the integrity of Vodou. This signals a deepening of one's relationship with his or her primary lwa and the initiate's growing knowledge of the mysteries of Vodou. The *haussement* concludes with the vesting of the ason (the symbol of priestly authority and the sacred emblem for directing and controlling the energy of a lwa), thus marking the final level of initiation. A senior 'oungan or mam'bo confers the investiture of the ason, the symbol of the priesthood that legitimizes the priest and priestess to perform initiations and divinations, provide healing and other therapeutic services, invoke the lwa, and preside over ceremonies.[43]

The ason, covered in a bearded mesh, is made from a small, empty, pear-shaped gourd, on the outside of which is drawn the vertebrae of Damballa, the Rada spirit it represents. Carrying the ason on ritual occasion gives visual evidence that the priestess occupies a high position of authority in a Vodou community and that the ason is indispensable for working the spirit. The ason plays such an important role in the cultus that the elaborate rituals that accompany initiation to the priesthood are "commonly referred to as 'taking the ason.'" Ascent to an even higher level of the priesthood comes through an initiation rite called the *asogwe* or *prise des yeux,* "taking or controlling of the eyes."[44] The secrecy of this order is closely guarded by the limited number of priests who have knowledge of it. Persons who undergo the experience are recognized for their knowledge of the traditions and mysteries of Vodou, their insights into the invisible world, and their ability to harness the powers of the lwa on behalf of the community.

Avenues to Spiritual Energy

If the lwas are the life-giving force of Vodou, rites, ceremonies, and rituals are its heart and lungs. Through these performances, the Vodou mythological spirit breathes and is preserved, reenacted, and perpetuated. Bonds are cemented and spiritual energy is brought to bear on the problems and affairs of the worshiping community. The purpose of a Vodou ritual is to align participants with the lwa whose power and energy are responsible for the events and activities of the world. This alignment takes place first through initiation, in which candidates prepare for and receive the presence of the lwa in spirit possession. Several rites may be subsumed under the category of initiation, varying from one ounfo or *lakou* to the other. Devotees and enthusiasts have various levels of involvement in the rites and rituals of the ounfo. At the outer limits of participation in a Vodou fraternity are the uninitiated: visitors, well-wishers, newcomers, and curious observers interested in Vodou works. Some may consult the priests as one would consult a doctor or a psychiatrist. Consultations are prompted not only by health concerns but also by issues of relationships: love, money, and other human needs. Most followers who attend ceremonies make use of the priests' service and may perform some minimal task for the community. However, they have not undergone a ritual initiation and are therefore called *bosal*, wild or not tamed, indicating that they have not become subjected to the controlling influence of a lwa. When a person decides to become a devotee, he or she is declared an *ounsi bosal* or wild one in training to be a servant of the lwa. The *ounsi* must be brought along a path of knowledge in the ways of the spirit by completing an initiatory rite called the *kouche* rite or *lav tèt* that signals the beginning of a relationship with the lwa. An *ounsi* who completes the *kouche* and undergoes the *kanzo* can perform rituals in the ounfo.[45]

KOUCHE

The cycle of initiation starts with the *kouche* and ends with the *kanzo*, the undertaking of which may be influenced by one or more factors. The candidate may desire to fulfill family obligations to the lwa, may be expected to become a spouse of the family lwa, or may receive a dream or a vision in which the lwa of departed family members instructs one to take on the obligation of serving the lwa. Others interpret their experience of sickness or misfortune as a result of their neglecting to serve their lwa. In many cases, recovery from illnesses is attributed to intervention of a lwa and can serve as a catalyst for entrance into a relationship and grateful service to the spirit. Still others are called to undergo the initiation while under possession. This is one of the strongest bits of evidence that the spirit desires a "marriage" with the individual.[46] Once the person is clear about the call to serve the lwa, plans are made with the 'oungan or mam'bo for the *kouche* to be performed. Preparation involves a significant outlay of money by the initiate. In addition to initiation fees paid to the officiating priest, initiates pay for the ritual paraphernalia necessary for the ceremony—something most Haitians find unaffordable. The prohibitive cost often forces indigent clients to combine their resources and have a joint initiation ceremony.[47]

When all of the preparations are made and the appointed day arrives, an initiate undergoes multiple cleansing rituals. The *kouche* requires a head-washing ritual designed to placate and make restive any unsettled spirits in the head of the initiate so that he or she can be receptive to the lwa. To strengthen the head to receive the lwa, an application of a poultice made of special ingredients is placed on the head of each inductee, where it remains for a week. The *kouche* is called the "lying down" or "sleeping" rite because it involves a lengthy period of isolation in which the initiate is said to go to sleep ritually and mentally. The primary significance of this period of isolation is a psychological and spiritual rebirth in which one is said to "die" in order to become attuned to the workings of a lwa, in whose image he or she is reborn. Here, the initiate receives instructions on the rules and etiquette of the ounfo and on how to greet elders and the lwa and how to care for and serve them. After the period of isolation, the lwa manifests itself in the head of the initiate. The investiture of *pot tèt,* or ceremonial jars, follows and represents the new relationship between the individual and the lwa. Symbolically, the *pot tèt* act as repositories of the individual's soul and of one's guiding lwa—a gesture that "seats" a lwa in the head of the newly initiated. A procession follows with the newly initiated *ounsi* marching with the priests and senior members of the ounfo with their *pot tèt* balanced on their heads. The sacred receptacles are finally placed on altars to become the property of the *ounsi,* who will eventually place them on their own altars.[48] The initiate is now ready for the next stage of initiation, the *Kanzo.*

KANZO

The *kanzo* is a culmination of the elementary education of *ounsi lav tèt,* those who have undergone the cleansing of the head, and the reception of the *pot tèts,* a fiery ordeal designed to convert suffering and hardship into spiritual energy. Often the *kouche* and the *kanzo* rites combine the ritual cleaning of the head, performed during a confinement in the initiation chamber of the ounfo for seven to fourteen days and followed by a fire dance in public. Those being initiated dance over boiling pots and handle items taken from the caldron without being burned. As Brown notes, for example, "hot dumplings are snatched from the boiling pots and placed into the palm of the initiate's left hand and the sole of the foot."[49] Surviving this ordeal demonstrates one's self-mastery and possession of *konesans,* the ability to acquire knowledge of the workings of the spirit world. Progressive acquisition of *konesans* signals a person's growth in the mysteries of Vodou and gives him or her the ability to understand and deploy spiritual forces for personal and communal benefits. *Kanzo* initiation qualifies the *ounsi* for an advanced leadership position in the ounfo, excluding that of 'oungan or *manbo.*[50] The reception of the lwa in the head marks the adoption of a new personality and indicates that the spirit has now become the controlling force in the devotee's life. This initiation creates a mystical bond between devotee and the lwa and makes the spirit into a guide for the individual. Metraux argues that "later, other spirits may possess the initiate, but the one who first made him his 'horse' remains his particular patron and protector."[51] The successful initiate who wishes to be a priest must undergo the final initiation, called the "giving of the ason," which qualifies one to perform all of Vodou's works.

The feast of yams, the wake for the dead, and mourning rites are among the many rituals not reviewed here. Healing rites address the issue of human well-being and include diagnostic readings by 'oungan or mam'bo. These include playing the tarot cards, giving ritual baths and offerings for the lwa, the preparation and application of various herbal concoctions, and the deploying of charms and protective potions or *wangas* and *gardes*—some of which are not regarded favorably by practitioners. Death and burial rites, called *dessounen*, relate specifically to the soul or spirit. Vodou accords each person a multiplicity of realities; in addition to the physical body, which decomposes after death, the individual has as many as four souls; two of these may be called the "big soul" and the "small soul." In Vodou psychology, the head contains two faculties: *petit bon anj* or *ti bòn-anj*, "little good angel," and *gwo bòn-anj*, "big good angel." *Ti bòn-anj* equals the individual personality and the faculty of self-reflection and thought. As Desmangles explains, "It is the personality, conscience, the moral side of one's character which reveals itself through one's general deportment."[52] This is the source of dreams, affect, and consciousness. The *gwo bòn-anj*, called a "shadow-corps, is the double of the material body . . . but is understood as the shadow cast by the body on the mind. The *gwo bòn anj* can easily be detached from the body"[53] and is responsible for such faculties as memory and intelligence as well as different bodily functions. In the ritual cleansing of the head at initiation, the *gwo bòn-anj* is prepared to receive the guidance of the lwa, who becomes the *mèt tèt* or master of the head of the devotee. The seating of the *mèt tèt* in the initiate's head occasions a mystical merger of the *gwo bòn-anj* and the *mèt tèt*.[54] The departure of the *gwo bòn anj* as animating force of the body signals a person's death, which must be ritualized through the death rite *desounen*.

DESOUNEN RITES

Various rituals like *desounen*, *manjé-lèmò*, and *boule-zen* are performed in connection with death and burial to ensure that the spiritual forces are disengaged from the body, retire to their resting place, and do not remain on earth to disturb the living. The rite that separates the individual's *mèt tèt*, or seated lwa, from the physical head also retires the *gwo bòn-anj* to its final resting place. It ushers body and spirit to their final destination and commences the ancestral rites for persons who are made ancestors. On the day of an individual's passing, the 'oungan or mam'bo is called to the house to perform the *desounen*. This rite ensures that the constituents of the individual's personality are dispatched to their rightful destinations: the *ti bòn-anj* to *Grand Mèt* or heaven; the *gwo bòn-anj* and *mèt tèt* to *Ginen*, the watery abode beneath the earth; and the body to the earth. The priest performs various ablutions, shakes the ason, and speaks into the ear of the deceased, all while commanding the *gwo bòn-anj* and the *mèt tèt* to leave. As a sign that the elements have been successfully exorcized from the body, the officiating priest becomes possessed by the lwa that is the deceased's *mèt tèt*.[55]

Following the *desounen*, the body of the deceased is washed in preparation for burial. The "bather" speaks to the deceased and conveys messages that family members would like the dead to take to the ancestors. A *prèt savann* accompanies the body to the cemetery, where he performs final Catholic rites. After the burial, the family goes to the ounfo for the ritual breaking and burial of the *pot tèt* or *case kanari*, a vessel that symbolically contains the *gwo bòn-anj* and *mèt tèt* of the deceased. A year and a day after death, family members are expected to sponsor a ceremony called *ouete mò nan ba dlo* and invite the spirit of the dead back into the community of the living as an active ancestor. This is done so that the deceased's knowledge, power, and access to the world of the lwas can be deployed to empower the living in negotiating the exigencies of life. Since this ancestral rite requires considerable expense, it is often delayed while family members tap various resources. However, failure to carry out this obligation is a bad omen and may result in affliction of family members and even of the community.[56] In addition, this failure could deprive the family of the protection and good fortune that the ancestor is able to provide.

SERVICES

Vodouisants hold a number of other ceremonies that are collectively known as "the services." The purpose of these is to honor and feed the lwa and draw on their power to enable members to deal with life situations. These services, convened on annual holidays in the Catholic liturgical calendar and on special saints' days (St. Patrick's Day, Our Lady of Fatima's Day), are observed with feasts given to the corresponding lwa. Along with the holiday observances, a lwa may demand that a feast be held in its honor. A family may sponsor a service to honor and feed its lwa and ancestors. As an expression of gratitude for healing or some other good fortune received, an individual may sponsor a service to honor the lwa.[57]

These Vodou *seremoni* in honor of the lwa generally proceed in several stages. They begin with the perfunctory Catholic prayers and a litany of the saints performed by the *prèt savann*. This is followed by the rites of entry, during which the sacred space is made hallow in preparation for the lwa's visitation. The consecration begins with the officiating priest performing a rite of orientation by saluting the four cardinal points of the earth with ablutions. The 'oungan or mam'bo then makes the important ritual drawings of the veves on the ground. To the accompaniment of drumming and singing, a ritual assistant or *la place* leads a parade of the flags of the ounfò and the lwa that are honored and served there. After the parade, the various sacred objects of the ounfò are greeted; special attention is given to the sacred drums, the rhythms of which invite the lwas to manifest themselves. The rites of entry conclude with the 'oungan or mam'bo invoking the lwa and the ancestors in a series of incantations.

At this stage, the sacrificial animal is offered to the lwa as a *manjè-lwa*, an offering to the lwa. During the playing of the rhythms, the lwa arrives and mounts one of the "horses" in whose head it has been seated during the initiation. Once the lwa leaves, the "horse" has no memory of what took place during the possession trance.

Rhythms of the Spirit

Vodou worship is inspired by what one writer calls a ritual orchestra. The most important of the musical instruments in this orchestra are the *ogan* ("triangle"), the ason, and the drum. The *ogan*, or iron, is a crude percussion instrument struck rhythmically with a piercing sound as it introduces the other instruments. Musicologist Lois Wilcken notes that the *ogan* "is the most steady and unchanging of all the rhythmic patterns, and a mistake on the *ogan* is more painfully noticeable than a mistake on a drum. . . . Even though the *ogan* is not always physically present in the Vodou drum ensemble, musicians and dancers feel its rhythmic pattern."[58] Some magic is associated with this instrument, the triangular shape of which symbolically opens the path of the air to the spirit world and puts practitioners in touch with the divine. The ason also sets the musical and liturgical tempo in the ceremony by giving drummers a signal to begin and end. Wherever there is Vodou, there are drums. In Vodou's rhythm and dance, the drum is king of all musical instruments, the center of gravity of all ceremonies, and a unique means of communication. The drums remain both a ritual conduit of the spirit and a main attraction for outsiders. There are Rada drums and Petwo drums, all made from a log carved into shape with a machete, hollowed out either by burning or digging out the inside, and covered at the ends with cowhide or goat skin soaked in locally brewed rum. According to Wilken, around Port-au-Prince, three Rada drums—*maman*, *segon*, and *boula*—play for all the divinities of the Rada family, and the Petwo drums serve the Petwo spirits, which include the Djouba, Ibo, Kongo, and Gede nations. The drums are mystical and are said to make occasional trips to Africa "in order to renew their magical force."[59] Without the drums, a Vodou ceremony loses its compass, its rhythm, its pulse, its magical force, and its power.

Conclusion

Vodou as a religious philosophy and as a system of communication is an expression of authentic spirituality to many Haitians. As a religion operating sui generis ("in its own right"), it has successfully weathered centuries of stormy attempts at obliteration by Christianity, the Catholic Church, or both; Haitian leaders; and even foreign governments. After more than two centuries as the most dominant and resilient symbol of religion for independent Haiti, Vodou has now become a numerically dwindling minority religion. Where Catholics tried to convert Haitians through coercion for three centuries and failed, modern versions of American Protestant Christianity are now succeeding. The African-derived religion survived a turbulent colonial history in Saint Domingue/ Haiti by adapting to Catholic cosmology and new world culture. Now, the future of Vodou no longer lies only in its ability to survive persecution but also in adapting once more to a new Christian competitor and in its relevance in the twenty-first century. Do I mean to suggest that Vodou has outlived its usefulness in Haiti, or agree with those who say Vodou serves no useful purpose in Haitian society? Patrick Bellegarde-Smith rephrases the question with disapproving sarcasm: "Might we conclude that populations of primary African descent were hopelessly confused and that, indeed, their beliefs are *un Catholicisme indigeste,* an undigested Catholicism?" Or that "by borrowing from the Catholic pantheon instead of from [ARTs or] Hinduism, Vodou might have acquired some respectability!"[60] Vodou's role in sustaining the struggle for freedom and dignity and its contribution to cultural and artistic expression in Haiti is beyond question.

My study of this intriguing religious philosophy was not informed by those who continue to regard it as a cabal of evil fit for the sinister entertainment in Hollywood. As Bellegarde-Smith says: "The slave owners feared their slaves' traditions not because they believed in them . . . but because of the revolutionary potential of elements that unified persons of a same ethnic group or from diverse groups."[61] Since the days under plantation slavery, Vodou has played a vital role in the political, cultural, and religious experiences of the Haitian people; it is a wellspring of Haitian artistic and literary expressions. Metraux writes, "The useful and productive role of Voodoo in the domain of arts is there for all to see. In music and dancing it has allowed the Haitian peasantry to maintain and develop its African heritage—and develop it to a very high level of excellence. A well-conducted Voodoo ceremony is something worth seeing: drummers and dancers are often virtuosos of their craft."[62]

Vodou is appreciated when it is viewed in its historical cultural context and in light of its significance in the lives of its practitioners, seen as paralleling that of its main competitor, Christianity. On the issue of Vodou's contribution to Haiti, the thirteen Haitians who, in 1997, signed the "Declaration" of the Congress of Santa Barbara called KOSANBA should have the final word: "The presence, role, and importance of Vodou in Haitian history, society, and culture are unarguably a part of the national ethos. The impact of the religion qua spiritual and intellectual discipline on particular national institutions, human and gender relations, the family, the plastic arts, philosophy and ethics, oral and written literature, language, popular and music, science and technology, and the healing arts is undisputable."[63]

Long live the religion of Vodou.

PART III

Santeria and Palo Monte

Cuban Religion of the Orisha and Drums

5

Caribbean Santeria

Judith Gleason and Elise Mereghetti's ethnographic film, *The King Does Not Lie: The Initiation of a Priest of Shango* (1992), brought Santeria to the big screen as a religion sui generis, appealing for understanding on its own terms after centuries of suppression and persecution. The documentary takes one on an exciting journey through the eight-day initiation of a Santeria priest in Puerto Rico, where more than five hundred thousand Santeria and Santerismo devotees (and many more in Cuba and the United States) are said to follow Orisha as a genuine form of spirituality. In part, this movie is a response to a constitutional battle over First Amendment rights that engulfed U.S. animal rights organizations, New York and Florida law enforcement and health departments, and exilic Cuban and Puerto Rican Santeria communities in the 1980s. It made its way to the U.S. Supreme Court in 1992 over the right to perform animal sacrifice in Santeria churches in the United States.[1] Santeria again stole the spotlight during the Elian Gonzalez saga, when a Cuban boy (rescued at sea on Thanksgiving) and the Santeria religion were thrust into the eye of a stormy tryst between religion and American politics. Exilic Cubans, the media, and politicians fought a nasty political and judicial battle over the fate of the juvenile while Catholic devotees saw apparitions of the Virgin Mary hovering over Elian's home and others declared him a Cuban Christ. Adding to the intrigue, followers of *la regla de ocha* in Florida were absolutely convinced that the deity Oshun saved Elian to show Cubans of the diaspora that she is still their mother goddess[2] and patron saint, the Most Holy Virgin Mary. Afro-Caribbean religions, Christianity, and U.S. politics have not had a stranger marriage relationship.

Santeria, also called regla de ocha and Lucumi, is the most dominant African-based religion brought to colonial Cuba, emerging on the island as a

Oshun, La Virgen de Caridad del Cobre.
(Illustration by Kelly Hawes.)

spiritual force that spread among Cuban exiles in Puerto Rico, Venezuela, and the United States.[3] It evolved as a system of spiritual communication containing beliefs and practices associated with the worship and veneration of African orishas in Cuba and in Puerto Rico's creole African and Spanish cultures; there it blended with Catholic Christianity and native traditions in ways that allowed Santeria to keep its religious system intact.[4] Among believers, regla de ocha is a religion of ashe (power) that enhances communication between humans and the divine for empowering the powerless in order to assuage the problems and contradictions of everyday life. It employs sacred space and symbolic signifying, as well as belief in supernatural powers, the potency of rituals, spirit mediation, divination, herbal healing, and human agency as vehicles of spiritual, psychological, and physical wholeness. The product of a needed sacred space that Afro-Cubans created as a refuge in the storm of enslavement, Santeria was a way to find meaning in, and a divine reality that could answer the contradictions and miseries of, a slave society and life's hopelessness among oppressed peoples of African descent. In modern times, devotees of various ethnic backgrounds and class structures find this faith attractive because they believe its practitioners possess special power and intuition to provide protection, explanations, and solutions to problems in life.[5]

The name *Santeria* is a derogatory creation imposed on the religion by white Cuban Catholic clergy to ensure that it is distanced from their Christian faith. According to Miguel De La Torre, the term was popularized in the 1940s in Cuba's La Habana and Matanzas, both home to large numbers of Yoruba settlers.[6] As a result, scholars disagree on what to call the religion and Santeria inherited different aliases: la regla de ocha, *la regla Lucumi*, Lucumi, *la regla de Ifa*, *Abakua*, *Ayoba*, and others, each of which reflects a perception and a significance of its essential nature and origin. The name originated from the Spanish-Cuban word *santos*, meaning worship of the saints, and may have been a term given in mockery. Later Santeria came to represent an Afro-Cuban spirituality called worship of the orishas of the Yoruba religion. Closely associated with Spanish Catholicism in Cuba, *Santeria* is the most common word used to describe the faith in Spanish and English. The terms *Lucumi* (rule of lucumi, a Yoruba self-designation) and *la regla de ocha* (order of the orishas) often replace the word Santeria and show Cuban attempts to correspond saints of Catholic hagiography with the spirituality that Africans brought to Cuba.[7]

The designations *la regla lucumi* and *la regla de ocha* both point to Santeria's Yoruba cosmology. But as Cuban-American linguist Isabel Castellanos said, the origin of the word *lucumi* or *locumi* to identify the Afro-Cuban Yoruba is mysterious. The word may have derived from the people of Ulkamy (also called Ulcami, Ulcama, Ulkami, and Ulkumi), located in ancient Benin. *Lucumi* may have also evolved from *oluku mi* as a friendly greeting among the Yoruba in colonial Cuba.[8] Whether this greeting was an ethnic identification or an expression of solidarity, it pointed to the religious beliefs and practices of Yoruba religion in predominantly urban areas in Cuba.[9] In both la regla de ocha and *la regla lucumi*, adepts affirm that the beliefs and practices of their religion are rooted in African culture and that, although the popular name *Santeria* associates the religion with Catholic sainthood, the African orishas are its dominant references, not the saints.

Cuba is home to many Afro-Caribbean religions. De La Torre, who grew up as both a *hijo de Ellegua* (child of the spirit Ellegua) and a Catholic in Cuba, said, "Four African religious cultural structures live within the overall national Cuban culture: the *palo monte* of Kongo origin; the *regla Arara* of Ewe-fon origin; the *Abakua* Secret Society containing Ejagham, Efik, Efut, and other Calabar roots; and the regla de ocha of the Yoruba. The latter, as Santeria, is the most popular in Cuba."[10] Cubans, especially in Havana and Santiago de Cuba, understood and spoke Yoruba and kikongo as late as the early 1900s. Cuban ethnic designations like Lucumi, Carabali (Efik), Arara (Fon), and Kongo (kikongo), and others later took on ritual significance rather than ethnic descriptions. Santeria is well known as part of the Yoruba orisha tradition that has millions of followers in the Americas, most of whom are in Brazil. Cuban ethnographer Miguel Barnet thinks that "Yoruba mythology offers the only consistent body of ideas about the creation of the world to be found among the treasures of Cuba's traditional popular culture."[11] As the most dominant Afro-Cuban religion, Yoruba beliefs and practices emerged with distinct features that subsumed elements of the other religious structures under what is now called Santeria. Although Palo Monte is very strong in Cuba, Lucumi-Santeria became the most widespread and dominant force in Afro-Cuban spirituality.

Because of the vicious persecution of its followers in the past, the stigma attached to the religion, and the allegation that it is a satanic cult that abuses animals in sacrifices, not all devotees readily admit their connections to the faith. Therefore no one knows precisely how many Lucumi or Santeria followers exist in the Americas, although the estimates are very high. In 1999, my wife and I interviewed two Cuban female Santeria devotees in their thirties (from Havana), whom I call M One and M Two because their first names begin with M. M One said to us, "The orisha faith (Santeria) is more alive in Cuba now than it ever was before. Lots of people follow the orisha way. Since the Communist Glasnost, it has become even more popular but we still have to be careful and keep it a secret because of Fidel."[12] As Mary Ann Clark says, "Hundreds of thousands of Americans participate in this religion. Some are fully committed priests and priestesses; others are 'god-children' or members of a particular house tradition."[13] Estimates suggest there are a few million Santeria devotees and sympathizers in U.S. cities, most of whom are female.[14] Something other than the usual cult psychology magically draws followers to the Santeria faith. Its charismatic leaders neither occupy a focal place of worship in the religion nor do they brainwash devotees into blind obedience and psychotic fantasies. Puerto Rican-American anthropologist Megine Gonzalez-Wippler reported that priests and priestesses she encountered in Cuba during her research are respected *only* as proxies of the orishas and as teachers in the mysteries of Santeria. *Santeros* or *santeras* who become *endiosados*, or self-deifying or gratifying, are discredited by the community.[15] Whatever sustains interest in this magnet called Santeria, its survival in colonial Cuba comes against tremendous odds.

The African Experience in Cuba

The first Africans brought into Cuba, both slave and free, came from Spain via Santo Domingo in 1511, after King Ferdinand decided slavery was essential for American colonization. The island's slave trade continued until 1873. For about 250 years of this period, Spain focused its economic interest on the Spanish Main and neglected its island colonies' struggling economies; therefore the importation of Africans into Cuba remained comparatively low, totaling about one hundred thousand people between 1511 and 1774. As a colony of Spanish artisans, petty bureaucrats, frontiersmen, and small-scale farmers, Cuba was a kind of backwater of the big Atlantic slave trade, but the coming of plantation sugar and several related events revolutionized Cuba's economy and brought vast numbers of Africans into Spain's new "Pearl of the Antilles" in the next one hundred years. When Britain captured Havana during the Seven Years War (1756 to 1763), it occupied Cuba for less than a year but it brought into the colony close to eleven thousand Africans and significantly increased the slave population. As a condition for its return of the island, Britain secured an agreement from Spain to allow British trade and capital in Cuba. A 1779 Spanish decree conceding free trading in slaves prepared the island for filling the vacuum in the world sugar market left by Saint Domingue following the Haitian Revolution.[16]

Supported by British-American capital, Cuba's new economic fortune was based largely on its cultivation of huge tracts of virgin land, use of new technology such as the steam engine and the locomotive, improved techniques for large-scale sugar production, and vast quantities of cheap slave labor.[17] Between the 1760s and the 1860s, Cuba experienced a second boom in which sugar production was the cornerstone of the colony's new economic prosperity. The building of hundreds of new mills for mass production of sugar demanded large numbers of field and factory workers for the huge *ingenios*, big mills supporting the sugar revolution, and led to the massive importation of Africans as slaves into Cuba until the 1870s. Between the 1760s and 1873, when the last officially recorded "slaver" arrived in Cuba, close to eight hundred thousand Africans were imported to Cuba.[18] After Britain made slave trading illegal in 1807 and signed a treaty with Spain against slave trading in the Americas in 1818, the clandestine trade continued, and African captives continued to pour into Cuba in large numbers long after 1820. Between 1790 and 1821, about 240,000 blacks were brought in, and from 1821 to 1865, Cuban slave imports well exceeded two hundred thousand. It is argued that about a million Africans were forced into Cuba. By 1840, Cuba was about 60 percent black, and Africans remained as high as 70 percent of the population today.[19] Strangely enough, most Cubans who found haven in the United States because of Castro's revolution were whites.

African Cultural Origins

African cultural traditions that survived slavery suggest that the number of Yoruba people brought into Cuba at the height of the sugar boom was substantially higher than that of other ethnic groups. Many slaves arriving in Cuba came through Dahomey. Most of the early arrivals came from the Gulf of Guinea, the Bight of Benin, and the Kongo region. Various subgroups of Yoruba and Kongo peoples constituted the majority of Cuba's slave population and came to exert the greatest influence on the development of Afro-Cuban culture (religion, music, dance);[20] they played a dominant role in Cuba's colonial creole society. Cuba's population first consisted of native peoples, Africans, and Europeans.

Although most of the natives found in Cuba in the early 1500s died in a very short time, remnants of native Ciboney, Arawak, and Taino peoples contributed to the island's creole culture through such things as techniques for the growing of native foods, the production of tobacco, herbal medicine, and a small human pool for labor and for intermarriage mainly with early Spanish colonizers. In addition to constituting the main labor force, Africans, by their sheer numbers, made a substantial impact on Cuba's religious culture, second only to Catholicism.

Although the names of its divinities vary from one region of Cuba to another, the Yoruba religion is observed in cities named by Afro-Cubans as homes of their ancestors, and in the Yoruba language spoken by older followers. William Bascomb found that certain objects—such as sacred stones and herbal plants—as well as animal sacrifice played a very important role in Santeria rituals.[21] Initiates believe that sacred stones increase their powers when the blood of sacrificial animals flow over them. "As in Nigeria, the special herbs mixed with water serve to cleanse, refresh, and prepare devotees and ritual objects for contact with the orisha. Striking similarities exist between two forms of Afro-Cuban divination—Ifa, which uses an *opele* ("divination chain") and *dilogun* ("sixteen cowrie shells")—and Yoruba divination[22] in Africa. Other African traditions from Kongo, however, also surfaced in Cuba under different aliases. Afro-Cubans of Yoruba and Kongo ancestry participated in their traditions first through ethnic association and later by means of initiation. As Joseph Murphy puts it, they maintained their African identity through initiation into *la regla lucumi* or *la regla conga*. "With the disintegration of the ethnic *cabildos* toward the end of the nineteenth century, Yoruba institutions increasingly took on the liturgical forms of the rites of private 'houses' rather than the civil or 'national' assemblies of African ethnicity. The house of Santeria is a community related purely by kinship of initiation into Yoruba rites"[23] and rituals.

Yoruba groups intermixed with others from different parts of West and Central Africa and grouped themselves into *naciones* ("nations") in different countries in the Americas, each group having a distinctive name. George Brandon and others noted that descendants of many of those emerged as the Lucumi nation, a secondary Afro-Cuban phenomenon within the heterogeneous Yoruba mix within Cuban slavery. Yoruba dominates Lucumi in the rituals of Santeria—especially in its prayers, chants, and songs—and Lucumi descendants often claim Yoruba origins. Since *naciones* represented various ethnic groups of African peoples with distinct languages, cultural traditions, and other features, the presence of numerous persons from the same cultural cohorts made it less painful for Africans to adapt to their harsh and unfriendly environment. The Lucumi group had the strongest influence on what was called the cabildos ("fraternities"), and members of different *naciones* often converted to Lucumi. Santeria's African traditions are derived mainly from Yoruba beliefs and practices, especially Lucumi, but the religon accommodated other elements as well. Because of their shared sacred cosmology and space, Yoruba, Catholicism, and other religious entities strongly influenced Lucumi.[24] Its avatars associated African deities with the idea of sainthood in Catholicism, not as human objects of worship but as parallel spiritual imitations of convenience. As Murphy says, Cuban Yoruba and their descendants preserved "a number of African religious practices by developing complex parallelisms among their experiences with their Yoruba society, the other African traditions that were brought to Cuba, and . . . Catholicism that was the official religion of the island"[25] colony.

Scholars disagree on the nature of the process through which the parallelism occurred and describe the phenomenon variously as syncretism, transcultural adaptation, intrapenetration, symbiosis, and intersystems. The nature of Santeria itself and the way it survived in the Spanish Caribbean indicate that all of the above were involved in the process and therefore best fit the description "creolization." Barnet sees a clear transformation in the evolution that gave rise to Santeria and says that elements of Yoruba culture that were much richer than others "served as paradigms for the birth and adaptation of transcultural expressions that are still today an integral part of Cuba's cultural legacy. . . . Transplanted to Cuba at various historical moments . . . [Yoruba] underwent crucial alteration when it clashed against other African religions and Catholicism."[26] Although the religions blended and adopted other elements, Yoruba still retained its African identity. The most obvious and common creole feature of Yoruba in Cuba is the paralleling of African divinities with Catholic saints, represented by chromolithographs and New World rituals. Since the late 1700s, the Santeria-orisha pathway has been paved with Spanish Catholic hagiography, sacred images used to facilitate the orisha worship of the African Yoruba. Afro-Cubans used the iconography of Catholic sainthood to express and often conceal their devotion to their African orishas, as they construed their religious identity in response to the Christianity of their oppressors[27] and other creolizing forces in Cuban society. Instead of abandoning their traditions to adopt Christianity, Afro-Cubans mediated the two systems, a process made easier by the facts that African religions were open to new influences and that numerous parallels existed between those religions and Catholic mythology. For example, many saints and orishas have similar functions, so the Africans had little difficulty identifying each saint with an orisha. The adoption of Catholic elements in Yoruba was both the result of physical proximity and functional similarities. Thus, while Yoruba remains the root of Santeria, the rituals and practices of the Afro-Cuban religion show many instances of cultural borrowing from Catholicism, other African traditions, and spiritism.

Confraternity and Identity

African religions survived in a Cuban plantation society dominated by a colonial, capitalist Christian culture; Christianity gave its blessings to various aspects of the sugar culture, and in a system of symbols, myths, and rituals protected its importance in colonial society. The Catholic Church christened sugar estates with Catholic rites and blessings and graced parishes and planta- tions with the names of its saints. Through its holy rituals, the Church as- signed plantations heavenly patrons who could go to their aid in times of stress or need. To give it legitimacy, the Church sanctified slavery. It blessed new build- ings and sugar mills on the estates, planters and their families, livestock, slave ships bound for Europe and Africa, and even slave whipping posts. The priests prayed and sprinkled holy water on factories, slaves, and machines and pro- nounced Christian benediction so that the planters would prosper in the name of the God of the Church. As soon as the ritual was over, enslaved Africans joined teams of oxen as fellow beasts of burden to haul the cane to the mills. Accord- ing to Brandon,

> At one level, Catholic hegemony was alienating and coercive. Whether through naked force . . . or through control of the definitions of reality and the ability to bestow or negate the significance of things, ideas, and events, it remained compulsive and separating. At another level, though, it bound together those who were, in reality, opposed. Despite their re- sistance, the powerful and the powerless, the master and the slave, the oppressors and the oppressed were tied together in a veil in which their relative positions were simply facts of life.[28]

So any initiative the church took in the interest of the slaves was out of both economic and religious self-interest and comes as no surprise.

Slavery shattered traditional African tribal, ethnic, and family relations, forcing survivors to forge a new kind of gemeinschaft in captivity. The ethnic "nations" by which Africans grouped themselves in Africa had to be replaced by something Africans could use in their Babylonian-like American captivity. One such institution was the confraternity established in Spanish and Portu- guese Catholic colonies. The cabildos, or Catholic Brotherhoods, united "god- parents (*padrinos*) and their godchildren (*ahijados*) in a series of close inclusive horizontal relationships that extended beyond blood ties"[29] and ethnic notions. The Catholic Church encouraged and supported more than a dozen *naciones* ("ethnic nations") established for Afro-Cubans as associations or fraternities (the cabildos or *cofradias*). These brotherhoods consisted of Africans from roughly the same ethnic background who were placed under Catholic patronage. Ethno- historian Katherine Hagedorn noted that from the mid-sixteenth century, the Church organized the cabildos to facilitate control of slave communities in Span- ish colonies. With the dramatic increase in slave populations in the nineteenth century, the "membership and visibility of the cabildos"[30] grew.

The cabildo, a form of local town council, has its origin in fourteenth- century Spanish church-state municipal initiatives to regulate and provide for the rapidly growing African population in southern Spain and to incorporate it into the Church. As historian Jane Landers says, Spanish "church officials approved the earliest documented religious confraternity *cofradia* for Africans," which "provided fraternal identity for their members and critical social services for their communities" in several urban cities in Spain.[31] Iberian Africans also founded their own fraternities in Valencia and other cities. This Medieval ecclesiastical institutional model was transplanted into Spanish and Portuguese colonies in the Americas by colonial church-state governments that saw in the organizations an opportunity to regulate and Christianize Africans and to infiltrate their culture with European values. Afro-Cubans, however, used the cabildos to preserve their ethnic identity, African worldview, and adaptation to life in a hostile environment. The cabildos provided a safe place for Africans to obtain relief—even if only socially and psychologically—from the wretched colonial slave life, preserving and discreetly nurturing African identity and culture.

During the 1800s, the cabildo gradually expanded its functions and prerogatives: its membership came to include both enslaved Africans and *criollos* (Cuban-born slaves), as well as free blacks. The cabildos served as fraternal mutual aid societies and social clubs; they provided support for the aged and infirm, assisted members with social services, raised funds for the manumission of some of its members, acquired real estate for its operation, and organized celebrations and festivals. The cabildos sponsored carnivals, fiestas, dances, and other cultural activities on Christian religious holidays such as the Epiphany of Jesus. They also kept their culture alive by preserving and transplanting African religions in Cuba. Castellanos says, "If the *barracon* ("communal slave household") promoted cultural sharing and intermingling among slaves of widely diverse origin, the cabildos were places where people of similar cultural and linguistic origin could worship, relax, and interact."[32] Religious holiday celebrations were marked by grand processions decorated with African colors of their *naciones*. Masked dancers performed to the beat of African drums as free and enslaved blacks marched through the streets with fanfare and pride and without fear of punishment from their slave masters.

Some groups of cabildos became quite dominant in colonial Cuba. The Arara group, made up of Fon people, was popular among Haitians who fled to Cuba during the Haitian Revolution or migrated there to work on the sugar plantations. The Abakua, an all-male secret society called *ñañigos*, was associated with the Efik people from the Niger Delta. The secrecy of the Abakua caused white Cubans to label them underground criminals and advocates of satanic practices. Reglas Congas, called Palo Monte and Mayombe, comprised several sects of people of Kongo origin and were the most well-known cabildo groups. These Kongo cabildos proliferated in the 1800s, especially in the northwestern part of Cuba, known for its huge *latifundi* sugar plantations. Under the antiblack sentiments of U.S. Jim Crow culture and a general fear of African ascendancy in Cuba, whites accused cabildo groups of practicing sorcery, witchcraft, and spells in their religious rituals[33] and attempted to shut them down. The cabildos, however, were a vital social outlet where Afro-Cubans preserved their religious and cultural traditions while adapting them to creole Cuban Christian culture. David Brown, who produced one of the most extensive and sophisticated treatments of the cabildos in print, contends that Santeria owes its strength and survival to the confraternity that functioned as its early temple.[34]

In the second half of the 1800s, Afro-Cubans were forced to find new ways of preserving the religion they practiced under the auspices of cabildos, which lost their cultural hegemony to a series of bad fates. Brandon listed these main challenges as (1) the deterioration of relations between the government, the church, and the cabildos after the 1860s; (2) the movement to abolish slavery, which affected the social composition of the groups and also made some whites nervous; (3) the declining influence of the Catholic Church on political power; (4) the destruction caused by the Cuban wars for independence; and (5) deep-rooted fear of the Africanization of Cuba.[35] As Stanley Urban explains, because of the increasing threat of the U.S. sectional furor over the Kansas-Nebraska Act of 1854, which intensified northern opposition to the expansion of slavery in the western United States, many southern planters saw Africanization in Cuba as an attempt to undermine slavery and their "good southern ways" in the United States and on the island. In 1854 the Louisiana legislature attacked the Africanization of Cuba by urging the U.S. government to prevent it by any means necessary. Spanish Creoles also saw the numerical predominance of Africans in Cuba and the scare of 1853 to 1855 as threatening to "lead to uprisings of slaves such as occurred in the neighborhood of Matanzas in 1843"[36] or following Haiti's more tragic example. During this period, Christianity fell out of favor with the government and the progressive movement, both of which saw the Church as preserving the status quo and as being reactionary and anti-independence. This weakened the Church's ability to help and protect the cabildos as a religious institution. Each cabildos had to be registered with its local parish church and receive an assigned space in religious processions and festivals. Growing Afrophobia or fear of black solidarity, fear of revolt, and the need to develop a means of controlling the swelling African population drove the Church and the government to legalize the cabildos[37] in order to register them, and by so doing proscribed them.

Viewing the cabildos as social clubs that lost their original ethnic and religious character, the government instituted laws in 1877 regulating their operation. In 1882, authorities required the cabildos to obtain licenses that prohibited them from functioning on the basis of ethnicity. By 1884, the "Good Government Law" further prohibited cabildos from meeting without a government representative present and banned drumming and street parades held on the eve of the Christian epiphany. The old-style cabildos were essentially outlawed in 1888. New cabildos of the 1890s had to show an open membership policy. Legally constituted cabildos, such as Arara Magino and El Cabildo

Africano Lucumi, continued practicing their religions secretly and remained active mainly to manage what was left of their mutual-aid organizations. African culture and ethnic distinction, kept alive by the presence of new African arrivals in Cuba, waned because of the abolition of slavery and state policy. The ethnic notions on which cabildos were established earlier became obsolete because of government regulations and group intermingling. Among other results, "the secret religious practices ceased to be solely the property of Afro-Cubans" (they were "passed on to people with mixed ancestry"), and membership into their religious order shifted from ethnic heritage to initiation rites.[38] Afro-Cuban religious culture also came under attack from the establishment as the government censured the cabildos, even confiscating religious items, under the pretense of eliminating sorcery and witchcraft from Cuban society. With the formation of the Cuban Independence Party of Color and its agitation for social and political change, repression of Afro-Cuban religions reached an all-time high in the 1912 massacre of thousands of blacks. Influenced by the spirit of Jim Crow from the United States, stereotypical portrayal of blacks and prejudice against what remained of the cabildos created ugly images and attitudes toward Afro-Cuban religious groups, with deadly consequences.[39]

After a white girl died in mysterious circumstances in 1919, the media blamed Santeria for her death, and a *brujo* ("witch-doctor") madness swept Cuba. This led to mass U.S.-type lynching fueled by outrageous rumors of santeros kidnaping white children and using their blood and entrails in satanic rituals. Angry lynch mobs descended on black Cuban communities with a vengeance. After the violent mayhem in which several blacks were murdered, the mob was praised for taking a brave step to make blacks civilized. Even famous Cuban sociologist Fernando Ortiz was caught up in unscientific racial profiling and damnation. He produced so-called research to argue that blacks were morally inferiority to whites and that their cultures and religions were the source of Cuba's crime problems. According to De LaTorre, "Ortiz insists that African immorality was 'in the mass of the blood of black Africans,' a contamination affecting lower-class whites. The fetishism of Santeria had to be eliminated; hence he suggests the lifelong isolation of its leaders."[40] To counter the anti-African pariah, an ethnically mixed group of Cuban intellectuals organized a cultural movement known as Afro-Cubanism, which celebrated creole culture and resisted the attempt to "whiten" Cuba. The movement was short-lived but it challenged the ugly stereotypes and attracted more Cubans of different ethnic backgrounds to African religions than before. Whites and creoles who were secretly involved in Santeria before the 1930s now brought their involvement into the open in greater numbers.

Scholars noted that during Castro's Revolution both government and revolutionaries sought help from Santeria powers. In 1958, Cuban dictator Fulgencio Baptista turned to Santeria to obtain help from the orishas to ward off young Castro's revolutionary movement, but perhaps his bad political karma

was too great for the orisha to overlook. At the same time, Castro and his gue-
rilla army identified themselves with Santeria and established their base
in Oriente, a hotbed of Afro-Cuban culture and the Yoruba religion. In 1959,
guerillas from Oriente marched into Havana wearing necklaces and waving
the red and black flag of Ellegua, Santeria's trickster orisha.[41] A national legend
has it that both the Christian Holy Spirit and the Santeria orisha Obatala
blessed Castro's rise to power when they symbolically rested on his shoulder in
the form of a dove during his appeal for peace in a speech given at Camp Colombia in January 1959.[42] As a celebration of African heritage, revolutionary
Cuba elevated the status of black religion in 1960 and 1961 in the *Conjunto
Folklorico* performances, which were part of a Cuban folklore movement. Within
a year, however, Castro's government officially distanced itself from religion by
declaring its intent to eliminate education supported by religious sources. The
government saw religion as a source of possible destabilization or an avenue for
counterrevolutionary ideas.

Since blacks supported Castro during the revolution and thought they had
little to lose, they continued supporting the government, hoping for a brighter
future. They soon realized, however, that Afro-Cuban religion, also regarded
as an *opiate* of the people, is an enemy of the Marxist-Leninist philosophy. The
regime began silencing religion at the institutional level and saw Afro-Cuban
religious traditions as a backward and primitive residue of capitalism and
slavery—a nonprogressive reality dispensable in the new Cuba. Castro resumed persecution of Santeria followers in the 1960s and imprisoned santeras
and santeros, at least one of whom devotees claim was executed; the evidence,
however, is not corroborated, and it is not clear whether he was killed for political reasons. To hold ceremonies, followers need authorization from *Comites
para la Defensa de la Revolucion* ("the Committees for the Defense of the Revolution"), an arm of the State Police ubiquitously placed throughout every city
and routinely declining such authorization. "Degraded as 'folklore' rather than
religion, Santeria became subject to a growing number of restrictions, including bans against practicing the rituals or participating in the festivals,"[43] to the
utter dismay of its followers.

My Santeria informant M Two said, "The blacks who helped Castro during
the revolution were greatly disappointed when they discovered that their freedoms were taken away and they could not practice their religion freely. Even as
late as the eighties, you could not let anyone know you were a follower of the
orisha. Things are changing and it is becoming fashionable to celebrate African culture in the open; but one still has to be careful discussing their relationship with the religion."[44] In the late 1980s, the Cuban government again began
showing tolerance of Afro-Cuban religions, although it packaged it as a folklore
and exotic Cuban culture of the African past. As Hagedorn says, "In twentieth-
century Cuba, the term *folklore Afro-Cubano* ("Afro-Cuban folklore") has come
to eclipse the potential divinity of Afro-Cuban performance, focusing mainly
on isolated and decontextualized songs and dances originally meant to evoke

specific deities, but now dramatized and choreographed to evoke audience applause."[45] After its history of persecution and suppression, Santeria survived and became recognized officially as a religion in Cuba, but it continues to require authorization to perform certain ceremonies and rituals.

Orisha Mythology

In its fundamental view of the world, Santeria shares with other Afro-Caribbean religions the same African cosmology or structure of beings in the universe and the forces that sustain it. God heads the invisible world and has many agents, called orishas, who act as intermediary beings or servants. Santeria practitioners serve a multiplicity of spirits in the orishas but it is, nonetheless, strongly monotheistic; it holds to the existence of one God as the central creative force in the universe and a supporting cast of spirits who are God's extensions. These spiritual entities are often called gods only because they function as deities. They are multidimensional mythological beings with human-like characteristics and personality. They represent forces of nature but function as sacred patrons or guardian angels of devotees. They are not construed as remote distant deities, as is Olodumare, but as beings who participate in and govern the daily routines of their devotees;[46] they defend, deliver, console, and come to the aid of their followers the same way relatives do.

The orishas provide a critically important nexus in Santeria whose traditions show variations in their interpretation of the divine-human relationship. According to one legend, Olodumare created all of the intermediate beings and endowed them with his power to work on his behalf in the natural and spiritual worlds. Issuing from Olodumare through the orishas and ancestors, therefore, is the cosmic energy ashe, which links and animates everything with the spiritual force necessary for accomplishing difficult tasks. In other legends, Olofi or Olofin is a manifestation of Olodumare's creation, Olorun is the creator of the material world, and Eleda is the source of all things, including a spark of the divine in humans.[47] A third *patakis* ("legend") has it that God designated creation of the natural world of humans and physical things to orishas, who now supervise their harmonious working through a system of rewards and punishments, life and death, and health and sickness. Since orishas are responsible for the quality of life, natural phenomena, and activities of the natural realm, they personify elemental forces and are the source of natural disasters as well as good fortune. Rank-and-file santeras or santeros worship both Olofi and orishas, the primary objects of their ceremonies and devotions, and often equate Olofi with Jesus in Christianity. Olodumare is honored as God the mighty creator, mainly during initiation rites or other special occasions. So, as in African Yoruba, many santeras and santeros do not make the Supreme Being their axis mundi in worship. Their objects of ritual actions are orishas who, in return for devotion, mediate powerful ashe to their human devotees.[48] Orishas receive prayers, sacrifices, and other worship, and they respond to devotees through oracles, spirit possession, and mediumship. The ritual means of communication are designed to make more potent ashe in the world to aid human accomplishments and the work of spiritual entities.

In Santeria beliefs, one can obtain superior ashe by gaining access to special knowledge about one's destiny and about the intricate workings of the visible and invisible world. This knowledge is accessible through oracles or divination, initiation, and a deepening personal relationship with one's orisha in order to affect one's destiny. As Murphy notes, practitioners believe Olodumare gives everyone a destiny or road map in life. By understanding this destiny, one grows with it rather than suffers from its predetermination. By cultivating a healthy relationship with the orishas, a devotee can realize "complete fulfillment of their destinies . . . worldly success and heavenly wisdom."[49] Complementing these spiritual entities are the spirits of the living dead or ancestors who also mediate between the human and the divine. In fact, an orisha is often seen as "a divinized ancestor who during his lifetime established connections guaranteeing him control over certain forces of nature."[50] Although ancestral spirits occupy the invisible realm, they are made present and active in the lives of their "family" through blood relations and rituals. After they departed this life, the ancestors joined the privileged Ara Arun, residents of the heavenly skies, but they live in the community among their relatives, whom they are able to council and protect. The ashe of the ancestors is available to the religious community through acquired knowledge and ritual activities performed in honor of the spirits. As a result, devotees recognize and venerate the ancestors in rituals and rites, and invoke their presence at special ceremonies.

Divine-Human Agency

Because they are spiritual beings, the existence of the orishas is an unfalsifiable phenomenon; one cannot prove they exist any more than a Hindu can prove Brahma exists. Yet, Gonzalez-Wippler argues that orishas are real and that their power is not "an intangible, mystical force" that believers nurture in their faith or imagination. The orishas are "raw energy, awesome power visually and materially discernible," and one communicates one's needs directly to them to receive quick results. Since they are direct manifestations of God, they can say immediately if a petitioner's request will be granted. The worship of the orishas demands "strict obedience and total surrender to their will."[51] These orishas have retained most of the characteristics accorded them in Africa relative to their roles in society, representations of the elements of nature, special likes and dislikes, ritual actions, sexuality, and adeptness at diplomacy. A corresponding set of "material symbols" appropriate to each orisha (and a prominent orisha for every important action or concept) exist. Clark states, "The signification of the Orisha can be approached from either side of these statements: one can choose an Orisha and attempt to determine all the material symbols associated with it, or one can move through the physical and conceptual world associating an Orisha with each object found there."[52] Of the hundreds of orishas in African Yoruba mythology, relatively few survived in the Caribbean; and even among those, a few are prominent in some places whereas others seem extinct or obscure. About twenty of the orishas that survived on the island are significant; all of these have their own "paths" and characteristics, called *caminos*, and are seen as having great influence on human life. The following twelve orishas are the most prominent and popular Santeria divinities.

SHANGO

Shango, or Chango, the romantic, flamboyant entity and fierce god of thunder, lightning, and fire—symbolizing power, sexuality, masculinity, and passion—is the most revered and well-known orisha among santeras and santeros. Legend has it that Shango, the fourth African king of the Oyo Empire, was immortalized and became an orisha because he was a courageous warrior and a ruler of distinction. Orisha Shango is also the creole version of a sacred priesthood order, as dramatized in the film *The King Does Not Lie*. Shango doubles as St. Barbara, whose special feast day is observed on December 4. He likes the numbers four and six and is associated with bright red, purple, white, satin, and chevron colors. Devotees must display the appropriate colors at an initiation or ritual sacrifice, where Shango is expected to appear and "perform." According to George Eaton Simpson, "In a ritual, he manifests himself like a bull as he butts with his head. He opens his eyes widely, sticks out his tongue as a symbol of fire, shakes his sacred axe, and holds his genitals in his hands. No other orisha goes through such violent contortions or stages such an unusual pantomime."[53] Shango has an appetite for dry red wine. He likes ram goat, sheep, turtle, turkey, rooster, and bull meats prepared with okra and bananas or *amala* made from cornmeal and palm oil, and he has numerous sacred herbs. Shango is a great dancer and drummer.

OGUN

Ogun (Oggun), among the oldest of the orishas, is a symbol of primal force and divine energy. He is the brother of Eleggua, Ochosi, and Shango, with whom he competes fiercely for the goddess Oshun. Legend has it that after Ogun attempted to rape his mother, he was exiled to the forest and only Oshun had the charm and power to coax him back into society. More commonly, Ogun is associated with the blacksmith's shop and is the god of iron and steel. His symbols are metal tools (shovels, chains, hammers, machetes, picks, and so forth), automobiles, railways, and tanks. He is also the source of minerals. Ogun crossdresses as St. Peter, whose holiday is June 29, and carries the symbolic keys to the kingdom of heaven. He is a shrewd and mischievous deity also associated with St. John the Baptist, and characteristically wields a machete, with which he clears underbrush. He wears sacred beads of purple, scarlet, black, or green, his favorite colors. His temple representations are a pot containing various types of iron objects. He lives in the hills and has many followers. Ogun loves roosters, kola nuts, white beans, smoked fish, palm oil, corn, rum, and cigars. He has more than a dozen sacred herbs and is the first orisha to eat at a given feast when there is an animal sacrifice. Because he is loved by police officers, doctors, and farmers, he has a professional air.[54]

ORUNMILA
Orunmila, also Orula or Orunla, is regarded as the master of all knowledge, divination, and concentrated magical science and powers. As ruler of the realm of the divine, he is father of the mysteries. He is the owner of Ifa divination, entrusted to him by Olodumare at the creation of the world, and the repository of knowledge about the destiny of all. He was the only orisha to witness the creation of the universe and the establishment of human destinies. Devotees believe that Orunmila is present in heaven as each *ori* chooses its destiny, then he comes to earth to be incarnated in individual human beings.[55] He "cross-dresses" as Saint Francis of Assisi, whose special day is October 4, and is known for his piety. Legend has it that the *tablero* of Ifa, the chief instrument used in divination of the future, belongs to him. Orunmila is therefore ascribed mythological abilities for interpreting devotees' future. He has limitless power for which he is revered and respected, but people have little communication with him directly. Sometimes the wise and intuitive Orunmila gets cantankerous and, with an iron will, may make rash decisions. But he is a greatly loved orisha who favors the number sixteen, wears yellow and green, drinks coconuts, eats black hens, and has many sacred herbs.

ELEGGUA
Eleggua (or Elegbara and Eshu), the trickster orisha, had Cuban revolutionaries from Oriente marching into Havana wearing his necklaces and waving his red and black flags. Ochosi, Oggun, and Eleggua form the triumphant mythological trio of warrior *santos* that have held a prominent position in the Cuban Santeria psyche. As Barnet states, "Fate, the unexpected, forgetfulness, tragedy, good and bad luck, any sort of triumph, and even our own actions and hopes depend on Eleggua [or] Echu. He is indisputably the most influential of the Lucumi santos who have exerted their authority over Cuba."[56] Eleggua is the fearless deity ruler of roads, who opens and closes paths and masters crossroads and the future. Santeria ceremonies begin and end with an incantation to him in request for his permission to perform initiations. His blessings must be sought before executing magic spells, and he must be given first place in a sacrifice. Eleggua cross-dresses as St. Martin, St. Anthony, and St. Serita, and is especially fond of children; often he is represented by a boyish stone headpiece carved with bulging eyes and with ears made of cowrie shells. Eleggua is a great magician whose spells are not easily broken, and he can divine the future without sacred tools. According to Simpson, "In Cuba, this restless god

personifies destiny or luck, and his attitude can make it easy or difficult for a devotee to realize a particular desire. Eleggua tells jokes, often harsh ones, and engages in mischievous caprice."[57] He smokes a large cigar, loves alcohol, and prefers pork, male chicken, smoked fish, roasted possum, palm oil, and toasted corn for food.

Female Orishas

OSHUN

Oshun, or Oshun-Kole—the gifted, beautiful, affectionate, sensual goddess of luxury, and pleasure, ruler of oceans and fresh waters—is one of the most popular and venerated orishas. She is called the giver of life, mother of the orishas, and possessor of feminine virtues; she guards women during pregnancy. Oshun walks many paths: she is given to industrious intuitions, manages finances, and loves music and dancing. As Kole Kole, Oshun represents children and the poor and needy. She typifies the "sensuous saint" and controls the knowledge and art of sexuality and lovemaking in human pleasure and marriage. Legend has it that Oshun used her charm to lure Oggun out of his wild forest life into the city. She seduces other male orisha lovers, although her main consort is Shango. Ogun loves everything yellow and her ornaments and *elekes* ("necklaces") reveal expensive tastes. Her favorite foods are peacock, rooster, turtle, canary, and duck meats. She also eats spinach, pumpkins, oranges, yellow fruits, and sweet potatoes. Cross-dressed as Cuba's patron saint and mother, la Virgin (Our Lady of Regla) de la Caridad del Cobre, whose feast day the church celebrates on September 7, the public statue of this goddess of love represents the graces of Cuban women. She willingly helps people in times of need and shows great patience and kindness but will viciously defend her integrity and honor when assailed. Oshun has become a national identity symbol of hope in a distressed Cuba and, since 1959, a metaphor for peace and reconciliation among ethnic Cubans in the diaspora.[58]

YEMAYA

The sister of Oshun and a favorite orisha, Yemaya is also the model mother and giver of life, protector of maternity, goddess of the oceans, and patron of mariners. As if to debunk stereotypes of black inferiority, ignorance, and low IQ in Cuba, the black Yemaya is seen as the goddess of rational thinking, good judgment, and superior intellect. Her temperament is as complex as her wisdom: she wears seven alternate blue and red beads; she dances as vigorously as angry waves of the sea; she is like a wild tempest but is often calm and peaceful; she is majestic, haughty, and sensual but protects her children with motherly grace.[59] Since her face is always masked, she is revealed only in dreams. The anchor, the half moon, and the silver sun announce her presence. Like Oshun, Yemaya is also one of Shango's wives and cross-dresses as Our Lady of Regla. Blue and white are her colors and she loves fruits, bananas, male goats, poultry, and fish. Her statue is a beautiful matron with a prominent and voluptuous breast that bespeaks fertility.

OBATALA

Obatala, or Oddua walks many paths: the creator of the world, source of all beginnings, supreme judge, principal messenger, husband and wife. Obatala is androgynous; he is Olofi's son and Olodumare's wife. He has multiple personalities and appears in as many as sixteen female and male forms. While he has these different personae, his feminine personality, Oddua, is dominant. She (he) cross-dresses as the Holy Our Lady of Mercy; she is regarded as the goddess of purity, truth, justice, mercy, wisdom, and peace, and is represented as a white dove. Obatala's special day is September 24, the birthday of Our Lady of Mercy. She has a lucky number, 8, and is obsessed with the color white. The hills and mountains of Cuba are his; there one finds most of his special herbs. In Santeria rituals, Obatala is number one. Of him Barnet says, "He is the head, birth, that which stands high, pure, and clean. For this reason, in the rites of initiation the color white is used as a symbol of what is born pure in life, and an *iyawo*, an initiate, spends an entire year dressed in white as a sign of being reborn or a new life within the Santeria world."[60]

BABALUAIYE, OSANYIN, AND OCHOSI

Three orishas thought to be important to devotees but less prominent in the orisha cultus are Osanyin, Babaluaiye, and Ochosi. Babaluaiye (Babalu-Aye), Cuba's creole name for the Ewe-Fon-Dahomey Shopona, or Chankpana, god of illness, who can punish and kill through disease, cross-dresses as St. Lazarus. This deity reigns supreme in Santeria houses and requires submission to his authority. As a sign of his most characteristic work and association, he dresses in jute and sackcloth to replicate the ancient biblical symbol of distress and pain. He also has a bag strung across his chest in which he carries his favorite food, corn, and has a dog (or dogs) who frequently cleans his wounds. As the orisha of illness and disease, he is associated with a wide variety of sickness and their agents. For this he is at once dreaded, loved, and respected for what he can do to anyone who antagonizes him. Babaluaiye works miracles and is strict and unforgiving to devotees who disobey him or break their pledges. This unkempt and dreadful-looking creature is said to be a womanizer and has a growing cult following in Cuba. According to Barnet, "Devotees of St. Lazarus or Baba are given to . . . performing the great sacrifice of flagellation. On the seventeenth of every month, they dress in sackcloth. . . . On December 17, his feast day, they fulfill a pledge that is now traditional in Havana"[61] in his honor.

Osanyin, or Osain, the spirit-owner of forest leaves, often associated with St. Raphael, St. Joseph, and St. Jerome, is the possessor of knowledge that sprang from the earth. As a result, he is the head herbalist in healing rituals. To show his connectin to illness, Osanyin's statue has one eye, one leg, and one arm. A santero or santera must obtain permission from Osanyin before enter-

ing the forest to collect the twelve sacred leaves for the ritual to make an initiate an *iyawo*. He has an appetite for tortoise meat. Ochosi, a member of the
triune orisha warriors or *guerreros*, is an extremely skillful hunter and scout
invoked for the protection of warriors. Legend has it that he became the orisha
who protected and sustained the Maroon communities. He protects those who
are on the wrong side of the law as well as persons whose rights are violated. In
more recent times, followers of Santeria associate Ochosi with legal matters as
well as with governance of cities and homes. He "becomes excited when he
attends a ceremony and shouts like a hunter during the chase. In the panto-
mimic dances of hunting his emblem is the bow and arrow."[62] Ochosi also has
healing powers and is an orisha of herbal medicine. He cross-dresses as St.
Norberto, loves the colors blue and yellow, and is fond of fruits and candies.

Regency of Orisha

The orishas operate in a spiritual family relationship with devotees; an initiate
is married to a specific orisha and becomes a *hijo de orisha*, or child of the orisha. The orishas and humans are linked through a large extended family that
reaches back to a single African ancestor who encompasses the living and
the dead. Barnet says that out of this system of African "familial lineage" came
the religious brotherhood made up of godfather and godchildren in a kinship
relationship that goes beyond blood relations to form an inclusive common
lineage. "This family system has been one of the most genuine characteristics
of Santeria in Cuba. The godmother or godfather becomes mother or father of
a brood of children, forming a group popularly known as a *linea de santo*, a line
or lineage of initiates."[63] This relationship between humans and orishas is cultivated through the different *ebbos*—ceremonies, rites, and rituals of the
cultus—without which one can neither obtain power from the orishas nor accomplish anything positive. In the divine-human relationship, devotees say
they do not choose their own orishas the way they chose the religion; the orishas choose and claim them prenatally. One's life and destiny are preordained,
and a parent can tell who their child's protecting orisha is while it is yet unborn. As Murphy observes, "Sometimes the orishas indicate that the child is
meant to be a santero or santera, and that it must be initiated before birth" in
a ritual called *medio asiento*, "medium" or "half of the asiento."[64] This regency
of the orishas can be likened to a horoscope reading; persons are born under
the sign and protection of orishas who affect what the stars predict for them;
the stars are guardian orishas who control human fate and destiny. In the
world of Santeria, nothing happens to humans outside the realm of the orishas,
who influence every good or bad fate. One cannot escape the orishas and must
therefore accept them as part of their reality and learn to live out one's destiny
through their agency. This is made possible through the cultus in the Santeria
religious community.

6

Energy of the Ashe Community
and Cultus

Key Topics

*Fundamentos-Initiation • Custodians of Ashe •
Ebbo and Animal Sacrifice • Ewe Pharmacopeia • Fiestas de Santos*

In the world of Lucumi worship, ashe and ebbo form the basis of cultic performances and services at the *iles* and are the magnet for their many rites, rituals, ceremonies, consultations, and pharmacopeia. These activities represent the works of ritual specialists, acts of devotion by the faith's most committed followers, a community of inquiring needy clients, and a veritable system of communication between human agents and the orishas. An ebbo is a tribute offered to the spirit in the form of sacrifices, offerings, and purificatory oblations. It requires participants to part with something of great value, often a victim, in order to release ashe from its spiritual source into the community. Ashe is the all-pervasive cosmic divine energy with which the gods endow and empower humans. With it, the world was created and sustained; through it, everything is empowered; and with it, all things are made possible. With ashe, the santeros and santeras ("priests" and "priestesses") believe "problems can be solved—illness can be cured, enemies can be subdued, lovers can be brought back"[1] together—and wars can be won.

Participation

Even though you do not expose your relationship to the orisha, it is a living faith that gives you *power*. The orisha is always with you. Most Cubans know about it and respect its power. I follow the orisha! My brother is a *hijo de orisha* (child of the orisha) and I have many friends and relatives who follow the orisha. I cannot give you their names because Fidel made it illegal to follow the orisha way. You have to keep what I tell you in strict confidence because . . . my husband, who works

Drums of the spirit.
(Illustration by Kelly Hawes.)

for the Cuban government, could be in great danger and I could lose my job at this hotel where we are now. (Interview, 1999)

The history of proscription, discrimination, and bad press that santeros and santeras sustained in the past drove their ceremonies into secrecy and closed them to suspicious outsiders, and membership in the faith was carefully monitored and kept confidential. A practitioner who "made the saints" and became a priest had to introduce a *registro* ("inquirer") to Santeria, undercover, and orishas were consulted on whether that inquirer was an agent of the government or if he or she should be allowed membership in the religion. Although this was still relatively true when I interviewed my informants in 1999, Santeria culture had already become popular, locally and internationally. Becoming a santero or santera in today's Cuba is no longer seen as the superstitious backwardness of the ill informed. Erica Moret (an ethnobotanist) states that Santeria is now regarded as a way of making economic progress. Initiation into an Afro-Cuban religion is today "one of the most secure, lucrative, and relatively legal means with which to improve one's material well-being." It is made more popular by the recent "commercialization of ritual activity under the pressure (and oppor-tunities) of mass tourism and the economic crisis in post-Soviet Havana, where a "highly competitive market has developed . . . catering to visiting tourist and expatriate-Cubans."[2] Santeria is a big beneficiary of this development.

Although many people are kindling the fires of tourist curiosity, a sig-nificant clientele enjoys the ashe (powerful magic) associated with Santeria through consultation and healing. A high percentage of Cubans and Puerto Ricans, many of whom are not members of the faith, at some point in their lives visit the ile and have a consultation or seek help from a professional priest. They believe in the power of the orishas and use the priests' services to their advantage. My Cuban interviewees said, "We know Cubans who are Chris-tians and orisha 'seekers' and others who are not orisha followers but who seek out the priest when they have a problem or sickness." They come from different walks of life and for sundry reasons: some seek consultation for the healing of ailments after modern medicine fails to bring them relief from pain and suf-fering, whereas others pursue solutions to domestic, legal, and economic prob-lems. The unemployed obtain blessings and good-luck charms to find jobs, and some politicians, including past presidents Fulgencio Baptista and Fidel Cas-tro, are said to have sought the help of spiritual leaders during their political campaigns and the Revolution.[3]

Fundamentos-Initiation

In this faith, regarded as a religion of dance, divinities, and initiation, devotees' ability to dance their way (progress) through various levels of the rites and ritu-als to the spirits determines their degrees of participation, knowledge, protec-tion, and status. Members "must accept the god-parenthood of a *santera* or *santero* and fulfill minimum responsibilities of service to the orisha"; this entails attending and supporting the feasts of "the godparent's patron *orisha* sponsored by her or his *ile*,"[4] and undergoing the necessary levels of initiations. Entry-level rites are the conferral of the *elekes* ("beaded necklaces"), the making of the *Eleg-gua* (an image of Eleggua), the receipt of warrior orishas of protection, and the making of the saints (undertaking the *asiento* initiation). Santeros and santeras often claim to have received a call to follow an orisha, or were chosen to be devo-tees, but most are brought to the faith by personal recruitment, curiosity, family connection, crisis, and trauma. Whatever their mode of entry, they must experi-ence the important rites of initiation to be a bona fide *aleyo* ("member"). *Aleyos* are persons who have completed the *fundamentos*, or "basic initiations," and are invested with the *elekes* and *los Guerreros*, "necklaces" and "guardian spirits."

In the *fundamentos*, an inquirer undergoes two subsidiary rites: the *col-lares*, or Eleggua, and the *los Guerreros*, or "warriors." In the *collares*, the initi-ate receives a graven image representation of Eleggua, orisha of destiny, and in the *los Guerreros*, an investiture of five major orishas symbolized in five colorful *elekes*. "In a babalawo's house, his Ifa godchildren receive the collares—four to six color-coded oricha necklaces—from an Ocha priest or priestess, often the babalawo's wife, who becomes their padrina or madrina in 'santo.'"[5] Color combinations in necklaces represent and correspond to five orishas, any one of which can later be the person's chief orisha. The necklaces, consecrated in a washing ritual called the *omiero*, symbolize and transmit the blessings and protection of the orishas; the *elekes* may increase in number as a devotee rises to higher ranks through initiation,[6] and are associated with different orishas. Devotees should wear their necklaces at all times, except while showering, sleeping, during sexual intimacy (out of respect for the jealous orishas), and (for women) during one's monthly menstruation.[7] This last is a Santeria taboo on female sexuality not seen in African Yoruba. Loss or damage of these sacred implements could be a bad omen; it leaves an initiate unprotected—a state requiring immediate ritual action.

Most participants rarely go beyond the level of *fundamentos*, but some take the ultimate step, the asiento, and get crowned as wives of the orisha. During our interview, M One lifted her necklaces from under her lapel and said, "You see these *elekes*? I got them at my *fundamentos* but I am not crowned, I did not move up to asiento. I am an open-minded Cuban. I believe in trying different religions, including Christianity, though I am not a Christian. If I take the asiento and marry to the orica, I will not have that freedom." A santera conferred M One's necklaces during her *limpieza*, a ceremonial clearing of her head in a ritual herbal bath. Her purification rite lasted seven days and concluded with the *rogacion de la cabeza* or "prayer for the head." She said that on the final day she wore all white clothes, including personal effects and undergarments. When the priestess prayed on her head, she invoked the name of God, ancestors, and several orishas while anointing different parts of her body with herbs and oils (Interview). The santera inquired of the chief orisha whether the spirit was pleased with the rite and, after a sign in the affirmative, completed the *collares* by adorning M One with the orishas' necklaces. These are usually done in the order of importance: the first for Eleggua, the orisha of pathways and doors; the second for Obatala, ruler of the head; and the others for Yemaya, Chango, and Oshun.[8] M One could have been invested also with Orunmila's necklace and bracelet, but only if a babalawo priest had performed her initiation; all of Orunmila's priests are male.

In M One's purse was kept a little stone of Ogun, which she said protects her from negative energy and evil forces. This shows she participated in the *los Guerreros*, the second part of the *fundimentos*, in which she was invested with the symbolic implements of three warrior orishas: Eleggua, Ogun, and Ochossi. M One said to me that if you became interested in following the orisha,

> After you enter into the Yoruba religion and become a *fundamentos*, you are later crowned with the saints to become a santero and get the protection of the warrior orisha. You are crowned with orisha and the orisha warrior protects you from harm. There are many orishas in Yoruba

religion and guerrerra, the warrior, fights for you. Eleggua protects your ways and Ogun, the orisha of iron, defends you at all times. This stone I carry with me belongs to Ogun. The stone has lots of things inside which protect me wherever I go. Oshun protects my head. Ologun, orisha of the ocean, protects me in water. I wear her necklace also when I go to the hospital or anywhere I think I will meet negative energy. (Interview)

About three weeks following the warrior investiture, the initiate receives a visit from the priest who performs the "entry" ritual. At this ceremony, the initiate provides articles for another sacrifice to the orisha. The priestess again offers prayers and divines an *obi* in dilogun—orishas speaking through their own mouths[9]—to confirm that the warriors were properly conferred. If "a diviner encounters a problem in Dilogun or Obi divination, a *babalawo* or Ifa priest may have to be consulted."[10] The priest instructs the newly initiated on the various responsibilities of her new status as a child of the warriors who will protect her against evil and danger if she follows the protocol. The elementary levels of participation give initiates the first part of the asiento that will qualify them to enter into a conscious lifelong relationship with an orisha. Men receive the *mano de orunla,* while on women *cofa de orunla* initiations are conferred by a senior priest. Mary Ann Clark suggests that these ritual offices have little to do with gender relations.[11]

Custodians of Ashe

Santeria's rich array of rituals and diversified leadership take the place of the hierarchy and creedal dogma of an institutionalized organization. However, the religion has structure, and a relationship with its orishas carries with it responsibilities that senior devotees must perform to be in tune with the divine, increase their ashe, and serve their spiritual communities as santeros or santeras. Miguel De La Torre contends that while there may not be official statistics, there might be as many as "4,000 resident Cuban *babalawos,* in contrast to about 250 Roman Catholic priests. According to a study done by the Catholic Church of Cuba in 1954, one out of every four Catholics occasionally consulted a *santera/o*."[12] De La Torre used the term *babalawos* here as a general description of a complex system of more than four thousand male and female priestly personnel, the visible rulers of Santeria who mediate the power of the invisible army of orishas in the community to meet a variety of needs. They are the total living symbols of the religion and not just the male priests; although babalawos claim to be the highest level of priests, they are just one of many different castes in Santeria priesthood.

SANTEROS AND SANTERAS
Santeria has as many as nine different categories of priestesses and priests, called *olosha* or santeros and santeras; each has a specific rank, responsibility,

title, authority, and mythological association. The most popular santeros and santeras in the spiritual houses are *iyalorisha* (priestesses, wives or mothers of the orisha) and *babalochas* (priests of a specific orisha). Santeras and santeras carry the titles *iyaloricha* or *iyalosha* and *babaloricha* or *babalosha*, based on whether they initiated someone, presided over an asiento, or are male or female.[13] These, as Gloria Rolando notes, "by way of the oral tradition and zeal for keeping the secrets of the religion, made it possible to bring the legacy of Africa down" to the present day.[14] Some priests and priestesses receive the *pinaldo* initiation and others the *kariocha* (ceremonies that induct initiates into the priesthood), both of which are forms of the asiento, or spiritual pact with the orishas. A santera, called a mother in the orisha, works in and with the spirit, and a santero, although a father in the spirit, is also a wife of an orisha.[15]

Other classes of santeros and santeras are the *oriate* (an officiating priest, master of initiation ceremonies, and head of divination); the *italero* (one who is skilled in reading of the cowrie shell divination); the *ayugbona* (an assistant at the asiento ceremony who is in charge of an *iyawo*, or one being initiated into the priesthood); and the *cuchillo* (a man or woman who received the sacrificial knife). According to Miguel Raymos, the position of *oriate* among the *oloshas* (owners of orisha), historically occupied by men, is often sought by women as one of prestige. The *oriate* ensures that the ritual is performed according to conventions, and, at the opportune time (the *ita* ceremony) determines the mind of the orisha, during initiation, by interpreting the oracles, an act "in which all *orishas* the novice receives communicate with the person through the dilogun or cowrie shells consecrated for the new *orisha*."[16] Clark suggests that "there have been some powerful female oriate" in the past, and women are in training in the United States for the office.[17] Among the highest priests are babalawos, men said to have received the consecration and wisdom of Ifa divination. Since "initiation into Ifa is limited to men" and "women cannot become Ifa priestesses,"[18] this is portrayed as a largely a male order. Again, Clark argues that "a female divination priesthood, whose priests are called either *iyalawo* (mother of secrets) or *iyanifa* (mother of Ifa), parallel to the babalawo, is becoming institutionalized in some religious communities."[19] So the dateline of divination authority and power does not remain in a distinctly male babalawo meridian.

All priests and priestesses are santeros and santeras but not all santeros and santeras are priests or priestesses; after becoming a santero or santera, one must graduate from certain levels of initiation to occupy the office of priest. The santeros and santeras are indispensable to the proper functioning of the ile in the Santeria community; they far outnumber the babalawos (whose female equivalent is *Iyanifa*) and maintain closer ties with the rank and file than the babalawos do.[20] Often filling roles as counselors, diviners, herbalists, medicine men or healers, and mediums, the priests mediate between devotees and orishas, dispense blessings and curses, divine problems and provide solutions, broker social and political power in local villages, and manage their iles as nonprofit charities. The *olosha* perform the *fundamentos*, the rite that initiates adherents into the worship of the orishas, produces many followers known as godchildren, and trains iyawos to be wives of the orishas.[21] Santeros and santeras serve many orishas, although each claims to be committed to the one orisha who has chosen him or her at birth and called him or her into spiritual service. They work, however, on their own initiatives, often found their own iles, exercise authority in leading their spiritual houses, and are answerable to no one but themselves and their orishas. As Joseph Murphy correctly notes, the Santeria priesthood requires the ability to perform initiations and create one's own family of followers, called godchildren. "Thus priest and priestesses can establish more or less independent *iles* of their own or join existing ones to form large extended families of initiates under a particularly powerful godparent."[22] Since everyone in the religious community must access the spirits via priestesses and priests, one can arguably say, "No santero or santera, no Santeria activity."

ASIENTO/KARIOCHA

Followers who become spiritual leaders undergo the asiento, or *kariocha*, initiation. An asiento is a pact with the spirit involving the conferral of a spiritual office, referred to as the "seating" in the head or in someone's throne, and the making of an agreement with an orisha. The ceremony is variously called the "crowning," *el dia de la coronacion*, or "sitting an orisha in the head," which is the seat of consciousness, personality (*ori*), and thought. This metaphor of making, crowning, and seating the orisha in one's head is reserved only for those who contemplate the asiento as entry into the priesthood.[23] The initiates enter a total lifelong relationship with the spirit in exchange for a life of spiritual power (ashe) and guidance. The mythological (or theological) belief is that the asiento clears the head of the initiate to allow the orisha to take up residence and subsequently guide the initiate through his or her destiny and vocation. To be effectual, the rite requires its initiate and sponsors (*madrinos* or *padrinos*) to attend to much detail throughout the eight days of the intense initiation.[24]

The cost of the asiento puts it beyond the reach of many participants. Initiates pay fees for the services of the priests, the ritual costumes, the animals and other items for the sacrifices, and the specially chosen herbs that the priests must use in the rituals. Performing the crowning in Florida or New York costs more than five thousand dollars, depending on the orisha being "seated." Some U.S. initiates make the trip to Cuba for their initiation, where they hope it will be less costly. But, as Erica Moret discovered, "*santeria* initiation costs, since the 1990s, have risen to such an extent that they become prohibitively expensive for the majority of Cubans without access to foreign capital (roughly equivalent to between three to twelve years' worth of an average state salary)." This is particularly acute "for those who find it difficult to gain access to the tourist or CUC market."[25] Hagedorn conjectures that "estimates of Ochatur initiations range from U.S. $6,000 to $8,000, including round trip airfare and

hotel accommodations, before and after the initiation"[26] in Cuba. My informants told me in 1999 that they could not afford the asiento in Cuba because,
even with their "exchange job" in Jamaica, they did not have the resources.
They could combine resources with other initiates in the same plight but said
they had no intention of become priestesses. Moret attributes the sharp rise
in initiation cost in post-Soviet Cuba to the recent "highly competitive market
in Afro-Cuban cultural activities," the surge in popularity of Afro-Cuban religion, the premium placed on initiation into its priesthood as babalawos and
santeros or santeras, and the economic crisis pushing Cuba's tourism.[27]

This ceremony takes days of preparation in which the iyawo abstains from
human desires for at least three days and engages his mind in healthy thoughts.
He spends the first five days of the asiento in an isolated chamber in the ile,
which is often at the home of the priest. During his sequestering, the iyawo
("wife of the orisha to be") dies to his old self and prepares for rebirth in a form
of reincarnation. The ritual act transforms his personality to endow him with
characteristics of his ruling orisha, in spite of the spirit's gender. As Clark observed, "Every fully initiated Santeria priest is crowned to a particular Orisha
with whom he or she is often understood to share character and personality
traits," but "an orisha devotee is as likely to be crowned to a male as a female,
regardless of the priest's own gender (or sexual orientation)."[28] The transformation is complete after the initiate's rebirth, and he is "married" and totally
devoted to his orisha for life. During the last three days of the ceremony, the
officiating priest must perform various rituals on the iyawo that end with a divination to ask the orisha of the initiate's destiny.[29] Purificatory rituals of sacrifices
plus the confession of past sins (probably a Christian influence), washing the
iyawo in river water while making an offering to Oshun, and cleansing of the
head (*rogacion de cabeza*) with coconut juice must be completed in preparation
for "crowning" on the last day.

At his initiation, an iyawo is disrobed, bathed like a child void of inhibition,
seated on the sacred stool (*pilon*), and balded by a santero or santera. Like a
young Buddhist does during his balding initiation into the *sangha*, the iyawo
holds a piece of cropped hair in his or her hand to symbolize the death of the old
personality. The initiate's shaved head becomes a symbolic orisha *otano* (stone
of the spirit), and thereafter is said to contain the deity's ashe. After the iyawo's
head is anointed with the *omiero* (a bath made of an herbal mix and blood from
the sacrificed chicken, which the initiate also tastes), the ritual team chants a
prayer while the priest crowns the iyawo by holding the *otanes* (stones) of different orishas over his or her head. Within minutes, the spirit appears and approves the crowning by "riding" his horse, possessing the iyawo, who goes into a
stuttering convulsion as if shaking something out of his or her mouth. The
crowning is completed with the pronouncement *"eroko ashe!"* (a benediction
that means "it is done, with your blessings"). During the coronation of a Shango
priest, devotees paint the floor in red and white pastes in preparation "to receive
the imprint of Shango's 'cloud mortar.' The iyawo, now dressed in white and

with the head still wet from the *omiero* bath, is seated on the *apoti*, Shango's cloud mortar-throne."[30] Then the priest places the sixth necklace, representing the iyawo's principal orisha, around the initiate's neck to signify that he or she is now permanently married to the orisha, an act that must not be revoked or there will be consequences.

An observer can lose count of the number of ritual actions done in this initiation. After the necklace investiture is completed, the priest must still take special herbs and consecrate, for the initiate's official use, the symbolic emblems and tools of Santeria. Among these are the sacred stones that contain the ashe of the orishas and the cowrie shells the iyawo needs for his divinatory science. Having completed the asiento, the newly wedded "wife of the orisha," seated on his throne, is robed in the colors of Shango, his or her patron orisha, whose symbols and emblems the initiate showcases.[31] Members of the family, friends, and other well-wishers pay their respects and genuflect before the initiate, who pats them gently on their shoulders with a blessing. After greeting and congratulating the initiate, the santeros or santeras prepare the *bembe*, a happy time of singing, dancing, and feasting on the sacrificial foods for the newly initiated. On the final day, a senior priest gives a dilogun reading that ascertains the initiate's new name, destiny, and vocation. It also determines whether other initiations are warranted. Oracles of the readings are recorded in the *libreta* and given to the initiate when he or she exchanges the title *iyawo* for *senior santero* or *santera* a year later.

BABALAWOS: JUST FOR MEN

The babalawo (male) priests (whose female equivalent is the Iyanifa) place themselves at the highest level of the priestly practice and next to the orishas and ancestors in Santeria's sacred hierarchy. These divinatory specialists, fathers of the secrets, are seen as the tradition's most trusted custodians, who claim a superior form of initiation into the mysteries of the Ifa divinatory knowledge of Orunla (Orunmila). These men have creolized Africa's babalawos' office by denying its gender-neutral character. In African Yoruba, women called "mothers of the mysteries of Ifa," or *Iyanifa*, serve in the role of babalawo. In January 1985, an African Yoruba babalawo initiated some American women into the sacred profession of Ifa in Oshogbo, Nigeria. In the diaspora, babalawos and Ifa divination are seen as the sole prerogative of men. For this reason, Ifa Yemi Eleguibon's (of Oshogbo) initiation of women, including Patri Dhaifa, a Jewish New York practitioner, into the babalawo office sent such angry shock waves throughout Santeria's leadership in the Americas that the debate continued for decades over its legitimacy.[32]

There was strong international condemnation of the initiation; the Latin American babalawos were the most vehement in their opposition to and outrage against female priests holding that "male" title. Elders in the Americas believe that the orisha of Ifa divination calls only men to be babalawos; they possess attributes that come only from Orunla, who will not accept sacrifices and rituals from anyone other than his babalawo, a male. A strong legend of Yoruba past has it that Orunla handed down the mysteries of Ifa and its divination to his sixteen spiritual sons who, in turn, bequeathed them to the babalawos. Another *patakis*, however, claims just as strongly that "the worship of Orunmila and the initiation into the mysteries of Ifa were once female endeavors."[33] An authority on Santeria, David Brown sees the incongruity originating from two opposed ideological "ritual fields" among the Yoruba—"an 'Ifa-centric' ritual field, and 'an Ocha-centric' ritual field . . . based in divergent cosmological models and structurings of ritual authority."[34] He explains further that "structurally, La Regla de Ifa, with its male babalawo and his tutelage *oricha*, Orunla, 'feminizes' La Regla de Ocha (the collective *orisha* priest and their pantheon),"[35] and the two are in tension. Brown thinks the *oriate*, as feminized, is the counterbalance to the babalawo. Clark argues that the babalawos "manipulate sacred symbols that are understood to be female entities who do not want to be seen (in the case of the *odu* of the babalawo) or touched . . . by women."[36]

Annually, babalawos assemble at regional convocations during which they make their authoritative prophetic predictions for the immediate future or, as Miguel Barnet calls it, execute "the rituals of prophecy through the use of the *tablero of Ifa*; a series of configurations drawn on special sawdust in accordance with the casting of the *opele*, or *okuele* chain."[37] Babalawos generally should not perform initiation rituals for santeros or santeras, but they officiate at some asientos, perform *fundementos* ceremonies, and do Ifa divinations or advance dilogun (*diloggun*). These leaders introduced the Ifa divinatory system into Cuba and are regarded as, or made themselves into, experts in the mysteries. At least four categories of priests exist among babalawos: (1) *omokolobas*, ones on whom was conferred the initiation of Olofi, or "God's mysteries"; (2) *cuanaldos*, ones on whom was conferred the babalawos' sacrificial knife and who also received the *cuchillo*; (3) *oluwos* ("owners of secrets"), priests who are coronated during their asiento ceremony to the priesthood; and (4) the more respected babalawos, or *babalaos*. Some babalawos seem to violate the rules of ordination; they receive Ifa divination without an asiento initiation ceremony when they join the elite fathers of the mysteries.[38]

Some babalawos claim that the rigorous training to the priesthood limits the number of santeros who progress to this ultimate level of Ifa spirituality. Santeros train for many years beyond their asiento, at the end of which they are enabled to recognize many *odus*, or "meanings," of readings in Ifa divination. They must know special Ifa prayers, wise sayings, a large number of Yoruba *patakis*, and cures for the many maladies that plague the community. The divine must also call a babalawo to the office. At some point, a santero is identified for service when an Ifa oracle determines that Orunla is calling him to be a babalawo. In a ceremony known as the "hand of Orula," a santero receives a mark allowing him to enter the sacred path and begin years of training in the techniques and ways of Ifa with his *padrino de Orula*, his tutor and godfather babalawo. Over a period of ten to fifteen years, the trainee learns the prayers and legends of hundreds of *odus* of Ifa divination and gains extensive knowledge of healing pharmacopeia. One must learn the 256 *odu*, or sacred letters, "that embody the oral scriptures of Ifa."[39] The training ends in an elaborate, intense, and costly rite of initiation to which are privy only babalawos who claim the ability to read Ifa and divine for the people who consult them.

Diviners in the Craft

Highly proficient santeros and santeras can perform dilogun, through which they obtain knowledge of the workings of orishas and their desires, wishes, and effects on human fortune. Dilogun is a system of ritual actions that provides tools and strategies for solving problems; it is understood as a mediation between a client's misfortune and the spirit world. Dilogun divination also determines someone's calling and is necessary as a person goes through rites of passage that determine the path to be taken in various stages of life and initiation. In dilogun, the practitioner ritually performs divination based on what, to an outsider, looks like luck and chance magician tricks. Clark contends that "many santeros use one of the European divination systems when dealing with clients. They may read cards, use a crystal ball, or gaze into a candle. However . . . they use cowrie shells" when they want to communicate directly with the orisha. Clark explains, "More complicated problems might be addressed through cards of various types. Questions or problems addressed directly to a particular orisha use a set of cowrie shells dedicated to that orisha."[40]

The sixteen and seventeen cowrie shells are the primary divination tools that speak for the orishas. They do so through the special designs or color patterns, called *odus,* that the shells form when tossed on a mat; these patterns are then deciphered. As Murphy records, each shell is so shaped that when it is thrown, it must land convex- or concave-side up. "This arrangement results in 256 possible combinations, each representing a basic situation in life. The combination that falls at any particular time is the purest expression of fate, and thus of the God-given destiny of the querent."[41] The priest begins the dilogun with a ritual cleansing in which he sprinkles water on the cowrie shells, then offers a series of prayers and incantations to invoke the orisha. He touches the client several times with the shells before tossing them onto the mat. Based on the color combination of shells that settle with their opening or "mouth" turned up, the priest divines the mind of the orisha. A priest can discover as many as sixteen readings, all of them giving an oracle that could be good news, a bad omen, or an unclear response. If the reading of the design is unclear, the priest has five divination aids (*igbo*) at his disposal to interpret the oracle.[42]

The simplest form of divination in Santeria is probably the coconut rinds divination, used "to get answers to yes/no questions" and confirm an action. The "coconut divination uses four pieces of un-peeled coconut, white meat on one side, dark rind on the other. When the pieces are dropped on the ground, they fall in one of five dark/light patterns: all white, one, two, three, or four dark sides showing."[43] This lot-casting divination is always read as *yes, no,* or *discard.* The *obi,* or the reading of the four coconut rinds, is used mostly in ceremonies to get answers from the orishas or to determine if the spirits are pleased with a ritual action. Doing the *obi* follows the same path as the dilogun. After the ritual libation and incantation prayers, the practitioner drops the number of pieces of coconut rind on the orisha's sacred stones to correspond with a specific orisha's number. The santero or santera casts the rinds to the floor in such a manner that they too form several possible patterns based on the number of pieces with the white or brown side facing upward. Each pattern suggests a positive or negative oracle.[44]

When the obi or reading is inconclusive, the performer again reads the patterns. This may necessitate repeating the actions to obtain the desired results. When the dilogun reveals that the *odus* reading is difficult, the santero or santera is required to refer those cases to an Ifa specialist, a babalawo, the only one qualified to decipher them.[45] A babalawo performs Ifa divination using several methods, three of which are *opele, opon Ifa,* and *ikin* (ikine). He follows a path similar to the reading of the *odus,* but his ability to discern the patterns, understand legends associated with them, and know special prayers distinguishes him as the master of the mysteries of Ifa. The babalawo performs the *opele* during consultation when malevolent forces or his clients' own failure to honor the orisha can bring them harm. The *opele* begins with a litany of invocations known as the *moyubbar,* in which the priest pays homage to orishas and the ancestral spirits in return for their blessing in performing the rites of divination.[46]

To diagnose a patient's case and prescribe a remedy, the diviner solicits the aid of the client's guiding spirits, gently touches the person's head with the sacred *opele* chain, throws it down repeatedly, and records the patterns it forms. To be sure that he has the correct *odou,* or to get clarification on the reading, he may consult the *igbo.* After determining that the *odou* is one of good luck, the babalawo prognosticates his client's problems—probably on the basis of his knowledge of tradition, Yoruba legends, and the art of suggestion. The result often requires nullifying the power of negative influences in a client's life with positive force. This is done, usually, by offering a sacrifice to one's patron orisha and taking an herbal bath. When the diviner needs a "deeper reading" of a difficult *odou,* or to determine what to offer the orisha in a special sacrifice, he uses the *opon Ifa* or *ikin Ifa.* With the *opon Ifa,* he makes readings of different patterns drawn on a tray sprinkled with a sacred powder called *eyeroson.* In *ikin,* a diviner uses sixteen sacred palm nuts to determine the destiny of clients with high social status. This follows the practice in Yorubaland of performing the *ikin* during the coronation of a chief, king, or other royal personage. This act is regarded as the most important method in Ifa divination and is reserved for special occasions.[47]

Ile and Sacred Cultus

The Ile

In Santeria, the ile or *casa de santo* (house of saints) is more than a material structure. "It refers not merely to the physical domicile of a priest, but to a rit-ual 'family' of priests initiated by an elder of Ocha (*babaloricha* or *iyaloricha*) or Ifa (babalawo)."[48] An ile is also a single santero or santera assembly made up of his or her extended family, "godchildren" of other families, and well-wishers. As a santero or santera becomes known as a diviner, healer, mediator, and coun-selor in his or her community, clients seek out that santero or santera for consultation and guidance, leading to the formation of a new ile.[49] In many communities, the local physical ile is little more than a room or rooms, the low-income home of a spiritual leader, a patched-up shack, or as is the case in the United States, a basement or concealed chamber.[50] However, it serves multiple purposes: it is the center of rites, ritual celebrations, and consultations; it is a place of employment for some Puerto Rican and Cuban santeros and santeras; it is the hub in a web of relationships among orisha avatars and followers; and it supports an informal extended network of santeros and santeras sharing cer-emonial kinship in a village with its own support system. The ile contains much sacred paraphernalia: altars, shrines, flags and emblems of popular ori-shas, ritual objects, religious symbols, adornments, and the throne called the *apoti* or *pilon*. As shown in *The King Does Not Lie*, the *apoti* is a pedestal or stool where an iyawo sits during his or her initiation. In larger iles, these ob-jects are kept in a separate room, the main ceremonial area of which is known as the *ile igbodu*.

Each Santeria ile is run by a sponsoring santero or santera or by a babalawo, also called a *padrino or madrina,* who, as is often noted, is also under the non-binding authority of his or her spiritual elder. This spiritual elder, in Nigerian Yoruba, may also have an *Ooni*, a spiritual figurehead.[51] The priest is supported financially and morally by his or her "godchildren" or *ahijados* (followers); these are initiates that the priest "gave birth to" in the faith and are among the ile's most committed devotees. Great respect exists in each house for senior mem-bers who attained high levels of initiation; junior members show their respects by bowing to their elders, who, in turn, give them their blessings. In return for the respect and support of the ile, leaders provide guidance, protection, in-struction, consultation, and mediation to members and visiting clients, many of whom are Christians. Those initiated into the priesthood can remain with their ile as other "godparents," or venture out to start new iles and initiate their own "godchildren" after attracting a following. In such cases, the new iles be-come part of the extended family of the "godparents";[52] they operate indepen-dently but are closely linked to their mother. Although autonomous, the close-knit ile cohorts support each other morally through collegiality, mutual respect, and occasional collaborations; they collaborate in financial crises or disaster, in festivities like ebbos and bembes, and annual cultural celebrations, but express their autonomy in interpretation of traditions, ceremonies, and rituals that are important to their community.[53]

Ebbo and Animal Sacrifice

EBO EJE OFFERINGS

Santeria thrives on the performance of ceremonies and sacrifices, the objects of which are to appease the orishas and enlist their aid in addressing human problems or procuring initiation. Two important aspects of those ceremonial rites and rituals are the ebbo (*ebos*) "offerings" and the *ewes*, or "healing pharmacopeia." As Roberto Nodal suggests, "Ebbo is best understood as a religious act consisting of ritual procedures for establishing communication with spiritual and supernatural beings in order to modify the condition of the persons on whose behalf it is performed, or objects with which they are concerned."[54] Most ebbo sacrifices, offered as gifts and peace offerings to propitiate the divine, are done so that the orishas can overlook the devotees' shortcomings and grant them divine protection or good health. Clark explains the mythology this way: "Through sacrifice, it is believed, one restores the positive processes in one's life and acquires general well-being. One gives to the Orisha and the ancestors what they need and want in the expectation that they in turn will give what one needs or wants."[55] If this giving to get is not "buying off" or bribing the spirits (Clark), it is certainly a form of religious magic—that is, the act of influencing the gods to act favorably on one's behalf.

De La Torre found nine types of ebbos—unrelated to the nine types of Santeria priests and nine leading male orishas: (1) food offerings made for the nourishment of talismans in which ashe is housed, (2) thanksgiving offerings to orishas for good fortune or a resolution to problems, (3) votive offerings enticing the kindness of a divinity, (4) propitiatory offerings to appease irate spirits, (5) animal sacrifices as substitution offerings (in place of human victim), (6) preventive offerings that ward off the evil eye, (7) initiatory offerings that also require blood for the orisha in an ordination, (8) offerings offered as groundbreaking rituals for a building, and (9) sanctification offerings that make holy profane items used in ceremonies.[56] An ebbo for the *rogacion de cabeza*, the cleansing prayer for the head, is made before an initiation can be performed, or to remove negative force from a person's life or body. On an orisha's anniversary, cakes and wines may also be part of the offerings. Often when a practitioner does a *registro* using seashells, the orisha may ask for an ebbo requiring only some fruits, rum, vegetables, candies, or one of the special foods of the orisha.

All theistic religions recognize the value of sacrifices to the gods. Regardless of the form and substance of the sacrifice (human, service, animal, plant, monetary, or manufactured goods), it is an essential means of religious magic; it is not a characteristic of only "backward" cultures, as some allege. In Santeria theology, ebbo offerings are requested by the divinities or seen as necessary during divination, and are undertaken with great gravity. They function on a reciprocal principle; they strengthen one's relationship with the orishas who, in turn, make their ashe available to the santero or santera to help them deal with life's challenges.[57] In these offerings, devotees feed the orishas their special foods, which consist largely of fruits and vegetables. Since most of the sacrificial offerings given to the orishas deal with common domestic and social situations, an ebbo does not always require the shedding of an animal's blood. When a major initiation (for example, an asiento or pinaldo) is performed,[58] or a serious problem arises and a person's life is at stake, however, animal sacrifice to the orisha is imperative; to be effectual and efficacious, the major ceremonies must be performed with divination, prayers, animal sacrifice, and other rituals. In santeria, human life is valued above animal blood.[59]

ANIMAL SACRIFICE

On the practice of animal sacrifice, U.S. media, public institutions, some Christians, and animal rights supporters draw swords with Santeria. Opponents of the practice charge that the ritual is barbaric and promotes gratuitous violence against defenseless animals. Since the 1980s, police harassment and law suits have threatened Santeria practice in the United States with extinction. This is exacerbated by the fracas over, as De La Torre observes, the carcasses of animals—offered in cleansing ritual sacrifices for different orishas—that were left decaying in the open at various points in a Florida county—for example, at railways (for Oggun), in a cemetery (for Oya), at a fork in the road (for Eleggua), and on river banks (for Oshun). The carcasses are usually pungent, unsightly, and pose a health hazard for the communities. So in Florida, "every morning civil servants at Dade county Courthouse must dispose of the numerous dead animals, burning candles, and food items left on the building steps as pleas to Ochosi for assistance"[60] in court cases. Of course, the question of how economically strapped Cuban communities could afford to waste such an important and needed food source in rituals is not forgotten in the debate; under Castro's government, most followers of Santeria in Cuba live in depressed economic conditions and could use the foods given to "waste" in Santeria ceremonies in the United States.

In 1980, this debacle was heightened by the infamous New York case involving the American Society for the Prevention of Cruelty to Animals (ASPCA), the New York Health Department, the New York Police Department, and the Cuban–Puerto Rican Santeria community in the United States. The litigation that ensued was settled in favor of a Santeria church, with the court recognizing the members' right to freedom of religious expression. When the city government of Hialeah, Florida, passed a hasty ordinance in 1990 against the torture and killing of animals, it aimed at folding its Santeria churches; it made it illegal for the Lukumi Babalu Aye church to perform animal sacrifice. This led to the 1992 ruling of the U. S. Supreme Court that recognized the rights of the followers of Santeria to express their freedom of religion in the practice of animal sacrifice.[61] That, however, is not the last word on this controversy. Clark has shown that this contentious harangue on sacrifices encompasses a range of issues associated with the debate on religion and violence.[62] Most of these are not featured in the debate and, for lack of space, are not treated here.

Santeria supporters argue that animal sacrifice is not performed recklessly and is more humane than America's slaughterhouses; performance is done with utmost respect for the animal, and the religion has strict rules governing the killing and disposing of an animal. The meat is used for food in the ceremonies, where raw carcasses are converted into a delicious feast[63] and only the ritually impure portion or "forbidden" parts are discarded. Larger animals are always chopped into pieces and devotees get to take a chunk of meat home after a portion is reserved for the bembe feast. Avatars contend, too, that Santeria's sacrificial system is African in origin and the practice is common to many cultures. During the initiation of a priest, the African Yoruba people offer a week of continuous animal sacrifice. On the first day of the week, the babalawo sacrifices a male goat to Eleggua (Eshu), and Ifa receives a female goat on the third day. On the fourth day, a guinea hen is sacrificed to Orisa-Ori, the protector deity of the head.[64]

The orisha being honored and the nature of the request being made, on behalf of the initiate, predetermines the type of sacrifice and the selection of the animal species, its gender, color, and size. A santero or santera divines what the orisha wants through the dilogun of the cowrie seashells. When an animal sacrifice is required, strong forces are at work and stakes are high, because the destiny and life of someone is at a crossroad or the community sees itself engaged in a battle. In this situation, the animal's blood, seen as a repository of potent ashe, is indispensable to the community, whose propitiatory foods offered to the deity must be of great value and sanctified with blood in the sacrificial rite. The stronger the blood, the more efficacious the sacrifice and the more prestigious the cult.[65]

A santera or a babalawo may divine that a ritual cleansing is needed to remove negative or evil forces from a person, a premise, or a situation and may thus recommend an animal sacrifice. The animal is washed and passed live around, or over, the client, as a part of the ritual of purification. This is done also in healing rituals, so that the spirit of the person's illness symbolically passes into the animal; this is similar to what the ancient Hebrews believed occurred in the "scapegoat" propitiation in the Torah. Blood is sprinkled over the *otanes* (stones) and other emblems as an offering to the orishas, and the animal takes on negative vibrations, said to surround an individual. In this case, the meat should not be eaten after the blood is offered to the deity. An initiation offering is used for the asiento when one "makes the saints," or joins the priesthood; in that case the devotees are allowed to eat a portion of the meat. Another kind of sacrifice functions as a gift of appreciation that participants offer to the eggun, or to the orishas (the ebbo).[66] Since quadrupeds are costly, most animals used in the ritual sacrifice are poultry.

Blood contains the ultimate spiritual ashe. As a life-sustaining property, shed sacrificial blood symbolizes the act of substitution and atonement. People of many descriptions find efficacy in the shedding of animal blood, the ultimate sacrifice and source of life. The animal's life is taken to save a human life believed to be in grave danger at the hands of the gods for breaching a pact, failing to perform a duty, or being defenseless against a malicious spiritual or human power. As Frederick Case argues, the life-giving force of the animal, killed in an offering to God, is a way of officially returning life to its source, the Creator. The earth absorbs the animal's blood and integrates into itself a nourishing substance of transcendence. Central to the African sacrificial ritual is the idea of returning vital energy to its original source as a way of reinforcing one's chances of protection and aid from the spirit. This is "a coded mediation that of itself brings about transformation. It is at one time enunciated in discourse that sometimes elevates the person offering sacrifice to a state of epiphany"[67] or human ecstasy.

Ewe Pharmacopeia

Pharmacopeia plays such an important role in Afro-Cubans' religious life and culture that it outrivals sacrifices. Very few ritual performances occur in Santería without the use of sacred herbs. Herbs function as an insignia, a putative language, and a conduit to the spirit world. In traditional medicine (hereafterTM), sacred plants provide the medical capital for physical and psychological healing; they form the basic ingredients in all healing prescriptions, magic spells, protective potions, and other "works." For both the application of physical healing and spiritual health, traditional healers have, over centuries, studied, experimented with, and endeavored to perfect the art of herbal medicine. During periods of repression, especially under Castro's regime, when Afro-Cuban religions were proscribed, herbalists preserved and protected knowledge of the medical plant use that was often done in secret, and as a result prevented this knowledge and the practices of Cuba's plant-based traditional healing from becoming extinct. According to Moret, the director of the island's largest medical plant farm (based in the Cienfuegos province), for example, argued that 'if it weren't for the *santeros, babalawos,* and *espiritistas,* nobody would remember how to use plants to heal anymore.'"[68] The hyperbole notwithstanding, the role of the herbalist is central in the preservation of TM internationally.

As in Africa, Caribbean peoples do not only visit medical facilities and physicians; when they are affordable and available, they often rely on herbalists and ritual professionals as a line of first defense, or as a last resort. This is so whether they consult Christian clergy, a Vodou hungan, a Cuban palero (of Palo Monte), a santero or santera or a babalawo, or a Spiritual Baptist healer in Trinidad. "A major portion of the work done by santeros in the course of their religious practice is the diagnosis and healing of physical, mental, and interpersonal ills."[69] As Moret concurs, treating disease is a principal function of most

"Afro-Cuban ritual specialists, and a sound knowledge of magico-medicinal pharmacopeia is as vital as the knowledge of ceremonial languages, songs and practices."[70] In African-based religions, physical ailments are treated with the view that a rupture or discord has occurred in a person's spiritual and physical life; like an imbalance between Chinese yin and yang, the need for spiritual healing portends lack of physical health. The effectiveness of prescriptions of herbal brews, baths, ingested portions, ointments, and therapy for various ailments depends on the practitioners' knowledge, skilled application, and faith. They provide cures for general discomforts such as skin irritations, the common cold, throat and nose infections, stomach aches, coughs, minor burns, asthma, and rheumatism. Since colonial times, herbal teas and inhaled herbs like hemp and ganja (marijuana) have been effective in treating rheumatism, asthma, and some other bronchial and nasal ailments in Africa, India, and the Caribbean. Until recent times, healing with spells and potions "was the best medical care available not only to slaves, former slaves, and other members of the lower classes in the Americas but to rich and poor throughout the world."[71]

Traditional healers have begun combining their craft in herbal medicine with medical science. Since much of modern medicine is derived from plants and animals, scientists and governments are rediscovering the importance of herbal medicine, and even traditional healing, in today's tough economic times. In the late twentieth century, staggering health-care costs and medical crises have forced Ghana, Uganda, Cuba, and several other developing countries to incorporate herbal and traditional medicine into their health provisions. In the 1990s, when the post-Soviet Cuban regime decided to find solutions to its critical health crisis in plant-based medicine, it found a natural resource in its tropical flora and herbal medicine. Since then, a high level of sharing exists between government-sponsored plant use and the religious pharmacology in Cuba. Moret reports that of the sacred herbs used by traditional healers and Cuban government's plant, "at least 93 percent of the same species are used in secular and ritual contexts for healing purposes."[72] Since TM was integrated *ad extra* into Cuba's internationalization program, "foreign medical students and doctors can now visit Havana to attend internationally acclaimed medicinal plant conferences and to receive training in the field" of herbalism.[73] "The stone the builders rejected" has not yet "become the capstone" (Acts 4:11), but what was once damned and forbidden as "superstition," incompatible with Marxism, now has a role in Cuba's health and economic salvation.

Santeria is second only to Candomble in the vastness of its repertoire of floral sacred substances whose efficacy makes *ewe* most effective; *ewe* is a collective naming of herbs and herbal dispensary practiced widely in Santeria ceremonies and medicines.[74] In Cuba and the rest of the Caribbean, *ewe* herbs are found readily in wild tropical flora, gardens, practitioners' backyards, and botanicas.[75] *Ewes* are categorized as either sweet or bitter; sweet attracts the good and the positive and bitter dispels the bad or the negative. As pharmacopeia, they fall into one of three general classifications: (1) remedies for physical health conditions, (2) medicines designed to treat spiritual and psychological problems, and (3) counteractive medicines intended to nullify the effects of unwelcome or evil powers or to punish personal detractors and offenders. An herbalist works with various kinds of plants and herbs in his or her orisha's *ewe*.

Practitioners believe that magical-working properties are produced in the interactive chemistry between plants, animals, other natural substances, and the spirit world; when ritually prepared, they are infused with supernatural ashe and spiritual "science," the result of which is sacred medicines of many descriptions. To herbalists, plants have individual temperaments and personalities and are "guarded by a spiritual entity" that infuses them with powerful ashe to "communicate to humanity their healing properties."[76] Not only are special leaves needed for treating a special ailment, each orisha also has its sacred leaves (some have more than a dozen species of sacred herbs), and some leaves are designated for special ceremonies. Practitioners must have extensive knowledge of the properties and spiritual force of the large variety of substances and plants in their sacred herbal arsenal. During an initiation ceremony, the right herbs must be used for the cleansing bath as well as to seat the orisha in the head of the initiate. Various levels of initiation into the priesthood also require the appropriate floral ensemble.

In keeping with their spiritual craft, santeros and santeras use a variety of *ewes* to prescribe herbal baths (*despojos*) as good-luck charms, protective potions for warding off the evil eye, and procuring treatment for their clients' many social and psychological problems. To induce love or good luck, for example, a priest may recommend a bath with a mixture of sweet herbs—"honey, cinnamon, and some perfume"—and take practical steps to make the love relationship happen or improve.[77] Some plants, especially the *ceiba pentandra* ("silk-cotton tree"), the palm tree, and the elm tree, which grow to a magnificent size, are considered very sacred and potent; they supposedly contain strong ashe effective in traditional healing and casting magic spells. Some santeros and santeras believe *bilongos* and *ebbos* are buried at the foot of the ceiba tree. Hence, they cover the ground around the tree with fruit offerings, money, and animals sacrificed to the spirit; the roots receive the offering and the blood of the animal sacrifice. The earth around the roots are used in magic, and medicine from the leaves cast love spells and prepares the *omeiro* performed in the asiento initiation.[78] From the roots, bark, and trunk of this sacred tree, herbalists produce teas, strong medicines, and magic to serve their constituency. Whatever the ritual, whatever the ailment, and whichever method of healing is employed, the orisha is always consulted through sacred leaves.

Fiestas de Santos

It is quite clear that Santeria is a religion of ritual action; the actions of the community make present the *orishas* who, as Murphy contends, do not exist without human thought and action. They are made by African herbs, ceremonies, rhythms, songs, and "shared manifestation of the spirit in common dance."[79] The life of Santeria is dramatized visually, not only in its spirit-filled performances, but also in the festive celebrations that climax the ceremonies. These provide a vital means of communication with the orishas and enrich the spirit of the participants. "The most dramatic form of communication between orisha and devotee occurs in ceremonial dances called *bembes*, where the community gathers to praise a spirit with drum music, feasting, dance, and song."[80] The *bembes tambors*, or *fiestas de Santos*, is the most popular and important feast on Santeria's sacred calendar. Bembes are given for a variety of reasons: to honor an orisha, mark an anniversary, celebrate an initiation or birthday, show gratitude to a guardian orisha, or recognize an important accomplishment in the community.[81] Since many popular orishas who "cross-dress" as Catholic saints also need to be honored on their special saint's day, a Santeria ile rarely sees a dull month in its liturgical calender. Although hosted in the home of a santero or santera, the bembe feast gives an open invitation to the community and offers opportunity for good public relations and for a leader to proselytize for the ile.

BEMBE TAMBORS

As an African tradition, the Santeria bembe is a festive eating, drumming, and dancing ritual performed as a thanksgiving in honor of the orishas or as a repayment, supplication, or redemption to the orishas.[82] The *bembe tambores* takes its name from the sacred drums, *tambors,* used to summon the spirit. The drums invite the orishas to join the community in song and dance. The type of drums being used often signifies the nature of the celebration; their rhythm reflects the pulse of the religion and provides a vital means of communication with the orishas. Three sacred drums, or *bataa*, provide rhythms for the feast. The mother drum, or *iya*, determines the tempo of the celebration, communicates with the orishas, and invites them to the bembe. The *itolele* and the *okonkolo* play the secondary but important role of keeping the beat. At the beginning of the bembe, just before the singing and dancing begin, percussionists drum for the gods; drummers skillfully salute and honor, in order of importance, major orishas invited to the feast by beating the special rhythm of each orisha. This is "a litany of unaccompanied rhythms for each of the *orishas* of the house, in strict sequence," culminating with those of the particular orisha.[83]

Led by a song leader and the percussionists, devotees sing and perform the special songs, dances, and antics characteristic of different orishas. If an orisha so chooses, it descends on the celebrants and seizes the head of a devotee through possession. In this state, an orisha that is incarnated in a medium can perform such magnificent dances that the participant would find it very difficult to replicate a spirit's capering in his or her ordinary consciousness. As Murphy notes, "More important, an incarnated *orisha* will deliver messages, admonitions, and advice to individual members of the community, bringing their heavenly wisdom to bear on their devotees' earthly problems."[84] After this, the spirit-guest is fed its special foods, which the devotee eats on its behalf. Attendees at the bembe feast greet important persons and celebrants with a ritual bow while honoring them with monetary and other gifts. In the *The King Does Not Lie*, the iyawo who has just had his asiento, an elder of the ile, and the priest that hosted the feast are the first to receive such gifts.

Conclusion

Santeria is a living example of how, under arduous conditions, resilient African religions survive through the process of creolization, or adaptation to their local cultural environment in the Americas.[85] Representing the fusion of several West African cultural traditions and "nations" or ethnicity, dominated by the Yoruba religious world view and numerical strength, Lucumi emerged in various traditions and groups in colonial Cuba. After clashing with the dominant colonial Christianity, it found breathing space in the Christian Catholic culture, spirituality, and mythology to exhale its African cosmology and adapt to its unfriendly environment. Because of political ideology, misunderstanding, and cultural distance under colonialism, Santeria operated mainly among Afro-Cubans, outside the comfort zone of most Cubans of European ancestry. In modern times, however, Santeria has become a multiethnic and multiclass religion in which people of all description find social and spiritual upliftment, a pathway to the divine, and a psychological refuge in the thunder of life.

During the twentieth century, and especially since the Cuban Revolution, Santeria was internationalized and now has a substantial following along the eastern half of the United States. In post-Soviet Cuba, Santeria became an important economic factor in the country's financial rescue as tourists flocked to the Spanish Antilles to savor Afro-Cuban religious culture and "medicine." This trumps the notion that the religion is responsible for Cuba's economic woes, low standard of living, alleged backwardness, alleged "corruption of its poor whites," and the crimes of Cuba's underworld, as some charged in the early twentieth century. No truth exists to the European-American myth that religions of African origin impoverish Haitian and Cuban peoples and keep them uncivilized, poor, and ignorant. African peoples practiced their religions while making Cuba and Saint-Domingue wealthy sugar kingdoms before the Haitian and Cuban Revolutions and before the countries' political disasters. As Gonzalez-Wippler concludes, "Contrary to popular belief, the practice of Santeria is not the exclusive domain of the ignorant and the uneducated. Some of the most devoted followers of the religion are people with extensive educational and cultural background."[86] Long live Lucumi for the healing of the Cuban nation.

7

Palo Monte Mayombe

KEY TOPICS

*Delimitation and Origination • Spirits of Fragments •
Receptacles of Power • Symbolic Oracles*

Regla de Ochaö (Lucumi/Santeria) is the most well known and investigated Afro-Cuban religion, locally and internationally, but its correlatives—Abakua, of the Efik-Ibibio; Regla Arara, from Ewe-Fon Dahomey (the modern People's Republic of Benin); and Regla de Palo Monte, of the Bakongo and Bantu-speaking peoples—are perhaps equally important to the practice and study of Afro-Caribbean religions. I intimated in Chapter 1 the importance of the Kongo to the Afro-Caribbean experience. The Bakongo and Bantu culture of Central Africa (especially in the Congo, Cameroon, and Angola) resonates in Cuban religions, Brazilian Candomble de Angola and Candomble de Congo, Haitian Vodou, and to a lesser extent, Jamaican Kumina and Obeah. During her decades of research in Cuba, art historian Judith Bettelheim found that practitioners of "Palo Monte Mayombe . . . refer to their homeland as Ngola (Ngola a Kilunje, 'the land between the lower Kwanza and the Dande'), from which derives the Europeanized 'Angola.'"[1] The cadre of names used for Palo Monte (see the section that follows) suggests that the religion encompasses other subsets of Kongo traditions, of which little might be known. Palo Monte is said to have spread among Afro-Latinos in the Dominican Republic, the United States, Venezuela, Colombia, and Puerto Rico (said to have more than five thousand followers),[2] a claim not corroborated herein.

Although Paulo Monte plays an important role in the religious culture of Afro-Cubans, it is still not well known or studied by many people outside of Cuba. Some religion researchers[3] correctly charge that recent upsurges of interest in Afro-Cuban religions among anthropologists, religionists (like myself), and other ethnographers focuses much too narrowly on the Yoruba-based Lucumi at the expense and neglect of other creole religions like Arara, Ifa, Abakua, and Palo Monte.[4] Unfortunately, space and cost constraints prevent coverage of all Afro-Cuban religions in this work. This brief survey on Palo Monte is written as a complement to some of the important recent ethnographic works published on the religion by Lydia Cabrera (1979, 1986, and 2000), Stephen Palmie (1995 and 2002), Arturo Lindsay (1996), Judith Bettelheim (2001), Miguel Barnet (2001), Fernandez Olmos and Paravisini-Gebert (2003), David Brown (2003), Jesus Fuentes Guerra and Armin Schwegler (2005), and Erica Moret (2008) in the hope of inspiring further examination.

Delimitation and Origination

Palo Monte is one of the leading Afro-Caribbean creole religions of the largest Spanish-speaking Antilles. It took its language, beliefs, and most of its ritual practices from the Bkango and Bantu culture of Central West Africa and decoded them in the multiethnic, multilingual, and diverse religious environment of colonial Cuba. The religion operates in concord with nature and the environment and places strong emphasis on the individual's relationship to ancestral and nature spirits. Its practitioners specialize in infusing natural objects with spiritual entities to aid or empower humans to negotiate the problems and challenges of life. Palo Monte is referred to often as Reglas Congas ("Kongo religions"), and has accrued more symbolic names than one wishes to countenance: Palo Monte Mayombe, Congas Reglas, Regla de Palo, Regla de Conga, Regla de Palo Monte, Las Reglas de Conga, Palo Kimbisa, and Santo Cristo Buen Viaje (or locally Palo, Kongo, Bantu, and Conga Regla), among others. These locutions share a common accent; they are creole (African-Spanish) historical significations of an African spirituality.

Palo and *monte* ("sticks of the forest") are creole-Cuban creations. Onlookers probably labeled the religion "palo monte" facetiously, because followers used numerous wooden sticks to prepare their artistically designed imposing sacred altars for the spirits, perhaps near the forest. Palo and Mayombe also are said to have a distinct connection to the religious import of trees for the Bakongo people; *palo* is a Portuguese word for "tree" while Mayombe is a deep-forest area in the Central African region. Fu Kiau Bunseki is recorded as saying that, in the Kongo, most judgments and "courts are held under trees, and debate, marriage, and initiation, are done under a tree. The tree is seen as the symbol, the pipe through which the *miela* comes to us."[5] Palo Monte (hereafter, Palo) also points to the reputation of Kango people in rural Cuba as being as resilient and intrepid as the spirits of their religion.[6] Worthy of note is the fact that Afro-Spanish designations define Palo (Regla de Conga) practitioners as *paleros, ngangeros,* and *nganguleros,* terms that augur the religion's dual Kongo and Cuban reality.

Provenance of Palo

Although the actual dating of Palo's advent remains imprecise, Bantu-speaking people from central Africa were taken to Cuba starting with the sixteenth century.[7] Palo began with the Kongo religious traditions among Afro-Cubans (the *bozales* and *esclavos, or* "newly arrived" and "enslaved"; the *gente de color,* or "free population of color"; and the *Ladinos,* or African-born Spanish-speaking Cubans[8]) around the eighteenth century. In more modern times, it is preserved and embraced by Cubans of mixed ethnicity who often identify themselves as being of Yoruba, Carabali, Kongo, or other ethnic nations; Palo's adherents are "a fusion of not only very mixed African background, but also Spanish, Asian, and Amerindian"[9] peoples. *Criollos* ("creole")—Cuban-born Africans, Europeans, and Asians—now constitute its primary supporters.

A recent etymological study of the language and vocabulary used in Palo, by Jesus Fuentas Guerra and Armin Schwegler, claims that much of the religion's cultural content, ritual language, and tradition are traceable, lexically and unambiguously, to one location in Africa, the area of western Congo called Mayombe. The study argues that a significant number of Africans sold into slavery in Cuba originated from that narrow region (circa fifty kilometers in width), from which they preserved a "lingua sacra" for Palo. Guerra and Schwegler conclude that "the esoteric vocabulary of this religious tradition (as exemplified by the names of its divinities) is derived in its entirety from a single Central African language, Kikongo."[10] This, as Kenneth Bilby argues, "contradicts previous scholarship, most of which represent the ritual vocabulary of Palo Monte as a diverse amalgam of terms from a . . . variety of Bantu languages."[11] Bantu languages, cultures, and peoples are still common throughout the huge expanse of Central Africa, not just within a region in Angola. As W. van Wetering and H.U.E. Thoden van Velzen argue, the so-called lingua sacra may not account for cultural turbulence and historic demographic dislocations in the area. Hawks of the Atlantic slave trade and their agents scavenged deep into the interior of West Central to Southern Africa to forage for their desired quantity of human cargo. "It seems improbable that Mayombe would have remained exempt from these tribulations," and thus one should not take the isolation of the region for granted.[12]

The work of Guerra, Armin, and Schwegler is very fascinating. However, scholars observe that "Kikango-derived ritual vocabulary of Palo Monte in Cienfuegos" is inseparable "from [the] broader Afro-Caribbean cultural matrix with which it is enmeshed, as evidenced by the complex semantic associations its practitioners perceive between their own terminologies and concepts, and those of other forms of Cuban religions such as Santeria and Catholicism."[13] Given the widespread presence of Bantu culture in Central Africa, it may be difficult to prove, with any certainty, that Palo represents cultural traditions from only one Angolan or Kongo region rather than from the broader Bakongo and Bantu geographical reach. Although Palo is indebted to Kongo for its conceptual language and may "boast a ritual vocabulary that seems to be derived exclusively from Kikongo," Bilby asserts, "it appears to have emerged and taken on many of its fundamental and distinctive meanings in relation to other locally developed religious systems, with which it now shares a certain broad cultural 'logic'"[14] in Cuba.

The Kongo peoples of Cuba originated from many ethnic communities, each with its own culture, dialect, and concept of religious reality. Names of local Congo, Cameroon, and Angolan communities still identify groups in Cuba. Barnet suggests that "the names Briyumba, Kimbisa, and Mayombe are recognized as three sources of culture and religion. These have become the principal terms for the Kongo religious cults of Bantu origin, at least in the western part of the island";[15] Benguela, Musundi, Kunalungo, Loanga, Ngola, Kabinde, Basongo, Quimbanda, and Bukumba nations show imprecise places of origin, but they constitute African "signifiers" of Palo. Partially for this reason, the religion became a melting pot of "Conga" spiritual traditions from the Bantu and Central Africa. The Bantu, a large linguistic group of people, and the "Bakongo inhabit a broad area of sub-Saharan Africa stretching from the southern part of Cameroon through northern Angola" and running diagonally "to Mozambique in the southeastern coast of Africa."[16] J. Lorand Matory observes that Central and Southern African cultures of Bantu-speaking peoples, "including the BaKango, are the products of a demographic and cultural expansion within Africa that dwarfs the transoceanic influence of the Yoruba's ancestors. By the eighth century A.D., the Bantu languages had spread from a small nucleus in what is now Nigeria to Zanzibar, off the coast of East Africa."[17] Among the close to one million Africans taken from about forty-five different ethnic groups and inserted into Cuban plantation slavery, many embarked at depots in West Central Africa.[18]

In captivity in Cuba, the Bakango-Bantu peoples held on to their cultural traditions—perhaps as strongly as their Yoruba counterparts did[19]—as a resource for mitigating their harsh life conditions in the Americas. No evidence exists of a nineteenth-century Afro-Cuban return to the Congo or Angola to reauthenticate a "pure" Palo religion, as the female founders of Candomble did, reexperiencing the religion in West Africa in the 1800s, and as Orisha avatars in Trinidad and Tobago did in the late 1900s for the same purpose. Slavery, however, was not abolished in Spanish Cuba before the last decades of the nineteenth century: the last officially recorded slave ship was said to disembark in Cuba in 1873,[20] or more likely in 1886,[21] and many new arrivals from the Kango and Bantu regions kept the religion alive. Because of Cuba's commerce with Africa in the very late nineteenth century and the fact that Palo does not emphasize a pantheon of divinities as Lucumi does, the stamp of Catholicism on the religion is not as indelible as it is in Vodou, Santeria, Candomble, and Trinidad and Tobago Orisha. The African traditional religions (ATRs), however, morphed into different creole forms as Africans struggled to preserve their traditions in a hostile foreign land.

Symbiotic Creole Filaments

Historically, Palo was influenced more by Lucumi practices than by external traditions. However, it is more open to the outside, and accommodating of other beliefs, than its counterpart, resulting in some of its African beliefs and practices becoming somewhat attenuated. This could be due also to the fact that, through political and ecclesiastical actions, Kongo people lost some of their traditional religious knowledge between their forced transition into slavery and the period following the deterioration of the cabildos. Barnet suggests that "the flexibility of the religious beliefs, together with their remote and imprecise origins, awakened an imagination that is less dogmatic, more fanciful and creative than that of the Yoruba."[22] Practitioners of Palo are not reticent in identifying their own divinities or spirits with those of the Yoruba and the sainthood of Catholicism,[23] although they do not have a pantheon of divinities to shadow the Catholic saints. They even chant to the spirits using the names of Bantu, Yoruba, and Catholic origination, and employ terms used in Santeria to identify some ritual activities and religious titles. Both Lucumi and Palo leaders, for example, use the affectionate title *tata*, the category *bozales*, and the initiation term *fundamentos*. Stephen Palmie reasons that "ocha and palo stand to each other like religion and magic, expressive and instrumental forms of human-divine interaction."[24] Palmie's preference for Lucumi, as religion, to Palo, as "magic," reflects his cultural preconception against a religion that exist sui generis, whose practices he sees as "morally ambivalent and potentially malignant."[25] The cultural borrowing between Palo and Lucumi is as common as it is in other African religions of resistance in Haiti, Jamaica, Brazil, and Trinidad.

Altars and sacred objects carrying African names (nganga, nkisi) and Spanish names (*el caldero, la prenda*) have become visual symbols of Palo. The religion comprises a diversity of practices, passed down in what might be termed *fragments of bone* (the term is borrowed from Bellegarde-Smith, 2005[26]), that have been redefined as its newer elements continue to merge with the remaining knowledge of ATRs and culture. It is argued that one should speak of Kongo religions in Cuba because several strands are "subsumed under the general rubric of 'Regla de Palo Monte Mayombe"; this includes also "Regla Biyumba, Regla Musunde, Regla de Quirimbaya, Regla Vrillumba, and Regla Kimbisa del Santo Cristo del Buen Viaje ('of the Holy Christ of the Good Journey')."[27] How these strands differ one from the other, whether each one still constitutes a religion sui generis, and how much of these filaments are incorporated in Palo rituals make for an intriguing further study. Religions of African originations, as Matory notes, adopted "new contrasting moral valences" that are unique to their Caribbean setting. Yoruba-related Lucumi practices and those of West Central Africa identified with Palo, "draw their primary meaning not only from their respective African cultural precedents, but from the moral contrasts between them as they are perceived in Cuba."[28] Palo was facilitated by the memory of Kongo languages, conceptions, and cultures.

Palo may constitute a putatively unique religion, but it operates in a geo-graphical space and in multireligious communities with many competing cultural traditions. This allows some Cuban devotees of Palo to expand their religious appetite. David Brown explains the eclectic phenomenon this way: since the beginning of the twentieth century, one could make the saints through the rite of initiation into Santeria. One could also become a priest (tata nkisi) of Palo, "worship Arara deities of Ewe-Fon (Dahomey) origin, become an *abonekue* (member) of the Abakua society, the sacred brotherhood of Old Calabar origin, as well as rise through the ranks of the Masons, rely on Rosicrucian geomancy, and take communion in the Catholic church."[29] The dual induction into Palo and Santeria would entail one being initiated into Palo first, and later into Santeria; the opposite is usually not allowed, because of the jealousy of the orishas. This religious envy could be likened to the vigilance in the Catholic Church over its ministry. If one is ordained a Catholic priest, it is easier for him to be an adept in the rituals of ATRs simultaneously than the other way around. A clear exception is early nineteenth-century Haiti, where Vodou *oungans* served freely as priests in abandoned Catholic parishes in the wake of the revolution.

While seeking spiritual guidance through the use of both Palo and Santeria services, initiates generally keep the Palo spirits at a great distance from the orishas, because it is believed that the ancestral and nature spirits are fierce; they are considered fearless and unruly entities of the forest. As Brown notes, in pictures with Palo insignias, "the Warriors' rustic and fierce iconography of war, hunting, and the countryside is made up of implements analogous to those carried by their forest counterparts in the 'strong' Palo Monte religion (hooked staffs . . . knives, machetes, and 'charged' animal horns . . .)."[30] Be-cause it is a stronger earth energy, for example, the prenda or nganga receptacle is kept outside in a shed, in a cellar, or close to nature, whereas the orisha is kept largely in the house, probably in the bedroom. It is not unusual for a palero (leader) to follow both Palo and Santeria, utilizing the myths and imple-ments of each faith as complements in his practice.[31] How much intermixing is allowed between the two groups depends completely on who is involved as well as their personal interpretation of what is correct or appropriate.

As its practitioners cross the religious lines, Palo incorporates concepts, terms, names, practices, and devotees of Santeria. Maria Teresa Velez's infor-mant, Felipe Garcia Villamil, whose father strictly practiced Palo, said, "My father didn't believe in Santeria, he only believed in the pot (prenda or nganga) and nothing else. And I made santo [became an initiate of Santeria] quite late because of him."[32] The relation between Santeria and Palo in a devotee is there-fore dynamic; some avatars freely mix the two in a religious eclecticism typi-cally shared by Palo followers. Cuban curator Gerardo Mosquera puts it this way: in Cuba, along with one's own religious tradition, "every *santero* considers himself also a Catholic, and in addition he may be a palero, an Abakua, and a

Freemason, without contradictions, in a system of coexisting fragments."[33] These eclectic fragments are important features of multiethnic Palo.

Instances such as these, where one person finds harmony by blending the two Afro-Cuban traditions whereas another strictly forbids it, are representative of the reality present in the acephalous structure of each faith. Neither Palo nor Santeria has a central authority who controls what is accepted and what is not. The only notion of hierarchy rests inside a single temple, with the priest, and not among the following as a whole. This is another reason why such great diversity exists within the religion. As these intricacies have intensified over the years, it is not surprising to find people (such as Velez's Felipe) with a heterogeneous mixture of backgrounds who still remain loyal to their religion and traditions in their own eclectic way. With the clear spirit of individuality at the heart of Palo, the diversity within its defining features continued to expand as assimilation between Kongo groups became more widespread. Likewise, within local Cuban communities, borrowing from the many groups surrounding the religion's practitioners added to the complexity of the groups' beliefs and ritual traditions.

Marshaling Spirits of Fragments

During the period of Atlantic slavery and ensuing colonialism, enslaved Africans from the Bantu-Kongo region were able to bond, in various ethnic enclaves, to form survival and cultural groups within Cuba. Although they hybridized in what Fernando Oritz calls an *ajiaco*,[34] a "rich soup of varied ingredients," some of their traditions remained somewhat distinct, and different ethnic "nations" blended with those who had original traditions and languages most closely resembling their own from Africa. As with Santeria, the first large organized groups of a general nature, the cabildos, allowed Africans of Kongo and other ancestry to collaborate in celebrating their cultural traditions and addressing social concerns. This cooperation afforded them an opportunity to express themselves publicly through ritual, music, and dance, with the reluctant blessings of the Catholic Church and the Spanish Government; the latter became increasingly more disinclined than the church in the later colonial period. Afro-Cubans were able to perform initiation rites, wakes, and other ceremonies[35] that, in the hostile Cuban plantation environment, kept their religion alive through cultural appreciation. This was often done secretly but, more often than not, under the umbrella of church-state initiated or endorsed brotherhoods or cabildos. Barnet observes that throughout the colonial period and "for sometime afterwards, there were numerous *cabildos* of all nations in Havana, the smaller towns and provincial capitals. Among these were: the Congas which comprised: Basongo, Mumbona, Bateke, Mundemba, Bakongo, Musabela, Kabinda, Bayaka, Benguela, Mondongo, Myombe, Ngola and so forth."[36] The African Kongo connection in this multitude of ethnic names is unmistakable.

Accommodation and Organization

Cabildos established in the Havana and Matanzas provinces had both socio-cultural and political functions, serving as clubs and mutual aid societies (see Chapter 5) for Kongo peoples. David Brown records that urban slaves, especially, "had the advantages of mobility, greater labor options, wider liberty in social and sexual conduct, access to certain legal protections . . . and the organized presence of the African nations in the *cabildo* system"; these resulted in much stronger African institutions in those centers.[37] Among the cabildo groups that became famous and well known throughout Cuba during the colonial period, perhaps the most notable was the "Congas Reales." It had some of "the most striking regalia and musical performance at the traditional epiphany festivities in Havana."[38] Kongo cabildos, in some communities, were referred to euphemistically as "kingdoms of the forest" because, on their Day of the Kings, the "festivities were exceedingly good, the best; no expense was spared on items of luxury. The King wore a frock coat and a sword and sat on a throne beside his Queen, surrounded by [their] courtiers. There, they ruled in the African style";[39] this, notwithstanding their captive condition and the fact that Kongo "royal and military attributes and processionals were regarded as mere imitations, as if the participants were impostors and buffoons playing at prestige and authority on their one day of the year to be king—their 'only day of freedom'"[40] and revelry.

Like the cabildos of Santeria, these allowed Kongo peoples to remain organized and unified in true African fashion, yet still distinct in their various groups. This was the people's main outlet for cultural spontaneity, creativity, and identity. Through the organized cabildos, the Congas were better able to reconstruct, enact, and remember their lost cultures, religion, and "ethnic nations." According to Matory, "The late 18th and 19th centuries were in fact a time when both American territorial units (such as Brazil, Cuba, and British colonial North America) and transoceanically dispersed black ethnic groups (such as the Nago, Jeje, Angola and Congo) were becoming 'nations' for themselves,"[41] but they did so in a context of distress. Accommodated since the sixteenth century as an extended arm of the Catholic Church, Conga *cofradias* were in their heyday in the eighteenth to nineteenth centuries. At that time, the "sticks" or fragments of the spirit of Palo thrived under the pennant of African culture, the church, and the Spanish flag. On days of celebration, Cuban Kongo Flag bearers, dancers, and singers paraded in jubilation, honoring country, god(s), and African culture.

In spite of the measurable success and role of the cabildos (see Chapter 5), Afro-Cuban identity and religious expressions were complex and tenuous peculiarities in a highly stratified colonial Cuban society. Brown captures the essence of this anomaly when he writes of Havana's leader of the Kongo cabildos, the enslaved King Siliman, who, during the French War of 1808, addressed his *afrocubanos* constituency as men (Senores) of "*Conga, Luango, Lucumi,*

Arara, Macua, Fanti, Mandinga, Mina, Brichi, Mondongo, and *Intuanza*," passionately urging them to support Spain, Cuba, Christianity, and their ATRs against Napoleon's imperialistic ambitions:

> The esteemed royal head of a *cabildo* of the Congo nation (*nacion*), Siliman. . . . A historically conscious participant in a global struggle for the New World, Siliman officially identified himself as a passionate royal subject, the servant of a vast, divinely sanctioned chain of authority called the Bourbon Empire (Spain, God, Jesus Christ, The Church, King Ferdinand VII, along with Cuba . . . and its African nations), which seemed threatened by Napoleon and his godless armies. Yet, Siliman's unique vision of future freedom carefully balances a series of goods and rights on parity with the whites, with specific markers of African cultural and social continuity. . . .[42]

This is reminiscent of African Americans being spurred to defend the Union and to preserve its religious, cultural, and political traditions in 1776, 1812, and 1861 while the said institutions held them enslaved. Both African groups saw their future freedoms intertwined with the preservation of the sovereignty and liberties of the state—that is, preserve the one to obtain the other.

On the eve of the Wars of Independence, however, ATRs were forbidden, and Palo, like Lucumi, lost an important cultural, spiritual, and political forum and vehicle. State censorship and persecution followed the wars. After a short hiatus (about three decades), the state resumed its persecution of Afro-Cuban religions. Brown notes:

> After 1875, increasingly in the 1880s, and with an unprecedented ferocity between the first American occupation of the island (1899—1902) and the early 1920s, the government not only scrutinized but also attacked the "internal essence" of Afro-Cuban organizations. This took the direct form of state "persecution against *naniguismo* and other religious customs of African origin." . . . Havana's Lucumi and Palo practitioners did not fare well. From the end of the nineteenth century, the houses of Lucumi and Palo Monte priests . . . were the special targets of ferocious police raids intended to stamp out *brujeria* (witchcraft).[43]

In addition to the bad fate Kongo fraternities suffered, the "specter of *cabildo* royalty may have provoked a certain anxiety in observers who could not reconcile" it with the participants' servitude.[44] The despised institutions therefore languished under political, ecclesiastical, and other restrictions and persecutions. As a result, Palo and other African religions went underground.

In modern Cuba, Africans again contend with their tenuous situation and unpredictable accommodation within restrictions imposed by Castro's Revolutionary Government. At first, the revolution advocated elimination of all class structures and institutional and cultural racism through the promotion of *cubanidad*, a single Cuban identity regardless of class, race, national origin or ethnicity, as propounded earlier by the nationalist "hero/institution" Jose Marti. Afro-Cuban religions and cultures were, on the surface, assimilated as, according to Palmie, "creolised manifestations . . . into the project of building a synthetically conceived national identity"[45] early in the revolution. This welcomed accommodation was very brief. Shortly after 1959, and well into the mid 1990s, as Erica Moret discovered, faith-based practices were disinclined and greatly restricted, "largely because of a supposed incompatibility of religion with Marxism"; the "restrictions on religious practices extended to prohibitions on the use of plants in Afro-Cuban religions and cults—typically suppressed through arguments relating to the use of 'witchcraft' or *brujeria*."[46] Practitioners of Afro-Cuban religions, again, had to find innovative means for their religious expression; so they formed smaller "houses" that could survive away from the watchful gaze of Castro's political informants.

In post-Soviet Cuba, intimates Moret, the Government took a reverse course, as it was forced to initiate "widespread economic restructuring" in the late 1980s and 1990s to deal with a crisis of unprecedented proportion in Cuba's health-care system. Led by the head of the Armed Forces and the Ministry of Health, Rual Castro, the government—as did the World Health Organization and the Ghanian government in the mid-1980s—sought to utilize "domestic and 'traditional' forms of knowledge" to address its medical crisis.[47] Cuba's government initiated a nationwide shift in health-care provision that would embrace traditional medicine. Moret reports that "as a consequence, ethnobotanical knowledge underwent a dramatic process of state-ordained validation . . . throughout the island. The government began to encourage the use and cultivation of medical plants in homes, schools, hospitals, work places and medical facilities."[48] Although the Castro regime kept African religions on its restricted list, the knowledge of pharmacopeia by African ritual specialists' was suddenly at a premium and the religions had a respite.

Palo Cosmology

ZAMBI (NSAMBI)

No pantheon of divinities cross-dressing as Catholic saints exists in Palo. Followers venerate and court the help of one god and many spirits of ancestors, nature, and the dead— summoned in special ways, depending on the occasion and on what ceremonies Kongo groups and individual practitioners are observing. God, or *Zambi*, who created and governs the world, is the highest and most powerful spiritual entity. Outside of this central deity is the diverse array of ancestral and nature spirits termed *minkisi inquics* and *mpungas* (also called *mfumbe*, *fumbe*, or *muertos*), each of which has a special name designation.[49] Minkisi are powerful spirits of ancestors resembling the orisha and the Vodou lwa. Palo does not entertain a pantheon of deities, but some avatars and their spiritual communities give their nkisi divine characteristics adopted from Cuban orishas. The most popular minkisi are *tiembla tierra* (a spirit who helps rule the world); *madre agua* (a female spirit who mothers waters and new life); *mama chola* (a spirit of beauty, libidinous love, and rivers); *lucero* (a joker or prankster messenger of God); *zarabanda* (a spirit of metal and conflict or battle); *centella* (a spirit of grave yards); and *siete rayos* (a spirit of fire, lightning, electricity, and other dangerous elements). This cosmology is not common in all Palo houses, or *munaso(s)*. The nature spirits and the ancestral spirits inhabit, or are lodged in, various vessels given the multivalent name nganga, which possess nkisi charms and divine force or spiritual power, the equivalence of *axe* in the Yoruba-influenced religions of Santeria, Orisha, and Candomble.

MPUNGUS
It is a tribute to their resilience that, despite the borrowing and sharing that took place—and that involved the characteristics of the Yoruba pantheon of spirits, the forms of spiritual practice in Santeria, and the influence of the surrounding Catholicism—the Cuban Kongo people kept their cosmology separate from that of their African counterparts and different from that of colonial Christianity. Palo's cosmology incorporates God, spirits of nature and of the dead, humans, and other creatures and things in the phenomenal world. The Palo spirits are generally referred to by several names: a name in the Palo tradition, a creole or Kongo-Cuban name, a name in the Yoruba-based Lucumi, and a name in Cuban Spanish. For example, *mpungas*, "spirits of deceased ancestors and forces of nature," are given names such as *Nsasi*, *Sarabanda*, and *Baluande*.[50] These have characteristic traits that give them the aura of individual deities. Some *mpungu* are associated with objects, like a clay pot, iron and steel, and colors. The mpungu is awakened and summoned, by the smoke from lighted gun powder, to participate in a ceremony. When mpungu and nkisi "axe"—drawn from animals, herbs, fossils, or a special type of soil—combines with the nganga, they are said to produce or channel powerful forces to be harnessed by the palero in magic and healing.

TATA-PALERO
A practitioner of Palo who communicates with God, the spirits, and the phenomenal world is known as a palero; the term denotes someone who follows the religion as well as one who functions as a leader. Initiates affectionately called the priests *tata* ("papa") and *yaya* ("mama"), and the place of their ritual activity is a *munanso* ("house"). *Palero* is a Cuban creole designation that parallels and replicates the roles of the Kongo *kitomi*, a public religious leader, and the nganga, the private spiritualist.[51] Not much difference exists between the Cuban palero and the West African traditional priest, who are both adepts at employing receptacles of power in rituals and at procuring healing for the well-being of clients. Conga groups are lead by a master of divination, known affectionately as tata nganga, essentially the palero, a keeper of the traditions.

This avatar directs the spiritual operation as the village shaman or priest would. Although there is a spiritual hierarchy within each temple, ultimately practitioners function independently of each other or in accord with oral traditions inherited from their forebears or ancestors. Since Palo, as "sticks of the forest," envisions different spirits thought to inhabit sacred objects from nature, or the forest, its leader "works with the earth, forest branches, stones, animals and all kinds of plants and objects. They assist him in the spells that he uses to save his clients. . . . These elements are the vehicles through which the palero can articulate his ritual language"[52] both to communicate with the spirit and to mystify or aid adherents.

Most paleros command a limited Kikango vocabulary, used in the weekly rituals and divinatory sessions they conduct. According to van Wetering and van Velzen, the fact that adepts have to perform ceremonies to the spirits provides paleros and priests opportunities to give speeches using "sacred" Kikango words. Their competence in the language may vary and the words they speak are often equivocal, "glossed over, or unduly accelerated, but a command of the sacred idiom is nevertheless a way of gaining prestige and a sign of belonging to this network of male devotees."[53] In the same vein, the names of the deities, "sacred objects, and the recurrent phrases of invocation are made common knowledge through songs that resound through the three wards in the town where most adepts live"[54] and operate in Cuba. Paleros do not form a distinct group like santeros "in any strict sense, but are recruited as individuals, and they are predominantly men. They come from diverse social backgrounds, often do not know each other, and are highly mixed ethnically"[55] and socially.

Summoning the Spirits

A palero has a different relationship with the spirit than that of a santero or santera. Palo spiritualists attempt to control the actions of spiritual powers (except the Creator God), including spirits of the deceased. While Santeria requires a continuous commitment or marriage to a divinity, Palo negotiates a "more occasional and intermittent sacred pact with a spirit. The spirit is summoned when needed, being a magical enforcer who carries out one's will."[56] When required, paleros call directly on the spirits of nature and the dead to do their bidding: these spirits can be summoned for healing purposes, considered either nocuous or beneficent. Palo's spirit engagement shares a similarity with Santeria in that its magic can be either constructive or malicious, but the manner and frequency with which the paleros call on the spirit constitutes a significant difference between the two. They summon the spirit more erratically and, although possession plays an important role in Palo's ceremony, its leader, representing the Kongo nganga, does not seek to be possessed or controlled by a spirit, as do priests and priestesses in Santeria. Instead, *perros* (mediums called "dogs" or servants) are the ones that experience possession. Similar to Santeria, temples have members who are initiated to become *perros* or *criados* ("servants") of the spirit.

Paleros control and dominate the small spiritual world signified in the nganga (the cauldron made of clay or iron). Legend has it that the *kiyumba,* or human skull, regarded as essential and a most potent aspect of many ngangas, controls all the herbal plants and animals that are associated with the receptacle. "The *mayombero* or palero, in turn, rules the kiyumba, who obeys his orders like a faithful dog. The kiyumba is the slave for the mayombero and it is always waiting inside the cauldron or the *macuto* to carry out his commands."[57] This master-servant-dog relationship seems to echo a lingering vestige of the slave colonial culture in Cuba. The characterization shows also a view of the palero as a sorcerer, manipulating the spirits in order to get his way. Other sources reveal a complex relationship between the palero and the spirit; or go a step further and describe an act of veneration of the various divinities with which they are in contact. Thus, the palero exhibits at least three dispositions: (1) he has mutual relations with the spirit, (2) venerates the highest being, and (3) dominates the spirit housed inside the nganga to his own ends. A palero specializes in performing healing with the use of magic charms and is regarded as the owner of the nganga (in fact, he is often called the nganga) that produces the magical charms. After a ritual ceremony, it is believed that a spirit of the dead is captured in this caldron of charms; the owner of the pot becomes the master and the spirit does the master's will, performing either good or punitive deeds.

Participation / Initiation

PARTICIPATION

Palo has evolved into a loosely organized institution with great fluidity in the constituency of its membership. Groups are formed around a temple house (*munanso*) and a tata or palero, but one "adopts the religion and its values in an individualistic manner, relying on his own personal viewpoint, and on the traditions of his family or clan."[58] A follower establishes a relationship directly with the power he or she venerates. Implicit in this design are ways in which individual perspectives function in interpreting exactly what it means to become a follower of Palo. A tata nganga may be involved in the process of attracting someone to the traditions, and one's family ancestry may influence one's participation, but in the end, the personal relationship between a practitioner and the spirit is of paramount importance. As Bettelheim records, "The 'rayados,' those sworn into the Congo Reglas . . . consider themselves united by a sacred bond of mystical kinship and, like them, speak and pray in their language," both Yoruba and Kongo.[59]

It has already been noted here that Palo and Santeria participants cross the religious lines with ease. Some paleros are knowledgeable of Santeria's ritual practices and its veneration of Catholic saints, and participate in both religions. Often, little difference is seen among followers of both faiths. As Brown records, tata gaitan, "a priest of the Lucumi hunter-deity, Ochosi," was "also a powerful Tata Nkisi, a priest of the Regla de Congo or Palo Monte. During the late nineteenth century, . . . 'many *babalawos* had their *prendas* [Congo sacred cauldrons] in order to protect themselves'"[60] from harmful forces. Brown interjects that tata gaitan has a huge property and a home with guest quarters

> for scores of *babalawo* colleagues, and Ocha, Ifa, and Palo godchildren, who [travel] from as far as Palmira, in Cuba's interior, to undergo initiation and work the religion in Guanabacoa. Undoubtedly, Tata was multilingual: he not only spoke Spanish, but also utilized the Lucumi, Congo, and Abakua Bricamo languages, as well as communicated in bozal with living African-born inhabitants or creoles and the spirits of the dead who would posses their mediums.[61]

This fluidity of membership in various African religions poses no problem to one's participation in Palo. Juan Boza, a priest in Kongo religion and an artist from Camaguey, Cuba, reports that he, like many others, grew up with a variety of religious influences and traditions that formed his ritual and cultural "aesthetics" and identity. Boza confesses, "The patrimony of my religion through the language of Yoruba, the Congo, and Carabaldi are united and incarnated through different rituals. The bilingualism compounded by existential secretiveness is inevitably called upon at the time of sacred creation."[62] As Arturo Lindsay records, Jose Bedia, another Cuban American artist and emblematic Palo initiate, acknowledges that, like other Cubans, he also experienced Lucumi[63] without any conflict of interest or concerns. Participation in Palo is open to followers of other faiths, but initiation is essential for avatars.

INITIATION

As practiced in most religions, initiation is the most fundamental and important ceremony for a *rayado* or *ngueyo* in Palo; a *rayado* or ngueyo is sometimes labeled a "*bozal.*"[64] Among the important ritual symbols that Palo adopted from Santeria, and which are employed in initiation, the *ndungui* ("coconut rind") and *chamalongos* ("shells") oracles stand out. Like santeros, paleros employ those symbolic oracles for divination: to arrive at answers to questions they inquire of the spirit, to prognosticate or reveal hidden secrets, and to divine one's condition, fate or destiny. A Santeria ritual expert occasionally refers clients to a Palo specialist for consultation or healing therapy. At an initial meeting before initiation, the tata performs a consultation by tossing the four pieces of coconut rinds. This is one of three types of divinatory oracles, employed on the basis of the kind of questions posed on behalf of an initiate-to-be. Cowrie shells (adopted from Lucumi) and gunpowder are also used as divinatory oracles. "This initial divination session determines if one is going to become a ngueyo, the first level of initiated participation in Palo, or a tata, the highest level."[65]

Often, the tata-palero's divinatory science, called Kongo magic, is little more than guesswork; it is a luck-and-chance tossing of the coconut rinds, or objects catching fire from other objects. For the practitioners and clients, however, they are efficacious enough to engage the tata in performance. The tata performs the initiation of the ngueyo or *bozal*, which requires necessary preparation and ritual paraphernalia. During the periods of state persecution, followers greeted each other in codes, the initiation was performed in secrecy, and the area of the *munanso* or *casa-templo* ("temple house") had to be protected from the police and political informants. The *casa-templo* must be guarded ritually against contamination. This is done by situating small packets called *makutos* and *masango* at the four corners of the sacred precinct. *Masango*, made of corn husk, earth from the four cardinal directions, and extract from the nganga cauldron, are ritually cleansed before they are lodged in the four corners of the sacred property.[66]

Before the initiation ceremony commences fully, the *munanso* and *casa-templo* are made sacred through a symbolic ritual of the drawing of a *firma* ("a signature, a composite name, a cosmogram") on the wall or the ground floor of the house, in front of the cauldron.[67] "These firmas often incorporate Kongo-derived references to the circling of the sun around the earth and to the Kalunga line, or horizon line," as symbolized in the Kongo yowa cross, and "to the Kalunga line, or the horizon line, the division between heaven and earth."[68] The firma includes a combination of arrows, circles, crosses, lines, and other parts representing the physical universe, such as the sun and the moon. These symbolic designs come together to give the firma its ritual power. The firma, resembling "the veve of Haitian Vodou in form and function, is an essential act in the ritual. Without the firma, the *mpungus* do not have a path into the ceremony, and communication with them will not occur";[69] therefore worship will not be effectual.

Firmas seem pervasive. Each *casa-templo* has a specific firma to be used by a ngueyo initiated into that house. Every *mpungu* has its personal firma, which is appealed to when the spirit or its nganga is actively summoned. Each palero also has his own firma representation. Other firmas are personal and must not be copied, or else negative consequences result. The devotees believe that the act of drawing firmas on the back and chest of an initiate during the ceremony puts the ngueyo at the center of life's force and power. As is done in a Santeria initiation, the ngueyo must learn the signs and complex meanings of the firmas and other receptacles of power. The initiation ceremony, which last at least seven days, is fraught with rituals and symbolism. The initiate is purified with a ritual cleansing bath called the *limpieza* or *omiero*, made of seven, fourteen, and twenty-one special herbal leaves mixed in water; the multiples of sevens and the naming of the bath are patterned after the Santeria iyawo initiation ritual. During the herbal bath, the ngueyo is stripped, and walks in a circular motion while he or she is washed from the neck down. The tata-palero rips the initiate's clothes and ritually discards them, as a sign of the dying of the old self. According to Bettelheim, twenty-one "palos" are "placed around the circumference of an nganga"; and "twenty-one paths of energy" are said to emanate from firmas "drawn as an arrow with twenty-one intersecting marks."[70]

A stick and a machete are used to mark the location of incisions that the initiate will later receive on the chest and back. Then the ngueyo is led into the initiation room proper for the next phase of the ceremony, the *rayamiento,* which he submits to while blindfolded to prove sincerity, commitment, and courage. When the ngueyo opens his eyes at the conclusion of the ceremony, the first thing he should see is a reflection of his new self in a mirror. The ngueyo rises from his knees to be greeted by the tata-palero and those who assisted him. In Jose Bedia's initiation, which Bettelheim narrates, the tata and his assistants welcomed their new member "with the special Palo handshake, saying: Salaam malekum! malekum salaam!" This Muslim greeting opened and concluded the ceremony,[71] in that *casa-templo.* The initiate is admitted to the faith at the climax of the initiation and accepts a spirit of the nganga pot or prenda; this is a vital receptacle of spiritual power in which his very personal nkisi is lodged.[72] The tata-palero prepares the newly initiated for service as a medium who allows the spirit to use him or her as a vessel of communication and a source of spiritual power.

Receptacles of Power

An interconnectedness between spirit, nature, ancestors, and flesh, or humans, is at the heart of Palo and is contained in, as well as communicated through, many spirit power-generating receptacles. All spiritual activities and actions—whether initiations, divinations, healings, spirit possessions, or the procuring of charms—are channeled through these sacred objects. They function as indispensable mythic and putative symbols of the religion. The most popular receptacles of power are nkisi or minkisi (objects of sacred charms); nganga (a pot or cauldron); *funza* (sacred medicines); *fula* (gunpowder); *ndungui* (a coconut); firmas (magic symbols); prenda (a divination receptacle); *vititi mensu* (a small mirror); *miyumba* (a human skull); and *macuto* (a form of pot), among others. Practitioners and initiates own objects which, in turn, provide them with a source or avenue to power and a means of spiritual communication.

Negotiating Palo Power

NKISI
Among the African Kongo, nkisi (plural minkisi) or *masango* were object-charms that practitioners held sacrosanct because they were charged with spiritual power for defense.[73] Wyatt MacGaffey notes that their visible form, intended to signify the presence of controlled masked forces, took the form of "an anthropomorphic or zoomorphic figure, an animal horn, a clay pot, a basket, and many others. The container itself is a mere object, until animated by 'medicines,'" and can adopt personal mannerisms: it can be flattered, petitioned, actuated, insulted, and humiliated.[74] According to African scholar T. J. Desch-Obi, in pre-

colonial Africa these were used as charms that offered protection against certain forces and misfortune. Among these were "group charms, such as the Imbangala *maji minkisi*," and sacred medicines "given by God the creator"; Africans took these "to protect themselves from sorcerers (*ndoki*) who used witchcraft to effect evil in the world."[75] Legend has it that "the first *nkisi* called Funza originated in God, and Funza came with a great number of *minkisi*, which he distributed throughout the country [of Congo], each with its respective powers, governing" its specific domain.[76]

Desch-Obi believes that enslaved Africans and their descendants, trained in the martial arts, "held on to this understanding of spiritual preparation for combat" in the Americas. "Group combat preparation rituals were an important part of many slave revolts such as the Haitian Revolution"; they were "influenced by Kongo-Angolan martial technologies" used in battle. It "began with spiritual preparation, referred to as *wanga* charms, and ritual specialists accompanied the troops."[77] A Palo nkisi object is a symbolic representation and metaphor for the harnessing and use of spiritual force to avenge hostile acts or to defend one against such malicious actions. This scheme is often effectuated by psychological angst, rather than by actual medical harm, because minkisi are not always noxious; a good nkisi brings good fortune.

NGANGA

As for the physical manifestation, where flesh meets spirit in Palo, the nganga (or *cazuela*) or prenda, the cauldron that supposedly houses the spirits, is at the epicenter of spiritual force. This Kongo signifying object is Palo's main receptacle of power; here, "poles, grasses, earth, animal and human remains, pieces of iron, stones, signs, objects, spirits and deities are arranged in a sort of summoning up of the cosmos."[78] Back in the Kongo, a nganga was a private individual spiritualist, or diviner, who had sacred powers to work secret magic and sorcery but could function occasionally in public roles (see Chapter 1). In addition to assisting individuals in dealing with hardship, the nganga often acted as a rainmaker, supposedly procured cures for epidemics, gave assurances of good luck, and performed other functions on behalf of the community at large. He was seen as a type of priest, although there were "differences in ceremonial usage between a *nganga a ngombo's* activities for private persons and those of the public."[79] Since a nganga could make foreboding magic, he was kept at a distance and treated with respect as well as dread. Beatriz Morales holds that "Congolese magicians and sorcerers developed a powerful role. . . . The ability to communicate with the dead, and to use medicine to cure and harm, made them major figures in maintaining social harmony, but also in disrupting the social order."[80] For this they were greatly feared. Christian missionaries to the Kongo viewed minkisi with derision and prohibited converted nganga from possessing or retaining the sacred objects, which were believed to be symbols of evil African paganism and witchcraft.

In Cuba, nganga amassed a baffling array of significations and meanings. The name symbolizes the spirit itself, the pot used to house the spirit, the objects that act as "signifiers," and the symbols of a religious role and role player in the religion, among others. Nganga is a spirit, a deceased individual, a supernatural power or force, a receptacle, ornamental rapping around the cauldron, and even "a sack of Russian cloth . . . in which is deposited a skull and human bones, earth from the cemetery . . . sticks, herbs, bowls, bones of birds and animals."[81] Nganga is also the precinct where the practitioners house and ritually utilize the objects they have collected; they arrange them in a symbolic manner that will aide in summoning the spirit to action. While the nganga refers to the pot itself, as well as to "the power of the pot," it is also the one who owns the pot. "It is a word in miniature, and when one is initiated into the final level in Palo, one receives a personal nganga. Thus, initiation makes nganga—both the priest and the pot."[82] In Cuba, "the most carefully preserved, and the most respected and feared Kongo element, is that of magic. The main source of this magical power is the palero's ability to make contact with the spirit of a dead person and to control it and make it work for him,"[83] or his client and *perros*, with the use of nganga.

The nganga is the most focal point of the palero's practice. From one perspective, the Cuban prenda represents the knowledge that paleros acquired from those who initiated them into the Palo religion. A Cuban tale holds that these ngangas or prendas were the only inheritance the ancestors could leave their children because they "had no wealth, land, or property. . . . The only possession they had was their culture—the knowledge of their rituals, the use of herbs," and the divination systems that are "symbolized by the prenda."[84] Prendas and ngangas are unique to each individual practitioner; once one is initiated, the initiate is given an individually owned nganga, which can be "born" only from a previously existing one. According to Bettelheim, "In the service of Palo Monte, the initiate accumulates power through the objects he or she deposits in the nganga."[85] By creating and using a nganga, a practitioner is entering into an agreement with the spirit held therein. Although the nature of the relationship, and the way it is interpreted, differ from person to person, there is a general understanding that the spirit will be helpful, or will "work" for the palero in some unique ways. The Cuban nganga fits the profile of the Kongo private spiritualist as well as the sorcerer, but his work and role in Palo are creole; they are best seen in the palero and in the healing and making of magic charms.[86]

Symbolic Oracles

CUBAN COSMOGRAPHIC *YOWA* CROSS
Perhaps the most intriguing ritual signification in Palo is its preservation of the multivalent Bakongo cross. This cosmographic symbol, prominent in African Kongo death rites, portends a cosmological reality and existence in the world of

the deceased, guided by the spirits, for the extension of life in the beyond. MacGaffey records that in Palo, as in the African Kongo, practitioners symbolize the cosmos as this encircled spherical cross showing four equal portions cleaved and clearly marked and having a time clock at the fulcrum. They label the four points of the cross in cardinal and elemental directions, exactly as was done in Mayombe Congo. The position pointing upward to the sky is *nsulu* (*ku zulu*). The *ensiafua*, or *kumangongo*, points to "the deep of the earth," or the "land of the dead." The *nototo*, "the earth," is the position on the cross that corresponds to 6:00 P.M. on the clock. The *kalunga*, "the ocean," is the opposite point of the cross that corresponds to 6:00 A.M. on the clock.[87]

Since the cross predates the Christian era, and is present in the ancient Greek and Roman civilizations, Dianne Stewart thinks it is probably one of the oldest religious cultural icons in Africa. It "symbolizes the holistic spiritual and philosophical orientation regarding [the] visible-invisible sacred cosmos, which is normative for many classical African societies."[88] Of the cross in Kongo religion, Robert Ferris Thompson writes: "The simplest ritual space is a Greek cross [+] marked on the ground, as for oath-taking. One line represents the boundary; the other is ambivalently both the path leading across the boundary, as to the cemetery; and the vertical path of power linking 'the above' with the 'below.'"[89] Thompson proffers the view that the circle around "the Kongo cross refers to the everlasting continuity of all righteous men and women" in the mystery of life.[90] The special import that the *yowa* cross served in Mayombe Kongo seems preserved in Cuba, although creole elements have been added to its multivalent meaning. Scholars suspect that the taking of oaths in some Afro-Caribbean religions was influenced by the Kongo *yowa* cross signification. In addition to being used in the swearing of oats and the pledging of allegiance, the cross as symbol points to the memory of ancestral spirits in the land of the beyond and represents the summoning of invisible mystical powers in the visible world through ritual. Thus the cross may function to attract and focus the spirit in the ceremonies, the same way that drawing the firma in Palo and the vive of Haitian Vodou focus the power.

VITITI MENSU
Other oracles unique to Palo are the *fula* ("gunpowder"), the *vititi mensu* ("small mirror"), and the *macuto*. Maria Valez explains how the *fula* is used: the priest places a number of "small piles of gunpowder over a board, or over the floor, in a ritually separate space. A question is formulated, and the palero sets one of the pile bundles on fire; according to the number of piles that catch fire, the answer to the question is considered positive or negative."[91] The other oracle, *vititi mensu* (*mpuka mensu*)—a receptacle of the "power of Kongo, made of an animal horn filled with religious substances and covered by a mirror"—is said to "reproduce . . . the flesh of the spirit"[92] that situates the palero in contact with the world of spiritual power and gives him a glimpse into the other world. The palero reads the *vititi mensu* by filling the mirror with smoke soot

from a candle, and proceeding to interpret the various shapes formed from it.[93] Descriptions like these demonstrate the diverse practices in Palo as a whole, but they also illuminate some similarities and differences between it and Santeria.

MAKUTOS

Other components of Palo important to its ritual function are those of music and two sets of magical symbols called *macuto* or *makuto*. Music plays a significant role in the religion's celebrations, initiations, funerary rites, and rituals, where its sacrifices are performed to feed the *mpungas*, or the spirits associated with objects made from iron or steel.[94] As the ceremonies themselves are generally less elaborate than those of Santeria, the music is also less complex; it does not revolve around special rhythms, chants, and dances for each spirit or deity. The palero has a collection of *mambos* ("chants") that are sung by a leader during rituals, as well as special drums unique to Palo ritual music.[95] As in other religions, the drums summon the spirits, announce their arrival, and dispatch them at the appropriate time.

A Palo *macuto*, like the nganga, is a complex symbolic oracle. In its simplest form, it is a small sacrosanct bundle made of vegetable and other ingredients ritually sanctified and imbued with protective medicines. In its superstitious world, many taboos surround the *macuto's* efficaciousness. A *macuto* is also an individually owned receptacle of the spirit of empowerment that manifests in ways pertinent to an initiate's pressing circumstances. Commenting on Marta Maria Perez's *macuto* receptacle of power, demonstrated in a 1991 art photo of a woman clasping an object across her unclothed breast, artist Gerardo Mosquera writes, "She gathers within the object the two dolls she has used in earlier works to represent her twin girls, using her chest as a hierophanic space, sacralized by means of one of those ritual drawings of Palo Monte," seen "so often in Bedia's works."[96] Mosquera concludes, "In this case, it is the 'sign of the four moments of the sun,' 'sign of signs,' foundation of everything: a graphic synthesis of *yowa* or Kongo cosmogony, which serves to activate the center of power, marking the very eye of the cosmos, [a uniquely] privileged point where the object that is prepared may acquire force."[97] Here symbol and auricle converge in ritual space to generate spiritual power and deep religious meaning.

Conclusion

Palo and its Cuban cognates are undoubtedly among the most distinctly Kongo religious traditions in the Caribbean. The religion's language and vocabulary, philosophical concepts, and religious practices are so different from Yoruba-based religion (and Christianity) that for a long time it remained less popular, less known, more suspect, and more greatly suppressed as *brujeria* than Lucumi was. Like other Afro-Cuban religions, persecution sent Palo underground and contributed to its national isolation, but also to its cultural preservation. After

Castro's regime lifted its ban on Afro-Cuban religions as a means of dealing with its mammoth economic and health crises at the end of the last millennium, the religion reemerged to be among the now popularly sought "forbidden African religions." As Moret observes, Cubans and foreigners alike seek initiation and pharmacopeia from *"paleros, santeros, babalawos,* and *espiritista."* Under state-organized "folkloric" tours, tourist are now enthusiastically ferried to the once damned Palo *casa-templo* in Palmira (as elsewhere) "to experience mocked-religious ceremonies, or, according to a *Ruta del Esclavo* [slave route] museum guide, a consultation with a local babalawo"[98] or palero. Because of practitioners' creative artistic expression, the religion is also a huge source of attraction for "culturalists" and art historians' articulation of Cuban culture. Art exhibitions on Palo and other Afro-Cuban religions are now educational staples of diversity in our cultural diets, brought into most world communities through the omnipresent Internet and the economic gods of international cooperation. In Cuba, Palo Monte Mayombe and Congas Reglas will continue to compete for cultural space and appreciation with the well-established Santeria and more newly arrived traditions, such as Espiritismo and Rastafari.

PART IV

Creole Religions of the Southern Caribbean

8

Dancing to Orixas' Axe in Candomble

KEY TOPICS

*Cultural Space • Catholic Irmandades • Candomble Structure
and Ethos • Ethnic Nations • Male and Female Divinities •
Sacred Space • Initiation into Candomble • Sacred Medicine*

Is it a coincidence that one of the most African of the African traditional religions (ATRs) in the diaspora is found in the land of the samba (the electrifying festive dance and symbol of Brazilian culture), the world's biggest Catholic country and largest African society outside of that continent? Candomble is a complex religion of the diaspora characterized by ritual dance, spiritual healing, divinatory science, spirit possession, sacrificial offerings, spiritual powers, and the celebration of living religious memories in Afro-Brazilian communities. Candomble is so internationally known as a vibrant and enduring legacy among African cultures in the Americas that it is called the locus classicus in the study of African "collective memory" and the historic debate over the survival of African cultures in the diaspora.[1] Scholars have established that the academic argument that Africans were completely stripped of their social heritage and retained no African language, social organization, or religious culture, and that "the nature of the slave trade and the socially disruptive immigration process of the Yoruba essentially precluded any wholesale transfer of African religion to the New World,"[2] cannot be true of Brazil.

Candomble emerged from high colonial times with some of the strongest African traditions in the Americas. Scholars[3] studied and measured Africanisms in the religion and clearly differentiated them from Indian, Roman Catholic, Macumba, and spiritualist cultural elements in Brazil; the cosmological system of gods and spirits, the ceremonies and ritual performance, the music, dance, and sacred medicine are all African in origin. Also identified are several features that distinguish Candomble as uniquely African among religions of Brazil: the active and systematic worship of a number of sacred entities, the feeding of the spirits and maintaining of sacred liturgical objects that represent spiritual forces,

Oxum, goddess of sweet, fresh waters.
(Illustration by Kelly Hawes.)

the wearing of ritual garments in sacred precincts of Candomble *terreiros*, the initiation of new members and ritual performers, and the practice of trance possession as an important cultic phenomenon.

Experience and Cultural Memory

Afro-Brazilian religions emerged in the throes of (1) the assiduous European colonial enterprise and the resulting transatlantic slave trade that facilitated contact among Africans and other peoples, (2) Portuguese Catholic Christianity in Brazil, (3) the tenacious West Central African religions (especially Yoruba, Fon, and Bantu), and (4) Amerindian culture. Geographically, Brazil was a strategic economic and political vantage point for the European West African slave trade; it received the first Africans to arrive on the South American continent and was the last to abolish the trade in the West (1888). Of the millions of captives taken from Africa as slaves, more than one-third came through Brazil, mostly to Bahia (labeled "Black Rome"), the largest slave depot and the face of black Africa in the Americas.[4] Portuguese traders had an early asiento to trade in slaves in Brazil by virtue of the imaginary line that Pope Alexander VI (Roderigo Borgia) drew by Papal Bull in 1492.[5] Brazil offered a huge land mass, with unlimited acreage for a plantation economy in sugar, tobacco, cocoa, and coffee. Colonists found that sugar cane required large plantations, the profitability of which demanded a massive supply of cheap labor. As elsewhere in the region, planters looked first to the natives for the labor supply, but Africans gradually replaced Amerindians on the plantations following the decimation of native peoples through brutality, forced labor, and European-borne disease. Jesuit priests captured thousands of Amerindians, whom they crowded into mission villages to be made Christians and provide labor by force, but they became helpless victims of the smallpox epidemic of 1562 to 1563[6] as well as of confinement.

Supporters of Brazil's slave trade claimed that Africans made a superior labor force to the rapidly disappearing natives and could be had cheaply and in abundance. Brazil took in more slaves in the 1800s than in the previous three centuries; huge numbers of Africans from Nigeria, Togo, Benin, and Ghana[7] (called Sudanese), as well as the Angola-Kongo-Zaire (Democratic Republic of the Congo) Bantu civilization, were brought to Bahia. Clandestine trafficking from the parallel slave market (called black market) inserted hundreds of thousands of Africans into the Brazilian coastal market before the 1850s. Ascertaining accurate statistics on the undocumented human cargo is nearly impossible,[8] but evidence shows that the slaves were ethnically diverse and that they have had a lasting impact on Afro-Brazilian culture. Roger Bastide contends that they comprised "representatives of round-house and square-house civilizations, totemic civilizations, matrilineal and patrilineal civilizations, blacks familiar with vast kingships and others who knew only tribal organization, Islamized Negroes and 'animists,' Africans having polytheist religious systems and others who worshiped chiefly their lineal ancestors."[9] Bastide's designations are outdated but his perception of African diversity is correct.

Social anthropologist Robert Voeks classifies slave arrivals in Bahia into several cycles that show their country of origin, ethnic grouping, and influence on Brazil. The Guinea Cycle brought mostly people from the Guinea coast. The Angola and Kongo Cycle brought mainly Bantu peoples living just south of the equator, among whom were blacks from Mozambique. The last cycle came from the Bight of Benin or the coast of Dahomey. The demand in old Dahomey/ Benin for Brazilian-Bahian tobacco, on the one hand, and Brazil's preference for "Sudanese" blacks to work in the mines, on the other, influenced the Mina Cycle. Therefore the wave of Africans to Brazil from the late 1700s to 1851 were mainly from this Central West African region (Yoruba, Dahomey, and Fanti-Ashanti) and were Islamized (Mandingo and Hausa) peoples. During the 1600s, Bantu Africans were dominant because the Brazil-Angola route was easier than that of countries north of the Congo, and planters preferred Bantu workers. Mina/Sudanese blacks were later replaced by Bantu people when gold-bearing sand was discovered and labor reinforcements were required to replenish the slaves killed by a smallpox epidemic raging through Angola. Wars between the Yoruba and Fon/Dahomey also furnished thousands of prisoners, causing Dahomeans to send "a series of embassies to Bahia and Lisbon asking that their country be granted a monopoly of the slave trade."[10] This had an impact on the number of Africans brought to Brazil from that region of Africa with their religious and cultural traditions.

Religious and political authorities sought to suppress African culture in Brazil because they feared that the so-called fetish priests of the Batuques religion (with its *autabaque* practices) would follow Boukman's example in Haiti and lead revolts against Christian whites. The notorious Inquisition ordered a municipal council in Bahia to investigate whether Batuques harbored "any persons utilizing fetishism or who may be witches—healing animals by blessing them, making use of diabolical relics, or having made a pact with the Devil."[11] Protest was both individual and collective and ranged from fleeing brutality to joining one of the many armed revolts. Having knowledge of revolts and abolitionists activities in the northern hemisphere, slaves planned dozens of uprisings against their masters on Brazilian plantations. Denmark Vesey's slave uprising in the United States in 1822 influenced the enacting of Brazil's first judicial ordinance in slave laws; it prohibited slaves from using religious assembly or gathering with African *autobaquis* drums, seen as a pretext for revolt or social action. Yet, a most infamous slave revolt in Bahia occurred in January 1835, led by Islamic and Yoruba rebels.[12]

For very different reasons, the white citizenry and the Afro-Brazilians both saw a connection between African religions, African ethnicity, and slave resistance. In the 1800s, Candomble and Macumba followers were constantly under persecution. Portuguese authorities and slave owners used penal measures, the splitting of tribal groups and families, forced conversion to Christian faith, and other means to eliminate African culture and thwart attempts at slave solidarity and revolt.[13] Afro-Brazilians, however, continued to sow seeds of rebellion and to resist the political and religious hegemony perpetrated on them by the planter class. Murphy says: "Their large numbers, the currency of their contacts with Africa, and their dedication to . . . freedom made for a remarkable continuity with the traditions of their ancestors and nurtured in Afro-Bahians a force of resistance to the brutal system of oppression that they endured."[14] Slaves endured wretched working conditions, harsh punishment, poor health, short life expectancy, and the affliction of many tropical and European diseases. As Rachel Harding notes, "In the nineteenth century, Bahia endured recurrent epidemics of cholera and yellow fever— during which slaves suffered disproportionately due to the precarious conditions under which they lived."[15] Although deprived of their humanity and freedom, slaves retained the memory of their African culture.

Notwithstanding the most concerted efforts to suppress slave gatherings and Batuques dances, slaves preserved African culture in their memory and through varied fraternities. Resistance to European cultural values contributed to black solidarity and the preservation of African religions in many creole forms. The numerical strength of Dahomey and Yoruba slaves gave them religious dominance in Afro-Brazilian culture. Especially in the 1800s, the appearance in Bahia of large numbers of Africans over a short period created what is called the cultural hegemony that distinguished Bahia as being very prominent in the nineteenth-century African diaspora. Both the country of origin of incoming Africans and the time of their arrival had a great impact on the dominance of Yoruba over other religious traditions in the African-dominated region of Bahia.[16] Late arrivals from Africa brought with them fresh memories of religions of their homeland to be infused into Brazilian culture. This allowed African populations to continue replenishing their religious knowledge and experience. Brazil's most densely populated areas were the large coastal cities of Rio de Janeiro, Recife, Salvador de Bahia, and Porto Alegre, which functioned as slave depots. The sheer density of the populations there created conditions favorable for maintaining African cultural traditions.[17] Afro-Brazilian religions first developed their vitality in these heavily populated black centers; there, Africans continued their religious practices covertly on the plantations and in communes with members of the same tribes who were familiar with the religion and the language.

This vital religious African culture in Brazil is creole. George Eaton Simpson observes that in Yoruba-derived houses in cult centers in Sao Luiz, most deities with Brazilian names are of Christian and native South American origin. At Dahomey houses, songs are sung in Fo, and dance rhythms are distinctly African. At Yoruba centers, the songs are sung either "in mixed Nago and Portuguese, or Portuguese. . . . In Sao Luiz . . . religious rituals closely parallel African patterns only in the 'orthodox' Dahomean and Yoruban cult groups, with the Dahomean house adhering to purer forms of African ritual than the Yoruban."[18] The beliefs and ceremonies of Batuques, found in Belem, show Yoruba and Dahomey traditions, American Indian shamanism, and Portuguese and local Brazilian folk traditions.[19] In time, Yoruba would dominate the African cultural religious landscape in Brazil as it did elsewhere in the region.

Cultural Space

African religions in Brazil survived as oral traditions transported out of Africa in the memories of specialists and religiously savvy chiefs and kings from Kongo, Yoruba, Ashanti, Fon-Dahomey, eastern Bantu, and other areas. An iconographic document called "Engraving no. 105 in the *Zoobiblion*" was recorded by Zacharias Wagna, who lived in the Dutch section of Brazil from 1634 to 1641. The inscription tells of Sunday meetings of slaves of all ages who assembled in specially designated places and spent the day dancing "wildly" to the sound of drums and flutes. They made frequent libations, "often until they are too deafened and inebriated to recognize each other."[20] African worship and spirit possession rituals, however, were not a party leading to drunken stupor. They were the vibrant African spirituality that helped the slaves bear the harsh punishment of slave life.

As anthropologist Yvonne Maggie noted, the earliest accounts of these religions show activities in fairly small Candomble and Macumba communities in costal regions. Later, African cultures and religions quietly emerged throughout Brazil in many forms under many different names: Candomble, Xango, Tambor de Mina and Nago, or Tambor das Minas, Pajelanca, Catimbo, Macumba, Batuques, and, more recently, Umbanda.[21] Forced into being clandestine operations on plantations at first, Afro-Brazilian religions did not flourish readily until the eighteenth and nineteenth centuries. According to Voeks, "Early houses of African worship offered perhaps the only viable alternative to the European social and religious order, to which slaves and freedmen had little or no access."[22] The rise of African religious centers as organized institutions in Brazil is dated to 1822, when the country obtained its independence from Portugal. Major centers preserved a range of African cultural traditions and practices known by different names in various regions of Brazil. Candomble is dominant in Salvador de Bahia and Reconcavo, Xango is popular in the regions of Pernambuco and Alagoas, Tambor de Mina thrives in Maranhao, Batuques survives in Porto Alegre and Belem, and Macumba is well established in Rio de Janeiro. These diverse traditions are grouped in families of religions: Candomble, a part of Afro-religious fraternities that comprise four ethnic "nations"; Macumba, a creole religion that Brazilians vilify; and Umbanda, an African religion de-Africanized within Brazil's populous culture of the middle class.[23]

Not all black religions were brought to Brazil by the unwilling hands of enslaved Africans, nor did the cultural migration move in one direction only. By the 1930s, Afro-Brazilians who were financially able traveled between Africa and the Americas and renewed family and religious ties. Joseph Murphy states, "A number of Africans freely emigrated to Brazil, often at the behest of emancipated members of families and congregations of [c]ondamble. Two large colonies of Brazilian Nagos returned to Africa to establish communities that continue to maintain their Brazilian identity."[24] Several realities contributed to keeping African culture alive in Bahia, especially among the Yoruba people: Africans made a conscious effort to stay in close contact with Africa and to spread and practice the cultural traditions of their ancestors in Brazil with an African worldview. In the decades following abolition, Africans in Bahia maintained more direct cultural connections with West Africa than did other African peoples in the diaspora. Afro-Bahians who repatriated to Africa engaged in transatlantic trade businesses with family and acquaintances back in Brazil, thus keeping contact alive. A few made the long commute to Africa for educational and cultural reasons. One of the most often cited examples is the story of Isadora Maria Hamus of Cachoeira, Bahia, who studied Yoruba and English in Lagos, Nigeria, for eight years and then returned to share her knowledge with a house of Candomble that she led. After 1850, absence of a forceful program of indoctrination by the Catholic Church and open hostility toward African religions (as seen among French Catholics in Saint-Domingue) created space for African cultural and religious traditions to thrive in Bahia.[25]

Catholic Irmandades

In Spanish, French, and Portuguese America, the Catholic Church initiated confraternities for enveloping the colonial Africans in its bosom for religious, social, and political reasons. Under cover of providing for the slaves' social and spiritual welfare, Portuguese colonial authorities of the 1800s encouraged Africans to form Catholic Brotherhoods called *irmandades*. The Spanish transplanted their *cofradias*—first designed in the mid-1400s to cater to the general welfare of black parishes in Valencia, Seville, Barcelona, and other cities—to colonial Catholic America.[26] In Brazil, these were organized according to their ethnic groupings, nationality, color, and even occupation, to serve a number of social and religious functions. They were to function as an arm of the Church and, as Harding notes, "were responsible for sponsoring annual festivals in honor of their patron saint and for other regular ritual activities of veneration, such as masses and votive offering."[27] Bastide says that black-mulatto brotherhoods reflected the Church's policy of uniting Africans, or their descendants, "under the cross in order to incorporate them as a distinct entity in the vast religious community of Brazil. It is within these organizations, the Brotherhood of . . . Saint Benedict the Moor, or of Our Lady of the Rosary, that assimilation and religious syncretism would develop"[28] nationally.

In one sense, nineteenth-century lay Catholic brotherhoods were a tool of the Portuguese government's political strategy for controlling Africans. The government sought to reestablish the "nations" with the intent of encouraging ferment among ethnic rivals so as to preempt unified slave revolts or the creation of class consciousness among blacks—the divide-and-conquer philosophy. By encouraging divisions of slave groups into ethnic nations, the government indirectly encouraged cultural diversity among Africans and increased the chances of slaves practicing much of their culture. The *irmandades* benefited their sponsors. Through the Brotherhoods, the Church obtained institutional access to Africans and imposed what Bastide calls a nonthreatening veneer of Portuguese Catholicism over the religious life of the slave. This allowed the Church to claim a large membership among Africans and expose them to the teachings of colonial Christianity with its many contradictions.

Although brotherhoods were different from the Candombles, they made it possible and legal for Africans to preserve and practice their sacred traditions openly and without reprisal. They preserved languages, religions, and culture. The religious orders also allowed some blacks to find acceptance in a slightly higher social class in colonial society than the one to which slaves were confined.

Membership was not based on accessibility, and the lay brotherhoods became the most widespread form of black mutual aid society in colonial Brazil. It is held that in the 1850s, almost every Bahian belonged to one or more *irmandades*. Like cabildos in Cuba, brotherhoods also helped slaves secure their emancipation and have access to the Church. As a result, African traditions, cloaked under and adapted to Portuguese Catholicism, emerged in the early nineteenth century in specific sects that succeeded the *irmandades* phenomenon. Brotherhoods provided an important institutional framework that enabled African religious practices to survive in most urban areas in the colonial period[29] under the Christian banner.

The impact of Christian teachings on most slaves was negligible and an inconvenience at best. Slaves were baptized into the Portuguese Catholic faith and given a Christian blessing upon arrival in Brazil, but rather than abandon their faith to become Christians,[30] they superimposed Catholicism on African religious practices and used the former to their own advantage. They associated their divine pantheon with saints of Catholic hagiology by ascribing each orixa characteristics of Christian saints and names.[31] As authority on Candomble Mikelle Smith Omari states, the conflict that originated from pressure to assimilate into modern Portuguese Brazilian society also led some sects to incorporate Catholic altars and various religious symbols into sacred spaces, ritual dances, and other activities of the cultus in Macumba, Candomble,[32] and Umbanda. Based on what Voeks calls a hagiology of "hands-on, miracle-working saints," white colonials invoked St. George, St. Sebastian, the Virgin Mary and others for good health and other blessings for their families. "It was this cult of the saints, the adoration of a pantheon of spiritual entities that solved earthly problems," that Africans knew as Catholicism[33] and used in their creole religions.

How should this adaptation be understood? Was the Afro-Catholic syncretism really superficial, an intentional strategy designed to deceive whites into believing that Africans were Christians? Were Catholic altars in the terreiro, for example, only extraneous decorations for camouflaging the fraternity's true ritual intent? Is it true that the altars' chromolithographs in the terreiro had no real spiritual function in Candomble ceremonies because daughters of the *santos* do not salute Catholic statutes of the saints? Voeks argues that the apparent deception required "a calculated tolerance on the part of the authorities, a feigned ignorance meant to lull Africans into conversion."[34] As Bastide contends, however, if this was the only reason for the adaptation, it does not explain why the priests closed the terreiros and sent the orixas away during the Christian Holy Week. This also does not explain why, during the month of May, practitioners of the Engenho Velho Candomble at Recife and other fraternal centers recite litanies of the Blessed Virgin and bow before her altar. Centers adopted characteristics of Catholic sainthood and reinterpreted and transformed its rituals, litanies, words, and name identification in their ceremonies. This shows that Africans intentionally creolized Brazilian Christianity to their spiritual needs. The African cosmology and system of myths, rites, and rituals found a home in the cracks of Catholic hegemony[35] in Brazil, for social, political, religious, and other reasons. Traces of Africanism in the Christian-influenced Caboclo and Catimbo cults of colonial Brazil show that creolization of African religions occurred in the shadow of the Christian cross.

Candomble Structure and Ethos

Paul Christopher Johnson is correct: "It is impossible to encapsulate the rich complexity of Candomble, a religion notorious for its elusion of firm boundaries or systemic closure, in a single chapter."[36] The origin of the word *Candomble*, which has a multiplicity of meanings, is debated, but the name is creole, derived from African Kongo-Bantu *Kandombele,* meaning "musical festival." Although derived from the Bantu language, the Yoruba-based religion, as Yvonne Daniel points out, is itself evidence of the infra-African syncretism of Nago, Ketu, and other nations, so that "a West African religion came to be known by a Central African title."[37]

Candamba was the name of a leading slave port and a large Bantu slave station in the Kongo.[38] Portuguese colonists used the word *Candomble* to describe African religious practices brought to Bahia. According to Smith Omari, Candomble came to denote individual sects and sacred places of the religions, and in the past represented huge festivities and parties that slaves held on their free days while honoring their African deities. As it is currently practiced in Bahia, Candomble is the ideology of the group—its religious myths, values, belief system, and rituals that honor and enshrine deities.[39] Candomble means many things as a religious field: It is the socially extended units in which cultic allegiances take precedence over family ties in terreiros that form a loose federation of independently operated creole fraternities. It is the ritual enactments and dispensing of sacred medicines in communities of worship embodying creole divinities. Candomble is a signifying act of exchange in which gods ride humans, humans feed gods, and gods empower the weak through axe while drums speak to and for them both through rhythms—all done in houses of secrecy and power where the eating, speaking and acting[40] are filled with meaning and vivaciousness.

Afro-Brazilian religions also have their own fluid organizational structure; cult leaders have made unsuccessful attempts to organize thousands of *centros, tendas,* and terreiros into working federations.[41] The most sustained attempt was made in the 1930s by Edison Carneiro, a trained Bahian journalist and ethnographer. He attempted to unite some seventy-five to one hundred Candomble houses, serving almost three hundred thousand people, into a self-supporting union. This was a way of marshaling Afro-Bahian political and economic power. This federation could have served an estimated 1600 diverse and fluidly organized Candombles with a huge following from among more than two million Bahians.[42] Although autonomous, Candombles are related cosmically, theologically, and culturally to each other; they receive their support from a predominantly African clientele, belief system, social conventions, and cultic practices.

Ethnic Nations

The diverse nations of the Candombles in Brazil number more than eight when Xango, Tambor de Mina, Catimbo, Batuque, and Pajelanca are classified as separate groups. They are usually reduced to a few larger ones: Candomble Nago (Anago) or Iya Nasso, Candomble Jeje or Gege, Candomble Angola or Congo, Candomble Ketou (Ketu) or Queto, and Candomble Caboclo. Each of the big Candombles comprises subgroups—called houses of nations—that have similar names: Oyo, Ketu, Angola, Alaketo, Mina Jeje, Congo (Kongo), Tapa, Xamba, Mozambique, Mina, Nago, Eba, Ijexa, Efan, Jebu, Jexa, Mucurumin, and Hausa. According to Matory, "The oldest, largest, and wealthiest Bahian Candomble houses tend to identify themselves as members of Queto, or Nago, nation"[43] and to form what he called Candomble elite. "In Bahia, the dying Jeje nation (whose worship of the *vodum* . . . gods identifies it with the Ewe, Gen, Aja, and Fon speakers neighboring Yorubaland) is closely associated with the Queto/Nago nation."[44] Since Jeje, Angola or Kongo, and Caboclo are not as influential in Afro-Brazilian religions as Nago, less is said about them. "Nago Candomble is centered at the sacred sites of Engenho Velho, Gantois, and Axe (de) Opo Afonja in Salvador (Bahia), which trace their founding lineages to the early nineteenth century."[45] Jeje Candombles are said to have evolved from Fon-Ewe (Dahomey) ritual practices, whose cosmology, ritual dances, characteristics, and dialects are similar to Yoruba.[46]

ANGOLA/KONGO

Candombles Angola and Congo (Kongo) trace their ancestry to a fairly large mix of Bantu-speaking peoples from what is now the Democratic Republic of the Congo (DRC) or Zaire, Angola, Cabinda in central West Africa, and Mozambique, Zanzibar, and other Central, East, and Southern African countries. As a result, symbiosis and intra-African creolization are evident. For example, deities in these Candombles use Bantu names, although most of their attributes and ritual paraphernalia show Yoruba origin. Their dance and music show Yoruba patterns but their rhythms differ substantially from Yoruba rhythms. Smith Omari reports that, at festivals she attended in Bate Folha and Bogum, Brazil, Yoruba gods had to be summoned, danced to, and dismissed before the festival could conclude successfully.[47] The modern Candomble is no longer a mysterious mystical sect veiled in secrecy, about which Paul Johnson writes so eloquently.[48] Bastide's poetic summation is sentient: "Among banana plants, bougainvilleas, breadfruit trees, and gigantic fig trees . . . or beside golden sandy beaches edged with coconut palms, stands the *candomble*, with the huts for the gods, the living quarters, the roofed shelter where at night the beating of drums summons the ancestral deities. . . . Half-naked children frolic under the fond eyes of mothers adorned with liturgical necklaces"[49] and flaunting Candomble culture.

NAGO

By far, the most numerous and powerful African religious associations in Bahia are Candomble Nago. They are so influential that Candomble in general is often called Nago and other Candombles have duplicated some of Nago's rituals, cosmological concepts, liturgical vestments, and other sacred paraphernalia.[50] The word *Nago* has its origins in Benin vocabulary among Fon-Ewe and Yoruba-speaking peoples and is currently used to describe all Yoruban Afro-Brazilian descendants and religion, although other nations like Oyo, Ketu, Eba, Jebu are still very distinct. Scholars see 1830 as the most credible date for the founding of the first Candomble Nago. Three free African women, Iya Deta, Iya Kala, and Iya Nasso, founded the first modern houses of Candomble in Barroquinha, Bahia, in the early nineteenth century. Engenho Velhos became the mother of Bahian Candombles; it was clearly established by 1830, and some accounts placed its origin in the mid- to late 1700s. The Candomble ancestors (Engenho Velho, Gantois, and Axe Opo Afonja) are models for the many current ones in Bahia. A dispute over leadership succession between two *Ialorixas* led to the founding of two new Candomble houses. Omari says, "Gantois in Engenho Velho . . . and the Beneficent Society of Sao Jorge, more commonly known as Axe Opo Afonja" were founded around "1918 by Aninha in Sao Goncalo do Retiro."[51] This is the site where Omari did her field research.

Nago houses usually claim the house of Iya Nasso, also known as Casa Branca, as their ancestor, and, as Murphy records, "most of the Nago candombles of Bahia can trace their origins to one of the priestesses of Casa Branca, Gantois, or Opo Afonja." After the death of Iya Nasso's daughter, Mercelina, "arguments about her successor led one of Casa Branca's senior priestesses, Maria Julia da Conceicao, to found the Ile Iya Omin Axe Iyamasse, a house best known today as Gantois after the Bahanian neighborhood in which it is located."[52] This practice of tracing a group's African roots and establishing the authenticity of Candomble rituals encouraged frequent travels to and from Africa to obtain a better understanding of the Nago spirituality at its source. The establishment of Candomble institutions contributes substantially to their superior sacred space and ritual cultus. Often, a Candomble house inherits the name of its founder, predecessor cultic center, or an outstanding leader whose roots go back to Africa. As Murphy attests, "Today every large Nago house of [c]andomble has sent members to Africa, and the question of the *pureza* or purity of Bahian practice in relation to African standards continue to stimulate the most lively debate among the houses."[53] Although there is evidence of Sudanese, Bantu, and other elements in various regions, they are dominated by the Yoruba worldview and cultus. Bahia's ethnic groups reconstituted their own

African religious beliefs and practices in the framework that Yoruba created. As Voeks says, "The Yoruba provided the central structural text within which various ethnic and cultural messages could be retained."[54] The Yoruba cosmology, cultic practices, musical rhythms, and language had an advantage over those of other Afro-Brazilian religions.

Mortal Creole Gods

Yoruba preserved the worship of the West African orisha (orixa) which, although creolized with Portuguese Catholic and native spirituality, remains the heart of Afro-Brazilian religions. The Yoruba world view is kept alive in the structure, beliefs, and practices of Candombles whose patron deities called orixas or *santos* are given names of male and female African Yoruba deities. Orixas of the Yoruba pantheon, serving as Olorun's diplomats and a direct link to the profane world, form a most important element of the Candomble cosmos. About seventeen of the hundreds of mythological orixas are well known, and an even smaller number are worshiped under different labels in most terreiros. The orixas personify the forces of nature and, as nature deities, are associated with certain geographical spheres and elemental forces like storms, wind, rivers, mountains, seas, and forests. The spiritual forces have mortal characteristics; they are neither omnipotent nor omnipresent. They are made in human thought, stationed in Africa, and must be subpoenaed to Brazil, aroused, fed, clothed, and pampered, via rituals, so they can manifest in individuals of their choosing.[55]

Orishas are guardian deities, two of which guide and control each adept. Like Chinese yin and yang, they represent what Voeks termed "dichotomous force" with "opposing energies, hot and cold, apparent and transparent. One is masculine; the other is feminine. They are temperaments constantly in conflict: one revealed, the other hidden; one dominant, the other recessive."[56] These opposing energies are signified in their adepts. For example, a person who is intelligent but has facial pimples is regarded as a devotee of Omolu, the god of smallpox. An aggressive and jealous person who is a good leader is associated with Xango, the male god of lightning and thunder. At the same time, forces of the deities maintain their individual state of equilibrium: "Xango is aggressive, Oxala is peaceful, and Iroko is plodding."[57] As in Yorubaland, an intricate symbolic system identifies each orixa by special songs, drumbeats, a series of dance steps, color combinations, costumes, liturgical implements, herbs, foods, and sacrificial animals.[58]

To Candomble functionaries, orishas are an essential reality, a living source of power, and indispensable means of communication. Religious ritual activities are directed to the orixa as the primary object of worship, but because the deities have different personality traits and characteristics, liturgical details differ in style from one terreiro to another. Some Candomble ceremonies open with an offering to Exu; others do not. Sacrifice is an important feature of

African rituals, but Candombles within Nago, Tamba de Mina, and Xango deemphasize animal sacrifice and spirit possession rituals in worship designed to bring assistance to those in need.[59] These mythic orixas have special traits, taboos, iconography, days, spherical location, antics, likes, and prohibitions. Each orixa also has personality descriptors that double with those of Catholic saints; they have name designations tied to special regions; and they are influenced by social, political, racial, and class-struggle realities in Brazil. The complex African-Catholic designations of the following entities signify this mythological world of the gods.

Male Powers

EXU (OR ELEGBA)

The all-important mythic divinity Exu appears in twenty-two creole forms, some of which are determined by race. In parts of Bahia, Maranhao, Recife, and Alagoas, Exu is the malicious Satan, but in other areas of the same region he is St. Bartholomew, St. Anthony, or St. Gabriel. In most of Bahia, Exu and Ogun are identified with St. Anthony. In Recife, Porto Alegre, and Rio de Janeiro, where blacks and whites have not had good relations, Exu could be the Rebel Angel, St. Gabriel, St. Bartholomew, St. Anthony, or St. Peter. In his devil persona, the male Exu is the master of tricks or magic. In the persona of St. Anthony, who was tormented by a demon, Exu's evil thoughts and actions could disrupt a cult's ceremonies and also cause an unguarded person to yield to temptation. When he is St. Peter, Exu opens and closes doors, opens the gates of heaven with his heavy bunch of keys, and acts as keeper of Candomble fraternities. Exu lets loose demons on August 24, St. Bartholomew's feast day. He is such an important entity in Yoruba mythology that nothing is done unless he is placated or appeased; he is the messenger of the orixas. His malicious character and love for creating chaos in people's lives make him an object of fear in the African community in Brazil.[60]

OGUN AND OXOSSI-ODE, BROTHERS

Oxossi, the masculine god of hunting, quite naturally likes the outdoors and wanders in the forest; he is worshiped on Thursdays, the day of the forest. Ogun, brother of Oxossi, is the male god of iron, steel, war, and revolution. He is depicted in Brazil as a conquering hero who rides his horse, slays the evil dragon and, like Exu, opens gates and opportunities. Ogun has become so popular in the Americas that his cult and mystique charm artists and scholars as they do his devotees; from Canada to Argentina, California to Nigeria, his literature proliferates. According to Bastide, in Bahia Ogun is St. Anthony and St. Jerome. In Recife, Porto Alegre, Alagoas, Maranhao, and Rio de Janeiro, Ogun is St. George, St. Paul, St. Michael, or St. John, but he is Sebastian, St. Onophrius, or St. Anthony in other places. In his St. Anthony persona, Ogun is believed to have defended the city against outside invasion and was rewarded with the title of lieutenant, an appropriate symbol of his warrior spirit. Since St. George took part in the Corpus Christi processions, riding on a horse, and was highly acclaimed, blacks have their own African St. George who protects revolutionaries and upholds black cause.[61]

XANGO

The most prominent Yoruba male deity is Xango (Shango). Once king of Oyo, the largest and most popular city-state in ancient Yorubaland,[62] Shango became a mythological powerhouse in signifying Yoruba. It is held that Xango's pervasive presence in the Americas is the result of the fall of Oyo in the early 1700s to Muslim Fulani and Dahomean Fon armies. Defeated leaders and priests of Oyo who were loyal followers of Shango were taken as war booty and auctioned off to eager European traders. Voeks says that Shango "personifies the indefatigable strength and aggression of his mortal followers. So great was his influence that in Trinidad and Tobago as well as Recife, Brazil, the religion of the Yoruba came to bear his name." Also, "Xango's furious temper is reflected by the bright reddish-purple floral display of some of his species. . . . Xango's flora is further distinguished by its abundance of trees and treelets" and their arborescent flora.[63] Simpson agrees that the fact that Xango predominates among orixas and other entities in the Americas is a tribute to his fearsome personality as god of iron, steel, fire, thunder, and lightning. Xango has an aggressive personality, strong leadership ability, loftiness, and a very hot temper; he has little patience for weakness, hesitation, and cowardice. He can be jealous, macho, and ruthless at times and has many wives, chief of which is Iansa.[64] This mythological figure typifies the Africans' battle against colonialism and slavery.

OMOLU/OBALUAYE

Omolu, or Shopona, the male god of smallpox and infectious disease, is identified with healing, sickly persons, and a dog that licks wounds. In Bastide's study, Omolu is St. Benedict, St. Roche, and St. Lazarus in black Bahia, but he is St. Sebastian in mainly white areas of Recife, Alagoas, Para, and Maranhao. In Rio de Janeiro, Omolu is associated with the holy Eucharist and Lazarus. He is also St. Jerome and St. Anthony in Porto Alegre. Omolu is a hot-tempered deity who is so feared in Candomble that devotees rarely mention his name audibly for fear that it might incite his wrath. Omolu combines creative and destructive energies of African peoples and has domestic currency for blacks; myth has it that he descended from Nana, owner and creator of lands, and therefore is owner of the land. Omolu's image is one of physical handicap but not to be pitied. Although he is quiet and reserved, he is uncompromising, tense, brusque, self-centered, and rigid. Myth has it that he unleashes misery on anyone who fails to offer him appropriate propitiation. Outbreaks of tropical disease among Brazilian slaves made Omolu a notorious but sought-after deity.[65]

OXALA/OBATALA

Oxala, son of Olorun in Yoruba mythology, is sometimes called Christ and the Holy Spirit (in Bahia, Recife, and Porto Alegre), but he is also the Eternal Father and St. Anne of the Holy Trinity (in Alagoas and Recife). Oxala is chief of the Candomble Yoruba pantheon and father to the orixas. He dresses always in white and detests wearing black. He seeks out lofty locations, has Friday as his consecration day, and loves eating chickens, ewe goats, and doves. Oxala is regarded as the deity of peace and love, and his white colors are said to be part of the organizing force in his sacred pharmacopoeia. Voeks says, although male, "Oxala is most intimately associated with the female entities, spiritual forces that serve to soothe and cool. One of the healing roles of this deity and of his associated flora is to counteract illness associated with overheating, a condition that frequently troubles adherents and clients who are connected to the hot deities."[66] These hot and cool orixas that correspond to hot and cool Vodou lwas are distinctly creole.

IFA-ORUNMILA AND OSSAIN/OSSAIM

Other male divinities grace the cultus. In the regions of Recife and Rio de Janeiro, Ifa-Orunmila, a beloved orixa, is St. Francis, one who supervises the holy sacrament, but in Porto Alegre he is St. Joseph, St. Bonfim, St. Jerome, or St. Anthony. As Voeks observes, in Salvador a huge crowd participates in the *lavagem do Bonfim*, or the "washing of the Church of Bonfim," during the month of January. This celebration, which dates back to the nineteenth century, involves spiritual leaders and members of their terreiros, hundreds of thousands of tourists, and local people in an impressive procession to the church.[67] Ossain/Ossaim, god of sacred leaves, is known in Porto Alegre as St. Manuel and St. Onuphrius, and in Maranhao he is worshiped as St. Francis of Assisi. Ossaim is ritualized on Thursday; a day on which his devotees are encouraged to avoid contact with dogs.[68]

Female Divinities

The idea of weak, submissive spiritual powers and priests led and dominated by patriarchal gods and babalawos is foreign to Candomble, whose gender signification is rather complex; gods are both male and female, men and women serve as wives of the spirits, and terreiros have been largely the domain of women since the 1820s. The gods are free of any male inferiority complex and marry men and women alike. Of the many female Candomble deities, the following four are among the most popular.

OXUM (OXUN) AND OBA

Oxum (or Oxun) is the goddess of sweet, fresh water as well as sensual love. In Africa she was associated with the River Niger, so when she emerged in Brazil she became protector of all rivers and streams. Said to be the most beautiful and glamorous of all orixas, Oxum loves riches, material excess, and perfume. She wears golden yellow and, in her serpent persona, represents coolness and a calm spirit. As Oxumare, she "is the deity of rainbows and good weather."[69] Oxum is the patron saint of the city of Recife, but in other regions of Brazil she has fifteen other forms and represents different Catholic saints. As Bastide noted, in Bahia, Alagoas, Recife and Porto Alegro, Oxum doubles as the Virgin Mary, Our Lady of Candlemas, Our Lady of Immaculate Conception, Mary Magdalene, Our Lady of Carmel, Our Lady of the Rosary, Our Lady of Sorrows, and Our Lady of Bantu houses or Lourdes. She is regarded as Saint Anthony, who defended the city in colonial times. Oxum has made her way across the Caribbean Sea to Cuba as the Virgin of Charity. She is usually identified with Oba, the patron of prostitutes and is called Our Lady of Pleasures. In Bahia and Recife, Oba is St. Joan of Arc, Our Lady of Perpetual Charity, and St. Martha. In Alagoas, Oba is also Our Lady of Pleasures, but in Porto Alegre she is St. Catherine. Oba finds her way into Cuba as Our Lady of Candlemas. Like Yemanja, Nana, and other feminine deities, Oxum and Oba are cool, earthly, and mild mannered.

YEMANJA AND YANSAN-OIA

Yemanja is a widely revered deity-saint in Brazil and the Greater Antilles; she is known as Virgin de la Regla in Cuba and Puerto Rico and as Our Lady of the Immaculate Conception and Lady of Grace among Haitian Catholics. In Recife, Rio de Janeiro, Alagoas, Bahia, and Para, Yemanja has other Catholic doubles—for example, Our Lady of Sorrows and Our Lady of the Rosary. In Bahia she carries the titles the Virgin Mary, Our Lady of Compassion, Our Lady of Lourdes, and Our Lady of Candlemas. In Porto Alegre, Yemanja is Our Lady of Navigators and of the Good Journey, but in Maranhao she is Our Lady of Good Childbirth.[70] Yansan-Oia does not have a large repertoire and is generally recognized in many parts of Brazil as St. Barbara. Occasionally she is associated with St. Catherine.

Male-Female Brides

PRIESTESSES AND PRIESTS

Although Candomble lacks the ecclesiastical structure of its Catholic counterpart, the social hierarchy of its religious centers nonetheless is well defined. Each Candomble terreiro is an entity unto itself, with its own spiritual leaders, sacred space, and variations in interpretation of African traditions and symbols. Mother of the saints, *maes de santo*, and Father of the saints, *pai de santo* (also called an "overseer" or *zelandor*), hold the highest office in the terreiro. Priests and priestesses, or *bablorixa* and *iyalorixa*—creole versions of the *babalawo* priest of the African Yoruba—perform the same function as the babalawo. Historically, strong women priestesses of African descent, with a rather imposing stature and unquestioned authority, led the Candombles and had an aversion to male leadership. The well-established women-dominated Candomble usually claim to be a purer form and closer to their original African source. Before the 1900s, *Bablorixa* served in auxiliary or supportive roles, but the winds of change have increased the percentage of male priests, mediums, and attendants significantly. Some Candomble nations, however, resist the change and still maintain a rigid matriarchy. The de Ketu nation is generally matriarchal; its priesthood and other high offices are firmly in the hands of women. Men, on the other hand, are prominent in the leadership of de Angola and de Jeje Candombles.[71]

In elite Nago Candomble houses in Bahia, leaders pass leadership authority of the terreiro to their juniors, often by inheritance. However, for a new priestess to serve, she must lay claim to a call from an orixa. This call could come during a crisis in the devotee's life that was resolved by another *iyalorixa* or *babalorixa*. The response could also be made after discovery of one's obligations to the orisha or out of a sense of guilt for a family member's suffering. Some initiates choose the orisha as an alternative religion and lay claim to a call to service. As is the case of African diviners and priests, a devotee also could dedicate herself to an orixa in gratitude for the deity's perceived help in resolving a crisis. After the call is confirmed, the uninitiated priestess begins the long and costly initiation ceremony to become an *iao*, a bride or spouse of the orixa.[72]

In most Candomble houses, initiation to become an *iao* climaxes with observing the Christian Mass at the Church of Bonfim, a creolized ritual intended to officially integrate the *iao* fully into the city's life. As Murphy says, "The process of initiation is long, and the outward ceremonies are only markers of a deepening inner relationship with one's orixa. After seven years, an *iao* may need to make an *abrigacaco* (a dance ceremony) to receive *deka*, and become a senior initiate, an *ebomin*."[73] Finally emerging as a religious leader, the *iyalorixa* unquestionably becomes a functionary chief. She maintains the spiritual secrets, fundamental precepts, respect, financial operation, and cultic and sociocultural life of the terreiro. According to Voeks, her primary goal "is the maintenance and cultivation of axe, the vital force of existence" and "the fulcrum upon which the success of the terreiro turns. Nurtured and properly tended, axe grows like a sacred flame, imparting strength, prosperity, and health to its mortal attendants,"[74] some of whom are mediums of the spirit. The leader also gives *consulata* ("consultations") to clients and devotees, prescribes medicine or advises an appropriate course of action a client should pursue.

Within a Candomble fraternity, social relations and conventions exist that may run counter to Brazilian moral codes. Since legal marriage akin to that of white society was not readily available to slaves in the nineteenth century, Afro-Brazilians who did not observe Catholic rites in marriage continued the African tradition of polygamy, or continued the dysfunctional familial relations they learned in slavery. It is not uncommon for a priest to have an *apetebi*, a second wife, along with his legitimate wife. The second wife assists in divinatory rites, accepts the blessings of the first wife, is regarded as her daughter, and is valued and respected in the fraternity. This sanctioned polygamy is not a license for concubinage; priests are required to observe strict rules and taboos related to sexuality, and may not fraternize sexually with young women or men indiscriminately. Women also observe certain taboos and rules. During initiation a woman must remain sexually inactive while she stays in the *camarinha* of the terreiro. One who is married to an orixa must avoid sexual relations during times of rituals and ceremonies honoring that deity. Devotees must also avoid spiritual incest, marrying a sister or brother who belongs to the same orixa. Instead, they are encouraged to seek partnership with a person belonging to another orixa, except those devotees of Shango and Yansan who are husband and wife in Candomble mythology. The matriarchal system in the fraternity also encourages a woman to have an income independent of her husband so that if he abandons her for another, she is not left with her children indigent and destitute.[75]

A HORSE RIDES HER

Mediums, devoted sons and daughters who are often lower in the pecking order of authority in the terreiro, are named variously *filhos* and *filhas* of the orixas, *iya kekere, iya mero,* and *ebomins*. They receive and interpret communication from the spirits and may later become priestesses. To become a medium, brothers and sisters of the saints also undergo the intense initiation, which, until recently, could last a few years before they got the spirit or experienced for the first time a full possession trance from their patron deity. Like a priestess or a priest, a medium must be called by the spirit during a ceremony or in a life-crisis situation. The more serious the crisis, the more authentic the call. Once the call to serve an orixa has been confirmed, ritual prayers and offerings are made to "seat" the orixa in a number of sacred objects and on the head of the *abian*,[76] or "initiate." The initiate gets two guardian deities, whose identity must be determined through the *jogo de buzios*, or "cowrie shell toss." The priestess has the duty of communicating between *aie* and *orun*, "the human realm" and "the divine realm," in this important ritual by interpreting the positions of the shells and giving the verdict of an orixa. Mediums of the orixas are recognized by the special dances, music, or songs performed for their personal deities. Each medium is consecrated to a deity of the pantheon whose name and characteristics the initiate adopts[77] and signifies.

A medium gives his or her body as a conduit for the orixas' manifestation and cognitive communication to the community. Upon possession, the medium speaks with authority and can allegedly diagnose mysterious evils and afflictions, find lost objects, give advice on or predict future events, and resolve puzzling enigmas or problems. These can cover a range of things: unemployment, a failing business, sickness, broken relations, victimization from someone through witchcraft,[78] the lost affection of a lover, or demon possession. As

Smith Omari saw during her research, possession functions as an emetic religious means of communication for members of the Candomble and "reinforces the solidarity of the group in addition to having cathartic, emotional compensation, or social power functions for individual devotees. . . . Great prestige and admiration accrue to an individual who can easily become entranced by . . . her *orixa*."[79] The mediums wear elaborate costumes and the colors of their orixa, which add to their sense of importance as well as to the prestige and aura of the terreiro. In spite of their power, mediums are expected to obey the orders of the Fathers and Mothers of the saints who lead the faith in the sacred space.

Sacred Space and Cultus

Sacred Space

The sacred spaces of Afro-Brazilian religions vary considerably but, as the religions of mainly blue-collar workers, most terreiros are modest. During his field research in Brazil, Omari observed class differences between rural Nago Candombles and urban ones; he distinguished between elite Candombles and proletarian ones, differences he found as obvious in the terreiros' structures and adornment. More affluent Candombles attract followers from the middle class and have better financial resources; they build much better structures on private lands in open space. The building walls are painted lavishly in the deity's symbolic colors, and elaborate liturgical paraphernalia adorn its inner core. The "holy place," where the sacred objects embodying the force or axe of the spirit reside, is occupied by privileged persons: the *iyalorixa* or *bablorixa* responsible for sacrificial animal slaughter; the *axogun*, senior adepts of particular orixas; and the medium through whom an orixa incarnates.[80] Axe is energy, a vital force or manifestation involving the "actualization of a ritual utterance" that "effects change or to call for the materialization of a given desire"[81] in the operation of cosmic force.

Centers of poorer Candombles, usually the homes of priests, consist of a few tiny rooms in a small house. In rural areas, these are surrounded by green vegetation whose flora are invaluable for the Candomble's pharmacopeia. In spite of the modest resources of poor Candombles, their members feel a sense of pride and empowerment through various levels of participation. Sons and daughters of the orixas represent the working black peasantry of Brazil, but in the religion they have access to axe or power and self esteem. Performing sacred tasks at the shrine of a divinity, no matter how menial, is viewed as having earned privileges that bring honor and prestige. The *iya kekere*, or "little Mother," assists Mothers of the saints in maintaining discipline in the Candomble; a Mother often becomes the successor priestess. In the Menininha Gantois house, an *iya moro* assists the little Mother while an *iya base* is responsible for preparing appropriate foods for the spirits. At large Nago terreiros, experienced elderly "sisters," or *ebomins* of an initiatory family, act out liturgical rites, perform rituals, and function as mediums. Omari confirms that "Candomble Nago also offers Afro-Bahians a channel through which they can achieve a significant measure of self-esteem, social solidarity, prestige, and social mobility within a system which celebrates African values, behavior patterns, ideas, and dark skin color."[82] These values continue to be cherished by Afro-Brazilians today.

Initiation into Candomble

A Candomble terreiro is a center of spiritual action and power: sacrifices, initiation, spirit possession, consultation, divination, dance, and celebration leave hardly a dull moment. The will of the deity concerning one's calling and fortune is sought through divination and rituals. When a diviner indicates that an initiation is warranted, a client begins to secure funds to pay for professional services and appropriate ritual paraphernalia. The initiation of a *filha* includes room and board for the time she spends in the *camarinha* ("chamber"), a sacrificial animal, the liturgical clothing she wears, and a "gift" (fee) for the priestess. Scholars have noted that when relatives cannot defray these expenses, godparents assist, the initiates' clothes are homemade, and after the ceremonies the initiates visit friends who bestow small monetary gifts on them. In some cases, the priestess combines several initiations so that expenses can be shared.[83] During annual initiations and festival rituals, which last for months, initiates may sleep overnight at the terreiro, referred to as their residence or *roca*, and wear specially prepared sacred uniforms. Initiates go through a ritual death and rebirth in seclusion for a period that could last up to twelve months. According to Margaret Drewal, "This spiritual retreat serves to dedicate the devotees to their deities and to prepare them for receiving the vital force of their god through possession trance."[84] They are stripped of their clothes, which must not be worn again, and like a devotee of Shiva, receive an immolation on the front of their shaved heads. Into that sacred scare is infused the vital force of their deity. The initiates' heads are washed regularly in a solution of ingredients that include sacred leaves.

In his experience of Candomble Nago initiations, Omari tells of the protracted drama performed at three levels. The primary initiation called the *bori* ("worship") occurs in the shrine, where the candidate is seated on a ritually prepared mat and dressed in a sacred white performance costume. The neck of a white dove or pigeon chosen for the sacrifice is wrung and the head of the initiate is anointed with the blood. Also being anointed are items such as kola nuts and favorite foods of the orixa who owns the initiate's head. Initiates and other assistants to the priestess dance to the beat of drums and sing special songs throughout the roughly three-hour ritual. During this period, initiates are given new names of the spirits and are taught the songs and dances of their own orixa. During Candomble Ketu and Nago initiation, drums accompany the dance procession, called an *abrigacao*, while the daughters of the deity enter the ceremonial house, called a *barracao*, led by the *mae de santo*. The will of the orixa is divined with the kola nut cut into four pieces and used periodically throughout the ritual. As Omari observes, the priest places small samples of each of the sacrificial foods on different parts of the novice's body, applies small bits of food on the crown of his head in the orixa's food ward, and the initiate's head is then wrapped tightly with white cloth.[85] Novices are isolated for up to seventeen days, kept on a special diet, communicate only through a series of specially learned hand claps, and are taught sacred songs, history, and the personality traits of their orixa. During the second stage, the novice receives a special necklace made out of tubular beads that carry the deity's scarlet colors. The isolated initiate lives in silence, sleeps on his or her own mat, and uses special utensils. He or she leaves the room only before sunrise and after sunset for ritual baths.

During this spiritually volatile period, a novice's only relief comes in the form of the possession trance called *ere*, or "infantile trance."[86] At this stage, devotees form a circle and begin to invoke the deity with three chants, each of which begins with an invocation to Ogun. In an attempt to coax the deity from its otherworldly domain into the profane world, devotees enter the *xire* ritual, known in Yoruba as *sire*, as a Mother of the saints leads the parade and sings, "We play for Ogun oh! We play for Ogun oh!" while daughters enter with horse-like strides in single file, with arms outstretched, holding the reigns of their invisible horse. The riding of the horse also dispatches Exu, messenger orixa of crossroads, to open up new communication lines between deity and initiate. Accompanied by drums, devotees join in the chant and dance as they honor and invoke their deities, one at a time, male first. Ogun leads the way, followed by Oxossi, who is trailed by Osanyin and Omolu. Nana leads other female deities: Oxumare, Yewa, Yemanja, and Oxum, in that order. Iansa precedes Xango, while the great Oxala brings up the rear flank. This ritual parade of mythic action is repeated until devotees successfully invoke the deities and fall into a trance. When the spirit arrives, the initiate is possessed instantly, as though hit by a bolt of lightning. Possession is communicated visibly by a sudden burst of energy that appears to thrust the initiate into space, body frozen in time, while attendants scramble to prevent him or her from falling on other participants or becoming hurt. Fully possessed, the medium prostrates himself or herself "before the drummers and the *mae de santo* and, as the manifestation of the deity," greets spectators.[87]

The complex and intricate system of rituals is made public through rhythm, song, and *abrigacao* dance. This performance in Brazilian Yoruba initiation is dominated by Ogun rhythms, practices, and paraphernalia. Mediums perform a variety of rhythmic dances that are distinctly in the style of Ogun while waving various instruments in the air to showcase their deity's power. During the performance, Ogun and his drummers receive money from spectators, who get blessings and recognition in return. Dynamic initiation dances mimicking the hot, aggressive temperaments of Ogun, Xango, and Oxossi are the signature of Candomble ceremonies and worship. At the honoring of an important orixa, rhythm and dance summon, carry, and dispatch the spirits of the rituals and preserve the life force of the Candomble; they begin ceremonies and end them; they petition health and announce the presence of death. Through the language of drums, spirits bring messages from the deity and the dead, give consultations to worshipers, advise individuals on personal problems, and purify members of evil influences.[88] This dynamic ritual activity is characteristic of most African religions in the diaspora.

Sacred Medicine

In African cosmology, a direct relationship exists between most human tragedies and the ability of mortals to live in concord with the immortal world. That is, few human misfortunes happen by chance. Instead, they result from what African and Chinese spiritualists call false balance or disequilibrium between humans and the world of nature, or a dysfunctional relationship between the divine and mortals. As a result of human weaknesses, Voeks says "rapid descent into disequilibrium, into the territory controlled by Exu, represents an invitation to physical, emotional, and material problems. Reestablishing spiritual harmony may be a simple process or may require the employment of the full arsenal of spiritual medicine available to the *pai-* or *mae-de-santo*."[89] Equilibrium with the world of the spirits in Yoruba is maintained by attracting and harnessing axe via the divinities. Axe is the vital life-giving force of the material and spiritual worlds; it supplies the power, energy, and strength necessary to deal with life's problems and is seen as present in animal parts, blood, and plants. Negotiating this vital force is done through the dispensing of medicines. Herbalists and medicine women and men brought to Brazil used sacred leaves to cure illnesses among slaves and in free black communities, where medical care was nonexistent.[90] Candomble pharmacology is a spiritually cohesive medical system whose theory of causation and practice are well defined. Herbal specialists use certain symptoms to diagnose specific illnesses, which they then treat on the basis of their knowledge of the healing properties of herbs as well as a belief in the power of the spirit.

An important objective in Candomble healing is creating and maintaining a state of harmony with the spirit world. Much of the sects' medicine is preventive or protective, therapeutic, and restorative in nature. More often than not, medicine specialists must dispense preventive medicines along with the appropriate sacrificial rituals as a preemptive strike against illness caused by malicious deities. When administered in certain ceremonies, "the combined forces of individual and group axe serve to immunize those who have given themselves to the deities against ill health and the other misfortunes of life."[91] Usually, treatment is recommended during a *consulata* and involves divination by tossing of cowrie shells or other paraphernalia to identify the deities of the

uninitiated and divine a message or medicine appropriate to the client's problem. Medicine may come in the form of drinking potions, inhaling substances,
or rubbing the body with special herbs. These may involve an *ebo* or animal
sacrificial offering, a leaf whipping, or an *abo* or leaf bath. The bath is made of
sacred leaves, raw eggs, and small animals passed over the client's body, done
in a private-home ritual or in the terreiro. The leaf bath is a primary purification ritual administered to clients and, especially in Candomble de Angola, is
combined with shell tossing for divining a range of problems related to finances,
relationships, and health. The *limpeza*, or discharge bath, done along with animal sacrifice, rids the body of negative fluids and energy. The *sacudimento*, or
leaf whipping bath, neutralizes negative energy and restores equilibrium with
the spirit. The development bath attracts good fortune.[92]

The corresponding relationship between orixas and sacred leaves is an indispensable element in Candomble healing rituals. Most commonly associated
with this pharmacopeia is Ossaim, the orixa of fields and forests; every leaf is
owned by an orixa and exhibits special features that link it with its corresponding spirit on the basis of the latter's temperament. For example, sacred flora
with cooling and soothing effects—associated with Oxum, Yemanja, Iansa and
other female deities—are used to treat a wide range of problems, ailments, and
attitudes specifically related to women. Leaves with the cooling properties of
Oxala are used to treat illnesses and conditions associated with overheating of
the body in general. Flora with healing properties ascribed to Omolu, Xango,
Oxossi, Exu, and Ogun are used to treat a variety of stubborn sicknesses with
"male characteristics" or problems related to men. For this reason, the macho
Xango dominates Candomble's sacred floral medium of special species of trees
and plants associated with healing orixas. Herbalists are not only versed in an
herb's healing properties, they also know what deities manifest in the sacred
leaves. These priests possess knowledge and skill to treat social and psychosomatic disequilibrium and ills in the family. They can prevent a man from leaving his wife for another woman, or cheating on his partner. Their herbs can
arouse love and allay disputes. Punitive medicine is also an important part of
the herbalist's craft. Special herbs, animal parts, beverages, and human personal
effects[93] are but a few of the potent items in the arsenal used to aid, bless,
curse, or punish offenders on behalf of the client and the orixa.

Candomble's herbal medicine attracts as many skeptics as it does believers.
Many Euro-Brazilians and Christians regard it as the hocus-pocus of uneducated Africans, filled with devil worship and macumba. Voeks points out that
the Candomble system of plant classification seems to be based much more on
morphology or conceptual religious forms of the medical properties attributed
to individual personalities of the orixa than to the properties of the flora themselves. Deities and their personal flora are divided into the ones regarded as hot
and those seen as cool, and between male and female. "Hot *orixas* exhibit fiery
personalities" associated with men, whereas feminine deities with cooling influences "are maternal, sensual, fecund, and materialistic."[94] How much of this

system of healing is medical, how much is faith, how much is prophylactic, and how much is psychosomatic one can only tell from careful ethnographic study of a wide variety of samples taken from diverse Candomble communities across Brazil.[95]

Conclusion

Although situated on the South American continent, the story of the survival of African religions in Brazil is a most fascinating one in the study of Afro-Caribbean religions. These religions consist of the memories of Africans rein-terpreted and lived out in Portuguese-Catholic Brazil; they constitute a variety of traditions known for their African world view, cultic practices, diverse cultural identity, and fraternal unity. As Bastide says, the African sects unite people into a coherent and functional fraternity through common beliefs and like feelings. The "sects mound their passions, desires, attractions and jealou-sies, according to a series of mythic models that enable them to coexist, join forces, or cooperate in a communal task"[96] and that helped them survive in the unfriendly environment of colonial Brazil. The religion that began as an unwel-come malaise among the suffering class in the early 1800s is now culturally popular in the land of the Samba and first-class world football.

9

Umbanda and Its Antecedents

KEY TOPICS

Tumor-Bakos Macumba • *Umbanda Phenomenon* •
Catimbo • *Caboclo* • *Batuques*

Outside of Candomble communities, many creole religions exist in Brazil, with varying degrees of Africanism: Batuques, Caboclo Pretos Velhos, Catimbo, Zango (Xango), Tambor de Mina, Umbanda, and Macumba. In the socially and ethnically mixed environment in which Africans worked, they reinvented their traditions with new cultural and religious signification. In Umbanda, for example, blacks worship spirits unknown in Candomble. John Burdick shows that this is true of "Zumbi, one of the chiefs of Palmares, the great maroon society that survived for almost a century in the black lands of Alagoas until it was finally destroyed by the Portuguese in 1697."[1] Roger Bastide points out that in the 1800s, Mozambique's cult of the dead and its system of ancestral worship made it easy for the Bantu to accept and adapt the Amerindian *pagelanca* and *catimbo* spirits of Brazil. The Dahomey and Yoruba worshiped a pantheon of divinities and had a dualistic religion based on lineage and community. Yoruba-Dahomey's worship of nature deities survived in some regions because it accommodated itself to the system of nations that were known in Africa but modified in Brazil.[2] Each Yoruba divinity in Africa had its own fraternities, priests, and shrine. In some regions of Brazil, however, individual nations often lacked the numeric and cultural strength to preserve their religion intact. Many religious sects thus became diminished replicas of the African cosmogony. Africans also resurrected sects in which family ancestors were held side by side with Amerindian nature deities. This was the case with beliefs and practices of *Casa das Minas*, one of the oldest temples of the Tambor de Mina religion in Maranhao, the second-largest state in northeast Brazil.

Rachel Harding notes that *Tambor de Mina, Catimbo, Caboclo, Batuques, Macumba,* and *Umbanda* "are among the terms used to denote black religio-cultural manifestations at various points and places in colonial Brazil."[3] Tambor, for example, is a creole syncretistic group that was founded by slaves in Marahanao, encompassed a strong African population in the city of Sao Luis, and was concentrated on Brazil's northern coast in river valleys known for their sugar and cotton plantations. Tambor survived as a distinct tradition because, until the 1800s, Maranhao and the Amazon region had a government separate from the rest of Brazil and remained isolated. Bastide holds that "here three 'families' of gods were worshiped: the family of Da or Danbira (smallpox), the family of Kevioso (thunder), and the family of Davise or Dahome, i.e. the ancestors of the royal family of Dahomey, to which the founders of the *casa* belonged."[4] They represent the different strands and strengths of African religious cultures in Brazil, a few of which are reviewed here.

Tumor-Bakos Macumba?

Before Afro-Brazilians founded their Candombles in the early 1800s, a religion of choice was Macumba—one of the earliest but most suppressed and least respected religion in the world's most African diaspora. Followers of Candomble and Umbanda go to great lengths to disassociate themselves from Macumba because of its alleged caravel of evil works. Repressed and demonized as a devilish tumor, the religion was forced underground. As late as the 1960s, its followers suffered severely at the hands of local, state, and Brazilian governments. After every wave of persecution, it resurfaced throughout Sao Paulo, Rio de Janeiro, and other regions of Brazil[5] with new strength. Some scholars ignore Macumba as insignificant to black religions in Brazil; when they mention it, their remarks are perfunctory or disparaging portrayals of so-called undesirable elements in Afro-Brazilian religions. Arthur Ramos labeled Macumba in Rio de Janeiro an odd mixture, an adulteration and the least interesting of African religions in Brazil. Donald Pierson claims that Macumba's rituals have disintegrated into unwholesome and vicious practices. Bastide's view, although less vitriolic, regards Rio's Macumba as a phase of African culture made degenerate by Brazilian capitalism. He cites the following as evidence of the degeneration: the distance of the Macumba cult from Dahomey or Yoruba centers of the northeast; the absence of clear African mythology in the erosion of religious institutions; the disappearance of initiation rites from some centers; the lack of African socialization; the inability of poor peasants to afford animal sacrifices; and poverty among the rural masses with no health providers. Many of these force priests to be preoccupied with healing and consultation rather than to focus on religious rituals.[6]

As a result of its secret magical rites, Macumba is used often as a pejorative label for all Afro-Brazilian religions; in the past, to "make Macumba" was to engage in devilish African juju. National attitudes toward Macumba have changed in recent decades, and it is now peddled for profit; it is seen as African folklore in "tourist *macumbas*" (commercialized Macumba culture). As Bastide suggests, profit motives in the capitalist economic system dominate sectors of the religion, making it "Macumba for sale." Priests in this caricature of Macumba are untrained, have not been initiated, possess only a limited understanding of the religion's secrets, violate important traditions and taboos of the faith, and make money the main motivation for their ritual performances and spiritual tours. Bona fide Macumba regards the activities of tourist Macumba as sacrilege. Tourist Macumba becomes Africa's "Exu," the spirit identifying with "evil" elements in African religions, associated with the uneducated, poor, predominantly black peasants in rural Brazil. Because of how rural Macumba is organized and developed, it is alleged that it degenerates into criminal activity. Bastide records this pejorative tale, often associated with the religion:

> In Itapeva, Vicencia da Sila Melo was ordered by God and the Blessed Virgin to kill her grandmother, who had been turned into a snake, and then walk about naked, carrying the banner of the Holy Ghost. To cure his sick father and drive out his demon, the black healer Joao Martins da Buri dragged him out of bed so violently that he killed him. He inflicted burns on a neighbor to exorcize him, and finally organized a purification procession that ended with the drowning of many members of his family.[7]

Whither Macumba?

Macumba, the religion most Brazilians despise, is "a black thing," an eclectic African creole spirituality founded largely in the southeastern cities and now prevalent in Rio de Janeiro, Espirito Santo, and Sao Paulo. It began as a religion of slaves and Brazil's poorest blacks; then, concentrated in urban centers, it evolved into various traditions, even influencing the beliefs of the more recent Candomble and Umbanda. It blends a Bantu cosmology, spiritual leadership roles, and ritual activities with a Catholic Christian hagiography of saints and creole Amerindian cultic traditions in what is referred to as a spiritist metaphysics of divine reality. Macumba got its Bantu name from its ritual worship "altars of the *macumbas*, with their stones, rum-bottles, crosses, statues of saints, pots containing the souls of the dead, wax candles, specially blessed rosaries,"[8] and so forth. Its ritual professionals accept trance possession by African spirits; the participation of adepts in divination consultation; healing by *macumbeiros*; ancestral veneration of departed spirits; a largely male leadership; *caquis* ("witch doctors") who practice medicine to fight negative force (called evil works); and more creole African traditional religious beliefs.

The existence and manifestations of Macumba sects are somewhat regionalized. In Rio, spirits are said to incarnate themselves during Macumba ceremonies, where they establish what is known as special "lines" or *linhas*, one of which is called the line of Mussurumin. Bastide argues that a special type of magic practiced in that region was considered effective and dangerous; its spiritual "line consists entirely of evil spirits who come down to earth to wreak vengeance" on offending parties. The head of these spirit lines is called Alufa, Father Alufa, or Uncle Alufa. As in Vodou's practice of tracing veves on the ground to commence Vodou rituals, the lines of Macumba spirits are invoked by tracing circles of gunpowder surrounding cigarettes, drinks, pins, tobacco, and chickens on the ground. A priest lights the gunpowder and spirits descend in the explosion. In central Brazil, where African Bantu and other religions have become syncretized with Amerindian traditions, Macumba has priests called *ngangas/ugangas* and witch doctors known by the native name *caquis*. They worship gods of the Angola, Opungo, and Kongo in the person of Zambiapungo, who represents a syncretization of Zambi, Angana-Nzambi, Calunga (the goddess of the sea and of evil spirits), and Cariacariapemba, who is mistakenly identified with the devil by Christian missionaries.[9] In Bahia, Macumba teachings, rites, and rituals resemble those of Candomble, but stigmas attached to manipulations of evil through magical rites called *Quimbanda* give Macumba a bad name in Afro-Brazilian spirituality.

At the turn of the 1900s, two African nations were said to be dominant in Rio: Yoruba and the Bantu cult known as *cabula*. Macumba was originally *cabula* and contained a mixture of orixa and Yoruba rites. A Carioca-type Macumba that retained elements of *cabula* (especially titles of priests like *embandas* and *umbandas*, and their assistants, *cambones*), has replaced the *cabula* of Espirito Santo. Bantu nations have ceremonies known as *macumba*. Bastide tells us that a sample of these show they were basically the *cabula*, in which *enbandas*, or *cambones*, directed the cults and *cafiotos* were initiates. "Like *cabula,* this cult was celebrated outdoors, the assistants standing or sitting on benches in a circle around the *canzol* or sanctuary. Candles were burned and hymns were sung asking the spirits' permission to begin the ritual." There was vigorous dancing "with some episodes of possession by the *tatas*," who also were regarded as guardian spirits.[10]

Spirits and Macumbeiros

Macumba gods, who descend on devotees in different forms, correspond to deities of the Yoruba pantheon, but Catholic names associated with them differ from those of Candomble. For example, the Christian Christ is the counterpart of Oxlala; Saint George is Ogun; Saint Jerome is Shango, Saint Sebastian is Oxossi, and Our Lady of Aparecida is Oxun. Each Macumba divinity has its own characteristic color, adornments, favorite foods, drinks, songs, dances, and mediums. They protect devotees but can also punish offenders. Priests reinvent and create new ritual forms, and sects compete for aesthetics, creativity, and innovations. The highest priest carries the Bantu title *embanda* or *umbanda*, derived from the Angolan *kimbanda*. Associates, called *cambones*, assist priests in performing cultic ceremonies; and mediums, called daughters of the *orixa*, are primary vehicles for divine communication to members of the sect.

These mediums are said to embody souls of the enlightened dead, gods, and spirits of Africa. The senior daughter in each sect, or *samba*, performs functions similar to those of a priest or priestess in Candomble. One becomes a member of the sect through initiation and its purification bath. A symbolic lock of hair is cut from the initiate's head before he or she retreats into seclusion in the *camarianha* for three to seven days. During this period, an initiate learns the songs, dances, special characteristics, and the likes of the spirits and the sect. To bring the initiation to a climax, a priest conducts a public ceremony in which he or she traces crosses on an initiate's back and other parts of the body. If the initiate can afford the animal sacrifice, it is performed during a public ceremony.[11]

In Rio, Macumba transformed Candomble worship and rituals as it coalesced with Bantu, native traditions, and spiritism. Priests in sacred precincts perform rituals and run the terreiros in non-Candomble-like fashion. In rural areas of Rio, folk medicine and magic are so common that the priest is both a medicine man and a healer. Peasants of different ethnic backgrounds regard these healers, mediums, and priests as *macumbeiro*, individuals endowed with supernatural powers. Their dispensary of blessings and medicines is designed to solve myriads of health-related and psychological problems. These *macumbeiros* are often former patients who were cured by another *macumbeiro* and later decided to dedicate themselves to serving the healing spirit. Healers can also be persons who, while attending a spiritist meeting, learned that they are mediums.[12] These persons may do a series of consultations, use herbal medicine to treat snake and insect bites, seek protection and good fortune from a deity, and punish an enemy or offender of their client. When economic stress exaggerates the plight of the poor, these African spiritual services take on new significance and increased importance.

Between the 1940s and 1950s, Brazil saw the coming of modern industrialization. The economic train of post-World War II industrialization that rolled into Sao Paulo and other large cities, according to Bastide, left many Africans at the "station of poverty" with its disadvantages. Because of racial prejudice and stiff economic competition from immigrants and poor whites, urbanization made little room for the black masses to share in the industrial enterprise. Overcrowding in urban centers, caused by huge migrations of peoples seeking employment opportunities, exacerbated the problem. Between 1900 and 1950, the population of Rio and Sao Paulo jumped from roughly 692,000 and 240,000 to 2,413,000 and 2,227,600, respectively.[13] Industrialization brought whites and some blacks employment but undermined traditional values, worsened social disintegration, and helped dissolve the traditional bonds and social institutions that were based on ethnic associations and ancestral traditions. For example, traditional African nations were replaced by smaller cultic sects that were preoccupied with meeting the everyday needs of its clientele. Bastide believes that the "superseding of the 'nations' by organized sects was the first erosive effect of the big city. Within the colored masses, ethnic and cultural bonds were dissolved. Another solidarity emerged—not yet the solidarity of class, but the solidarity of misfortune, of comradeship in the struggle to adapt to the New World and in loneliness."[14] This had an impact on the practice of Macumba and other African religions in Brazil's developing industrial cities.

In later decades, Macumba began to appeal to poor whites caught in the same economic strait and who soon became almost as numerous as blacks. To consolidate itself socially and politically, this emerging class required, at minimum, an effective homogeneity and intellectual support—one that Bastide believes it could achieve only by incorporating into the new framework of industrialization the mystic and mythic experiences that were characteristic of each of its supporters or constituencies. Macumba represents that minimum of cultural unity required for achieving solidarity in a world of instability, insecurity, disorder, and mobility. The new creole admixture of Kardec intellectualism and Macumba created a tertium quid, *Umbanda*, a word derived from the Bantu *embanda* and *umbanda*, derivations of the Angola *Kimbanda* brought to Brazil. So the ugly tumor-Macumba gave birth to Umbanda, which shifted its emphasis to the Kardec spirituality that drove Macumba "out of Rio suburbs into the small towns that form a kind of proletarian ring around the city."[15] What strange bedfellows, friends, and foes!

A new movement is under way to re-Africanize Umbanda by restoring to its religious ethos the African rites, rituals, and ceremonies for which it was known. To say Macumba is in Umbanda is to express the forbidden and paradoxical truth about a religion that is popular neither among Africanists nor among scholars and Umbanda society. However, both religions encourage individual participation in rituals by means of divinatory consultation; they conjure spirits of the deceased in possession rituals, mostly through female mediums; their men have high visibility in leadership roles; and they deemphasize African ethnic allegiance. They both show "the intermingling of Angolan-Congolese religious symbolism and terminology with populist Catholic theology and Kardecism, and the broadening of the membership base across racial ethnic lines."[16] Therefore, long live the African tumor in Umbanda and Candomble.

Umbanda Phenomenon

Umbanda is an Afro-Brazilian religion that assimilated Native American and European traditions in its earlier days and became a modern religious cultural phenomenon whose emphasis shifted from its African roots and black consciousness to the eclectic spiritist orientation of its middle-class supporters. This modern movement began exploding onto the Brazilian cultural scene in Rio de Janeiro and other southern towns in the 1920s, and by 1970 it had an estimated national following of about twenty million, drawn from many sectors of the urban population. Diana Brown remarks that Umbanda, acclaimed as the fastest-growing religion in Brazil, in 1980, had more than twenty thousand centers in Rio alone, and now dominates annual celebrations such as the New Year's Eve Festival of Yemaja on Copacabana Beach.[17] In 1997, Umbanda's large following was estimated to have reached over thirty million people, mainly white middle-class supporters. A more generous but less reliable estimate puts the number of Ubandists at fifty million in 1980.[18] Brazilian sociologist Renato Ortiz says that charting the academic course of Umbanda reveals a multicultural community called "the organic intellectuals," who gave form to the religion; it "emerged as the *bricolage* of intellectuals who 'pieced' together elements of the past, including elements of Afro-Brazilian origin"[19] and black consciousness to create a new reality.

Since Umbanda is not predominantly black, it is debatable whether it is the result of urban Afro-Brazilians' attempt to boost their self-esteem and improve their race by "civilizing" Bakos Macumba with European culture. It is also up for discussion whether the religion is the end product of a class-conscious Eurocentric political project in Rio de Janeiro. As Denise Da Silva notes, however, "The idea that Umbanda was a 'de-africanized' African religion"[20] is so well established, Ortiz could conclude that Umbanda is not an African religion because its roots are neither black nor African, they are Brazilian.[21] Ortiz's view represents an influential voice in the revisionist enterprise to make Umbanda African-free and bring it in line with its Kardecian progenitor, discussed in the next section. Other scholars,[22] who ascribe to Umbanda the status of African religion, acknowledge its mixed intellectual and cultural heritage and political agenda, but see it as one of the most popular spiritist folk religions in Brazil.

Bastide writes, "It is difficult to draw a hard-and-fast line of demarcation between the *caboclo, candomble,* the *macumba* of Rio de Janeiro, and the so-called 'spiritualism of Umbanda,' presently flourishing throughout almost the whole of Brazil." What distinguishes them is their "relative extent and development . . . of syncretism."[23] In spite of its spiritism, Umbanda is a cousin of Candomble and recognizes some orixas in its cosmology. Christopher Johnson visited a house labeled "Umbandomble" in Brazil that "practices both Umbanda and Candomble in the same terreiro, alternating formats weekly."[24] As anthropologist Patricia Lerch notes, Umbanda is "a vehicle of 'social urbanization' whereby rural people are drawn into the urban institutional nexus to become part of the urban system."[25] Blacks, whites, and mulattos are drawn together culturally in thousands of Umbanda ritual centers throughout the country. Brazilians, many of whom are not devout followers of Umbanda, go to centers for a variety of experiences and, through its spiritual leaders, obtain advice (*consulata*) from a wide range of Brazilian spirits, including those of deceased slaves and American Indians. Although an urban phenomenon, Umbanda is not confined to the cities; some of its centers, built from very modest or meager means, are found in rural neighborhoods in the "interior,"[26] which is often referred to as "the jungle."

Eclectic Umbanda

Umbanda owes its origin to two very different religious traditions—Frency Kardecism and African Macumba—but Dahomey, Yoruba, and Bantu were predecessors of the Umbanda cult, which combines several different religious elements and influences. Notwithstanding its middle-class clientele, some Brazilians saw Umbanda as a religion of the uneducated lower classes because of its African Macumba features. The spirits of Umbanda that possess mediums are said to be of four different types; three of those are regarded as spirits of light and one a spirit of darkness. The so-called positive spirits battle against the "evil" spirit of darkness, associated with the *Pretos Velhos* of black slaves, on behalf of human supplicants.[27]

In many ways, Umbanda is a popular heterodox religion whose devotees are in search of a new reality and identity. This identity is forged from a religious and cultural mix of French "Kardec spiritualist beliefs," Afro-Brazilian religions, native traditions, other world faiths, and the nationalist consciousness that swept through urban centers in Brazil in the early decades of the twentieth century. The eclectic Umbanda uses literature from the occult, Hinduism, Jewish-Kabbalah, and Rosicrucian teachings.[28] Brown found that one of the centers she visited in Brazil was made up exclusively of Jewish Umbandists. It was devoted completely to interpreting the Jewish mystical Cabalistic (Kabbala) traditions, and spirits from the Hebrew Bible were welcomed along with those of Indian Caboclos and African Pretos Velhos.[29] As a departure from Yoruba-Candomble traditions, Umbanda is regarded as the most Brazilian of the African religions. By drawing on Amerindian, Jewish, Hindu, African, Christian, Kardec, and other traditions, it gives itself a distinct ecumenical flavor.

According to Brown's important study on Umbanda, a French schoolteacher named Rivail, who adopted the alias Allan Kardec, claimed he received special communications from the spiritual world over a period of fifteen years and used them to form the basis of the belief system known in France as Spiritisme and in Brazil as Espiritismo/Kardecismo. Rivali's book, published in 1855, proposed a philosophical theology and an appealing spiritism. Within thirty years of the book's mysterious arrival in Brazil, a network of organized Kardecist federations made Rio their national center for the rapid spread of Kardec teaching. It appealed to a middle class that highly valued an intellectual understanding of faith and spiritual experience. Kardecism earned a reputation for being charitable to the poor but used its charity as a means of infiltrating lower sectors of urban communities, not only to attract followers to the movement but also to reinforce class distinctions between the urban poor and middle-class professional sectors. It dominated and shaped Umbanda in such a way that it defined the general character of the religion as one oriented to solving individual problems rather than those of the community. In the same spirit, "lower spiritism" and Afro-Kardecism were kept out of the mainstream of the movement. As Brown surmises, this "position is expressed internally within Kardecist ritual and belief: less educated and cultured spirits who clearly symbolize the lower sectors of the population are rejected rather than incorporated into rituals, and beliefs stress the class standards of intellect, education, and culture"[30] of multiethnic Brazil.

The Catholic Church labeled Umbanda "a den of ignorance, magic, sorcery," superstition and devilism—an image that the movement's non-African Kardecist supporters are determined to stamp out. Kardecist Umbanda organizers made it a highly political institution and use it to broker power in urban politics; they fostered a political following linked to individual Umbanda centros, through which politicians can gain access to Umbanda voters. At the same time, Kardicists used different religious traditions to promote their version of racial harmony in Brazil. According to Brown, "The organizers used Umbanda's syncretic background and cosmology, in which African deities and Catholic saints mingle with the spirits of Brazilian Indians and African slaves, to promote its image as a major national symbol of Brazilian religious and cultural unity and racial harmony."[31] Kardecists developed a belief system that had a strong influence on Umbanda cosmology and on the interpretation of Umbanda's world view, expounded in its formal ideological political structure. Umbanda is closely tied to Kardec teachings and follows evolutionary theories and a dogma of reincarnation. The doctrines produce a panoramic view of spirits who evolve and move through a state of upward mobility, from a plane of spiritual ignorance to great enlightenment. This is made possible through successive incarnations of spirits who move slowly away from the earth's orbit. Brown suggests that the "formal structuring of the Umbanda cosmos" reflects Kardec views—a highly structured, bureaucratic, regimented, and ordered world in which military language and metaphors abound.[32]

Many controversies have dogged Umbanda followers over efforts to create a "purer" form of religion, one influenced by Kardec spiritualism, which cajoles the faithful to eliminate Afro-Brazilian elements from the sect. Portrayed as a yuppie, mulatto, and middle-class crusade, it appeals to intellectuals and attempts to rid the faith of so-called sorcery, the Satanism of the lower class, and, characteristically, Macumba and Batuques African practices. Umbandists, however, want to be regarded as preservers and custodians of all of Brazil's rich cultural heritage. Their search for a new identity therefore produced several faces of Umbanda: Purer Umbanda, White Umbanda, Kardec Umbanda, and African Umbanda. All "Umbandas" form a creole religious and cultural phenomenon that is African and Brazilian.[33] Umbanda developed a syncretistic tendency that allowed it to embrace participants from different sectors of society with multicultural religious expressions. These include the despised Macumba that many Umbandists detest because of its Africanism and mysterious magical powers. Umbanda leaders held two spiritist congresses for all followers of the movement. The first congress, staged in 1941, was intended to organize the religion and formalize its primary rituals,[34] a goal that is yet to be achieved. The second congress aimed at uniting all elements of Umbanda, which continues to fight with its own identity under the label of "Afro-Brazilian religion."

Structure and Ethos

An Umbanda origin myth showcases its universalist, interracial, and ecumenical nature. It claims that its religious teachings first "emerged with the human race, were influenced by ancient Hindu laws, continued by the Mayans and by Greek, Egyptian, and Jewish priests, and preserved in Africa until its revival through the reuniting of three branches of humanity—Indians, Europeans, and Africans—in Brazil."[35] Umbanda's sacred beings differ significantly from Candomble's spiritual entities. The Umbanda pantheon comprises four different types of divinities, categorized as spirits of light (Caboclos, Pretos Velhos, *criancas*) and spirits of darkness (*exus*, associated with Africans and evil). The Caboclos, native ancestral spirits, represent spiritual energy and vitality. Pretos Velhos, who represent humanity, are spirits of African slaves who lived to a ripe age. Each Umbanda functions autonomously but shares certain common motifs with others. Prominent are Brazilian Amerindian spirits and the use of tobacco and herbal medicines. Central tenets are Portuguese-Catholic theological ideas of salvation, immortality, the equating of saints with native and African divinities, and benevolent divine-human relations.[36]

Eclecticism, crises of identity, and ideological conflict within Umbanda created what Brown refers to as internal contradictions in its cosmological system. It is so eclectic and relies so heavily on other religious traditions for its thought forms that lines become blurred between Umbanda and Candomble, Umbanda and Macumba, Umbanda and Caboclo, Umbanda and Kardecism, and Umbanda and Catholicism. Brown was able to locate most members of Yoruba and Bantu pantheons of Candomble, Caboclo, and Pretos Velhos in Umbanda's divinity system; often these show only slight variation. So strong is Umbanda's association and cross-creolization that, in some scholarly discourses, the religion has either replaced Candomble or has become a synonym for it. The major differences between the cosmology of Candomble and that of Umbanda, of course, are the vertical sevenfold division of *linhas* ("lines"), the five major types of Umbanda spirits, and the complex formal system containing a three-level cosmos: astral spaces, the earth, and the underworld. George Eaton Simpson writes:

> Members of a typical Umbanda cult center in Sao Paulo believe in five major types of spirits: the Caboclo spirits of the dead Brazilian Indians; the *preto velho* (gentle spirits of dead Afro-Brazilian slaves); and the *orixas* (spirits who represent a merging of West African deities and Catholic saints). Umbandists organize their spirits into seven *linhas* (lines), each headed by an *orixa* and divided into seven *falanges* (phalanxes). Each phalanx is in turn divided into seven *legitoes* (legions) of spirits. A common organization of lines in Sao Paulo includes those headed by Oxala (Jesus Cristo), Iemanja (virgem Maria), Oxossi (Sao Sedastiao), Xango (sao Jeronimo), and Ogun (Sao Jorge).[37]

GOD AND THE SEVEN LEVELS

At the head of Umbanda's cosmic order is the creator God, the source and destination of all spirits, good and bad. Subordinate to God is the complex system of beings organized around the mysterious number seven. Powerful personages with African and Catholic identities occupy "astral spaces," which they share with Caboclos, Pretos Velhos, and other less well-known spirits. In this cosmology, the earth forms an intermediate sphere that provides a temporary habitat for spirits that pass through different human incarnations as they move from lower to higher stages in their spiritual evolution. Evil and ignorant spirits from the netherworld visit the earth and become the primary source of harm and bad fate that Caboclos and Pretos Velhos seek to correct. Then there are the centros, "led by ritual priestesses and priests under whose guidance mediums accept possession by disembodied spirits in order to enhance personal spiritual development."[38] Umbanda's complex cosmos containing seven lines of spirits resembles the spiritual cosmos of Macumba deities, all of whom show the dual creole personalities of Catholic saints and African deities. Most of these deities carry the same names as they do in Macumba. These rather complicated lines of spirits are further divided into seven sublines and legions, which are again divided and subdivided into sublegions, *falenges* ("phalanxes"), and subphalanxes.[39]

The system of a sevenfold grid organizes and ranks the great Umbanda pantheon. In these lines, the highest intermediary power is the Creator's son Oxala, associated with Christ. Umbanda's characteristic African cosmology comprises a celestial court with four categories of incarnate and nonincarnate spirits that communicate to the faithful through mediums. Many of these are spirits of deceased Brazilians, African slaves, children, and malicious persons— the latter especially of European origin.[40] Within the Umbanda divine cosmos, orixas are placed next to God in the hierarchy. With the powers of Catholic saints, they combine all of the forces of nature that are answerable to the major African deities. Like the great African supreme God, these Umbanda powers occupy dual roles and are distant from human activity. Having "evolved beyond the point of returning to earth, they have become permanent inhabitants of the astral spaces and therefore no longer descend to visit Umbanda centros. Instead they send their lower ranking emissaries, the Caboclos and Pretos Velhos"[41] to do their bidding. To this worldview is added the Hindu doctrine that an evolving soul in the human body reincarnates according to the laws of karma and is thus subject to misfortune. This bad fate can be positively altered by study, meditation, prayer, ritual oblations, and charity. In this creole cosmology, African deities lead and direct "battle lines," spiritual hosts grouped and arrayed as spirits of light versus spirits of darkness. Operating as a buffer between spiritual forces and humans is Exu, the African messenger,[42] known to have diverse personae in Vodou, Santeria, and Candomble.

Perceptions of the role of Caboclo and Pretos Velhos spirits in Umbanda are colored by racial and cultural bias, and as Johnson argues, the distinction made in some centros "between light and dark spirits leads to a rigid compart-mentalization of the world into good and evil,"[43] evil signifying Africa. Um-bandists locate Pretos Velhos spirits at the ranks of legion leaders, who consti-tute the lower tier of the Seven Lines division of its cosmology. Caboclo spirits have been incorporated into the orixas' saints to form "their lower ranks," but the Pretos Velhos occupy the seventh and lowest-rank line, called the "Line of Dead Souls," also referred to as the African Line. This is so because they share a common historical experience as enslaved and exploited peoples. The reason given for their lower ranking is the belief that "unlike Orixas, who are com-monly interpreted as deities, the Caboclos and Pretos Velhos are disincarnate spirits of individuals who lived during the Brazilian colonial and slave peri-ods."[44] Prejudice is also present in other areas of Umbanda cosmological struc-ture. Catholic saints in the Umbanda pantheon who appear in rituals are given the strategic position of being patrons of a higher order; they become models and direct the various activities of Caboclos and Pretos Velhos intermediaries. As Brown observes, consultations and healing done with Catholic orixas are weighted more heavily than those of African ones, whose "miraculous work-ings" are called magic; in some quarters they are called black magic.[45] Pretos Velhos spirits represent a sector of black Brazil and serve important functions in ecumenical Umbanda, whose priests incorporate them into their ceremo-nies and act with authority when possessed by a Pretos Velhos spirit.

Umbandists learn about the Caboclos and Pretos Velhos spirits through personal encounter as well as through tradition, especially in texts of sacred songs, called *pantos,* sung at some ceremonies. The main cultic operation of Um-banda consists of its rituals, which are performed two or three times a week in very spirited services in centros and terreiros. Rituals performed in the latter emphasize African elements and reflect Candomble features. Umbanda cen-tros have different spheres of organization and hierarchal power. Brown calls one of these spheres a ritual hierarchy; it comprises everyone who participates in the ceremonies and supplies the social structure for the religious cultus. The other sphere she refers to as a secular or administrative hierarchy that attends to issues of managing the center's activities. Umbanda's *giras,* or "dance," the most important ritual led by the local *chefe,* is very spirited. The *chefe,* leader, or priest of the center occupies both spheres of power and resembles the *mae* and *pai de santo* in Candomble.[46] The leader of a center may be one of the origi-nal founders or owners and has ultimate authority over all of its activities and functions. Immediately below the leader in authority and importance are the mediums.

MEDIUMS
An Umbanda spirit medium is an individual whom the ritual community rec-ognizes as the conduit of a spirit; she is in tune with, and is a vehicle for, the operation of the orixa. The different types of Umbanda mediums are similar to the daughters and sons of the *santos* in Candomble. They prescribe remedies

for ailments, give consultation or advice, offer help to those who need it, and function as mediators between the deity and the people. Women dominate Afro-Brazilian religious leadership, as they do other Caribbean regions.[47] That dominance is well represented among Umbanda mediums. From her ethnographic study on Umbanda in Porto Alegre, Brazil, Lerch observed that "approximately 80 to 85 percent of the mediums were women."[48] At some centers, female mediums outnumbered male mediums more than two to one. For example, in forty-seven centers in Sao Paulo there were about 135 women to about seventy-two men. In fourteen centers in Rio de Janeiro there were sixty-seven women and only thirty-three men. The ten centers in Porto Alegre had seventy-five to eighty women as opposed to twenty to twenty-five men. From the pattern she observed at most centers, Lerch finds that "males dominate the external, public affairs of Umbanda and females handle the internal affairs, especially the individual relationships between mediums and clients."[49] What accounts for this socioreligious phenomenon?

Several explanations are suggested for this feature of female dominance in Umbanda. Followers believe that a woman possesses the innate quality called *mediunidade* that causes her to excel in this leadership role. Women seem to have natural attributes that make them especially suited to this office; the attributes used to describe a good mother or good wife in Brazil are characteristic of the spirit medium. The women are seen as sensitive, caring, devoted, industrious, and in tune with spirituality. Perhaps more important, the role of medium offers a position of advantage, power, and psychological fulfillment to women. Many of them are either unemployed or underemployed housewives or are in some disadvantaged situation in life. The industrialization of the 1950s did not benefit the majority of Brazilian women, black or white, all of whom are often outside the modern work force. The role of a medium therefore offers women opportunity and prestige. As Lerch concludes, "Since the medium is possessed by a spirit, she becomes the repository of super-human wisdom. Clients come seeking this wisdom. Besides wise counsel, clients may also receive practical help from the spirit mediums who stand at the center of a network of clients."[50] These streams of power are sent by God to Afro-Brazilian women. As is true of African diviners, Umbandists believe that the mediumistic ability is not learned but innate. Although this gift may not be acquired, it has to be nurtured or developed and the recipient has to learn its use and mode of operation.

A woman may spontaneously discover she possesses this gift during a spirit possession trance. Umbanda spirit possession takes three important forms: (1) the *incorporado*, in which the medium's body and faculties are under the full control of the possessing spirit; (2) the *encostado*, in which the spirit coasts or moves alongside the medium and places messages in her heart rather than taking complete control of her body or faculties; and (3) the *en transe*, in which the medium experiences a completely altered state of consciousness and wakes up later feeling she was in a different world. Senior mediums who are "ritually purified and specially attired" dance to achieve a trance state in the ritual, during which the spirits may descend. "Bearing positive messages from the higher celestial ranks, the possessing spirits consult with members of the congregation, offer advice on personal problems, and cleanse the members of evil influences."[51]

The completely voluntary membership in the fraternity brings its privileges, and is often promoted by word of mouth among family, friends, and business associates. Other devotees carry out various ritual functions in the fraternity, and a caretaker cares for the building and grounds. The congregation in attendance at a ceremony is at the lowest end of the totem pole, but its members constitute important entities in the worship and consultation activities. Entrance into the public ritual is free, but regular members of the center are assessed an initial registration fee or small monthly dues to defray the expenses[52] of the centros.

CONSULATAS AND CEREMONIES

Ceremonies and rituals are held in the centros, which can be makeshift buildings, tents, or private homes. The rituals are conducted on special nights each week and facilitated with songs that summon the deities as well as dismiss spirits that have the potential to cause disturbance. The centros are decorated with statues or chromolithographs. At a center that Brown visited, statues of Catholic orixas, Indian Caboclo, and African Petros Velho deity-saints lined the Umbanda ritual altar, before which devotees arriving for worship were expected to genuflect in reverence. Ritual specialists, all dressed in white robes, wore white socks and tennis sneakers and displayed insignias of the particular center visibly on the left side of their garment. Worshipers who entered the center also paid respect to the leader and the mediums who accompanied her. At the entrance, some people paused to collect a token to be used for their consultation at the appropriate time in the ceremony.

In most centers, an Umbanda ritual follows a typical pattern. When it is time for a ceremony to begin, the leader makes an oblation by scattering incense over the altar and those in attendance. The congregation then joins in singing spirited hymns in celebration of the spirits being invited to work charitably among the people. The *chefe* greets the spirit deities and someone offers a Catholic prayer in honor of the saints. After this, the leader reads an excerpt from a Kardec text in Christian liturgical fashion. Another round of singing continues, accompanied by hand clapping as the "ritual party" dances and moves around the room in a circular fashion. The dance signals the imminent appearance of an orixa invited to possess the medium on the spirit's special nights of ritual activities in the center. Possessed mediums often display strange eye and hand movements as well as facial contortions, utter intermittent shrieks, and engage in other actions symbolic of their special spirit. Through the medium and leader, the spirits greet one another and the worshipers in attendance. As a mark of distinction, the *chefe* is almost always possessed by one of the highest and most respected Pretos Velhos spirits. Through the medium, the spirit symbolically smokes a pipe, looks quite elderly, and gives and receives special greetings.[53]

Once the special greetings, singing, and clapping cease, the important *consulatas* begin. Initiates who are high-ranking spirit consultants take up key positions in the center of the meeting room in preparation for giving consultations. Here too, the racial prejudice of Kardec Umbanda raises its ugly head in the public ritual as it seeks to marginalize its African elements. For example, the Kardec-Catholic orixas are displayed more prominently than the genuine African spirits. Orixas-spirits are paid homage by initiates and Caboclo and Petros Velhos spirits. Consultations offered by Catholic orixa spirits and Kardec spiritists are respected more highly than those offered by African ones. Brown argues that "the rational bureaucratic process of the formal cosmological system permeates the organization of the consultations, by numbers, with tokens, according to an orderly process. This is reflected as well in the tone of this public ritual, which is generally sedate, decorous, restrained, and controlled."[54] However, spontaneous spirit possession can occur during consultation and may not be related to a diagnosis of a client's problem. Consultation can continue past midnight or until all those with tokens have been attended to. The activities end with a ritual garb being exchanged for regular clothes and the *chefe* and ritual party taking their exit.

Catimbo

Catimbo and Caboclo sects are the least African and perhaps the most native-creole of early Afro-Brazilian religions. They comprise an odd mix of Christian, African, and Amerindian traditions and are found mainly in northern Brazil. Blacks assimilated Caboclo and Catimbo cultures that were not dominated by African traditions. Catimbo is a healing sect known for its smoking of tobacco and its Amerindian roots. It is said to be the oldest of Brazil's creole cults, practiced as early as the sixteenth century in Indian villages that were influenced by Portuguese Catholic beliefs and African traditions. According to Bastide, Catimbo's adherents appeared in the early colonial era as *santidade* and are mentioned in the confessions and denunciations of residents of Bahia and Pernambuco who went before the Inquisition tribunal of 1591 to 1592.[55] Catimbo spread to Recife, Rio De Janeiro, and Salvador and flourished in coastal regions around the Amazon River. It inherited mainly Christian and African Caboclo traditions from Amerindian culture. Social scientist Roberto Motta writes that "*Catimozeiros* (i.e., practitioners of *Catimbo*) generally see their rites as Indian or *Caboclo*. Even if much of what they believe and practice does have undeniably native roots, it is equally clear that Catimbo was affected significantly by European and African influences, both in the origin of many of its supernaturals and in its styles of singing and dancing."[56]

The Amerindian spirits of Catimbo, scattered throughout villages and states in Brazil, are called upon by strictly localized groups with no centralized organization. Catimbo groups are small and loosely organized around a practitioner-healer and his or her clients rather than a known cultic center with a priest.

A stone idol called Mary the Mother of God was apparently the central focus of the sect, which was led by a "pope." Admission to the sect was done through an initiation resembling the Christian sacrament of baptism. Catimbo's rites were heavily synchronized with Christian practices: it had a church building where the idol was worshiped, its adherents carried rosaries and small crosses, and men led processions of the faithful, with women and children in the rear. Bastide notes that their practices also had Indian elements: "polygamy, singing and dancing, and the use of the 'sacred herb' tobacco as it was used by Indian medicine-men; the smoke being swallowed to produce the mystic trance known as the spirit of Santidade."[57] The buildings of modern Catimbo centers are simple, housing only a few statues, an altar, and some seats. Its rituals are also simple. The healer, or *curandeiro*, leads the cult in a ritual invoking the spirits' help for healing and good fortune. The healer also leads the group in drinking the famous intoxicant *jurema* to induce visions and a form of spirit possession. A component of *jeruma* is the root juice of the *jurema preta*, a hallucinogen to which practitioners add raw rum (*cachaca*), thus making it more potent.[58] The use of this drug is a native Brazilian tradition found among Caboclo-Catimbo sects. When an Amerindian spirit possesses a medium, or *Mestre* ("mistress"), she is empowered to give advice and perform healing. The possessed medium performs a simple healing ritual of blowing tobacco smoke upon the needy devotees seeking the spirit's aid. In most of the Catimbo groups, spirit possession is experienced through the leader alone; this is the medium upon whom any one of a number of spirits may descend during a ritual designed to welcome the spirits. Spiritual powers invoked on such occasions include the "gods Tupa and Ituapa, [the] stereotypical Indian spirit Iracema, [the] Master Healer, [the] Christian saints Antonio and Josaphat, and some African deities worshiped elsewhere."[59] These spirits are much less African than those found in Caboclo culture.

Caboclo

Caboclos are peoples, religions, and spirits of native Brazilians and African slaves; the Africans are called Pretos Velhos, and the Amerindians call themselves Caboclos. Historically, people have classified these religious cultures with a race and class construction of society. Slaves were aware of the dominant ideology that blacks were no more than a subhuman species and chattel. This undergirded the deep psychological pain that the dominant society inflicted on blacks. Many colonial Brazilian whites shared with northern counterparts the belief that blacks were mere animals, without souls. As Bastide records, the following lines of an antiblack poem, in Brazilian folklore, were characteristic of white sentiment in Brazil, as late as the early 1900s:

*The white man: God made him. The mulatto: God painted him.
The caboclo is a pig's fart. And the Negro's the Devil's shit.*[60]

This unabashedly wretched view of Africans was quite widespread among colonists, especially the heartless slave masters who sought philosophical reasons for enslaving, exploiting, and brutalizing Africans.

As the Brazilian Mundicarmo Ferretti shows, this ideology bred the myth of three formative races of society in Brazil, a myth responsible for the categorization of African and non-African spiritual entities worshiped in Afro-Brazilian religious centers as "1) *Caboclos*, representatives of . . . indigenous populations or the popular classes of Brazilian society living in rural areas; 2) *Pretos Velhos*, blacks representing enslaved Africans in Bahia; and 3) *Senhores*, white gentlemen or noble folk, representatives of the European colonizers."[61] As the oldest of the three groups, Caboclos first emerged in the regions of Bahia and Maranhao, in Nago, and in Bantu-influenced centers. Since the 1890s, these regions have seen the rise of new, distinctly Caboclo centers. Pretos Velhos, closely linked to Umbanda, are popular in Rio de Janeiro and Sao Paulo. Caboclos and Pretos Velhos spirits in Umbanda act as intermediaries between powerful spirit entities and humans. Pretos Velhos are said to be good-hearted and are addressed by affectionate familial names such as Grandpa, Grandma, Aunt, Uncle, and Father. These so-called "white gentlemen spirits," also recognized in Umbanda, represent ancestral spiritual entities in Tambor de Mina, where they blend with African divinities.

Caboclos include a subcategory of spirits called cowboys (*baiadeiros*), which are popular African elements in Umbanda. These are both domesticated spirits in the Umbanda pantheon of deities and Indian ancestors, who inhabit the interior and are summoned during ceremonies. Ferretti concludes that "in the Afro-Brazilian religions in Maranhao the term Caboclo does not apply exclusively to indigenous entities, such as *Cabocla Jurema* (female Amerindian spirit) and Caboclo Velho, nor only to those involved in the raising of cattle, such as members of the important Maranhao spirit family of Legua-Boji-Bua, an entity who commands the Codo forest."[62] *Caboclo* also designates Turkish spirits, high-class European spirits, and wild scary entities of the forest. As Brown observes, Caboclos are generally regarded as "unacculturated Indians" who inhabit the Amazonian forests. These are hunters and brave tribal warriors who appear vain and arrogant to their detractors. "The individual details and lore of their identities are learned and transmitted in the beautiful *pontos* sung to them in Umbanda ceremonies, accompanied by hand-clapping or drums."[63] The characteristically proud, free Caboclo leaders and warriors are mobile, were not enslaved as Africans were, and are said to derive their power from the spiritual forces of nature. Caboclo spirits share features of Amerindians and are associated with certain heroic acts and adventures. These spirits are said to utter loud cries, move in aggressive ways, smoke large cigars, and call for Indian ritual paraphernalia such as beads and headdresses made of feathers. The proud Caboclos, however, were likened pejoratively to the noble savage, in contrast with Pretos Velhos, who are seen as the humble, patient, subservient, faithful slaves.[64]

Caboclo and Pretos Velhos are equally eclectic; they combine native, Christian, and African elements in their rituals and beliefs. Those rituals are further blended with Candomble Angola-Congo and Jeje, and their songs are sung in Portuguese. This accents their unique creole character, but often eclipses their African features. According to Omari, Caboclo's dances are similar to the popular national Brazilian *samba* and *encantados* dances, which imitate the deities whose name they bear; these are also the only deities recognized in Caboclo. The dances show the non-African practice of dancing with eyes open, smoking cigars, and offering healing advice and consultation during public festivals; the wearing of feathers and multicolored costumes, derived from Amerindians, are prominent in annual festivals, and the yellow and green colors of Brazil's national flag are conspicuous in devotees' liturgical garments and house decorations. Omari adds, "Fruits and vegetables are the most common sacrifices, rather than animal sacrifices most common in Yoruba and Angola Candombles. These fruits and vegetables are present in abundance during public ceremonies for Caboclo"[65] and their use is no less controversial.

Batuques

Batuques is the name given to a variety of African religious traditions in the southernmost part of Brazil. Defined as part cult, part funeral ceremony, part entertainment, and part culture, the Batuques have survived to modern times with a strong African tradition. When Bastide did his research on religions in the 1950s, he found that the number of Batuques registered with the police was relatively high and increasing annually. The oldest center dates back to the 1890s; ten new houses opened in the 1920s, more than twenty in the 1930s, and eighteen more in the early 1940s. "There were fifty-seven African religious societies in Porto Alegre, thirty of which were named after Catholic saints, two after African Gods, one after a *caboclo* spirit, and ten after historic dates."[66] Batuques religious societies were known for their much maligned ritual dances, which they saw as authentic expressions of their African religion and culture. Brazilian planters, who insisted that slaves must work every day, believed Sunday Batuques infringed on their rights of property, but the government saw the institution as a tool for defusing slave anxiety and rebellion. Batuques dancers indirectly helped Africans rekindle instinctive feelings of ethnic antipathy that many African nations had for each other, but gradually extinguished in their common colonial suffering. Nina Rodrigues writes: "If the different 'nations' of Africa were totally to forget the furious resentment which by nature has divided them, if the Agome were to become the brothers of the Nago, the Gege of the Hausa, the Tapa of the Ashanti, and so on, a tremendous and inescapable danger would descend upon and destroy Brazil."[67] Batuques centers were located in dense black populations of the suburbs of Sant' Ana, Petropolis,

Floresta of Rio Grande do Sul, and elsewhere. In Porto Alegre, Yoruba and Dahomey nations had many Batuques centers, which functioned much like those of Candomble. Each center was directed by a father or mother of the saints and had a predominantly female leadership.[68]

Conclusion

During Brazil's long colonial history, government and local authorities saw African religions as a threat to the religion of the dominant Portuguese class. This forced many Afro-Brazilians to practice their religion underground and, as a result, made accessing African beliefs and practices a challenge.[69] In more modern times, Brazilians openly follow Candomble and Umbanda as cherished cultural and religious experiences of the country's multiethnic population. Umbanda has attracted a large following and shown noticeable political strength. The more affluent among Candomble and Umbanda initiates trade votes and political favor with politicians. The growing Brazilian middle class, bent on the "whitening" of African traditions and culture, has also contributed to the new face and popularity of Umbanda. Yvonne Maggie holds that "many religious celebrations are now supported by state governments and have been included in the official calendars of tourist festivities. At the ritual celebration for Iemanja, the goddess of the sea waters, the beaches of Sao Paulo, Rio de Janeiro, and Bahia are crowded with thousands of people bearing offerings for the deity."[70] Although popularizing Afro-Brazilian religious culture has its disadvantages, Candomble and Umbanda benefit appreciably from increased national attention and popular attraction.

African religions that survived in the collective memory of the slaves are represented not only in Umbanda and Candomble, but also in Macumba and the Caboclos. As Bastide suggests, the existence of African sects is based largely on faith in the omnipotence of the *orixas*, those supernatural powers that sanction taboos and punish those who violate them. This faith rests on myriads of religious actions, resulting in "children of the gods punished for their disobedience, profane men healed by sacrifices or by 'giving food to the head.' A primal faith inherited from the ancestors and transmitted from one generation to the next."[71] Rene Ribeiro argues that the roles of African religions in Brazil are to offer to their adherents systems of beliefs and practices, as well as a type of interpersonal relationship that helps relieve tensions while allowing devotees to maintain the traditional values and styles of a Luso-Brazilian civilization. Many of these marginal peoples, whose exclusion from the global economy often affords them no chance of realizing their dreams or achieving even modest goals, find in these religious centers a "type of relationship with the supernatural and of apparent control over chance that enables them to satisfy their indispensable psychological needs."[72] This religious empowerment is socially invaluable for surviving the harsh realities of Afro-Brazilian life.

10

Orisha Powers

Creole Religion in Trinidad and Tobago

KEY TOPICS

Foreground • Symbiotic Orisha • Orisha Cosmology •
Yards and Shrines of the Gods

The numerical strength of African-derived religions in the Republic of Trinidad and Tobago (locally called Trinidad and Tobago) pales against that of the dominant Christianity, Hinduism, and Islam, but the African-derived religions are arguably as resilient as the country's steel-band-calypso-and-carnival culture. The most vibrant African religion in the Caribbean's southernmost islands is the small but lively creole Orisha, one of the region's various African spiritualities consisting of different forms of African religious beliefs and practices as influenced by Christian and other traditions. This religion of the "spiritual powers" or "lineages" of Africa adopted its name from the African traditional religion (ATR) Yoruba/Orisa (Orisha) and its leading divinity Shango, god of thunder and lightening. It first began in early nineteenth-century British colonial Trinidad as a collection of practices and observances among African families and small "nations"—ethnic groups such as Kongo, Mandingo, Egbo, Ebo, Yoruba, Efik, Calabari, Rada, Kramanti, and Kroomen. The unorganized religious practices facilitated unobtrusive performance of ancestral rites, rituals, and celebrations like marriage, naming ceremonies, and Emancipation Day. This was especially true of funeral rites in communities where Africans were not afforded Christian burial in church-related cemeteries; one such cemetery designed for the burial of all Africans was reportedly donated in the 1840s to an ethnically mixed black community in Deigo-Martin, northwest Trinidad, by a first-generation Yoruba[1] "Good Samaritan."

In the mid- to late 1800s, this nascent religion morphed into Shango, retaining that name for well over a century as a secretive religion under great restrictions.[2] Emboldened by sympathy from the world-renowned historian and highly respected Prime Minister of Trinidad and Tobago, Eric Eustace Williams,

Symbols of Orisha.
(Illustration by Kelly Hawes.)

and under the influence of America's black-consciousness movement of the late 1960s—as well as of Rastafarian culture and the Black Power movement that directly impacted Trinidad and Tobago in the 1970s (all harbingers of black identity and African affirmation)—avatars at last affirmed their religious culture, shed Shango's pupa, and went public.[3] After the Orisa World Congress in 1981, Shango became Orisa (Orisha), its current and preferred name. With the influence of the Rastafarians, Shango shrines were renamed Orisha *yards* (a yard is a Rastafari home). Because of its close association with the proto-Christian Spiritual Baptist (sometimes labeled "Shouter Baptist" and even "Shango Baptist") group, outsiders often attach one of those labels as well as the label "Obeah" to Orisha. In this chapter, I occasionally use the term *Orisha-Shango* only to keep in memory its historical nexus before the 1960s and 1970s.

Trinidad and Tobago's Orisha-Shango was related to the Congo, Chimbundu, Igbo, Yoruba "Fon-connected Rada," and Mina-Jeje, as well as to other nations characteristic of black Atlantic religions in the Caribbean and Brazil.[4] The Caribbean received about 35 percent of its slaves of various origins from the huge depot in Bahia. Brought into what became the Republic of Trinidad and Tobago by slaves, free blacks, and indentured workers of West Africa, Orisha-Shango incorporated elements of ATRs, Islam, Christianity, Judaism, and Sanatana Dharma (Hinduism), becoming a creole spirituality. It claims to be distinctly African and has recently begun to divest itself of its non-African religious embellishments; *mangbas* ("priests") are Africanizing their shrine and yard rituals, adopting the Yoruba language in the liturgy and commuting to Nigeria for initiation in order to make their religious practices more authentically African.[5] Like other African-Caribbean faiths, Orisha-Shango was a religion in confrontation with the colonial Christian cultural hegemony, race differentiation, economic deprivation, oppression, and persecution. It survived as an oral tradition, but because of its past history of repression, avatars are attempting to preserve its sacred myths and traditions in written texts for perpetuity.[6]

During Trinidad's late colonial history, Yoruba-Shango and other expressions of African culture were repressed and outlawed as surreptitious cults of African heathens among an ignorant underclass. Africans in Trinidad and Tobago suffered legal restrictions, ethnic discrimination, and social stigma for, among other things, their association with the Orisha-Shango, Spiritual Baptist, and Obeah religions well into the late 1900s. Until recently, yards (shrines) had to obtain a license from the Ministry of Cultural Affairs before hosting a feast, and several acts enforced political and judicial restrictions on religious practices. Ordinance No 6 of 1868, designed to prohibit Obeah in Trinidad, and the Canboulay Riots Act of 1884 (a canboulay is an African cultural celebration) prohibiting African religious practices, have existed for more than one hundred years; they made African religion illegal in the British colony, which had an overt preference for Christian culture. These pieces of legislation, incorporated into the Summary Offences Act of 1921 to suppress African culture, allowed the government to ban from public places the following, all of which are sacred to Afro-Trinidadian religion: ". . . the carrying of any lighted torch, the beating of any drum, the blowing of any horn, or the use of any other noisy instruments; any dances or processions; and any assemblage or collection of persons armed with sticks or other weapons of offence and numbering ten or more" (Act of 1921 No 17: Clause 59).

The police were authorized to (1) confiscate any objects, instruments, and religious reliquaries and their paraphernalia; (2) enter forcefully any building or residence; and (3) arrest or disperse persons in any gathering for forbidden or suspicious activities involving African dance, procession, singing, drumming, feasting or other practices.

> Anyone without a license under the hand of a Gazetted Police Officer, who permits any persons to assemble and play or dance therein to any drum, gong, tambour, bangee, chac-chac, or other similar instrument of music, at anytime between the hour of ten o'clock in the evening of one day, and the long hour of six o'clock in the morning of the next day . . . Or permits any persons to assemble and dance therein the *dance*

known as bungo or any similar dance, shall be liable to a fine . . . and it shall be lawful for any constable . . . to enter any house, building . . . and stop such dance or seize and carry away all such . . . instruments of music, and the same shall be forfeited (Act of 1921, No 17: Clause 69).[7]

Of special concern were the beating of African drums and assemblage in Orisha-Shango worship, both of which the colonial government linked to black revolts. Police regularly seized Orisha-Shango drums and arrested suspects for the alleged practice of Obeah. Only after the Ministry of Legal Affairs reviewed the offensive legislation did the government rescind the prejudicial restrictions and consider a draft bill to legalize religious and other African cultural associations in Trinidad and Tobago. Pear Eintou Springer, an Orisha leader, notes that in 1981 Ebge Orisa Ile Wa was incorporated by an Act of Parliament; the organization was led by the eighty-four-year-old priestess Iyalorisa Melvina Rodney, head of the National Council of Orisha Elders in Trinidad, and "the spiritual heir to the most famous Orisa high priest . . . Babalorisa Ebenezer Elliot."[8] In 1991, the yard (shrine) of Opa Orisha was also incorporated and its annual Oshun festival in August continues to draw hundreds of enthusiasts.[9]

Since the founding of the International Congress of Orisa Tradition and Culture by the organization Orisa World in 1981, Trinidad and Tobago Orisha leaders have seated very active "Permanent Delegates" in the Congress. Through those delegates, the Republic hosted the third World Conference on Orisha Tradition and Culture in 1987, following its Second World Conference in Salvador de Bahia in 1983. At the third conference, more than two thousand participants[10] from Brazil, the United States, West Africa, and the Caribbean showcased their Yoruba Orisha religion with international flare and celebrated African culture with ethnic pride. In 1988, the Ooni of Ife, Nigeria—head of the worldwide Orisha religion—visited Trinidad and Tobago and, as Emperor Haile Selassie's visit to Jamaica did to Rastafari in 1966, stimulated a new interest in the faith and a steady rise in its membership. In spite of the cultural and political defamation it has endured and the fact that the most recent national census classified most adherents to African religions as Christians, the ancestral African Orisha religion attracts a growing cross-section of members throughout the country. Devotees find spiritual fulfillment, self-worth, meaning, and pride in their culture. Black Power advocates and other young nationalists turn to Trinidad and Tobago's ATRs (Orisha, Obeah, and Rastafari) as signifiers of identity and African ideological self-expression. Others celebrate Orisha as folk tradition and a means of affirming their ethnic roots in the cosmopolitan Republic.[11]

Foreground

The emergence of Orisha-Shango in Trinidad and Tobago is a recent phenomenon created by late Spanish and British colonialism. For almost three hundred years after Columbus claimed the larger island for Spain, naming it and two adjacent islands the Trinity (for the rows of three hills), it remained a deserted colony in the vast Iberian American empire; it was little more than a retooling dock for weather-beaten and war-torn ships of the Spanish Armada in the angry Atlantic. The natives of Trinidad (approximately forty thousand in 1498) were decimated by disease and by Spanish enslavement in the Capuchin mission camps designed to convert them to Christianity; by 1762, demographic returns showed a population of only 2,475 natives, about half of which were labeled "Christianized Indians." The island remained unexploited by the colonial enterprise, retaining only a fledgling settlement at San Josef de Oruna (St. Joseph) until the 1780s.[12] In 1783, King Charles III instituted a new initiative, the Cedula of Population, a decree that offered lucrative incentives to planters to settle in the colony.[13] Since planters accepting the Spanish offer to invest in the island had to be Catholics, most of those who seized the opportunity were French whites and mulattos fleeing the Haitian Revolution or escaping British Protestant rule in former French colonies in the Windward Islands. Madrid's initiative, therefore, brought thousands of French Catholics and their African slaves into the "Land of the Hummingbird." By 1796, Trinidad's population jumped from about 2,600 to more than 17,700. Of these, 6,630 were free whites and mixed-race inhabitants, about 10,100 slaves, and 1,075 indigenous people.[14] Most of the slaves coming via Haiti and the eastern Caribbean were "re-cycles," originally from West and Central Africa.[15]

Britain seized Trinidad from Spain in 1797 and for decades afterward debated the island's fate as a slave colony. The abolition of the slave trade in 1807 spared the youngest (and shortest-lived) slave plantation culture in the region from the massive importation of African captives that had been inflicted on its Caribbean neighbors. That, however, did not stop the flow of Africans into the colony. Among 31,000 inhabitants in 1810, about 67 percent were slaves, most of them born in Africa; 20 percent were free blacks; and 13 percent were whites and indigenous people.[16] Maureen Warner-Lewis found, in the 1813 Register of Slaves, that about 41 percent came from the Bight of Biafra, a depot for the Igbo, the Ibibio, the Efik from the Niger Delta, the northwestern Bantu of Cameroon, and other peoples. About 19 percent came from the Central Atlantic coast, Angola, and the Congo. Another 12 percent originated from Senegal, Gambia, the Bight of Benin, and the Gold Coast, and the rest from the Windward Coast.[17] In addition to the Africans who landed under the Spanish Cedula (1783 to 1797) and British slavery (1798 to 1834), a much larger number arrived because of different circumstances. Under an immigration scheme designed to solve labor shortages on plantations in British colonies, thousands of workers were imported as indentured laborers from Sierra Leone, St. Helena, Nigeria, Benin, Ghana, Senegal, Gambia, Ivory Coast, and Central Africa to join other blacks from the same region between 1842 and 1867. Many of the indentured workers were "recaptures" confiscated from condemned vessels seized by the British Naval Preventive Squadron, which policed the Atlantic starting in 1808 to enforce the Prohibition of the Slave Trade Act of 1807.[18] Liberated Africans from Sierra Leone and Liberia also joined blacks who were already indentured in other Caribbean islands. Serious disturbances in Venezuela in the 1850s sent a flood of Venezuelans into Trinidad. Other Africans came, too, as a result of crises in the region and in Africa (the Ashanti Wars of the 1870s and the Boer War of 1899 to 1902) involving the British navy.[19] By far, the largest number of African immigrants to Trinidad migrated voluntarily from Anglo-Caribbean islands after the official abolition of slavery. From 1842, economic hardship sent about 68,000 blacks to the Trinidad mecca from Jamaica and the eastern Caribbean. By imperial acts of fiat, Tobago was annexed to Trinidad in the1880s and 1890s, adding to the number of Africans in the new Trinidad and Tobago. Most of these immigrants arriving from the north flocked to the cities of Port of Spain, San Fernando, Arima, and Point Fortain to seek jobs in the ports, the civil and domestic services, and later the oil refinery at Point-a-Pierre. These late "birds of opportunity" gathering in the land of cocoa, sugar, and oil formed the backbone of the country's African population in the racial creole mix of Portuguese, Spanish, Dutch, French, English, Chinese, Venezuelan, Middle Eastern, and East Indian peoples. Trinidad and Tobago's huge ethnographic shift was "tilted East" when Britain, between 1842 and 1917, brought about 145,000 indentured Indian workers to field plantations.[20] Almost all indentured Indians remained among the working peasantry on or near the estates and became a significant block of small land-owing or propertied peasants; they were able to live in their own settlements, thus providing "the basis for the emergence of a settled Indian community with its own social organization."[21] This ethnic rainbow created what would become the most heterogeneous country in the Caribbean and signaled the character of its emerging religions and cultures.

The nineteenth-century Trinidad Crown Colony was highly polarized by ethnicity, color, class, and creed. The plantation colony based on African slaves was controlled by a Spanish system, a powerful French planter class, and the British government from 1783 to 1838. The period of heavy population growth and rapid economic development (1840s to 1917), built on indentured labor, was dominated by the privileged French propertied class and by a British administration and culture, as evident in areas such as religion and education. The white European elite, brokers of political and economic power, propagated the notion of race pedigree as well as class distinction and color stratifications. Warner-Lewis writes that "color was the visible and popularly accepted manifestation of the economic and political power that created the society and that shaped the goals and values of the colony. Although wealth was not always the collateral of whiteness, whiteness was the passport to privilege."[22] Here, "European culture, and especially all things British, were considered superior to all other cultural forms in the island."[23] White Creoles, the ruling propertied class, dominated life in Crown Colony nineteenth-century Trinidad and Tobago. They were recognized as the elite "legitimate upper class," and many citizens "accepted and subscribed to the color stratification"[24] they proffered.

Whites preferred East Indians (except for their "strange" religions) to Africans because of their work ethic, alleged "docile predisposition," thriftiness, and "good manners." To Africans they assigned a position of inferiority by virtue of ethnicity. To the opulent European Christians, Africans were pagans trapped in tribal customs and heathenish ways; they lacked facility with English; and they were avaricious, suspicious, and savage barbarians. Even the official British Church in Trinidad and Tobago thought Africans lacked the capacity for any spiritual formation[25] and had no religion of their own. In the late 1800s, however, a small black and colored middle class—part of the Creole educated class—emerged, consisting of professionals, civil servants, property owners, and labor-union leaders.[26] These became the forefathers of political agitators that took Trinidad and Tobago into the halls of West Indian federation and independence in the twentieth century.

To provide low-wage labor for the thriving cocoa and sugar industries, African former slaves, squatters, and especially newly landed indentured workers from West Africa and India were settled conveniently in villages strung out along the plantations. According to Warner-Lewis, the Africans "were tools of the planter class that organized their immigration. They worked on sugarcane and cocoa estates . . . and driving carts. Some males were artisan carpenters, masons, and smiths. Many of the young women were hired by Europeans as domestic servants."[27] Some blacks, however, like Indians, got the opportunity to be peasant owners of parcels of "crown land" (state-owned land) on the fringes of the plantation. The communities in which large numbers of these and other peasants lived were grouped as villages called wards. For example, the Montserrat Ward, made up mainly of squatters on nonarable land, survived into the mid-twentieth century and was known for its African dialects and culture. Its peoples used the African titles *nations, Hausa, Congo* (or Chumundu), Fon, and Yoruba,[28] as was done in Haiti, Brazil, and Cuba. British historian Bridget Brereton—with whom I studied at the University of the West Indies, St. Augustine, Trinidad (1981–1983)—noted that in the late 1800s "the Rada, Yoruba, Ibo, Congo, and Mandingo peoples in Port of Spain lived in separate wards and the Rada cult was an integral part of life for those who traced their ancestry to Dahomey"[29] (Benin and Togo), Nigeria, and Sierra Leon. The Yoruba were found in Belmont, Diego Martin, east Port of Spain, Barataria, St. Joseph (where I lived for several years), Petit Valley, and along the Eastern Main Road, as well as in Gasparillo, Claxton Bay, Oropuche, Princess Town, Couva, and Freeport. Africans and East Indians mistrusted each other, lived in ethnic enclaves with separate cultures and associations, and thus had limited social interaction for more than seventy-five years. The villages of Caratal, Maryland, Gasparillo, Mayo, and Sangre Grande, for example, were predominantly African while the East Indians were concentrated in the Bon Aventure, Caroni, Narima, and Poona villages.

Among the African emigrants, those of Yoruba extraction constituted the most prominent block;[30] where they lacked a numerical majority, their social organizational structure and belief system made them influential. French Creole writer Louis A. de Verteuil wrote in 1858 that the Yoruba are guided "by the sense of association; and the principle of combination for the common weal has been fully sustained wherever they settled in any number. . . . The whole Yarraba race of the colony may be said to form a sort of social league for mutual support and protection. [On the whole, they] are laborious, usually working for day wages on estates, but preferring job labor."[31] De Verteuil's colonial spelling of the word *Yoruba*, notwithstanding, he verified the prominence of the ethnic group among the many others that existed in Trinidad villages. In Gasparillo, the earlier Shango was based largely on Yoruba, although Christian elements modified the ritual over time. Near Point-a-Pierre's oil refinery in south Trinidad, Yoruba (Orisha) still thrives in its creole form in Afro-Trinidadian communities. Studies in the early 1900s[32] show that Yoruba is without doubt the ancestor of Shango and that it was especially strong in northern Trinidad, where many orisha divinities are worshiped. The religion became an important factor in Trinidad and Tobago's Afro-Caribbean culture after the 1840s, when immigrants of Yoruba descent began forming ethnic associations in the British colony. These groups would combine their traditional beliefs with elements of the Christian, Muslim, and Hindu faiths[33] of East Indian immigrants who, in some villages, were greater in number.

Since the Yoruba were hard-working and thrifty, some were able to become small land owners (although they were often denied arable crown lands) and integrated well into communities where they were accepted as a social group.[34] As in Yorubaland, where ancestral lands were held jointly in lineages and considered communal rather than individual property, the Yoruba kept property within the family clan. J. D. Elder explains that "the sentiments which opposed transfer of land among these 'Africans' stem not only from . . . economic considerations but also from emotions associated with the idea of transferring to 'the stranger' the *aura* of the dead ancestors whose presence on such land is commonly asserted by the villages."[35] Legend has it that the spirits of the ancestors of one of the largest Gasparillo families often appear to relatives at their property called Twin Mangoes. Early 1900 research found among Gasparillo Africans special cultural and ethnographic traits, which underlie the Yoruba and their African identification of different "nations," into which various groups had formed themselves. Such traits were found in language, mythological relics, African place names, Yoruba religious practices, and ancestral cultic musical rhythm and dance. Elder notes several ethnic characteristics that apply to Africans as a whole: common racial ancestry, strong African identity, and an African cosmology of spiritual powers and ancestral spirits related to family descendants; also, "patrilocal residence rules, the patrisib kinship system . . . Christian allegiance with Roman Catholicism, ancestor cult with Olympian type pantheon of 'powers' . . . and peasant agricultural economy."[36] The paternal, religious, social, and other arrangements among the Gasparillo Yoruba were also noted, with slight variations, among the Kongo people, who used the ancient art of magic to fight African droughts. African "nations" are represented at a feast for Shango, which is also attended also by non-Yoruba family members.[37]

Symbiotic Orisha

The Yoruba religion that emerged in the cosmopolitan colony of Trinidad and Tobago is the creole Orisha-Shango religion that, over time, became embellished with elements of other religious traditions. First called Yoruba, then Shango, and finaly Orisa, this religion is a mixture of African culture and spirituality in which many strands of traditions synchronize. The older Kongo-Yoruba religion acquired aspects of Jewish Kabbalistic mysticism as well as a variety of elements from Catholicism, Spiritual Baptist practices, Rastafari, and Hindu and Islamic cultural traditions. The Rastafarian presence at Orisha (shrine yards) also influenced its religious practices; some of the drummers in the Orisha ritual are Rastas who play authentic African rhythms and prefer the name Orisha to Shango and Baptist. Many followers attend Christian Churches while holding membership in a Spiritual Baptist shrine or Orisha yard. This makes an accurate count of the number of Orisha followers in the Republic of Trinidad and Tobago difficult to determine. A 1995 study shows that there were about 160 Orisha yards with about thirty-five heads of major shrines and more than fifty well-established *palais* (also called yards) in Trinidad.[38] Clients come to Orisha for sundry reasons: to find medicines for various conditions and psychological healing; to search for good luck in a new venture; or to deal with disappointment, hardship, trauma, and pain. Some Christians attend Orisha rituals out of a spiritual or physical need and participate in the ceremonies undercover. Others frequent the worship out of curiosity, ethnic pride, or because of the healing and conjuring that the faith practices.

In Spiritual Baptist and Orisha, traditions assimilate and synchronize with such freedom and latitude that lines of distinction between the two are often blurred. A symbiotic relationship existing between Orisha adherents and Spiritual Baptists is evident in the constant sharing of sacred space, devotees, ritual paraphernalia, and practices. It is noted that in addition to the conflating of Orisha and Baptist elements in the same ceremonies, "some leaders carry on *orisha* and Spiritual Baptist rites separately, either at the same location or at different places."[39] Orisha shows its Christian symbiosis by equating African deities with Roman Catholic saints, the ritual use of water, the widespread use of charms, death rites, and belief in witches. George Eaton Simpson notices that almost "all of the objects on the altar and on the upper half of the wall space in the chapelle" of Orisha are Catholic symbols. Other elements include "the Bible, Catholic prayers, books of magic, 'spontaneous' prayers of the 'Baptist' type, candles, the cross and crucifix, incense, and divination by gazing into a crystal ball, a glass of water, or the flame of a candle,"[40] among other things.

The Spiritual Baptist church located not too far from where I lived in Grenada had a very busy internal decor. Its colorful flags swayed in the breeze, inviting one to see the many strange objects in the sanctuary: numerous crosses and crucifixes; lighted candles at the four corners of the church; communicants' white robes and black gowns; mourning chairs or stools; different bowls and vases of flowers; sacred leaves and roots of plants; calabashes, pots, pans, and goblets with water or some other liquid substance; and vials of oil. The smell of incense permeated the air. We kept the back door and windows of our home closed to keep out the unwelcome incense odor and the loud noises of the shouters, especially late at night when, as we referred to it, "the spirits hit someone"—a euphemism for spirit possession. The Baptist's immaculate white dresses and white and black gowns, head ties, ringing bells, hymn-singing queue, and slow march to the Annandale Waterfall (Grenada) for baptism by water early on some Sunday mornings never escaped my curiosity as a child. To many people in the southern Caribbean, Spiritual Baptist is also called Shouter Baptist, and the religion is not easily distinguishable from Orisha-Shango.

Although Yoruba descendants held distinctly African views of Shango, Ogun, and other Orisha–Ile-Ife mythology, they embellished them with Hindu, Jewish, Muslim, Christian, and other practices and beliefs. Practitioners use "saints," "powers," and "orisha" (orisa, orishe) in reference to their Yoruba deities and the creator.[41] Simpson says, however, that ritual activities of "animal sacrifice, dancing as a part of religious ceremonies, the use of drums and rattles, use of thunder stones, emphasis on rhythm," head washing and incising rites, the idea of intermediary supernatural beings intervening in human affairs, and "revelation by the gods of procedures that will be helpful in dealing with illness and other misfortune" show the full retention of African elements in Orisha. Practitioners reinterpreted and recreated religious myths symbiotically, but African distinctions are seen in the "characteristics and powers of Yoruba deities, initiatory rites, multiple soul concept, the ritual use of blood, the use of [sacred] leaves, divination by throwing *obi* seeds, public possession by the spirits, and utilization of the spirits of the dead."[42] The distinctly African elements of Orisha show that it is an authentic Yoruba religion made creole in Trinidad and Tobago's cultural calaloo.

Outsiders' association of Orisha with Obeah, sorcery, and other aspects of religion they regard as dubious or antisocial has caused followers of Orisha to refer to themselves by the more socially acceptable name Spiritual Baptist. Others use the more inclusive term Baptist, to the displeasure of traditional Baptist Christians. Significant differences between Orisha and Spiritual Baptists, however, persist. As Simpson notes, the meaning of some rituals varies among groups, within the same group, and between Orisha and other sects. Unlike a Spiritual Baptist leader, an Orisha priest gives orders and makes announcements during his ceremony but does not preach, and makes little use of the Bible. There is no "groaning" or "grunting" (hyperventilating or overbreathing sounds) at Orisha ceremonies, but this method of facilitating spirit possession is followed by devotees in Spiritual Baptist groups. Rum is always offered to Ogun and to a few other powers at Orisha ceremonies but it is not used in the Spiritual Baptist ritual. A number of spirits with African names are expected to "manifest" in the participants during an Orisha rite,[43] but not during a Baptist rite.

Simpson correctly notes that Shango (Orisha) drums, thunderstones, daggers, hatchets, wooden knives, fake guns, rattles, whips, *shay-shay* brooms, anchors and oars, large wooden keys, stools and shrines for the gods, and statues of saints are conspicuously absent from a Spiritual Baptist church. On the other hand, "one would not find in an Orisha chapelle a large brass handbell, religious mottoes and placards, or a chariot wheel (a bicycle wheel, suspended from a center post, which is spun from time to time during the service)."[44] Most of these were part of the Spiritual Baptist church's ritual paraphernalia. In his important fieldwork in Trinidad on the Orisha, James Houk surveyed thirty *chapelles* and found Shango's (the spirit) stools in all of them.[45] As much as ten dominant Orisha deities manifest themselves and receive special adoration during a ritual. There are probably as many Orisha yards in Trinidad as there are Spiritual Baptist shrines. Combined, these yards have thousands of followers, clients, and spectators but a smaller number of actual devotees. Although they remain faithful to their own local shrine, Orisha devotees attend the big annual feasts performed at various yards around the country.

Orisha Cosmology

In Orisha's Yoruba cosmology, believers are kept in constant communication with nature and the spiritual world. Giving meaning to life in the world is Olodumare (called Elemii, Elefon, and Eledaa), creator of the universe and owner of all that lives. Assisted by a host of powers, God works in a motif of three with Obatala and Oshala in imitation of the godhead of Father, Son, and Holy Spirit of Christianity[46] or of the Hindu trimurti Brahma, Vishnu, and Shiva. Elefon created life sacred, and creation testifies to the divine presence and being in the world. God gave humans the privilege of enjoying and caring for the earth, with choices to be exercised in view of suffering consequences for their actions. Positive consequences include rewards or blessings, such as good health, prosperity, or material success. Punishment—in the form of affliction, suffering, disaster, and death—may result from poor human judgment and bad karma. Karmic actions are monitored by a consort of African powers called orisha (orisa) who represent God in the world. Functioning just like emendations of Brahma (Lakshmi, Vishnu, and Shiva), the intermediaries of Elefon link God to humans and the world and are directly involved in peoples' lives. They control destiny, natural phenomena, and plant and animal life while maintaining the balance of life's forces (like yin and yang) and assist devotees in coping with life's stresses and needs.

Devotees have their individual family orisha but also revere a number of other powers, including Shango, Ogun, Orunmila, Oshun (Osun), Eshu, Obatala, Mama Latere (Mama Lata), Yemoja (Yemanja, Iemanja), Osayin (Osain/

Ozain), Shopona (Shakpana), Ibeji, Oya, Erele (Erinle), and Emanjie. The orisha were placed in symbiotic relationships with Roman Catholic saints as spiritual mediators. Syncretists ascribe attributes of Christian saints to African
divinities to mask Orisha practices by feigning devotion to entities such as
St. Jonas (or Erinle), St. Peter and St. Paul (Ibeji and Ibeja), and Jesus (Obatala).
These orisha, however, have their own personalities, likes, idiosyncrasies, and
ways of manifesting their presence in their devotees; devoted mediums become avatars (embodiments) of their bodily manifestation. Houk observes that
the orisha can be "stubborn, demanding, moody, proud, ostentatious, stoic,
merciful, loving, caring, concerned and matronly."[47] The fact that orishas defy
monolithic descriptions, can be unpredictable, and have a great sense of humor
shows imaginative thinking in African cosmology.

Black-Eyed Peas and Rice Powers

Do spirits dine, give performances with speeches, wear special apparel, carry
weapons, ride horses, sing, and dance? Orisha powers are made present in "educational toys," or implements, consisting of signs, symbols, tools, songs, colors,
as well as in action dances, weekdays, and foods they love; each orisha has a
special gourmet palate but also eats the staple peasant diet of black-eyed peas,
rice, and corn. The powers have their own mediums, called horses, whom they
ride or manifest through with regularity. These powers are both male and female actors who appear in performances and direct life in the Orisha community. They constitute an arbitrary hierarchy, and Frances Mischel claims their
ranks influence the status of their devotees.[48] The faithful conduct themselves
in such a manner as to render praise to the orisha and Olodumare, show respect
to the ancestors and elders of the community, and become persons of good
character. All aspects of life are under the control of the powers who are responsible for all human experiences—that is, tragedy or fortune.

OGUN AND SHANGO, CHIEF POWERS

Chief of the orisha and the archangels is Ogun (Ogoun), the all-powerful divinity, father of truth and justice, owner of roads, and protector of followers.
This fearless god of metal, war, technology, labor, sacrifice, and politics—whom
legend claims can move any mountain and is unconquerable—mimics battle
and aggression in menacing action. As the double of St. Michael, Ogun spends
much of his time diagnosing sickness, finding solutions to problems, and blessing devotees and the palais (sacred space) with the use of lavish amounts of
olive oil. He must be first at every ceremony; when he is too busy to attend, he
sends another in his place. He is the first manifestation) in a possession, and
many orisha songs are directed to him.[49] To devotees, Ogun's shrine is the first
among equals and is therefore the most frequented. In it, a cutlass is driven
into the earth or an iron tip protrudes. Frances Henry states, "This is a reference to the Yoruba myth of Ogun's use of an iron tool to carve out a path to link

the gods with mankind."[50] Ogun's other educational toys are a machete, a sword, red and white colors (he has a red flag on a bamboo pole), and rum. Ogun manifests in robust women as his avatar (bodily form) who, like him, command respect, fear, and reverence in the yard (house). He eats his black-eyed peas, rice, and corn with mutton (ram) and chicken.

The skilled and powerful warrior Shango (Chango, Nago Shango)—god of storms, lightning, fire, and thunder—has three impersonations: John the Evangelist, John of the Cross, and John the Baptizer. Shango is one of the two most dominant entities among the orisha and plays a prominent role in the faith; he is so highly respected that the Orisha religion bears his name. He also has his own religious cult, called Opa Orisa, which honors other Orisha spirits. Shango receives his full complement of adoration during special Orisha shrine rituals as worshipers sing to him and the other entities while a medium dances around a fire in one of his impersonations. On ritual occasions, when his help is being solicited, devotees display his colors while singing and dancing to his special song. Shango is also the recipient of various sacrifices, all of which consist of male animals and birds according to his special taste: bulls, rams, cocks, pigeons. He represents male sexuality and power and is hot-tempered and unpredictable, but he guards his devotees; he wills his double-headed ax and machete, which are to be kept as sharp as a razor's edge to show his protective power.[51]

SHAY-SHAY BROOM POWERS

The quiet power Osayin (Osain)—healer-god of the *omiero* (herbal medicines obtained from a liquid produced from sacred herbs), owner of the forest and bushes—is guardian and keeper of herbs needed for all ceremonies. Finding his double in three persona (St. Francis of Assisi, St. Francis Xavier, and Metaphi), Osayin is very protective of children and is sought by families for pediatric healing and blessing. His educational toys are the *shay-shay* broom, a cross, a lance, a turtle carapace, and a lit candle; he is present wherever a fire is lit. A morocoy and a white goat are Osayin's favorite animal sacrifices, and he manifests in physically trim devotees, wears yellow, and eats his black-eyed peas, rice, and corn with turtle and mutton.

Master of the sea Alreelay doubles as Jonah who, according to Hebrew legend, survived in a fish's belly. Like Jonah, he preaches with urgency and gives orders to maintain the cleanliness of the palais. Alreelay carries much authority, and one of the three horses he rides is a leader of the Shango cult. He carries olive oil for healing, a symbolic blue belt, and eats his black-eyed peas, rice, and corn with guinea bird.

Shakpana (Shoponna, Shakpata), also called Omolu and associated with Babalu Aye, is the son of Iemanja and the god of diseases like AIDS, leprosy, smallpox, and other epidemics. He is also the deity of health and of the earth's environment and doubles as St. Vincent, St. Jerome, St. George, or St. Raphael. His devotees must wear red when he is to manifest his presence. Because of his connection with sickness, evil, and prophetic utterances, many followers fear him. His representative swishes around with his *shay-shay* broom and eats his black-eyed peas, rice, and corn with male chicken and pigeon.[52]

FEMALE POWERS

In Trinidad and Tobago, followers of Orisha venerate three times as many male divinities as female ones. The most prominent female orisha are Yemanja (or Yemoja), Oshun, Omela, and Oya. Doubling as St. Anne, Yemanja (spelled twelve different ways and called by four different names), a derivative of Yemoja in Yorubaland, is the motherly side of the divine and the most powerful female orisha. She is the daughter of Obatala, the wife of Aganju, and the mother of all living people. As goddess of the hydrosphere, Yemanja governs streams, lakes, rivers, and oceans, where all life is said to begin. She is as calm and peaceful as the Caribbean Sea but can be as turbulent as its angry waves. She is naturally associated with ships, mariners, and piers and claims wealth as vast as the ocean. Yemanja's devotees wear the colors blue and white and carry the numeral seven. She has a special love for children and fiercely protects women. In one myth, she is one of Shango's concubines, but in another she is his mother. Yemanja's symbols and educational toys are an anchor, a harpoon, and a boat, but her medium or representative carries a calabash of water and an oar, with which she makes wave-like motions. This female power eats her black-eyed peas and rice with duck and pullet.[53]

Oshun (Osun, Oschun), another river goddess of love, sexuality, and intimacy, doubles as St. Philemon and St. Anne. She is said to be one of Shango's consorts and is a lover of the fine arts, especially ceremonial dance and drama. Women look to her for fertility and beauty, and she cautions against polluting her rivers and lakes. During the Oshun festival held in August every year, she is immortalized for her great powers as adherents praise her with drumming, dancing, singing, and votive offerings. Dressed in her favorite colors of yellow, white, blue, or pink, a female Trinidad representative of Oshun is a dazzling beauty. Her educational toys are a *coryal*, or "canoe," a goblet of water on her head, a ship's anchor, and symbols of wealth—expensive clothing, perfume, jewelry, and gold-plated items. Oshun likes her black-eyed peas, rice, and corn with a yard fowl or pigeon.

Less well known than Yemanja and Oshun are Oya (St. Catherine) and Omela (St. Michael), both consorts of Shango and Ogun. Oya (Oia, sometimes Iansa, Yansa, Iansan) is a warrior goddess of angry elements (hurricanes; wind, hail, and dust storms; inclement weather), and has a boisterous or Amazonian temperament that earns her masculine characteristics. Legend says she is a formidable sorcerer and a goddess of underworld entrances who keeps evil beings in confinement. A representative of Oya must be an accomplished dancer who is said to move as gracefully as the wind. Green and red objects and a hatchet are among her educational toys, and she too eats her black-eyed peas, rice, and corn with chicken and pigeon.

Omela, Mother of the Earth, has no special saint double but is represented as a stooped old woman. She carries a brown calabash of water to quench the thirst of devotees or to wash the unclean in the palais. She too eats the staple orisha dish.[54] Sought occasionally in domestic relations (family, marriage, common-law unions, and divorce) is the goddess Oba (Obba), the daughter of Yemanja and the possessive wife of Shango.

PEACEFUL POWERS

Elofa (Aba Lofa), Eternal Father, is a patron of the chief Orisha-Shango leader. He is much revered, and gracefully manifests only on his horse (an old man). He dresses in white but carries blood from a cow's head to anoint and bless followers in the chapelle. Elofa holds a ritual for children, to whom he gives gifts. His toys are a cane, a cattle head, candles, and olive oil. Elofa eats black-eyed peas, rice, and corn with beef.

Orunmilla (also Erunmila, Orunla, and Ifa) is the orisha of divinatory wisdom, foresight, and destiny, who guides his priests with the power of knowledge. He ordains the babalawo priests, to whom he commits the sixteen kola nuts or cowrie shells of divination, and is therefore one of the most influential orishas. The green and yellow colors won by his devotees announce his sought-after presence.

The little-known Omira, a chief archangel, doubles as St. Raphael and is a friend of hunters. His educational toys are a wooden gun, the colors pink and lilac, a ham sack over his shoulder, and a flambeau or oil lamp made of bamboo. He eats his black-eyed peas, rice, and corn with yard chicken.[55]

Also, among the peaceful powers is Eshu (also called Elegba and Elegbara), the trickster or ritual prankster mistakenly identified with the devil. As the gatekeeper to the spirit world, Eshu doubles as St. Peter, but he is flirtatious around women, who often seek physical contact with him as well as his blessings to bring on fertility and good luck. He eats his black-eyed peas and rice with an assortment of meats. Myth has it that he impersonates other orisha, among whom he can cause mischief and discord; therefore he must be ritually dismissed or ejected before other powers arrive at a ceremony.[56] After Eshu's ejection, Ogun is invited to the meeting, followed by other powers in a male-then-female pecking order.

In Yards (Shrines) of the Gods

Unlike African shrines that can be carried as small objects, a Trinidad and Tobago Orisha shrine or yard is a court (or sacred space) in which can be found equipment for the leading powers, a chapelle (one or two ten-foot-square rooms), an adjoining room or church-house, a kitchen, and tombs. The chapelle contains many altars and symbolic implements of the saints and gods. It also shelters the palais, an annexed tent or open part of the building where rituals and ceremonies are performed and where most of the singing, dancing, and drumming take place; in some cases, the palais is the center or the church. Candles burn at the four corners, where libations and offerings of olive oil and water are made to the deities as necessary. At the other end, facing the drummers, Ogun's sword is planted in the earth, with candles, bottles of olive oil, and water positioned around the blade. Wooden structures house an array of sacred paraphernalia that reveal the symbiotic relationship between Orisha and Christianity: statues and lithographs of Catholic saints, thunderstones, crucifixes, rosaries, and many vases of flowers. Also among these are tools and weapons of the powers: swords, axes, cutlasses, clubs, hatchets, daggers, whips, fake guns and spears, bows and arrows, boat paddles, anchors, banners, wooden crosses, *shay-shay* brooms, *chac-chacs* (rattles), and even shepherds' crooks. In a corner of the yard or shrine is the *perogun*, an open triangular structure housing statues of the orisha. Here the faithful plant several twenty-foot bamboo poles bearing a number of multicolored flags that are considered "a conduit through which spirits may visit the shrine. It is here in this corner too that the slaying of any sacrificial animal takes place"[57] during the feast.

Participation in the cultus is loose, and followers frequently make pilgrimages from one yard or shrine to another, often traveling a long distance to celebrate a feast. Confirmation as a devotee is done through initiation, which is the most important rite of membership. Followers may hold dual membership in the Spiritual Baptist or another Africanized faith. Social organization of a yard or shrine consists of a *mongba or iya* (male or female) called *baba olorisha* ("priest and spiritual head") supported by elders, mothers, and children or servants of the yard. Male babas, sometimes pejoratively called Pa Neezers[58] (obeah-men), outnumber female ones about five to one, and each one has his or her own yard. The responsibility is theirs to generate economic resources to found new yards and to maintain old ones; founders of new yards or shrines usually have the means or property to create the cultic centers. A shortage of leaders in Orisha may force two or three yards into a loose association or circuit served by one baba and brought together in the annual feast. This allows a small group of leaders to govern the larger body and provides a stream of revenue to support the babas.

Myth and Rituals

Most babas claim to have received a call, through a dream of vision, to leadership in the yard or shrine. As Frances Mischel observed, some leaders designate their spouse to succeed them; others appoint whoever is second-in-command. The successor must be a follower of the same "power" (spirit) as her predecessor. If a leader appointed no one as successor, a baba from another group conducts a succession rite during which the spirit of the deceased is dismissed ritually. Whoever gets a message from the "power" of the dead leader assumes leadership of the yard. If no one takes on the leadership role, the sacred objects in the chapelle are given to another yard and the community and shrine disband.[59]

Babas oversee ritual activities and worship at the yard or shrine, direct the annual feasts, give consultations, and perform healings. Equipped with an array of symbols of the spirits, tools for divination, and colorful candles in the yard, priests lead devotees in worship to communicate with their orisha. They say Yoruba prayers and dance to spirited music with the *chac-chacs* and African drums, three of which must always be present in every ritual. Trinidad and Tobago Rastas love to beat Orisha drums to authentic African music.

Orisha's liturgical calendar is never uneventful. Rites and rituals are performed routinely and include the initiatory rituals of head washing and head gashing, the "laying" of (installing) a stool for an orisha, "planting" a flag near a stool, relocating a stool to another site, consecrating a new set of drums, making a feast, dismissing an orisha power, installing a new baba, and spirit possession. Most of these require the making of a sacrifice, animal or otherwise. Ceremonies mark various ritual cycles: birth, marriage, death, and initiation into Orisha. These are open to people of all faiths, without discrimination on the basis of ethnicity, gender, class, or creed. However, foreigners, law enforcement, and other government agents are held suspect and may be prevented from entering ceremonies, which are often marked by a period of intense rituals, fasting, and prayer. Orisha prayers are offered at all ceremonies and often begin with the Lord's Prayer, the Hail Mary, and the Apostle's Creed. The leader may also say a prayer to St. Francis, St. George, or another saint while the drum beats softly to prayerful music, either African or Christian. When the drum changes beat from a Christian to a Yoruba song or chant, the leader offers African prayers inviting an orisha to visit the shrine.[60] Since the 1970s, prayers have become more African as the faithful attempt to make the faith distinctly Yoruba. During the prayers at the Ebo feast, songs are sung to Eshu, Ogun, Shango, Osain, Shakpana, Emanje, Oshun, and Erele, in that order.

The Ebo Feast

Each Orisha yard or shrine stages a major ceremony at about the same time each year. Established yards celebrate the annual *Ebo* (called the Feasts) in honor of the orisha who are summoned to the community for action. At some yards, the feast celebrating different occasions may last an entire week and is followed by the dilogun ritual two weeks later. The week-long *Ebo* attracts many participants and visitors and is a time to pray, make sacrifices, show gratitude to the orisha, celebrate with song and dance from midnight till dawn, and see the spirits manifest themselves in possession trance. The feast begins on Sunday night with the lighting of Eshu's fiery flame as a signal for the opening prayer. Eshu, the messenger deity and trickster, is fed and symbolically dismissed outside of the ceremonial area to make room for other deities. This is followed through the night by drumming (ogun drums), singing, and dancing that are accompanied by spirit possession.[61] In the morning, the Obi, or priest, climaxes the ritual with a sacrificial offering for Yemanja (Yemoja) and Erunmila. Ogun-

Kangun-Dangun is the recipient of the offering made on Monday night in a ritual that lasts until Tuesday morning. Devotees salute the African ile and earth spirit, Mama La Terre, who mothers us all and to whose bosom we all return in death. From Wednesday night through Thursday morning, Osayin, Ibeji, and Erinle receive their offerings while the faithful greet the great healer spirit who knows the secret of herbs. On Thursday night, a white sheep sacrifice is made to Shango while drums speak his language. On Friday, followers celebrate, cook, and offer heavily salted foods to the spirits, relate stories of the deeds of the orisha, learn and sing new chants, and receive oracles through possessed mediums. On Saturday, most celebrants depart the Ebo feeling energized by the powers, but some may visit other Ebos in neighboring yards.[62]

Possession Trance

In Orisha, spirit possession is an indispensable ritual for the functioning and credibility of the cult. In spirit possession, transcendent deities become immanent among the people; the sacred is made manifest in humans, and claims made about the gods are substantiated. Deities accept the sacrifices, answer prayers, control the heads of possessed mediums, bring a sense of awe and reverence to worshipers, and may reveal the fate of an individual or of the group. Spirit possession is filled with ritual drama, strange and unpredictable behavior, surprises, and suspense. As Henry notes, highly respected mediums under possession show much aggression, give orders in the manner of drill sergeants, trod the ceremonial space, and make themselves the center of attraction. Others of little importance are so subdued that their possession occurs with little notice. This shows that this spiritual activity is a vehicle of social stratification within the faith. The frequency of possession, the number of orisha that possess the medium, their rank in the divine hierarchy, the speed with which they possess devotees, and the value of one's spiritual gifts and resources all converge to bring them more attention and a higher status in the religion.[63]

The ritual of possession reaches an important stage when it is time for a medium or a ceremonial assistant to pour water, incense, or alcohol in all four corners of the palais. The drumming, dancing, chanting, and moaning-type prayers charge the air with heightened expectation. In a frenzied moment, an orisha arrives to take possession of the head of its horse, the medium. As possession sets in, the medium runs to the appropriate spot in the chapelle, takes hold of the important symbols of his or her primary deity, and brandishes them with movements and facial expressions mimicking the specific orisha. Women dressed in white clear the way for the horse being ridden by the spirit, divest him or her of any sharp-edged jewelry around the neck that might cause harm to anyone in the service, and tie a full length of red cloth around the horse's waist and shoulder. The red indicates that he or she could be in danger of the spirit or could be dangerous as a vessel of the orisha. An orisha medium may fall and writhe on the ground in uncontrollable spasms, even slash his or her garment, and dance or sing an appropriate deity's song. Myth has it that some men dance on live coal and broken glass without feeling pain. At the height of possession, the medium moves in a flash from a state of suspended consciousness and speaks with authority and gesticulation.

According to Mischel, "The specific behavior of a power is said to be a function of what activity he or she was engaged in at the time of being summoned."[64] The medium may speak a prophetic word to the shrine, reveal some unknown problem, warn of disaster, or suggest an appropriate course of action to be taken.[65] If the riding spirit is Shango, he examines his flock with emotive facial expression while the ritual Mother brings forward a candlelit dish containing his sacred thunderstone and sweet olive oil. She stands before Shango while members take turns kneeling before him and receiving his blessings. Since Shango is the spiritual leader's deity, respect for the shepherd's authority is reaffirmed in the ritual and in the presence of the spirit. The ceremony may continue all night with blessing, dancing, singing, drumming, and repeated outbursts of spirit possession until dawn. The exhausted, sleep-deprived medium is elated over her great spiritual experience but she neither remembers any of her actions during possession nor feels any pain or injury. The ritual ends with the sacrifice of an animal or a bird (a pigeon, dove, chicken, or duck), depending on the client's means and resources and on the occasion.[66]

Divination Healing

They come for exorcism, for medication, for divination, for help in financial and other matters, to get new cars or houses blessed. They come in a never ending stream; the Hindu Pundits, the holder of Kali Pujas, the French Creole business men, the bank clerk wanting to trap a man into marriage. They all come [as Christian, Muslim, African, Hindu]. They come to make dry or blood offerings, they come to learn about the religion, and they come out of curiosity.[67]

Like spirit possession, divination healing (through conjuring, folk medicine, and consultation) is the trademark activity in Orisha; the practice is a necessity for the cult's esprit de corps and survival. Healers perform this ritual to prevent sickness and tragedy, cure illness, assure good luck, and even punish malevolent persons and spirits, but the ritual also provides material support for the center; patrons provide revenue in the form of fees and gifts in exchange for good consultations and through the purchase of healing paraphernalia from the center. Clients of diverse faiths in rural areas, especially those with limited access to medical care or who receive little help from modern medicine, seek out healers as their last lifeline in times of desperation. Some boast of their refusal to consult modern physicians; others seek both nontraditional healers and modern medicine for a specific illness or the same condition.[68] In New Hampshire (Grenada), where I grew up, patrons (even from Christian churches) discreetly paid nocturnal visits to the leader or "shepherd" (healer, herbalist, and obeah specialist) who lived in my neighborhood. The well-known Spiritual Baptist healer received clients from different parts of the island in droves. Some clients traveled long distance and found accommodation at his oversized home as they waited their turn for a healing consultation.

The healer's office and knowledge allows him or her to exercise sole prerogatives in healing performances. He claims his healing powers come from God and were received through personal communication with the spirits in dreams, visions, divination, or a traumatic experience. The spirits also give the healer the gift of knowledge and reveal the diagnoses, types of healing pharmacopeia, spiritual counsel she should give, and the kind of sacrifice clients must offer for their healing ritual. As Mischel notes, however, healers inherit the art from their families or learn it from others in the cult, as well as through a variety of secular and religious sources. The proper preparation of some herbal medications is common knowledge among the working class. Healers also use the Bible, prayer books, Napoleon's *Book of Fate*, the *Home Physician's Guide*, and exotic texts to aid them in their craft.[69]

Orunmila, the god of Ifa divination and wisdom, does not play as significant a role in Orisha in Trinidad and Tobago as he does in Santeria. Simpson holds that in the absence of direct access to knowledge, from Ifa techniques, of causes and cures for sickness and problems, priests substitute the art of "looking," "seeing," or "reading" with crystal balls, cards, sacred leaves, "dreams, visions, and prophecy," and possessed mediums to pursue their craft. Herbal medicine is rarely performed without sacred leaves in its healing formula. The leaves are boiled, ground, or mixed with water and one of many oils for ingestion, baths, or potions. The beating of drums hastens the arrival of the spirits "when a healer undertakes to cure a person who is seriously ill, especially one who is thought to be possessed by an evil spirit."[70] Whether the medicine formulae are innocuous or dangerous, the faithful swear by them.

Healing takes many forms, the most common of which are (1) consultation or counseling and pharmacopeia, (2) anointing with oil, (3) petitioning the spirit's aid while vigorously hand-stroking the patient in the affected area, (4) exorcising an evil spirit, (5) making protective potions or "bundles for retributive justice," and (6) "reading" or "seeing" into one's circumstances. Healing may address psychological, physical, social, or emotional problems and often involves ingesting medicines and taking herbal baths intended to cleanse a patient of negative influences, protect him or her from the evil eye or an imminent danger, and cure a specific malady or mental imbalance. All of these require an offering or sacrifice of gratitude to the spirit in return. Healing methods differ among Orisha, Shouter Baptists, and Christian healers. Christians use no drums or animal sacrifice during healing performance, make anointing with oil optional, and use no water, candles, or special healing garments. They emphasize, instead, prayer, faith, belief in Christ and biblical texts, and the laying on of hands. In Orisah, a consultation is necessary to determine the diagnosis and remedy, which may be revealed during spirit possession. Followers claim that multiple healing occurs during worship and feast celebrations,[71] but claims of healing results may be regarded askance.

Conclusion

Orisha, like other Afro-Caribbean religions, is an institution of resistance—not to slavery, with which Trinidad and Tobago had a relatively short experience, but to colonial cultural hegemony, race discrimination, and economic deprivation. The religion came into prominence through free blacks of West African origin working in the emerging cosmopolitan British colony with its cultural diversity, multiplicity of faiths, an economically and socially stratified society, racial prejudice, and the political and religious elitism of the ruling class. Surviving many attempts to silence it as *religio ilicita* up to the 1900s, Orisha survives as a vibrant alternative spirituality to the dominant classical religions in Trinidad and Tobago (Christianity, Hinduism, and Islam) and claims to be the country's most authentic African religious expression. In recent times, Orisha followers in Trinidad and Tobago have attempted to make the religion more African by requiring a Yoruba standard in their ritual. Yoruba prayers are given prominence over Christian prayers at Orisha ceremonies and at the Ebo feast for the gods. At the feast, the spiritual leader (*mongba* or *iya*) sings a Yoruba litany and leads Yoruba prayers. As James Houk observes, prayers offered to Shango and Ogun were "taken from a collection of Yoruba prayers with English translations compiled by Orisa (sic) Youth Organization."[72] Also, the Yoruba language is used extensively in Orisha. For example, "worshipers recited much of the liturgy in languages other than Yoruba, such as French patois and English. Today, many worshipers are emphasizing Yoruba and consider it the proper language of orisha worship"; whereas in the past only the leader could conduct worship in Yoruba, "the goal of some individuals is to popularize a Yoruba liturgy so that all worshipers can follow the rite."[73] Even if it is reduced to mere folk traditions, Orisha promises to remain an important part of the culture of Trinidad and Tobago. Long live Orisha (Shango).

PART V

Jamaica's Creole Religions

Culture of Resistance and Rhythms

11

Obeah

Magical Art of Resistance

The village where I was born in Grenada was rife with Obeah paranoia. Two Spiritual Baptist Shepherds known to be Obeah priests, Shep and Sister Oglala, lived in my little hamlet. As kids we were taught to avoid going near the Shepherds' home and never to accept gifts from them or their followers. In seventh grade, Shep's eighth-grade daughter, Monica, and I had an after-school street brawl, which she initiated and won. With the help of three bully friends, Monica beat me mercilessly with moccasins and school bags and left me with black eyes and a bloody nose; but I was not ready to roll over and lick my wounds. Later that evening, I waited in ambush for her return from a Girls' Guide meeting and stealthily greeted her with a swinging gourd whip. Monica's torn uniform and swollen arms, back, and legs showed the results. When my mother learned of my altercation, she was petrified and scolded me soundly: "You are bringing the wrath of the Shepherd on our family." In fear and trembling, Mom hastily took me over to the Obeah-man's house to apologize to Monica before, as she said, "he jinx us with a curse." I was so horrified that my knees buckled, my heart pounded in my chest, and I wet myself. Imagine how relieved I was when Shep accepted my apology for whipping Monica. He merely scolded me, "Keep your distance from her!" Nearly everyone in New Hampshire kept their distance from the Obeah-man; although he was a Spiritual Baptist leader and was held to be a good healer and diviner, he represented a menacing sciénce (connection to the spirit world).

Constructs of Obeah

I grew up in an environment in which we believed the more than two-hundred-fifty-year-old colonial myth that Obeah is an evil, antisocial magic practiced by

The spirit of Obeah.
(Illustration by Kelly Hawes.)

uneducated, religiously misguided, or mentally imbalanced people of African origin—colonial snobbery held widely by the offspring of colonizers and by us, descendants of the colonized, who knew precious little about Obeah. It was only after I began graduate studies in Caribbean history and culture at the University of the West Indies (Trinidad and Tobago) that I saw Obeah, like other African spiritualities, as an art or practice with which Caribbean peoples access streams of mystical power to negotiate the historical contradictions of their lives. The words *Obeah*, *Obeah-woman*, and *Obeah-man* are still foreboding; they represent the practice of a deadly science and "evil magic, from a "heathenish" African people. In colonial culture, *Obeah-man* signified the iniquitous divination of uncivilized Africans, despised traditional healers, "Vodou works," and any African religious activities that gave colonists consternation and threatened their socioeconomic base.[1]

Alan Richardson notes that since the Romantic era, the British ascribed to Obeah Vodou characteristics, viewing it as an evil mysterious cult of obscure African provenance that employed the demonic as well as erotic indulgence. Before Vodou entered the English vocabulary, Obeah portended any religious beliefs or practices among Africans that did not fit the Euro-Christian ilk and gave colonists nightmares of revolt; this included most African religious be-liefs.[2] In the postslavery era, Obeah remained a serious Caribbean preoccupa-tion and was given sinister characteristics regionally in British colonies, where it is still banned. Today, Obeah continues to be perceived as a mysterious cult and a menacing conduit to harmful spiritual powers in popular Caribbean thought. Religionist Leonard Barrett mused that Obeah is "the most dreadful form of Caribbean witchcraft plaguing both Blacks and Whites in the days of slavery and continuing to haunt Jamaicans today."[3] Obeah still rivals Vodou as an object of fear and a symbol of evil in modern Caribbean culture.

Caribbean people have a love-hate relationship with Obeah; they secretly embrace its herbal medicine, divinatory practices, and mystical power (magic spells) in times of critical need and crisis but publicly deride and shun it as a cabal of evil. This makes it a satirical pariah in pop culture. The Carnival hit song "Melda" by the Mighty Sparrow, the Trinidad King of Calypso (born in my home country, Grenada), is a classic satire on the power and character of Obeah in the southern Caribbean. In "Melda," a desperate, sensual, but unkempt woman uses Obeah magic to try to induce her intimate partner into a connu-bial relationship. Sparrow, representing the diffident lover, responds with great confidence in the magical protection he gets from his own Obeah-man to as-suage Melda's Obeah works. He tells Melda that by searching throughout the country for Obeah until her perspiration smells like cow's dung, she is turning herself into a "pappy show" and a "bloody clown" and that she is only wasting her time, because she will never be able to make her Obeah wedding bells chime by trying to trap him with necromancy (Mighty Sparrow, "Melda," 1960). Sparrow's "Melda" is colored by the typical Caribbean cultural male androg-yny, as are most calypsos, but it highlights the pervasiveness of Obeah in the region and the conceptions of its powerful spells and magic, which, in our his-torical memory, have been a source of much foreboding, disdain, controversy, and confusion.

Sparrow's "Melda" is colored by the typical Caribbean cultural male an-drogyny, as are most calypsos, but highlights the pervasiveness of Obeah in the region and the conceptions of its powerful spells and magic, which, in our his-torical memory, have been a source of much foreboding, disdain, controversy, and confusion.

The lyrics of the song "Obeah-man" ("I am not an Obeah-man, I am a Rasta-man, I am the righteous one. . . . I do not study iniquity") highlight the long-standing perception of Obeah as iniquitous. Leonard Howell, one of the founders of the avant garde Rastafari, gave credence to the myth in the early 1930s. His notoriously slanderous monograph, *The Promised Key* (1935)—perhaps the most poorly written book in the Caribbean—launched as scathing an attack on Obeah as it did on Catholic Christianity. Howell exemplifies the Rastafarian disdain for Obeah[4] and comically associates it with the sins of Babylon and the epitome of the evil governments of Jamaica and the West. Kevin Aylmer observes that in the more recent Rastafarian movie *Countryman*—a tale of duplicity, betrayal, and "good triumphing over evil"—Obeah becomes the source of evil and poverty. Countryman, who represents the good forces, battles the forces of Babylon, especially "the Obeahman whose cultivation of the occult upsets the elemental lifestyles of 'the sufferahs,' the poor masses. These sufferahs are attuned to the rhythms of nature, reggae, custom, and community,"[5] true elements of the good, as a way of overcoming evil Obeah.

I am not surprised that an Afro-Caribbean religious avenue of spiritual empowerment and means of resistance to oppression should be maligned by Caribbean artists chanting liberation rhythms from subjugation. There are varied and conflicting views and definitions of Obeah among Caribbean people, many of whom know little about its true provenance. The religion is influenced by two strands of African beliefs and practices: one connected to sorcery and witchcraft and the other to esoteric magic.[6] Then there is the evil paradigm and public disdain for the practice and the art, influenced by both European and African views. One African view of Obeah regards it as "essentially the worship of evil as formerly represented by the Ashanti devil, *Sasabonsam*— a monster, grotesque and malicious," a character "associated with the woods and, in particular, the odum tree which he uses as headquarters from which he captivates unwary hunters"[7] and persons who get lost in the forest. According to legend, such creatures fly through the air, suck the blood of their victims from a distance, radiate light from their anus, turn into animals, and cannibalize children. Legend has it that to recognize them "it is necessary to carry around their corpses after death, hints here of divination from the appearance of the body, such as we have found surviving in Guiana."[8] These myths of evil Obeah and the idea of its use as a dreaded science in black resistance to slavery were enough to make it the object of legislative prohibitions, satire, and racial and religious stereotypes.

Many scholars (Barbara Bush, Werner Zip, Joseph Murphy, Barry Chevannes, and so forth) accept the Obeah versus Myal tradition—that is, the idea that Myalists who reasserted their authority over the proper use of spiritual power sought to stamp out Obeah from the community by exposing what they saw as Obeah's illegitimate uses. Like religious purists, anti-Obeah Myal followers are said to have launched attacks on Obeah-men, destroyed their ritual paraphernalia, and developed a system of finding antidotes to Obeah. As a result, postemancipation Jamaican communities saw Myal-men as the "good guys" who helped people fight and find cures for the "bad works" of Obeah. Whenever the Obeah practitioner was seen as violating moral codes of society with "destructive works" by "putting Obeah" on someone, the Myalist was said to "pull the Obeah" and reversed "the consequences of obeah actions as a counterforce."[9] Chevannes contends that when anti-Obeah feelings reached the point of hysteria in the community, Myal-men led followers on Obeah hunts at night. During the "Great Myal Procession of 1842," spirit-possessed devotees followed their leaders in a frenzy reminiscent of the great witch hunts in Europe, harassing Obeah-men, seeking out sacred places and objects of Obeah, and destroying them while symbolically releasing duppy ("ghost" or "spirit") shadows of persons in the community believed to be bewitched by Obeah. Practitioners thus hid their craft from whites and from black Myal purists, but occasionally they were ordered to dig up obeah medicines from their premises[10] and burn them to destroy Obeah.

Based on her extensive study of Jamaican religions in 2005, Dianne Stewart sees in this tradition a Myal fight not against "evil Obeah," but against the misuse or evil use of the practice. "The Myalists of this 1842 movement were actually combating the evil manipulation of Obeah, that is, *obeye* (natural mystical power)." Stewart continues, "In ancient Akan societies, the struggle between good and evil was a struggle between good and ill human will, between persons who accessed *obeye* for beneficent ends (*obirifo or okomfo*) and those who accessed *obeye* for malevolent ends (*obayifo*)."[11] The U.S.-Jamaican scholar describes Obeah elegantly as a set of religious practices (oath taking, prayers, divination, healing, sacrifices) exercised to negotiate mystical spiritual powers. It is an institution with "capacity to use energy dynamically" and requiring special knowledge gained naturally or through training. "As the sum of its parts, Obeah is a religious institution reflecting not one particular continental ethnic African religion but the synthetic institutionalization of Pan-African religious institutions on Jamaican soil."[12]

This view of Obeah is admittedly revisionist; it sets out to recast the paradigms of the dominant historical view of the art perpetuated in the region *via negativa*. Stewart contests "established meanings and assumptions associated with each tradition and thus reassesses the cultural, theological, and historical rubrics for conceptualizing Obeah and Myal"[13] in Caribbean religious experience. Obeah enables powerless Africans to access forces that could aid them in regaining control of their lives. "It also allowed them to exercise control over other people and invisible forces, functioning . . . as a system for checking and balancing power";[14] with it, one could unleash retribution against any offending party in the larger society. As was done with Vodou at the onslaught of the Haitian Revolution, the Obeah oath was a well-known signifying tool used in rallying the troops for slave revolts, in Jamaica, Trinidad, and the Guyanas.[15]

Obeah is a set of religious practices designed to help persons in distress deal with foreboding circumstances, respond to tragedy, or fight for their survival and freedom. The art and practice are based on a belief that mysterious and powerful forces inhabit the phenomenal world and that they can be seduced to work for the benefit, or harm, of a needy individual; they can affect a person's life and destiny for good or ill. Although Obeah is a self-centered and self-preserving religious magical art performed with the use of charms, spells, prayers, and other spiritual services, it has often been deployed for corporate social action. It was used first by slaves, and later by their descendants, to secure justice and revenge on other Africans and colonists who controlled,[16] exploited, or abused them. This religious system is neither inherently evil nor completely innocuous; it provides services to clients who believe in its efficacy but may also affect others negatively. As Ivor Morrish explains, through this art, one can seek personal desires, treat poor health, secure good fortune, "turn the affections of the objects of his love or lust towards himself, evince retribution or revenge upon his enemies, and generally manipulate the spiritual forces of the cosmos in order to obtain his will."[17] To effect this erstwhile manipulation, a practitioner uses medicine endowed with sacred powers that can be harnessed for both healthy and punitive purposes.

Obeah operates with coded[18] magic and healing pharmacopeia and also may deploy esoteric artilleries of sorcery, prescience, and witchcraft to accomplish its purposes. Practitioners work undercover and at nights because they are seen as evildoers working against the harmony and welfare of community life and dabbling in iniquity. They work in the realm of the mysterious, and their craft appears supernatural, but it is not miraculous; its magic art and spells are learned tricks to bring about a desired action. Obeah is fluid and operates outside of constricted boxes of traditional ways of being and of conceiving the religious life. The invisible institution is largely an oral tradition,[19] without its own sacred space, religious organization, and ritual professionals; it functions within other religious traditions and among varying ethnic groups and is not restricted by race, class, or creed.

Obeah Africana

The African origination of Obeah is not in question, but its precise country of origin and meaning are the subject of ongoing discussion. The art was common among the Efik, Akan, Edo, and Twi ethnic groups[20] of West Africa; and scholars say it is derived from the Twi word *obeye*, a minor deity associated with the Fanti-Ashanti *Obboney*, the malicious spirit of the Rada or Dahomey sacred powers.[21] The use of the word *obayi* or *obaye* is seen as evidence of the influence of the Ashanti people in Jamaica and other Caribbean states; the most well-known "freedom fighters in the British colonies were . . . the Ashantis."[22] Ashanti and Twi-speaking peoples whom slave-traders labeled Koromantyns were taken from the Gold Coast to the British colonies rather than to French islands or the Spanish main. Koromantyns were freedom fighters, and British slave markets accepted them when other depots did not. Morrish adds that "*obayi*, or the practice of witchcraft among these tribes, was taken to Jamaica and became an esoteric possession of the slaves which they did not share with the whites but which, nevertheless, they could use for personal advantage against their captors. The word *obayi* was creolized into *obeah, obiah or obia*, and the form *obi* was also used.[23] This, of course, is not an airtight argument. Obeah is associated also with two Ashanti root words: *oba* ("child") and *yi* ("to take or snatch"). An *obayi*'s practitioner is said to be an *obayifo*, a "child snatcher." Legend has it that the last stage in becoming a witch is the snatching of a child from a distance and then killing it by simply dispatching an evil spirit in its direction.

In western Africa, Obeah is associated with the use of magical powers, derived from both good and evil African spirits. A sorcerer or necromancer is not always an Obeah-man and may or may not be different from an African priest or priestess. In Ghana, for example, the Akan okomfo (priest) who works like a cleric, religious social worker, and counselor, is held to be more acceptable socially than the obayifo. The okomfo also is said to counteract the evil works or malfeasance of the obayifo, who is regarded as a worshiper of the evil spirit Sasabonsam. Africans "guarded themselves against the machinations of the obayifo by wearing *suman* (amulets or charms) which were often provided by the okomfo. Sometimes the aid of a *bonsam komfo* (witch doctor) was enlisted to unearth the obayifo and to render his work ineffective."[24] Thus, according to Roger Bastide, "The term signifying magic, *obeah*, is quite certainly derived from the Ashanti word *obayifo*, which bears the same meaning. 'Obeah-men' are generally male, but there do exist a few 'obeah-women' too. Their business is to prepare objects that are meant to kill, or cure, or procure someone's love. Such objects are called *obi* (we should not forget that the Ashanti priest in Africa is known as *Obi O Komfo*).[25] These arguments differentiate an obayifo from an okomfo and give the former a negative character and origination.

I find no absolute certainty, as Bastide and others claim, that the obayifo works only on behalf of individual clients for a fee, works mainly with evil magic to bring others harm, and takes revenge on those who are in an antagonistic relationship with him; any African spiritualist could do that. The priest or priestess, for example, is a mediator between the divinities and the tribal peoples, fills social roles, and officiates at religious ceremonies that are public or communal affairs, but who works for individuals. *Obi, obeye,* okomfo and obayifo are geographical (not moral) African sources in the evolution of the word *Obeah-man,* and the art evolved in interaction with other Caribbean religions with no special appetite for evil works. Stewart and others correctly challenge this, apparently sure notion of the West African origination of Obeah that causes it to be labeled strictly evil or antisocial magic. Stewart finds in the Twi word *obeye* "a more fitting cognate in that it signifies the concept of 'moral neutrality' in its original usage and because it is closer in terms of pronunciation to the Jamaican term 'Obeah' than *obayifo*"[26] it has the potential for both good and evil.

Stewart has received much applause for taking "the lead in expanding interpretive discourse on Obeah in academic and popular imaginations, to at least include competing construals of the Obeah phenomenon" to expunge "the older paradigm of Obeah amounting to evil magic"[27] from Caribbean peoples' consciousness. Given the peculiar nature of the practice—as an oral tradition tied to colonialism and popularized in our people's mythology—it will always be open to interpretation and new constructs in Caribbean culture. The idea of an *obi,* when combined with *okomfo,* often describes a priest who works magic with fetishes; a sharp distinction between the Obeah-man and the priest has never been clear to Caribbean people of any ethnic group. In Afro-Caribbean religions, practitioners often combine the roles of the priest, the medium, the herbalist, and the medicine woman or medicine man who works with herbal recipes. The Obeah-men I encountered in northern Trinidad and in Grenada seem to have occupied all four offices, even when other persons qualified for these roles were in their religious circles. The healer and the Obeah-man are often one and the same; some Obeah-men are more renowned for healing than others. Clients seek the same practitioner for consultation on cures for sickness, solutions to social problems, help to avenge their enemies, and obtaining charms and amulets so that they can ward off spells cast by any evil spirit. Priests often practice works associated with Obeah-men. In the past, both the okomfo and the obayifo wielded powerful influence over Africans, but the African *Sasabonsam*, or invisible *sasa*, became synonymous with Obeah-men in the Caribbean.

Obeah is clearly an African religious art and practice that survived colonial Caribbean culture. In 1794, Bryan Edwards wrote, "As far as we are able to decide from our own experience and information when we lived in the island . . . professors of *Obi* are . . . natives of Africa, and none other; and they have brought the science with them from thence to Jamaica where it is so universally [practised], that we believe there are few of the larger estates . . . which have not one or more of them."[28] Elaine Savory holds that the practices "were transformed in the crucible of slavery into spiritual support for the Afro-Caribbean community"[29] and continue to be a living curiosity in creole religions in the region. Obeah carriers who were brought to the Caribbean preserved their skills by passing them on orally to the younger generation. In the early period, slaves learned new herbal remedies by sharing the same plantation or cabin space, where they covertly sought advice of known medical specialists and healers. Obeah slave practitioners used the art to intimidate others who had a habit of plundering huts, hog sties, and garden plots. British colonists laughed at these benign gadgets "contrived by the more sagacious for deterring the more simple and superstitious blacks, and serving for much the same purpose as the scare-crows" used among English farmers and gardeners.[30]

Obeah Colonial

During colonial times, Obeah was practiced in Maroon communities among free Africans, poor whites, and slaves on plantations. Maroons who absconded to the mountains after 1655, during Britain's occupation of Jamaica, used Obeah and Myal magic while enlisting the help of African spirits in their resistance to the colonists. For decades, these independent Maroons resisted British culture, celebrated their African traditions, and developed their own religious beliefs[31] away from the gaze of whites. Steadman recalls a Guiana Maroon who, trusting in the power of his Obeah amulet, believed he was invulnerable. He climbed a tree and fired several rounds at approaching militia-men until he was shot down. "The soldier instantly advancing, and putting the muzzle of his musket to the rebel's ear, blew out his brains, while several of his countrymen, in spite of their spells and charms, shared the same fate."[32] Ac-cording to a Jamaica legend, the Maroon slave revolutionary leader Tacky was "invested with the further power of catching shots which were fired at him and of returning them to his opponents. The obeahmen themselves held they were immune to injury and even to death on the battlefield."[33] In these cases, Ma-roon faith conflicted with reality and the results were fatal.

As Richardson notes, Obeah facilitated "resistance and revolt among the slaves: it provoked an 'ideological rallying point' in sanctioning rebellion, af-forded meeting places and leaders, and formed a repository for the collective memory of the slaves by preserving African traditions which could be opposed to the dominant colonial culture."[34] Obeah's peculiar acts of resistance occa-sionally required violence: aiding slave revolts, poisoning a master or a slave snatcher, and "fixing" an overseer with a fatal illness or paralysis. Practitioners of Obeah cultivated psychic powers of aggression and prepared poisons that planters and overseers dreaded.[35] The subversive influence of Obeah was evi-dent in the slave revolts of the 1700s. In the 1760 Maroon uprising led by Tacky, the influence of those who professed the art of Obeah was so strong that it in-duced many slaves in the parish of St. Mary, Jamaica, to rise up in a rebellion. Tacky, a freedom fighter of the Koromantyne group, claimed that he was an African chief and had secured the help of an Obeah-man in the struggle. As Bisnauth contends, after 1760 "it was alleged that Tacky, the leader of the in-surgents, had furnished the slaves with a magical preparation that was sup-posed to render them invulnerable to the weapons of the authorities. Inspired by the belief that they were immune to injury, the slaves created havoc in St. Mary."[36] The group's sworn secrecy; its night rituals, practiced in hideouts and largely inaccessible to outsiders; its powerful and deadly herbal medicines; and the supernatural power claimed by its leaders made Obeah a weapon of choice in slave resistance in colonial Jamaica.

Regarding Obeah works as detrimental to Caribbean society, colonial au-thorities made the practice a primary target for legal regulations and control. Between the 1760s and 1780s, the Jamaican legislature enforced a series of laws prohibiting Obeah practices on penalty of death upon conviction.[37] In passing the laws, the government hoped to discourage the practice of Obeah because it was known to support slave revolts. The 1792 Consolidated Slave Act of Jamaica again targeted Obeah leaders and prohibited "fanaticism," which was associated with Obeah practices. The Act reads, "In order to pre-vent the many mischiefs that may hereafter arise from the wicked art of Negroes going under the appellation of obeah men and women. . . . Be it there-fore enacted [that] any slave who shall pretend to any supernatural power, in order to promote the purposes of rebellion, shall, upon conviction thereof suf-fer death, transportation, or such other punishment."[38] Edward Seaga claimed that practitioners of Obeah "sometimes infringe the Night Noise Prevention Law of 1911 and the so-called Obeah Law of 1898—the latter . . . proscribes the practice of Obeah, the consultation with practitioners of Obeah, and the publication and distribution of any material 'calculated to promote the superstition of Obeah.'"[39] The prohibition extended throughout the English-speaking Caribbean, which followed Jamaica's lead in legislating against Obeah.

Bush affirms that despite their legislation and instruments of torture, colonials were unable to control Obeah actions. British law and the threat of punishment failed to suppress "the secret and highly influential magical practices of the slaves"; in spite of the many severe penalties, Obeah continued to play a significant role in slave culture. In her extensive research on Obeah, Stewart found more than a dozen government litigations against Obeah practitioners. Court papers cited the offenders as possessing a variety of forbidden objects, trinkets, and "fetishes" (the term is mine) and participating in alleged "illegal evil" Obeah works.[40] Whites feared Obeah because of its subversive activities, sinister association with poison, potential for the secret deaths among whites and blacks, and the fact that it was incomprehensible to a European world view. Bush says, "They viewed obeah and other mystical beliefs as something to be feared, as something always harmful and destructive. . . . The planter's fear of poisoning, often marked by paranoia, exemplified this irrational and often inaccurate view of African religious practices."[41] During slavery, this fear often worked to the advantage of slaves on smaller plantations, who were able to garner better treatment from their masters when the masters were overcome by fear of Obeah. The conditions of oppression that allowed slaves little opportunity to practice their African religions in public could not prevent this black religion from surviving as a source of strength for resistance. Morrish believes that the laws that forbade slaves' religious assembly "inevitably had the effect of encouraging individual and undiscoverable face-to-face relationships with the obayifo. Thus obeah became an established practice in Jamaica from the earliest days of slavery, and the Obeah-man—or the Obeah-woman—became a powerful individual within any slave community"[42] and in the postemancipation Caribbean.

Obeah and Maroon were the earliest African Jamaican religious cultures that colonists named in official documents and other literature. The two complemented each other as mediums of resistance against the common enemy of oppression and rallied other African traditions to the cause. Zip notes that the Obeah, Maroon, and Myal religions were important elements of a larger religious system that combined similar African heritage and formed a basis for organizing an African counterculture in the underground of colonial Jamaica. "Likewise, as starting point of cultural resistance and mainspring of the open rebellion against tyranny, they ensured the psychic survival of the majority of Maroons and runaways, whose struggle was crowned with success."[43] Practitioners of Obeah and Myal united in the fight against oppressive slave culture and, in Maroon communities, formed tools of defense against external forces.

Because of their collaboration, colonists regarded Obeah and Myal as one and the same and described them as a form of witchcraft or sorcery brought to the island by African slaves;[44] both religions communicated with supernatural powers and aimed at bettering the lives of their believers.

In spite of colonial perceptions, Obeah was not the same as the Myal religion. Bush holds that "Obeah was worked by individual priests who dealt in magic, poisons, herbs, and folk medicine and were highly secretive. Myal was concerned more with group worship and was used as an antidote against the harmful aspects of Obeah."[45] Both healthy and punitive Obeah and Myal existed concomitantly, but eventually Obeah was demonized as evil in colonial culture. Colonists conveniently but erroneously labeled all African religious practices in the Caribbean as Obeah, whether they understood them or not, and often mistook one for the other. As a result, proscriptions enacted against the practice of Obeah spirituality affected other Caribbean religions as well.

Features of Obeah

Obeah practice transverses ethnicity and social class. Elizabeth Nunez-Harrell's novel *When Rocks Dance* shows that the use of Obeah magic cuts across race and class in times of need or crisis. Set at the turn of the century, the novel opens with Emilia, Marina's mother, being ostracized for forsaking the ways of her Ibo ancestors and shacking up with an Englishman named Horthgar. Emilia's pregnancies result in repeated stillbirths of male twins. In desperation, she visits both an Indian chief and an Obeah-man for answers to this mystery and is told she has breached her racial ethnic mores. Succumbing to guilt, Emilia takes the practitioners' advice to make a human sacrifice of her next set of male twins in order to save future pregnancies. Karla Frye states that Emilia's turn to Obeah and her willingness to perform a human sacrifice are signs that she again believes in the efficacy of her ancestral ways; when Marina turns eight, her mother tells her about the realities of life that she can experience only through Obeah.[46] Thus Obeah is practiced not only in remote and impoverished communities, where alternative medicine is the only lifeline; it is also practiced in upscale middle-class society. Caribbean people of all hues visit Obeah-men—to be protected by their blessings, "fixed" trinkets, beads, necklaces, and other good luck charms. Politicians discreetly visit them during their political campaigns; business people and other professionals, some of whom are Christians, seek their spiritual baths for protection from the evil eye or to receive blessings for good fortune.

Obeah appeals to descendants of indentured immigrants and slaves, persons of both high and low society, the propertied class, people of African and European descent, and other creole peoples—a reality overlooked in the portrayal of Obeah as a religion of maladjusted poor blacks.[47] It is a cause-and-effect religious art; believers place magic potions around their premises and wear "fixed" charms and fetishes to protect themselves against other peoples' evil works. They take precautions not to offend Obeah practitioners, and suspect them of foul play in mysterious tragedies in their communities. Bryan Edwards claims that among slaves who believed completely in Obeah's supernatural power, the bravest "tremble at the very sight of the ragged bundle, the bottle, or the egg-shells, which are stuck in the thatch, or hung over the door of a hut, or upon the branch of a plantain tree, to deter marauders."[48] The reality of this dreaded art shows two important features in colonial times.

Literary Fascination

Following Morrish's example, scholars categorize Obeah as African and literary; the two reinforce one another but also compete with each other. In literary Obeah, practitioners facilitate their works with the use of esoteric writings as texts on astrology, the occult, mysticism, and other religious subjects. Among these, Olmos and Paravisini-Gebert identified the Bible, *The Sixth and Seventh Books of Moses, Moses Books of the Kabbalah and the Talmud for the Good of Mankind,* James Dillet Freeman's *Prayer, the Master Key,* Lewis de Claremont's *Seven Steps to Power: A Study of Beliefs, of Customs, of Traditions of People in Various Ages,*[49] and *The Black Arts.* Myths from extracanonical biblical literature, especially the *Wisdom of Solomon, Ben Sirach,* the *Maccabees, Enoch, Additions to Daniel, Tobit,* and *Bell and the Dragon* are also sources upon which practitioners are said to draw religious concepts and practices for Obeah. Some of these books provide magical techniques that are different from the religious practices of nonliterary Obeah, which is akin to African pharmacopeia. In the latter, "the specific African elements in obeah are concerned in the main with the use of animal and herbal substances, and with the casting of spells in African dialects"[50] as well as with healing.

Since the late 1700s, literature portrayed Obeah as an insidious evil magic that originated from a devilish African source: the *Ob/Aub,* or African-Egyptian serpent, and a pagan African mind.[51] Writers saw Obeah as the most grotesque and uncivilized African activity and regarded its practitioners as the worst of Caribbean slave society. Europeans who believed that Africans had no religion and were incapable of expressing religious sentiments[52] but for the redeeming graces of Christianity saw Obeah as the natural behavior of heathenish superstitions and pagan African practices. Obeah became so notorious that it held the British playwrights and their reading audiences spellbound for decades. In the early 1800s, many short stories, plays, novels, and other fictitious writings fed the British public a steady diet of writers' conceptions of Obeah's world. The ferocity of the Haitian Revolution, its psychological and economic impact on Western powers, and the fact that it was largely a "black thing" made Obeah a ready subject of satire for writers who saw Haitian Vodou as African barbarism and Obeah superstition.

Richardson found such aberrations in Thomas Campbell's "Wild Obi" (published in *The Pleasures of Hope,* 1799), William Shepherd's "The Negro

Incantations" (published in *The Monthly Magazine*, 1797), and other tales. The play *Obi, or Three-Fingered Jack*, Charlotte Smith's "The Story of Henrietta" (1800), and Maria Edgeworth's "The Grateful Negroes" (in *Popular Tales*, 1801) added to the Obeah conundrum. These share many characteristics: an anti-African philosophy, the stereotyping of the unknown and unfamiliar, a phobia of Afro-Caribbean religions, and defense of European cultural or political and economic power. In Richardson's words, "The Romantic concerns with Obeah, which De Quincy calls a 'dark collusion with human fears,' grows out of British anxieties regarding power: the fluctuations of imperial power, the power of slaves to determine their own fate, the power of democratic movements in France, in England, and in the Caribbean."[53] This literary portrayal of Obeah shows how powerful its representation was in generating "Afro-phobia" in colonial times; as Stewart holds, Afro-phobia is both the fear and the hatred of things African and of Africa's people.[54]

The dominant perceptions of Obeah as devil worship and evil works are changing slowly as modern society becomes more knowledgeable of the nature and function of this practice and art. It is now portrayed with intriguingly positive images in a variety of twentieth-century novels by writers of different nationalities. Since the 1960s, Edward Seaga, Maureen Warner-Lewis, George Eaton Simpson, Ivor Morrish, Barbara Bush, Joseph Murphy, Barry Chevannes, Kenneth Ramchand, Werner Zip, Dianne Stewart, and others have raised awareness of the many misconceptions and prejudices against Obeah in colonial and popular literature and thus have added much to an understanding and appreciation of this religious art.[55] Literary critic Ramchand shows that in the childhood novel *Christopher* (1959), Geoffrey Drayton, a Euro-Caribbean novelist, correlates his main character's growing-up process with experiences in the black world around him.[56] He learns to relate to Obeah on a cerebral level rather than on an emotional one and thereby understands the true workings of the art. V. S. Naipaul, the Trinidadian Nobel Prize winner who has been dubbed the Dean of Caribbean literature, gives a comical but apt portrayal of Obeah in *The Sufferage of Elvira* (1958). Elvira's "bib big dog" meets a "drunken Baksh" at night and is turned into a little puppy by morning. Everyone around Elvira fears the sinister power of Obeah. Even the cultured Elviran king-maker and his wife believe that the Obeah-dog is an evil agent called Preacher, so they are led to an Obeah-man who is able to counteract Preacher's evil. To counter the belief that Obeah is the machination of poor, illiterate blacks who practice African cults in depressed communities, Naipaul shows that Obeah cuts across economic structures and racial ethnic lines.

Interreligious Ethos

As a religious practice, Obeah has an ethos that cuts across creed as much as it does race and class. It is receptive to Islamic, Hindu, Christian, and other faiths. Practitioners can be Jamaican Myalists, Pocominists, and Kuminists; they can be Spiritual Baptists, Orisha, and Kabbalists; or they might be Guyanese Hindu Kali Mai Pujah or a Muslim sect. The Obeah-man in my hometown was pastor (shepherd) of a Spiritual Baptist church which, like other Afro-Caribbean spiritualities, relied heavily on Judeo-Christian traditions for its religious lyrical tradition, teachings, theology, and liturgy. There is both a continuum and a disconnect between the Christian culture of the colonial Caribbean and Obeah. Like Vodou, Candomble, and Santeria, Obeah—especially outside of Jamaica—shares with Catholicism a fluidity on such things as the burning of incense in various types of services, the use of sacred altars, the performance of many of its feasts, and the robing of priests. According to Frederick Case, when the Guianas formed one colonial Dutch colony, the spirits that manifested themselves in black religion were often "aboriginal, African, Indian, European, Jewish, Christian, or Muslim. . . . In order to survive on the plantations, African systems of spirituality had to be versatile and to put in practice their ability to be inclusive."[57] The results of that versatility are creole practices and cultures that draw on a rich variety of religious traditions.

Obeah practitioners "Africanize" and reinterpret Christian scriptures with the help of other religious experiences that speak to Afro-Caribbean spirituality. The ceremonial laws, Levitical priesthood, and liturgical system in the Jewish Torah form a common source of information for Obeah teachings on defilement and healing cures in the southern Caribbean. Practitioners of Obeah support their claims to access supernatural works of "spiritual magic" by referencing popular biblical myths that deal with mysterious deaths, disappearances, and miraculous phenomena. For example, when the Philistines cornered Saul and his armies in battle, the king, in a last-ditch attempt to save himself and his Hebrew nation, solicited the help of a medium, the Witch of Endor, who used "Obeah magic" and allegedly brought the dead prophet-priest Samuel back to life to speak to Saul (1 Samuel 27:3–19). The body of Moses disappeared on Mount Pisgah, opposite Jericho, after the deliverer made Joshua his successor (Deuteronomy 34:1–9). Elijah was caught up to Heaven in a whirlwind and thereby defied gravity, death, and burial traditions. Jesus used spiritual magic to turn water into wine and also defied the laws of physics by descending into Hades to release prisoners from the bowels of the earth on the night of his crucifixion (1 Peter 3). Thus, as an African creole religious system, Obeah makes itself at home in western Judeo-Christian culture and scriptural traditions and mimics these ancient stories.

Case finds, in Guyanese culture, a truly creole interreligious symbiosis that evolved in Obeah's encounter with Abrahamic religions, with Aboriginal culture, and especially with the Kali Mai Pujah, the synchronizing of two different forms of worship of the god Kali from northern and southern India with Obeah and other traditions. The will and power of the fierce Hindu god finds correspondence in the god of wrath, justice, and destruction in the Hebrew Bible and Jewish faith. At the same time, a Guyanese religious myth of Kali Mai Pujah allows the Indian deity to be also an African mother to Obeah practitioners, thus facilitating interreligious spiritual communication between the two systems and easing cultural tensions between African and Indian ethnic groups. Case believes the myth is a conceptual way of understanding a highly sophisticated cultural process: it allows the deity Kali to be an international Hindu maternal reality, a Tamil village god who cures certain diseases "and at the same time the mother of all Africans torn from their ancestral home. . . . In Obeah, references to the black water, the black triangular *jhandi*, and the use of black candles are frequent codes that give coherence to a sacred discourse that the uninitiated see but do not understand."[58] Such is the ecumenical ethos of Obeah, especially in the southern Caribbean.

The dominant perception of Obeah practice is one of defilement, grotesque evil, and satanic rituals. Nonetheless, this religious system has its code of ethics, purification rituals, healing balms, and penchant for justice. Obeah priests require clients to undergo a period of purification before a major Obeah work is performed. This purification often consists of special prayers, baths, and abstinence from foods, alcoholic drinks, and some types of sexual activities. To enter into the work of the spirit in an impure state, or in an unworthy spirit and body, is considered dangerous for both practitioner and client. The divine could respond with swift retribution for a careless act of uncleanness, irreverence, and defilement of the sacred rituals. Obeah seeks to obtain protection, good health, and personal success as well as retributive justice. Its magic prescriptions have more good intent than ill will. Problems for which people seek Obeah works are classified as sociological and psycho-physiological. Sociological problems include forcing a harmful person out of a neighborhood or property, stopping a stalker in a fatal attraction, settling a score in a love triangle, punishing a malicious enemy, getting even with a landlord or employer, fighting a lawsuit, increasing one's business chances, or salvaging a broken relationship. Psycho-physiological problems are health related: paralysis, septic ulcers, sterility, stomachaches, contagious disease, psychoses, and a range of other maladies.[59] Of course, only the faithful claim that the Obeah-man can cure these serious medical conditions.

Can Obeah, on the other hand, cause sickness or anything harmful? Alleged Obeah afflictions involve losing one's sight or hearing; getting "the big foot" (finding one's feet mysteriously swelling until walking becomes painful or impossible); suddenly developing large, protruding varicose veins; huge facial growths; malformation in one's fingers; and contortions, the cause of which may result from poisoning. Obeah's power resides as much in a psychology of fear and belief as it does in its magic potions. One of our neighbors who saw her legs doubling its width almost overnight and confining her to her home believed she was "Obeahed" for giving false testimony in court against another woman. When another neighbor lost a goat to a thief who was pilfering animals in the community, she quickly enlisted the services of the Shepherd, who sent the word out that Obeah was set for the thief. Within days, the kleptomaniac heard the news; fear and a guilty conscience sent him in a state of panic. He returned the goat in the dead of night, tying it to a tree behind my neighbor's house. This is reminiscent of Brian Edwards' observation that when one discovers he is afflicted by Obeah, he spares no resource seeking help from a more eminent Obeah-man to counteract the magical operation. If no one is found of superior ability "or if after gaining such an ally he should still fancy himself afflicted, he presently falls into decline, under the incessant horror of impending calamities. The slightest painful sensation in the head, the bowels, or . . . any casual loss or hurt, confirms his apprehensions, and he believes himself the devoted victim of an invisible and irresistible agency."[60] Cardiac arrests are known to follow a few traumatized victims of Obeah.

The mystique that an Obeah-man carried in my hometown served as a deterrent to the acts of nefarious persons who otherwise would have committed violence against people who were not Obeah-fixed. In this way, Obeah works as a code of conduct in communal morality; it is used to catch thieves and criminals and punish liars, especially in litigations. Some women use Obeah to inhibit the conjugal deviance and unfaithfulness of their partners. Others, like "Melda," use Obeah to seal a desired relationship. Hence, the belief in Obeah serves as a good function in a believing community and may be a source of good luck as well as misfortune. As Chevannes says, "Through obeah, spirits and duppies are invoked or [exorcised], witnesses in litigation silenced, predial thieves intimidated or hurt, employers forced to re-employ, or business ventures ensured success"[61] if not effectively derailed. Might there be fewer criminal activities in the Caribbean if more people believed in and feared Obeah?

Avatars of Obeah

Obeah practitioners inherited several names and dreaded titles in the Caribbean: Obeah-man, Obeah-woman, Shepherd (Shepad), Obeah-priest, sorcerer, conjuror, and, as in the Mighty Sparrow's calypso "Melda," necromancer and Papa Niser. In the French Caribbean they are associated with Vodou priests (in Haiti) and *quimboiseurs,* or "magicians" (French Antilles).[62] *Obeah-man* is not an exclusive gender description as much as it a role, symbol, and office of a spiritualist, whose claim to supernatural powers and the use of pharmacopeia make him or her a force to reckon with. Edwards gave a classic account of the most crafty among the workers of Obeah and of the power and influence their magic exerted in colonial times. Such power was seen in the fear and respect they commanded, which often worked for the good of slave society:

> The oldest and most crafty are those who usually attract the greatest devotion and confidence; those whose hoary heads, and a somewhat peculiarly harsh and forbidding [look] . . . together with a skill in plants of the medicinal and poisonous species, have qualified them for the exercise of this art. The [negroes] . . . revere, consult, and fear them; to

these oracles they resort, and with the most implicit faith . . . whether for the cure of disorders, the obtaining [of] revenge for injuries or insults, the conciliating of favor, the discovery and punishment of the thief or the adulterer, and the protection of future events.[63]

In Roger Mais's novel *Brother Man* (1954), the main character, Bra' Ambo, is known as a powerful Obeah-man who reads the *Book of the Dead* and shows everyone he has "high science." But he is seen as a Jamaican *ginal*, a swindler of the resources of simpleminded and unsuspecting persons;[64] this is an image of Obeah practitioners common in the southern Caribbean. The most important function of an Obeah practitioner is to provide what their customers desire; Obeah "is concerned with the individual and his appetite as opposed to the total good and welfare of the society."[65] Through their charms and amulets, practitioners offered slaves assurance in their struggle to survive the brutal slave system. They allegedly unleash spiritual entities through magic and exercise control over duppies or zombies troubling their clients.

Obeah Women

Among Obeah practitioners who exerted great influence over the slaves, a significant number of them were women. Women have always featured prominently in Obeah rituals, leadership, magic, and herbal medicine, and they have used the system to their own economic and social advantage. In the postslavery era, Caribbean women were more likely to turn to Obeah for social and economic support in the face of the inequities they experienced because of unemployment, underemployment, and domestic abuse. In the novel *When Rocks Dance*, one of Nunez-Harrell's lead characters, Emilia, embodies what Frye calls "the fractured nature of African identity in the New World" and a path to freedom and power for women via Obeah. *When Rocks Dance* is a story of heroine Marina Heathrow's quest for land, an extension of her mother Emilia's desire to gain power and security as a black woman. As Frye suggests, "Through Hrothgar and Emilia's relationship, Nunez-Harrell constructs black female subjectivity in colonial society and intertwines the quest of African women for power and freedom from domination with the acknowledgment of 'African ways' symbolized by Obeah."[66] In this art, women create their own religious space and identity, demand respect, provide a source of revenue, and attempt to control their own social and political destiny and spirituality.

Bush records British army captain John Steadman's 1796 description of a ceremony in Surinam and of the role an Obeah-woman played in the movement:

[The slaves] also have amongst them a kind of sybilis, who deal in oracles; these sage matrons [are found] dancing and whirling round in the middle of an assembly with amazing rapidity until they foam at the mouth and drop down convulsed. Whatever the prophetess orders to be done, during this paroxysm, is most sacredly performed by the surrounding multitude which renders these meetings extremely dangerous, as she frequently enjoins them to murder their masters, or desert to the woods.[67]

The nomenclature *Obeah-woman* represents something far more sinister and loathing than *Obeah-man*. The women corral a mystique around them that is quite foreboding. To British colonials, Obeah-women epitomized the wicked African witch who works dangerous magic, the fierce Nanny Maroon leader, and the evil Queen Jezebel in ancient Hebrew tradition who used deception and violence to accomplish her ends. These have exacerbated the fear of Obeah-women in society. Partly because of their skill in Obeah magic, their knowledge of plant pharmacopeia and other medicines, and partly through their strong leadership role in African religions, Obeah-women are still respected and feared in the Caribbean. The more physically robust, curvaceous, and oversize the woman, the more foreboding her appearance, the more effective her remedies, and the more respect she commands.

Women's prominence in Obeah often exposed them to greater risk than men; they became scapegoats for many of the evils of slave culture. They were frequently blamed for slave poisonings, seen as part of the great black conspiracy, and were severely punished, often fatally, for various acts. Women were often suspected of "subversive activities," including encouraging and plotting revolts. The accusation is not completely false, for Obeah-women played a critical role in the resistance efforts against slavery in the Americas; not the least of these Obeah-women was Nanny, the fearless Maroon leader in Nanny Town, Jamaica. Women used the secret weapons of Obeah through poisoning and sorcery in their fight against slavery. As Bush explains, "Poisoning was an act of individual resistance to slavery. Female domestic servants in particular, because of their close proximity to whites, were able to disguise poison in food and drink with the minimum of personal risk. Poisons used often induced a slow death which was difficult to detect from natural illness"[68] in a victim in colonial times. Of course, not all poisons were Obeah driven or administered by women.

Practitioner and Craft

Whether male or female, Obeah avatars are the sole arbiters of their magical craft; they are answerable to no one, fear none, but respect one another. Practitioners are often leaders of other Afro-Caribbean religions or work under an Afro-Christian camouflage. The Obeah initiate undergoes an informal apprenticeship period to develop knowledge of the craft. The pharmacopeia and balm-yard works of the Caribbean are vast, and one takes several years to master the art of producing and applying the right herbal medicines. Myth has it that an

Obeah scientist must be four-eyed, "having developed the gift to see both the visible and the invisible world";[69] he must see in front and behind, in the future and in the past. Practitioners divine problems, illnesses, conditions, and situations affecting clients and prescribe treatment based on a range of acquired information. They depend on psychology and the power of suggestion for their success, mesmerizing believers with their mystic spells and medicines. Bisnauth suggests that the Obeah-person's magic operates on three principles: similarity, contiguity, and unusualness.

> The principle of similarity was based on the belief that there was a similarity between an act that was performed and the result that was to be achieved. Thus, if the effigy of the victim was sprinkled with "guinea" pepper, the victim himself was expected to burn with a fever that was like the heat of pepper. . . . The principle of contiguity was based on the belief that things which were in contact with each other at one time would continue to interact although the contact was broken. . . . Thus, if the victim's foot-print was lacerated with a poisoned knife, it was believed that the foot which had made the print would itself become poisoned.[70]

There is the belief that practitioners can use certain body fluids, discharges, hair or nail clippings, clothing, and other personal effects to produce protective medicine, concoct potions, and place hexes on enemies. In communication with malicious spirits, they even claim the ability to jinx detractors through the art of sympathetic magic.

In Caribbean legends, Obeah practitioners can cause disease and misfortune (if not death), through the use of sympathetic magic[71] and potions. Bryan Edwards writes this of blacks and Obeah: "When at any time sudden or untimely death overtakes any of their companions, they impute it to the malicious arts of some practitioners in Obeah. . . . The practice of this art has a very powerful effect on the Negroes; for, in a considerable degree, it gives a bias to their general conduct, dispositions, and manners."[72] Obeah works are said to involve seances, communication with a variety of spirits, and the use of magic spells and poisonous substances; they represent what Murphy accurately calls "the disintegrative forces of a society under stress."[73] Myth has it also that an Obeah practitioner's primary preoccupation is catching people's shadows or duppies, with which they can inflict harm on victims. Duppies are often blamed for mysterious tragedies in society and have made the headline news several times in the Jamaican press. "The duppy has an unpredictable character, sometimes helpful, sometimes harmful."[74] Most Obeah practices, however, are benign and cause harm to no one except through poisoning and psychological mirage—such things as displaying chickens' feathers and other paraphernalia in windows to scare or frighten suspects and would-be thieves; the use of such things as parrots' beaks, the teeth of a dog or alligator, a bone, empty bottles, grave-dirt, and egg-shells to make fetishes and keep away the evil eye.

Obeah healers are consulted for what are called readings, or "tellings"—that is, seeing what the stars predict or foretelling one's fate through magic. Seaga is of the opinion that Obeah-men use two basic methods of reading-magic:

> The first is an intellectual method which deduces the diagnosis from pre-formulated beliefs. An example of this is the card-cutting technique in which a card is selected to suit the individual's features and complexion, for example, the Jack of Spades for a young black man of powerful thick features; its position is noted as the pack is dealt out in rows of nine. All cards above the chosen card are the consultant's danger cards and the specific forms of danger are interpreted according to the cards; those below this card signify that he can control whatever they represent.[75]

The use of intuitive impressions is a more popular method of reading than the use of intellectual deductions. In this method, the priest usually "reads" a glass that contains water into which he dropped a silver coin. Set close to a candle or the direct light of the sun, the glass of water reflects light. The reader concentrates on the coin until his eyes begin to see diverging images from the light, at which point he deciphers a message for the client. The reader-interpreter makes a diagnosis and proceeds to prescribe treatment for the problem. Such treatment usually falls in the category of the magical-religious. For example, if an unrequited lover wants another's affection, the priest might instruct him or her to clandestinely put a charm or a specially treated (Obeahed) object in the admired's clothes or drink. A practitioner might treat the problem by requiring the client to perfume himself or herself with the "oil of love," a pharmaceutical compound that carries a very pleasant odor. This perfume is supposed to attract the spirit, who then loiters around, like a fly on the wall, to aid the couple in their romance.[76] Herbalists claim to use an array of herbs to allegedly cure a variety of sicknesses as goiter, gangrene, pneumonia, and the common cold. Then, spiritual healing may follow. A woman consulting a healer for advice on increasing her chances for success in business might receive advice based on common sense to put a mirror or some important object in her shop to attract more customers. The healing and other services an Obeah-man or Obeah-woman offers are usually sought as a last resort. Few Caribbean people who are ill turn first to a healer or Obeah-man, even when their illness is diagnosed as having a spiritual source and nature. Like other folk healing, Obeah consultation is used as one's last lifeline. A patient first applies bush remedies, then modern medicine, and only when these fail he or she searches for a spiritual cause and cure.[77]

Conclusion

Obeah is alive and well in the twenty-first-century Caribbean. As Frye feels avers, "The pull of Obeah remained strong enough to foster doubt in the minds of even the staunchest disbeliever and naysayer,"[78] and its tools—spirits, natural objects, pharmacopeia, fear, and faith—continue to maintain their efficacy in peoples' religious consciousness. Chevannes tells of an extreme situation that occurred in April 1983 in a district in St. Catherine, Jamaica. A healthy middle-aged man fell ill and was bedridden for several weeks with an illness that produced a progressively acute pain that moved from one part of his body to another. Instead of seeking medical attention, his family—who believed that his symptoms were indicative of a spirit-influenced or extraordinary condition— took him to see an Obeah-man, who confirmed their suspicion. The practitioner said the patient's partner in a small business venture put evil spirits on him to control the business. The Obeah-priest, therefore, proceeded to ritually remove a doll that had been placed on the roof of the sick man's house. A few days before the man expired, his family finally took him to the hospital, where doctors diagnosed his condition as leukemia in its advanced stage, for which they could offer no help. The deceased received the proper Christian rites and the minister assured the bereaving community that the man died of cancer of the blood, but nothing could dispel the belief that the man had been Obeahed.[79] Obeah as a belief, a practice, an art, a consciousness or seance, and a black resistance movement has been used for both good and ill purposes. Many things have contributed to pejorative conceptions of Obeah in both colonial and modern societies, but the colonial aversion to African religions also shaped the creole Caribbean perception of Obeah and other religious systems. Colonial suspicion of the practice of Obeah exacerbated modern contempt for Jamaican religions and their African heritage.

12

Myal and Kumina in Jamaica's Past

KEY TOPICS

*Colonial Foreground • Obeaed Myal • African Orientation •
Obeah Beliefs and Rituals • Kumina's Genesis • Mythology and
Ritual • Sacred Kumina Drums*

For its relatively small size and population (fewer than one million people during its heyday of African religions), Jamaica has seen an impressive school of religious traditions of African provenance since the 1700s. The story of Jamaican creole religions is a fascinating narrative of a people's erstwhile search for identity, freedom, and justice through their battle with colonialism and slavery. Black resistance, kindled by the fires of African religions and Africanized Christian thought, was the primary avenue of social and political change of historic significance for that Caribbean country. It is noted that even in areas of social life, where resistance is no longer significant, having contributed to the demise of colonial domination, religion still remains the source "of public and private morality"[1] and an important fount of folk culture. Africans sought to recreate and preserve a coherent worldview from the fragments of their home institutions, from their broken lives, and from the contradictions of the Jamaican colonial Christian culture. This was done over centuries of peoples' enduring the unrelenting constrictions of capitalism and slavery. Joseph Murphy claims that in these straits, "Afro-Jamaicans found their equilibrium in a variety of neo-African religious institutions, elements of which have come down to present day"[2] even as new ones are being created.

The tenacious Yoruba, Akan-Ashanti, and Kongo religions of West and Central Africa are progenitors of Jamaica's rebel Maroon, Obeah, Myal, Kumina, and other creole religions. As movements and institutions, these represented an antithesis to the colonial culture as they nurtured the spirit of resistance to enslavement, oppression, and human suffering in the British colony. Some of the African-derived spiritualities were active in Jamaica in the late 1700s; as historian Bryan Edwards writes, "Evidence of the cultural tenacity of religious [Africanisms] was much stronger in the slave cultures of the Caribbean and South America than on the plantations of the American South."[3] After emancipation, other religions arrived with indentured workers whom the British, strapped for a supply of labor, imported from West Africa to its Caribbean colonies. Today, those religions are less evident on the island, since their numbers and influence have waned considerably; the ones that survived the twentieth century are so strongly creole that they are barely distinguishable from local versions of popular Christianity in spiritual churches, Revivalism, and folk traditions.

Determining the numerical strength of any Afro-Jamaican religion is a guessing game; those mentioned in the 1943 national census accounted for less than 1 percent of the population. The religions are not named in Jamaica's 1982 census; after it listed fourteen thousand Jamaicans (only 0.6 percent of the population) as Rastafarians, the census gave a numerically indeterminate category: "Other." In the census, a puny fraction of the population publicly identified itself with Afro-Jamaican religions. This contrasts with the hyperbole that among the lower classes of Jamaican society African religions "can claim more adherents than all the mainstream traditions combined"[4] and with Newell Booth's 1977 claim that Poco (a shortened form of Pocomina) can claim about 15 percent of Jamaicans. W. F. Elkins, however, is correct that "in Jamaica, [Pokomania] and Zion Revivalism are major folk religions."[5] Jamaica's former Prime Minister and sociologist Edward Seaga reports interesting statistics on membership in revival cults he studied: 50 Poco "bands" with an average size of 25 serving 1,250 members; 240 Zion bands with an average size of 25 serving over 6,000. With regard to the percentages of followers of these two religions in Jamaica, Seaga records Poco as having .06 percent of a population of 1,240,000 in 1943 and only .01 percent of 1,610,000 people in 1960.[6]

A 1963 ethnographic study shows that in Jamaica's 1943 and 1960 censuses the percentage of Revivalists was underestimated. These religions received little mention in the earlier census because devotees identified themselves as Christians while secretly practicing African religions; participation in those traditions was looked on with disdain. To enhance their social status, Jamaicans claimed membership in one of the established churches while disguising their ancestral faith. Because of suspicion and mistrust, very few readily admitted to being a follower of Poco or Convince; some listed their religion as Revival, which bears an affinity to Christianity, but few publicly embraced Obeah, Myal, or Kumina. Centuries of Protestant Christian influence, sustained repression, and condemnation of these creole spiritualities drove them underground, but in situations of imbroglio they reemerge and show that the obscure and remote sects are the expression of a much deeper consciousness.[7] By the mid-1900s, when Afro-Jamaicans had become more overt about their spiritualities, these sects had already seen substantial decline; although traces of their earlier presence exist in a revival complex, most of the religions have been consumed by a modern brand of Christianity in indigenous churches. In many local communities, the Rastafari movement and Jamaican-American Christian sects have replaced the Myal, Kumina, Convince, Revival Zion, and Poco[8] resistance tradition.

Colonial Foreground

The African culture of resistance in Jamaica has its earliest origins in the Spanish settlement of the island. As it did in other colonies in the region, after decimating the native population through disease, brutality, and slavery, Spain turned to Africa for cheap labor. The first Africans arrived in Jamaica in 1509; a 1511 census showed 107 free and 558 enslaved Africans in a population of 1,510.[9] Of the small but steady stream of early captives deposited in Jamaica, many resisted slavery by escaping to rugged terrain, where they were called *cemarons*, Maroon runaways. More than a century later, these Maroons were a formidable source of resistance to colonial slavery after the British seized the "forgotten, ill-managed, and often-corrupt Spanish colony"[10] in 1655. Taken as a face-saving and defenseless consolation prize for the defeat of Britain's attempt to capture Hispaniola and Cuba from Spain, Jamaica proved invaluable to Britain's penetration of Spanish America and became the most important English colony in the Caribbean. When Spain reluctantly ceded the island to Britain under the Treaty of Madrid in 1670,[11] Jamaica's Anglo colonial destiny was sealed. Private colonists immediately followed and staked their fortune in whatever goods Jamaica's fertile lands proffered. The land-scratching settlers and opportunists were soon overpowered by better-prepared sugar planters seeking an alternative to Barbados, where the real estate value had become too inflated while its sugar production declined.

British planters converted Jamaica into a profitable colony whose mercantile economy depended on large sugar estates and exports to Britain that were based solely on cheap labor. Most of the poor whites on the island came as indentured workers in payment for their passage from Britain, or, in lieu of punishment, for hard crimes and larceny; but that labor supply was limited and expensive. The backbone of the sugar kingdom, therefore, was the Atlantic slave trade that brought almost a million Africans, with their religions and cultures, to Jamaica. By 1673, Jamaica's population had jumped to 17,300, about ten thousand of whom were Africans laboring in more than seventy "sugar works" and producing about eight hundred tons of sugar annually. The slave population exceeded forty thousand in 1700, and over the next one hundred thirty-five years, almost eight hundred thousand Africans who survived the hellish Middle Passage were enslaved in Jamaica. When Britain abolished the slave trade in 1807, it had about 320,000 slaves in Jamaica. Among these captives was a huge representation of Akans from the Gold Coast. Jamaica became such a sugar Pearl of the British Antilles that one hundred years after the Treaty of Madrid, sugar cane still made up 76 to 80 percent of Jamaica's exports[12] to Britain.

"Dem slaves on ah de Jamaican plantation saw nuf" hell (enough misery).[13] These human livestock and disposable chattels worked under the most ghastly exploitation that encouraged macabre punishment for minor infractions. The majority of enslaved Africans labored under slave masters or their representatives, called overseers, who extracted every ounce of energy from their African captives in order to maximize their profit margin. They showed concern for their human chattels only insofar as they were an economic means of production. On larger plantations, the health of slaves, family ties, and African religions were cadaverous casualties of the pecuniary system. Because of its high percentage of white plantation owner absenteeism, the Caribbean saw more brute force exerted on slaves than did many other parts of the Americas. Brutal oppression, regimentation, anti-African prejudice, and Christian-based religion were distinguishing features of colonial Jamaica.[14] With theological arguments based on Scripture and natural religion, in defense of the institution as God-ordained, the whip brokered the orderly working of slave society; it justified relationships of oppression rooted in the social and economic power of the planter class in a Caribbean where, as historian Barbara Bush explains, philosophical, legal, "religious, biological, and scientific reasons were used to instill the notion of inferiority into black people"[15] and ensured the psychological and social cadaverous state of Africans and their traditions.

British slave codes (enacted in 1808 and 1818) attempted to regulate the masters' whips and make the penal system less nefarious, but laws designed to ameliorate the appalling condition of the slaves were largely ignored by the planter class, who silenced the public's ethical conscience with political and economic clout in the colony. Under this unforgiving system, slaves were punished mercilessly for serious offenses and leaders of slave uprising were routinely hung. A number of legal injunctions in the penal system stipulated severe punishment for African religious activities. Dianne Stewart cites "legal codes against the use of poisons (1684), against the beating of drums and the congregating of enslaved Africans for 'feasts' or 'revel' (1699), and against beating drums, barrels, gourds, and boards, the blowing of horns, and other noisy instruments (1717)."[16] More prohibitions "against African gatherings, drumming, music of all kinds, and Obeah were passed in 1781 and 1784" as well as in 1788, 1826, and 1827.[17]

The British Government and missionary societies encouraged planters to make Christians of their alleged "heathen" slaves, but most Africans resisted the religious contradictions of colonial culture that allowed their bodies to be enslaved while seeking to save their souls; they felt they were doomed to double jeopardy. As a consequence, the role of Christianity in the lives of Jamaican slaves was paltry. For psychological reasons and a means of discouraging slave revolts, some masters allowed slaves to celebrate their African folklore tradition, especially through singing and doing the Jonkunnu dance, in off-crop season. The celebration of this African folk culture continues today in modified forms in Barbados's Crop Over Festival in July and in the Carnival Fiesta in Trinidad and Tobago in February and March. Some slaves became the trusted confidants of masters, a few of whom had a tradition of freeing a "well-behaved" slave at Christmas time, as a good example to the other miserable wretches. Cronyism, brown-nosing (being an "Uncle Tom"), and compliant hierarchies within the slave population benefited a lucky few,[18] to the hellish damnation of the gang.

The colonial system constructed a sharp class and social distinction between master and slave and between free whites and free blacks in Jamaica. After emancipation in 1838, European ethnicity and privilege remained the distinguishing badge of the ruling class. A runty number of blacks and mulattoes found room for proscribed upward mobility in the tiered society, but the lines of privilege and class were rigidly drawn. The minority tenaciously held onto their Englishness and grotesquely flaunted their pedigree as they attempted to create another "Little Britain," in which blacks were needed only as beasts of burden in a colonial economy. Class consciousness and racial prejudice became so systemic that as late as the 1920s a historian unabashedly profiled Afro-Jamaicans as racially inferior, simplistic, deceitful, "suspicious, inefficient, irresponsible, lazy, superstitious and loose" in their morals.[19]

The dehumanizing of Africans was an essential ingredient in black-white relations in the postemancipation culture, but being cast as a social pariah was not the greatest irritant to the impoverished ex-slave. The huge, underemployed, free but landless black peasantry suffered busted hopes for emancipation, decades of poverty, natural disasters, and starvation. Their economic plight was made acute by the drastic decline in colonial agricultural production. Even with the importation of foreign labor, emancipation signaled the imminent fall of "king sugar"—and the declining of the planter class with it—followed by sky-rocketing unemployment in its wake. With no franchise or say in the colonial government, the hungry and powerless masses were driven in desperation to violent uprisings in 1831, 1865, and 1938 at the cost of many lives. Marked by political incompetence, internal factions, British prejudice, and malfeasance—while battling economic hardship exacerbated by the Northern Union blockade of the Southern Confederacy of the 1860s as well as by the Great Depression of the 1930s—Jamaica's Victorian government was inert and pusillanimous but reckless in its prejudicial and insensitive attempts at dealing with these veritable social and economic crises.

The story of the African fight for survival and dignity in colonial Jamaica is one of black resistance to a culture of negation and oppression in every aspect of life. The much maligned and hated African religions provided a most valuable tool in the struggle. This epoch of culture building, as Jean Besson holds, "drew on the African baseline beliefs in witchcraft, medicine, ancestral cults, and a pantheon of gods and spirits, re-molding them within the slave plantation system. At the heart of this recreated worldview were the magical-religious cults of Obeah and Myalism."[20] Obeah, prevalent in the early religious phase, coexisted with Myal in the late 1700s and created an ideology around which broad cultural and organizational ties were made. To this African religious mix, other creole religions were added; they were influenced by American Christianity (especially the Great Revival of 1860 to 1861) from nonconformist missionaries and became different from the religion of the planter class. Thus came about the rise of the religious variants of Convince, Poco, Revival Zion, and black Baptist Christianity.

Myal Religious Culture

Myal, one of the Afro-Jamaican religious traditions practiced during colonial rule, is the creole version of an ancestral West Central African traditional religion (ATR). It is a religious institution with a belief system, a dance ritual, an initiatory rite tradition, and a pharmacopeia for herbal and spiritual healing. Myal functioned as a fraternity modeled after a West African secret society and operated away from the watchful eyes of colonial authorities. Stewart argues that this synthetic Pan-African-type "freestanding institution of African derivation" had "its specialized language and rituals unknown to White observers, whose proclivity was to stamp a generic 'Obeah' label on diverse African religious cultures in Jamaica."[21] Myal may not have been an anti-Obeah movement with "healthier practices" than Obeah, as is generally believed. In pre-emancipation Jamaica, all African religions were dubbed Obeah or were associated with that art. Therefore, lines of distinction between these religions are blurred or often removed.

Obeahed Myal

Some colonists thought of Myal as a form of Obeah and sorcery practiced under the spell of narcotics. Edwards represents the sentiment: "Myal-men, or those who, by means of a narcotic portion, made with the juice of an herb (said to be the branched *calalue* or spices of *Solanum*) which occasions a trance or profound sleep of a certain duration, endeavor to convince the spectators of their power to re-animate dead bodies."[22] Other British visiting Jamaica in the late 1700s registered a stereotypic contempt for Myal. Legislator and historian Edward Long was the brusquest: "Not long since [the war of 1760], some of these execrable wretches in Jamaica introduced what they called the Myal-dance, and established a kind of society, into which they invited all they could. The lure hung out was, that every Negro . . . would be invulnerable . . . and, although they might, in appearance be slain, the obeah-man could, at his pleasure, restore the body to life.[23]

Long's knowledge and view of Myal and its relationship to Obeah are suspect since they serve well his colonial propaganda against African religions. However, his identification of Myal in 1774 shows the emergence of ATRs in Jamaica in the second half of the eighteenth century. As Murphy correctly notes, "Our first records of the religious life of Afro-Jamaicans came to us from planters and colonial officials, who by the end of the eighteenth century began to recognize, if not understand, two related religious institutions among the slaves, *obeah* and *myal*,"[24] as a subject of interest. Leonard Barrett claims that "for the first time Africans began to practice their rites in public. The legitimate priests were now beginning to assert themselves and to organize" their Myal religion.[25] How public early Myal was, its true nature, and its relation to other religions of African origin are the subjects of much academic discussion. The unfriendly environment in which Myal was born influenced its character when it appeared in the second half of the 1700s, especially among slaves near Maroon settlements.

Soon after the 1760 rebellion, Myal emerged as a secret society "taking its name from the possession dance which accompanied it"[26] and, in 1774, was described by Long as an accompaniment of Obeah.[27] Myal seemed to have merged with other Afro-Jamaican traditions by the time of emancipation (1834 to 1838), and was associated with herbal medicine and funerary rites.[28] After 1860, Myal was identified with possession trances and a special dance that was important to the Kumina ritual; its spirit possession catalepsy is still referred to as "catching the Myal spirit."[29] With Kumina, Myal formed a cultural matrix in which succeeding African traditions were nurtured in Jamaica and is believed to have provided a means of communication for drawing ethnic groups into slave rebellion and to its culture. The religions supplied the spiritual impetus and political framework for the psychological struggle against slavery and were seen as enabling Tacky (Tacki) to organize a major slave rebellion on pan-African lines for the first time in Afro-Jamaican history.[30] Besson suggests that, consistent with these perspectives, "'Myalism was the broadest reference of slave religion in Jamaica, and serves as a cover term for all religious observances that developed from African religions,"[31] the same as Obeah was conceived as representing all African religions.

In 1843, a missionary to Jamaica, James Phillippo, named Myal in a pejorative description of African religions on the island. He claimed that Myal and "fetishism" were essentially parts of Obeah "and included a mystery of iniquity which perhaps was never fully revealed to the uninitiated. The votaries of this art existed as a fraternity composed of individuals from the surrounding neighborhood, who were regularly inducted into it in accordance with certain demonical forms."[32] This characterization of Myal and Obeah as iniquitous and demonic served well Phillippo's British political and religious purposes but besmirched the character of the religions. His discussion of Myal is not unimportant since he corroborates accounts of its rituals and recruitment strategies as using every possible means to increase its numbers and since it proffered, as advantages of such membership, "exemption from pain and premature death . . . or certain recovery from its influence when life was actually extinct."[33] Phillippo also supported the Myal versus Obeah thesis that postemancipation literature and recent scholars have followed in portraying Myal as having strong anti-Obeah tendencies and serving different purposes.

It is held widely that a Myalist, as herbalist and bush doctor, was sought for healing and neutralizing the power of Obeah and what was perceived as its evil entities and omens. Barry Chevannes claims Myal was "anti-obeah. The doctor, or Myal-man, is resorted to, that he may neutralize the power of the Obeah-man."[34] Slaves looked to Myal for protection from the negative works of Obeah and the brutality of whites on the plantations. In this regard, Afro-Jamaicans believed Myal brought them revelations of the invisible world: a state of mind that allowed the initiates to see Obeah works and to transmit messages from that other world to their community. Further, it is held that Myalists performed initiation ceremonies and health-related services as reinforcement rituals. They attracted large gatherings to their worship and actively resisted Obeah practices in their community. Therefore, although a Myal priest knew the Obeah-man's art and made both "good and evil" medicines, he was a worker of good magic. A "Myal-man" was especially interested in liberating shadows and spirits of the living trapped by the magic of Obeah. While counteracting injury conjured or invoked by Obeah, Myal-men allegedly also had the ability to interpret the mind of the spirits. Chevannes and others relate the story of the great Myal outbreaks and destruction of evil Obeah works of the late 1850s, now established in Jamaican folk tradition as "canon."[35]

This long-held view of Myal has not gone unchallenged. The religious practices equipped blacks psychologically and spiritually for survival in colonial society and, as a result, are seen as complements rather than antagonists in the fight against oppression. Stewart surmises that "from Long's, Edward's, and Lewis's descriptions, Myal is characterized as a distinguishable class of Obeah religious leaders with a particular specialization called 'Myal,' or at least . . . one of the chief components of the Obeah religious practice."[36] In addition to seeing Myal-men as specialized Obeah-men, Stewart contends that "the most significant distinction between Obeah and Myal was not moral but possibly structural. While Obeah is often described as a practice for individuals as well as groups, Myal is only described as a religious ceremony, an association based upon corporate duty, which featured charismatic leaders with identifiable groups of adherents."[37] This supports the view that while Myal was more cooperative and community centered than Obeah, the two are much more closely akin than was thought. The fight that whites saw between Obeah and Myal was not about for the undoing of Obeah, but about addressing the system of oppression.[38] Our revisionist view of Myal has come full circle: preemancipation colonialists conflated it and Obeah *via negativa*; postemancipation colonials and modern scholars placed them in antagonistic roles; now, we have brought them together again with a new idiosyncratic formula, as cohorts with differences only in design.

African Origination

The view that the word *Myal* originated from a Jamaican plant referred to as "myal weed" is not convincing, since the use of the weed may have gotten its name from its frequent ritual use in the religion. Because of the significant number of Akan-Ashanti descendants and their linguistic patterns that survived in Jamaican parishes, Myal traits were thought to be of Akan origin.[39] Myal was prominent in the parish of Trelawney, and it was argued that the religion originated among the Akan or Fanti-Ashanti of Ghana known in that part of the country. Myal was also seen as the first West African religion to appear among large numbers of Akan slaves on the plantation. Myal, however, flourished in St. Thomas and other parishes where many residents are descendants of Central African peoples; they commonly speak about "catching Myal spirit" and being possessed by their ancestral spirits, who have Kongo characteristics. Their culture also has the capacity and tendency to incorporate foreign influences—a characteristic of Central African religions. Therefore, recent studies have argued more convincingly that Myal roots are located in Central Africa.

Stewart and many others support the view that Myal's origination is found within Kongo and Central African religious culture. Based on her extensive study and the credible work of Maureen Warner-Lewis and others on African-Jamaican linguistic and cultural formation, Stewart confirms that many of the terms, rituals, beliefs, and practices of Myal point to a Central West Africa origin, and that the religion arose in concert with the African Jonkunnu (John Canoe) dance.[40] Warner-Lewis points out that "the Jamaican term *mayaal* (generally spelled *myal*) derives from *mayaala*, the physical representations of power. In a secular context, *mayaala* are agents of paramount chief authority."[41] Research on Jamaican religions in the 1970s and 1990s, done in several parishes by Kenneth Bilby, found that the Jonkunnu dance, the beating of the gumbay drum (rectangular and benchlike in shape), the Gumbay Play ceremony (one of the most African of Jamaica's traditions), and other African practices substantiate Myal's Congolese origin.[42] Most recently, Stewart showed that Bilby's finding corroborating Martha Beckwith's earlier discovery that Myal originated from the Kongo Jonkunnu "masquerading [the] institution and its *gumbay* drumming rituals in modern southwestern Jamaica" is credible.[43]

The precise date on which Myal appeared in Jamaica will remain a secret like that of Obeah's. It was first identified or named after the Tacky rebellion of 1760; it surfaced in Long's work in 1774 and in Edward's *An Abridgement of Mr. Edward's Civil and Commercial History of the British West Colonies in the Indies in Two Volumes* in 1794. Before 1800, Myal was identified also as a different religion from the Jamaican indigenous Baptists and again associated with Obeah in 1843. One account notes that followers of the Myal movement of the 1840s were called "angel men" and "Myal people," and that they often preached Africanized Christian beliefs.[44] Chevannes holds that "it was clear that, by what the missionaries referred to as 'Myal outbreaks,' beginning not long after the turn of the century and appearing as late as 1860, there was a fairly uniform system of beliefs widely distributed" in Jamaica[45] called Myal. Before 1873, William Gardner, a missionary to Jamaica, bewailed the influence of Myal on black Christian culture, writing, "With few exceptions, native

Baptist churches became associations of men and women who . . . mingled the belief and even the practice of Myalism with religious observances, and who perverted and corrupted what they retained of these."[46] Myal probably began as a secret society before 1760, became popular among slaves before emancipation, and reached the peak of its influence in the late nineteenth century, when it was associated with Kumina.

To say the least, to Afro-Jamaicans Myal was not a corrupting religion but one of survival, identity, protection, and support. It was "a mechanism of social responsibility and control, and an independence and militancy in the face of white power."[47] Chevannes notes that the role Christ plays in Christianity—as mediator between God and humans—and the enabling power of the Holy Spirit appealed to Myal followers, for whom the work and place of the spirit in a devotee's life was essential. They sought dreams and spirit possession, which became a typical experience of Myal religion, an experience ritualized in secret circular gatherings away from the master's gaze, where the devotees danced and lamented until possessed by a spirit. It is said that the prearranged sacred meeting place varied but that it was often under a large tree, with music and singing employing the African-American call-and-response style. "Slaves danced until they attained a state of ecstasy and a state of suspended consciousness after which they had to be revived"[48] with a remedy or spirit.

Mythic Beliefs and Rituals

Records of the beliefs and practices of Myal as an oral tradition have only recently been reconstructed by Bilby, Stewart, Chevannes, and others, but without infallibility or absolute certainty. So these must be supplemented with eyewitness accounts of the beliefs and practices of the religion for some measure of accuracy. Such accounts point to some common themes: communal religious activities, the offering of sacrifices,[49] a dance ritual with an initiation structure involving enthusiastic singing, consciousness of Obeah works, shadow catching, pharmacopeia or healing rituals, loosely structured circles of practitioners, and spirit possession trances labeled as "getting wild" or "senseless madness." As Murphy notes, Myal had its own ritual dance, music and drumming style, worship, dreams and vision quest, offerings to the divinity, pharmacopeia or herbal healing, and spirit possession trance.[50] J. H. Buchner's 1854 report of Myal gave this description of its cultus:

> As soon as darkness of evening set in, they assembled in crowds in open pastures, most frequently under large cotton trees, which they worshiped, and counted holy; after sacrificing some fowls, the leader began extempore song, in a wild strain, which was answered in chorus; the dance followed, grew wilder and wilder, until they were in a state of excitement bordering on madness. Some would perform incredible revolutions while in this state, until nearly exhausted, they fell senseless to the

ground, when every word they uttered was received as a divine revelation. At other times, Obeah was discovered, or a "shadow" was caught; a little coffin being prepared in which it was to be enclosed and buried.[51]

In Jamaican mythology, Myalists honored the creator God and departed ancestors or African-derived spirits. These divinities and ancestors, able to possess the faithful, were invoked to guide and protect the ritual community against harm, especially from Europeans. Devotees believed that each person has two souls or spirits: one spirit, referred to as the *duppy*, departs the body at the moment of death and remains in the grave for several days before journeying to take its place among the ancestors. This special occasion was marked by elaborate funeral rites and rituals, which attracted a crowd of people who often were unrelated to the religious cultus. The second spirit was seen as a living person's shadow that needed to be protected from harm caused by evil spirits, witchcraft, and sorcery. It is alleged that when the Myal leader suspected the work of another Myal priest or Obeah-man affecting the person's shadow, a counter-ritual was prescribed and administered.[52] Myal followers emphasized the receiving of dreams and visions as a prerequisite for initiation into the cult, and some practiced water baptism. Ritual dancing and healing, however, were their trademark preoccupation.

DANCE AND HEALING
As a dance religion, Myal kept alive an important African tradition of connecting the impersonal spirits with the body and feelings of the participant. During the dance ritual, worshipers formed the famous circle in which Hope Masterson Waddell, a missionary to Jamaica, claims women "performed a mystic dance, sailing round and round, and wheeling in the center with outspread arms, and wild looks and gestures. Others hummed, or whistled a low monotonous tone, to which the performers kept time, as did the people around, by hands and feet and swaying of their bodies."[53] Music and dance with wild gesticulations expressed a militant defiance and independence in the face of unmitigated hardship. The ring circle-song-and-dance ritual is an African religious practice usually tied to healing and possession trance. The ring circle provided a sense of touch and symbolic connection with the ancestral spirits, but was replaced by the laying on of hands for initiation and healing purposes.

The most popular and indispensable facet of healing was herbal. Myalists are adept in pharmacopeia and used a variety of herbs, vegetables, and other plants in their medicine arsenal. Early accounts of the elaborate initiation into Myal describe the ingestion of an herb extract that produced a trance imitating the death of a devotee. Murphy wrote, "Another herbal preparation resurrected the initiate from this state, and he or she became a member of the *myal* society, immune to the invisible coercions of Africans and Europeans alike."[54] A Myal cultus, centered around community rituals rather than individual fetish, made healing a three-way activity: it connected the supplicant with healing objects and the divine. A Myal-woman or Myal-man (Myal Daddy) functioned like a medical practitioner treating patients in one-on-one conferences.

DADDY-WORKS

The Myal "Daddy," leader, or shaman followed a similar path to the priesthood that was pursued in African religions. One had to receive a call from an appropriate source—a spirit, another Myal shaman, a dream or vision, an illness, a tragedy, or a near-death experience. After a call was established, the initiate underwent an informal but important apprenticeship period in which the trainee first learned the healing potentials and potency of herbs, trees, and various plants, as well as other types of spiritual medicines. During slavery, this training was secretive and irregular and varied greatly in quality. Knowledge of an array of plant pharmacopeia and their use in specific cases qualified the apprentice to advance to the next stage of preparation, which involved soul and spirit conditioning. An apprentice was required to do a dance ritual with great intensity until possessed by the right spirit. Under spirit possession, the initiate was said to be "slain by the spirit"—that is, thrown to the ground by a divinity in a suspended state of consciousness. The initiate convulsed and gave out a moaning or groaning sound. He or she remained in that trance state for several hours and claimed to have been elevated into the spirit world to communicate with the divinity, who bestowed on the new shaman the powers to heal and to see unusual things in the sacred and profane worlds.

The final stage of initiation to the level of shaman, marked by an elaborate ritual bush bath with special sacred herbs, signified to the community that the initiate was no longer an apprentice but was qualified to prescribe healing, give spiritual advice, and dispense medicines. Charismatic leadership, as a spiritual gift, was another important characteristic of Myal-men; they enticed devotees with their style and mesmerized clients with their medicines. Myal-men had many allegiances; they remained firm to African spirituality, often held eldership in their Christian church, and embraced the antislavery and antiestablishment stance taken by their nonconformist missionaries. As Chevannes notes, this dual affiliation made it possible for freedom fighter Sam Sharpe, for example, "to be both a Native Baptist Daddy and at the same time a deacon in the Baptist church, and for tens of thousands of people to retain what subsequently became known as 'dual membership'"[55] in Christian churches and Myal.

Myal did not stage a successful revolution like the Haitian revolt, and its political role in the struggle against slavery and colonialism in Jamaica is not comparable to that of Vodou,[56] but it was a significant spiritual resource for Afro-Jamaicans under stress. It appears to have been a factor in the great slave rebellion of 1760 and a force for social integration and political mobilization among Jamaicans, both bound and free. The oppressive colonial environment in which Africans were thrown warranted appeal to any source of spiritual power available to the "down pressed." According to Besson, "In the post-emancipation period, Myal and the Great Revival were central to the counter-culture of resistance that emerged against the persisting plantation system, which retained its stranglehold in Trelawney."[57] During its interaction with Christianity, Myal fashioned an ideology that held to a sense of African moral and cultural integrity and gave followers a feeling of community. It valued individualism and respected human achievements, especially when communal values were also upheld. Members who achieved success but by their actions and attitudes rejected the community's values were sanctioned.[58] In this context, Myal held a moral canon by which slaves chose to govern their lives in bondage. By the 1830s, the Myal religion had instilled certain ethical and moral codes in Afro-Jamaicans that continued in Kumina and the more recent Rastafari.

Kumina Culture

Like other African religions of Jamaica, Kumina has seen a sharp numerical decline in the last century because of natural attrition, twentieth-century urban migration, a change in the economic and social conditions of rural workers, and the impact of other faiths. Poor economic conditions encouraged African drummers to migrate from their rural dwelling places to cities in search of employment. Many of them eventually settled in what became the slums of west Kingston, where later they would influence Rastafarian practices. As a result of the impact of Christianity and Rastafari on Kumina culture, followers are found today only among a few families scattered in Jamaica's most eastern parish. Notwithstanding its decline, Kumina's influence on Jamaican culture is significant, but as "an oral-based transgenerational tradition"[59] it continues to suffer misrepresentation.

From her intensive study of this religion in 1995 and 1996, Stewart concludes that Kumina "is perhaps the most misunderstood African-Jamaican religious tradition, in part because [its] practitioners produced no liturgical or theological literature pertaining to their beliefs and practices."[60] Because of the spirit-possession trance with which Kumina is associated, colonial critics labeled it "African madness." Kumina's intense drumming ritual ceremony was regarded also as subversive. Horace Campbell contends that "the Jamaican planters had good reason to fear these religious practices because Africans who possessed training as spiritual leaders commanded great respect, and they were usually the ones in the forefront of revolts" regionally.[61] Kumina was also regarded as an ancestral cult, with a neutral or pacifist political consciousness on social and economic conditions in Jamaica.[62]

Kumina is a way of life permeated with religious or cultural tradition. Scholars see Kumina as "a complex and cogently nuanced expression of religious ideas and ritual that govern the lives of adherents as they negotiated experiences that promote or compromise human potential for health . . . productivity, and fulfillment"[63] This creole religion, largely family-based among peasants of eastern rural Jamaica, is "a worldview, a living cultural presence," an African dance tradition.[64] It operates through a system of spiritual communication with the divine and with ancestral spirits as a tool for negotiating life's struggle and contradictions, and is aided by a variety of sacred rituals. Key to this spiritual communication is the ritual cotillion; Kumina avatars dance to the collective memory of their African past as they attempt to deal with their harsh social condition. This creole faith is neither the first African religion in Jamaica, nor the progenitor of Myal and Obeah, and it did not give birth to Rastafari, whose rituals it influenced.

Kumina's Genesis

Since no record exists of the precise date Kumina took root in Jamaica, speculation runs wild. Barrett mistakenly thought the practice of Kumina,[65] as a family ritual, was the first African religious tradition practiced among large numbers of Akan peoples and Maroons in Jamaica. Kumina meetings were held among the Maroons who lived in the hilly country. Later, plantation slaves living near Maroon settlements adopted Kumina practices. Barrett assumes that following the 1760 revolt, Kumina became Myal, which took its name from the spirit-possession dances that accompanied Kumina. The social, matrilineal arrangement in Kumina is seen also as evidence that the religion has an Akan origin. Further, in the beginning, Kumina "was a secret society that supplied the impetus and framework for the psychic struggle against slavery. About the middle of the eighteenth century it emerged as the Myal society; [and it] grew until the middle of the nineteenth century, when it merged again with Afro-Christian cultism and became known as Pukkumina"[66] (Pocomina or Poco). To support this argument, Barrett assumed also that the word *Kumina* is an etymological corruption that combines the Ashanti *Akom*, "to possess or be possessed," and the Akan *ana*, the "ancestor."

Notwithstanding Barrett's assumptions, Kumina succeeded Myal and was neither the first African religion in Jamaica nor does it have a sure Akan origin in slavery. George Eaton Simpson, whose 1970 study had linked Kumina and Convince to Blue Mountain Maroon religion and suggested that Kumina's earliest presence on the island is traceable to enslaved Africans, later agreed with Monica Schuler, Kenneth Bilby and Elliott Leib, and others that Kumina does not have its origin among eighteenth-century plantation slaves; it came to Jamaica with Central African immigrants in the postemancipation era.[67] It appeared in the mid-nineteenth century and represented living evidence of a vibrant religion among descendants of slaves[68] and indentured laborers from West Central Africa; indicators point to a Kongo-Bantu origin for Kumina. As Stewart contends, "The Kumina community was established in eastern Jamaica only through the settlement of post-emancipation African immigrant indentured laborers," so it surfaced in the eastern parish of St. Thomas, among contract immigrant workers, between 1841 and 1865;[69] this is one hundred years later than Barrett claimed. Kumina's rise is attributed to the presence of the fairly large number of Bantu-speaking peoples brought there from the Congo-Angola region.

Much of what is known of Kumina practices and beliefs in late colonial Jamaica were found among immigrant settlers on the island after 1840. The settlers were hired laborers that the British government brought to the Caribbean from the Congo, Nigeria, and elsewhere to help solve the labor shortage on West Indian plantations after 1838. As Laura Tana states, there was an "influx of over 8,000 Yoruba and Central African immigrants who came to Jamaica between 1841 and 1865 as indentured laborers, particularly after 1844."[70] In this period, thousands of Nigerians found work and homes in the British Caribbean. Bantu groups from the Congo also settled primarily on the leeward side of Jamaica, where from the 1840s onward they formed a strong Kumina community with Kongo traditions. Bilby and Leib affirmed that "a great many aspects of the Kumina tradition, including the ritual language, music, and dance through which contact with the ancestors is maintained and fostered, are derived primarily from Central African (and particularly Kongo) cultural traditions."[71] The word *Kumina* also is Bantu in origin, and some of its rituals and ethnic affiliations have their roots in Kongo culture.

Kumina followers refer to themselves as "Bongo" or the "Bakongo nation"; an ethnic designation for Kongo, as well as Bakongo thinking, is central to Kumina tradition. As the name of the African homeland, *Kongo* represents also the most important Central African group to settle in eastern Jamaica. Like the followers of Convince Cult who are led by a Bongo Man, devotees of the family-oriented Kumina religion also share the common understanding that they are Bongo people originating from the Bakongo of the Kongo. In the 1950s, Donald Hogg and Joseph Moore found that Kumina was still alive in the parish of St. Thomas where, in the 1970s, Monica Schuler witnessed the smoking of cannabis in Kumina rituals. This African practice of smoking ganja is common in Kongo nightly healing ritual dances that are designed to attract the spirit and enhance healing powers of devotees.[72] During his research in the parish of St. Thomas in the late 1970s, Bilby also found that Kumina devotees commonly smoked cannabis for spiritual guidance and inspiration. Many adherents used Central African terms to describe cannabis and the pipes in which they smoked it. "Oral traditions passed down by post-emancipation Kikongo immigrants to their offspring also bear witness" that cannabis smoking in Jamaica among Rastas may have a Central African origin.[73]

Kumina Mythology

Although most African deities have not survived by name in Jamaican creole culture, Kumina has not lost the basic theology of West Central Africa; believers hold to the African cosmology of a created universe operated by a divinity and spirits who affect the daily lives of humans. According to Stewart, "Although Jamaican Kumina emphasizes continuity between the visible and invisible domains of the human and ancestral world, practitioners claim to worship one Deity, whom they call Zambi or King Zambi"[74] (from Kongo Nzambi, not zombi spirits). Followers recognize the great creator God, Zambi, and hundreds of ancestral spirits, among whom are roughly forty sky divinities. Some of these include Jubee, Belgium, Bebee, Fasha, Fee, Flash, Obei, Otto, Twiss, and Shango, the Yoruba god of thunderstorms and fire (perhaps the only African divinity whose authentic name is retained and venerated). Simpson and Moore identified sixty-two other earthbound deities, many of whom had ancient Hebrew names, and twenty-one ancestral spirits.[75] As Simpson reports, some Kumina deities in Jamaica "serve groups which appear to belong to the tribes of 'nations,' among which the most frequently mentioned are *mondogo, moyenge, machunde, kongo,* and *mumbaka.* Other groups sometimes mentioned are *gaw, ibo,* and *yoruba.*"[76] Since Kumina is largely a family religion, each group or cell honors special divinities and family ancestral spirits.

Kumina followers posit the existence of good and bad spirits, duppies, and shadows or ghosts that have the power to aid or harm human beings. There are also spiritual entities divided into three ranks: "sky gods, who rank the highest; then earthbound gods; and last, ancestors. All three types of spirits possess their mortal followers and can be identified by African rituals associated with them: by their food preferences, drum rhythms, and style of dancing"[77] mediums. Devotees generally invoke the spirits of deceased family members, some of whom are referred to as duppies. Myth has it that there are twenty-one ancestral duppies, regarded as the spirits of male and female devotees who, during their lifetime, experienced spirit-possession in the dance ritual and so were either dancing spirits, drummers, or Obeah-men. Some of these ancestral spirits have attained the status of divinities.

According to Stewart, Kumina devotees "believe that each human being is essentially who she is due to the unique combination of her *kanuba* (spirit), *deebu* (blood), and *beezie* (flesh). The *kanuba* shapes the human personality and is patrilineally derived. The *beezie,* on the other hand, is matrilineally derived, and the *deebu* can be derived from either side."[78] The individual's three component parts are also perceived as body, soul-spirit, and duppy-ghost or shadow. As in Egyptian religion, a person's ghost or shadow is not the image that the body casts in light but a spiritual entity or one's twin self. In this mythology, one's duppy, which could haunt the living after death, operates in an inverse way to humans. It sleeps during the day and roams the community at nights, lurking in dark alleys, abandoned buildings, and under trees, but must be back in its tomb before daybreak. Its feet never touch the ground (some are said to have feet with cow hooves); it talks with a clogged nasal accent, laughs in a shrill juvenile tone, and is able to count only to four. Villagers who know the duppy's traits and habits keep the undesirable entities at bay by performing certain rituals—for example, reciting the Lord's Prayer, making the sign of the cross when one gets a duppy sensation, and counting beyond the number four.[79] This is creole (Africanized-Christian) mythology at its best.

At death, the soul or spirit journeys to the heavens and returns to the supreme Creator, where it joins with other spirits. The ghost or duppy traipses for several days, after which the family must lay it to rest through a special funeral rite. If these rites are not performed, the duppy could tramp indefinitely and carry out evil acts by manipulating sorcerers or natural and psychic phenomena. Elizabeth Pigou states, "During the interval between clinical death and the time the duppy is laid to rest, the individual is not fully dead. The purpose of the funeral rite is to secure the safe journey of the spirit as well as to placate the duppy."[80] This belief in a world of spirits, duppies or ghosts, death rites, and funeral practices in Kumina, Convince, Obeah, and Myal have had a profound impact on Jamaican culture. Older Jamaicans have a great respect for the spirits of the dead and value communication with them in some fashion. On the other hand, Pigou writes that "because of the potentially evil nature of duppies, there is a distinctive fear of the dead. The greatest evil duppies are considered capable of is the infliction of death. So there is a wide range of ritual acts designed to protect the individual and community from duppy-inflicted death"[81] that are part of Jamaica's folklore traditions.

Kumina Rituals

Membership in this family-based religion is obtained by inheritance rather than through the rite of incorporation—although, in some cases, the rules have changed to allow inquirers from other ethnic groups and families to join if they meet conditions established by the community. Matrilineal arrangements determine one's membership in that the spirits possessing a member are ancestral spirits of that member's mother's clan or cell. Kumina has small sect cells whose organization imitates the African ethnic "nation" structure seen in Candomble. Each cell has its own chief and queen, or mother, who are responsible for the ritual life of the cult;[82] they conduct ceremonies to mark a variety of important community and family events. Devotees memorialize deceased relatives and ancestors, whose help they seek in addressing domestic needs, sickness, and tragedies. According to Stewart, these elevated departed loved ones "acquire power and use it to assist their living descendants in the visible world"; therefore devotees "are in constant communication with ancestors who validate and replenish their steadfast communication with Africa." In this regard, "through ritual possession and other acts of devotion, Kumina Africans constantly strengthen the metaphysical continuity between the living and the dead, the visible and the invisible, the Bongo nation and the Bongo ancestors" (the name of the Kumina ancestral homeland and ethnic identity).[83]

RITUAL DANCE
Kumina ceremonies, done nocturnally and held on different holidays, are always performed with ritual dances. They begin with a leader greeting the

spirits with special rhythmic drumming while welcoming and feeding them before beginning the ceremonial dance held to honor a long-deceased family member. Dances mark the end of a memorial celebration and a "wake" during a time of mourning. Entombment dances involve cotillions appended to a memorial services. During a memorial ritual, participants do circular dances around the graves of their ancestors and recently deceased family. They perform these rituals so that the ancestral spirits can reappear through a possession trance. The African ring dance requires participants to move in time with the beat of *banda* drums. As Joseph Moore explains, "Dancing is always counter-clockwise around the ring, and can be done alone or with a partner. . . . Ancestral zombies each have distinct dance styles more closely related to the basic African dance."[84] Crop-over dances are sometimes tied to these memorial capering. Crop-over, held in late July, also survived as a very festive holiday in Barbados and elsewhere in the Caribbean and has marked the end of the harvesting of the sugarcane crop since colonial times.

The Kumina ceremony, which could attract small gatherings and up to hundreds of participants, begins on late Friday evening and lasts through Saturday night. Worshipers sing two types of spirit-inducing songs: *Bilah* (Bilo, Bailo) and country. The former is sung in Jamaica English, whereas the other uses patois, the local Jamaican dialect. A prominent member of the group leads by singing each line of the song while the audience follows in call-and-response fashion. Women in Kumina are both leaders and singers, just as in Africa. On slave plantations, "women sang songs of their 'own composing' which were answered in the same manner by men. Slave women sang so-called 'wild choruses of joy' at crop-over but also expressed through song the sorrow of enslavement."[85] Jamaican Kumina avatars were not slaves but were influenced by slave traditions. A Kumina tradition holds that male singers are usually drummers while female singers are dancers. A female singer is called Mother of the Kumina, or the "black and white girl" because the master of ceremonies wears a black and white cord around her neck as the badge of her office. The female singer wears the official insignia, also, if the male leader is absent or is under spirit possession. Ancestral spirits generally possess devotees during Kumina ceremonies that involve drumming, dancing, and singing. Possession "takes place at funeral rites as well as all other important community events, particularly as an aspect of worship"[86] in the cult.

SACRIFICE AND HEALING
Animal sacrifice is an indispensable Kumina ritual. The life of an animal, caught in the dripping blood of the sacrifice, is an essential means of communication with the divine. Before dawn, on the day of a festival, Kumina avatars sacrifice a goat or a chicken while a Queen and her "train," or procession, dance to the arrival of ancestors that are being honored. The Queen is often a relative of the family that sponsored the Kumina dance and sacrifice and the slaughterer is spiritually designated to perform the sacred act. The animal's blood

must be mixed with rum as an offering to the spirit. After the sacrificial act is completed, no part of the meat is left to waste. Devotees get portions of meat to take home or, more commonly, a meal is prepared with the meat for all in attendance, so that the sacrificial offering involves an act of feasting in a tight communal fellowship. Foods prepared for sacrifices are unsalted because, in Kumina mythology, ancestral spirits do not consume sodium. Africans who do not eat salted foods acquire the power to see and interpret secret things and are enabled to fly back to Africa. Before the appearance of Kumina, plantation slaves saw salted foods as a European entrapment; it was designed to jinx them and corrupt their minds with colonial ideas and thus thwart their plans and hopes of repatriating to freedom in the motherland.[87] Afro-Jamaicans now know that heavily salted foods are unhealthy for other reasons.

For the health of its supporters, all African ancestral religions practice healing and magic in an attempt to influence the cosmic powers responsible for human life to act favorably on behalf of a client. In the diaspora, colonial oppression, physical and mental abuse, ravages of disease, poverty, poor health, and the need for spiritual and psychological intervention make healing, both herbal and magical, indispensable for a people in trauma with meager access (if any) to modern medicine. As Stewart notes, Kumina ceremonies are performed to mark important events like births, deaths, and the honoring of ancestors, as well as to commemorate past struggles and achievements of forebears, but healing is Kumina's most popular ritual activity. In Kumina, healing takes the form of prayer services for the sick, herbal medicines, libations, ritual baths and sacrificial food offerings to the spirits, Myal-influenced possession, and other forms of benign magic. Kumina Queens are known for their balm-yard healing, special herbal teas, and spiritual consultation and magic. From personal observations, Stewart writes, "Kumina leaders, who are almost always female, are regularly sought out by the sick and troubled for their expert knowledge of therapeutic plants and access to ancestral power."[88] They augment their knowledge and skill in herbal properties, spring water, and other pharmacopeia with the elemental or cosmic forces to address a range of ailments in the Afro-Jamaican community, many of whose members are not members of the Kumina cult. Healing is most often sought during the Kumina ritual ceremony that involves animal sacrifice, drumming, singing, dancing, spirit possession, and the summoning of ancestors to the aid of sick clients.[89]

NINE-NIGHT VIGIL

On the night following a person's death, family members and friends hold a wake or "setup" that lasts all night. In some cases, the wake last several nights while the family makes funeral arrangements and awaits the arrival of relatives from abroad. The body may be kept for a maximum of nine days, at the end of which (that is, on the night before burial) the "Nine-Night" ritual is performed. Those attending the wake console mourners, sing African and Christian dirges, and liberally drink locally brewed Jamaican rum. The dirges are a carryover from slave songs, which had an African structure in their call-and-response mode. Several days might pass before the body is actually taken for interment to the family or community plot, where other rituals follow. In a Christian burial, the body leaves the parlor headfirst as a sign of honor and respect to the departed soul. In a Kumina funeral, the dead must exit a building feet first because of the belief that the duppy, or ghost, never travels backward and will not return to haunt the places it has left behind or torment the family. Graves must also be ritually sealed to contain the deceased spirit. "The sealing is done to the accompaniment of drumming, all to secure the final resting of the duppy and prevent its return to harm the community,"[90] and to mournful shrieking in honor of the deceased.

In a Kumina graveside ritual, the body is buried amid the singing of Christian and African hymns and the reading of scripture. At a funeral in the Plantain Garden River district that Monica Schuler attended, mourners sang in Kongo, telling their mothers that they were mourning because a Kongo man has gone, a good friend has gone, he has gone to the other side.

African man is mourning he has gone mother, mother, eh!
Kongo man is mourning a friend has gone.
Kongo man is mourning he has gone over there. . . .[91]

Respect for the deceased fuels many myths and folk tales. Three days after a person is buried, a cloud of smoke is said to rise from the grave, signaling that person's return in the form of a duppy. When a duppy reenters the house, occupants must burn cow's dung, a rosemary bush, and an animal horn to ensure its prompt departure. Myth has it that the duppy can catch the voices of persons who talk loudly at night and injure them, so one should speak softly at night and, before throwing things out through a window in the dark, one must give a warning to the spirits. These practices and beliefs have a long history in an ancient African-Egyptian religion. In the death rites and rituals of Jamaican peasants, they underscore the fact that things associated with death "are harmful and contaminating."[92] However, they also speak to the African belief in the afterlife and the precariousness of life in colonial Jamaica.

Sacred Kumina Drums

African cultural traditions in the Caribbean are heard most audibly in music, at the base of which are the omnipresent and sacred drums. During slavery, a special beat of the drums indicated the time to abscond to the hills, situations of danger, a call for freedom fighters to rally and resist the enemy, or a call to celebrate African traditions; celebrating those traditions became the dominant role of Kumina drums after emancipation. In addition to their cultural functions, drums speak the language of the sprit; mark the beginning and the ending of ritual actions; control the activities of the ancestral spirits, ghosts, or duppies; set rhythmic tones in spirit-possession dances; summon and announce the arrival or departure of the spirits; and signify a divinity's acceptance or rejection of sacrificial offerings. Instruments such as scrapers and shakers accompany ritual singing, but the rhythmic drumming remains indispensable. As Barrett observes, in Kumina two drums are necessary but as many as six "can be used along with the African trumpet, the triangle, and other instruments for beating out rhythms"[93] of the spirit in rituals. The Kumina two-drum duet comprises the beating of the *baandu* and the *cyas*.

There is a widespread pattern of cross-pollination between Kumina drumming styles and other Afro-Jamaican drums played in Burru music. In urban centers, like Kingston's shantytown, Burru and Kumina drumming and musical styles fused into more secular forms than the ones found in rural areas of Jamaica. A Kumina drumming style, found in crime-ridden west Kingston, was associated with celebrating a person's release from prison. The drumming style, according to Bilby and Leib, "had no association with ceremonies connected with the dead, and thus, its stigma would be reduced for Rastafari musicians seeking inspiration from African-derived drum-related musical forms"[94] that had a significant impact on the evolution of Rasta-reggae music. The cross-fertilized form of Kumina and Burru drumming created one of the foundation beats that later became Jamaica's famous reggae music.

Conclusion

Although Kumina is no longer a numerically significant religion in Jamaica, it remains an important complement to Jamaica's cultural and religious history and has had a significant impact on the formation of other creole religions on the island. The rituals have almost disappeared in the burgeoning urban environment, but the drumming continues to be heard on special occasions in sections of west Kingston. Aspects of Kumina ceremonies "have gained considerable publicity as an art form," and the religion "is seen as a vivid, active, and creative form of cultural expression."[95] The Jonkunnu dance, still popular in Jamaica's annual cultural festivals, had Kumina influences and may have originated from the West African yam festival or the Kongo gumbay masquerading dance. In the 1930s, Rastafari founder Leonard Howell incorporated Kumina practices as well as drumming techniques into his movement's rituals. When he fled St. Thomas under police persecution, his hardcore supporters, who helped him establish Pinnacle Commune in St. Catherine around 1940, were Baptist-Kuminist. A number of Bilby and Leib's informants state that Howell's "original group at Pinnacle was composed primarily of persons originally from St. Thomas, the parish where Kumina is most strongly represented"; hence, Kumina "became an important source for Rastafari's rituals."[96] Chevannes maintains that after their Sunday dinner, Howell followers at the Pinnacle commune gathered in a parade, "dancing and singing to the rhythms of the *baandu* and the *funde*, two Kumina drums."[97] Rasta Howellites have retained many Kumina-based practices and demonstrate knowledge of Kumina-Kongo language, history, and songs. Bilby and Leib conclude that "through such interchange, the invigorating rhythms of Kumina, meshed with those of Burru and perhaps others have indirectly been able, via [Nyabingi], to enter the Jamaican musical mainstream."[98] Long live the influence of Kumina.

13

Poco, Zion, and Convince

KEY TOPICS

*Poco and Zion Origination • Stewed in Different Cauldrons •
Functionaries and Performance • Sacred Space and Rituals •
Convince Cult • Afro-Colonial Christianity*

In the late 1800s, Jamaica saw several creole religious movements appearing under the nomenclature of Revivalism, a name given to groups affected by the experience of Jamaica's Great Revival of 1860 and 1861. The religious signification Great Revival describes a period of religious fervor fueling activities and manifestations that were influenced by the Great Revival of the 1850s in the United States. The U.S. revival phenomenon was largely Christian, but in Jamaica it effervesced into new Afro-Caribbean expressions that blended African spirituality with elements of Christianity and spiritism (the practice of employing ancestral spirits to reinforce existence). Revivalism also identifies the rituals associated with the revival ethos and the values that informed it. Under this caption is grouped the diverse creole Jamaican religious movements of Convince, Poco (Pocomina), Zion, Bedwardism, Spiritist Baptist, and Rastafari, some of which have faded into Jamaica's recent past while others have only recently arrived. These religions succeeded Myal and Kumina, which appear to be the antecedents and the probable source of Poco and Zion, but they show the impact of Protestant Christianity on Jamaica's African religious culture. Like all Afro-Caribbean religions, they have their roots in African ancestral traditions but were germinated (or reborn) in a colonial Protestant Christian culture and share many features among them.[1] While the eighteenth- and nineteenth-century Myal and Kumina were rural and distinctly African, the others are largely eclectic urban phenomena that began in the throes of the economic and social dislocation of postemancipation Jamaica.

Poco and Zion

Poco and Zion are traditions of charisma, "a set of shared ways of working the spirit in the tradition of the Great Revival and the African traditions which underlie it."[2] As two of the most creole religions in Jamaica, they represent a stage in the African-Christian flowering of religious syncretism in the Caribbean. Dianne Stewart regards as "dubious" scholarship and colonial religious "bias" the view that these revival religions have been heavily influenced by Christianity,[3] but I contend that none of the creole religions in the Caribbean are or have been completely African; none have escaped the influence of Christianity. Some traditions evolved into sects so far removed from their ancestry that they bear only diminished resemblances to African traditional religions (ATRs). Zionists, for example, are so Christian in their beliefs that members have to change little of their theology to fit into nontraditional Spiritual Baptist and some revival Christian churches. Poco, the more African of the two, was labeled a corruption of Christianity. Stewart may be correct in contending that "orthodox beliefs, doctrines, and rituals of Western Christianity are either absent or superficially present in Revival Zionism,"[4] but the Christianity of Afro-Caribbean peoples, especially Jamaicans, has a long-standing tradition in heterodoxy. Poco and Zion are Christian influenced, but they represent what Barry Chevannes calls "bits and pieces of evidence of a worldview" that differs from the Euro-Christian cosmology and that stands in some contradiction to it.[5]

Poco is a Jamaican creole spirituality with a dynamic African ethos, but its origin is debated. Attempts have been made to connect the African *kimbundu kumona*, meaning "spiritual insight," to Pocomina. Another view regards Poco as a corruption of the Hindi word *pukka*, meaning "reality" or "real," used by indentured Indian workers in Jamaica. It is also suggested that Myal characteristics may have been added to the Twi words *po* ("shaking" or "trembling") and *kom* ("dancing wildly") to designate a new religion, Pocomina. The words *poco* ("small") and *mania* ("madness"), said to be of Spanish origin, are also proffered as the genesis of the poco religion. Edward Seaga, who links *poco* semantically to *Kumina* to defend its African rendering as *Pukkumina*, contends that it survived as an African religious sect that absorbed Myal practices before becoming popular in the late nineteenth century.[6] More recently, Stewart and others have given more credence to the Myal-Kongo connection of Poco and Zion; they argue that the designation *poco* is an actual derivative of the Kikongo term *mumpoko*, one of the most powerful components in the Kongo pharmacopeia used in the rituals of healing and blessing. The plant has the potential to send one into a trance and to induce reactions that are not unlike some experienced in Poco and Zion. Stewart notes that studies show practices that appear to parallel those of Kongo religious culture. "We know that Myal is the parent source of the movements emerging from the Great Revival of 1860–1861. Consequently, any connection drawn between Myal and Africa is plausibly a connection between Revival Zion and Africa."[7] This Kongo origination of Poco and Zion links them more closely to Kumina and Myal than was originally thought.

The 1959 novel *A Quality of Violence* correctly places Poco in the social and economic reality of the early 1860s. Andrew Salkey locates the novel in a time of drought and great hardship in Jamaica, and gives clear indications that, as Kenneth Ramchand observes, he has a "larger artistic purpose" for the Poco follower than the depiction of "frenzied manifestations."

> Pocomanians find the substance of their lives breaking up beyond control in the endless drought. Dada Johnson, their leader, sees their faith in him collapsing, and the deputy is looking around for the right moment to make a bid for primacy. These motives operate in the spectacular dance ("the Giant X") in which the dancers equate their bodies with the land, each whipping himself in an attempt to banish the barrenness of the land and that of the earthly body. [They shout] "We must lash the devil out of the land. We must lash good water into the land."[8]

Sylvia Wynter's 1962 novel *The Hills of Hebron* comically depicts Afro-Jamaican religions and is even more direct than Salkey's book. Wynter shows great concern for the emptiness and misery in the lives of the impoverished, depressed, and hopeless Poco followers, and suggests social and economic adjustments as a solution. Wynter's angry labor leader, Moses, one of her lead characters, uses antireligious language to urge his people to forget organized religion and to contemplate the extent of their misery, their poverty, and the dark and hopeless future of their children.[9] They must believe not in the gods but in humans and in their organized labor union.

Poco began in 1861 among African immigrants to Jamaica. It is referred to locally as "Sixty-one," pointing to the date of its founding, whereas Zion is called "Sixty." In the 1870s and 1880s, Poco quietly spread to a few rural communities. In 1909 it came to public attention in the parish of St. Mary, where one newspaper referred to it as a distinctly new endeavor, and again in 1912, when an Anglican clergy reported in an article that Poco had spread to St. Catherine and St. Ann among the working class, calling it a "new superstitious cult" and a "cousin of Myalism."[10] As expected, mainline Christians regarded this new "thing" as bizarre, fanatic, wild, childish, and pagan. One reporter's hyperbole stated that, at meetings, Poco followers tore off their hair, beat their chests, and engaged in weird ejaculations. They also made a barking sound that distinguished them from their predecessors. Poco followers worked themselves into a frenzy and "cut their bodies with pieces of tin" while citing a "scriptural text saying there can be no remission of sin without the shedding of blood."[11] If these practices existed, they were probably not widespread or common among all Poco groups.

Because of the disapprobation they have received in Jamaican society, adherents of Poco refer to themselves as Baptist (Nativist Baptist), Zionist, or Revivalists. Poco has been labeled as debased Christian superstition mingled with Obeah, and its followers as comical illiterates whose lack of Christian values contributes to their lives of suffering. Poco's ceremonies have been said to have a propensity for loud and unusual behavior. Its followers are shunned even by other revival groups; Zionists, or children of Revival Zion, "distinguish themselves from *pocomina* by pointing out the biblical foundations of all their activities and citing the failures of *pocomina* churches to do the same."[12] They also disassociate themselves from Poco followers and are proud to be Sixties instead of Sixty-ones; Sixty-ones supposedly dance and bow to the earth, the home of Satan, Rutibel, and the other fallen angels, whereas Sixties claim to worship good spirits, prophets, saints, apostles, and the Christian trinity. There is no evidence that the belief in fallen angels and Satan are African in origin.[13] In Revival Zion, the idea that fallen angels who were cast out of heaven by God are bound to the earth and the underworld is certainly influenced by Christian Scriptures, especially the apocalyptic literature, rather than by African religion.

Stewed in Different Cauldrons

Jamaican Zion is not related to the post-World War II political movement devoted to the preservation of the state of Israel, and is not affiliated with Africa's traditional and proto-Christian church of Zion in Natal South Africa (although the latter shares revival and ancestral beliefs and practices). Revival Zion also was unaffiliated with the African Methodist Episcopal Zion (AMEZ) church, founded in New York in 1796. In spite of the attempt to give it a U.S. origin, its modern interaction and affiliation with U.S.-based revivalist churches came about one hundred years later.[14] Notwithstanding their Great Revival Baptist influence and their tightly knit Afro-Christian syncretism, significant points of departure exist between Christianity and revival Zion and Poco thinking, which are influenced by Myal and Kumina cosmology. Christians take exceptions to the polytheistic elements in ancestral worship, as well as to animal sacrifice. The practice of spirit possession in Zion and Poco is not cherished in mainline branches of Christianity. Christians frown upon the Revivalists' "emotional manifestations of the spirit, and even if the fundamental division of exclusiveness and inclusiveness were somehow to disappear, a cultist would get little satisfaction from a service where his participation is restricted to hymn singing and responses from a prayer book."[15] As Stewart puts it, Zionist and Poco's "classical African communotheism" associates spirit messengers with forces of nature that manifest the "Creator or representative Supreme Divinity"; and natural creation—whether moon, sun, waters, or fire—"are sources of power, healing, cleansing, and harmony"[16] as well as being destructive.

To outsiders of the faiths, both Zion and Poco are *poco*-stew cooked in the same revival cauldron. Their avatars, however, use various markers to differentiate between their two traditions. The tall conspicuous flag pole at the "meeting house" is one distinguishing feature. Zionists showcase a red flag, a pair of scissors, and the Bible to symbolically cut and clear away any evil or malicious spirits that attempt to infiltrate their ranks; leaders with special spiritual gifts are said to be able to detect the presence of those spirits before they strike. Followers highlight differences in ritual styles between the groups and point to the different ways in which Zionists "trump," or breathe rhythmically during their ritual dance under spirit possession. Pocos trump upward and take a groan (heavy, course breathing) down, whereas Zionists groan upward and trump down. According to one myth, all Zionists came directly from Mt. Zion, their spiritual or mythological church. Another myth states that all children of God came from Zion, which is God's Holy City.[17]

Poco and Zion also share differences in beliefs and practices. Christian symbols and the Bible are central to the beliefs and rituals of Zionists; charismatic leaders around whom Poco is centered show some familiarity with the scriptures but are more influenced by Kumina and Myal traditions than are the leaders of Zion.[18] Especially in west Kingston, Poco followers place emphasis on singing and ritual dance and give less time than Zionists do to explaining and preaching from the Bible. Zionists show little respect for any of the African spirits they recognize as existing realities; they "deal primarily with Heavenly spirits and with apostles and prophets of the 'earthbound' group. They believe in the existence of other spiritual powers but consider them evil, and therefore useful only for evil purposes."[19] Both religions show belief in the existence of evil spirits, but Poco followers respect good and bad spirits alike. Adherents of Poco seek the help of earth-bound spirits, while Zionists invoke Christian saints, angels, biblical prophets, and the Holy Spirit. Chevannes claims that "all spirits are powerful in Pukumina, which is closer to traditional African religions in which there is no equivalent of the evil spirit Christians call Satan; all spirits can possess believers and therefore deserve respect, an attitude also found in Vodun and Orisha (Shango)."[20] Zionists use neither alcohol nor ganja in rituals, whereas Poco believers use both for religious purposes and are also said to practice Obeah.

Revivalists acknowledge a three-level divine pantheon: heavenly divinities, earthbound spirits, and ground spirits. The Christian trinity, archangels, and saints constitute the first category. A Hindu deity, who descends only on the Mother leader, is also in this pantheon. God—the leading power of the trinity, the force and creator of the world—is "Big Massa" and "Massa God" (both colonial designations), who manifests himself in such phenomena as lightning and thunder. It is believed that this God does not play a significant role in the daily running of the revivalists' life; he is distant, dwells in the highest heaven, and is not in direct communication with humans. God does not descend on worshipers during ceremonies, nor does he possess anyone. God may receive prayers and worship, but spirits of the lesser orders are the ones who are "propitiated, exorcized, remunerated, and contacted for advice and protection for specific purposes."[21] Jesus occupies an important role in Zion as an object of prayer and worship. According to Chevannes, the benevolence of Jesus "earns him the frequently heard appellations 'Father Jesus,' or 'Papa Jesus,' and at times one is unsure whether he is thus being identified as the incarnation of

Big Massa. He is also the same spirit as the 'Lamb.'"[22] During services, Jesus visits the faithful, who hold a love feast in his honor and remember deceased members.

The second category of Zion spirits consists of fallen angels or evil powers, biblical prophets, and apostles. These spirits possess Zionists and receive worship and propitiation. In Zion and Poco, rituals culminate in spirit possession, but the possessing spirits are not only African divinities; they could be those of Hebrew prophets, evangelists or apostles, archangels, and the Holy Spirit. All dead humans, other than those mentioned in the Bible, constitute the third category of spirits. Zionists do not worship fallen angels and evil spirits, although they can use them for malicious purposes. Poco believers communicate chiefly with "ground" spirits (probably of Hindu influence), African spirits, and fallen angels, whom they do not regard as necessarily evil and whom they find more accessible than the ones Zionists recognize. Poco spirits are stronger than Zionist spirits, who are considered too cautious in action and too busy to render personal attention to devotees. Spirits of deceased relatives, called duppies, complete the revivalist pantheon. Myth has it that these duppies can roam the community at night and terrorize the living. "They may also be used by obeahmen to harm people. The most feared are East Indian, Chinese, and baby duppies. To relatives, however, duppies may assume protective roles, communicating with them in sleep"[23] through dreams and visions.

Functionaries and Performance

No institutional structure unifies Poco or Zion groups and no religious authority exists beyond the leader of the local "bands" (used as a singular as well as plural word). Revivalist leadership, however, is not chaotic. In their urban setting, Poco and Zion developed a stable leadership structure of both men and women. In Poco, shamans—called Shepherds and Shepherdesses— give spiritual direction to their bands and have almost complete control over their followers. Serving under the direction of these shepherds are "undershepherds," shepherdesses, and a band's Mother, who functions in various capacities. Bands recognize such titles as the "wheeling shepherd," who is responsible for leading the ritual dance; the "watchman shepherd," who maintains order at meetings; and the "spying shepherd," who ensures that the spirits function in an orderly fashion in the meetings and that unwelcome spirits keep their distance or at least do not disturb proceedings. Like-minded bands engage in fellowship and informally share mutual attendance at ritual celebrations and spontaneous occasions that allow leaders to collaborate reciprocally. Elders (older leaders) pass on ritual ways to new leaders, who freely improvise upon them.[24]

Followers of Zion are classified as leaders, post-holders, and floor members but also have other functional positions, such as Mother, Shepherd Boy, Governess, and Armor-bearer. All members of revival bands are called brothers and sisters. The highest-ranking leaders in Zion are called Fathers and Mothers; male leaders are also called captains. The functions of Mothers within the groups are equivalent to those of the men; they serve as herbalists, medicine specialists, and healers. Often, a man and a woman lead a "bands." The leader's assistant, called an Armor-bearer, holds the next high position in the bands, but in groups headed by males, it is Mothers who are often the next in rank. Deacons and Elders (Christian titles), most of whom are women and who assist with the ritual and ceremonial activities of the bands, are third in leadership rank. Other participants, called floor members, consist of both those who "have the spirit" and those who do not. It is not absolutely necessary "for certain of the post-holders to have the spirit."[25] They have varying degrees of authority and responsibility in the bands. A bands is a "unit group" in both Poco and Zion. According to Seaga, "Some bands are branches of other groups within their respective cult. The branch groups in such cases . . . do not pay financial dues to the major body. The leader of this latter bands has authority over the members of the branch group, but such authority is usually exercised with more restraint than in the case of his own bands"[26] for political reasons.

The leader of each bands maintains sole responsibility for the harmonious functioning of the cult and the disciplining of its members, which may range from imposing a sanction to requiring physical punishment. The leader is the custodian of information on matters related to rites, rituals, teachings, the spirits' power, pharmacopeia, and important financial and business matters. The effective functioning of the leader and the efficacy of his or her craft are shrouded in secrecy and confidentiality within the bands. Hence, there is a significant gap between a leader's knowledge in spiritual matters and the knowledge of those in the lower ranks. After examining some revival groups in his research, Seaga discovered that in most cases, cultic functionaries such as Mothers, Shepherd Boys, and Armor-bearer can provide only elementary information on spirit matters. Leaders regard these as their personal prerogatives; they share information at their convenience and only to those persons whom they deem worthy to receive them. Such worthy persons include functionaries, the next-in-command to the leader, and others whose enthusiasm, trustworthiness, and spiritual gifts are proved.[27]

Followers of Poco and Zion are largely washerwomen, unskilled seasonal workers, unemployed homemakers, and the underemployed; unemployment among women in many parts of Jamaica borders on a stupefying 75 percent. Following emancipation, many people faced busted hopes, homelessness, hunger, starvation, and disfranchisement. Women found, in the religious community, strength and support to fight depression, poor health, and other social or economic disadvantages.[28] Some men visit Zion sects for social reasons, whereas others take a genuine interest in the cult; nonmembers perform perfunctory tasks and serve as drummers. The fact that Zion and Poco bands (especially Zion) are frequently headed by women is explained by the dominance of women in the membership of both cults, as is the case in most Afro-Caribbean religions. Seaga found that "only about ten percent of the Zion membership is male in contrast to about 35 percent in Pukkumina."[29] In Poco, a female head (called Mother) retains a Governess as second-in-command. Together, they control all affairs of the Poco bands and only the degree of their authority differentiates them one from the other. Serving at a lower level are many other functionaries: Dove, Cutter, Hunter, Sawyer, Planner, Messenger, Nurse, Bell Ringer, Time Keeper, River Maid, Earth Cleaner, Engineer, Coal Maid, Surveyor, Postman, and Acolyte. Each one has specific duties. "Below these post-holders are those with no positions and often without the spirit. There are very few positions in Pukkumina for which having the spirit is not essential."[30] During worship, many of those who are possessed get repeated experiences or visitations from spiritual powers.

Each Zionist group, or bands, averages between forty and sixty bona fide members who attend meetings regularly, although a larger number frequents the bands. The bands actively recruit, but becoming a communicant of the bands begins with a process of conversion that requires an introduction to special ways of working the spirit. Here, one is led into deeper spiritual experiences through purification and initiation rituals. The initiate is stripped and sponged with an herbal and pharmaceutical concoction that may include water, a coconut beverage, milk, sodas, herbs, and (in the case of Poco) blood from a sacrificed animal. The liquid used for bathing the inductee is allowed to dry on his or her body to attract the spirits. If a sufficient number of members are in attendance during the initiation, singing, Bible reading, and prayer accompany the ritual. One can become a member also through a call, a dream, and a vision. The visitation is confirmed and sealed with possession by the spirit. Reception of messages from the spirits is one of the first signs that one has entered Zion. The initial experience of spirit possession transforms the initiate and provides access to the world of spiritual power. The new status enables one to communicate frequently with the spirits, and the spiritual gifts received are used to enrich the bands through corporate worship, which is encouraged in the rituals of singing, dancing, prayer, and praise.[31]

Sacred Space and Rituals

SEALS AND MISSION GROUNDS

Most members of the bands reside at their private homes, but a few live on the "seal grounds" or "mission grounds," so called because each site has a "mission house" that provides limited accommodation for some women devotees. The mission grounds are marked with a number of seals or sacred objects and spaces designed to attract the spirits. They are consecrated colorfully with lighted candles and an assortment of sacred objects; they occupy a portion of the "yard space" on the leader's premises and vary in shape and size but rarely exceed four thousand square feet. The area accommodates the mission house, which averages about six hundred square feet; a small garden of sacred herbs for pharmacopeia; and sacred spots. Seaga writes, "Most Revival grounds have huts which are large enough to accommodate two or three people. These huts, called 'offices,' are for private consultations with clients seeking healing or aid. . . . Spirits particularly efficient in such matters are said to reside at these 'offices'"[32] to serve the faithful.

The mission house is furnished with bench seats and a long rectangular table, called the Feasting Table, placed at one end near an altar. A seal that comes in the form of a pole is made visible at the entrance to the mission. The tall pole, erected in the center, or most sacred corner of the "seal ground" of the sacred precinct flies a multicolored flag designed to mark the sacred precinct. The pole also supports an ark that honors and attracts spirits that pass by. The three-tiered altar in the sanctuary is the most sacred seal; all sacred rites and rituals are performed around it. Altars serve the important function of focusing the feast and other spiritual activities of the cult. There, leaders offer prayers, administer healing rituals or balms, and supplicate the spirits on behalf of the sick and needy. From the altars, spirits are dispatched to treat persons afflicted with Obeah and other curses.

The "inner seal," or station, is another sacred space in the mission that holds a small table on which a large container of holy water is placed, as well as fruits, grains of corn, candles, a coconut, herbs, a grapefruit, and salt. From this sacred seal in the sanctuary, the Revivalists commence ceremonies and do their ritual dance. A seal consisting of a small, round plot of land marked off by whitewashed stones encloses sacred herbs with familiar plants and with figures representing saints and known by Bible names. Dedicated to the "Dove" and situated in the backyard, another seal, resembling a birdbath and consisting of a white basin with water, sits on a pole that is approximately seven feet tall. At night, all seals and sacred places of the spirits are lit with candles and "tilley" lamps. "The belief behind this custom is quite simple and may be traced in western culture to the symbolizing of evil by darkness and God by light. . . . For this reason, the lights burn all night."[33] These lights serve a practical use. Peasants in rural communities with no electricity must walk dark streets and alleys at nights where, according to a Caribbean myth, scary creatures and duppies lurk in dark shadows and under trees, waiting to pounce on unsuspecting victims.

Zionists have weekly ritual performances, some of which are given on demand and driven by spiritual revelations and the needs of the bands. Murphy observes that frequently there are "calls to bring the spirit into the 'streets and lanes of the city,' and the congregation will process through the streets, stopping to testify, sing, and draw converts back to the church. There are also a variety of 'tables,' feasts 'laid under the scripture' in intricate symbolic displays in the church."[34] Their special ritual calendar notes the Feasting Table celebration, baptisms, initiations, and funeral rites. The latter include the wake, the "ninth night," the forty days' observance, and memorial services. To these are added balm-yard or healing rituals and the dedication of other sacred places or missions.[35] Ceremonies held at the mission are open to the public, but persons regarded as hostile to the group are kept out. Revivalists are suspicious of law enforcement, government personnel, Christian intruders, and anyone who might be an informant.

THE FEASTING TABLE

Feasting Tables, the origin of which is unclear, are special ritual events, the purposes of which are varied: they render gratitude to the spirits in thanksgiving; they solicit prosperity, healing, and deliverance from social conditions; they provide a service to memorialize the dead (a mourning rite); they facilitate the annual sacrifice; they conduct fund-raising and food drives in response to disaster and other pressing needs of the community;[36] and they provide times of fellowship in the bands. The Feasting Table is also offered for consecration, pole-planting, and farewells. During the feasting ceremony, Bibles, hymn books, candles, and floral arrangements decorate the long, colorful, rectangular table (placed in a conspicuous spot in the sacred temple), along with an assortment of alcoholic and carbonated beverages, breads of many descriptions, colorful fruits and vegetables, cooked foods, and water pitchers. (Ganja is also present among Poco sacred table paraphernalia). The number of water containers on the table highlights the importance of ritual baths and purification and of oblations offered in the sacred place.

The Pocoists' Feasting Table affair begins late Sunday night with speeches explaining the purposes of the table, the singing of hymns, the reading of a biblical text, and the offering of prayers. The pace of the meeting accelerates during the late hours of the night. When a midnight rooster crows, the leader "breaks" the table, distributes much of its content to attendees, and sets apart a portion for the spirits. Devotees then go into spiritual labor or "drilling" for the spirit, until morning, after which they return to their daily routine. They come back on Monday night to continue the spirit-possession activity of "traveling" until the wee hours of the morning. On Tuesday evening, the bands offer an animal or vegetable sacrifice to the spirits and resume traveling until Wednesday morning. Zionists break the table and conclude their activity before midnight. They offer their sacrifices, either before the meeting begins or during the breaking of the table. Drilling takes place on the same night of the sacrifice, and the feast concludes the ceremony at midnight.[37]

DRILLING FOR THE SPIRIT

In Revivalism, a principal activity of the community cultus is spirit possession; it is a means of enabling and empowering the devotee, to whom the spirit becomes a counselor and protector. Analogous to "tarrying for the spirit" in Pentecostal churches, the practice is influenced by the Myal and Kumina spirit possession of African heritage. Seaga argues that in African beliefs, "the spirit world was not separate and apart from the temporal world but formed one unified whole; and this belief in the unity of the spirit world has persisted to the present day among those sections of the population whose cultural formation remains Afro-Christians."[38] At the onset of possession in Zion, devotees "drill for the spirit" through praise, worship, and prayers, as was done in the Pentecostal church, where I was first introduced to Christianity. Preparatory rituals to possession are confession, contrition, and supplication in the form of groaning, lamentation, vigorous dancing, and singing. Seaga notes that Zionists do a simultaneous sidestepping and groaning (rapid, heavy, guttural breathing) drill on the threshold of possession. "The body is raised a tip-toe on one foot and then[,] vigorously 'stomping,' lowered on the other; at the same time the downward foot is usually moved sideways with a slight hop in that direction. At some stage of this side-step and groaning drill, possession is said to occur."[39] The initiate receives a trance possession experience called "being slain in the spirit," and is believed to receive empowerment from the Christian Holy Spirit, an archangel of the spirit, a biblical prophet, or an apostle—all trimmings of Christianity superimposed on ATR culture.

The possessed Zionist makes polyrhythmic groans called laboring, which indicate the intensity and genuineness of the possession. One may roll, shake uncontrollably, or fall into an immobile trance. Under possession, the medium begins "spiritual journeying" (a state of ecstasy) and receives messages from the spirits, which are regarded as a call to service or to performance of a special, one-time task. According to Murphy, the "journeyings on the ground" often last for a few hours, but the spirit may seize a devotee for a few weeks. When a medium is "put on the ground by the spirit," the congregation can do little but bathe and feed the "traveler" and stand vigil with prayers. After the traveler returns to the temporal world, worshipers gather for a special feast called a "rising" or a "coming up" table, where the possessed relates aspects of the experience and brings a message from the spirits.[40]

A Poco worshiper genuflects with each breath exhaled, using a type of stressed breathing called "laboring." This act might continue for more than an hour, during which the possessed dances around as he or she goes into "labor" before "delivering himself or herself," that is, performing an act appropriate to the position he or she occupies in the bands. The leader takes the necessary steps to ensure that he or she is the one to transmit the received spiritual messages to the rest of the bands. To make transmission possible, the leader first organizes, in a circle, members who have the spirit, taking them through a drill in the rhythmic sidestepping and groaning ritual until he or she believes everyone in the circle is spirit-filled to the same degree as he or she is. The group is believed to be, at that point, cosmically in sync and able to communicate with each other in the language of the spirit, thus aiding transmission of the message. Meanwhile, other members of the bands sing continuously to a rhythmic beat that the possessed echoes through groaning and laboring.[41]

Music and dance provide a language for the spirits; the beating of drums initiates the capering ritual and invites dancer and spirit to "tango." When worship commences, worshipers form a circle around the most visible holy seal and center of power, the flag pole, and move around in a counterclockwise manner to the beat of the drums. The rhythm and pace of the movement gradually intensify as possession becomes imminent. In Zion, a special spirit-person called the "bands messenger" delivers the spiritual message to the leader and the community. In Pocomina, a character known as the "journey prophet" or "journeyman," who resides at the "mission ground," leads the journey in the spirit world. Members pledge to serve the bands in certain capacities and offer an annual sacrifice in the spirit's honor. Revivalists maintain that "the spirits usually demand more than their share and if they are gratified, it would only serve to encourage further demands. Therefore, it is necessary to discipline the spirits without angering them and thereby running the risk of being disciplined by them"[42] and incurring serious consequences.

HEALING, MAGIC, AND DIVINATION

Every religion of African origin depends on the arts of healing, magic, and divination to centralize the activities of its cultus and maintain its usefulness and vitality among patrons. While spirit possession puts members of the group in touch with the source of spiritual energy, healing and divination provide the movement with two vital resources that aid in sustaining interest, enthusiasm, and support of cult members and in working for their betterment and health. Healing, magic, and divination consultations also provide a source of revenue for the upkeep of the cultus. In those essential activities, adherents and well-wishers get something in return for their participation and support: help in dealing with mental and physical illness and with problems of a spiritual, social, domestic, and economic nature. Different levels of responses are detected in this treatment of the community's problems: the spiritual, the physical, and the magical. At the physical level are both herbal healing and modern medicine, often administered in a sequence or simultaneously. At the spiritual-magical level, revivalists apply balm-yard or herbal healing, prayers, and, in the case of Poco, anti-Obeah works. The healers learn the properties and potencies of herbs for healing certain conditions.[43] Balm-yard healing is the major ritual function of Poco. In this ritual, shepherds administer herbal and other types of medicines for physical and psychosomatic conditions. The patient is generally given a bath in an herbal mixture whose recipe, myth claims, was received only through divine revelation. Some conditions require that the herbal medicine be taken in liquid form and ingested with food.

The third level requires the preparation of ritual baths and the use of special powders and oils to treat maladies. "The specialists may be a trained dispenser of medicine who combines knowledge of plants and herbs with that of poisons and drugs. More often than not it is his knowledge of the plants and herbs which forms the mainstay of his clientele."[44] The difference between the first two levels of healing is seen as one only of degree. For example, nothing magical exists in the use of fever grass. A medicine man is expected to be an expert in herbal remedies and, in most cases, clients accept the diagnosis that the problem has supernatural causation. This is often the case after the healer has worked on the assumption that the malady is the result of natural causes and was unable to prescribe a solution.[45] Zionists use water from the special spring that flows into the Hope river to perform healing baths. This is done in an atmosphere of prayer and supplication to the spirit, and may entail the laying on of hands, the massaging of the affected area of the client's body, and giving the patient a special drink. The more well known the healer, the more elaborate the ritual and the more public the performance. When a client's problem requires supernatural intervention, he or she either reveals the nature of the problem to the consultant (healer) or allows him or her to diagnose the conditions through magical reading, which is the art of diagnosing a condition through prescience, suggestion, or divination and deductive reasoning. One form of reading diagnoses the condition from beliefs and knowledge already understood about the patient. A common method of reading is based on intuition, in which the healer or consultant receives impressions from communications with the spirit but essentially relies on magic.

Convince Cult

Convince is an Afro-Jamaican spirituality that has a small following, scattered among peasants, in mainly the parishes of St. Mary, Portland, and Saint Thomas.[46] It is often listed among Jamaica's Afro-Christian cults because of Christianity's impact on its creole thought forms and practices. In spite of its Christian features, the cosmology of Convince is African; its chief spiritual powers have their home in West Africa but represent the spirits of deceased individuals believed to have been members of the cult. African religious traditions are at the heart of Convince practices: the use of animal sacrifice, the worship of ancestral spirits, bodily convulsion and vocal contortions in worship, spirit possession, belief in good and evil spiritual powers, the housing of spirit-ghosts, African-style religious dances, the concept of horses riding mediums, and the practice of guarding against malevolent beings. Simpson suggests that the strong African elements in Convince exist because the sect developed among the Maroons and therefore remained in greater isolation than other faiths.[47]

Convince belief rests on the premise that humans and spirits are part of a unified cosmic structure, where they interact with each other while influencing one another's behavior. According to Donald Hogg:

> The principles of cooperation and reciprocity govern the relations between cult members and certain of the spirits who are neither potentially dangerous nor immediately useful. God and Christ, whom they consider too benevolent to worry about and too remote and other-worldly to be of much practical value, therefore merit little attention from them. Bongo Men focus their concern instead on lesser more accessible

spirits who take an immediate interest in material human affairs and have greater influence upon phenomenal events. They deal exclusively with ghosts. . . .[48]

These ghosts are among the ancestral spirits in the African pantheon of lesser divinities. The most powerful ghosts originate in Africa; the next in rank are those of Jamaican slaves and Maroons, who were active participants in the sect. The ghosts of Jamaicans whose deaths occurred more recently, however, are less potent. Older spirits are revered highly and feared if they are associated with the practice of Obeah.[49] As a result of their widespread belief in ghosts, followers of Convince were once thought to have worshiped evil spirits of the recent dead. However, closer investigation reveals that they venerate the good, strong, and courageous spirits of their African ancestral heroes. These ghosts are regarded as more powerful than those of Obeah and are given an animal sacrificial offering at least once annually.

Practitioners of Convince adopt the spirit named Bongo, or Bungo, and are called Bungo-men/ Bongo-men.. They trace their religious roots and authorization back to West Africa, the slaves, and the Maroons. Each Bongo-man functions independently of others but occasionally attends the meetings of fellow Bongo-men. The visiting Bongo-man is expected to induce his favorite spirit through a dance ritual. He must also assist his host Bongo in seeing that spectators behave in an orderly fashion. The Bongo-man has several assistants, called apprentices or grooms, who are the most devout members of the group, but he also attracts a number of less devoted followers and admirers to his cell group, some of whom are Christians of different ethnic background in historic churches who attend the Bongo rituals out of curiosity. Participants include women who serve as cooks for the Bongo-men and their visitors, men who take care of the animals used for the annual sacrifice, and a helper who serves as an usher collecting admission fees from visitors. Since most Bongo-men are illiterate yet must use the Bible as their liturgical source, a youth, usually a girl, reads the biblical selections for the occasion. She also follows the practice, common in the black Church in the Caribbean and the United States, of reading aloud each line of the Christian hymns as part of the liturgy, before the audience sings[50] in response.

Bongo-men make their animal sacrifice annually, perform Convince rituals as the need arises, and conduct memorial services for each deceased member once a year. These services give Bongo spirits an opportunity to recruit new followers. Some rituals are designed to pacify the spirits or to show them gratitude for help they have provided to the family or community. Each Convince ceremony follows the same pattern. As a prelude to the ritual, followers conduct an evening vigil where they sing Christian hymns, read Bible passages, and offer prayers to God. When the Bongo-men arrive, the ceremony begins in earnest. They sing African Bongo songs and do a slow handclapping and feet-stamping ritual to invoke the spirit's presence. During ceremonies that involve no sacrifices, spirit possession occurs and a spirit can ride its horse for several days. As is done in the Shango Saraka feasts in Grenada, Bongo-men "throw" a feast to the spirits at an appropriate time in the ceremony. After feasting, followers can dance to more spirit possessions for another two or three days.[51]

The spirit possession ceremony is one of the most important features of Convince. It encourages group solidarity and brings rejuvenation and spiritual vitality to the cult. Comparison has been made between Convince and Winti, the Afro-Caribbean religion in Guyana, in which both good and evil divinities exist and whose followers believe no spirit is either perfectly good or absolutely evil. Albert Raboteau holds the idea that the absence of a spirit that is totally "good or completely evil enters here in a more subtle way. For while it generally follows that a spirit is friendly if it is worshiped, unfriendly if it is neglected, and evil if it has been sent to do evil, a spirit may be temperamentally as inconstant as human beings are inconstant."[52] These traditions are much stronger in Vodou, Santeria, and Candomble than in Convince, which, however, shows greater African influences than do Revival Zion, Poco, and Rastafari. The strength and popularity of the cult has declined sharply since the 1950s, and it is valued mainly as folklore celebration and African cultural appreciation. The decline of Convince is attributed to several causes, among them being the impact of Protestant Christianity on the cult, the lack of interest in ancestral traditions among younger generations, competing forms of modern entertainment, competition among Bongo-men for power, and the rise of the Rastafarians.[53] Rastafari's protest against revivalism in Convince and other Afro-Jamaican religions has been quite sustained, notwithstanding the impact of those religions on the Rastafarian movement itself.

Afro-Colonial Christianity

British missionaries to Jamaica had little success in their earliest attempt to convert Africans to Christianity, but the planting of the U.S.-Baptist faith in the colony set the stage for the rise of new creole religious movements and black solidarity. In the late 1700s, George Lisle, Thomas Gibb, and Moses Baker, black Baptists preachers from what later became the United States, along with local Jamaican blacks (the term *African Americans* has no currency in the Caribbean), stimulated a new religious consciousness and eclectic spirituality that was critical to the struggle against slavery and oppression in Jamaica. Lisle, the first Baptist to convert Jamaican blacks to Christianity, was a freed slave taken to Jamaica by loyalist British Tories who fled the American Revolution and relocated to the island during the 1780s. Former slaves from what were the American colonies accompanied the defeated British and brought their special brand of antislavery Baptist preaching, adding to the anxiety of the Jamaican colonists. Other North American blacks who migrated to Jamaica during the American Revolution furthered Lisle's missionary efforts. Before long, blacks established independent churches with unorthodox interpretations of Christian beliefs opposed to slavery. The Baptist Church became very popular among Jamaican blacks as a result of this antislavery stance.[54]

By the mid-1800s, African and Baptist beliefs fused into the Native Baptist movement, the precursor of Jamaica's revivalism. Lisle and others emphasized the Christian and African foundations of their movement and named their assembly the Ethiopian Baptist Church. By adopting the names Ethiopian Baptist and Native Baptist, blacks registered their embrace of Christianity but also a simultaneous indifference to the colonial culture. Scholars note that by 1860, blacks accounted for 50 percent of Kingston's churchgoing population but that "their success did not go unchallenged by white missionaries, who were quick to find evidences of heathenism in the unsupervised embrace of Christianity by black flocks."[55] The British, who saw black religion as a movement of resistance to colonial values and a corruption of Christianity through the practices and beliefs of African religions, attempted to silence Lisle and his supporters. Lisle was imprisoned, once on a charge of inciting insurrection through his preaching and another time for alleged unpaid debts, but he and his supporters persisted in their spirit of resistance and new religious signification, establishing several Baptist congregations throughout Jamaica.

The Native Baptist movement, heavily influenced by the Myal religion that directed its ire against the planter class and missionaries alike, was without serious competition. During the period between 1780 and 1820, Myalist-influenced Baptist Christianity sustained its appeal among the slaves and became an important factor in postemancipation wages, land, and rent disputes. Myal inspired (1) anti-establishment preaching of the early 1840s; (2) measures adopted by the authorities against the movement; and (3) a reinterpretation of Christianity among blacks that was colored by social, economic, and religious circumstances. As Murphy notes, "This 'mingling' of belief and practice, pioneered by independent black Christians, among the Native Baptists, would become general, among the black population of the island, in a great Christian revival, which occurred from 1860 to 1862."[56] In the 1860s, Afro-Jamaicans were reeling under economic depression, busted hopes of social and economic change following emancipation, and food shortages resulting from the American Civil War. Harsh conditions encouraged different religious affiliations among the black masses, who found the millenarian and apocalyptic message of Baptists and revivalists appealing, especially in times of crisis. Blacks also found the Baptist polity and the ritual of baptism adaptable to their African spirituality, which emerged in Poco and Zion.

While the Afro-Baptist missionary message appealed to Myalist Jamaicans before emancipation, the Great Revival of the 1860s is credited with transforming African religions into Poco and Zion religious variants under the term *Revival*.[57] A strong wave of evangelicalism from the British Isles swept through Jamaica, resulting in an influx of blacks into traditional Christian churches. Roots of the revival were both African and Christian; Baptist missionaries who, for many reasons, were inclusive in their membership policies, gave the revival its impetus. The means of achieving spirituality implicit in the "Great '61 Revival,'" however, were more African than Christian. Missionaries who saw the phenomenon as the hand of God and as the fruit of their years of toil soon discovered that the newcomers in their churches had their own definition of spirituality and that what they thought was truly Christian proved to be the successors of Myal and Kumina in Convince, Poco, and Zion traditions.

Although, at first, Jamaicans from all strata of society embraced the revival, which provided a displacement for the country's famine and bad economic times, the ruling class condemned it; they saw it "as the manifestations of African religious survivals," which had "intensified and swept through the population, signifying to the planter class a loss of control."[58] To some missionary pastors, the "extravagances" of their African members seem to have swept away the effects of European Christianity derived from the revival. Much to the missionaries' chagrin, when the Great Revival subsided, a spirituality expressed in African rituals became a permanent feature of the Afro-Jamaican religious experience. Popular interest in missionary churches, stimulated by the Great Revival, soon waned, but the hybrid Myalist-Baptist religion, characterized by drumming, dancing, and spirit possession, reappeared in the 1860s as Poco.

Missionaries sought to de-Africanize blacks and make them into European Christian carbon copies by suppressing the emotional expressions that are essential to the African spirit. Blacks, however, saw in the church an opportunity to address their social and economic concerns. They remained suspicious of the church's traditional forms of Christianity[59] and held onto their African traditions. This religious ethos created a consciousness in which traditional ethnic identities were challenged and a new ethic emerged in which each black person was viewed, by both blacks and whites in the religious tradition, as human and as culturally and morally equal to a white person. The black Baptist tradition became a national religion for the Jamaican working class, regardless of ethnic or religious particularity, and constituted the dominant ideological vehicle for defending black people's interests during the Baptist War of 1831 and in the immediate postemancipation period. This was the period when the problem of having "freedom" without political power, land, employment, or a means of survival became a long-lasting crisis. This problem extended to the struggle led by Paul Bogle and George Gordon in 1860 and down to the time of Alexander Bedward and Marcus Garvey in the early twentieth century.[60]

At the turn of the 1900s, the lingering effects of the economic depression, the millenarian hopes of the Great Revival, and African spirituality converged in the apocalyptic messages of another revivalist group called Bedwardism. Bedward was a successful, unorthodox Jamaican charismatic preacher and healer who led revival groups as well as a movement that had affiliations throughout Jamaica and in Panama. Between the 1890s and 1921, he fired up his movement with sermons against oppression, calling on his black followers to rise up and shake off the "white wall" that had them caged in—a euphemism for overthrowing British domination. According to Chevannes, Bedward stirred up painful memories of the Morant Bay Rebellion of 1865 and, as a self-styled prophet, offered social and political criticism of the white power structure and its dealings with the poor masses.

Bedward's congregations had a hierarchy made up of followers whom he called ministers, angels, and elders (there were seventy-four elders). Like Baptists, he practiced water baptism by immersion as an act essential to salvation, but added African ideas of the spiritual properties of water to this Christian rite. Using as a prototype Jesus's forty-day fast before facing his spiritual battle and trial, Bedward required his followers to fast and pray in preparation for war with spiritual and political forces in Jamaica. He practiced healing through prayers, herbal medicine, and the use of healing spring water. Bedward consecrated, bottled, and dispensed water that sprang from underneath a large rock and flowed into Jamaica's Hope river. Curious foreigners visited August Town to see the prophet and to receive healing vials. He attracted the poor masses as well as the Jamaican middle class and political hopefuls, including the first creole political leaders of Jamaica. Bedward, however, is remembered mostly for his apocalyptic predictions that his admirers believe came to pass in 1907, when Jamaica experienced a series of earth tremors and some people thought the world was, indeed, coming to an end.[61]

The Jamaican government declared Bedward insane, arrested him on sedition charges, and committed him to a mental asylum. On his release, he continued his preaching and healing activities, and in 1921 led about eight hundred supporters on a resistance march to Kingston "to do battle with his enemies," but his strategy was pitiful. The police and the militia routed his march and had him incarcerated, along with many of his supporters.[62] As Murphy contends, "Though Bedward's Jamaican National Baptist church is no longer an incorporated entity today, his influence is still strong in the revival churches, particularly around Kingston. His emphasis on the healing properties of his holy water from sacred springs . . . continues to be a major feature of the revival churches of the area."[63] Revivalism helped fire Bedward's vision, sparks of which survived in Poco and Zion, in the thinking of Marcus Garvey, and with the Rastafarians. In his early preaching and writing, Leonard Howell, one of the pioneers of the Jamaican Rastafari, devoted much time and energy to launching a sustained attack on Pocomina and its so-called Obeah rituals, seeking to distance his Rasta group from this revivalist tradition. Rastafari, however, never succeeded in freeing itself of Revivalism.[64]

14

The Rastafari Chant

KEY TOPICS

*Messianism and Formative Years • Jah Rastafari,
the God-Man • City of Zion and Repatriation • Reggae
Freedom Chant • Dawtars Dare to Trod • Houses and
Missions • Livity and Ital Rituals*

Princes shall come out of Egypt; Ethiopia shall soon stretch out her hands unto God (Psalm 68:31).

Ethiopia is now really stretching out her hands. This great kingdom of the East had been hidden for many centuries, but gradually she is rising to take a lead place in the world and it is for us of the Negro race to assist in every way to hold up the hand of Emperor Ras Tafari (Marcus Garvey on Haile Selassie's coronation day, 1930).

Give thanks and praise to Jah Rastafari, His Imperial Majesty, Haile Selassie I, Elect of God, King of Kings of Ethiopia, Lord of Lords, Conquering Lion of the Tribe of Judah (Rastafari leader on Haile Selassie's visit to Jamaica in 1966).

The emperor was not God to the Ethiopian people and other nations. He was a religious man who was elected king of Ethiopia. While one can appreciate the respect, love, and devotion given to him, as a clergyman, it is my duty to speak the truth. . . . Beware of the commandment of God: "Thou shall have no other gods before me—for I am a jealous God."

—ARCHBISHOP ABUNA YESEHAQ,
THE ETHIOPIAN TEWAHEDO CHURCH

W ho are the eccentric renegades claiming to be earthly spiritualists, nurturing an alternative consciousness, embracing a religious Ethiopian ideology swathed in Africanized Christian beliefs, deeming themselves ambassadors of African identity and liberation and proxies for social, political and economic change in society? Rastafari, the most well-known Caribbean new religious movement, is Jamaica's only vibrant indigenous spirituality. Rising as a social and political religious sect from Jamaica's

The lion of Judah/Jah Rastafari.
(Illustration by Kelly Hawes.)

underclass, the movement evolved into an influential heterogeneous religious phenomenon, has become one of the most popular cultural icons of the twentieth century, and has fueled an international cultural revolution embraced in countries where it is barely understood. This religion attracts a diverse patronage: sympathizers, reggae enthusiasts, "designer-dread wannabes," Hollywood cultural fads, ganja rascals or drug opportunists, and profiteers from the pickings of Rasta accessories and music. The broad cultural appeal of this emergent faith is surprising; Rastafarians number fewer than a million worldwide. In Jamaica's censuses they are unclassified, and estimates run the gamut from 20 percent to less than 1 percent of the population.[1]

Foregrounding

Although born in Jamaica's depression of the 1930s, the Rastafarian ideology finds its early roots in international soil during the convergence of social and historical events on opposite sides of the globe. In November, 1930, Haile Selassie I was crowned Emperor of Ethiopia. Within a year he was declared a god in a nascent religious vision by a people of whom he had little knowledge. On Selassie's coronation, which constituted the most colorful ten-day pageantry in Addis Ababa's history, the British Crown presented him with a scepter of solid gold that had been taken from Ethiopia in early colonial times. On one side of the scepter were inscribed the religion-making words "Ethiopia shall make her hands reach unto God"; on the other side was the inscription "King of Kings of Ethiopia." The *New York Times* front-paged the event: "Amid barbaric splendor and lavish pageantry, the 39-year-old Emperor Haile Selassie I, who claims [descent] from King Solomon and the Queen of Sheba and bears the title Lord of Lords and King of Kings Conquering Lion of the Tribe of Judah, the Elect of God, Defender of the Christian Faith and the Light of the World, was crowned at dawn today."[2] The sight of world dignitaries paying respect to the diminutive black king of the only independent African country in the League of Nations, and Haile Selassie's acceptance of the illustrious titles, inspired Africans in the diaspora, already expecting a messiah, to "go tell it on the mountains" that wise messiah Ras Tafari has come from the east.[3]

Messianic Vision

Conceived as a proto-Christian Ethiopian vision in the Caribbean, United States, and Central America—all hotbeds for the social struggle of the underclass—the Rastafarian ideology was nurtured in a messianic hope that had been held for centuries within the African diaspora.[4] In the 1790s, for example, the missionary and former U.S. slave George Lisle used the Bible to spark Jamaicans' interest in this Ethiopian vision. During the 1800s, African-American freedom fighters and church leaders preached a gospel of a coming African-Ethiopian redemption through a black god. When Abyssinia defeated Italy at Adowa in 1896, preachers connected the victory to a biblical text stating that "princes shall come out of Egypt, Ethiopia shall stretch forth her hands unto God" (Psalm 68:31). Jamaican prophet Alexander Bedward foretold of a millennium in which Ethiopians will be specially favored by an African messiah. James Lowe wrote of the "Revealed Secret of the Hamitic Race" in Ethiopia,[5] and James Webb announced the coming of a black king out of Ethiopia, who would obliterate British power and liberate Jamaicans from oppression. Followers of the Jamaican-born Garvey movement promised that liberation would come from the blessed homeland of Ethiopia. On the eve of Selassie's coronation, the vision inspired several pro-Ethiopian writings in the diaspora, among them *The Holy Piby* (1924), *The Royal Parchment Scroll of Black Supremacy* (1926), and *A Blackman Will Be the Coming Universal King, Proven by Biblical History* (1924). Like the *Kebra Nagast* (an epic apology on Ethiopia first written in 700 C.E.), these aspired to shape the dream into an Ethiopian theology of black pride, the glorification of Africa-Ethiopia, and a black messianic deliverer.

THE GARVEY VISION
Among the Ethiopian visionaries of African redemption, Jamaica's Marcus Mosiah Garvey provided the strongest impetus for the founding of Rastafari. The young traveler and newspaper publisher vowed to find deliverance for his

people, who were "hemmed in by every economic barrier" in the region. In 1914 he founded the Universal Negro Improvement Association (UNIA) to unite Africans and empower them to deliver themselves from their economic plight. The UNIA was stunted in Garvey's homeland, but among New York's dislocated and destitute blacks fleeing the oppression and violence of the United States' Jim Crow states, Garvey found a receptive audience. From his Harlem base, he organized hundreds of chapters of the UNIA in the early 1920s and boasted of close to two million members[6] internationally. Under the motto "Africa for Africans . . . one God, one Aim, and one Destiny,"[7] Garvey promoted his ambitious agenda: fight racial and economic oppression and free Africa from colonialism, strengthen the bonds of unity among the races,[8] unite diasporic Africans with their roots, establish a superempire on the continent, and help Africans control their own destiny. Advancing his political vision in Afro-Christian thought, Garvey urged the need for a black conception of God and affirmed that a deliverer will indeed come out of Ethiopia to save the race.

Garvey's own weaknesses and some malicious American gadflies turned his dream into a nightmare. CIA chief J. Edger Hoover and U.S. president Calvin Coolidge had him incarcerated in Georgia on questionable charges of mail fraud, then deported to Jamaica in 1927. His vision crashed, but among his protégés, who bristle with hope about the idea of an African messiah-liberator, "truth crushed to the earth will rise again." The deported prophet had high hopes that Selassie I would be Africans' Simon Bolivar. On the emperor's coronation, Garvey dispatched a cable from Jamaica commending him on his rise to power and wishing him success in carrying out his great vision to develop Ethiopia and lead Africans out of colonialism. Garvey exclaimed, "Ethiopia is now really stretching forth her hands. This great kingdom of the East has been hidden for many centuries, but gradually she is rising to take a lead place in the world and it is for us of the Negro race to assist in every way to hold up the hand of Emperor Ras Tafari."[9] This prophecy inspired several Rasta pioneers who embraced Garvey's Afrocentric signification as a prophetic warrant on the messiah and, to his dismay, turned his political vision into a Caribbean-Ethiopian religious movement.

THE PIONEERS
All of the pioneers of Rastafari had connections to Christianity and to the Panama-United States-Jamaica axis of the vision. Before World War I, the Panama Canal attracted thousands of desperate workers seeking a fortune on the isthmus. These workers were Pan-Africanists, national liberationists, Afrocentric prophets, messianic dreamers, and socialist thinkers. In spite of the treacherous work and acute health problems, Panama, as Helene Lee notes, became a marketplace for a cross-fertilization of ideas among immigrant workers who were en route to industrial cities as well as the social climate for seeding religious dreams. Annie Harvey, a preacher from Central America and New York and

leader of the Black Israelite Church in Jamaica, pursued the vision along with her husband as missionaries to Ethiopia. Five years later they returned, spreading a message: "Zion waits in Ethiopia" for oppressed Africans. In New York City, Harvey's message touched would-be Rasta pioneer Leonard Howell, the first acknowledged leader of the movement.

Robert Hinds, who visited Panama for a short period, was an admirer of Garvey and a loyal follower of the prophet Alexander Bedward, whom he regarded as a black Christ. Hinds joined Bedward in prison as a result of their social protest march in Jamaica.[10] On his release, he founded the King of Kings Mission (KKM), which boasted a substantial membership and became one of the earliest Rastafarian "churches."

The Jamaican Joseph Hibbert lived in Costa Rica and Panama from 1911 to 1931, where he was ordained Master of The Ancient Mystic order of the Ethiopia Masonic Lodge. He returned to Jamaica shortly after Selassie's coronation and created the Ethiopian Coptic Church, through which he announced the coming of the Ethiopian messiah. After joining forces with Hinds to conduct street meetings in the parish of St. Andrews, Hibbert collaborated with Howell in spreading the emerging Rastafari doctrine. Hibbert's church became the Jamaican Ethiopian Orthodox Church,[11] a Rastafarian center. Archibald Dunkley, who worked for The Atlantic Fruit Company and visited Panama several times, started a religious ministry in Port Antonio and later was drawn to Kingston, where he chanted the Rastafarian beliefs about Selassie I based on the Bible. Claudius Henry, founder of the African Reformed Church in Kingston, followed Dunkley and Leonard Howell as an early exponent of Selassie as messiah.

Leonard Percival Howell was the most articulate Rastafarian pioneer. The Jamaican mystic, who made several trips to Panama and migrated to the United States two years before the opening of the Canal in 1914, was adept at mythmaking; he claimed to be divine and, although born in 1898, said he fought in the Ashanti War in 1896, studied African languages, and met King Prempeh of Coute de Voire. In Harlem, Howell operated a tearoom for herbal medicines used in balm-yard healing, which included Hindu rites and Kumina rituals.[12] It was in the United States that he acquired his revelations of Haile Selassie's divinity; he told the media he joined the "Ras Tafarites" in New York before returning to Jamaica to preach the sect's basic tenets. Of course, no such group existed in the United States at the time. With help from Hinds' KKM, Howell established his "Ras Tafarite" cult in Jamaica in 1932. He attracted sizable crowds among the rural underclass, which was drawn to the gospel of anticolonialism, an African messiah, and repatriation. To fund his ministry, he sold as passports to Ethiopia duplicates of Selassie's picture, which he obtained from Annie Harvey in New York.

Along with Paul Erlington, Ferdinand Rickets, and Vernon Davis, these pioneers piloted a political-religious movement based on the conviction that Selassie I is in fact the black people's messiah.[13]

Formative Years

FIRST RASTA CHANTS

Preaching under the influence of Garveyism, Ethiopianism, and Christian scriptures, Howell declared Haile Selassie I as the divine deliverer and "the blessed and only Potentate" (1 Timothy 6:16). Selassie I was said to be the messiah promised in the Bible and foretold by Garvey and other prophets, the King of Kings and Lord of Lords (Revelation 19:16), Lion of the tribe of Judah (Revelation 5:5), the only one worthy to open the great seal of divine secrets about the day of judgment and the end of the world (Revelation 6:5). In 1933, Howell chanted, "The Lion of Judah has broken the chain, and we of the black race are now free. George the Fifth is no more our King. George the Fifth has sent his third son down to Africa in 1928 to bow down to our new king Ras Tafari of Ethiopia."[14] The preacher narrowly escaped ambush, but he was eventually arrested and imprisoned for chanting "rebellion and seditious doctrines"—that is, the superiority of the black race over whites, retaliation against all white devils for the wrongs they did to blacks during slavery, the call to switch Jamaicans' allegiance from the King of England to Emperor Haile Selassie I, the notion that God is black, and the idea that Christ is not a meek and mild blue-eyed blond dying on a cross but rather the fearsome black messiah, Ras Tafari. In 1934, Howell observed the 100th anniversary of Emancipation with a demonstration during which he promised repatriation to Ethiopia to his followers.

In 1935, using a pseudonym, Howell put his chant into an infamous ephemera, *The Promised Key*, the most controversial fourteen-page booklet to appear in the Caribbean. In this rueful diatribe, Howell took unlimited freedom with the Bible and several other sources, botching Christian theology to such an extent that the booklet was banned in Jamaica. As a voice for irate Africans against Italian aggression in Ethiopia, the book launched an assault on Italy's Papacy. When Benito Mussolini (with a papal blessing) invaded Ethiopia to bring the continent's only independent nation under fascism, Howell declared Italy the seat of the Antichrist and the home of the Great Harlot of Babylon, whom Haile Selassie I, Conquering Lion of the Tribe of Judah, would vanquish. In 1936, after the League of Nations turned a deaf ear to Selassie's plea for help, the Italians pulverized Ethiopia's defense and forced the Emperor into exile in Britain. Outraged, Howell and other Africans in the diaspora demonstrated against the fascist invasion and raised funds for the resistance effort.[15] Italy's entrance into World War II in 1941 with an attack on France and Britain, however, proved Howell's prediction true. After the United Nations granted Ethiopia allied status, Haile Selassie I led Allied forces in a decisive defeat of the Italians and became *Time* magazine's Man of the Year. His triumphant re-entry into Addis Ababa after the war buttressed belief in him as the eschatological messiah of the black race, and Howell's prophetic status was validated.

PINNACLE COMMUNE

In the 1940s, Rastafari spread throughout Jamaica in small groups, the same way early Christianity did in the first two centuries of its existence. Howell organized widespread recruitment drives that enlarged his camps. He secured an abandoned estate in Spanish Town, where he established the Ethiopian Salvation Society on Pinnacle Hill. It was reported that there were as many as two thousand members in the commune. As the undisputed cult head, Howell ran Pinnacle as an efficient military camp. Members adhered to a code of conduct and Howell inflicted punishment for various infractions. Families inhabited small cooperative arrangements and were required to contribute free labor to the support of the cultic commune by growing specific crops on their plots of land. This gave birth to the growing of ganja for rituals and for use as a cash crop.[16] A flamboyant leader, Howell had many incarnations that gave a cue to his mental health: President General of the KKM; Gong or Gangunguru Maragh, lord of the universe; Wise Teacher; King; Counselor; and Prince Regent.[17] He maintained that he was endowed with supernatural healing powers, prophetic gifts, and knowledge of God, and even saw himself as another Selassie, a second messiah. Chanting a persistent war on the colonial culture and economic system of the corrupt society Rastas called Babylon, Gong pressured his neighbors to switch their allegiance by paying taxes to Pinnacle, in the Emperor's name, rather than to the Jamaican government.

Police busted the commune in 1941, arresting seventy members on charges of sedition, harassment, and cultivation of a dangerous drug. When the prophet escaped, members attributed the feat to his divinity, but he was caught promptly and again incarcerated. On Gong's return to Pinnacle, he placed guards with vicious dogs at the gates, but this failed to deter police raids on the commune and so he endured additional imprisonments in the 1950s. On his final arrest in 1954, about two hundred followers were detained, police razed the commune, and members absconded to Back-O-Wall, Kingston's most impoverished ghetto. After the authorities committed Gong to a mental asylum in 1961, the forlorn pioneer faded into oblivion, and Claudius Henry, Mortimo Plano, and Count Ossie (founder of Rasta music) snatched the spotlight[18] in the cult. Pinnacle was a short-lived experience but had a lasting impact on the religion. Many Rastas live communally, use ganja as an essential sacrament, fly Rasta colors and flags, wear the trademark dreadlocks, observe practices and teachings initiated by Howell, nurture a lasting odium for the Babylon police, keep women as second-class citizens, and hold *Nyabinghi* gatherings (first adopted at Pinnacle),[19] which became a staple liturgical feature of the movement and later became a major sect. Rastafari became a largely urban phenomenon practiced under derelict conditions because of the police closing down Pinnacle and other rural communes.

Battling Babylon

JAH-JAH PEOPLE RISE UP

By the 1950s, Rastas had become a critical voice of resistance against the race and class structures that fueled inequities in Jamaica and that had been sources of the 1938 uprising. The minority class controlled Jamaica's economic means and political structure, to the destitution of the "wretched of the earth," on whom they imposed their colonial values and will. Fortunate mulattos and the Anglicized middle-class Jamaicans glorified European culture, treated black-African traditions with utter disdain, and saw Rastafari as a social distraction and pariah. Rastafarians countered by trumping the colonial ideology that "nutten black nuh good"; they rejected the white man's ways and refused to beg for crusts that fell from his table. Katrin Norris states, "While the conformist still looks on a white man as a source of financial assistance and few would hesitate to beg from him . . . , the Rastafarians prefer to live in appalling squalor"[20] rather than sacrifice their African pride and dignity. The government, finding in Rastas a perfect scapegoat for attacking growing nationalist anticolonial feelings over harsh economic conditions among the masses, flexed its postcolonial muscles to silence the movement.

In response to persecution and police and public harassment, a new Rasta sect, the "Youth Black Faith," showed its defiance toward the dominant Babylon culture and oppression of Rastas in a radical cultural counterpoint; it used ganja publicly, groomed dreadlocks, wore ragged clothes, grew long beards, and abandoned English for Rasta talk, called I-an-I consciousness. Their new natty hair, unkempt clothes, and painted screw face gave them a menacing Mau-Mau warrior look that symbolized confrontation and warned that peaceful Dreads will defend themselves by appropriate means. The paranoid state government enacted the Dangerous Drugs Law against the cultivation and use of ganja, drove Rastas from squatted lands, and razed many of their urban camps and "squaller-housing yards." Riots broke out and Rastas were indiscriminately rounded up, forcibly shaved, beaten,[21] and incarcerated. Driven to despair, a few Rastas accelerated preaching of repatriation to Ethiopia as a divine intervention to escape hellish Babylon. Some migrated to other islands—Canada, Britain, and the United States—while a minority contemplated the warpath.

Leader Claudius Henry claimed to be the "Repairer of the Breach" and "Moses of the Blacks" in order to allay political tension between Rastas and law enforcement, but he too lost faith in the Babylon system; his repatriation plans to take Jamaicans to Ethiopia on October 25, 1959, and his increasing militant posture set him on a collision course with police. In 1958, leader Prince Emmanuel rallied Rastas at a Nyabinghi convention held at the Coptic Theocratic Temple headquarters in Kingston to unite the movement into one organization for peaceful resistance. His effort failed, but the excessive ganja smoking of one of the Nyabinghi groups and the Rastas' anticolonial rhetoric and criticism of the police received wide press coverage. Violent clashes between the police and Rastas, as well as the publicity of the convention, emboldened three hundred misguided, bearded Rastas to gather at Victoria Park in Kingston during which they announced plans to oust the government of Jamaica. A paltry number of the three hundred Rastas came three months later and occupied Old King's House (the governor's house) in the name of King Negus Negusta of Ethiopia, to the amusement of onlookers. However, the militant front unnerved authorities, who launched another offensive against the "miscreants." A police assault team set a Bobo Shanti commune on fire and arrested Claudius Henry for selling fake tickets for repatriation passage to Africa. At his headquarters, they seized a stash of weapons[22] and two letters addressed to Fidel Castro that promised to assist him in invading Jamaica on the eve of the Rastas' departure to Africa.

Before Henry could be convicted of sedition and imprisoned for his quixotic coup idea, his son Ronald led radical Rastas in mounting a retaliatory assault on police. Jamaica's Babylon government suppressed the riot swiftly, and the revolutionaries were executed. To stem the tide of further violence, Rastafari leader Mortimo Planno and a small delegation convinced the University of the West Indies to undertake a study of Rastafari to educate the public on its philosophy. The 1961 study, by Smith, Augier, and Nettleford, produced the first substantive publication on the religion and made these recommendations to government: educate the public on the Rastafarian faith, end police brutality of Rastas, address the dereliction in Jamaica's shanty-town, provide opportunities for social expression for youths, and send a fact-finding mission to Ethiopia to investigate the Rastas' claim of Haile Selassie's land grant for repatriation. The government's positive response to the report paved the way for better relations between Rastas and the public, one that reached a watershed in Selassie's follow-up visit to Jamaica in 1966.[23]

JAH GOES TO JAH-MAICA!

The emperor's visit in April 1966 drew the largest crowd in Jamaica's history and gave Rastafari such extensive press coverage that national interest in the movement was sparked. "Jah ah come to h'ert (earth) in ah Jah-maica!" shouted Rastas. As Chevannes says, Jamaicans greeted the emperor with such enthusiasm that mounting vocal devotion to him and his country seemed to threaten Jamaica's rising nationalism and its relations with Britain. Haile Selassie I was humbled by the euphoric adulation but befuddled by the idea that he is the Rastafarian god. He acknowledged privately the Rastas' right to their beliefs but saw their deifying him as amusing and misguided. Rastas, hearing no divine utterance from their messiah, put their best spin on His Majesty's reticence, and took advantage of the publicity to strengthen their political base. After Selassie's visit, several Rasta "houses" with sociopolitical agendas became prominent: the Human Rights Brethren Association of Barbican; the Rastafari Movement Black African Recruitment Center; the Rastafarian Repatriation Association; the Ethiopian African International Congress (or Rastafarian

Melchizedek Orthodox Church); and the Rastafari Brethren United Front, which led the Selassie visit.

With their national image at an all-time high, Rastas seized the moment to become a catalyst for political change. They contested the 1972 general elections and, although the paltry political support for Ras Sam Brown's ticket[24] was largely in-house, Rastas gained publicity; one of Jamaica's two national parties co-opted and politicized Rastafarian symbols and slogans to the advantage of both. This Rasta respite was checkered. In the 1970s and 1980s, they experienced a new wave of violent persecution on both sides of the Atlantic. Sensational tabloids, media hype, and the posturing of political hopefuls stereotyped Rastas as unkempt derelicts of society, West Indian Mafia in England on the war path, Jamaican criminals on the prowl, New York Rastas in cahoots with the Colombian coca cartel, and drug traffickers, all threatening peaceful neighborhoods under the guise of religion. These created a sinister Rasta phobia that yielded deadly consequences.[25] Law enforcement in Britain, the United States, South Africa, and the Caribbean, associating Dreads with unsolved homicides and as a cause of civil unrest, placed many under false arrest and incarceration for alleged drug dealing;[26] others were beaten or murdered.

Ideological Orientations

Internationally, Rastafari is identified most often with reggae music, dreadlocks, and ganja smoking. These are but a few of the many orientations associated with the beliefs and practices that constitute Rastafarian sects (houses). Ostensibly, Rastas believe in an Ethiopian messiah as JAH (God), an Ethiopian-Zion vision, black repatriation ideology, an apocalyptic hope, patriarchal leadership, a reticulate organizational structure (Edmonds), "livity" (mores, lifestyle, dietary habits, and ritual assembly), dread talk (I-talk) or "I-an-I" consciousness, a diffused system of beliefs,[27] and an infatuation with the Bible and Afro-Christian thought. Some of these orientations are discussed in the sections that follow.

Jah Ras Tafarl, the God-Man

"Sing unto God, sing praises to his name: extol him that rides upon the heavens by his name JAH, and rejoice before him" (Psalm 68:4, King James version). The "bredren" chant this as they hijack scripture and the God of their oppressors to redefine them in their image. For its first forty years, Rastafari claimed its quintessential tenet to be that Selassie I is Jah RastafarI, its God and messiah. The exclamation *Jah* (a Hebrew synonym for God) *RastafarI* (uppercase I), the creator who sustains the universe, is the powerful, incarnated black God-man. He came to earth to bring deliverance to the poor and oppressed and functions as a successor to Christ. The concept of God-man recalls Jesus's being called "Son of Man" in Mark's Gospel, but points to the oneness of being between the divine and humans. Jah is not the inaccessible, otherworldly, indifferent god of the "Babylon religions," but a black human Christ. Jah lives within I-an-I (a Rasta), and suffering humans, especially oppressed blacks, live in Him. No alienation exists between God and humans because "God shares a part of his being with those who were once poor"[28] and oppressed. The evocative chant "I-an-I Selassie I Jah RastafarI" has the force of the Muslim *Shahadah*: "There is no God but Allah and Muhammad is his Prophet." However, it crosses the lines of Abrahamic monotheism to "communotheism," or the sharing of divinity;[29] I-an-I is divine the same way the suffering Christ was human and divine. Rastas who identify with Selassie experience shared divinity expressed in the "I" in RastafarI, pronounced Rasta-for-I (for me).

Before 1975, many Rastas held the belief that since they are one with Jah, they are divine, they cannot die; Jah never dies, and death contaminates body and soul. After departing earth, I-an-I continue with Jah, enjoying a new existence, but not in a Hindu state of reincarnation; Rastas say they have "always existed in the distant past with Jah"; they need no rebirth. The Emperor's horrific death in 1975, however, moved the faithful to invent new mythologies to account for his disappearance (or assassination). Bob Marley immortalizes Selassie I in his song "Jah Lives" and claimed that he is still alive—that his alleged death was fabricated by his enemies or that he staged it to mystify Babylon. In another myth, Selassie I died but rose from the dead as Christ did; he is the Christ who was to come. Yet another Rastafarian view holds that Haile Selassie I, like the first Buddha, is an extraordinary man and the most spiritual of leaders; he fulfills the prophetic role of Christ as the greatest black man and Christian King who lived. He is a descendant of David and Solomon, and he died a martyr for the faith, but he is not a deity.

A reigning Archbishop of the Ethiopian Orthodox Church (EOC), puzzled by Rastas' advocacy of Selassie's divinity, pleaded, "The emperor was not god to the Ethiopian people. . . . He was a religious man who was elected king of Ethiopia [and] it is my duty to speak the truth and to strongly advise my brethren and sisters . . . to be aware of the commandment of God: 'Thou shall have no other gods before me—for I am a jealous God.'"[30] Selassie I remained tutelary head of the EOC until his death, carrying the appellation *Protector of the Faith of Christ*; a 1955 constitution made him the church's leader and legitimate authority. Article 5 of Ethiopia's 1974 Draft Constitution also shows the Emperor as professing the faith and calling on Ethiopians to recognize his role in the EOC.[31] At a World Evangelism Conference in Lausanne, Switzerland, in 1966, Selassie I urged fellow delegates to be diligent in spreading the Christian faith by preaching the gospel to all nations.[32] This religious man of royal hue showed no interest in being a god to Caribbean "sufferers"; but to most Rastas, he was too humble to acknowledge his divinity.

Selassie I's nobility contributed to his ascribed divinity. Makonnen, his father, was king of the city of Harar and Ethiopian ambassador and emissary to Europe. Emperor Menelik II was Ras Tafari's second cousin. He grew up *Lij* (child of a nobleman) and, while still a teenager, was made a provincial governor. On Menelik II's death, his granddaughter, Empress Zauditu, replaced his Muslim rival, Lij Yasu, and made Makonnen's son, *Lij* Tafari, her trusted advisor, regent, and heir apparent to the throne. From 1916 to 1928, he held the military title Ras (head and prince) and became Negus (King) Tafari. After two years as king, he was crowned Emperor and, at his coronation, was given the supreme judicial-political rank Negusa Nagast (King of Kings). As Clinton Chisholm notes, the titles Selassie I held, of course, were not unique; they were used commonly by past emperors as insignias of authority, political status, and power. The titles *King of Kings of Ethiopia* and *Elect of God* were used territorially in the 1800s to assert dominance over rival regional rulers and kings. Emperors inscribed, on their official seals, the words *"The Lion of the Tribe of Judah hath prevailed."* A Negus of Shoa addressed his correspondence "The Lion of the Tribe of Judah has conquered"; and Menelik II used *Elect of God, King of the Kings of Ethiopia* as bragging rights.[33]

Ithiopia, City of Zion

Rastafari's' orientation to Ethiopia claims to be historical, but it is largely mythological. From the Bible and other sources (for example, Kibra *Nagast, The Holy Piby, The Promised Key,* and Ethiopian messianism), Rastas came to see Ethiopia as an extension of favored Israelites and the city of Zion. According to the biblical story, Ethiopia's close association with Israelites dates back to Moses, who married an Ethiopian (Numbers 12:1). Many Ethiopians were conscripted in the Hebrew military (2 Samuel 18:21); and Jeremiah, who spoke figuratively of Ethiopian's color and leopard's skin (Jeremiah 13:23), was rescued from danger by an Ethiopian Ebed-melech (Jeremiah 38:4–14). Ethiopians claimed royal descent from the Hebrew King Solomon and Queen Makeida of Sheba. According to a biblical story, the African Queen visited Solomon in Jerusalem to experience firsthand his wealthy kingdom and great wisdom (1 Kings 10:1–13; 2 Chronicles 9:1–12).[34] In early Christian writings, Jesus is credited with giving prophetic credence to the story: "The Queen of the South shall rise up in the judgment with this generation and shall condemn it; for she came from the uttermost parts of the earth to hear the wisdom of Solomon and behold a greater than Solomon is here" (Matthew 12:42). Therefore Ethiopia finds a popular orientation in the Bible, a source of Rasta teachings.

The *Coptic History of the Patriarchs* (circa 500 C.E.) portrays Ethiopia as the kingdom of Sheba, out of which came the Queen of the South to see Solomon. Legend has it that during their encounter, Solomon and Makeida cohabited and sired a son, Menelik I, patriarch of Ethiopian kings, now ancestors of Emperor Haile Selassie I. According to the legend, Makeida—impressed by King Solomon's wisdom and God—admitted she was a worshiper of Egypt's sun god Re and quickly converted to worshiping the God of Israel. *Kebra Nagast* (called the "Lost Bible of Black Man's Wisdom") established Ethiopia's sacred history by glorifying the myth of the lineage of Ethiopian kings and emperors connected to King Solomon, Makeida, and ancient Hebrew religion. Another legend claims that the Hebrew Ark of the Covenant, taken from Jerusalem and transferred to Menelik I, resides in Ethiopia, the ancient empire of Aksum, where the famous Queen had her capitol around 1000 B.C.E. "Today the Ark of the Covenant lies in the St. Mary of Zion Church in the ancient city of Aksum . . . birth place of Ethiopian civilization."[35] Excerpts from *The Promised Key* and the *Holy Piby*, recorded later in this chapter, further propagate these myths and serve to glorify a spiritual Ethiopia as the City of Zion.

This saga with Solomon and the Ark of the Covenant became an essential orientation in Rastafari' mythological history. Ethiopia, having become the sacred land and special people, is the seat of Jah and the home of blacks, who are made a superior race through their connection to Selassie I. In this historical connection, Rastas equate themselves with Falashas, black Jews in Ethiopia, many of whom were airlifted to Israel in the 1980s. In the mythic blending of their political and theological narratives, diaspora blacks who suffered in captivity became Israelites. Throughout the history of blacks in the Americas, this mythology held up Ethiopia as the pride of Africa, a symbol and historic glory of the continent, and Ethiopians as being among God's chosen ones. Africans took solace in the discovery that the Bible spoke well of Ethiopia, to which they looked with pride as their future home. They cherished the fact that they were called "Ethiopians" and drew on biblical themes related to Ethiopia to lift their psyche and sense of "some-bodiness" and to work for freedom from slavery.[36] In postemancipation liberation narratives, "Ithiopia" is a vision of human dignity; religious struggle for equal rights and justice; "the transcendence of a negative self-image, racism, religious hegemony"; and freedom from economic and political exploitation. To God's new Children of Israel, who suffered "four hundred years of the Babylonian Captivity in plantation America," Selassie I has become "the agent of an imminent liberation that entails a return to Ethiopia," the blessed and wise promised land.[37] Ethiopia is Zion, a symbol of hope for a new social order for the black race.

Repatriating Evil Babylon

REPATRIATION

"We know where we're going, we know where we're from, we're leaving Babylon, we're going to our Father's land," sang Rasta Marley in "Exodus," his paradigmatic appeal to the biblical memory of the Hebrew exodus and Babylonian exile, to express the Rasta notion of liberation and repatriation. Rastafari maintains no consistent doctrine on repatriation, which it has only sporadically emphasized. Influenced by the back-to-Africa movement, the strong, early repatriation message of the 1930s to the 1960s advocated the physical return of large numbers of oppressed blacks to Ethiopia and Africa. However, less than three dozen Rastas actually overcame the mammoth financial hurdle of migrating to

Ethiopia; those who did settled to an arduous life in Shashamane in the Goba Valley. In 1955, Selassie I granted the American-based Ethiopian World Federation a five-hundred-acre lot of land in Shashamane as a kind gesture intended to benefit a few Western blacks "who supported Ethiopia in the war against Mussolini."[38] The emperor invited skilled Jamaicans to Ethiopia to continue the rebuilding effort in his country but had no place for a mass migration of unskilled peasants under the banner of repatriation. Rumors spread that Selassie had reserved a large settlement for repatriates and was building ships to transport them to Ethiopia. The following year, hundreds of the persuaded assembled at a Kingston port awaiting in vain the arrival of the "promised ships." In 1958, a little-known Rasta, Prince Emmanuel Edwards from a Back-O-Wall camp in Kingston, called on Rastafarians to prepare for imminent repatriation to Ethiopia. The following year, Claudius Henry bamboozled a number of people into selling their possessions and purchasing from him phony passage-tickets that were stamped October 25, 1959, for their imminent repatriation to Ethiopia.

After 1966, Rastas linked repatriation with reparation and retributive justice owed to blacks during colonialism. One repatriates Babylon by fighting for justice and freedom from oppression in the system[39] or by contributing to the impending apocalyptic fall of Babylon and a realization of the kingdom of Jah. Repatriation also involves an attitude and consciousness that rejects Babylon's culture and values things African; most Rastas "step out ah Babylon" culturally and ideologically in their lifestyle and practices. The voice of resistance to oppression urges that liberation from political control and economic deprivation[40] begin within, "for only we can free our mind from mental slavery" (Bob Marley, Redemption Song).

BABYLON

No orientation is as consistently held by all Rastas as the belief that life in the African diaspora is under the curse and domination of agents of Babylon. The use of this apt typology draws on the biblical memory of the ancient Babylonian empire as the symbol of evil in its invasions and oppression of the Hebrews and other peoples. The multivalent metaphor first symbolized colonial rule in Jamaica, with its menacing police, race and class prejudice, and twisted socioeconomic system. Later it included world political systems and cultural traditions that contribute to the impoverishment and oppression of African peoples. Babylon is Leviathan the Beast in governments, whose almighty power defends the interest, ethical mores, values, and institutions of the wealthy against the wretched of the earth. These Rastas find the culture of Babylon demonstrated also in the waste of the earth's natural resources and in the greed of multinational corporations from the world's richest nations.[41] Rastas' persistent chant against Babylon in reggae rhythms symbolically "delegitimizes" those Western values and institutions. In "Ride Natty Ride," Marley sings, "All in all you see wa g'wan. It is to fight against the Rastaman. So they build their world in great confusion to force on us the Devil's illusion, But we refuse to be what they want us to be; we are what we are, that's the way its going to be" ("Babylon System"). The battle against Babylon is construed in apocalyptic terms: evil arrayed against Jah and his people in a final showdown. To Howell, Western governments and Christianity constitute the evil powers of Babylon, which are set against oppressed Africans. The complicity of the Catholic Church in the European exploitation of African countries makes the Pope the Antichrist and the Vatican in Rome the "great harlot" of Babylon, spoken of in terms of the Apocalypse (Revelation). Jah will bring to a disastrous end the world's corrupt Babylon system that one Rasta intellectual claims "conspire" to create for the masses "busted hopes, broken dreams, the blues of broken homes, and of disjointed tribes of people trapped by history."[42] When Babylon falls, Jah will create a new society, where Rastas—God's true Israelites—and the poor will rule the world in peace and love.

Reggae Freedom Chant

Music, especially reggae, is the most well-known Rastafarian orientation. In the earliest Rasta meetings, their music consisted of Christian hymns and choral chants. At the Kingston ghetto camp, Burru drumming was added and consisted of the bass, fundeh,and repeater drums. Although the African Burru, played during Nyabinghi celebrations, remains the most authentic and distinct Rastafarian music, reggae, a latecomer, is its chief vehicle and the most universally recognized cultural form. Since the early 1970s, Rastas have used this scintillating art as an effective communication tool, and it earned for them a broad international cultural appeal. Music is one of the movement's greatest means of diffusion, especially from artists of the reggae revolution— the nonviolent artistic revolt against the Babylon system and its colonial legacy. Rastafari's message is spread and legitimized in the music of "the masters," who sound its beliefs in dynamic rhythms and flash its culture in the media. The most notable among the masters were Desmond Decker, the late Nesta Robert Marley (his first name is Nesta), Peter Tosh, Toots and the Mytals, and Burning Spear;[43] a few of these artists were actually diehard Rastafarians.

After many years of experimenting with various musical styles and forms, the destitute Marley and the Whalers made history; they created reggae after Bob "cited up Rasta" in the historic post-1966 visit of Haile Selassie I. At the peak of Bob's short career as arguably the most popular musician of the second half of the twentieth century, he became Rastafari's proxy and evangelist to the world. His fans found his colorful dance parties[44] and reggae hits (for example, "Stir It Up," "No Woman No Cry," and "We Jamin") irresistible, but they also heard that Selassie I is Jah the divine, incarnate in living flesh; that the black man is suffering in a "War in Babylon"; and that Rastas must chant down the system because "Jah's Kingdom Goes to Waste." To resist Babylon, we must follow our "internalized alternative consciousness"[45] and not let anyone fool us, or try to school us, because "we got a mind of our own" ("Can You Be Loved").

Some try to brainwash us to make us into fools, hating us while telling us about their god above but we must "chase those crazy baldheads right out of town" ("Crazy Baldheads").

In his revolutionary hits "Confrontation," "Babylon System," "Duppy Conqueror," "War," "Rebel Music," "Burning," "Catch a Fire," "I Shot the Sheriff," "Africa Unite," and "Get Up Stand Up," Bob waged a peaceful political war, chanting to the world the black struggle for dignity, economic justice, and inclusion. When he performed "Zimbabwe," before a massive audience at the nation's independence celebration in Harare, he inspired black dignity and a call for freedom in many countries in Africa. In his cool rhythms—"Could You Be Loved," "One Love," and "Is Dis Love"—Bob is an ambassador for brotherhood and interracial harmony around the world. The death of the King of Reggae, similar to the murder of Selassie I six years earlier, was a great loss to the movement and the world. He died from a neglected soccer injury in 1981, but his death became the object of myths and conspiracy theories, implicating the Babylon police, the Federal Bureau of Investigation, and the Central Intelligence Agency.[46] Some fans mythologize that Jah took Marley to heaven, because a strange specter was seen in the sky over his home the minute he died. Some Rastas say Marley, like Jah, lives. He climaxed an epoch in Rastafari history, put Jamaican culture on the map, and changed the world for the better through music and Rastafari.

Dawtars Dare to Trod

Caribbean religions of African origin are dominated by women and have a proclivity toward female leadership. Rastafari, however, broke that mold. Although it is now open to anyone, from its inception it was a male-dominated order where men outnumbered women three to one and "sistren" had no say. Mirroring its belief that it is made up of the new Israelites, the movement built its social structure on ancient Hebrew regulations found in the Torah. Like the Hebrew and Catholic priesthood, or like Buddhist's *sanghas* ("orders"), Rastafari groups were perceived as male cultic orders; the men hung out together and assembled at private yards ("homes") for ritual activities. Few "dawtars" ("women") "trod" ("followed") the movement; most of those who "cited up" ("joined") were brought in by their kingmen ("Rasta men"). "Bredren" ("men") were leaders and "sistren" or dawtars, although called queens, served their kingmen and their "youths" ("children") as good caretakers of the home.[47] The bredren were head of all sistren in the "house"; all women in the Bobo Shanti sect are still lower in the pecking order than the kingmen's sons; that is, male youths hold a higher status than their mothers and other women. A female can trod the path of Rastafari only through a male and cannot expect to attain the highest level of Rastafari wisdom without having a kingman as her head; he has the responsibility of balancing her thoughts, which are perceived as inferior and limited.

In the Caribbean, except in East Indian communities, women have a strong rebel tradition and are authority figures in most homes.[48] Especially since the 1960s, they also have outpaced men academically: girls now account for more than two-thirds of co-ed high school populations in Jamaica. Literate women are better providers than men and hold the social fabric of the family together, to the chagrin of their underemployed men, to whom they must play a proscribed role in the Rastafari communes. In "mansions," women may perform important tasks where their academic skills are needed, but the treasurers and leaders are all male. Sistren cannot lead or direct rituals in the mansion (Rasta "church" meetings). At a binghi I attended with some students in Barbados in 1998, women were not allowed to take a lead role in the chanting of hymns or testimony. They are not denied "grounding" ("reasoning") among themselves, but this cherished activity of the body politic was for males.[49] Under the influence of Revivalism, the Rastas' reading of myths about the fall of Adam and Eve, the Delilah story, and ancient Hebrew ceremonial codes all generated many taboos that typecast women as unclean and dangerous. Rastas claim that men lose spiritual force during sexual intimacy and that they are most vulnerable during the menstrual flow of women, who must be temporarily quarantined from the rest of the family. The idea of women being hazardous to men recalls the secret societies in West Africa where women use their feminine resources as magical tools of empowerment to keep irresponsible men in check.[50] Rastas who know of this African tradition feel discommoded by the idea and have one more reason to keep women "downpressed."

Maureen Rowe and Imani Tafari-Ama (both Jamaican), Obiagele Lake from the United States, U.S. Lauretta Collins at the University of Puerto Rico, and other Rastafari scholars[51] note that women's role in Rastafari is no more proscribed than it is in the Babylonian culture in which the religion emerged. Jamaica has been patriarchal and has historically abridged women's role in established religions. Rastas did not see women's liberation and equality as their movement's priority. As violence, economic disadvantage, discrimination, and racism were more pressing issues than sexism and patriarchy during the long night of the African American struggle, so too early Rasta women accepted their proscribed role to fight the more sinister causes of liberation from economic slavery and bigotry. Not immune to winds of change in the Caribbean, Rastafari saw a period of accommodation, when a significantly larger number of women began "citing up" the movement. Many dawtas committed to the faith by trodding the Twelve Tribes of Israel, whose houses allowed sistren an active social role in the cult. For example, at official functions, twenty-four members comprising equal numbers of men and women officiate. Women wear the Rasta colors, head wraps, dreadlocks, and tams, share in the challis, participate in reasoning, and assert themselves at various gatherings.

Under the influence of the Caribbean Women's Movement (CWM) in the 1970s, sistren were emboldened to initiate new changes in the movement by challenging its gender relations and ideology. CWM held several important conferences and initiatives in Jamaica, some under the international feminist umbrella, and had a significant impact on Rastafari women, who began organizing their own groups and associations regardless of the threat they posed to men. King Alpha and Queen Omega's Theocracy Daughters, International Twelve, Dawtas United, and other women's groups were formed in the 1980s to advance the cause of the sistren. They articulated their own perceptions of Rastafari in reasoning sessions; debunked social taboos of feminine sexuality; redefined Rastas' beliefs about women's spirituality; and collaborated to establish spiritual, social, and economic circles of association within the movement. Ostensibly, they brought Rastafari patriarchy a new orientation on women.[52]

Structure and Cultus

From its inception, Rastafari formed from different cells led by its pioneers and remained a structurally loose reticulate movement, consisting of a network of heterogeneous circles of associations. These range in size from groupings of three or four families to several hundred who live in small shacks within "camps" ("squatting settlements"); "yards" comprising several poorly maintained small structures enclosed in a city community or ghetto; and regular homes. Most Rastas affiliate with one of many small camps, and others are "own-built" ("unaffiliated"); they follow Rastafari as individualists, with little interest in group association. As Makeda Lee explains, the "believers are of many kinds . . . there are the holy men, the patriarchs of the faith, and the sages, who can be found living in small shacks in . . . encampments on the hillsides and seashores, and in the heart of the ghetto."[53] Since the late 1950s, groups of Rastas, called "mansions," and "houses" formed as autonomous sects and developed specific practices and beliefs. Houses are small, informal groups of ten to eighteen Rastas whose members sustain an ongoing relationship. A mansion (often called a house) is a commune-type settlement or a sect of hundreds of Rastas led by a charismatic leader. Prince Edward's Ethiopian National Congress, Abuna Fox's Church of Haile Selassie, Rastafarian Theocratic Government, Peacemakers Association, Rastafari Movement Association, Sons of Negus Negusa, and Count Ossi's Mystic Revelations of Rastafari are among the popular houses in Jamaica.[54] They form an amphictyony, or loose federation, with no centralized authority.

Houses and Mansions

Notwithstanding their reticulate structure, camps, houses, and mansions form quasi-organizations that facilitate their orderly function. Their informal associations allow houses to communicate, collaborate, and socialize spontaneously. Some mansions are well organized; their founders are leaders and senior elders of the commune. These elders certify anyone who is "citing-up Rasta" before they are considered legitimate, perform ceremonial rites, and officiate at funerals in houses, where the dead are ritualized. An elder travels, as a delegate, to international Rastafari gatherings and reports to his house. He may also plan Nyabinghi and other ritual activities of the sect.[55] The following houses, whose names have changed several times, are run by founding elders and represent the broadest cross-section of the faith: Bobo Dreads (Bobo Shanti), House of Nyabinghi (called variously Rastafari Theocratic "Issembly," Theocratic Priesthood and Livity Order of Rastafari, Prince Emanuel Edwards Ethiopian International Congress, and Ethiopian African International Congress), and the Twelve Tribes of Israel.

BOBO DREADS

Bobo Dreads form the most recognizable sect within Rastafari; the tightly wrapped turbans covering matted locks is a most conspicuous Rasta cultural symbol. On special occasions, Bobos can be seen dressed in long black or white robes and sandals, with staff in hand, conducting evening prayers and paying tribute to their holy trinity.[56] In the 1950s, disagreement among Rastafarians, caused by the dissident Youth Black Faith, over the necessity of growing dreadlocks resulted in a split in the order; one faction formed the House of Dreadlocks and another, which saw no need to "locksup," formed the House of "Combesomes." The House of Combesomes faded into other groups, but the House of Dreadlocks carried the distinguishing Rastafarian trademark. It further divided into regular dreads and Bobo Shanti, named after the Ashanti of Kumasi, Ghana. The Bobos eke out an existence from the most humble of circumstances—government's displacement action forced many into Trench Town and other ghettoes of Kingston—but they are a very proud and self-assured group. These landless peasants originally squatted on "crown lands," which allowed for the growing of sustenance food crops. As an important means of survival, they make and barter arts and crafts for the small tourist trade. Some Bobos escaped the ghetto and settled in Bull Bay in western Jamaica, establishing another Rasta community and living communally and self-reliantly after Howell's Pinnacle model. The Bobos are peaceful and denounce violence of every kind.

Bobo mythology is rich in symbolic meaning and typology. Embellishing an annual Roman Catholic tradition, Bobos view their "Ithiopian" African Black Congress Church, settled during state persecution, as Stations of the Cross everywhere; the locations are named after an important place where Jesus walked. They named the Bull Bay settlement Mt. Temon, regarded as a sacred site from which Israel's God originated, and claim to be the new biblical Israelites. Bobos are one of the few Rastafarian sects to develop a strict social code with taboos based on the Bible. They observe Sabbath from sundown on Friday to sundown on Saturday, follow sabbatical restrictions given in the Torah, and uphold rigid disciplines and female taboos on social relations in their commune. Their ceremonial observances often exceed the forms found in the Christian Old Testament. For example, male and female living quarters are separated for ritual purposes; sistren must observe strict purification rituals, inspired by taboos associated with the female reproductive cycle. Every month, Bobo sistren spend a week in a hostel-type "sick house," during which they must not cook for men or approach a ritual gathering. They do not share the chalice with males—an act that excludes them from the essential Rastafarian "livity" and fellowship. After childbirth, a sistren is unclean for up to three months and must be attended to by a "nurse."[57] In the commune, all sistren must be properly clad so as not to distract the brethren. They should cover their heads during prayer and other public rituals, they should not wear "cross-gender" clothing, and must not straighten their hair. Bobo's houses are communities of social control and allegiances. At his own commune, Prince Emmanuel is the absolute authority; he is the divine prince of the holy trinity (son of God) and a reincarnated "Melchizedek." At the heart of this trinity are three constituent divinities in a triad of priest, prophet, and king: Selassie is Father of creation and King Alpha, Garvey is prophet, and Emmanuel is Priest. When Emmanuel died in 1993, Bobos claimed he left only for a short while; he returned[58] as a reincarnated black Christ, sent to earth, and is on par with Selassie I the divine.

NYABINGHI ORDER

Nyabinghi is a religious sect, an assembly, a ritual celebration, a musical or drumming style, and an ideology expressing a spirit of resistance to oppression. Associated with an uprising against European colonists in southwestern Uganda's Ndorwa-Kajara region, in the late 1800s, *Nya* and *Binghi* meant "death to oppressors." Among women who led the insurgence was the much-feared medicine woman Muhumusa. Myth has it that she possessed the spirit of a legendary Amazon Queen, Nyabinghi, which gave her supernatural powers. Rastas appropriated Nyabinghi as their liberation motto after *Jamaica Times* (1935) ran an article "Nya-Binghi," written by Italian journalist Frederico Philos and published as propaganda in a Vienna newspaper in August, 1934. Intending to justify Italian-European aggression against Ethiopia, Philos charged that African nations were leading a secret society called the Order of Nyabinghi, founded by the king of the Kongo to resist white colonial rule in Africa. Philos claims that at a congress in Moscow in 1930, the eighty-two African delegates unanimously gave Selassie supreme powers in the Nyabinghi. The emperor then swore to go to war against Europeans and "is regarded as a veritable messiah, a savior to colored people everywhere, the Emperor of the Negro Kingdom. . . . He is their god."[59] The sensational article, printed with a picture of the Emperor in an Ethiopian Amharic warrior's headdress, circulated throughout Kingston's shantytown at the beginning of Mussolini's invasion of Ethiopia and inflamed angry passion among Rasta pioneers.[60]

In 1949, Jamaican Rastas held a convention at Wareika Hills under a Nyabinghi banner to show their large rally's solidarity with the African struggle. Shortly thereafter, militants of the Youth Black Faith reappropriated the

Nyabinghi concept as a battle cry against persecution. Later, Rastas organized several orders under the name Nyabinghi. The House of Nyabinghi called TPLOR constitutes one of the largest sects in Rastafari.[61] It claims that Selassie I authorized the founding of the original House of Nyabinghi in the late 1940s. This is celebrated in a symbolic dance that is dedicated to the African struggle. TPLOR says its order began with the mysterious Bible character Melchizedek, King of Salem, the mythic biblical high priest who has no beginning or end of days and no father or mother (Genesis 14:17-24). Selassie I is the new Melchizedek, and elders of the house of Nyabinghi, the keepers of the faith, are inheritors of the divine order of Melchizedek. Leonard Howell also claimed to be Melchizedek, and the Ethiopian National Congress regards its founder and first leader, Emanuel Edwards, its Melchizedek. So the ancient mythic character of Mesopotamia has several Rasta impersonations.

Ras Pidow, a priest, poet, and theologian (born in 1931), and Ras Sam Brown (1921 to 1998), two of the most well-known elders of the Nyabinghi Theocratic Order, articulated its belief in this abbreviated manifesto:

- We strongly object to sharp implements used in the desecration of the figure of man, e.g., trimming. . . .
- We are . . . vegetarians, making scant use of certain animal flesh yet outlawing the use of swine's flesh in any forms, shell fish, scaleless fish, and snails.
- We worship and observe no God but Ras Tafari, outlawing all forms of pagan worship.
- We love and respect the brotherhood of mankind yet our first love is to the sons of Ham.
- We disapprove and utterly hate jealousy, envy, deceit, guile, treachery. . . .
- We are avowed to create a world order of one brotherhood, and adhere to the ancient laws of Ethiopia.
- Our duty is to extend the hands of charity to any brother in distress . . . to any human, animals, plants.[62]

TWELVE TRIBES OF ISRAEL

Twelve Tribes, a name adopted from ancient Hebrews, is the strongest and most progressive house in Rastafari. Made famous by Marley, the king of reggae, it has established branches in many Caribbean states, the United States, Europe, Canada, and Africa. Members of the Tribes consist of what is termed Rasta's ethnically diverse middle class. The sect has an organized leadership that is incongruent with the acephalous nature and antihierarchy philosophy of Rastafari. Vernon Carrington, Prophet Gad, heads the Tribes, which is served by an executive board of thirteen elders and a twenty-four-member body made of twelve male and twelve female representatives. Members on the board have a stated policy for filling their vacant seats, and the prophet Gad (Gadman) approves board appointees and decisions and maintains control of the sect. Gadman Carrington claims he founded the order in 1968, following Selassie I's visit to Jamaica in 1966, as the lost tribes of Israel. He also claims to have experienced a vision from Jah to organize the group under the name Twelve Tribes. Until the 1970s, however, the sect existed as Local Chapter 15 of the Ethiopian World Federation (EWF), located in Trench Town; it changed its name to Twelve Tribes during the reggae explosion of the 1970s.[63]

Revivalist leader Carrington synthesized the Bible with Egyptian and Ethiopian myths, African history, and Jewish mystical Kabbalah numerology to frame the sect's beliefs. Through Selassie I, Tribers claim to be descendants of King Solomon and the Queen of Sheba. His Majesty is the second-coming manifestation of Christ, as taught in the Bible. Members of the Tribes trace their roots to the twelve tribes of Israel and use the number twelve as a sacred wand for genealogical and metaphysical determinations. They replicate the twelve disciples of Jesus, and each member takes a biblical tribal name based on the twelve signs of the Zodiac and one's birth month. The Tribes are among the 144,000 whom Jah will save "from the four corners of the earth" (Revelation 7:3-8). Twelve Tribes freely showcase their middle-class values. Unlike vintage Rastas, tribesmen share roles with the sistren[64] and may choose not to wear dreadlocks and to groom facial hair. Strict adherence to a vegetarian diet is not required, and some members eat salted meat, forbidden in other houses. Tribes bury their dead and attend funerals, as they did at Bob Marley's passing.

Livity and Ital Rituals

An essential orientation of Rastafari is the integrative praxis—lived out in commitment to its rituals and social code—called livity, an all-inclusive idea that involves such things as beliefs, dietary choices, pharmacopeia, ritual ganja, Nyabinghi, lifestyle, and symbols of the faith. The livity mantra is multipurpose: it symbolically expresses Rastas' cultural alternative to social norms and a lifestyle they designed for themselves on the basis of their view of biblical teachings; it is an attempt to model a life that honors Jah while living in harmony with the natural order of things; and it is a path to true spirituality and holistic health. The complex livity concept incorporates elements of African culture that survived among Caribbean peasants and is a veritable rejection of Western consumerism, intrusive science and technology, postmodernist ethics, and the modern medicine of Babylon.

DREADLOCKS, SYMBOLS OF RESISTANCE
Most characteristics of the Rastafari livity are its symbols of resistance, chief among which are the darning of beards and dreadlocks; the wearing of tams (or ites); unkempt clothes; the Haile Selassie icon; and the lion-and-cross mascot cast against the colors of their flag, which are green, black, red, and gold.

Red symbolizes the triumphant faith of Rastafari and the blood of those who died in the cause of freedom for enslaved and oppressed Africans. Black represents the resilient African race, holiness, and wisdom. Green represents the holy herb and the beautiful vegetation of Africa and Jamaica. Gold is a symbol of the purity of Rastafari's philosophy and faith, as well as the "natural wealth" and hope of Africa and Jamaica;[65] Africans are impoverished, but the continent is rich in minerals, diamonds, gold, bauxite, fossil fuel, and rubber—all controlled by Babylon companies. Darning dreadlocks is not original to Rastafari and was not a dominant feature of the movement before the 1950s.[66] It was appropriated from several sources: Jamaican Hindu holy men, East African Galla, Somali or Masai tribesmen, and the Mau Mau of Kenya, all of whom grew matted locks. After a group of Rastas started wearing locks in western Kingston, they took the Hindi name Jagavi. "Locksingup" got popular after Rastas saw photos of Kenyan Mau Mau freedom fighters and of Jomo Kenyata's Reform army resisting colonial rule.[67] Pictures of Ethiopian monks wearing dreadlocks appeared in a 1970 issue of *National Geographic*, coinciding with the emerging worldwide appearance of reggae and its superstar Marley darning his locks. Since then, locks became the authentic Rastafarian icon[68] and pop cultural symbol of choice, internationally.

For Rastas, dreadlocks are both important elements in a lifestyle and an authentic symbol of resistance to Babylon culture. What could be a more powerful symbol of resistance than the locks that show Rastas' "lion-ness," or inner strength, as followers of the African lion of the tribe of Judah? The crown, formed by the matted hair, identifies with the crown of Selassie I and is a symbol of the king of beasts whose hairy mane warns enemies of its lethal strength. In Rastafari, the lion embodies moral fortitude, fearless resistance, "and wholesome integrity that come from self-realization."[69] Also, the grooming of the locks was a reform trend, intended to purge the movement of the revivalist elements it retained in its rituals. Dreadlocks and matted hair point to a staunch African identity and a way of expressing Rastas' natural lifestyle, in sharp contrast to the unnatural straightened hair glorified as a symbol of beauty in colonial society. Rastas grow locks also as a sign of their Nazarite vow to follow Jah, in appropriation of the biblical story of strongman Sampson (Judges 16 and 17), who single-handedly vanquished the armies of the enemies of the Hebrews as long as he kept his locks and obeyed his god. Dreadlocks heighten the brethren's psyche and improve their status in the house; the longer one's locks, "the greater his standing as a professor of the faith."[70] For many Rastas, wearing locks is optional, but it is an important orientation and symbol of the faith.

ITAL LIVING
Ital living is true to Rastas' Nazerite lifestyle, in imitation of an ancient Hebrew practice. Rastas grow long hair naturally, although many locks are superficial; they do not consume alcohol or smoke tobacco products; they avoid corpses and, with the exception of members of Twelve Tribes of Israel, do not attend

funerals—Rastafari is a religion of the living, not the dead. The bredren are opposed to war and the shedding of blood, especially human blood, even if the intent is to save lives; Jah is a god of peace and love, not violence and bloodshed. Rastas view, as taboo, family planning programs; divorce and remarriage (many replace traditional marriage practices with those of African traditions); and same-sex unions, which they regard as an abomination to Jah. Cosmetic makeovers and the straightening of kinky hair also dishonor Jah, since it shows enslavement to the Babylon culture and lack of African pride. The ital code also marks a time of purity when Rastas set themselves apart from natural pleasures.

Rastas believe in preserving the environment. In rural areas, they mostly live off squatted lands, which they attempt to keep free from pollutants. Their humble yards (homes) are built of wood and other environmentally friendly plant products. Although the harsh economic realities of the Caribbean make it impossible for them to live "strictly ital" (on organic foods), Rastas strive to consume homegrown foods in order to be independent of evil Babylon's "poisonous system," which is seen in the contamination of foods through processing plants, canning, and preservatives. Among meat foods, pork, certain species of marine life (shellfish and scaleless fish), birds, and animals—all regarded as earth's scavengers and predators—are on the forbidden list. Like Medieval Jewish teacher Moses Maimonides, Rastas claim that eating predatory or carnivorous animals makes one violent. Salted foods are also off-limits for many, because they are associated with slavery and with African-Maroon myths of salt interfering with human communication. Rastas say that salt clouds their vision and abridges their freedom in Babylon, just as slaves suffered in Jamaica.

Caribbean Rastas have limited access to health care and few of them trust Babylon's medical system, regarded as contributing to the pollution of the environment.[71] Furthermore, the performance of modern medical experiments on black human subjects is suspected. In most rural communities, Rastas rely strictly on ital medicines taken from a variety of plants. Ganja (known in non-Rasta society as grass, marijuana, hemp, and cannabis) is the most popular item in their pharmacopeia. Rastas call it callie (kali), Iley, holy herb, and wisdom weed and put it to multiple use, as has been done in Caribbean society for more than 150 years. Jamaican use of the herb is traced to many sources, among them India and western, central, and southern Africa. In the Democratic Republic of the Congo, for example, ganja pipes were smoked to the beat of drums and ritual chants and dances in ATRs. West African traditional healers use the herb to procure a variety of cures for aches and pains, spells, and to access spiritual power. In Kumina ceremonies in Jamaica, cannabis is smoked for health and spiritual reasons,[72] as is done in West Africa.

HERBS HEAL THE NATION
Smoking ganja was a Caribbean practice among the working class, influenced by colonial postemancipation Indian immigration. The use of Indian hemp was

popular among the indentured East Indian immigrants brought by the British into their territories in the second half of the 1800s. Those immigrant workers grew cannabis among their food crops, in garden plots, and on their host plantations for medical, spiritual, and recreational use. Like their African ancestors, Caribbean herbalists and medicine men use ganja as folk medicine, discreetly mixed with other herbs. Rastas cite Scripture: "Of the herbs that bear the various fruits, the leaf of it shall be the healing of the nation" (Revelation 22:2, King James version). The holy herb heals the Rasta nation. In Rasta mythology, "herbs feed the brain, prevent cancer," and suppress an overly active sex drive. As Amerindians do with tobacco, parents blow the smoke of the herb in the face of children to cure common colds and coughs. The herb is chewed, smoked, cooked in foods or brewed as a panacea for a variety of ailments, among them asthma, stomach disorders, fevers, cramps, and rheumatism. Rastas are well known for their ganja herbal teas and "roots-tonics";[73] this petit trade is used to subsidize their meager income, while at the same time one of the earth's natural sources provides cures for ailments.

Rastas' medical and culinary use of the sacred herb is less well known than their cultic sacramental use, which was neither widespread nor a sacred ritual until the late 1950s. It would be later still before biblical warrant would be summoned in support of a doctrine of the sacrament and the labeling of ganja as a "holy herb for the healing of the nation."[74] Hindu mystical ideas influenced the religion's sacramental use of ganja. The use of the chillum pipe—one of the two pipes used in "pulling the chalice" (the ritual smoking of ganja)—the manner in which it is used, and the method of preparing ganja for the chalice are East Indian in origin. The other pipe used is the Kochi. Howell made ganja use a ritual at Pinnacle Hill at the same time that he adopted East Indian titles. Following this, the Youth Black Faith institutionalized the herb as an integral part of their worship. As Chevannes explains, to ensure that they used ganja only "as part of their religious practices and beliefs, the Youth Black Faith" prohibited its members from carrying ganja paraphernalia on them as drug traffickers do. A myth of convenience says the holy herb received its sacredness and spiritual force from first appearing as a plant on the grave of King Solomon, who built the first temple to Jah, and therefore pulling the chalice renders "I-an-I" as wise as Solomon.[75]

The sharing of the single ganja pipe imitates Christ and his disciples celebrating the Jewish Passover sacrament with the sharing of a single cup of wine and thus enhances communal bonds. Brethren say the holy herb is a source of enlightenment and a means of spiritual nourishment; its ritual smoking enhances meditation, gives clarity of thought in reasoning sessions and Nyabinghi services, and soothes the troubled mind. It is also an expression of authentic individual freedom given by Jah as well as a symbol of resistance to Babylon's culture. Jah created and blessed the callie for I-an-I: "He causeth the grass to grow for the cattle and herb for the service of man, that he may bring forth food out of the earth" (Psalm 104:14); "and thou shalt eat the herb of the field"

(Genesis 3:18); "eat every herb of the land" (Exodus 10:12); "Better is a dinner of herbs where love is, than a stalled ox and hatred there with" (Proverbs 15:17 King James version). So what Jah-Jah blessed, let no Babylon curse as illegal. No legal infractions were committed in the use of ganja before Babylon made it illegal in the 1930s. The criminalizing of ganja began after the Egyptian government persuaded the League of Nations to place marijuana on its Dangerous Drugs list in 1924, after which Britain prohibited its use in all of its colonies, with exceptions made for medical and scientific use. After the 1938 revolt, caused largely by economic deprivation in Jamaica, authorities invoked the Dangerous Drug Law and declared marijuana a nuisance, erroneously claiming that its use influenced the uprising among Rastas. In spite of the political myths, no research has shown that ritual ganja makes Rastas violent.

RITUAL NYABINGHI
Rastafari's festive rituals find their fullest expression in the Nyabinghi meeting, the most important of Rastafarian "Issemblies." Rastas initiated the binghi in the Warika Hills communes, Pinnacle Hill, and Kingston's shantytown as a symbolic worship event. As Chevannes notes, this was "a death-by-magic ritual in which an effigy representing the intended victim is consumed by fire while all the participants dance under a spell of *buru* drumming called 'tuokin [stoking?] the drum.'" At first, "the ritual was performed in the presence of Rastafari only,"[76] as a music festival, but today it is less secretive. It is enacted with a special drumming style known as "churchical" (religious) music and combines "instruments and rhythmic techniques of the African Burru drums and rhythms with Rastafarian Christian-based hymn singing and chanting"[77] lyrics. The African Nyabinghi music style survived in Revival, Pocomina, and especially Burru and Kumina drumming. Rastafari's three-drum set—called the *akete* (the bass), fundeh, and repeater—are Burru in origin and form the binghi's most authentic musical base. Although the binghi music emerged from Back-O-Wall in the 1940s and 1950s, it was unknown before the Rasta conference in 1958. Notwithstanding the popularity of reggae, Rastafari retains the distinctly African-Buru musical score that is unmistakable in the binghi celebration.

The ceremonial binghi can last for several days, and in addition to singing, drumming, and dancing, it consists of reading the scriptures, reasoning, testimony, and sharing the chalice. At two Rasta binghis I was privileged to attend (in Barbados and Trinidad), smoke filled the air around us as drums kept a deep and steady "haunting beat" and brethren sang lyrics, repeatedly, into the wee hours of the morning. Drummers and song leaders paused only to catch their breath before the next song began; it was as if Jah was not in a hurry for anything. The smoke that greeted my students and me at the Barbados camp came not from the holy herb but from a bonfire, symbolically lit to burn down Babylon. The Binghi Night lasted from 10:00 P.M. on Sunday to 6:00 A.M. on Monday, during which brethren danced around an altar-table that was covered with gifts (food, herbs, and so forth), pictures of Selassie, and

Bibles; the food on the table recalls the table in Revivalism. Brethren led chants in immediate succession as the fire burned continuously to the unceasing drumbeat.[78] When a voice signaled a long overdue intermission, one brethren at a time began reading passages from the Bible as a basis for the ensuing reasoning.

GROUNDATION

In the binghi, Rastas assemble for a spiritual grounding in the faith; this is the most common communal activity found in all Rastafari houses. Groundings are meetings where Rastas assemble for intellectual reflection, or reasoning, on a regular basis. They are also held during the commemoration of important events on the liturgical calendar, such as Groundation Day, which celebrates Selassie's visit to Jamaica in 1966. Although unstructured and informal, the meetings are used to instruct new adherents in the principles of the faith. Grounding occurs in the yards of leading brethren. Some Rastas ground in each others' yards daily as a social activity to build community politic. Grounding takes the form of biblical texts citations, exhortations, homilies, explanations, and commentaries on current events; Rastas share their views on theology, politics, and a variety of other issues. In most houses, groundation is accompanied by the ganja sacrament.[79] An unofficial calendar guides Rastafari's ritual occasions. Each April, Rastas observe the anniversary of the Emperor's visit to Jamaica; they celebrate his birthday on July 23 and commemorate his coronation on November 2. They honor founders of their houses and celebrate birthdays of national heroes like Marcus Garvey, Paul Bogle, and Maroon freedom fighter Nanny. Also commemorated are Emancipation Day (August 1), Ethiopian Christmas (January 7), and the beginning of the Ethiopian year on April 1.

Conclusion

Rastafari evolved as a despised and dreaded tumor among the downtrodden but has become Jamaica's most popular religious movement of modern times. The persecuted dreadlocks-waving, ganja-smoking, unkempt followers of the renegade cult chanting down evil Babylon are now the proud bearers of a commercialized Babylon culture. This is but another phase of the social struggle and misery that gave birth to the religion. Africanists combined their anticolonial liberation ideology with the black struggle for equality and dignity and grounded their Ethiopian messianic hope in an eschatology of a returned Messiah. The fact that Rastas chose a diminutive Haile Selassie I as that messiah must remain a paradox. His supporters, who saw him as special and as a leader who did great things for his country, say that he gave Ethiopia international recognition by getting it into the League of Nations in 1924; he also modernized the country with automobiles, electricity, postal services, and a world-class international airport; abolished elements of Ethiopia's cruel penal system;

made improvements in transportation and health; and gained respect for his country with his decisive defeat of Italy.

Ethiopia under Selassie I, however, was no paradise, and the emperor was not a merciful god to his political dissenters, especially from the breakaway country-state of Eritrea. He lived in opulence, lavishly entertaining dignitaries at the royal palace while giving beggarly handouts to starving peasants in order to keep their homage.[80] Selassie I surrounded his administration with unsavory characters, some of whom were "Babylonians" of Italian descent. Ethiopian masses lived in squalor, poor health, and backwardness. The illiteracy rate in the country was about 90 percent. These realities of Haile Selassie's ineptitude did not factor into Rastafarian theology, because religions are born of myths, new consciousness, and faith rather than truth, science, or logic.

EXCERPTS

The First Chant: Leonard Howell's *The Promised Key,* with Commentary by William David Spencer

THE MYSTERY COUNTRY

I wish to state to you my dear Readers, that Ethiopia is a Country of great contrasts largely unexplored and is populated by Black People whose attitude towards this so called Western civilization has not changed within the last six thousand years.

The people are Christians while retain Primitive customs. The result is that the Black People of Ethiopia are extraordinarily blended into a refined fashion that cannot be met with in any other part of the world.

In 1930 the Duke of Gloucester undertook one of the most interesting duties he had been called upon to execute up to this date. The occasion was the Coronation of His Majesty Ras Tafari the King of Kings and Lord of Lords the conquering Lion of Judah, the Elect of God and the Light of the world.

The Duke was to represent his father The Anglo Saxon King. The Duke handed to His Majesty Rastafari the King of Kings and Lord of Lords a Sceptre of solid gold twenty seven inches long of which had been taken from the hands of Ethiopia some thousand years ago.

The Duke fell down bending knees before His Majesty Ras Tafari the King of Kings and Lord of Lords and spoke in a loud tone of voice and said, "Master,

Excerpt: Selection reprinted from Nathaniel Samuel Murrell, William David Spencer, and Adrian Anthony McFarlane, *Chanting Down Babylon: The Rastafari Reader* (Philadelphia: Temple University Press, 1998).

Master my father has sent me to represent him sir. He is unable to come and he said that he will serve you to the end Master." See Psalm 72:9 to 11 verses, also see Gen. 49 chap. 10 verse.

On one side of the Sceptre was inscribed Ethiopia shall make her hands reach unto God, and on the other side the King of Kings of Ethiopia, the top of the shaft was finished with a seal and above was a clen cross in which a single carbuncle was set.

The Sceptre was a magnificent piece of workmanship and had been designed from an historic piece in which was the special ceremonies of His Royal Highness of Ethiopia, Earth's Rightful Ruler.

The Duke also handed to Queen Omega the Empress of Ethiopia a Sceptre of gold and ivory. The shaft being in the form of a spray of lilies and at the top a spray of lilies in bloom.

It was a brilliant ceremony, the church began to fill. The Ethiopians were brilliant in special robes having discarded their precious white robes, and wore Jewels of great value.

The men's swords being heavily ornamented with gems. On their heads they wore gold braided hats, in which the covered lion's manes were to be seen. In contraction then were the solar note struck by the women who were heavily veiled, and wore heavy cloaks.

His and Her Majesty King Alpha and Queen Omega the King of Kings drove to the Cathedral in a Coach drawn by six white Arab horses.

Queen Omega in a Robe of Silver and the escort on mules wearing lion's skin over their shoulders, forming into procession outside the Cathedral.

King Ras Tafari and Queen Omega the Royal pair, the escort and a line of Bishops and Priests entered, the guests rank obeisance.

King Alpha sitting on his Throne homage was done to him by the Bishops and Priests fulfilling the 21st. Psalm. The ceremony took 10 days from the second day to the eleventh day of November 1930.

King Alpha was presented with the orb spurs, and spears and many other mighty emblems of His High Office, Dignitaries of the world power presented King Alpha with the wealth of oceans.

The Emperor attended to most of his preparations for the reception of his thousands of guests himself, and day after day could be seen rushing about in his scarlet car seeing how the white labourers were getting on with the new road he had ordered that the lawns he had laid down be attended to and that the extension of the electric lights throughout the city were being hurried on.

THE FALSE RELIGION

All the Churches Religious system of today, claims to represent the Lord God of Israel; but the Pope who is Satan the devil, false organization, it is a hypocritical religious system that has three elements, first commercial political and ecclesiastical, to keep the people in ignorance of their wicked course.

. . . .

The Promised Key

The glory that was Solomon greater still reigns in Ethiopia We can see all the Kings of earth surrendering their crowns to His Majesty Ras Tafari the King of Kings and Lord of Lords Earth's Rightful Ruler to reign for ever and ever.

Upon His Majesty Ras Tafari's head are many diadems and on His garment a name written King of Kings and Lord of Lords oh come let us adore him for he is King of Kings and Lord of Lords. The Conquering Lion of Judah, The Elect of God and the Light of the world.

His Majesty Ras Tafari is the head over all man for he is the Supreme God. His body is the fullness of him that filleth all in all. Now my dear people let this be our goal, forward to the King of Kings must be the cry of our social hope. Forward to the King of Kings to purify our social standards and our way of living, and rebuild and inspire our character. Forward to the King of Kings to learn the worth of manhood and womanhood. Forward to the King of Kings to learn His code of Law from the mount demanding absolute Love, Purity, Honesty, Truthfulness. Forward to the King of Kings to learn His Laws and social order, so that virtue will eventually gain the victory over our body and soul and that truth will drive away falsehood and fraud. Members of the King of Kings, arise for God's sake and put your armour on.

Dear inhabitants of this Western Hemisphere, the King of Kings warriors can never be defeated, the Pope of Rome and his agents shall not prevail against the King of Kings host warriors you all must stand up, stand up, for the King of Kings.

All ye warriors of the King of Kings lift high King Alpha's Royal Banner, from victory to victory King Alpha shall lead his army till every enemy is vanquished.

Ethiopia's Kingdom

Dear inhabitants of this world King Ras Tafari and Queen Omega are the foundation stones of the resurrection of the Kingdom of Ethiopia.

Their prayer and labour for our resurrection is past finding out; no library in this world is able to contain the work of their hands for us, for they work both day and night for our deliverance.

As for this generation of the 20th century you and I have no knowledge how worlds are build and upon what trigger Kingdoms are set.

In King Alpha's Encyclopedia he will explain to us all, how worlds are being built and upon what trigger Kingdoms are set on. He will also explain to us the capacities of generations.

Speaking for the Universe and the womanhood of man Queen Omega the Ethiopian woman is the crown woman of this world. She hands us Her

Rule Book from the poles of supreme authority she is the Cannon Mistress of creation.

King Alpha and Queen Omega are the paymasters of the world, Bible owner and money mint. Do not forget they are Black People if you please.

Owing to the universal rend of our ancient and modern Kingdoms we are at this junction of our history scattered over the Globe into little sectional groups.

All our local bands throughout the globe are bent towards King Alpha's Royal Repository, the Royal Authority is to admit all Bands, Mission Camps, Denominations into this supreme Royal Repository.

Queen Omega being the balming mistress of many worlds she charges the powerhouse right now.

Ethiopia is the succeeding Kingdom of the Anglo-Saxon Kingdom. A man of greater learning and a better Christian soul, than King Alpha is not to be found on the face of the Globe. He makes the nations hearts rejoice with raging joy, we give him the glory. Ethiopia rule book leads us into different departments of the Kingdom, the records of the Kingdom are with us unto this day. The Regulations points us to the basis of the Kingdom.

Many will not see the truth, because they are spiritually blind. See Matthew 3:13. The woman of Samaria first re[f]used to obey the request of our Lord because she was spiritually blind. But when the great Physician opened up her eyes and healed her of her infirmities concerning her many husbands in the city of Samaria, she found out that her first teachers of denominations throughout the state or country of Samaria were false. Then she cried aloud unto the inhabitants of the city and said "Come see a man that told me all that I ever did" and is not a native of Samaria but an Hebrew, is not this man the very Christ. Our cities of today are inhabited with the same qualities of people as it was in the days of Jesus and the woman of Samaria.

The Holy Piby: Blackman's Bible and Garveyite Ethiopianist Epic in Commentary

The Second Book of Athlyi Called Aggregation

CHAPTER 1: HEAVEN GRIEVED

1. For as much as the children of Ethiopia, God's favorite people of old, have drifted away from his divine majesty, neglecting life economic,

Excerpt: From Hemchand Gossai and Nathaniel Samuel Murrell, eds., *Religion, Culture and Tradition in the Caribbean* (New York: St. Martin's Press, 2000), reproduced with permission from Palgrave Macmillan.

believing they should on spiritual wings fly to the kingdom of God, consequently became a convenient for the welfare of others.

2. Therefore the whole heaven was grieved and there was a great lamentation in the kingdom of God. Ethiopian mothers whose bodies have been dead a thousand years, weeping for their suffering generations and would not be comforted.

3. And behold two angels of the Lord resembling two saints of Ethiopia appeared before Athyli and he inquired of them what is the cry?

4. And they answered him saying, Ethiopian mothers who have been dead a thousand years pleading before Elijah for the redemption of suffering Ethiopia and her posterities who by the feet of the nations are trodden.

. . . .

Rejoicing in Heaven

19. There was great rejoicing in heaven and singing hosanna to Elijah; praise ye Douglas; blessed be thou Ethiopia forever and forever; the people at the end of the known world, and world unknown shall look for the coming of thy children with food and with raiment.

20. And when the two angels had joined the multitude and the mighty angel had finished his performance the said angel who was robed in colors turned to the heavenly host and said:

21. Mothers of Ethiopia, the convention has triumphed, your sorrows have brought joy to Ethiopia, your tears have anointed her soil with a blessing, your cries have awakened her children throughout the earth, yea in the corners of the unknown world are they aroused, and is prophesying, saying prepare ye the way for a redeemer.

CHAPTER 3: GOD'S HOLY LAW
TO THE CHILDREN OF ETHIOPIA

Great and manifold are the blessings bestowed upon us the oppressed children of Ethiopia, by His Divine Majesty, Lord God Almighty, King of all mercies, when by his most holy command his divine highness, Christ, Prince of the heavenly kingdom, descended and anointed us that we may be prepared to receive these noble men, servants of God and redeemers of Ethiopia's posterities, his honor, Marcus Garvey and colleague, his holiness the shepherd Athlyi, supreme minister of God's holy law to the children of Ethiopia, may we show gratitude to our God by being submissive to his teachings through these his humble servants, and submitting ourselves in obedience to his holy law that we a suffering people may reap the fruit thereof.

When as it was the intention of others to keep us forever in darkness, by our faithfulness to the law we shall in time prove to the nations that God has not forsaken Ethiopia.

The Holy Law-Commandments

I. Love ye one another O children of Ethiopia, for by no other way can ye love the Lord your God.

II. Be thou industrious, thrifty and fruitful, O offsprings of Ethiopia, for by no other way can ye show gratitude to the Lord your God, for the many blessings he has bestowed upon earth free to all mankind. . . .

. . . .

V. Be thou clean and pleasant, O generation of Ethiopia, for thou art anointed, moreover the angels of the Lord dwelleth with thee.

VI. Be thou punctual, honest and truthful that ye gain favor in the sight of the Lord your God, and that your pathway be prosperous.

. . . .

IX. O generation of Ethiopia, shed not the blood of thine own for the welfare of others for such is the pathway to destruction and contempt.

X. Be ye not contented in the vineyard or household of others, for ye know not the day or the hour when denial shall appear, prepare ye rather for yourselves a foundation, for by no other way can man manifest love for the offsprings of the womb.

XI. Athlyi, Athlyi, thou shepherd of the holy law and of the children of Ethiopia, establish ye upon the law a holy temple for the Lord according to thy name and there shall all the children of Ethiopia worship the Lord their God, and there shall the apostles of the shepherd administer the law and receive pledges thereto and concretize within the law. Verily he that is concretized within the law shall be a follower and a defender thereof, moreover the generations born of him that is concretize within the law are also of the law.

XII. O generation of Ethiopia, thou shalt have no other God but the Creator of heaven and earth and the things thereof. Sing ye praises and shout hosanna to the Lord your God, while for a foundation ye sacrifice on earth for his divine majesty the Lord our Lord in six days created the heaven and earth and rested the seventh; ye also shall hallow the seventh day, for it is blessed by the Lord, therefore on this day thou shall do no manner of work or any within thy gates.

CHAPTER 6: THE ATHLIAN'S CREED

. . . .

20. We believe in one God, maker of all things, Father of Ethiopia and then in his Holy Law as it is written in the book Piby, the sincerity of Angel Douglas and the power of the Holy Ghost. We believe in one Shepherd Athlyi as an anointed apostle of the Lord our God, then in the Afro Athlican Constructive Church unto the most Holy House of Athlyi. We believe in the freedom of Ethiopia and the maintenance of an efficient government recorded upon the catalog of nations in honor of her posterities and the glory of her God, the establishment of true love and the administration of justice to all men, the celebration of concord, the virtue of the Solemnityfeast and in the form of baptism and concretation as taught by our Shepherd Athlyi.

We believe in the utilization of the power and blessings of God for the good of mankind, the creation of industries, the maintenance of colleges and the unity of force, then in the end when earth toil is over we shall be rewarded a place of rest in the kingdom of heaven, there to sing with the saints of Ethiopia, singing Hallelujah, hosanna to the lord our God for ever and ever-Amen.

. . . .

CHAPTER 7

1. Now in the year of nineteen hundred and nineteen on the thirtieth day of the seventh month, when the Athlians were celebrating concord in the city of Newark, New Jersey, U.S.A., and on the third day of the period a paper was read by the Rev. Bonfield telling of Marcus Garvey in New York City.

. . . .

4. Raise not the weight of your finger on Marcus Garvey, neither speak ye against him.

5. In the year of 1921 Garvey spake, saying: I have no time to teach religion.

6. Because of this saying Athlyi took up his pen and was bout to declare him not an apostle of the twentieth century.

7. And it came to pass that the word of the Lord came to Athlyi saying, blame not this man, for I the Lord God, hath sent him to prepare the minds of Ethiopia's generations, verily he shall straighten up upon the map.

8. Nevertheless, in the year nineteen hundred and twenty-two Apostle Garvey issued a religious call throughout the world which fulfilled the last item upon the map of life.

9. Therefore, Athlyi yielded him a copy of the map, and declared Marcus Garvey an apostle of the Lord God for the redemption of Ethiopia and her suffering posterities.

10. And the word of the Lord came to Athlyi saying, I am the Lord God of Ethiopia, three apostles of the twentieth century have I sent forth unto Ethiopia's generations to administer the Law and the Gospel which I have commanded for their salvation, let not the hands of men ordain them.

11. For I, the Lord, hath anointed mine apostles that they may ordain and give authority to ordain.

Conclusion

Since the 1930s, scholars in different fields of the humanities have published many important works probing and documenting the history and character of African religions in the Caribbean. These works are drawn from personal experience as well as from field and archival research, and appear as anthologies, monographs, biographies, theses and dissertations, papers in conference proceedings, journal essays and articles, and audiovisual documentaries and recordings. This academic flowering is complemented by works of sculpture, displays in art galleries, musical repertoires, pop-culture music, commercial musical productions, and other artistic and literary media. The most commonly stated intent of these diverse enterprises is the attempt to provide a new or better understanding of and appreciation for the Caribbean people's cultural traditions than was previously available. I have the audacity to offer this book as a complement to this rich tradition as a new understanding of Afro-Caribbean religions. In it, I have analyzed many phenomena associated with African and Caribbean peoples and their religions; I have underscored their historical colonial experience, their struggle for life and liberty, the battle to preserve their religious culture as they preserved their own lives, areas where they have shown creolization or adaptation to the New World, and the basic structure and essential features of their religious cultus.

No attempt was made in this book to offer a systematic exposition of the religions and cultures of all of Africa. In Chapters 1 and 2, I presented stories about the history and cultures of some of the peoples of West and Central Africa because they are among the most important examples of, and the clearest connection Caribbean creole religions have to, the African continent. It was not also my intent to produce a pedagogical tool for a theological interpretation of African and Caribbean religions. These traditions have their own cosmological reality and ethos that do not fit neatly into theological *Weltanschauung* and preunderstandings—whether Christian, Jewish, or Muslim. This is largely a *Religionsgeschichte* (history of religions) and a religious studies undertaking. On the other hand, although I intended to treat all aspects of African-Caribbean religions under this cover, I had to be selective in the stories I told of the religions. Because of space and cost restrictions, completed chapters telling the stories of Maroon and Winti religions in Surinam and Guyana were eliminated from what had become an oversized manuscript. I excluded from the book some "fragments" of religions that once thrived in the region, and I could not offer the Espiritismo of Puerto Rico as a chapter separate from Santeria. The most obvious, but deliberate, omission from this introductory text are the stories of Afro-Caribbean religions transplanted to the United States and Canada; these are left for a subsequent volume.

Essentially, this book tells the story of peoples of the African diaspora throughout the long night of colonialism and slavery, but in a slightly different mold from those that preceded it. Lorand Matory is correct. Although this is a story about Africans in the Americas, "it is just as much a story about the Americas in Africa." Indeed, "the story suggests that life ways, traditions, and the social boundaries they substantiate endure not *despite* their involvement in translocal dialogues but *because* of it."[1] This story, which must remain unfinished business never punctuated with a period, tells of the disruption and radical change of life's fortune (or more appropriately misfortune) for tens of millions of African peoples on the continent and in the diaspora; it is a story of the devaluation and oppression of the lives of millions of African peoples in colonial slavery across the Atlantic; it is a recounting of the history of invasion, destruction and enslavement of the ancestors of native and African peoples. I tell the story of the hybridization and adaptation of Africans and their religions transplanted to the Americas. This is a story of the battle for life, survival, personhood, and human dignity of peoples originating from the continent; and it espouses the colonized, "forbidden, and damned," but amazing aesthetic adornment of religious ritual practices and beliefs of Afro-Caribbean peoples.

All Caribbean religions that have their roots, or the essence of their philosophy, in Africa and that emerged from an oppressive, colonial plantation economy are movements of resistance for human freedom and survival. They all existed in hostile Christian environments, which did not leave their beliefs and practices unscathed, but many—like Vodou, Santeria, Candomble, and Orisha—remain fairly intact. Others—like the Maroon and Winti religions of Guyana and Surinam, Abakua and Palo Monte of Cuba, Kumina and other African religions of Jamaica—exist in what Patrick Bellegarde-Smith calls "fragments of bone" as extant evidence of once thriving religious culture.[2] The people of these religions once comprised complex systems of ethnic houses called African nations, as well as *criollo-religio*, creole or Caribbean-bred African religions. Some houses have combined individual cults and many mediumistic and priestly roles. They are led by ritual professionals, who, in some of the religions, honor a divine pantheon of deities, spirits, or both. These are associated with diverse phenomena such as storms, water, war, love and sexuality, sickness, fertility, wisdom, and famine, and they are made present through rites and ceremonies with the blessings of the gods.

Afro-Caribbean peoples were not cudgeled into following their ancestral ways; the religions "were a natural" and, in many cases, an essential alternative to the Christian religion that dominated their colonial experience. Rastafari, for example, is a postcolonial, Afrocentric religion that emerged out of Jamaica's oppressive, but largely Christian, culture of the 1930s. The God of Jamaican Christianity seemed unmoved by the miseries and struggles that plagued Africans in the Caribbean. The God of the oppressor seemed *deus obsconditus* (hidden or unresponsive) to the needs of the "sufferers." Many Afro-Caribbean peoples ignored Christianity and creolized the gods and religious traditions of their collective African memory, the same way some African Americans did to Christianity.[3] So important were African religions to blacks in their long struggle against colonialism and slavery that for a long time the colonial authorities controlled slaves by targeting African religions and cultures and attempting to eradicate them completely from the slave population.

Temples and high church steeples with melodious chimes above magnificent sanctuaries do not demonstrate the presence of these Afro-Caribbean religions and their cultus. The religions are practiced in sacred spaces—shrines, palais, centros, and ounfos—hardly worthy of the name temple or chapel. Others are found among the people: in homes and tenements, apartments and basements, and even in sacred leaves of grass. The ringing of bells, the singing of spiritual songs, women parading in white headbands and dresses, the jingling of bracelets, and the beating of drums announce the hallowing of a sacred space for their ritual performance. In spite of their embarrassingly humble hallowed grounds, these are religions of high spiritual voltage that provide a pressure-release valve for life's miseries in Caribbean island-states.

Notes

INTRODUCTION

1. J. Lorand Matory, *Black Atlantic Religion, Tradition, Transnationalism, and Matriarchy in the Afro-Brazilian Candomble* (Princeton, N.J.: Princeton University Press, 2005), 5.

2. Peter Manuel, Kenneth Bilby, and Michael Largey, *Caribbean Currents: Caribbean Music from Rumba to Reggae* (Philadelphia: Temple University Press, 1995), 6.

3. Newbell Puckett, *Folk Beliefs of the Southern Negro* (1926; repr. New York: Negro University Press, 1968); Melville Herskovits, *Myth of the Negro Past* (Boston: Beacon Press, 1958); E. Franklin Frazier, *The Negro Church in America* (1963; repr. New York: Schocken Books, 1974); Lorenzo Turner, "West African Survivals in the Vocabulary of Gullah," paper presented at the Modern Language Association, New York, December 1938; Sidney W. Mintz and Richard Price, *The Birth of Afro-American Culture: An Anthropological Perspective* (Boston: Beacon Press, 1992).

4. Roger Bastide, *African Civilizations in the New World*, trans. Peter Green (New York: Harper and Row, 1972); George Brandon, "Sacrificial Practices in Santeria, an African-Cuban Religion in the United States," in *Africanism in American Culture*, ed. Joseph E. Holloway (Bloomington: Indiana University Press, 1990), 119–147; Herskovits, *Myth of the Negro Past*; Jessie G. Mulira, "The Case of Voodoo in New Orleans," in Holloway, *Africanism in American Culture*, 34–68; Anthony B. Pinn, *Varieties of African American Religious Experience* (Minneapolis, Minn.: Fortress Press, 1998); George Eaton Simpson, *Black Religions in the New World* (New York: Columbia University Press, 1978).

5. Sandra T. Barnes, "The Many Faces of Ogun: Introduction to the First Edition," in *Africa's Ogun: Old World and New*, 2nd expanded ed. (Bloomington: Indiana University Press, 1997), 1.

6. 'Wande Abimbola, "Ifa: A West African Cosmological System," in *Religions in Africa: Experience and Expression*, ed. Thomas D. Blakely, Walter E. A. van Beek, and Dennis L. Thompson (Portsmouth, N.H.: Heinemann, 1994), 102.

7. Edison Carneiro, Melville Herskovits and Frances Herskovits, Yvonne Maggie, Mikelle Smith Omari, Joseph Murphy, Robert Voeks, George Simpson, Pierre Verger,

Margaret Drewal, and others. Omari, for example, has researched Afro-Brazilian religions for almost twenty-five years since the mid-1970s as a graduate student at UCLA and is regarded as a leading authority on this subject.

8. Representative samples: Paul Christopher Johnson, *Secrets, Gossips, and Gods: The Transformation of Brazilian Candomble* (New York: Oxford University Press, 2002); Leslie G. Desmangles, *Faces of the Gods: Vodou and Roman Catholics in Haiti* (Chapel Hill: University of North Carolina, 1992); James T. Houk, *Spirit, Blood, and Drums: The Orisha Religion in Trinidad* (Philadelphia: Temple University Press, 1995); George Brandon, *Santeria from Africa to the New World: the Dead Sell Memories* (Bloomington: Indiana University Press, 1997); Barry Chevannes, *Rastafari Roots and Ideology* (Syracuse, N.Y.: Syracuse University Press, 1994).

9. Manfred Kremser's *Afro-Karibische Religionen*, an edited anthology, examines some Afro-Caribbean religions but includes neither Jamaica nor the southern Caribbean. Joseph Murphy's book *Working the Spirit: Ceremonies of the African Diaspora* (Boston: Beacon Press, 1994); Pinn's *Varieties of African American Religious Experience* and Margarite Fernandez Olmos and Lizabeth Paravisini-Gebert's *Creole Religions of the Caribbean: An Introduction from Vodou and Santeria to Obeah and Espiritismo* (New York: New York University Press, 2003) are priceless; so also are Patrick Taylor, ed., *Nation Dance, Religion, Identity, and Cultural Difference in the Caribbean* (Bloomington: Indiana University Press, 2001) and Dianne Stewart, *Three Eyes for the Journey: African Dimensions of the Jamaican Religious Experience* (New York: Oxford University Press, 2005).

10. I take the position that Caribbean Studies as a discipline has come of age and reserves the right to determine its curricular content, a theory of methods for investigating its diverse subject matter, and the nature of its cultural heritage with special reference to its religious traditions.

11. Kees W. Bolle, "Animism and Animatism," in *The Encyclopedia of Religion,* vol. 1, ed. Mircea Eliade (New York: Simon and Schuster/Macmillan, 1995), 296. Bolle references E. B. Tylor, *Primitive Culture,* vol. 2, chap. 14. According to animism, humans saw spirits possessing objects and elevated the spirits to the level of deity, to whom they attributed both human tragedies and human success.

12. Franklin W. Knight, *The Caribbean: The Genesis of a Fragmented Nationalism* (New York: Oxford University Press, 1990), 4.

13. Rachel E. Harding, *A Refuge in Thunder, Candomble and Alternative Space of Blackness* (Bloomington: Indiana University Press, 2000), 2. Eric Williams made a similar point in his book *Capitalism and Slavery* (London: Andre Deutsch, 1964).

14. Jan deCosmo, "Reggae and Rastafari in Salvador, Bahia: The Caribbean Connection in Brazil," in *Religion, Culture and Tradition in the Caribbean,* ed. Hemchand Gossai and Nathaniel Samuel Murrell (New York: St. Martin's Press, 2000), 37.

15. Manuel, Bilby, and Largey, *Caribbean Currents,* 14. The creole religions discussed in this book show hardly any influence from Chinese religion and culture.

16. Frank A. Salamone, "A Yoruba Healer as Syncretic Specialist: Herbalism, Rosicrucianism, and the Babalawo," in *Reinventing Religions: Syncretism and Transformation in Africa and the Americas,* ed. Sidney M. Green and Andre Droogers (New York: Rowman and Littlefield Publishers, 2001), 43. See also Louis Roniger, *Hierarchy and Trust in Modern Mexico and Brazil* (New York: Praeger, 1990).

17. Murphy, *Working the Spirit,* 121.

18. Newell S. Booth, Jr., *African Religions: A Symposium* (New York: NOK Publishers, 1977), 208.

19. See essays in Booth, *African Religions,* and Jacob K. Olupona, ed. *African Traditional Religions in Contemporary Society* (St. Paul, Minn.: Paragon House, 1991).

20. Simpson, *Black Religions*, 54, 58, 61. On the question of survival of African religions in the Americas, see also Bastide, *African Civilizations*.

21. Robert A. Voeks, *Sacred Leaves of Candomble: African Magic, Medicine, and Religion in Brazil* (Austin: University of Texas, 1997), 148.

22. See Holloway, *Africanism in American Culture*, 1–17.

23. Charles Long, "Assessment and New Departures for a Study of Black Religion in the United States of America," in *African American Religious Studies: An Interdisciplinary Anthology*, ed. Gayraud Wilmore (Durham, N.C.: Duke University Press, 1989), 34–49; Lawrence W. Levine, *Black Culture and Black Consciousness: Afro-American Folk Thought from Slavery to Freedom* (New York: Oxford University Press, 1977), 56–57.

24. Simpson, *Black Religions*, 286. See also Levine, *Black Culture and Black Consciousness*, 52–58; Long, "Assessment and New Departures," 40–47; Brandon, *Santeria from Africa to the New World,* 59–79; Murphy, *Working the Spirit*, 176–200.

25. Voeks, *Sacred Leaves of Candomble*, 62–63.

26. Knight, *The Caribbean*, 51.

27. See Simpson, *Black Religions*, for a reverse view, 57–58.

28. H. Hoetink, *Caribbean Race Relations: A Study of Two Variants,* trans. from Dutch by Eva M. Hooykaas (New York: Oxford University Press, 1971), 4–21.

29. Voeks, *Sacred Leaves of Candomble*, 53. See also 56 and 59 passim references.

CHAPTER 1

1. Robert O. Collins, *Western African History*, vol. 1 of *African History: Text and Readings* (New York: Markus Wiener Publishers, 1990), 147.

2. Noel Q. King, *African Cosmos: An Introduction to Religion in Africa* (Belmont, Calif.: Wadsworth Publishing, 1986), 6.

3. See Migene González-Wippler, *Santeria: The Religion* (St. Paul, Minn.: Llewellyn Publications, 1998), 8; Ulysses Jenkins's argument on the origin of Yoruba from *yo* and *rupa* in his *Ancient African Religion and the African American Church* (Jacksonville, N.C.: Flame International, 1978). See also Anthony B. Pinn, *Varieties of African American Religious Experience* (Minneapolis, Minn.: Fortress Press), 207.

4. Pinn, *Varieties of African American Religious Experience*, 56; Jacob K. Olupona, "The Study of Yoruba Religious Tradition in Historical Perspective," *NUMEN* 40 (1993): 240–271; E. Thomas Lawson, *Religions of Africa: Traditions in Transformation* (Prospect Heights, Ill.: Waveland Press, 1985), 50; John Pemberton III, "The Dreadful God and the Divine King," in *Africa's Ogun: Old World and New*, 2nd ed., ed. Sandra T. Barnes (Bloomington: Indiana University Press, 1997), 105–146; King, *African Cosmos*, 6.

5. Margaret Thompson Drewal, *Yoruba Ritual: Performers, Play, Agency* (Bloomington: Indiana University Press, 1992), 12. See also Roland Abiodun, "The Future of African Studies: An African Perspective," in *African Art Studies: The State of the Discipline, Papers Presented at a Symposium Organized by the National Museum of African Art, The Smithsonian Institution* (Washington, D.C.: National Museum of African Art, 1987), 63–89.

6. John Pemberton, "Yoruba Religion," in *The Encyclopedia of Religion*, vol. 15 (New York: Macmillan, 1995), 535.

7. Collins, *Western African History*, 149–150. See also F. K. Buah, *A History of West Africa from AD 1000* (New York: Macmillan, 1986), 48–51; Pemberton, "Yoruba Religion," 48–49.

8. Collins, *Western African History*, 149–150. See also Buah, *A History of West Africa*, 51–52; J. D. Y. Peel, *Religious Encounter and the Making of the Yoruba* (Bloomington: Indiana University Press, 2000), 27.

9. Buah, *A History of West Africa*, 54. See also J. B. Webster, A. A. Boahen, and Michael Tidy, *West Africa since 1800: The Revolutionary Years*, 6th ed. (Hong Kong: Longman Group, 1990), 62–66.

10. Buah, *A History of West Africa*, 47.

11. Pemberton, "Yoruba Religion," 535–536.

12. Lawson, *Religions of Africa*, 51, 54. See also John S. Mbiti, *Introduction to African Religion*, 2nd rev. ed. (Oxford: Heinemann, 1991), 35; King, *African Cosmos*, 7.

13. Robert B. Fisher, *West African Religious Traditions: Focus on the Akan of Ghana* (Maryknoll, N.Y.: Orbis Books, 1998), 8. See Michelle Gilbert, "Akan Religions," in *Encyclopedia of Religion*, vol. 1, ed. Mircea Eliade (New York: Simon and Schuster/Macmillan, 1995), 166; Larry W. Yarak, *Asante and the Dutch* (New York: Oxford University Press, 1990), 5.

14. Gilbert, "Akan Religions," 166; King, *African Cosmos*, 20.

15. K. Hart, "Annual Review of Anthropology of West Africa," *Annual Review of Anthropology* 4 (1985): 257. See Fisher, *West African Religious Traditions*, 32.

16. Yarak, *Asante and the Dutch*, 7. See also I. Wilkes, "Land, Labor, Capital," in *Rediscovering Ghana's Past* (London: n.p., 1982), 34; Fisher, *West African Religious Traditions*, 32, 45–46.

17. J. W. Tufuo and C. E. Donkor, *Ashantis of Ghana: People with a Soul* (Accra, Ghana: Anowuo Educational Publications, 1989), 27–31.

18. Mensah Sarbah, "On the Fante National Constitution," in *African Intellectual Heritage: A Book of Sources*, ed. Molefi Kete Asante and Abu S. Abarry (Philadelphia: Temple University Press, 1996), 462; Gilbert, "Akan Religions," 166. See also William E. Abraham, "Theory of Human Society," in *African Intellectual Heritage*, 457.

19. Abraham, "Theory of Human Society," 455

20. J. Casely Hayford, "Indigenous Institutions of Ghana," in *African Intellectual Heritage*, 185–186. See also Tufuo and Dunkor, *Ashantis of Ghana*, 8–9.

21. Agasu (ca. 1600), Dukodonu (1625–1650), Wegbaja (1650–1685), Akwamu (ca. 1685–1700), Agaja Trudo (1708–1740), Tegbesu (1740–1774), Abandozan (1797–1818), Gezo (1881–1853), Gelele (1858–1889), and Behanzin (1889–1894).

22. Roger Bastide, *The African Religions of Brazil*, trans. Helen Sebba (Baltimore, Md.: Johns Hopkins University Press, 1978), 47.

23. Michelle Gilbert, "Fon and Ewe Religion," in *Encyclopedia of Religion*, vol. 5, 386–387.

24. David Eltis, "The Volume and Structure of the Transatlantic Slave Trade: A Reassessment," *William and Mary Quarterly* 58, no. 1 (January 2001): 4–6. This twenty-seven-page article is a product of the *Trans-Atlantic Slave Trade: A Database on CD-ROM* project started in the 1980s and published by the Omohundro Institute of Early American History and Culture and accessed through the courtesy of the History Cooperative of the University of North Carolina, Wilmington.

25. David Eltis, *The Rise of African Slavery in the Americas* (New York: Cambridge University Press, 2000), 167. See the corresponding figures for this and other periods in Eltis, "Transatlantic Slave Trade: A Reassessment," 3–7.

26. Eltis, "Transatlantic Slave Trade: A Reassessment," 4.

27. Ibid., 9.

28. John M. Janzen, "Kongo Religion," in *Encyclopedia of Religion*, vol. 7, 363. See Anne Hilton, *The Kingdom of Kongo* (Oxford: Clarendon Press, 1985), xi.

29. Simon Bockie, *Death and the Invisible Powers: The World of Kongo Belief* (Bloomington: Indiana University Press, 1993), 2. See also John K. Thornton, *The Kingdom of Kongo: Civil War and Transition 1641–1718* (Madison: University of Wisconsin Press, 1983), xiv, 5.

30. Janzen, "Kongo Religion," 362.

31. Ibid., 363.

32. Hilton, *The Kingdom of Kongo*, 155–156.

33. Thornton, *The Kingdom of Kongo*, 57.

34. Ibid., 59.

35. Ibid., 63.

36. Wyatt MacGaffey, *Religion and Society in Central Africa: The BaKongo of Lower Zaire* (Chicago: University of Chicago Press, 1986), ix. See also Hilton, *The Kingdom of Kongo*, 3–48.

37. Bockie, *Death and the Invisible Powers*, 3. Cited from Henry Morton Stanley, *The Congo*, vol. 1 (London: Sampson Low, 1885), 281–282. See also MacGaffey, *Religion and Society*, 21–22.

38. Eltis, *The Rise of African Slavery*, 166; "Transatlantic Slave Trade: A Reassessment," 7.

39. Eltis, "Transatlantic Slave Trade: A Reassessment," 11.

40. Ibid., 8; Philip D. Curtin, *The Atlantic Slave Trade: A Census* (Madison: University of Wisconsin Press, 1969); Paul E. Lovejoy, "The Volume of the Atlantic Slave Trade: A Synthesis," *Journal of African History* 33 (1982): 473–501; J. E. Inikori, *Forced Migration: The Impact of the Export Slave Trade on African Societies* (London: Hutchinson, 1982); Per O. Hernaes, *Slaves, Danes, and the African Coast Society: The Danish Slave Trade from West Africa and Afro-Danish Relations on the Eighteenth-Century Gold Coast* (Trondheim, Norway, n.p, 1995), 140–171.

41. Janzen, "Kongo Religion," 363–364.

42. Ibid., 363. See MacGaffey, *Religion and Society*, 39.

43. MacGaffey, *Religion and Society*, 16. See Gilbert, "Fon and Ewe Religion," 386–387.

44. MacGaffey, *Religion and Society*, 24, 26; Hilton, *The Kingdom of Kongo*, 5–9; also Janzen, "Kongo Religion," 362. On "social security," see also Wesley H. Brown, "Marriage Payment: A Problem in Christian Social Ethics among Kongo Protestants" (Ph.D. dissertation, University of Southern California, 1971), 34.

45. Joseph Omosale Awolalu, *Yoruba Beliefs and Sacrificial Rites* (London: Longman Group, 1979), 34.

46. Gilbert, "Akan Religions," 166. See Mensah Sarbah, "Akan Religion," in *African Intellectual Heritage*, 107.

47. E. Bolaji Idowu, *African Traditional Religion: A Definition* (London: SCM Press, 1973), 135.

48. Hal Horton, "Yoruba Religion and Myth," Postimperial and Postcolonial Literature in English, available at www.stg.brown.edu/projects (Brown University, February 17, 1998), 1.

49. T. N. O. Quarcoopome, *West African Traditional Religion* (Ibadan, Nigeria: African University Press, 1987), 32. See also Mercy Amba Oduyoye, "The African Experience of God through the Eyes of an Akan Woman," *Cross Currents* 47, no. 4 (Winter 1997/1998): 494.

50. John Mbiti writes about God in the language of Christian dogmatic theology: sustainer, provider, ruler, father and mother, good, merciful, holy, omnipotent, omniscient, omnipresent, self-existent, first cause, immutable, etc. (Mbiti, *Introduction to African Religion*, 49–59). See Evans M. Zuesse, "African Religions: Mythic Themes," in *Encyclopedia of Religion*, vol. 1, 70–71.

51. Benjamin C. Ray, "African Religions: An Overview," in *Encyclopedia of Religion*, vol. 1, 62–63. See Tufuo and Donkor, *Ashantis of Ghana*, 71.

52. Thornton, *The Kingdom of Kongo*, 59. Cited from Wyatt MacGaffey, "The Religious Commissions of the Bakongo," *Man, New Series* no. 5 (1970): 28–36.

53. Thornton, *The Kingdom of Kongo*, 59.

54. Ibid., 60.

55. Ibid., 59.

56. Ibid.

57. MacGaffey, *Religion and Society*, 36–37. According to MacGaffey, "Ordinary ailments, if not blamed on witchcraft, might be blamed on charms. Either the victim had been selected by the charm itself to be the instrument of its powers, or he was considered to have violated the rules of the charm, deliberately or otherwise" (37).

58. Bockie, *Death and the Invisible Powers*, 16.

59. Ibid., 17. See also George Balandier, *Sociology of Black Africa* (New York: Praeger), 320; Agnes C. Donohugh, "Essentials of African Culture," *Africa* 8, no. 3 (1935): 330.

60. Janzen, "Kongo Religion," 362.

61. Bockie, *Death and the Invisible Powers*, 18.

62. Robert Farris Thompson, *Flash of the Spirit: African and Afro-American Art and Philosophy* (New York: Random House, 1983), 108. See also Dianne M. Stewart, *Three Eyes for the Journey African Dimensions of the Jamaican Religious Experience* (New York: Oxford University Press, 2005), 159–160, and Wyatt MacGaffey, *An Anthropology of Kongo Religion: Primary Texts from Lower Zaire* (Lawrence: University of Kansas Press, 1974), 34.

63. Stewart, *Three Eyes for the Journey*, 160.

64. MacGaffey, *Religion and Society*, 46.

65. Ibid., 158–160.

66. Mbiti, *Introduction to African Religion*, 34.

67. Marla Berns, "Agbaye: Yoruba Art in Context," *UCLA Museum of Cultural History Pamphlet Series* 1, no. 4 (Winter 1979): 1.

68. Gilbert, "Fon and Ewe Religion," 386.

69. Zuesse, "African Religions," 70–71. "The Ashanti . . . say that God, Nyame (also known as Onyankopon), withdrew heaven from the earth because he was annoyed when the low floor of heaven was knocked from below by the pestle of an old woman who was pounding *fufu*" (Zeusse, 71).

70. Horton, "Yoruba Religion and Myth," 1. According to Horton, some interpreters "considered Olorun and Obatala one and the same." See also Idowu, *African Traditional Religion*, 135f; Mbiti, *Introduction to African Religion*, 47–48.

71. Gilbert, "Akan Religion," 167. R. S. Rattray, *Religion and Art in Ashanti* (London: Oxford University Press, 1927), 11–12, 23. A fetish is an object that becomes the dwelling place of the spirits and is closely related to the control of the powers of evil or magic for the personal or communal well-being.

72. Joseph Murphy, *Santeria: An African Religion in America* (Boston: Beacon Press, 1988), 8. See Gilbert, "Fon and Ewe Religion," 386.

73. 'Wande Abimbola, "Ifa: A West African Cosmological System," in *Religion in Africa: Experience and Expression*, ed. Thomas D. Blakely, Walter E. A. van Beek, and Dennis L. Thompson (Portsmouth, N.H.: Heinemann, 1994), 102. See also Abimbola, *Ifa: An Exposition of the Ifa Literary Corpus* (Ibadan, Nigeria: Oxford University Press, 1976); Quarcoopome, *West African Traditional Religion*, 27.

74. Abimbola, "Ifa: A West African Cosmological System," 101. Legend has it that "Orisha was a single being who was struck by an enormous stone and shattered into millions of pieces. Many of these fragments were gathered together in ceremonial vessels, but

most remain unrecognized amid the objects of the world" ("Orisha," *The HarperCollins Dictionary of Religion*, ed. Jonathan Z. Smith and William Scott Green [San Francisco: HarperSanFrancisco, 1995], 819).

75. Quarcoopome, *West African Traditional Religion*, 71, 73; Idowu, *African Traditional Religion*, 169. See Mikelle Smith Omari, "Candomble: A Socio-Political Examination of African Religion and Art in Brazil," in *Religions in Africa*, 146.

76. Murphy, *Santeria*, 11. As Murphy says, "The testimony is ambiguous about the origins of the *orisha* themselves" (Murphy, *Working the Spirit: Ceremonies of the African Diaspora* [Boston: Beacon Press, 1994], 149). See also Idowu, *African Traditional Religion*, 169; Quarcoopome, *West African Traditional Religion*, 70.

77. Pemberton, "Yoruba Religion," 537. See also Ben Burt, *The Yoruba and Their Gods: Museum of Mankind Discovering Other Cultures* (London: British Museum, 1977), 6, 11–12.

78. Murphy, *Santeria*, 11. In Muslim- and Christian-influenced Yoruba, however, the orisha have become mere cultural icons and the objects of annual festive amusement and cultural appreciation. See also Berns, "Agbaye," 3.

79. Horton, "Yoruba Religion and Myth," 1; Burt, *The Yoruba and Their Gods*, 8; Murphy, *Santeria*, 11; Berns, "Agbaye," 10.

80. Abimbola, "Ifa: A West African Cosmological System," 102, and *Ifa: An Exposition*, 111; Quarcoopome, *West African Traditional Religion*, 71; Idowu, *African Traditional Religion*, 169; Lawson, *Religions of Africa*, 59.

81. Pemberton, "Yoruba Religion," 537. For a study on the etymology of Ogun, see Robert G. Armstrong, "The Etymology of the Word Ogun," in *Africa's Ogun*, 29–37.

82. Sandra T. Barnes and Paula Girshick Ben-Amos, "Ogun, the Empire Builder," in *Africa's Ogun*, 39. See also Lawson, *Religions of Africa*, 61.

83. Sandra T. Barnes, "The Many Faces of Ogun: Introduction to the First Edition," in *Africa's Ogun*, 2. As Barnes shows, the concept of Ogun has evolved over centuries. See also Sandra Barnes, "Africa's Ogun Transformed: Introduction to the Second Edition," in *Africa's Ogun*, xiii-xiv.

84. Marla Berns, "African Art in Context," 4; cited from Thompson, 7, 12.

85. Barnes, "The Many Faces of Ogun," 2, and Pemberton, "The Dreadful God and the Divine King," 107, both in *Africa's Ogun*. For a full discussion on ritualized art on body parts, see Henry John Drewal, "Art or Accident: Yoruba Body Artists and Their Deity Ogun," in *Africa's Ogun*, 235–260.

86. Pemberton, "Yoruba Religion," 537. "Humans have forgotten their fate," but this "knowledge can be recovered through the process of divination (Ifa)" (Lawson, *Religions of Africa*, 60).

87. Abimbola, "Ifa: A West African Cosmological System," 102, 105. It is not clear whether the terms *iwa* and *lwa* are cognates or name surface resemblance in Caribbean Voodoo.

88. Lawson, *Religions of Africa*, 61.

89. Burt, *The Yoruba and Their Gods*, 7.

90. Murphy, *Santeria*, 11, 39, 41–42.

91. Migene Gonzalez-Wippler, *Santeria: The Religion, Faith, Rites, Magic* (St. Paul, Minn.: Llewellyn Publications, 1998), 57

92. In earlier times, Yoruba, Ashanti, Fon, and Kongo peoples kept little shrines in their homes to these divinities and other ancestral spirits (Murphy, *Working the Spirit*, 70, 72–73, 95, 107–108; *Santeria*, 42–43).

CHAPTER 2

1. Joseph Omosale Awolalu, *Yoruba Beliefs and Sacrificial Rites* (London: Longman Group, 1979), 54; Jomo Kenyatta, "Religion and Ancestor Veneration," in *African Intellectual Heritage: A Book of Sources*, ed. Molefi Kete Asante and Abu S. Abarry (Philadelphia: Temple University Press, 1996), 88; Abu Shardow Abarry, "Recurrent Themes in Ga Libation," in *African Intellectual Heritage*, 92.

2. John S. Mbiti, *African Religions and Philosophy* (Garden City, N.Y.: Anchor Books, 1970), 107; T.N.O. Quarcoopome, *West African Traditional Religion* (Ibadan, Nigeria: African University Press, 1987), 128; E. Thomas Lawson, *Religions of Africa: Traditions in Transformation* (Prospect Heights, Ill.: Waveland Press, 1985), 62; Asante and Abarry, *African Intellectual Heritage*, 112.

3. Joseph M. Murphy, *Santeria African Spirits in America* (Boston: Beacon Press, 1988), 8; John M. Janzen, "Kongo Religion," in *The Encyclopedia of Religion*, vol. 7, ed. Mircia Eliade (New York: Simon and Schuster/Macmillan, 1995), 362.

4. Wyatt MacGaffey, *Religion and Society in Central Africa: The BaKongo of Lower Zaire* (Chicago: University of Chicago Press, 1986), 65–67.

5. Mary C. Curry, *Making the Gods in New York* (New York: Garland Publishing, 1997), 48–49; Murphy, *Santeria, African Spirits in America,* 10; Awo Fa'lokun Fatunmbi, "The Concept of Male and Female Polarity in Ifa Divination and Ritual," *Journal of Caribbean Studies* 9, nos. 1–2 (Winter/Spring 1992/1993): 77, 79.

6. MacGaffey, *Religion and Society*, 70.

7. Marla Berns, "Agbaye, Yoruba Art in Context," *UCLA Museum of Cultural History Pamphlet Series* 1, no. 4 (University of Southern California, Winter 1979): 14. See also Michelle Gilbert, "Akan Religions," *The Encyclopedia of Religion*, vol. 1, 166; 'Wande Abimbola, "The Place of African Traditional Religion in Contemporary Africa: The Yoruba Example," in *African Traditional Religions in Contemporary Society*, ed. Jacob K. Olupona (St. Paul, Minn.: Paragon House, 1991), 55.

8. Molefi Kete Asante and Abu S. Abarry, "Reflecting an African Heritage," in *African Intellectual Heritage*, 112. See also Simon Bockie, *Death and the Invisible Powers: The World of Kongo Belief* (Bloomington: Indiana University Press, 1993), 109.

9. Peter Sarpong, "The Akan Blackened Stool and the Odwira Festival" in *African Intellectual Heritage*, 251.

10. Gilbert, "Akan Religions," 166.

11. Murphy, *Santeria, African Spirits in America*, 8–9.

12. Ben Burt, *The Yoruba and Their Gods: Museum of Mankind Discovering Other Cultures* (London: British Museum Publication, 1977), 14.

13. Benjamin Ray, "African Religions: An Overview," in Gary E. Kessler, *Ways of Being Religious* (Mountain View, Calif.: Mayfield Publishing, 2000), 63.

14. "Traditional Religions in Africa," in *HarperCollins Dictionary of Religion [HCDR]*, ed. Jonathan Z. Smith and William Scott Green (San Francisco: HarperSanFrancisco, 1995), 18.

15. Janzen, "Kongo Religion," 364. See also John M. Janzen, "Drums of Affliction: Real Phenomenon or Scholarly Chimera?" in *Religions of Africa*, 167–68.

16. John S. Mbiti, *Introduction to African Religion*, 2nd rev. ed. (Oxford: Heinemann International, 1991), 130–146.

17. Ray, "African Religions," 62. "Oral tradition usually records the encounter between the conquering kings and the autochthonous cults, which sometimes put up resistance. This encounter was often memorialized in the form of annual rites that recalled the initial conquest and subsequent accommodation between the king and the autochthonous cults whose powers over the land were necessary for the welfare of the state" (ibid.).

18. Mensah Sarbah, "Akan Religion," in *African Intellectual Heritage*, 107. See also Lawson, *Religions of Africa*, 68.

19. "Traditional Religions in Africa," in *HCDR*, 17–18; Ray, "African Religions," 162.

20. See R. S. Rattray, *Religion and Art in Ashanti* (London: Oxford University Press, 1927), 41; Quarcoopome, *West African Traditional Religion*, 76; and Lawson, *Religions of Africa*, 56.

21. Lawson, *Religions of Africa*, 55–56, 68; John Pemberton, "Yoruba Religion," *Encyclopedia of Religion*, vol. 15, 537.

22. Rosalind Hackett, *Religion and Women* (Albany: State University of New York Press, 1994), 65; Paula Girshick Ben-Amos, "The Promise of Greatness: Women and Power in an Edo Spirit Possession Cult," in *Religion in Africa: Experience and Expression*, ed. Thomas D. Blakely, Walter E. A. van Beek, and Dennis L. Thomson (Portsmouth, N.H.: Heinemann, 1994), 130; R. E. Bradbury, *Benin Studies* (London: Longman Group, 1969), 155.

23. John S. Mbiti, "Flowers in the Garden: The Role of Women in African Traditional Religion," in *African Traditional Religions in Contemporary Society*, 62; Mbiti, *Introduction*, 116–117.

24. Denise Lardner Carmody, *Women and World Religions* (Englewood Cliffs, N.J.: Prentice Hall, 1989), 27–29.

25. Robert Ross, *A Concise History of South Africa* (Cambridge, U.K.: Cambridge University Press, 1999), 12; Mbiti, "Flowers in the Garden," 60–61. See also Herman Baumann, *Schoepfung und Urzeit des Menschen im Mythus der afrikanischen Voelker* (Berlin: Reimer, 1964), 138, 180, 204, 245–248.

26. Mbiti, "Flowers in the Garden," 63–64. See also G. Barra, *1,000 Kikuyu Proverbs* (London: Macmillan and East African Literature Bureau, 1960), 60–61.

27. J. W. Tufuo and C. E. Donkor, *Ashanti of Ghana: People with a Soul* (Ghana, Accra: Anowuo Educational Publications, 1989), 58–59.

28. Judith Hoch-Smith and Anita Spring, *Women in Ritual and Symbolic Roles* (New York: Plenum, 1978), 14. Also cited in Ben-Amos, "The Promise of Greatness," 130.

29. Ben-Amos, "The Promise of Greatness," 119, 121, 123–126, 130–133. Ben-Amos states, "Trance is a central feature of the weekly meetings of congregations. During these meetings one or more priestesses go into a trance and in this manner convey the requirements of Olokun to his followers" (125). Olokun, of course, is believed to be female rather than male.

30. Warren L. d'Azevedo, "Gola Womanhood and the Limits of Masculine Omnipotence," in *Religion in Africa*, 344–345, 349.

31. Simon Ottenberg, "Male and Female Secret Societies Among the Bafodea Limba of Northern Sierra Leone," in *Religion in Africa*, 363–387; T. O. Beidelman, "Circumcision," in *The Encyclopedia of Religion*, vol. 4, ed. Mircea Eliade (New York: Simon and Schuster Macmillan, 1995), 511–513; Carol P. MacCormack, "Clitoridectomy," in *The Encyclopedia of Religion*, vol. 3, 535–536.

32. Hanny Lightfoot-Klein, *Prisoners of Ritual: An Odyssey into Female Genital Circumcision in Africa* (Binghamton, N.Y.: Haworth Press, 1989), 31. Between 1988 and 1990, fifty-three women filed lawsuits against a physician by the name of Dr. Burt for performing female circumcision on them without their knowledge ("Female Circumcision: Human Rites," Video recording, Films for the Humanities and Sciences [Princeton, N.J.: Journeymen Picture Production], and "Fire Arms: Female Circumcision," Videorecording [New York: Filmmakers Library, 1994]).

33. Kwame Anthony Appiah, "Africana," *The Encyclopedia of the African and African American Experience* (New York: Perseus Books, 1999), 736; Jomo Kenyatta, *Facing Mount Kenya* (New York: Vintage, 1965), 137–141; Alice Walker, *Warrior Marks: Female Genital*

Mutilation and the Sexual Blending of Women (New York: Harcourt Brace, 1993), 367; Rosemary Romberg, *Circumcision: The Painful Dilemma* (Boston, MA.: Bergin and Garvey Publishers, 1985); Lightfoot-Klein, *Prisoners of Ritual*, 33–76; Awe Thiam, *Black Sisters Speak Out: The Trials of Black African Women* (Ann Arbor, Mich.: Pluto Press, 1986), 57–87.

34. Joseph Akinyele Omoyajowo, "The Role of Women in African Traditional Religion and Among the Yoruba," in *African Traditional Religions in Contemporary Society*, 74–75.

35. Mbiti, *African Religions and Philosophy*, 100–101.

36. Hilda Kahne and Janet Giele, *Women's Work and Women's Lives: The Continuing Struggle* (Boulder, Colo.: Westview Press, 1992), 51.

37. Janzen, "Kongo Religion," 363.

38. Rudolph Blair, "Diviners as Alienists and Announciators among the Batammaliba of Togo," in *African Divination Systems: Ways of Knowing*, ed. Philip M. Peek (Bloomington: Indiana University Press, 1991), 73.

39. As my colleague from Drew University says, people's history is also reconstructed from texts of divination and tradition (Peek, *African Divination Systems*, 2–3, 38).

40. Janzen, "Drums of Affliction: Real Phenomenon or Scholarly Chimera?" in *Religions of Africa*, 168.

41. Evans M. Zuesse, "African Religions: Mythic Themes," *The Encyclopedia of Religion*, vol. 1, 72–73; Peek, *African Divination Systems*, 37, 38.

42. Evans M. Zuesse, "Divination," *The Encyclopedia of Religion*, vol. 3, 375–376.

43. Michelle Gilbert, "Fon and Ewe Religion," in *The Encyclopedia of Religion*, vol. 5, 386–87; Blair, "Diviners as Alienists," 74–77, 79–80.

44. Peek, *African Divination System*, 24–25; 'Wande Abimbola, *Ifa: An Exposition of the Ifa Literary Corpus* (Ibadan, Nigeria: Oxford University Press, 1976); William Bascom, *Ifa Divination: Communication Between Gods and Men in West Africa* (Bloomington: Indiana University Press, 1969), 81–90; E. M. McClelland, *The Cult of Ifa among the Yoruba, Vol. 1, Folk Practice and Art* (London: Ethnographica, 1982), 85–95.

45. John W. Burton, "Nilotic Cosmology and the Divination of Atuot Philosophy," in *African Divination Systems, Ways of Knowing* (Bloomington, Indiana University Press, 1991), 45; Blair, "Diviners as Alienists," 78, 80.

46. M. Fortes and G. Dieterlen, *African Systems of Thought* (Oxford: Oxford University Press, 1966), 21; John Middleton, "Theories of Magic," *The Encyclopedia of Religion*, vols. 9–10, 82.

47. Mbiti, *Introduction*, 166; E. Bolaji Idowu, *African Traditional Religion: A Definition* (London: SCM Press, 1973), 195–196.

48. Idowu, *African Traditional Religion*, 193–195. See also James W. Fernandez, *Bwiti* (Princeton, N.J.: Princeton University Press, 1982), 144.

49. Abimbola, "The Place of African Traditional Religion," 57.

50. Ray, "African Religions," 150; John Middleton, *Lugbara Religion* (Washington, D.C.: Smithsonian Institute Press, 1987), 236; E. E. Evans-Pritchard, *Nuer Religion* (Oxford: Oxford University Press, 1956), 103. ATRs have complex but distinct criteria for what can be considered constructive and destructive magic and for whether a magician is a medicine man, a witch, or a sorcerer. While destructive magic is viewed as harmful to an individual or community, magic that is beneficial to the society at large and is not done out of self-interest is often called medicine and is seen as a primordial gift from God (Idowu, *African Traditional Religion*, 195, 197–199).

51. Evans M. Zuesse, *Ritual Cosmos* (Athens: Ohio University Press, 1979), 168; Evans-Pritchard, *Nuer Religion*, 101–103; Fortes and Dieterlen, *African Systems*, 22; Mbiti,

Introduction, 170; Walter E. A. van Beek, "The Innocent Sorcerer: Coping with Evil in Two African Societies (Kapsiki and Dogon)," in *Religion in Africa*, 203.

52. Janzen, "Kongo Religion," 364; Idowu, *African Traditional Religion*, 197.

53. Gilbert, "Fon and Ewe Religion," 386–387.

54. Kofi Appiah-Kubi, "Traditional African Healing System versus Western Medicine in South Ghana: An Encounter," in *Religious Plurality in Africa, Essays in Honor of John S. Mbiti*, ed. Jacob K. Olupona and Sulayman S. Nyang (New York: Mouton de Gruyter, 1993), 97–98.

55. Janzen, "Kongo Religion," 363. Janzen stated that "Kongo cultic history may be seen as a veritable tradition of renewal, either at the local lineage level, the national level, or in terms of a specific focus. Often the appeal is for restoration of public morality and order; individualized charms are commanded to be destroyed, the ancestors' tombs are restored, cemeteries purified, and group authority is renewed."

56. Ibid. Kongo prophet Simon Kimbangu was more fortunate. He effectively blended African traditional religion with Christian spirituality and enjoyed more religious tolerance and popularity for his medicines than some of his predecessors.

57. Ray, "African Religions," 59.

58. Ibid., 60.

59. Awolalu, *Yoruba Beliefs*, 72–73.

60. Appiah-Kubi, "Traditional African Healing," 98.

61. Mbiti, *Introduction*, 153–155, 171–172. See also Evans-Pritchard, *Nuer Religion*, 104; Idowu, *African Traditional Religion*, 199; Abimbola, "The Place of African Traditional Religion," 57; Quarcoopome, *West African Traditional Religion*, 77.

62. Joseph Omosade Awolalu, "The Encounter between African Traditional Religion and Other Religions in Nigeria," in *African Traditional Religions in Contemporary Society*, 111–117; Lawson, *Religions of Africa*, 51–52.

63. Mbiti, *Introduction*, 32–33. See also "Traditional Religions of Africa," in *HCDR*, 15–16.

64. Abimbola, "The Place of African Traditional Religion," 52.

65. Ibid.; Mbiti, *Introduction*, 33. See also Sandra T. Barnes, ed., *Africa's Ogun: Old World and New*, 2nd ed. (Bloomington: Indiana University Press), xiv.

66. Sandra T. Barnes, "The Many Faces of Ogun: Introduction to the First Edition," in *Africa's Ogun*, 1–2.

67. Robert G. Armstrong, "The Etymology of the Word 'Ogun,'" in *Africa's Ogun*, 29.

68. Abimbola, *Ifa*, 101.

CHAPTER 3

1. Leslie A. Desmangles, *Faces of the Gods: Vodou and Roman Catholicism in Haiti* (Chapel Hill: University of North Carolina Press, 1992), 1. In another expression of the myth, the people are 90 percent Catholic and 100 percent Vodou (Selden Rodman, *Haiti: The Black Republic* (New York: Devin-Adair, 1961), 61.

2. Karen McCarthy Brown, *Mama Lola: A Vodou Priest in Brooklyn* (Berkeley: University of California Press, 1991), 5; Robert E. Hood, *Must God Remain Greek? Afro-Cultures and God-Talk* (Minneapolis, Minn.: Fortress Press, 1990), 45.

3. Karen McCarthy Brown, "Mama Lola and the Ezilis: Themes of Mothering and Loving in Haitian Vodou," in *Unspoken Worlds: Women's Religious Lives*, ed. Nancy Auer Folk and Rita Gross (Belmont, Calif.: Wadsworth Publishing, 1989), 235; Brown states that 80 to 90 percent of the population is Vodou (Karen McCarthy Brown, "Voodoo," in

The Encyclopedia of Religion, vol. 15, ed. Mircea Eliade [New York: Simon and Schuster/ Macmillan, 1995], 296).

4. J. Gordon Melton, "Voodoo," *The Encyclopedia of American Religions*, vol. 2 (Wilmington, N.C.: McGrath Publishing, 1978), 268.

5. Mederic Louis Elie Moreau De St.-Mery, *Description Topographique, Physique, Civile, Politique et Histoirique de la Partie Francaise de l'Ile Saint-Momingue* (Philadelphia: 1958), trans. from the original ed. (Paris: Societie de l'Histoire des Colonies Francaises et Librairie Larose, 1789, 1798). Cited in Rodman, *Haiti*, 64–66.

6. Laënnec Hurbon, *Voodoo: Search for the Spirit* (New York: Harry N. Abrams, 1995), 13. See also Alfred Metraux, *Voodoo in Haiti*, trans. Hugo Charteris (New York: Schocken Books, 1972), 26; "Voodoo," in *HarperCollins Dictionary of Religion [HCDR]*, ed. Jonathan Z. Smith and William Scott Green (San Francisco: HarperSanFrancisco, 1995), 1125; Desmangles, *Faces of the Gods*, xi.

7. Sallie Ann Glassman, *Vodou Visions: An Encounter with Divine Mystery* (New York: Villard, 2000); Joan Dayan, *Haiti, History, and the Gods* (Los Angeles: University of California Press, 1995), 29ff; David P. Geggus, *Slavery, War, and Revolution: The British Occupation of Saint Domingue, 1793–1798* (Oxford: Clarendon Press, 1982); Francois Hoffmann, "Histoire, Mythe et Ideologie: La Ceremonie du Bois-Cai'man," *Etudes Creoles: Culture, Langue, Societe* 13, no. 1 (1990): 9–34.

8. Brown, "Voodoo," 297. See also Joseph Murphy, *Working the Spirit: Ceremonies of the African Diaspora* (Boston: Beacon Press, 1994), 17.

9. Dayan, *Haiti*, xvii.

10. Milo Rigaud, *Secrets of Voodoo*, trans. from the 1953 French ed. by Robert B. Cross (San Francisco: City Lights Books, 1985), 7. See also Desmangles, *Faces of the Gods*, 93.

11. Anthony B. Pinn, *Varieties of African American Religious Experience* (Minneapolis, Minn.: Fortress Press, 1998), 18. Pinn states that "the term *voudoux*, later *vodoun*, was first used by Mederick Louis Moreau de St. Mary, who described a dance he witnessed in Saint-Domingue among slaves" (19).

12. Demangles, *Faces of the Gods*, 2–3. See also Murphy, *Working the Spirit*, 16.

13. Brown, "Mama Lola and the Ezilis," 236; Brown, "Voodoo," 296.

14. Eric Williams, *From Columbus to Castro: The History of the Caribbean 1492–1969* (New York: Random House, 1984), 237–238; Eric Williams, *Capitalism and Slavery* (London: Andre Deutsch, 9th impression, 1990), 113–114; Brown, "Voodoo," 297; Sidney Mintz and Michel-Rolph Trouillot, "The Social History of Haitian Vodou," in *Sacred Arts of Haitian Vodou*, ed. Donald J. Cosentino (Los Angeles: UCLA Museum of Cultural History, 1995), 135.

15. C. L. R. James, *The Black Jacobins: Toussaint L'Overture and the San Domingo Revolution*, 2nd ed. (New York: Random House, 1989), 6, 10f; Hurbon, *Voodoo*, 34; Mintz and Trouillot, "The Social History," 135.

16. Pinn, *Varieties of African American Religious Experience*, 16–17; Desmangles, *Faces of the Gods*, 20–21.

17. "Voodoo," in *HCDR*, 1125–1126.

18. George Eaton Simpson, "Afro-Caribbean Religions," in *The Encyclopedia of Religion*, vol. 3, 90.

19. Donald J. Cosentino, "Introduction: Imagine Heaven," in *Sacred Arts of Haitian Vodou*, 38.

20. "Voodoo," in *HCDR*, 1126; Simpson, "Afro-Caribbean Religions," 96; Brown, "Voodoo," 297.

21. See also Hurbon, *Voodoo*, 42–43; Pinn, *Varieties of African American Religious Experience*, 26–27; Hood, *Must God Remain Greek?* 45; Joan Dayan, "Vodoun, or the

Voices of the Gods," in *Sacred Possessions: Vodou, Santeria, Obeah, and the Caribbean*, ed. Margarite Fernandez Olmos and Lizabeth Paravishini-Gilbert (New Brunswick, N.J.: Rutgers University Press, 1999), 23.

22. Carolyn Fick, *The Making of Haiti: The Saint Domingue Revolution from Below* (Knoxville: University of Tennessee Press, 1990), 92, 241.

23. Desmangles, *Faces of the Gods*, 45.

24. "Voodoo," in *HCDR*, 1126. See also Gerard A. Ferere, "Haitian Voodoo: Its True Face," *Caribbean Quarterly* 24, nos. 3–4 (September–December, 1980), 38.

25. Rodman, *Haiti*, 38–39, 62.

26. Dayan, *Haiti*, 14.

27. Hurbon, *Voodoo*, 51.

28. Desmangles, *Faces of the Gods*, 43–44. Rodman states, "The elite in revulsion against the pre-Concordat clergy who, it is said, would bless a boat or even a privy for a fee, had become open believers" of Vodou (Rodman, *Haiti*, 62).

29. Dayon, *Haiti*, 53. Dayan cited the Haitian scholar Thomas Madiou, *Histoire d'Haiti*, vol. 8 (Port-au-Prince: n.p., 1848), 318–319ou.

30. Rodman, *Haiti*, 62.

31. Hood, *Must God Remain Greek?* 46; also Pinn, *Varieties of African American Religious Experience*, 17–19.

32. Mintz and Trouillot, "The Social History," 142; Selden Rodman and Carole Cleaver, *Spirits of the Night: The Vaudun Gods of Haiti* (Dallas, Tex.: Spring Publications, 1992), 100; Hood, *Must God Remain Greek?* 46–47; Pinn, *Varieties of African American Religious Experience*, 18–19.

33. Ferere, "Haitian Voodoo," 38; Pinn, *Varieties of African American Religious Experience*, 18.

34. Mintz and Trouillot, "The Social History," 144–146; Rodman and Cleaver, *Spirits of the Night*, 102–102; Dayan, *Haiti*, 88, 125–126.

35. Brown, *Mama Lola*, 185–186; Dayan, *Haiti*, 125–126.

36. Mintz and Trouillot, "The Social History," 146–147; Rodman and Cleaver, *Spirits of the Night*, 104.

37. Gedes Fleurant, "The Ethnomusicology of Yanvalou: A Case Study of the Rada Rite of Haiti" (PhD Dissertation: Tufts University, 1987), xxi; Mintz and Trouillot, "The Social History," 147.

38. Zora Neal Hurston, *Tell My Horse: Voodoo and Life in Haiti and Jamaica* (New York: Harper and Row, 1938/1990); Maya Daren, *Divine Horsemen: The Living Gods of Haiti* (New York: McPherson, 1953); Alfred Metraux, *Voodoo in Haiti*; Roland Pierre, "Caribbean Religion: The Voodoo Case," *Sociological Analysis* 38 (1977): 25–36; George Eaton Simpson, *Black Religions in the New World* (New York: Columbia University Press, 1978); Wade Davis, *The Serpent and the Rainbow* (New York: Simon and Schuster, 1985); Robert S. McIntyre, "Neo-voodoo Economics: The Unkindest Tax Cut of All," *New Republic* (February 8, 1988): 19–21; Michael S. Laguerre, *Voodoo and Politics in Haiti* (New York: St. Martin's Press, 1989); and many others.

39. Desmangles, *Faces of the Gods*, 1; Joseph M. Murphy, "Black Religion and 'Black Magic': Prejudice and Projection in Images of African-Derived Religion," *Religion* 20 (1990): 326.

40. James Anthony Froude, *The English in the West Indies or the Bow of Ulysses* (New York: Scribner, 1888), 343. Cited in Dayan, "Vodoun," 13.

41. Hurbon, *Voodoo*, 52–57.

42. Joan Dayan, "Vodoun," 13–36; John P. Bartkowiski, "Claims-Making and Typifi-

cations of Voodoo as a Deviant Religion: Hex, Lies, and Videotape," *Journal for the Scientific Study of Religion* 37, no. 4 (December 1998): 559–580.

43. Dayan, "Vodoun," 13. Joan Dayan cited *Newsweek*, *Vanity Fair*, and *New York Review of Books* as modern perpetrators of the stereotypic vocabulary. See also William B. Seabrook, *The Magic Island* (New York: Harcourt, Brace, 1929), 43; Froude, *The English in the West Indies*, 343.

44. Desmangles, *Faces of the Gods*, 1.

45. Rene S. Benjamin, *Introspection dans l'Inconnu*, trans. Gerard A. Ferere (New York: French Publishing Corp., 1976), 18.

46. Metraux, *Voodoo in Haiti*, 269.

47. Patrick Bellegarde-Smith, ed., *Fragments of Bone, Neo-African Religions in a New World* (Chicago: University of Illinois Press, 2005), 62.

48. Cosentino, "Imagine Heaven," 47.

49. Demangles, *Faces of the Gods*, 15; Brown, "Voodoo," 297.

50. Louis Martinie and Sallie Ann Glassman, *New Orleans Voodoo Tarot* (Rochester, Vt.: Destiny Books, 1992), 5.

51. Simpson, "Afro-Caribbean Religions," 90. See also Brown, "Voodoo," 297; Roland Pierre, "Caribbean Religion," 27–28.

52. Brown, "Mama Lola and the Ezilis," 237.

53. Mintz and Trouillot, "The Social History," 127; Cosentino, "Imagine Heaven," 32; Rodman and Cleaver, *Spirits of the Night*, 54. Rodman and Cleaver suggest three Taino words as the possible roots of the name *Zaka*: *zara*, or "corn"; *azada*, or "hoeing"; and *maza*, from which we get the word *maize*.

54. Rodman and Cleaver, *Spirits of the Night*, 53–55; Gerdès Fleurant, in the Introduction to *Vodou: Visions and Voices of Haiti*, by Phyllis Galembo (Berkeley, Calif.: Ten Speed Press, 1998), xix.

55. Desmangles, *Faces of the Gods*, 15.

56. Dayan, *Haiti*, 36. Dayan says, "It is hardly surprising that when black deeds and national heroic action contested this mastery, something new would be added to the older tradition."

57. Ibid., 35–37.

58. Lydia Cabrera, "Religious Syncretism in Cuba," *Journal of Caribbean Studies* 10, nos. 1–2 (Winter/Spring 1994/1995), 85.

59. Brown, "Mama Lola and the Ezilis," 237.

60. Desmangles, *Faces of the Gods*, 8.

61. Pierre, "Caribbean Religion," 28–29.

62. Fleurant, "Ethnomusicology," xviii.

63. Brown, *Mama Lola*, 55–56, 197–199. See also 138–139, 197–198; Desmangles, *Faces of the Gods*, 74.

64. Desmangles, *Faces of the Gods*, 10–12, 15, 108, 159; Simpson, "Afro-Caribbean Religions," 91; Brown, "Voodoo," 298; Murphy, *Working the Spirit*, 28–31; Rodman and Cleaver, *Spirits of the Night*, 49, 53.

65. "Freemasonry," in *HCDR*, 368

66. Cosentino, "Imagine Heaven," 45; Beauvoir-Dominique, "Underground Realms of Being," 162–163; Fleurant, "Ethnomusicology," xxv. Interestingly enough, one of the symbols on the United States capitol is a masonic pyramid topped by the panoptic on an "all-seeing eye."

67. Brown, "Mama Lola and the Ezilis," 237.

68. Dayan, *Haiti*, 33.

69. "Voodoo," in *HCDR*, 1126.

CHAPTER 4

1. Robert E. Hood, *Must God Remain Greek? Afro Cultures and God-Talk* (Minneapolis, Minn.: Fortress Press, 1990), 48. As Anthony Pinn says, "This economy of energies is composed of several elements: Bondye (the supreme power), the manifestations of Bondye, the *lwas* (loas) or mysteries . . . ancestors (*les morts*), other spirits, earthbound humans, animals, plants, and other objects" (Anthony B. Pinn, *Varieties of African American Religious Experience* [Minneapolis, Minn.: Fortress Press, 1998], 20).

2. Joan Dayan, "Vodoun, or the Voices of the Gods," in *Sacred Possessions: Vodou, Santeria, Obeah, and the Caribbean,* ed. Margarite Fernandez Olmos and Lizabeth Paravishini-Gilbert (New Brunswick, N.J.: Rutgers University Press, 1999), 16; Leonard Barrett, "African Religion in the Americas: The 'Islands in Between,'" in *African Religions: A Symposium,* ed. Newell S. Booth, Jr. (New York: NOK Publishers, 1977), 200; Pinn, *Varieties of African American Religious Experience,* 20; "Voodoo," in *HarperCollins Dictionary of Religion* [HCDR], ed. Jonathan Z. Smith and William Scott Green (San Francisco: HarperSanFrancisco, 1995), 1126; George Eaton Simpson, "Afro-Caribbean Religions," in *The Encyclopedia of Religion,* vol. 3, ed. Mircea Eliade (New York: Simon and Schuster/Macmillan, 1995), 90; Karen McCarthy Brown, *Mama Lola: A Vodou Priest in Brooklyn* (Berkeley: University of California Press, 1991), 6; Gerard A. Ferere, "Haitian Voodoo: Its True Face," *Caribbean Quarterly* 24, nos. 3–4 (September–December, 1980), 39–41.

3. Joseph Murphy, *Working the Spirit: Ceremonies of the African Diaspora* (Boston: Beacon Press, 1994), 15; Ira Lowenthal, "Ritual Performance and Religious Experience: A Service for the Gods in Southern Haiti," *Journal of Anthropological Research* 34, (1978) 393; Lois Wilcken, *Drums of Vodou* (Tempe, Ariz.: White Cliffs Media, 1992), 21; Pinn, *Varieties of African American Religious Experience,* 24.

4. Wilcken, *Drums of Vodou,* 22. See also Murphy, *Working the Spirit,* 16; Leslie A. Desmangles, *Faces of the Gods: Vodou and Roman Catholicism in Haiti* (Chapel Hill: University of North Carolina Press, 1992), 94–95; Karen McCarthy Brown, "Voodoo," in *The Encyclopedia of Religion,* vol. 15, 298–299.

5. Milo Rigaud, *Secrets of Voodoo,* trans. from the 1953 French ed. by Robert B. Cross (San Francisco: City Lights Books, 1969), 46.

6. Alfred Metraux, *Voodoo in Haiti,* trans. Hugo Charteris (New York: Schocken Books, 1972), 39; Murphy, *Working the Spirit,* 16; Karen McCarthy Brown, "Systematic Remembering, and Systematic Forgetting: Ogou in Haiti," in *African-American Religion: Interpretive Essays in History and Culture,* ed. Timothy E. Fulop and Albert J. Raboteau (New York: Routledge, 1997), 437; Brown, "Voodoo," 298; Wilcken, *Drums of Vodou,* 24. Hurbon lists Kongo as a separate category of lwas (*Voodoo,* 71).

7. Wilcken, *Drums of Vodou,* 23.

8. Joan Dayan, *Haiti, History, and the Gods* (Los Angeles: University of California Press, 1995), 35. See also Desmangles, *Faces of the Gods,* 97; Pinn, *Varieties of African American Religious Experience,* 19; Brown, "Mama Lola and the Ezilis," 237–238.

9. Brown, "Systematic Remembering," 437–439. See also Brown, "Voodoo," 299. Instead of the benevolence associated with the Rada lwas, the malevolence of sorcery and magic is often attributed to some of the Petwo lwas. But Murphy warns that one must "distinguish these Rada rites from the infamous sorcery that 'voodoo' usually connotes to outsiders" (Murphy, *Working the Spirit,* 11–12, 16); Metraux, *Voodoo in Haiti,* 49.

10. Desmangles, *Faces of the Gods,* 95. Desmangles states that the "Petro lwas can still protect a person from danger" and beneficent lwas can also "inflict diseases on devotees who fail to fulfill their obligations toward them."

11. Dayan, "Vodoun," 28.

12. Brown, *Mama Lola*, 6, 24. See also Maya Daren, *Divine Horsemen: The Living Gods of Haiti* (New York: McPherson, 1984), 271–284; Mederic Louis Elie Moreau de Saint-Mery, *Description topographic, physique, civile, politique et histoirique de la partie francaise de l'Ile Saint-Domingue* (Philadelphia: n.p, 1958 trans. of the 1789 original), 69; Booth, *African Religions in the Americas*, 199. The Rada tradition has absorbed spirits from various West African ethnic groups or "nations" (Desmangle, *Faces of the Gods*, 94–95), but Dayan states that Petro lwas are all born in Haiti ("Vodoun," 21).

13. Dayan, *Haiti*, 56, 58–61; Brown, *Mama Lola*, 220–257, 246.

14. Brown, *Mama Lola*, 220–257. As Brown notes, "The chromolithograph Haitians most often use to represent Ezili Danto is a particular manifestation of Mater Salvatoris: a Polish black virgin known as Our Lady of Czestochowa" (228).

15. Dayan, *Haiti*, 59; also Pinn, *Varieties of African American Religious Experience*, 21.

16. Metraux, *Voodoo in Haiti*, 39; Murphy, *Working the Spirit*, 16; Brown, "Systematic Remembering," 437; Brown, "Voodoo," 298; Wilcken, *Drums of Vodou*, 24.

17. Metraux, *Voodoo in Haiti*, 90; Booth, *African Religions in the Americas*, 199; Pinn, *Varieties of African American Religious Experience*, 20.

18. A baron or bawon is the first man to be interred in a cemetery, and the first female is called a *Gran Brijit*.

19. Brown, *Mama Lola*, 360–361. Pinn states that in Gede's manifestation as Baron Samedi, "sensual gestures and rude comments are not lost with Baron Samedi, who is often associated with control over death and reanimation of humans and zombies" (*Varieties of African American Religious Experience*, 23).

20. Booth, *African Religions in the Americas*, 200.

21. Pinn, *Varieties of African American Religious Experience*, 21–22; Murphy, *Working the Spirit*, 20; Brown, *Mama Lola*, 274–275. To prevent devotees from drowning in the river, worshipers extend a circle of hands around those whom Dambala possesses while they are jumping and dancing in the water under his spell.

22. Metraux, *Voodoo in Haiti*, 90–91; Brown, "Systematic Remembering," 439–442.

23. Rigaud, *Secrets of Voodoo*, 90–91. Pinn, *Varieties of African American Religious Experience*, 22.

24. Murphy, *Working the Spirit*, 28–31. See also Rigaud, *Secrets of Voodoo*, 14–17; Dayan, "Vodoun," 17.

25. Pinn, *Varieties of African American Religious Experience*, 24, 203; Booth, *African Religions in the Americas*, 200. As Booth notes, "The vevers have inspired a marvelous art form in Haiti and are greatly sought after by tourists." Metraux says not all priests are gifted in tracing the veve (*Voodoo in Haiti*, 165–166).

26. Murphy, *Working the Spirit*, 28–29.

27. Pinn, *Varieties of African American Religious Experience*, 21–24. See also Rigaud, *Secrets of Voodoo*, 88–91.

28. Ibid.

29. Hurbon, *Voodoo*, 60–61; Dayan, *Haiti*, 67.

30. Metraux, *Voodoo in Haiti*, 58. Metraux thinks this phenomenon, like Vodou, is strictly lower-class "rural paganism and must be considered in its true setting" in the Haitian villages (ibid., 59).

31. Lizebeth Paravisini-Gebert, "Woman Possessed, Eroticism and Exoticism in the Representation of Woman as Zombie," in *Sacred Possessions*, 37–58.

32. Paravisini-Gebert, "Woman Possessed," 38. Also Dayan, "Vodoun," 31.

33. Melville J. Herskovits, *Dahomey, an Ancient West African Kingdom* (New York: J. J. Augustine Publisher, 1938), 243. Cited also in Dayan, *Haiti*, 36.

34. Dayan, *Haiti*, 36–37. See also Milo Rigaud, *La Tradition Voudoo et le Voudoo Haitien* (Paris: Editions Niclaus, 1953), 67.

35. Dayan, *Haiti*, 36–37. See also Daren, *Divine Horsemen*, 42.

36. Murphy, *Working the Spirit*, 29. Murphy states that "as the spacial representation of access to Guinen, all ceremonial activities take place" in the shadow of a great tree" called Loko.

37. Ibid., 186.

38. Wilcken, *Drums of Vodou*, 25; According to Metraux, "When a family is obliged to sell its land, the deed of sale will often stipulate that the cemetery must remain in the family's possession, likewise the right to use it for the burial of their dead" (*Voodoo in Haiti*, 257).

39. Rigaud, *Secrets of Voodoo*, 14. Pinn states that a special room is reserved for initiation and it is off-limits to nonspecialists; "non-ritual activities are never conducted in the altar room" (*Varieties of African American Religious Experience*, 30).

40. Murphy, *Working the Spirit*, 19. See also Rigaud, *Secrets of Voodoo*, 31–32; Pinn, *Varieties of African American Religious Experience*, 31.

41. Booth, *African Religions in the Americas*, 200. See also Pinn, *Varieties of African American Religious Experience*, 30–31.

42. J. Lorand Matory, *Black Atlantic Religion, Transnationalism, and Matriarchy in the Afro-Brazilian Candomble* (Princeton, N.J.: Princeton University Press, 2005), 6.

43. "Voodoo," in *HCDR*, 1126; Brown, *Mama Lola*, 351, 353–354, 278–279. See also Rigaud, *Secrets of Voodoo*, 33–38; Hurbon, *Voodoo*, 103–104; Murphy, *Working the Spirit*, 18–21, 24–25, 192, 196.

44. Brown, *Mama Lola*, 76; Murphy, *Working the Spirit*, 19; Pinn, *Varieties of African American Religious Experience*, 32–32.

45. Murphy, *Working the Spirit*, 17–35, 41–42; Hurbon, *Voodoo*, 106; Brown, *Mama Lola*, 220, 324–325, 351.

46. Murphy, *Working the Spirit*, 19–21; Brown, *Mama Lola*, 76–77, 320–321

47. Murphy, *Working the Spirit*, 20–21. For a list of other expensive items needed for the ceremony, see Brown, *Mama Lola*, 76. Initiates' fees may run up to one thousand U.S. dollars. On the Internet (http://members. aol.com/mambo125/kanzo01.html), fees for the ceremonies start at five hundred dollars and go all the way to twenty-five hundred dollars in Haiti.

48. Murphy, *Working the Spirit*, 24–24. See also Brown, *Mama Lola*, 265.

49. Brown, *Mama Lola*, 351.

50. Murphy, *Working the Spirit*, 17, 19, 26.

51. Metraux, *Voodoo in Haiti*, 244. Also in Desmangles, *Faces of the Gods*, 87.

52. Desmangles, *Faces of the Gods*, 67. See also Murphy, *Working the Spirit*, 23.

53. Dayan, *Haiti*, 67; Pinn, *Varieties of African American Religious Experience*, 28–29.

54. Desmangles, *Faces of the Gods*, 66–61; Murphy, *Working the Spirit*, 22–24.

55. Brown, *Mama Lola*, 61, 112–113, 351–352; Desmangles, *Faces of the Gods*, 69–73.

56. Desmangles, *Faces of the Gods*, 80.

57. Murphy, *Working the Spirit*, 28–31.

58. Wilcken, *Drums of Vodou*, 40.

59. Rigaud., *Secrets of Vodou*, 117, also 114; Wilcken, *Drums of Vodou*, 30–33, 41–42.

60. Patrick Bellegarde-Smith, *Fragments of Bone: Neo-African Religions in the New World* (Chicago: University of Illinois Press, 2005), 63.

61. Ibid.

62. Metraux, *Voodoo in Haiti*, 363–364.

63. Ibid.

CHAPTER 5

1. On *Church of the Lukumi Babalu Aye vs. City of Hialeah* see Mary Ann Clark, *Where Men Are Wives and Mothers Rule, Santeria Ritual Practices and Their Gender Implications* (Gainesville: University Press of Florida, 2005), 109–110; Miguel A. De La Torre, *Santeria: The Belief and Rituals of a Growing Religion in America* (Grand Rapids, Mich.: Eerdmans, 2004), xiv; Sonia L. Nazario, "Sacrificing Roosters to Glorify the Gods Has Miami in a Snit—But Adherents of Santeria Must Keep Their Orishas from Getting Riled Up," *Wall Street Journal* (October 18, 1984).

2. Miguel A. De La Torre, *La Lucha for Cuba: Religion and Politics on the Streets of Miami* (Berkeley: University of California Press, 2003), 1–13.

3. "Santeria," in *HarperCollins Dictionary of Religion [HCDR]*, ed. Jonathan Z. Smith and William Scott Green (San Francisco: HarperSanFrancisco, 1995), 960; Joseph M. Murphy, "Santeria," in *The Encyclopedia of Religion*, vol. 13, ed. Mircea Eliade (New York: Simon and Schuster/Macmillan, 1995), 66; Miguel A. De La Torre, "Ochun: (N)Either the (M)Other of all Cubans (n)or the Bleached Virgin," *Journal of the American Academy of Religion (JAAR)* 69, no. 4 (December 2001): 840.

4. Frank A. Salamone, "A Yoruba Healer as Syncretic Specialist: Herbalism, Rosicrucianism, and the Babalawo," in *Reinventing Religions, Syncretism and Transformation in Africa and the Americas*, ed. Sidney M. Greenfield and Andre Droogers (New York: Rowman and Littlefield Publishers, 2001), 47.

5. Maria Margarita Castro Flores, "Religions of African Origin in Cuba: A Gender Perspective," in *Nation Dance, Religion, Identity, and Cultural Difference in the Caribbean*, ed. Patrick Taylor (Bloomington: Indiana University Press, 2001), 54.

6. De LaTorre, *Santeria: The Beliefs and Rituals of a Growing Religion in America*, xii.

7. "Santeria," in *HCDR*, 960; Joseph Murphy, *Working the Spirit: Ceremonies of the African Diaspora* (Boston: Beacon Press, 1994), 81.

8. Isabel Castellanos, "From Ulkumi to Lucumi: A Historical Overview of Religious Acculturation in Cuba," in *Santeria Aesthetics in Contemporary Latin American Art*, ed. Arturo Lindsay (Washington, D.C.: Smithsonian Institution Press, 1996), 39–40; William Bascomb, "Two Forms of Afro-Caribbean Divination," in *Acculturation in the Americas*, vol. 2, gen. ed. Sol Tax (Chicago: University of Chicago Press, 1951), 14.

9. James R. Curtis, "Santeria: Persistence and Change in an Afro-Cuban Cult Religion," in *Objects of Special Devotion: Fetishism in Popular Culture*, ed. Ray B. Brown (Bowling Green, Ohio: Popular, 1982), 338.

10. De La Torre, "Ochun," 839.

11. Miguel Barnet, *Afro-Cuban Religions*, trans. from Spanish by Christine Renata Ayorinde (Princeton, N.J.: Markus Wiener Publishers, 2001), 18. Also, Migene Gonzalez-Wippler, *Santeria: The Religion, Faith, Rites, Magic*, 2nd ed. (St. Paul, Minn.: Llewellyn Publications, 1998), 9.

12. The term *Glasnost* ("openness") was used for reforms introduced by Mikhail Gorbachev into Russian society.

13. Mary Ann Clark, "No Hay Ningun Santo Aqui! (There Are No Saints Here!): Symbolic Language within Santeria," *JAAR* 69, no. 1 (March 2001): 23.

14. De La Torre, "Ochun," 840. See also Gonzalez-Wippler, *Santeria*, 9; Mary C. Curry, *Making the Gods in New York* (New York: Garland Publishing, 1997), 5; Martha Moreno Vega, "The Yoruba Tradition Comes to New York City," *African American Review* 29 (Summer 1995): 202.

15. Gonzalez-Wippler, *Santeria*, 12.

16. George Brandon, *Santeria from Africa to the New World: The Dead Sell Memories* (Bloomington: Indiana University Press, 1997), 43, 44.

17. According to Eric Williams, the costly eighteenth-century sugar plantation required "large capital investment for land, buildings, machinery, technologists, and livestock. The larger plantation offered the advantage of lower unit costs of production, greater facility for obtaining credit, easier terms on loans, more advantageous freight and insurance rates, higher profits, and a greater accumulation of surplus capital" to offset losses to natural and other disasters (Eric Williams, *From Columbus to Castro: The History of the Caribbean 1492–1969* [New York: Random House, 1984], 41, 121, 145, 264).

18. Cuba's population in 1774 was about 171,620, of whom roughly 25 percent were slaves. But by 1800, the island's total population increased dramatically to more than 705,000, about 40 per cent of whom were slaves (Franklin W. Knight, The *Caribbean: The Genesis of a Fragmented Nationalism,* 2nd ed. [New York: Oxford University Press, 1990], 126); Brandon, *Santeria,* 4; Joseph M. Murphy, *Santeria: African Spirits in America* (Boston: Beacon Press, 1993), 22.

19. Williams, *Columbus to Castro,* 311–312; David R. Murray, *Odious Commerce: Britain, Spain and Abolition of the Cuban Slave Trade* (New York: Cambridge University Press, 1980), 298; Katherine J. Hagedorn, *Divine Utterances: The Performance of Afro-Cuban Santeria* (Washington, D.C.: Smithsonian Institution Press, 2001), 22; Carlos Moore, *Castro, the Blacks, and Africa* (Los Angeles: University of California Press, 1988), 362; Miguel Willie Ramos, "Afro-Cuban Orisha Worship," in *Santeria Aesthetics,* 51–52.

20. Curtis, "Santeria," 337–338; Miguel Barnet, "La Regla de Ocha: The Religious System of Santeria," in *Sacred Possessions: Vodou, Santeria, Obeah, and the Caribbean,* ed. Margarite Fernandez Olmos and Lizabeth Paravishini-Gilbert (New Brunswick, N.J.: Rutgers University Press, 1999), 79; Murphy, *Working the Spirit,* 83.

21. William R. Bascomb, "The African Heritage and Its Religious Manifestations," in *Background to the Revolution: The Development of Modern Cuba,* ed. Robert Freedman Smith (Rhode Island/New York: Alfred A. Knopf, 1966), 113. Adapted from Bascomb's earlier essay, "The Focus of Cuban Santeria," *Southwestern Journal of Anthropology* 5, no. 1 (Spring 1950): 64–68.

22. Bascomb, "The Focus of Cuban Santeria," 64–68. Cited also in George Eaton Simpson, *Black Religions in the New World* (New York: Columbia University Press, 1978), 297; Fernando Ortiz, *Los Bailes y el Teatro de los Negros en el Folklore de Cuba* (Havana: University of Havana Press, 1951), 199–253.

23. Murphy, *Working the Spirit,* 83–84. *Ile* means "house" in Yoruba and functions, in some ways, like its counterpart, the Catholic Church.

24. Brandon, *Santeria,* 55–56; Joseph M. Murphy, *Santeria,* 32; David H. Brown, *Santeria Enthroned: Art, Ritual, and Innovation in an Afro-Cuban Religion* (Chicago: University of Chicago Press, 2003), 18–19, 274.

25. Murphy, *Working the Spirit,* 81.

26. Barnet, "La Regla de Ocha," 79–80.

27. Bascomb, "The African Heritage," 113; Barnet, "La Regla de Ocha," 79–80; "Santeria," in *HCDR*, 960; Murphy, "Santeria," in *The Encyclopedia of Religion,* 66.

28. Brandon, *Santeria,* 48–49.

29. Barnet, *Afro-Cuban Religions,* 22.

30. Hagedorn, *Divine Utterances,* 187. See also Barnet, *Afro-Cuban Religions,* 22.

31. Jane Landers, *Black Society in Spanish Florida* (Chicago: University of Illinois Press, 1999), 9. See also Brown, *Santeria Enthroned,* 35. Brown has the most impressive academic treatment of the cabildos I have seen in print.

32. Castellanos, "From Ulkumi to Lucumi," 44–45.

33. Brandon, *Santeria,* 55.

34. Brown, *Santeria Enthroned*, 70–71.

35. Brandon, *Santeria*, 82–85, 95–98.

36. Although blacks were important friends and a force in the wars of independence (1868 to 1878 and 1892 to 1898), the leaders of independence feared black ascendancy in Cuba and the breeding of black rebellion within the cabildos. See C. Stanley Urban, "The Africanization of Cuba Scare, 1853–1855," *Hispanic American Historical Review* 36 (1950): 29–30. Cf. *House Miscellaneous Documents*, 33 Congress, 1st Session no. 79 (Washington, D.C., 1854); Duvon C. Corbitt, "Immigration in Cuba," *Hispanic American Historical Review* 22 (1942): 283–284.

37. Rafael Ocasio, "Babalú Ayé Santeria and Contemporary Cuban Literature," *Journal of Caribbean Studies* 9, nos. 1–2 (Spring 1993): 30.

38. Brandon, *Santeria*, 82–83; Fernando Ortiz, *Los cabildos africanos* (Havana: La Universal, 1921); Murphy, *Santeria, African Spirits in America*, 28ff.

39. Michael L. Conniff and Thomas J. Davis, *Africans in the Americas* (New York: Garland Publishing, 1997), 275–276. See the interesting review in De La Torre, "Ochun," 841. Also helpful is Hagedorn, *Divine Utterance*, 173–175, 186–190.

40. De La Torre, "Ochun," 842–843. See also Hagedorn, *Divine Utterances*, 196–197; Curtis, "Santeria," 40–43.

41. De La Torre, "Ochun," 846; Hugh Tnomas, *Cuba: The Pursuit of Freedom* (New York: Harper and Row, 1971), 1122; Hagedorn, *Divine Utterance*, 20.

42. De La Torre, "Ochun," 846.

43. Ibid., 844; Hagedorn, *Divine Utterances*, 197. See also Margarite Fernandez Olmos and Lizabeth Paravisini-Gebert, *Creole Religions of the Caribbean an Introduction from Vodou and Santeria to Obeah and Espiritismo* (New York: New York University Press, 2003), 73.

44. At a hotel in Montego Bay in July 1999, my wife Joy and I conducted this interview with two Santeria followers who were on work assignment in Jamaica. Joy rolled the camcorder and tape while I raised most of the questions. The first names of both informants begin with M (we call them M One and M Two) and are withheld for confidentiality. M One had a "fundamentos," the first level of three major initiations in Santeria.

45. Hagedorn, *Divine Utterances*, 19–20.

46. Awo Fa'lokun Fatunmbi, "The Concept of Male and Female Polarity in Ifa Divination and Ritual," *Journal of Caribbean Studies* 9, nos. 1–2 (Winter/Spring 1992/1993): 67–68. Also Clark, "No Hay Ningun Santo Aqui!" 25. See also E. Thomas Lawson, *Religions of Africa: Traditions in Transformation* (Prospect Heights, Ill.: Waveland Press, 1985), 57; Gonzalez-Wippler, *Santeria*, 12–13.

47. Lydia Cabrera, "Religious Syncretism in Cuba," *Journal of Caribbean Studies* 10, nos. 1–2 (Winter/Spring 1994): 89; Barnet, "La Regla de Ocha," 81, 88; Gonzalez-Wippler, *Santeria*, 25–26; Fatunmbi, "The Concept of Male and Female," 68.

48. "Santeria," in *HCDR*, 961; Gonzalez-Wippler, *Santeria*, 25–26; Barnet, "La Regla de Ocha," 81; Murphy, *Working the Spirit*, 10.

49. Murphy, "Santeria," in *The Encyclopedia of Religion*, 66. See also Barnet, "La Regla de Ocha," 81–82.

50. Barnet, "La Regla de Ocha," 81.

51. Gonzalez-Wippler, *Santeria*, 24–74, 227; see also chap. 2.

52. Clark, "No Hay Ningun Santo Aqui!" 25–26.

53. Simpson, *Black Religions*, 89, 86.

54. Gonzalez-Wippler, *Santeria*, 45–47, 73–74; Barnet, "La Regla de Ocha," 90; Simpson, *Black Religions*, 89.

55. Gonzales, Santeria, 95; Fatunmbi, "The Concept of Male and Female," 77.

56. Barnet, "La Regla de Ocha," 89.

57. Simpson, *Black Religions*, 89.

58. Barnet, "La Regla de Ocha," 94–95. See also Simpson, *Black Religions*, 90; Gonzalez-Wippler, *Santeria*, 59–60, 73–74. See also "Santeria," available at webspinnerpress.com, 5; De La Torre, "Ochun," 849.

59. Barnet, "La Regla de Ocha," 92; Gonzalez-Wippler, *Santeria*, 57–59; 73–74.

60. Barnet, "La Regla de Ocha," 93; also Simpson, *Black Religions*, 89.

61. Barnet, *Afro-Cuban Religions*, 60, 58. Also Murphy, *Working the Spirit*, 109, 96; Gonzalez-Wippler, *Santeria*, 73–74.

62. Simpson, *Black Religions*, 89.

63. Barnet, "La Regla de Ocha," 81.

64. Murphy, *Santeria*, 87.

CHAPTER 6

1. Roberto Nodal, "The Concept of Ebbo (Sacrifice) as a Healing Mechanism in Santeria," *Journal of Caribbean Studies*, Special Issue 9, nos. 1–2 (Winter 1992/Spring 1993): 115.

2. Erica Moret, "Afro-Cuban Religion: Ethnography and Healthcare in the Context of Global Political and Economic Change," *Bulletin of Latin American Research* 27, no. 3 (2008): 343–344.

3. David H. Brown, *Santeria Enthroned: Art, Ritual, and Innovation in an Afro-Cuban Religion* (Chicago: University of Chicago Press, 2003), 84–86.

4. Joseph Murphy, *Working the Spirit: Ceremonies of the African Diaspora* (Boston: Beacon Press, 1994), 86. Also Migene Gonzalez-Wippler, *Santeria: The Religion, Faith, Rites, Magic*, 2nd ed. (St. Paul, Minn.: Llewellyn Publications, 1998), 85; "Santeria," available at www.webspinnerspress.com.

5. Brown, *Santeria Enthroned*, 152.

6. Michael Atwood Mason, "'I Bow My Head to the Ground': The Creation of Bodily Experience in Cuban American Santeria Initiation," *Journal of American Folklore* 107 (Winter 1994): 23–24.

7. Miguel A. De La Torre, *Santeria: The Beliefs and Rituals of a Growing Religion in America* (Grand Rapids, Mich.: W.B. Eerdmans, 2004), 108–109.

8. Ibid. See also Murphy, *Working the Spirit*, 75, 77–83; Gonzalez-Wippler, *Santeria*, 165–168; Mason, "'I Bow My Head to the Ground,'" 28–30.

9. Brown, *Santeria Enthroned*, 159.

10. Miguel "Willie" Raymos, "Afro-Cuban Orisha Worship," in *Santeria Aesthetics in Contemporary Latin American Art*, ed. Arturo Lindsay (Washington, D.C.: Smithsonian Institution Press, 1996), 70. See also Gonzalez-Wippler, 169; Mason, "'I Bow My Head to the Ground,'" 30.

11. Mary Ann Clark, *Where Men Are Wives and Mothers Rule: Santeria Ritual Practices and Their Gender Implications* (Gainesville: University Press of Florida, 2005), 26.

12. Miguel De la Torre, "Oshun: (N)Either the Mother of all Cubans (n)or the Bleached Virgin," *Journal of the American Academy of Religion* 69, no. 4. (December 2001): 840.

13. Clark contends that the ritual offices are not determined by gender (*Where Men Are Wives*, 26–27). On these priestly titles, see Joseph Murphy, *Santeria: An African Religion in America* (Boston: Beacon Press, 1988); Gonzalez-Wippler, *Santeria*, passim.

14. Gloria Rolando, "Oggun: Proposals Starting from a Video," in *Santeria Aesthetics in Contemporary Latin American Art*, 261.

15. Raymos, "Afro-Cuban Orisha Worship," 71. For a critical discussion on this, see Clark, *Where Men Are Wives*, chap. 2 and 3.

16. Raymos, "Afro-Cuban Orisha Worship," 70–71. Also "Santeria," available at www .webspinnerspress.com, 2.

17. Clark, *Where Men Are Wives*, 27

18. Raymos, "Afro-Cuban Orisha Worship," 70.

19. Clark, *Where Men Are Wives*, 27.

20. James R. Curtis, "Santeria: Persistence and Change in an Afro-Cuban Cult Religion," in *Objects of Special Devotion: Fetishism in Popular Culture*, ed. Ray B. Brown (Bowling Green, Ohio: Popular, 1982), 343.

21. Raymos, "Afro-Cuban Orisha Worship," 70–71.

22. Murphy, *Working the Spirit*, 85; Ibid., 71.

23. Murphy, *Working the Spirit*, 94, 112; See also Brown, *Santeria Enthroned*, 133–136.

24. Brown, *Santeria Enthroned*, 133–136.

25. Moret, "Afro-Cuban Religion," 343. Moret based her findings "on the estimated average yearly state salary in Havana of US$162 (Ernst and Young, 2006) and the average Cuban *santeria* initiation cost" (343). She cited Ernst and Young from "A Business Guide to Cuba II," available at www.walterlippmann.com/cuba-business-guide.pdf (accessed March 15, 2006). Also, M. Holbraad, "Religious 'Speculation': The Rise of Ifa Cults and Consumerism in Post-Soviet Cuba," *Journal of Latin American Studies* 36 (2004): 643–663.

26. Katherine J. Hagedorn, *Divine Utterances: The Performance of Afro-Cuban Santeria* (Washington, D.C.: Smithsonian Institution Press, 2001), 222. Also Murphy, *Working the Spirit*, 90–91; Cabrera, "Religious Syncretism in Cuba," 85.

27. Moret, "Afro-Cuban Religion,"343–344.

28. Clark, *Where Men Are Wives*, 26.

29. Brown, *Santeria Enthroned*, 167–168.

30. Murphy, *Working the Spirit*, 99, also 96, 98–104 on Shango's colors in Santeria and his role in the initiation of a priest exercises. See also Gonzalez-Wippler, *Santeria*, 184.

31. Ysamur M. Flores, "'Fit for a Queen': Analysis of the Consecration Outfit in the Cult of Yemayá," *Folklore Forum* 23, nos. 1–2 (1990): 47–78, 51.

32. Brown, *Santeria Enthroned*, 96; Gonzalez-Wippler, *Santeria*, 110–120.

33. Raymos, "Afro-Cuban Orisha Worship," 69. See also Gonzalez-Wippler, *Santeria*, 84–86, 94–96, 107–109.

34. Brown, *Santeria Enthroned*, 19.

35. Ibid., 19–20. Brown cited Andrew Apter, *Black Critics and Kings: The Hermeneutics of Power in Yoruba Society* (Chicago: University of Chicago Press, 1992), 33–34; James Lorand Matory, "Vessels of Power: The Dialectical Symbolism of Power in Yoruba Religion and Polity" (M.A. Thesis: University of Chicago, Department of Anthropology, 1986).

36. Clark, *Where Men Are Wives*, 27.

37. Miguel Barnet, "La Regla de Ocha: The Religious System of Santeria," in *Sacred Possessions: Vodou, Santeria, Obeah, and the Caribbean*, ed. Margarite Fernandez Olmos and Lizabeth Paravishini-Gilbert (New Brunswick, N.J.: Rutgers University Press, 1999), 83. See also Murphy, *Working the Spirit*, 89; Gonzalez-Wippler, *Santeria*, 106–107; Curtis, "Santeria," 343.

38. Brown, *Santeria Enthroned*, 75–76, 83–84.

39. Clark, *Where Men Are Wives*, 52.

40. Ibid., 54.

41. Joseph M. Murphy, "Santeria," in *The Encyclopedia of Religion*, vol. 13, ed. Mircea Eliade (New York: Simon and Schuster/Macmillan, 1995), 66. See also Awo Fa'lokun

Fatunmbi, "The Concept of Male and Female Polarity in Ifa Divination and Ritual," *Journal of Caribbean Studies* 9, nos. 1–2 (Winter/Spring 1992/1993): 81–81.

42. Raymos, "Afro-Cuban Orisha Worship," 70–71; Gonzalez-Wippler, *Santeria*, 80–81, 127–30. Scholars say each of the sixteen designs has a subset of sixteen, producing the 256 in total, just as the *opele* does.

43. Clark, *Where Men Are Wives*, 54.

44. For example, two browns and two whites are positive; all browns or three browns and one white are a negative answer. But the combination or four or three whites with one brown is inconclusive and uncertain (Gonzalez-Wippler, *Santeria,* 123; Murphy, *Working the Spirit*, 74–75).

45. Barnet, "La Regla de Ocha," 83–84; Brown, *Santeria Enthroned*, 159.

46. Nodal, "The Concept of Ebbo," 119–121.

47. Brown, *Santeria Enthroned*, 79, 132–34; Gonzalez-Wippler, *Santeria*, 17, 97–100; Murphy, "Santeria," 67–68.

48. Brown, *Santeria Enthroned*, 74.

49. De La Torre, *Santeria*, 102. Also, a documentary by Judith Gleason and et al, *The King Does Not Lie: The Initiation of a Santeria Priest of Shango* (New York: Filmakers Library, 1992).

50. De La Torre, *Santeria*, 102.

51. Ibid.

52. Fatunmbi, "Concept of Male and Female," 64; De La Torre, *Santeria*, 104–106.

53. Curtis, "Santeria," 344; De La Torre, *Santeria*, 104–105.

54. Nodal, "The Concept of Ebbo," 115; also Brown, Santeria Enthroned, 108–110.

55. Clark, *Where Men Are Wives*, 109.

56. De LaTorre, *Santeria*, 121–123.

57. Raymos, "Afro-Cuban Orisha Worship," 59.

58. Brown, *Santeria Enthroned*, 110.

59. Clark, *Where Men Are Wives*, 110.

60. De Latorre, Santeria, 126; Raymos, "Afro-Cuban Orisha Worship," 126; Brown, *Santeria Enthroned*, 108–110, 285.

61. See 1993 ordinances: *Church of the Lukumi Babalu Aye, Inc. and Ernesto Richardo, Petitioners, v. City of Hialea*, 508 U.S. 520; 113 Sup. Ct. 2217; Marta Morena Vega, "From the Altars of My Soul: The Living Traditions of Santeria," in *New Religious Movements: A Documentary Reader*, ed. Dereck Daschke and W. Michael Ashcraft (New York: New York University Press, 2005), 185; De La Torre, *Santeria*, 123–126; Clark, *Where Men Are Wives*, 109–111.

62. These issues are related to the shedding of blood and to relationships, gender relations in a male-dominated ritual, ritual blood and menstruation taboos, the celebration of ritual and sacrifice as essential to human life, and so forth (Clark, *Where Men Are Wives*, 112–120).

63. Clark, *Where Men Are Wives*, 112.

64. De La Torre, *Santeria*, 118; Nodal, 115–117.

65. Roberto Mauro Cortez Motta, "Meat and Feast: The Xango Religion of Recife, Brazil" (Dissertation: Columbia University, 1988), 309. See also Nodal, "The Concept of Ebbo," 117.

66. Gonzalez-Wippler, *Santeria*, 5–6, 156. See also De La Torre, *Santeria*, 123–127.

67. Frederick Ivor Case, "Intersemiotics of Obeah and Kali Mai in Guyana," in *Nation Dance, Religion, Identity, and Cultural Difference in the Caribbean*, ed. Patrick Taylor (Bloomington: Indiana University Press), 47; Nodal, "The Concept of Ebbo," 115–117.

68. Moret, "Afro-Cuban Religion," 340. She cited this from her interview of July 9, 2005.

69. Clark, *Where Men Are Wives*, 136.

70. Moret, "Afro-Cuban Religion," 345. See also Stephen Palmie, "Against Syncretism: 'Africanising' and 'Cubanising' Discourses in North American *Orisha* Worship," in *Counterworks: Managing the Diversity of Knowledge,* ed. R. Fardon (London: Routledge, 1995), 73–104.

71. Clark, *Where Men Are Wives*, 125.

72. Moret, "Afro-Cuban Religion," 340. Moret references Moreno Rodriguez, E. Bermudez, and P. P. Herrera Oliver, "Las plantas y el espiritismo cruzado ed Cuba Oriental," *Fontqueria* 42 (1995): 289–308, and others.

73. Moret, "Afro-Cuban Religion," 343.

74. Curtis, "Santeria," 347; Gonzalez-Wippler, *Santeria*, 133.

75. In the metropolitan United States, Caribbean Americans purchase herbs in their neighborhoods at various botanicas or small shops. These botanicas or shops may not have any African antecedent but instead import the tropical herbs mostly from Puerto Rico and the Dominican Republic; they specialize in implements, emblems, and substances used in herbal medicines (De La Torre, *Santeria*, 133).

76. De La Torre, *Santeria*, 130.

77. Gonzalez-Wippler, *Santeria*, 138–140.

78. Ibid., 134–35. De La Torre, *Santeria*, 133–135. Some santeros and santeras work with the orishas, ancestors, underworld agents, and a list of potent substances to produce punitive magic spells. Invariably, the santero or santera writes the offending party's name on a piece of paper, takes a personal effect or some object used by the victim, and wraps it in a sacred mixture of ashes and herbs. After asking the orisha to reduce the victim's life to ashes, the priest buries the deadly bundle, which, mysteriously is supposed to begin the demise of the individual.

79. Murphy, *Working the Spirit*, 110.

80. "Santeria," in *HCDR*, ed. Jonathan Z. Smith and William Scott Green (San Francisco: HarperSanFrancisco, 1995), 961.

81. Ibid.; Gonzalez-Wippler, *Santeria*, 190; Murphy, *Working the Spirit*, 105.

82. De La Torre, *Santeria*, 119.

83. Murphy, *Working the Spirit*, 106. See Gonzalez-Wippler on the three types of drums (*Santeria*, 190).

84. Murphy, "Santeria," 66.

85. Barnet, "La Regla de Ocha," 80.

86. Gonzalez-Wippler, *Santeria*, 226. See also Hagedorn's insightful explanation in *Divine Utterances*, 174–175.

CHAPTER 7

1. Judith Bettelheim, "Palo Monte Mayombe and Its Influence on Cuban Contemporary Art," *African Arts* 34, no. 2 (Summer 2001): 2; also available at EBSCOhost.com.

2. "Palo (religion)," available at Wikipedia.org/wiki/Palo-Myombe, 1 (accessed October 2, 2008). The popular but marginally reliable encyclopedia points to a study done by Eric M. Miletti on Palo Monte.

3. Dianne Stewart of Emory University (2005), Terry Rey (who gave a trenchant and insightful review of my manuscript), Kenneth Bilby (at the Smithsonian Institution), two other scholars who participated in the blind review process of my manuscript, and others.

4. Kenneth Bilby, "Review of Jesus Fuentes Guerra and Armin Schweler, *Legua y ritos del Palo Monte Mayombe: dioses cubanos y sus fuentes africanas*," *Journal of the Royal Anthropological Institute* (N.S.) 12: 957-1003 (2006): 979; also available at EBSCOhost.com, 979.

5. Fu Kiau Bunseki, interview with Dianne Stewart, Atlanta, Ga., April 23, 2004; Dianne M. Stewart, *Three Eyes for the Journey: African Dimensions of the Jamaican Religious Experience* (New York: Oxford University Press, 2005), 50–51, 256.

6. Bettelheim, "Palo Monte Mayombe," 2.

7. Mary Ann Clark, *Where Men Are Wives and Mothers Rule: Santeria Ritual Practices and Their Gender Implications* (Gainesville: University Press of Florida, 2005), 79; Stephen Palmie, *Wizards and Scientists: Explorations in Afro-Cuban Modernity and Tradition* (Chapel Hill, N.C.: Duke University Press, 2002), 162.

8. David H. Brown, *Santeria Enthroned: Art, Ritual, and Innovation in an Afro-Cuban Religion* (Chicago: University of Chicago Press, 2003), 29–30.

9. Erica Moret, "Afro-Cuban Religion, Ethnobotany and Healthcare in the Context of Global Political and Economic Change," *Bulletin of Latin American Research* 27, no. 3 (2008): 341.

10. Bilby, "Review of Fuentes Guerra," 979.

11. Ibid., 980.

12. W. van Wetering and H.U.E. Thoden van Velzen, "Lengua y ritos del Palo Monte Mayombe: Dioses cubanos y sus fuentes africanas," ed. Jesus Fuentes Guerra and Armin Schegler (Frankfurt am Main: Vervuert, 2005); Review in *Nieuwe West-Indische Gidsvol.* 80, nos. 3–4 (2006): 301.

13. Palmie, *Wizards and Scientists*, 25. Cited also in Margarite Fernandez Olmos and Lizabeth Paravisini-Gebert, *Creole Religions: An Introduction from Vodou and Santeria to Obeah and Espiritismo* (New York: New York University Press, 2003), 78.

14. Bilby, "Review of Fuentes Guerra," 980; van Wetering and van Velzen, "Lingua y ritos del Palo Monte Mayombe," 300.

15. Miguel Barnet, *Afro-Caribbean Religions* (Princeton, N.J.: Marcus wiener Publishers, 2001), 74.

16. Robert Farris Thompson, *Flash of the Spirit: African and Afro-American Art and Philosophy* (New York: Vintage Press, 1984), 103. Cited by Olmos and Paravisini-Gebert, *Creole Religions*, 78; also J. Lorand Matory, *Black Atlantic Religion: Tradition, Transnationalism, and Matriarchy in the Afro-Brazilian Candomble* (Princeton, N.J.: Princeton University Press, 2005), passim.

17. Matory, *Black Atlantic Religion*, 43. See also Jan Vansina, *African History* (Boston: Little, Brown, 1978), 25–30.

18. Erica Moret and others put the number at 850,000 enslaved Africans, most of whom came "from the Bantu-speaking region of western central Africa" ("Afro-Cuban Religion," 339–340).

19. Of course, Bettelheim found that "Oyo-Yoruba gods are the core of a . . . lingua franca" that dominates African religious thought in Cuba ("Palo Monte Mayombe," 2).

20. Barnet, *Afro-Caribbean Religions*, 73.

21. Moret, "Afro-Cuban Religion," 339.

22. Barnet, *Afro-Caribbean Religions*, 83.

23. Bilby, "Review of Fuentes Guerra," 979.

24. Palmie, *Wizards and Scientists*, 193.

25. Ibid., 165. Referenced by Mary Ann Clark (*Where Men Are Wives*, 80–81) as a precursor to discussing gender relations in Santeria and Palo Monte.

26. Patrick Bellegarde-Smith, ed., *Fragments of Bone: Neo-African Religions in the New World* (Chicago: University of Illinois Press), 2005.

27. Gerardo Mosquera, "Eleggua at the (Post?)Modern Crossroads: The Presence of Africa in the Visual Art of Cuba," in *Santeria Aesthetics in Contemporary Latin American Art,* ed. Arturo Lindsay (Washington, D. C.: Smithsonian Institution Press, 1992/1996), 226–227; Eugenio Matibag, *Afro-Cuban Religious Experience: Cultural Reflections in Narrative* (Gainesville: University Press of Florida, 1996), chap. 5; Jorge Castellanos and Isabel Castellanos, *Cultura Afrocubana 1 (El Negro en Cuba, 1492–1944)* (Miami, Fla.: Ediciones Universal, 1992), 3.

28. Matory, *Black Atlantic Religion,* 13. See also Palmie, *Wizards and Scientists,* 25.

29. Brown, *Santeria Enthroned,* 28, 71. See also Bettelheim, "Palo Monte Mayombe," 1–3.

30. Brown, *Santeria Enthroned,* 187.

31. Olmos and Paravisini-Gebert, *Creole Religions,* 86.

32. Maria Teresa Velez, *Drumming for the Gods: The Life and Times of Felipe Garcia Villamil, Santero, Palero, and Abakua* (Philadelphia: Temple University Press, 2000), 30.

33. Mosquera, "The Presence of Africa in the Visual Art of Cuba," 227.

34. Fernando Oritz, "Los Cabildos Afrocubanos," *Revista Bimestre Cubana* 16 (January–February, 1921): 5.

35. Miguel Barnet, *Afro-Cuban Religions,* trans. from Spanish by Christine Renita Ayorinde (Princeton, N.J.: Markus Wiener Publishers, 2001), 74, 76.

36. Ibid, 76.

37. Brown, *Santeria Enthroned,* 30, 34.

38. Barnet, *Afro-Cuban Religions,* 74.

39. Ibid., 78. Cited from Lydia Cabrera, *Reglas de Congo, Palo Monte, Mayombe* (Miami, Fla.: Peninsular Printing, 1979), 15–16.

40. Brown, *Santeria Enthroned,* 44. Cited of Fernando Oritz, *La antigua fiesta afrocubana "del dia de reyes"* (Havana: Ministerio de Relaciones Exteriores, Departamento de Asuntos Culturales, Division de Publicaciones, [1920] 1960), 15.

41. Matory, *Black Atlantic Religion,* 9.

42. Brown, *Santeria Enthroned,* 26. See also Isabel Mercedes Castellanos, "The Use of Language in Afro-Cuban Religion" (PhD Dissertation: Georgetown University, 1977), and her "Grammatical Structure, Historical Development, and Religious Usage of Afro-Cuban Bozal Speech," *Folklore Forum* 23, nos. 1, 2 (1990): 57–84; Fernando Oritz, *Los Negros Esclavos* (Havana: Editorial de Ciencias Sociales, 1916/1987), 40–59.

43. Brown, *Santeria Enthroned,* 57.

44. Ibid., 44.

45. Stephen Palmie, "Against Syncretism: 'Africanising' and 'Cubanising' Discourses in North American *Orisha* Worship," in *Counterworks: Managing the Diversity of Knowledge,* ed. R. Fardon (London: Routledge, 1995), 77, 96. Cited by Moret, "Afro-Cuban Religions," 341. See also G. Girardi, *El ahora de Cuba: Tras el derrumble del comunismo y tras el viaje de Juan Pablo 11* (Madrid: Nueva Utopia, 1994), 287.

46. Moret, "Afro-Cuban Religion," 340. See also Girardi, *El ahora de Cuba.*

47. Moret, "Afro-Cuban Religion," 340.

48. Ibid., 339.

49. Bettelheim, "Palo Monte Mayombe," 2.

50. Ibid., 2–3. On the idea of the absence of a pantheon in Palo Monte, see also Olmos and Paravisini-Gebert, *Creole Religions,* 79.

51. Bettelheim, "Palo Monte Mayombe, 2

52. Barnet, *Afro-Cuban Religions,* 95. Avatars of Palo Monte depend on the natural reserve for their ritual paraphernalia and are thus environmentally sensitive.

53. van Wetering and van Velzen, "Lengua y ritos del Palo Monte Mayombe," 301.

54. Ibid. The desire to impress communicants with linguistic acumen is a common pastime of clerics in most religions, especially those with sacred texts in an earlier language, whether written or oral.

55. van Wetering and van Velzen, "Lengua y ritos del Palo Monte," 300.

56. Olmos and Paravisini-Gerbert, *Creole Religions*, 78. Also van Wetering and van Velzen, "Lengua y Ritos del Palo Monte," 300.

57. Olmos and Paravisini-Gebert, *Creole Religions*, 80. See also Migene Gonzalez-Wippler, *Santeria: The Religion* (New York: Harmony Books, 1989), 246.

58. Barnet, *Afro-Caribbean Religions*, 79.

59. Bettelheim, "Palo Monte Mayombe," 2.

60. Brown, *Santeria Enthroned*, 71–72.

61. Ibid. Cited from Cabrera, *Reglas de Congo, Palo Monte, Mayombe* (Miami, Fla.: Coleccion del Chicheriki, 1979).

62. Ricardo A. Viera and Randall Morris, "Juan Boza: Travails of an Artist-Priest, 1941–1991," in *Santeria Aesthetics in Contemporary Latin American Art*, 171–172.

63. Arturo Lindsay, "Living Gods in Contemporary Latino Art," in *Santeria Aesthetics in Contemporary Latin American Art*, 216. See also Bettelheim, "Palo Monte Mayombe," 6–10.

64. In Cuba, *bozal* is a novice or new inquirer, but it also names a creole language: "arriving Africans who could not speak Spanish were called *bozales* ('raw')" or new (Brown, *Santeria Enthroned*, 30).

65. Bettelheim, "Palo Monte Mayombe," 6.

66. Ibid., 5.

67. Velez, *Drumming for the Gods*, 16.

68. Bettelheim, "Palo Monte Mayombe," 6.

69. Ibid., 4.

70. Ibid., 6–7.

71. Ibid., 7. Since Islam's influence in Central Africa was not prominent in the seventeenth and eighteenth centuries, this greeting was probably not Kongo in origin but learned from enslaved Muslim in Cuba.

72. van Wetering and van Velzen, "Lingua y ritos del Palo Monte Mayombe," 301. See also Jesus Fuentes Guerra and Armin Schwegler, *Lengua y ritos del Palo Monte Mayombe: Dioses cubanos y sus fuentes africanas* (Madrid: Iberoamericana/Frankfurt am Main, Vervuert, 2005).

73. John K. Thornton, *The Kingdom of Kongo: Civil War and Transition 1641–1718* (Madison: University of Wisconsin Press, 1983), 62.

74. Wyatt MacGaffey, "Art and Spirituality," in *African Spirituality, Forms, Meanings, and Expressions*, ed. Jacob K. Olupona (New York: Crossroad, 2000), 231–232.

75. T. J. Desch-Obi, "Deadly Dances: The Spiritual Dimensions of Kongo-Angolan Martial Art Traditions in the New World," in *Fragments of Bone*, 76. See also Thompson, *Flash of the Spirit*, 103 and passim.

76. Desch-Obi, "Deadly Dances," 76. Quoted also from Thompson, *Flash of the Spirit*, 117.

77. Ibid. Quoted from John Thornton, "African Soldiers in the Haitian Revolution," *Journal of Caribbean History* 25 no. 1 (1994): 71–72.

78. Mosquera, "The Presence of Africa in the Visual Art of Cuba," 230.

79. Thornton, *The Kingdom of Kongo*, 59. Thornton states, "The public role of mediating between society and nature belonged typically to the *kitomi*," whom missionaries likened to the Christian bishop. See also Wyatt MacGaffey, "The Religious Commissions of the Bakongo," *Man, New Series* 5 (1970): 28–36.

80. Beatrix Morales, "Afro-Cuban Religious Transformation: A Comparative Study of Lucumi Religion and the Tradition of Spirit Belief" (PhD Dissertation: City University of New York, 1990), 107–108. See also Olmos and Paravisini-Gebert, *Creole Religions*, 79.

81. Bettelheim, "Palo Monte Mayombe," 3. See Lydia Cabrera, *La medicina popular de Cuba: Medicos de antano, curanderos, santeros y paleros de hogano* (Miami, Fla.: Coleccion del Chichereku, 1984/1986), 126.

82. Bettelheim, "Palo Monte Mayombe," 3.

83. Olmos and Paravisini-Gebert, *Creole Religions*, 79.

84. Velez, *Drumming for the Gods*, 32.

85. Bettelheim, "Palo Monte Mayombe," 3.

86. Olmos and Paravisini-Gebert contend that "healing rituals of the *quimbandeiros* [healing sorcerer], are strongly linked to the mysteries of the jungle; and the preeminence of the sorcerer or *nganguleros* [makers of magic charms or *ngangos* of the villages in the interior zones of the Congo Basin . . .]. All of this is mixed together . . . gives rise in the Caribbean to a new product without necessarily in this case . . . a clash with Christianity as an indispensable condition" (*Creole Religions*, 229).

87. Wyatt MacGaffey, *Religion and Society in Central Africa: The BaKongo of Lower Zaire* (Chicago: University of Chicago Press, 1986), 46. See interpretation in Stewart, *Three Eyes for the Journey*, 158–159.

88. Stewart, *Three Eyes for the Journey*, 158. See MacGaffey, *Religion and Society in Central Africa*, 46–47; Thompson, *Flash of the Spirit*, 108.

89. Thompson, *Flash of the Spirit*, 108. Cited also in Stewart, *Three Eyes for the Journey*, 159.

90. Thompson, *Flash of the Spirit*, 108.

91. Velez, *Drumming for the Gods*, 15.

92. Mosquera, "The Presence of Africa in the Visual Art of Cuba," 253.

93. Velez, Drumming for the Gods, 15.

94. Bettelheim, "Palo Monte Mayombe," 3.

95. Velez, *Drumming for the Gods*, 16, 64.

96. Mosquera, "The Presence of Africa in the Visual Art of Cuba," 254.

97. Ibid. See also "Mosquera References Robert Farris Thompson and Joseph Cornet," *The Four Moments of the Sun: Kongo Art in Two Worlds* (Washington, D.C.: National Art Gallery of Art, 1981), 43–52; Thompson, *Flash of the Spirit*, 108–116; MacGaffey, *Religion and Society in Central Africa*, 42–51; A. Fu-Kiau Kia Bunsiki-Luminisa, *Le Mukongo et le Monde qui l'Entourait: Crosmogonie Kongo* (Kinshasa: n.p., 1969), 2, 8–11, 17–29.

98. Moret, "Afro-Cuban Religion," 343–344. See also Katherine J. Hagedorn, *Divine Utterances: The Performance of Afro-Cuban Santeria* (Washington, D.C.: Smithsonian Institution Press, 2001).

CHAPTER 8

1. J. Lorand Matory, *Black Atlantic Religion, Tradition, Transnationalism, and Matriarchy in the Afro-Brazilian Candomble* (Princeton, N.J.: Princeton University Press, 2005), 11, 38.

2. James T. Houk, *Spirit, Blood, and Drums: The Orisha Religion in Trinidad* (Philadelphia: Temple University Press, 1995), 116. Scholars regard the Yoruba religion found in Brazil as one of the most authentic forms of African traditional religion anywhere in the Americas (George Eaton Simpson, *Black Religions in the New World* [New York: Columbia University Press, 1978], 60; Melville J. Herskovits, *New World Negroes* (n.c.: Minerva

Press, Frank and Wagnalls, 1969); Matory, *Black Atlantic Religion*; Mikelle Smith Omari, "Candomble: A Socio-Political Examination of African Religion and Art in Brazil," in *Religion in Africa: Experience and Expression*, ed. Thomas D. Blakely, Walter E. A. van Beek, and Dennis L. Thompson (Portsmouth, N.H.: Heinemann, 1994), 135–159.

3. For example, Roger Bastide, *African Civilization in the New World*, trans. Peter Green (New York: Harper and Rowe, 1972); Robert A. Voeks, *Sacred Leaves of Candomble, African Magic, Medicine, and Religion in Brazil* (Austin: University of Texas Press, 1997); Simpson, *Black Religion* (1978); Joseph M. Murphy, *Working the Spirit, Ceremonies of the African Diaspora* (Boston: Beacon Press,1994); Matory, *Black Atlantic Religion*; Diana Deg Brown, *Umbanda, Religion and Politics in Urban Brazil* (New York: Columbia University Press, 1994); Rachel E. Harding, *A Refuge in Thunder: Candomble and Alternative Spaces of Blackness* (Bloomington: Indiana University Press, 2000); Mikelle Smith Omari, "Cultural Confluence in Candomble Nago: A Socio-Historical Study of Art and Aesthetics in an Afro-Brazilian Religion" (PhD Dissertation: Department of Art History, University of Michigan, 1984); Mikelle Smith Omari, *From the Inside to the Outside: The Art and Ritual of Bahian Candomble* (Los Angeles: Museum of Cultural History, UCLA, 1984); Paul Christopher Johnson, *Secrets, Gossip, and Gods: The Transformation of Brazilian Candomble* (New York: Oxford University Press, 2002).

4. The "Prevailing Winds" of the south Atlantic drift and the Benguela Current off the coast of southwest Africa escorted slave ships bound for the New World into Brazil. Many ailing and weather-beaten vessels short on food, water, and medical supplies drifted into Bahia much more quickly than into other ports of call in the region.

5. It was "one hundred leagues" to the west of the Cape Verde Islands and the Azores, and was expanded to 370 leagues at the Treaty of Tordesillas in 1494 (Eric Williams, *From Columbus to Castro: The History of the Caribbean 1492–1969* [New York: Random House, 1984], 71).

6. Voeks, *Sacred Leaves of Candomble*, 35.

7. Murphy, *Working the Spirit*, 45. Voeks put the number of Africans to arrive as slaves in Brazil at 40 percent and said they had technological and agricultural advantage over the natives (*Sacred Leaves of Candomble*, 41–42, 148–149).

8. Voeks, *Sacred Leaves of Candomble*, 150; Brown, *Umbanda*, 27.

9. Roger Bastide, *The African Religions of Brazil: Toward a Sociology of the Interpretation of Civilizations*, trans. Helene Seba (Baltimore, Md.: The Johns Hopkins University Press, 1978), 46.

10. Ibid., 47; Voeks, *Sacred Leaves of Candomble*, 148–149.

11. Bastide, *The African Religions*, 56.

12. Harding, *A Refuge in Thunder*, 5.

13. "Afro-Brazilian Religions," in *The HarperCollins Dictionary of Religion [HCDR]*, ed. Jonathan Z. Smith and William Scott Green (San Francisco: HarperSanFrancisco, 1995), 28; Murphy, *Working the Spirit*, 46, 152; Bastide, *The African Religions of Brazil*, 78–82.

14. Murphy, *Working the Spirit*, 47. Murphy states, "The 'autabaquis,' the drum ceremonies of the Nago, the Jejes, and to a lesser extent, the Hausas and various Angalon peoples, were the means by which the Afro-Brazilian identity was maintained amid the horrors of a slave society."

15. Harding, *A Refuge in Thunder*, 3–4.

16. Murphy, *Working the Spirit*, 145, 148; Voeks, *Sacred Leaves of Candomble*, 53; Pierre Verger, *Bahia and the West African Trade: 1549–1851* (Ibadan, Nigeria: Ibadan University Press, 1964), 31; Philip Curtin, *The Atlantic Slave Trades: A Census* (Madison: University of Wisconsin Press, 1969), 89, 268; and others.

17. Brown, *Umbanda*, 27–28.

18. Simpson, *Black Religions*, 295.

19. Simpson based some of his findings on Octavio Da Costa Eduardo, *The Negro in Northern Brazil* (New York: n.p., 1948).

20. Bastide, *The African Religions of Brazil*, 134.

21. Yvonne Maggie, "Afro-Brazilian Cults," in *The Encyclopedia of Religion*, vols. 1–2, ed. Mircea Eliade (New York: Simon and Schuster/Macmillan, 1995), 102; Brown, *Umbanda*, 102.

22. Voeks, *Sacred Leaves of Candomble*, 52.

23. Maggie, "Afro-Brazilian Cults," 29.

24. Murphy, *Working the Spirit*, 48. Murphy makes it clear that there were free African and Bahian (*emancipado*) merchants who traded tobacco, firearms, sugar, slaves, and other goods across the Atlantic and "established multiple contacts between Africa and Bahia so that African goods were readily available in Bahia."

25. Voeks, *Sacred Leave of Candomble*, 153–158.

26. Jane Landers, *Black Society in Spanish Florida* (Chicago: University of Illinois Press, 1999), 9–12.

27. Harding, *A Refuge in Thunder*, 123.

28. Bastide, *The African Religions*, 53.

29. "Afro-Brazilian Religions," 28. See also Harding, *A Refuge in Thunder*, 122; Bastide, *African Religions*, 56, 59–61, 127–129.

30. Tammy Todd, "Call of the Drums: Afro-Caribbean Religions," *Alternative Religions* 20 (November 2000): 1.

31. Voeks, *Sacred Leaves of Candomble*, 153–158, 161. According to Simpson, in Umbanda, "identification between African deities and Catholic saints is greater in the Yoruban cult than elsewhere in Sao Luiz (*Black Religions*, 295).

32. Mikelle Smith Omari, "Candomble," 139–140. Omari states, "Casa Branca in Engenho Velho has a Catholic altar to the right of the entry of the building (*barracao*) where public festivals are held" (156). Maggie believes the theory that "the original purpose of this identification may have been to prevent suppression of the African religions by white slave owners" ("Afro-Brazilian Cults," 103).

33. Voeks, *Sacred Leaves of Candomble*, 157. Reference to Pope Innocent III is in F. Guerra, "Medica Folklore in Spanish America," in *American Folk Medicine*, ed. W. D. Hand (Los Angeles: University of California Press, 1976), 169–175.

34. Voeks, *Sacred Leaves of Candomble*, 60. See also Bastide, *The African Religions*, 272–276.

35. Bastide, *The African Religions*, 274. See also Voeks, *Sacred Leaves of Candomble*, 153–158, 161.

36. Johnson, *Secrets, Gossip, and Gods*, 35.

37. Yvonne Daniel, *Dancing Wisdom: Embodied Knowledge and Haitian Vodou, Cuban Yoruba, and Bahian Candomble* (Chicago: University of Illinois Press, 2005), 3.

38. Omari, "Candomble," 156. Some scholars say "its etymology is presumed to be African and given as related to candomble from *ka* (custom, dance) and *nombe* (black)." (Brown, *Umbanda*, 32). The history of Candomble is uncertain, but colonial accounts of nighttime dances (*calundus batuques*) among enslaved Africans may have been its source ("Candomble," in *HCDR*, 178).

39. Omari, "Candomble," 135. See also Renato Ortiz, "Ogun and Umbanda Religion," in *Africa's Ogun: Old World and New*, 2nd ed., ed. Sandra T. Barnes (Bloomington: Indiana University Press, 1997), 90.

40. I thank Johnson for the "key vectors of signification" in my definition (Johnson, *Secrets, Gossip and Gods*, 35–36). Murphy often writes the word *Candomble* in lowercase, whether it is singular or plural; but I shall put it in uppercase throughout this work, as I have done with Voodoo, Santeria, and other religions.

41. Omari, "Candomble," 148. Also Maggie, "Afro-Brazilian Cults," 103.

42. Murphy, *Working the Spirit*, 50–51.

43. Matory, *Black Atlantic Religion*, 21.

44. Ibid., 23.

45. "Candomble," in *HCDR*, 178. See also Omari, *From the Inside*, 18; Murphy, *Working the Spirit*, 47. The same way Yoruba devotees like to trace the origin of their sacred space and ritual back to the mythic city of Ile-Ife, so too the Candombles trace their origins to mother Africa.

46. Omari, "Candomble," 136; Paul Mercier, "The Fon of Dahomey," in *African Worlds*, ed. Daryll Forde (London: Oxford University Press, 1954), 210–234; Pierre Verger, *Orixas: Deuses Iorubus na Africa e no novo mundo* (Salvador, Bahia: Corrupio, 1981), 155.

47. Omari, "Candomble," 136. Omari says "The grammar and vocabulary of these Candombles' ritual languages are basically Bantu yet also exhibit influences from Portuguese and from Amerindian languages such as Tupi or Tupinamba."

48. Johnson, *Secrets, Gossip, and Gods*.

49. Bastide, *The African Religions*, 224.

50. Murphy states, "If the name Nago may be accepted as referring to a generally homogenous culture, language, and religion, nearly every house in Bahia receives Nago spirits, if not exclusively"(*Working the Spirit*, 48).

51. Omari, "Candomble," 137. See also Voeks, *Sacred Leaves of Candomble*, 51; Murphy, *Working the Spirit*, 50.

52. Murphy, *Working the Spirit*, 50.

53. Ibid., 49. Also "Candomble," 178; "Afro-Brazilian Religions," 28.

54. Voeks, *Sacred Leaves of Candomble*, 53.

55. Omari, "Candomble," 141, 146. See also Murphy, *Working the Spirit*, 56; Voeks states, "Although he enters into Yoruba mythology, Olorun may be alien to the original Yoruba cosmology, a product of early Christian or Moslem influences" (*Sacred Leaves of Candomble*, 54, also 55–56).

56. Voeks, *Sacred Leaves of Candomble*, 74.

57. Ibid., 74–75.

58. Omari, "Candomble," 147.

59. Maggie, "Afro-Brazilian Cults," 103.

60. Bastide, *The African Religions*, 263; Voeks, *Sacred Leaves of Candomble*, 76.

61. Bastide, *The African Religions*, 263–264, 268–268; Voeks, *Sacred Leaves of Candomble*, 60–61.

62. Omari, "Candomble," 146.

63. Voeks, *Sacred Leaves of Candomble*, 55, 125.

64. George E. Simpson, *Yoruba Religion and Medicine in Ibadan* (Ibadan, Nigeria: Ibadan University Press, 1980), 73–79. See also Voeks, *Sacred Leaves of Candomble*, 125.

65. Bastide, *The African Religions*, 262, 264–265. Also Voeks, *Sacred Leaves of Candomble*, 79–80.

66. Voeks, *Sacred Leaves of Candomble*, 121, see also 157, 159; Bastide, *The African Religions*, 264–265, 270.

67. Voeks, *Sacred Leaves of Candomble*, 81. See Bastide, *The African Religions*, 266–267.

68. Bastide, *The African Religions*, 266–267.

69. Voeks, *Sacred Leaves of Candomble*, 59, 121–122.

70. Bastide, *The African Religions*, 68, 263, 266–268.

71. "Candomble," in *HCDR*, 179. Also Omari, "Candomble," 138; Murphy, *Working the Spirit*, 53; Bastide, *The African Religions*, 63; Voeks, *Sacred Leaves of Candomble*, 63.

72. Murphy, *Working the Spirit*, 53–54; Johnson, *Secret, Gossip, and Gods*, 55. Also Maggie, "Afro-Brazilian Cults," 103.

73. Murphy, *Working the Spirit*, 64.

74. Voeks, *Sacred Leaves of Candomble*, 65. Omari states that "key objects and implements embodying the sacred force, *axe* . . . of the *orixa* were located in a sacred inner core room" in the *terreiro* ("Candomble," 148).

75. Bastide, *The African Religions*, 225–228.

76. Murphy, *Working the Spirit*, 59–60.

77. Maggie, "Afro-Brazilian Cults," 103; Margaret Thompson Drewal, "Dancing for Ogun in Yorubaland and Brazil," in *Africa's Ogun*, 307; "Candomble," in *HCDR*, 179; Murphy, *Working the Spirit*, 59–60.

78. Maggie, "Afro-Brazilian Cults," 103.

79. Omari, "Candomble," 148, 150. See also "Medium," in *HCDR*, 696. Omari references Claud Lepine, "Os Estereotipos da Personalidade no Candomble Nago," in *Oloorisa: Escritos Sobre a Religial do Orixas*, ed. Carlos Eugenio Marcondes de Moura (Sao Paulo: Agora, 1981), 27; Bastide, *The African Religions*, 259; and others.

80. Omari, "Candomble," 137–140; Voeks, *Sacred Leaves of Candomble*, 67–68.

81. Niyi Afolabi, "Axe: Invocation of Candomble and Afro-Brazilian Gods in Brazilian Cultural Production." in *Fragments of Bone: Neo-African Religions in the New World*, ed. Patrick Bellegrade-Smith (Chicago: University of Illinois Press, 2005), 108.

82. Omari, Candomble," 140, also 137–139, 141; Omari, *From the Inside*, 18; Murphy, *Working the Spirit*, 54–56.

83. Bastide, *The African Religions*, 230; Omari, "Candomble," 141, 142, 143.

84. Drewal, "Dancing for Ogun," 220. Drewal drew on the works of Melville J. Herskovits and Francis Herskovits, "Afro-Bahian Religious Songs," and *Folk Music of Brazil*, issued from the Collection of the Archive of American Folk Song (Library of Congress Music Division, 1942), 10, 273; Donald Pierson, *Negroes of Brazil: A Study of Race Contact at Bahia* (Chicago: University of Chicago Press, 1942), 286–287; Omari, *From the Inside*, 23; Pierre Verger, "Bori, Premier Ceremonie d'Initiation au Coute des Orishas Nago a Bahia au Bresil," *Revista do Museu Paulista* (Sao Paulo, 1955).

85. Omari, "Candomble," 142.

86. Ibid., 143–144.

87. Drewal, "Dancing for Ogun," 220–223. See also Omari, *From the Inside*, 22; Melville J. Herskovits and Francis Herskovits, "The Negroes of Brazil," *The Yale Review* 32, no. 2 (1942): 277; Bastide, *The African Religions*, 377.

88. "Afro-Brazilian Religions," in *HCDR*, 31. Also "Umbanda," in *HCDR*, 1108.

89. Voeks, *Sacred Leaves of Candomble*, 89.

90. Ibid. Voeks says, "Native healers from Africa's Gold Coast, according to a Dutch observer in 1600, 'make use of green leaves' to cure what ails them" (see p. 44, for original references). In Africa, the herbalist, medicine man, and the babalawo are often three different persons. In Candomble, these offices are often united in one.

91. Ibid., 88. On life's disequilibrium, see also 70.

92. Ibid., 73, 90–91, 93–95, 115.

93. Ibid., 98, 118–119, 125, 227.

94. Ibid., 128. See also 69, 121–127.

95. A major hurdle here is that religion often, though not always, feels uneasy in the company of certain types of scientific methods and their results.

96. Bastide, *The African Religions*, 224–225.

CHAPTER 9

1. John Burdick, "Brazil's Black Consciousness Movement," *Report on the Americas: The Black Americans 1492–1992* 25, no. 4 (February 1992): 27.

2. Roger Bastide, *The African Religions of Brazil: Toward a Sociology of the Interpretation of Civilizations*, trans. Helen Sebba (Baltimore, Md.: The Johns Hopkins University Press, 1978), 59.

3. Rachel E. Harding, *A Refuge in Thunder: Candomble and Alternative Spaces of Blackness* (Bloomington: Indiana University Press, 2000), 22.

4. Bastide, *The African Religions*, 62.

5. Ibid., 30. Also "Macumba," in *HarperCollins Dictionary of Religion [HCDR]*, ed. Jonathan Z. Smith and William Scott Green (San Francisco: HarperSanFrancisco, 1995), 672.

6. Roger Bastide, *Les Religions Africanes au Bresil* (Paris: Presseus Universitaires de France, 1960), 297. See also Diana DeG. Brown, *Umbanda, Religion and Politics in Urban Brazil* (New York: Columbia University Press, 1994), 25–26; Arthur Ramos, *The Negro in Brazil* (Washington, D.C.: Associated Publishers, 1939), 92–94; Donald Pierson, *Negroes in Brazil: A Study of Race Contact at Bahia* (Chicago: University of Chicago Press, 1942), 305.

7. Bastide, *The African Religions*, 293. See also 228.

8. Roger Bastide, *African Civilization in the New World*, trans. Peter Green (New York: Harper and Row, 1972), 155. Also "Afro-Brazilian Religions," in *HCDR*, 30; Bastide, *The African Religions*, 295; Arthur Ramos, *O Negro Brasileiro* (Rio de Janeiro: Civilizacao Brasileira, 1934), 113.

9. Bastide, *The African Religions*, 152, 201–202; Bastide, *African Civilization*, 155–156.

10. Bastide, *The African Religions*, 204–205, 295; Bastide, *African Civilization*, 84–85, 105–112.

11. Bastide, *The African Religions*, 296–298.

12. "Afro-Brazilian Religions," in *HCDR*, 30; Bastide, *African Religions*, 216.

13. Bastide, *African Religions*, 295. See also 291–292.

14. Ibid., 295.

15. Ibid., 298. See also 295–296.

16. "Macumba," in *HCDR*, 672. See also "Afro-Brazilian Religions," in *HCDR*, 30.

17. Brown, *Umbanda and Politics*, xvi–xviii.

18. Robert A. Voeks, *Sacred Leaves of Candomble: African Magic, Medicine, and Religion in Brazil* (Austin: University of Texas Press, 1997), 2. Also John R. W. Stott, "Brazil: The Spiritual Climate," *Christianity Today* 24 (1980): 32–33. Stott is cited in Patricia Barker Lerch, "An Explanation for the Predominance of Women in the Umbanda Cults of Porto Alegre, Brazil," *Urban Anthropology* 11, no. 2 (1984): 257.

19. Renato Ortiz, "Ogun and the Umbanda Religion," in *Africa's Ogun, Old World and New*, ed. Sandra T. Barnes (Bloomington: Indiana University Press, 1997), 93.

20. Denise Ferreira Da Silva, "Out of Africa? Umbanda and the 'Ordering' of the Modern Brazilian Space," in *Fragments of Bone: Neo-African Religions in a New World*, ed. Patrick Bellegarde-Smith (Urbana: University of Illinois Press, 2005), 33.

21. Ortiz, "Ogun and the Umbanda Religion," 90. Ortiz has published six books and dozens of essays in his field and on the subject.

22. See "Umbanda," in *HCDR* and Yvonne Maggie, "Afro-Brazilian Cults," in *The Encyclopedia of Religion*, vol. 1, ed. Mircea Eliade (New York: Simon and Schuster/Macmillan, 1995), 103–104.

23. Bastide, *African Civilization*, 86, 87.

24. Christopher Paul Johnson, *Secrets, Gossip, and Gods: The Transformation of Brazilian Candomble* (New York: Oxford University Press, 2002), 52.

25. Patricia Barker Lerch, "Predominance of Women," 237–238. Lerch states, "This may occur when clients attend Umbanda sessions in the city and then return to their neighborhoods in the interior." See Louis Margolis, "Introduction: The Process of Social Urbanization in Latin America," *Urban Anthropology* 8, nos. 3–4 (1979): 213–225.

26. Lerch, "Predominance of Women," 238. Also Burdick, "Brazil's Black Consciousness Movement," 27.

27. Johnson, *Secrets, Gossips, and Gods*, 52.

28. "Rosicrucians," in *HCDR*, 937–938.

29. Brown, *Umbanda and Politics*, 88.

30. Ibid., 24–25. See also 17 and 93. Umbanda's clientele includes attorneys, physicians, politicians, political activists, schoolteachers, persons in the Brazilian military, college professors, the press corps, police officers, persons in commerce, and other members of the literate community (ibid., 15–16).

31. Ibid., xvi–xvii.

32. Ibid., 62. Brown cites the anonymous work *Primeiro Congress Brasileiro de Umbanda* (Rio de Janeiro: n.p. 1942), 101.

33. Maggie, "Afro-Brazilian Cults," in *The Encyclopedia of Religion*, 104. Kardec spiritualism, which took its name from its leader, sought to "purify" Afro-Brazilian elements of the religious cults (ibid.). To accurately represent the important elements of the major African religions in Brazil, I treat the Umbanda phenomenon as an African creole religion in a modern multicultural eclectic movement.

34. Ortiz, "Ogun and the Umbanda Religion," 91. See also Burdick, "Brazil's Black Consciousness Movement," 27, and "Umbanda," in *HCDR*, 1107.

35. "Afro-Brazilian Religions," in *HCDR*, 31.

36. Ibid., 30–31. Also Ortiz, *Ogun and the Umbanda Religion*, 95; "Umbanda," in *HCDR*, 1107–1108.

37. George Eaton Simpson, *Black Religion in the New World* (New York: Colombia University Press, 1978), 292–293. Simpson cited as a source Esther Pressel, "Umbanda Trance and Possession in Sao Paulo, Brazil," in *Trans, Healing and Hallucination*, ed. F. D. Goodman, J. H. Henney, and E. Pressel (New York: n.p., 1974), 116.

38. "Afro-Brazilian Religions," in *HCDR*, 30; "Umbanda," in *HCDR*, 1107.

39. Brown, *Umbanda and Politics*, 54–55.

40. "Afro-Brazilian Religions," in *HCDR*, 31.

41. Brown, *Umbanda and Politics*, 59. Also Armando Cavalvanti Bandeira, *Umbanda: Evolucao Historico-Religiosa* (Rio de Janeiro: n.p., 1961), 114–115.

42. Brown, *Umbanda and Politics*, 59; "Afro-Brazilian Religions," in *HCDR*, 31; Maggie, "Afro-Brazilian Cults,"103.

43. Johnson, *Secrets, Gossip, and Gods*, 52.

44. Brown, *Umbanda and Politics*, 55; Pedro McGregor, *Jesus of the Spirits* (New York: Stein and Day, 1967), 196, cited in Brown.

45. Brown, *Umbanda and Politics*, 55. Johnson says Umbanda was "perceived as elevating whitening over Africanizing moves" and "presented as a nationalist religion" (*Secrets, Gossip, and Gods*, 52–53).

46. Brown, *Umbanda and Politics*, 54–55, 64–69.

47. See Donald Pierson, *Negroes in Brazil: A Study of Race Contact in Bahia* (Carbondale: Southern Illinois University Press, 1967), 285.

48. Patricia Barker Lerch, "Spirit Mediums in Umbanda Evangelizada of Porto Alegre, Brazil: Dimensions of Power and Authority," in *A World of Women,* ed. Erika Bourguignon (New York: Praeger Specialist Studies, 1980), 129.

49. Lerch, "Predominance of Women," 244.

50. Ibid., 239, 250.

51. "Umbanda," in *HCDR,* 1108; "Afro-Brazilian Religions," in *HCDR,* 31; Lerch, "Predominance of Women," 245.

52. Brown, *Umbanda and Politics,* 103, 109.

53. Ibid., 79–80, 82.

54. Ibid., 85; also 83.

55. Ibid., 173.

56. Roberto Motta, "Ethnicity, Purity, the Market and Syncretism in Afro-Brazilian Cults," in *Reinventing Religions, Syncretism and Transformation in Africa and the Americas,* ed. Sidney M. Greenfield and Andrea Droogers (New York: Rowman and Littlefield, 2001), 73.

57. Bastide, *The African Religions,* 173–174.

58. Motta, "Syncretism in Afro-Brazilian Cults," 73.

59. "Afro-Brazilian Religions," in *HCDR,* 30.

60. Bastide, *The African Religions,* 129. Bastide cited Jose Lins de Rego, *Banque* (Rio de Janeiro: J. Olympio, 1934), 258, and Luis de Camara Cascudo, *Vaqueiros e Contadores: Foclore Poetico do Sertao de Pernambuco, Paraiba, Rio Grand do Notre e Ceara* (Porto Alegre: Livraria do Globo, 1939), 113, among others.

61. Mundicarmo Maria Rocha Ferretti, "The Presence of Non-African Spirits in an Afro-Brazilian Religion: A Case of Afro-Amerindian Syncretism?" in *Reinventing Religions,* 102. Cited in Roberto Matta, *Relativizando: Uma Introducao a Antropologia* (Petropolis: Editora Vozes, 1981), 59, 63.

62. Ferretti, "The Presence of Non-African Spirits," 104.

63. Brown, *Umbanda and Politics,* 65.

64. Johnson, *Secrets, Gossip, and Gods,* 52; Brown, *Umbanda and Politics,* 65–67.

65. Mikelle Smith Omari, "Candomble: A Socio-political Examination of African Religion and Art in Brazil," in *Religion in Africa: Experience and Expression,* ed. Thomas D. Blakely, Walter E. A. van Beek, and Dennis L. Thompson (Portsmouth, N.H.: Heinemann, 1994), 136–137.

66. Bastide, *African Religions,* 206.

67. Nina Rodrigues, *O Animismo Fetichista dos Negros Bahianos* (Rio de Janeiro: Civilizacao Brasileira, 1935), 234–235. Cited in Bastide, *African Religions,* 55.

68. Bastide, *The African Religions,* 211.

69. "Candomble," in *HCDR,* 179. Also "Afro-Caribbean Religions," *HCDR,* 31.

70. Maggie, "Afro-Brazilian Cults,"104.

71. Bastide, *The African Religions,* 221.

72. Rene Ribeiro, *Cultos Afro-Brasileiros de Recife: Um Estudo de Adjustmento Social* (Recife: Boletim do Instituto Joaquim Nabuco de Pesquisa Social, 1952), 142–143. Cited in Bastide, *The African Religions,* 221.

CHAPTER 10

1. Maureen Warner-Lewis states that this donation was necessary because "Africans who were known by Catholic clergy to have practiced African religions and whose burial

included related rituals were churched by laymen, not ordained priests, and were denied burial in church cemeteries" (*Trinidad Yoruba, From Mother Tongue to Memory* [Mona, Jamaica: The Press University of the West Indies, 1977], 41). Cited also in Ursula Raymond, "The Yorubas of Diego Martin" (St. Augustine, Trinidad: Unpublished typescript of University of the West Indies Library, n.d.)

2. As early as the 1850s, Yoruba-Shango was named in criticisms of African religions that claimed they were the "heathenish practices" of "semi-barbarians" (see L. A. de Verteuil, *Trinidad: Its Geography, Natural Resources, Present Condition and Prospects* [London: Ward Lock, 1858]).

3. I arrived in Trinidad and Tobago to study in 1973, just before Prime Minister Williams gave one of his captivating speeches in Woodford Square, Port-of-Spain, on the preservation of and respect for Trinidad and Tobago's cultural diversity, with special reference to African culture and traditions. *The Bomb*, a sensational tabloid, spread rumors that week that "The Doc," as he was called fondly, joined Orisha-Shango and the Rosicrucians.

4. J. Lorand Matory, *Black Atlantic Religion, Tradition, Transnationalism, and Matriarchy in the Afro-Brazilian Candomble* (Princeton, N.J.: Princeton University Press, 2005), 43.

5. James Houk, *Spirit, Blood and Drums: The Orisha Religion in Trinidad* (Philadelphia: Temple University Press, 1995), 9. Anthropologist Houk has written one of the most interesting, "must-read," and informative books on African religions in Trinidad in recent times.

6. Chief FAMA, *Fundamentals of the Yoruba Religion (Orisa Worship)* (San Bernadino, Calif.: Orunmila Communications, 1993). This text has been adopted in Trinidad but is largely about Nigerian Yoruba and is not yet accessible to English readers.

7. Cited in Pearl Eintou Springer, "Orisha and the Spiritual Baptist Religion in Trinidad and Tobago" (Port-of-Spain Public Library, Suriname: Unpublished paper presented at the Ecumenical Conference of the Caribbean Conference of Churches, May 1994), 5–7.

8. Pearl Eintou Springer, "The Orisha Religion and National Council of Orisha Elders of Trinidad and Tobago" (Public Library at Port-of-Spain, Trinidad: Unpublished report of Iyalorisa Melvina Rodney, head of Egbe Orisa Ile Wa, 1994), 1–2.

9. Ibid., 12. Also, Pearl Springer, "Orisha Oshun, the Heroine of Oshogbo Nigeria," *Trinidad Guardian* (August 23, 1990): 23

10. Molly Ahye, "Orisha Tradition and Culture: A Report on the Second World Conference in Bahia," *Sunday Guardian* (October 30, 1983): 8, 21.

11. David Tindall, "Drums and Colors," *Caribbean Beat* (November 2000): 1. Also, Tindall, "Caribbean Drums and Colors," available at www.caribbean.com.

12. Bridget Brereton, *A History of Modern Trinidad 1783–1962* (London: Heinemann, 1981), 3–4.

13. The Cedula, which granted tax concessions and rights to citizenship after five years, offered a white planter thirty acres of land for every member of his family and fifteen acres for every slave. Every free black planter was offered fifteen acres, while his slave fetched seven-and-a-half acres.

14. Brereton, *A History of Modern Trinidad*, 13–14. I had the privilege of being be a student of the history of Trinidad and Tobago under the tutelage of Professors Brereton and James Millette at the University of the West Indies, St. Augustine, Trinidad, 1981 to 1983.

15. Robert E. Hood, *Must God Remain Greek? Afro Cultures and God-Talk* (Minneapolis, Minn.: Fortress Press, 1990), 59; Philip D. Curtin, *The Atlantic Slave Trade: A Census* (Madison: University of Wisconsin Press, 1969), 170. See table in B. W. Higman, "African and Creole Slave Family Patterns in Trinidad," in *Africa and the Caribbean: The*

Legacy of a Link, ed. Margaret E. Crahan and Franklin W. Knight (Baltimore, Md.: Johns Hopkins University Press, 1979), 44–48.

16. Higman, "African and Creole Slave Family Patterns in Trinidad," 42.

17. Warner-Lewis, *Trinidad Yoruba*, 35.

18. Ibid., 28–31; Brereton, *A History of Modern Trinidad*, 96–98.

19. Warner-Lewis, *Trinidad Yoruba*, 26 –31.

20. Peter Manuel, Kenneth Bilby, and Michael Largey, *Caribbean Currents: Caribbean Music from Rumba to Reggae* (Philadelphia: Temple University Press, 1995), 183; Hood, *Must God Remain Greek?* 60; Brereton, *A History of Modern Trinidad*, 100–108.

21. Brereton, *A History of Modern Trinidad*, 108.

22. Warner-Lewis, *Trinidad Yoruba*, 37.

23. Brereton, *A History of Modern Trinidad*, 346–146.

24. Warner-Lewis, *Trinidad Yoruba*, 37.

25. Ibid., 37–38.

26. Brereton, *A History of Modern Trinidad*, 127–130.

27. Warner-Lewis, *Trinidad Yoruba* 37; Maureen Warner-Lewis, "Yoruba Religion in Trinidad-Transfer and Reinterpretation," *Caribbean Quarterly* 24, nos. 3–4 (September–December, 1978): 36–37.

28. In this ward, several "Amerindian kitchen-middens" were excavated by archaeologists (J. D. Elder, "The Yoruba Ancestor Cult in Gasparillo," *Caribbean Quarterly* 16, no. 3 [September, 1970]: 6–7). See also George Eaton Simpson, *Black Religions in the New World* (New York: Columbia University Press, 1978), 60; Maureen Warner-Lewis, "The African Impact on Language and Literature in the English-Speaking Caribbean," in *African and the Caribbean: Legacies of a Link,* ed. Margaret Crahan and Franklin Knight (Baltimore, Md.: Johns Hopkins University Press, 1979), 101–102.

29. Brereton, *A History of Modern Trinidad*, 55; Warner-Lewis, *Trinidad Yoruba*, 40–41.

30. David V. Trotman, "The Yoruba and Orisha Worship in Trinidad and British Guiana: 1838–1870," *African Studies Review* 19, no. 2 (1976): 2; and Houk, *Spirit, Blood, and Drums*, 51.

31. L. A. de Verteuil, *Trinidad*, 175 (cited in Simpson, *Black Religions*, 288). See also Leonard Barrett, "African Religion in the Americas: The 'Islands in Between,'" in *African Religions: A Symposium*, ed. Newell S. Booth, Jr. (New York: NOK Publishers, 1977), 206.

32. Melville J. Herskovits, "African Gods and Catholic Saints in New World Religious Beliefs," *American Anthropologist* 39 no. 4 (1937): 635–643; Peter. C. Lloyd, "The Yoruba of Nigeria," in *Peoples of Africa*, ed. James L. Gibbs, Jr. (New York: n.p., 1965), 575–576.

33. Melville J. Herskovits and Francis Herskovits, *Trinidad Village* (New York: Alfred Knopf, 1947), 46; Simpson, *Black Religions*, 74, 286; Houk, *Spirit, Blood, and Drums*, 52.

34. Warner-Lewis, *Trinidad Yoruba*, 35, 49.

35. Elder, "The Yoruba Ancestor Cult," 8; Hood, *Must God Remain Greek?* 60.

36. Elder, "The Yoruba Ancestor Cult," 8, 9–10. See also Barrett, "African Religions in the Americas," 207–208.

37. Elder, "The Yoruba Ancestor Cult," 10–12.

38. Simpson, *Black Religions*, 74, 75; Houk, *Spirit, Blood, and Drums*, 147, 185.

39. Simpson, *Black Religions*, 290, 295.

40. Ibid., 75, 78, 288–290.

41. Warner-Lewis, "Yoruba Religion in Trinidad," 18–20.

42. Simpson, *Black Religions*, 77, 288.

43. Ibid., 289.

44. Ibid., 288. See also George Eaton Simpson, "The Shango Cult in Nigeria and Trinidad," *American Anthropologist* 64, no. 6 (December 1962): 1204–1205.

45. Houk, *Spirit, Blood and Drums*, 151–152.

46. Warner-Lewis, "Yoruba Religion in Trinidad," 18–20.

47. Houk, *Spirit, Blood, and Drums*, 144. Also Simpson, "The Shango Cult," 1204–1205.

48. Frances Henry, "Social Stratification in an Afro-American Cult," *Anthropological Quarterly* 38, no. 2 (April 1965): 75; Frances Mischel, "African 'Powers' in Trinidad: The Shango Cult," *Anthropological Quarterly* 30, no. 2 (April 1957): 49–51.

49. Henry, "Social Stratification," 47–49, 53; Mischel, "African 'Powers' in Trinidad," 49–50.

50. Henry, "Social Stratification," 24–25. See also Simpson, *Black Religions*, 75–76; Rudolph Eastman, "Orisa: An Indigenous African Theology in Trinidad and Tabago," *Trinidad Express,* Emancipation Day (August, 1988): 27.

51. Cf. Houk, *Spirit, Blood, and Drums,* 138; Simpson, *Black Religions*, 74–75; Simpson, "The Shango Cult," 1204–1205.

52. Mischel, "African 'Powers' in Trinidad," 53, 54; Simpson, *Black Religions*, 75; Eastman, "Orisa," 27.

53. Mischel, "African 'Powers' in Trinidad," 57. Also Simpson, "The Shango Cult," 1205; Eastman, "Orisa," 27.

54. Mischel, "African 'Powers' in Trinidad," 58; Simpson, *Black Religion*, 75; Simpson, "The Shango Cult," 1205–1206.

55. Mischel, "African 'Powers' in Trinidad," 55–56. Also, George E. Simpson, *The Shango Cult in Trinidad* (Rio Piedras: Institute of Caribbean Studies, University of Puerto Rico, 1965).

56. Simpson, *Black Religion*, 76. Simpson writes, "A ritual assistant brings a calabash filled with water and ashes . . . into the palais and places it on the ground while a song is sung for Eshu. The calabash is then carried outside the palais and emptied, symbolizing the ejection of Eshu from the ceremony."

57. Tindall, "Drums and Colors," 2; Tindall, "Caribbean Drums and Colors"; Simpson, "The Shango Cult," 1205–1206.

58. In southern Caribbean culture, Pa Neezer is an Afro-Caribbean practitioner of high seance, often associated with Obeah works. Pa Neezer was popularized in the lyrics of the Mighty Sparrow's calypso song *Melda*, whose title character is a believer in Obeah.

59. Mischel, "African 'Powers' in Trinidad," 55–56. See also Simpson, *Black Religions*, 74–76.

60. George Eaton Simpson, "Caribbean Religions: Afro-Caribbean Religions," in *The Encyclopedia of Religion*, vol. 3, ed. Mircea Eliade (New York: Simon and Schuster/Macmillan, 1995), 92; Simpson, *Black Religions*, 74, 76. See also Tindall, "Drums and Colors," 4.

61. Simpson, "Afro-Caribbean Religions," 92; Simpson, *Black Religion*, 76.

62. Tindall, "Drums and Colors," 1; Springer, "Orisha and the Spiritual Baptist Religion," 5.

63. Tindall, "Drums and Colors," 72–76; Simpson, *Black Religion*, 77. See also Henry, "Social Stratification," 72.

64. Mischel, "African 'Powers' in Trinidad," 47.

65. This behavior was very common in the Pentecostal Church where which I was first introduced to Christianity in Grenada, where possession is called being filled with the Holy Spirit.

66. Tindall, "Drums and Colors," 2–3; Simpson, *Black Religion*, 77.

67. Springer, "Orisha and the Spiritual Baptist," 2–3.

68. Frances Mischel, "Faith Healing and Medical Practice in the Southern Caribbean," *Southern Journal of Anthropology* 3 (1960): 407.

69. Ibid., 408.

70. Simpson, *Black Religions*, 78, 79.

71. Ibid., 290.

72. Houk, *Spirit, Blood and Drums*, 158–159.

73. Ibid., 189–190.

CHAPTER 11

1. Dianne M. Stewart, *Three Eyes for the Journey: African Dimensions of the Jamaican Religious Experience* (New York: Oxford University Press, 2005).

2. Alan Richardson, "Romantic Voodoo: Obeah and British Culture, 1797–1807," in *Sacred Possessions: Vodou, Santeria, Obeah, and the Caribbean,* ed. Margarite Fernandez Olmos and Lizabeth Paravisini-Gebert (New Brunswick, N.J.: Rutgers University Press, 1999), 173; Orlando Patterson, *The Sociology of Slavery: An Analysis of the Origins, Development and Structure of Negro Slave Society in Jamaica* (Teaneck, N.J.: Fairleigh Dickinson University Press, 1975), 185.

3. Leonard E. Barrett, *The Rastafarians: A Study of Messianic Cultism in Jamaica* (Puerto Rico: Rio Piedras, Institute of Caribbean Studies, University of Puerto Rico, 1969), 18. See also Leonard E. Barrett, "African Religions in the Americas: The Islands in Between," in *African Religions: A Symposium*, ed. Newell S. Booth, Jr. (New York: NOK Publishers, 1977), 191.

4. Edward Seaga, "Revival Cults in Jamaica: Notes toward a Sociology of Religion," *Jamaican Journal* 3, no. 2 (1969): 5. See William David Spencer, "The First Chant: Leonard Howell's *The Promised Key*, with Commentary by William David Spencer," in *Chanting Down Babylon: The Rastafari Reader*, ed. Nathaniel Samuel Murrell, William David Spencer, and Adrian Anthony McFarlane (Philadelphia: Temple University Press, 1998), 372–374.

5. Kevin J. Aylmer, "Towering Babble and Glimpses of Zion: Recent Depictions of Rastafari in Cinema," in *Chanting Down Babylon*, 291–292.

6. According to Dale Bisnauth, witchcraft "involved a theory of causation that was concerned with the explanation of misfortune or evil" but it also represents the essence of evil. Sorcery is evil magic associated with the underworld or the dead (Dale Bisnauth, *A History of Religions in the Caribbean* [Kingston, Jamaica: Kingston Publishers, 1989], 91).

7. Ivor Morrish, *Obeah, Christ and Rastaman: Jamaica and Its Religions* (Cambridge, U.K.: James Clarke, 1982), 44. See also 24.

8. Roger Bastide, *African Civilization in the New World*, trans. Peter Green (New York: Harper and Row, 1972), 103.

9. Werner Zip, *Black Rebels: African-Caribbean Freedom Fighters in Jamaica*, trans. from German by Shelley L. Frisch (Princeton, N.J.: Markus Wiener Publishers, 1999), 194. See Barry Chevannes, *Rastafari: Roots and Ideology* (New York: Syracuse University Press, 1994), 19; Joseph Murphy, *Working the Spirit: Ceremonies of the African Diaspora* (Boston: Beacon Press), 120, 121.

10. Barry Chevannes, ed. *Rastafari and Other Worldviews*, (New Brunswick, N.J.: Rutgers University Press, 1995), 7. Duppies, African *dupe* or ghosts, are shadows of the deceased who are considered potent spiritual forces and allegedly can be either harnessed in the community's interest or ritually neutralized through funeral rites and rituals (Murphy, *Working the Spirit*, 121).

11. Stewart, *Three Eyes for the Journey*, 182–183.

12. Ibid., 41.

13. Ibid., 31.

14. Ibid., 42.

15. Ibid., 43; Gordon R. Lewis, *Main Currents in Caribbean Thought: The Historical Evolution of Caribbean Society in Its Ideological Aspects, 1492–1900* (Baltimore, Md.: Johns Hopkins University Press, 1983), 224; Richard Hart, *Slaves Who Abolished Slavery* (Kingston, Jamaica: Institute of Social and Economic Research, 1985), 236.

16. Murphy, *Working the Spirit*, 121.

17. Morrish, *Obeah*, 41. In modern academic studies of religion, magic is any act or action that attempts to influence the divine to act favorably in the realm of the profane.

18. Chevannes, *Rastafari: Roots and Ideology*, 32; Morrish, *Obeah*, 40; Richardson, "Romantic Voodoo," 173.

19. Frederick Ivor Case, "The Intersemiotics of Obeah and Kali Mai in Guyana," in *Nation Dance, Religion, Identity, and Cultural Difference in the Caribbean*, ed. Patrick Taylor (Bloomington: Indiana University Press, 2001), 41. This attribute, Case says, allows the art to be receptive to Islamic, Hindu, Aboriginal, Christian, and other faiths and practices.

20. Case, "The Intersemiotics of Obeah," 41. See Gerard M. Dalgish, *Dictionary of Africanism: Contributions of Sub-Saharan Africa to the English Language* (London: Greenwood, 1982); Morrish, *Obeah*; Joseph J. Williams, *Psychic Phenomena of Jamaica* (Westport, Conn.: Greenwood, 1979); F. G. Cassidy and R. B. Lepage, *Dictionary of Jamaican English* (Cambridge: Cambridge University Press, 1967).

21. Robert E. Hood, *Must God Remain Greek? Afro Cultures and God-Talk* (Minneapolis, Minn.: Fortress Press, 1990), 60. See also Barbara Bush, *Slave Women in Caribbean Society 1650–1838* (Bloomington: Indiana University Press, 1990), 74; George Eaton Simpson, *Black Religions in the New World* (New York: Colombia University Press, 1978), 52; Richardson, "Romantic Voodoo," 173.

22. Booth, Jr., *African Religions*, 191.

23. Morrish, *Obeah*, 23. The dominant Ashanti/Akan root *obayifo*, which means "wizard" or "sorcerer," offers a historical origin for the evil side of Caribbean Obeah.

24. Bisnauth, *A History of Religions*, 89.

25. Bastide, *African Civilization*, 103. See also Bisnauth, *A History of Religions*, 90; Morrish, *Obeah*, 23.

26. Stewart, *Three Eyes for the Journey*, 49; Patterson, *Sociology of Slavery*, 185–195; Cassidy and Le Page, *Dictionary of Jamaican English*, 326; Joseph J. Williams, *Voodoos and Obeahs: Phrases of West Indian Witchcraft* (New York: Dial, 1932), 120–121; Leonard E. Barrett, *Soul Force: African Heritage in Afro-American Religion* (Garden City, N.Y.: Anchor Books, 1974), 64.

27. Stewart, *Three Eyes for the Journey*, 42

28. Bryan Edwards, "African Religions in Colonial Jamaica," in *Afro-American Religious History: A Documentary*, ed. Milton C. Sernett (Durham, N.C.: Duke University Press, 1985), 20–21, 22. (Adapted from *An Abridgement of Mr. Edward's Civil and Commercial History of the British Colonies in the Indies in Two Volumes*, vol. 11 [London: J. Parsons and J. Bell, 1974]). See Michael S. Laguerre, *Afro-Caribbean Folk Medicine* (South Hadley, Mass.: Bergin and Garvey Publishers, 1987), 6, 16, 23; Morris, *Obeah*, 40.

29. Elaine Savory, "'Another Poor Devil of a Human Being' . . . Jean Rhys and the Novel as Obeah," in *Sacred Possessions*, 218.

30. Edwards, "African Religions," 20.

31. Simpson, *Black Religions*, 52. Cited in Donald Hogg, "The Convince Cult in Jamaica," *Yale Publication in Anthropology no. 58, Papers in Caribbean Anthropology*, compiled

by Sidney W. Mintz (New Haven, Conn.: Department of Anthropology, Yale University Press, 1960), 19–20.

32. Captain J. G. Steadman, "Guerrilla Warfare: A European Soldier's View," in *Maroon Societies: Rebel Slave Communities in the Americas*, ed. Richard Price (Garden City, N.Y.: Anchor Press, 1973), 307.

33. Morrish, *Obeah*, 141.

34. Richardson, "Romantic Voodoo," 173–174; Michael S. Laguerre, *Voodoo and Politics in Haiti*, (New York: St. Martins Press, 1989), 70; Eugene D. Genovese, *From Rebellion to Revolution: Afro-American Slave Revolts in the Making of the New World* (New York: Random House, Vintage Books, 1979, 1981 reprint ed.), 28, 47.

35. Murphy, *Working the Spirit*, 121. See Hart, *Slaves Who Abolished Slavery*, 236; Basil C. Hedrick and Jeanette E. Stephens, *It's a Natural Fact: Obeah in the Bahamas* (Greeley, Colo.: Museum of Anthropology, University of Northern Colorado, 1977), 10.

36. Bisnauth, *A History of Religions*, 83, 85. See also Bush, *Slave Women*, 74. Cited in Bryan Edwards, *The History, Civil and Commercial, of the British Colonies in the West Indies*, vol. 2 (Dublin: Luke White, 1793/1801), 118; Morrish, *Obeah*, 41.

37. Bisnauth, *A History of Religions*, 83. See also Murphy, *Working the Spirit*, 121; Williams, *Voodoos and Obeah*, 158–162. As early as the 1680s, laws prohibited the use of poisons on anyone and debarred slaves from assembling to celebrate African feasts with the beating of drums.

38. Law XLV (1792), quoted in Bush, *Slave Women*, 74, and Edwards, *The History, Civil and Commercial, of the British Colonies*, 177–178; Stewart, *Three Eyes for the Journey*, 36–45.

39. Seaga, "Revival Cults in Jamaica," 5.

40. Stewart, *Three Eyes for the Journey*, 37–46.

41. Bush, *Slave Women*, 75.

42. Morrish, *Obeah*, 40.

43. Zip, *Black Rebels*, 188.

44. Colonists associated all systems of African beliefs and rituals with Obeah and then rejected such manifestations of spiritual service as worship of the devil (Murphy, *Working the Spirit*, 115).

45. Bush, *Slave Women*, 73. See also Herbert G. DeLisser, *Twentieth Century Jamaica* (Kingston: *The Jamaica Times*, 1913), 108.

46. Karla Y. E. Frye, "An Article of Faith, Obeah and Hybrid Identities in Elizabeth Nunez-Harrell's When Rocks Dance," in *Sacred Possessions*, 198–200.

47. Morrish, *Obeah*, 42. See also Frye, "An Article of Faith," 199.

48. Edwards, "African Religions," 20.

49. Margarite Fernandez Olmos and Lizabeth Paravisini-Gebert, *Creole Religions of the Caribbean: An Introduction from vodou and Santeria to Obeah and Espiritismo* (New York: New York University Press, 2003), 138; Morrish, *Obeah*, 42.

50. Morrish, *Obeah*, 42; Olmos and Paravisini-Gebert, *Creole Religions*, 138.

51. Edwards, "African Religions," 20, 22, 390–396. Edward Long, *The Report of the Lords of the Committee of the Council Appointed for the Consideration of All Matters Relating to Trade and Foreign Plantation* (London: n.p., 1789), 353.

52. Bisnauth, *A History of Religions*, 82. Cited in Long, *The Report of the Lords of the Committee*, 353. Bisnauth also referenced R. Legion, *A True and Exact History of the Island of Barbados* (p. 47), but gave no publisher, place, or date.

53. Richardson, "Romantic Vodou,"173.

54. Stewart, *Three Eyes for the Journey*.

55. See also Edward Kamau Brathwaite, "The African Presence in Caribbean Literature," *Daedalus* 103, no 2 (Spring 1974): 73–109; Elaine Campbell, "Reflections of Obeah

in Jean Rhys' Fiction," in *Critical Perspectives on Jean Rhys*, ed. Pierrette Frickey (Washington, D.C.: Three Continents Press, 1990): 59–66. In Olmos and Paravisini-Gebert's *Sacred Possessions*, Karla Frye, Alan Richardson, and Elaine Savory have published fascinating essays spotlighting modern interest in Obeah in society.

56. Kenneth Ramchand, *The West Indian Novel and Its Background* (London: Heinemann, 1983), 123–131.

57. Case, "The Intersemiotics of Obeah," 43. See also Bisnauth, *A History of Religions*, 98–99; Frye, "An Article of Faith," 199–201.

58. Case, "The Intersemiotics of Obeah," 45; also 43, 47.

59. Seaga, "Revival Cults in Jamaica," 11. Also Laguerre, *Afro-Caribbean Folk Medicine*, 27–31.

60. Edwards, "African Religions," 20–21.

61. Chevannes, *Rastafari: Roots and Ideology*, 32.

62. Laguerre, *Afro-Caribbean Folk Medicine*, 26.

63. Edwards, "African Religions," 20. See also Long, *The Report of the Lords of the Committee*, cited in Murphy, *Working the Spirit*, 115, 224; Williams, *Voodoo and Obeahs*, 113.

64. Kenneth Ramchand, "Obeah and the Supernatural in West Indian Literature," *Jamaica Journal* 3, no. 2 (June 1963): 52–53. Rumors have it that Rastafari founder Leonard Howell practiced Obeah in New York while dispensing herbal remedies and teas.

65. Morris, *Obeah*, 41. Hood says that the Obeah-man, for example, "acted as a broker for a male slave trying to court a female slave as a means of revenge on a fellow male slave" (*Must God Remain Greek?* 68. See also page 72); Stewart, *Three Eyes for the Journey*, 182.

66. Frye, "An Article of Faith," 200.

67. John Steadman, *Narrative of a Five Years Expedition against the Revolted Negroes of Surinam, 1772–1777*, vol. 1 (London: n.p, 1796), 33–34. Recorded by Bush, *Slave Women*, 74.

68. Bush, *Slave Women*, 77.

69. Murray, *Working the Spirit*, 121; Chevannes, *Rastafari: Roots and Ideology*, 32.

70. Bisnauth, *A History of Religions*, 92.

71. Barrett says the ultimate test of whether one is a sorcerer or a witch is the act of snatching away a child (Barrett, *The Rastafarians*, 191; Morris, *Obeah*, 40–41).

72. Edwards, "African Religions," 21. See also Bastide, *African Civilization*, 103.

73. Murphy, *Working the Spirit*, 120.

74. Morris, *Obeah*, 44; Murphy, *Working the Spirit*, 116.

75. Seaga, "Revival Cults in Jamaica," 11.

76. Ibid., 11–12.

77. Chevannes, *Rastafari: Roots and Ideology*, 32; Laguerre, *Afro-Caribbean Folk Medicine*, 27. See also Seaga, "Revival Cults in Jamaica," 12.

78. Frye, "An Article of Faith,"199.

79. Chevannes, "Some Notes on African Religious Survivals in the Caribbean," *Caribbean Journal of Religious Studies* 5, no. 2 (1983): 19–20.

CHAPTER 12

1. Barry Chevannes, *Rastafari and Other African-Caribbean Worldviews* (New Brunswick, N.J.: Rutgers University Press, 1998), 1–2.

2. Joseph Murphy, *Working the Spirit: Ceremonies of the African Diaspora* (Boston: Beacon Press, 1994), 115. See also Karl Luntta, *Jamaica Handbook* (Chico, Calif.: Moon

Publications, 1991), 46–47; Leonard E. Barrett, *The Rastafarians: Sounds of Cultural Dissonance* (Boston: Beacon Press, 1997), 17–18; Leonard E. Barrett, "African Religions in the Americas: The Islands in Between," in *African Religions: A Symposium,* ed. Newell S. Booth, Jr. (New York: NOK Publishers, 1977), 189–190.

3. Bryan Edwards, "African Religions in Colonial Jamaica," in *Afro-American Religious History A Documentary,* ed. Milton C. Sernett (Durham, N.C.: Duke University Press, 1985), 19. Adapted from *An Abridgement of Mr. Edward's Civil and Commercial History of the British West Colonies in the Indies in Two Volumes,* vol. 2 (London: J. Parsons and J. Bell, 1794), 390. See also 91–96.

4. Murphy, *Working the Spirit,* 228.

5. W. F. Elkins, *Street Preachers, Faith Healers and Herb Doctors in Jamaica, 1890–1925* (New York: Revisionist Press, 1977), 31; Booth, Jr., *African Religions,* 198.

6. Edward Seaga, "Revival Cults in Jamaica: Notes Toward a Sociology of Religion," *Jamaican Journal* 3, no. 2 (June 1963): 5.

7. Barry Chevannes, "Some Notes on African Religious Survivals in the Caribbean," *Caribbean Journal of Religious Studies* 5, no. 2 (September 1983): 19–20; Barry Chevannes, *Rastafari: Roots and Ideology* (Syracuse, N.Y.: Syracuse University Press, 1994), 22f; Chevannes, *Rastafari and Other Worldviews,* 1–3; Seaga, "Revival Cults in Jamaica," 5.

8. George Eaton Simpson, "Jamaican Revival Cults," *Social and Economic Studies* 5, no. 4 (December 1956): 342; Barry Chevannes, "Revivalism: A Disappearing Religion," *Caribbean Quarterly* 24, nos. 3–4 (September–December 1978): 1, 4–5. Luntta's *Jamaica Handbook* includes among its "cults" Revivalism, Kumina, Convince, and Obeah magic.

9. Osei-Mensah Aborampah, "Out of the Same Bowl: Religious Beliefs and Practices in Akan Communities in Ghana and Jamaica," in *Fragments of Bone: Neo-African Religions in a New World,* ed. Patrick Bellegarde-Smith (Chicago: University of Illinois Press, 2005), 129.

10. Luntta, *Jamaica Handbook,* 18–19. Also Chevannes, *Rastafari and Other Worldviews,* 1–3.

11. Franklin W. Knight, *The Caribbean: The Genesis of a Fragmented Nationalism,* 2nd. ed. (New York: Oxford University Press, 1990), 53–54; Eric Williams, *Columbus to Castro: The History of the Caribbean 1492–1969* (New York: Vintage Books, 1984), 84. Knowledge of sugar production from Barbados invigorated sugar growing in Jamaica, and sugar planters became by far the largest purchasers of cheap slave labor.

12. Williams, *Columbus to Castro,* 102, 112, 114. Sadly enough, although the Europeans brought more than 750,000 Africans to Jamaica after 1655, when the slave trade was abolished in 1807 the black population was no more than 320,000; the demographics was a constant casualty of slave mortality (Abigail B. Bakan, *Ideology and Class Conflict in Jamaica: The Politics of Rebellion* [Buffalo, N.Y.: McGill-Queen's University Press, 1990], 19). Joseph M. Murphy, *Working the Spirit: Ceremonies of the African Diaspora* (Boston: Beacon Press, 1994), 115; Orlando Patterson, *The Sociology of Slavery: An Analysis of the Origins, Development and Structure of Negro Slave Society in Jamaica* (Teaneck, N.J.: Fairleigh Dickinson University Press, 1975), 113–134.

13. As quoted by a neighbor in Kingston, Jamaica.

14. According to Barbara Bush, "In the Caribbean . . . planters relied more on brute force than in the Southern USA and when they became absentee masters in England, leaving the running of the plantations to overseers and managers, society became more degenerate and cruel." Barbara Bush, *Slave Women in Caribbean Society 1650–1838* (Bloomington: Indiana University Press, 1990), 24, 52.

15. Bush, *Slave Women,* 3. See also Orlando Patterson, *Slavery and Social Death: A Comparative Study* (Cambridge: Harvard University Press, 1982), 35.

16. Dianne M. Stewart, *Three Eyes for the Journey: African Dimensions of the Jamaican Religious Experience* (New York: Oxford University Press, 2005), 77.

17. Ibid.

18. Don Robotham, "Development of Black Ethnicity in Jamaica," in *Garvey: His Work and Impact*, ed. Rupert Lewis and Patrick Bryon (Mona, Jamaica: Institute of Social and Economic Research and Development of Extra-Mural Studies, University of the West Indies, 1988), 32–33.

19. Lowell T. Ragatz, *The Fall of the Planter in the British Caribbean 1763–1833* (New York: Octagon Books 1928/1963), 27. See also Bush, *Slave Women*, 4; Knight, *The Caribbean*, 80.

20. Jean Besson, "Religion as Resistance in Jamaican Peasant Life: The Baptist Church, Revival Worldview and Rastafari Movement," in Chevannes, *Rastafari and Other Worldviews*, 56. See also Patterson, *The Sociology of Slavery*, 182–207.

21. Stewart, *Three Eyes for the Journey*, 47.

22. Edwards, "African Religions," 20. See also Maureen Warner-Lewis, *The Nkuyu: Spirit Messenger of the Kumina* (Mona, Jamaica: Savacou Publications, 1977), 59; cited in Robert Hood, *Must God Remain Greek? Afro Cultures and God-Talk* (Minneapolis, Minn.: Fortress Press, 1990), 66.

23. Edward Long, *The History of Jamaica*, vol. 2 (London: T. Lowndes, 1774), 416. Cited in Booth, Jr., *African Religions*, 192. See also Murphy, *Working the Spirit*, 116–117.

24. Murphy, *Working the Spirit*, 115.

25. Leonard Barrett, "African Religions in the Americas," 192. See also Stewart, *Three Eyes for the Journey*, 44–48, 100–103.

26. Barrett, "African Religions in the Americas," 195. See also Stewart, *Three Eyes for the Journey*, passim.

27. Edward Long, *The History of Jamaica*, 2, 416.

28. Matthew Gregory Lewis, *Journal of a West Indian Proprietor* (London: Paternoster Row, 1834; New York: Negro University Press, 1969), 354–356; Murphy, *Working the Spirit*, 225.

29. Chevannes, *Rastafari and Other Worldviews*, 7, 19. See also Monica Schuler, *"Alas, Alas, Kongo": A Social History of Indentured Immigration into Jamaica, 1841–1865* (Baltimore, Md.: Johns Hopkins University Press, 1980), 76; Leonard E. Barrett, *Soul Force: African Heritage in Afro-American Religion* (Garden City, N.Y.: Anchor Books, 1974), 71; Barrett, "African Religions," 192; Hood, *Must God Remain Greek?* 66.

30. Chevannes, *Rastafari: Roots and Ideology*, 17–18; Monica Schuler, "Myalism and the African Religious Tradition in Jamaica," in *Africa and the Caribbean: The Legacies of a Link*, ed. Margaret Crahan and Franklin W. Knight (Baltimore, Md.: Johns Hopkins University Press, 1979): 68–69.

31. Besson, "Religion as Resistance," 57. Cited in Mervyn Alleyne, *Roots of Jamaican Culture* (London: Pluto Press, 1988), 88–89. See also Robotham, "Black Ethnicity in Jamaica," 35.

32. James M. Phillippo, *Jamaica: Its Past and Present State* (London: Paternoster Row, 1843/ Dawsons of Pall Mall, 1969), 248.

33. Ibid. Similar views are represented in Lewis, *Journal of a West Indian Proprietor*, 354–356. Cited in Murphy, *Working the Spirit*, 117, 225.

34. Chevannes, *Rastafari and Other Worldviews*, 7.

35. Ibid., 7, 33; Chevannes, *Rastafari: Roots and Ideology*, 16–17; Hood, *Must God Remain Greek?* 68–69; Patterson, *The Sociology of Slavery*, 186; Besson, "Religion as Resistance," 57.

36. Stewart, *Three Eyes for the Journey*, 47.

37. Ibid., 48–49.

38. Ibid.; Patterson, *The Sociology of Slavery*, 188; Frederick Cassidy and R. B. Le Page, *Dictionary of Jamaican English* (Cambridge: Cambridge University Press, 1967), 313.

39. Stewart, *Three Eyes for the Journey*, 152–153.

40. Dianne Stewart, "African-Derived Religions in Jamaica," in *Encyclopedia of African and African-American Religions*, ed. Stephen Glazier (New York: Routledge, 2001), 165–169; Warner-Lewis, *Central Africa in the Caribbean: Transforming Time, Transforming Culture* (Barbados: University of the West Indies Press, 2003), 190–198; Martha Beckwith, *Christmas Mummings in Jamaica* (New York: American Folklore Society, 1923), 11; Kenneth Bilby, "Gumbay, Myal, and the Great House: New Evidence of the Religious Background of Jonkonnu in Jamaica," *ACIJ* 4 (Research Review: 25th Anniversary Edition, 1999): 64.

41. Warner-Lewis, *Central Africa in the Caribbean*, 190.

42. Bilby, "Gumbay, Myal," 64. See Stewart, *Three Eyes for the Journey*, 51–53.

43. Stewart, *Three Eyes for the Journey*, 52.

44. Murphy, *Working the Spirit*, 120–121.

45. Chevannes, *Rastafari and Other Worldviews*, 33. Chevannes states that much to the chagrin of George Liele and other Baptists missionaries, a Christianized version of Myal called Native Baptist was birthed in Jamaica and allowed them little control over converts, who taught and preached a Myal understanding of Christianity. See Chevannes, *Rastafari: Roots and Ideology*, 19.

46. William James Gardner, *A History of Jamaica from Its Discovery by Christopher Columbus to the Year 1872* (London: T. Fisher Unwin, 1873/1909), 357. Cited in Murphy, *Working the Spirit*, 123.

47. Murphy, *Working the Spirit*, 117.

48. Chevannes, *Rastafari Roots and Ideology*, 7-8; Murphy, *Working the Spirit*, 11–18.

49. As Chevannes says, "The description of Taki and his comrades drinking blood sacrifice and exacting oaths of secrecy from their coconspirators, parallels very closely the development of *vodou* in the Bois Caiman in Haiti" (*Rastafari and Other Worldviews*, 6–7). Vodou and Myal displayed violent responses to slavery and colonial oppression.

50. Murphy, *Working the Spirit*, 117–121.

51. J. H. Buchner, *The Moravians in Jamaica* (London: n.p., 1884), 139–140. Cited in Booth, Jr., *African Religions*, 192.

52. Besson, "Religion as Resistance," 57.

53. Hope Masterson Waddell, *Twenty-Nine Years in the West Indies and Central Africa* (London: Frank Cass, 1863), 189. Cited in Murphy, *Working the Spirit*, 117–118, 225. See Edward Long, *History of Jamaica* (London: T. Lowndes, 1774), 2; James M. Philippo, *Jamaica: Its Pastand Present State* (London: Dawson of Pal Mall, 1843, reprinted 1969), 248.

54. Murphy, *Working the Spirit*, 117.

55. Chevannes, *Rastafari and Other Worldviews*, 20. Also Hood, *Must God Remain Greek?* 69.

56. Chevannes, *Rastafari and Other Worldviews*, 39

57. Besson, "Religion as Resistance," 61. See also Robotham, "Black Ethnicity in Jamaica," 35–36

58. Chevannes, *Rastafari and Other Worldviews*, 25.

59. Stewart, *Three Eyes for the Journey*, 143.

60. Ibid., 139.

61. Campbell, *Rasta and Resistance: From Marcus Garvey to Walter Rodney* (Trenton, N.J.: Africa World Press, 1987), 26; Luntta, *Jamaica Handbook*, 47; Seaga, "Revival Cults in Jamaica," 4.

62. Maureen Warner-Lewis, "The Ancient Factor in Jamaica's African Religions," in *African Creative Expressions of the Divine*, ed. Kortright Davis and Elias Farajaje Jones (Washington, D.C.: Howard University Divinity School, 1991), 74.

63. Stewart, *Three Eyes for the Journey*, 142–143, 151; Kenneth Bilby and Fu-Kiau Bunseki, "Kumina: A Kongo-Based Tradition in the New World," *Les Cahiers du Cedaf* 8 (1983): 1, 8.

64. Stewart, *Three Eyes for the Journey*, 141; Bilby and Bunseki, *Kumina*, 1.

65. Leonard Barrett inaccurately claims that the word *Kumina* does not appear in Jamaican literature before Zora Neal Hurston's book *Voodoo Gods* appeared in 1938. Hurston had learned from informants that, although unrelated to Vodou, the word *Kumina* meant "power" and was associated with death.

66. Barrett, "African Religions," 196. See also 192–195. Also Stewart, *Three Eyes for the Journey*, 49–53 and passim.

67. George Eaton Simpson, *Black Religions in the New World* (New York: Columbia University Press, 1978), 55. See also Kenneth Bilby and Elliot Leib, "Kumina: The Howellite Church and the Emergence of Rastafarian Traditional Music in Jamaica," *Jamaica Journal* 19, no. 3 (August–October 1986): 22–23; Stewart, *Three Eyes for the Journey*, 49–53.

68. "Afro-Americans (Caribbean and South American), New Religions," in *The HarperCollins Dictionary of Religion [HCDR]*, ed. Jonathan Z. Smith and William Scott Green (San Francisco: HarperSanFrancisco, 1995), 26.

69. Stewart, *Three Eyes for the Journey*, 50. See also Seaga, "Revival Cults in Jamaica," 4; Bilby and Leib, "Kumina," 22–23.

70. Laura Tana, "African Retentions: Yoruba and Kikongo Songs in Jamaica," *Jamaica Journal: Quarterly of the Institute of Jamaica* 16, no. 3 (August 1983): 47.

71. Bilby and Leib, "Kumina," 23. See also Joseph G. Moore, "Religion of Jamaican Negroes: A Study of Afro-Jamaican Acculturation" (PhD Dissertation: Northwestern University, 1953; Ann Arbor, Mich.: University Microfilm Publication 7053); Warner-Lewis, *The Nkuyu*, 13; Edward Kamau Brathwaite, "Kumina: the Spirit of African Survival in Jamaica," *Jamaica Journal* 42 (1978); Cheryl Ryman, "The Jamaican Heritage in Dance: Developing a Traditional Typology," *Jamaica Journal* 44 (1984).

72. Schuler, *"Alas, Alas, Kongo,"* 78, 152; Donald Hogg, "The Convince Cult in Jamaica," Yale University Publication in Anthropology no. 58, in *Papers in Caribbean Anthropology*, comp. Sidney W. Minz (New Haven, Conn.: Department of Anthropology, Yale University, 1960), 3–24; Moore, "Religion of Jamaican Negroes," 115; See Neil J. Savishinsky, "African Dimensions of the Rastafarian Movement," in *Chanting Down Babylon: The Rastafari Reader*, ed. Nathaniel Samuel Murrell, William David Spencer, and Adrian Anthony McFarlane (Philadelphia: Temple University Press, 1998), 131.

73. Kenneth Bilby, "Holy Herb: Notes on the Background of Cannabis in Jamaica," in *Rastafari*, ed. Rex Nettleford (Kingston, Jamaica: University of the West Indies/United Cooperative Printers, 1985), 85; Neil J. Savishinsky, "African Dimensions," 131.

74. Stewart, *Three Eyes for the Journey*, 140. See also Simon Bockie, *Death and the Invisible Powers: The World of Kongo Belief* (Bloomington: Indiana University Press, 1993), 108.

75. Simpson, *Black Religions*, 98. Also George Eaton Simpson, "Caribbean Religions: Afro-Caribbean Religions," in *The Encyclopedia of Religion*, vol. 3, ed. Mircea Eliade (New York: Simon and Schuster/MacMillan, 1994), 93; Moore, "Religion of Jamaican Negroes," 116.

76. Simpson, *Black Religions*, 93.

77. Albert J. Raboteau, *Slave Religion: The 'Invisible Institution' in the Antebellum South* (Oxford: Oxford University Press, 1978), 16–17. Cited in George Eaton Simpson, *Religious*

Cults of the Caribbean (Rio Piedras: Institute of Caribbean Studies, University of Puerto Rico, 1970), 202; Simpson, *Black Religions*, 98, 290; Simpson, "Caribbean Religions," 93.

78. Stewart, *Three Eyes for the Journey*, 144. Referenced from Moore, "Religion of Jamaican Negroes," 115–117.

79. Chevannes, *Rastafari: Roots and Ideology*, 25.

80. Elizabeth Pigou, "A Note on Afro-Jamaican Beliefs and Rituals," *Jamaica Journal* 20, no. 2 (May–July 1987): 24.

81. Ibid.

82. "Afro-Americans," in *HCDR*, 26.

83. Stewart, *Three Eyes for the Journey*, 145, 277.

84. Moore, *Religion of Jamaican Negroes*, 99–100.

85. Bush, *Slave Women*, 158. Also "Afro-Americans," in *HCDR*, 26.

86. Pigou, "A Note on Afro-Jamaican Beliefs," 24. Also Simpson, *Black Religions*, 199; Joseph G. Moore and George Eaton Simpson, "A Comparative Study of Acculturation in Morant Bay and West Kingston, Jamaica," *Zaire* 11 (November–December 1957): 79–119 and 12 (January 1958): 65–87.

87. Nathaniel Samuel Murrell and Clinton Hutton, "Rastas' Psychology of Blackness," in *Chanting Down Babylon*, 46; Schuler, *"Alas, Alas, Kongo,"* 67, 95–96.

88. Stewart, *Three Eyes for the Journey*, 150–151.

89. Ibid., 151.

90. Pigou, "A Note on Afro-Jamaican Beliefs," 25–26. Also Chevannes, *Rastafari: Roots and Ideology*, 25.

91. Schuler, *"Alas, Alas, Kongo,"* 75; Pigou, "A Note on Afro-Jamaican Beliefs," 26. The second part of the graveside ceremony, called the "tombing ceremony," comes after the gravediggers are finished hollowing the spot and drinking Jamaican rum heavily in the process. During "tombing" rites, no singing of hymns is allowed.

92. Chevannes, *Rastafari: Roots and Ideology*, 25. See also Pigou, "A Note on Afro-Jamaican Beliefs," 26. Jamaicans have a great respect for the dead, although they see the dead as something to fear. Funerals are well attended; the larger they are, the "nicer" they are said to be.

93. Barrett, "African Religions," 196. See also Luntta, *Jamaica Handbook*, 47; Campbell, *Rasta and Resistance*, 126; Ennis Barrington Edmonds, *Rastafari: From Outcast to Cultural Bearers* (New York: Oxford University Press, 2003), 103.

94. Bilby and Leib, "Kumina," 24. Also Luntta, *Jamaica Handbook*, 47.

95. "Afro-Americans," in *HCDR*, 26. See also Simpson, *Black Religions*, 303.

96. Bilby and Leib, "Kumina," 26. See also Edmonds, *Rastafari*, 100; Schuler, *"Alas, Alas, Kongo,"* 95–96; Murrell, Spencer, and McFarlane, *Chanting Down Babylon*, 46. Barrett states that the Jonkonnu dance festival was widespread in some English colonies on the eastern seaboard of the United States, especially in the Carolinas ("African Religions," 196, 215).

97. Chevannes, *Rastafari: Roots and Ideology*, 123.

98. Bilby and Leib, "Kumina," 27. Cited in Savishinsky, "African Dimensions," 127–128.

CHAPTER 13

1. William Wedenoja, "The Origins of Revival, a Creole Religion in Jamaica," in *Culture and Christianity: The Dialectics of Transformation*, ed. George Saunders (Westport, Conn.: Greenwood, 1988), 106–108; George Eaton Simpson, "Culture Change and Reinvigoration Found in Cults of West Kingston, Jamaica," *Proceedings of the American Philosophical Society* 99, no. 2 (April 1955): 89–91.

2. Joseph Murphy, *Working the Spirit: Ceremonies of the African Diaspora* (Boston: Beacon Press, 1994); Karl Luntta, *Jamaica Handbook* (Chico, Calif.: Moon Publications, 1991), 46; "Afro-Americans (Caribbean and South American), New Religions Among," in *HarperCollins Dictionary of Religion [HCDR]*, ed. Jonathan Z. Smith and William Scott Green (San Francisco: HarperSanFrancisco, 1995). What some scholars label revival cults or revivalism, some Christians regard as authentic forms of spirituality or evangelical expressions of faith with African trimmings, hardly different from what one witnesses in a Caribbean Pentecostal Church.

3. Dianne M. Stewart, *Three Eyes for the Journey: African Dimensions of the Jamaican Religious Experience* (New York: Oxford University Press, 2005), 116.

4. Ibid., 117.

5. Barry Chevannes, "Some Notes on African Religious Survivals in the Caribbean," *Caribbean Journal of Religious Studies* 5, no. 2 (1983): 20.

6. Edward Seaga, "Revival Cults in Jamaica: Notes Toward a Sociology of Religion," *Jamaican Journal* 3, no. 2 (1963/1969): 4. See also Murphy, *Working the Spirit,* 1.

7. Stewart, *Three Eyes for the Journey,* 119, also 117–118; discussed in relation to Martha Bechwith, *Christman Mummings in Jamaica* (New York: American Folk-lore Society, 1923), 32.

8. Kenneth Ramchand, "Obeah and the Supernatural in West Indian Literature," *Jamaica Journal* 3, no. 2 (June 1963): 54.

9. Ibid.; Sylvia Wynter, *The Hills of Hebron: A Jamaican Novel* (New York: Simon and Schuster, 1962).

10. Barry Chevannes, *Rastafari: Roots and Ideology* (Syracuse, N.Y.: Syracuse University Press, 1994), 20; W. F. Elkins, *Street Preachers, Faith Healers and Herb Doctors in Jamaica, 1890–1925* (New York: Revisionist Press, 1977), 30; Stewart, *Three Eyes for the Journey,* 271.

11. Elkins, *Street Preachers,* 30–31. Also Chevannes, *Rastafari: Roots and Ideology,* 30.

12. Murphy, *Working the Spirit,* 125. See also Seaga, "Revival Cults in Jamaica," 5; Stewart, *Three Eyes for the Journey,* 107–109.

13. Barry Chevannes, "Revivalism, a Disappearing Religion," *Caribbean Quarterly* 24, nos. 3–4 (1978): 4. I loathe the notion that Satan and evil spirits somehow originate in Africa, for Africa has had her full measure of stereotypic representations in Western thought.

14. Chevannes, *Rastafari: Roots and Ideology,* 24; Murphy, *Working the Spirit,* 126; Elkins, *Street Preachers,* 30. The AMEZ became affiliated with Jamaica's Revival Zion only in the late 1960s after one of its leaders, C. D. Wright, a member of Parliament for the parish of St. Elizabeth, Jamaica, paid the New York AMEZ a visit. See also Chevannes, "Revivalism," 1.

15. Seaga, "Revival Cults in Jamaica," 4. See also Stewart, *Three Eyes for the Journey,* 108–111.

16. Stewart, *Three Eyes for the Journey,* 112. Cited in John S. Mbiti, *Introduction to African Religion,* 2nd ed. (Portsmouth, N.H.: Heinemann, 1991), 11–86, 131–143.

17. Elkins, *Street Preachers,* 9–110.

18. Stewart, *Three Eyes for the Journey,* 10,

19. Seaga, "Revival Cults in Jamaica," 10.

20. Chevannes, *Rastafari: Roots and Ideology,* 20–21.

21. Seaga, "Revival Cults in Jamaica," 10; Barry Chevannes, *Rastafari and Other African-Caribbean Worldviews* (New Brunswick, N. J.: Rutgers University Press, 1995), 23; Chevannes, *Rastafari: Roots and Ideology,* 23.

22. Chevannes, *Rastafari: Roots and Ideology,* 23. See also Albert J. Raboteau, *Slave Religion: The 'Invisible Institution' in the Antebellum South* (Oxford: Oxford University

Press, 1978), 28; George Eaton Simpson, *Religious Cults of the Caribbean* (Rio Piedras: Institute of Caribbean Studies, University of Puerto Rico, 1970), 169. This work was reissued as *Religious Cults of the Caribbean: Trinidad, Jamaica, and Haiti*, Caribbean monograph series vol. 15 (Rio Piedras: University of Puerto Rico, Institute of Caribbean Studies, 1980).

23. Chevannes, *Rastafari and Other Worldviews*, 23. See also Raboteau, *Slave Religion*, 28; Simpson, *Religious Cults of the Caribbean*, 169.

24. Elkins, *Street Preachers*, 30; Newell S. Booth, Jr., ed. *African Religions: A Symposium* (New York: NOK Publishers, 1977), 197; Murphy, *Working the Spirit*, 126.

25. Seaga, "Revival Cults in Jamaica," 8. "A well-known Revivalist leader of modern times was the late Kapo, originally Mallica Reynolds, a major Jamaican intuitive artist. He died in February, 1989. An eccentric man and fascinating artist, the largest single collection of Kapo's work, 65 paintings and sculptures, can be viewed at the National Gallery" (Luntta, *Jamaica Handbook*, 47). See also "Afro-Americans (Caribbean and South America)," in *HCDR*, 27.

26. Seaga, "Revival Cults in Jamaica," 12.

27. Ibid., 9.

28. Leonard Barrett, *Soul Force: African Heritage in Afro- American Religion* (London: Heinemann, 1976), 115–116; first issued in Garden City, New York by Anchor Books/ Doubleday, 1974; Leonard Barrett, "The Portrait of a Jamaican Healer: African Medical Lore in the Caribbean," *Caribbean Quarterly* 19 (September 1973): 9.

29. Barrett, "The Potrait of a Jamaican Healer," *Soul Force*, 9–10.

30. Seaga, "Revival Cults in Jamaica," 8. See Murphy, *Working the Spirit*, 126–27.

31. Seaga, "Revival Cults in Jamaica," 7, 10. See also Murphy, *Working the Spirit*, 127–29; Leonard Barrett, *The Sun and the Drum: African Roots in Jamaican Folk Tradition* (London: Heinemann, 1976), 57–58.

32. Seaga, "Revival Cults in Jamaica," 5, 6–7.

33. Chevannes, "Revivalism," 6. See also Chevannes, *Rastafari and Other Afro- Caribbean Worldviews*, 4. By smashing the coconut on the ground or against a wall or a brick, revivalists ward off unwelcome spirits.

34. Murphy, *Working the Spirit*, 127–128.

35. George Eaton Simpson, "Caribbean Religions: Afro-Caribbean Religions," in *The Encyclopedia of Religion*, vol. 3, ed. Mircea Eliade (New York: Simon and Schuster/ Macmillan, 1995), 95, 1956.

36. Murphy, *Working the Spirit*, 229; Simpson, "Jamaican Revivalist Cults," 371; Seaga, "Revival Cults in Jamaica," 9.

37. Seaga, "Revival Cults in Jamaica," 9–10.

38. Ibid., 3–4.

39. Ibid., 7. See Chevannes, *Rastafari: Roots and Ideology*, 24. Of course, Seaga contends that among Zionists, spirit possession is not very important because it often lasts no more than three hours at major revival functions ("Revival Cults in Jamaica," 12).

40. Murphy, *Working the Spirit*, 129. See also Simpson, "Jamaican Revivalist Cults," 375–376; Donald Hogg, "Jamaican Religions: A Study in Variations" (New Haven, Conn.: Unpublished PhD Dissertation in Anthropology, Yale University, 1964), 248.

41. Seaga, "Revival Cults in Jamaica," 7.

42. Ibid., 8. See also Barrett, "African Religion," 197–198.

43. Chevannes, *Rastafari: Roots and Ideology*, 32. In Obeah, "animate and inanimate objects take on sacred characters. For example, exudia such as hair or nail clippings can be used to hurt the owner and therefore are disposed of specially. . . ."

44. Chevannes, "Some Notes on African Survivals," 23. See also Chevannes, *Rastafari: Roots and Ideology*, 31.

45. Chevannes, *Rastafari: Roots and Ideology*, 32, 31. See also Chevannes, "Some Notes on African Survivals," 23.

46. Chevannes, *Rastafari and Other Worldviews*, 19; Simpson, "Caribbean Religions," 92.

47. George Eaton Simpson, *Black Religions in the New World* (New York: Colombia University Press, 1978), 102. For a proper citation from Hogg et al., see Simpson's endnotes: 133, 134, 135.

48. Donald Hogg, "The Convince Cult in Jamaica," Yale University Publication in Anthropology no. 58, in *Papers in Caribbean Anthropology*, comp. Sidney W. Minz (New Haven, Conn.: Department of Anthropology, Yale University, 1960), 3–24. See especially, p. 4. Cited in Raboteau, *Slave Religion*, 17.

49. Simpson, "Caribbean Religions," 93; also Simpson, *Black Religions*, 100, 291; Luntta, *Jamaica Handbook*, 47.

50. Simpson, "Caribbean Religions," 93. Also Simpson, *Black Religions*, 101; Raboteau, *Slave Religion*, 17; and Luntta, *Jamaica Handbook*, 47. See also Hogg, "The Convince Cult," 3–24.

51. Simpson, *Black Religions*, 101–102. Also Simpson, "Caribbean Religions," 93; Luntta, *Jamaica Handbook*, 47.

52. Raboteau, *Slave Religion*, 330. Raboteau cited Melville J. Herskovits and Frances Herskovits, *New World Negroes* (Bloomington, Ind.: Minerva Press, Funk and Wagnalls, 1969), 288.

53. Raboteau, *Slave Religion*, 303. See Hogg, "The Convince Cult"; also Hogg, "Jamaican Religions."

54. Don Robotham, "Development of Black Ethnicity in Jamaica," in *Garvey: His Work and Impact*, ed. Rupert Lewis and Patrick Bryan (Mona, Jamaica: Institute of Social and Economic Research, Extra Mural Studies, University of the West Indies, 1988), 35; Luntta, *Jamaica Handbook*, 46. See also, "Afro-Americans (Caribbean and South America)," in *HCDR*, 27.

55. Murphy, *Working the Spirit*, 123. See also Raboteau, *Slave Religion*, 28; Philip D. Curtin *Two Jamaicas* (Cambridge: Harvard University Press, 1955), 32–35; Martha W. Beckwith, *Black Roadways: A Study of Jamaican Folk Life* (Chapel Hill: University of North Carolina Press, 1929), 157–174; Edward Bean Underhill, *The West Indies: Their Social and Religious Condition* (London: n.p., 1862), 194–201.

56. Murphy, *Working the Spirit*, 123. See also Simpson, "Caribbean Religions," 95.

57. Curtin, *Two Jamaicas*, 30–38; Orlando Patterson, *The Sociology of Slavery: An Analysis of the Origins, Development and Structure of Negro Slave Society in Jamaica* (Teaneck, N.J.: Fairleigh Dickinson University Press, 1975), passim; Chevannes, *Rastafari: Roots and Ideology*, 20–33, 77–87; Chevannes, *Rastafari and Other Worldviews*, 22–26.

58. Chevannes, "Revivalism," 4.

59. Simpson, "Caribbean Religions," 95. See also Murphy, *Working the Spirit*, 124; Monica Schuler, "Myalism and the African Religious Tradition in Jamaica," in *Africa and the Caribbean: The Legacy of a Link*, ed. Margaret E. Crahan and Franklin W. Knight (Baltimore, Md.: Johns Hopkins University Press, 1979), 66, 68; Booth, Jr., *African Religions*, 196–197; William James Gardner, *A History of Jamaica from Its Discovery by Christopher Columbus to the Present Time* (London: E. Stock, 1873), 464.

60. Robotham, "Black Ethnicity," 36.

61. Chevannes, *Rastafari: Roots and Ideology*, 79–82, also 39.

62. Ibid., 39; Chevannes, "Some Notes on African Survivals," 25–26.

63. Murphy, *Working the Spirit*, 125.

64. Chevannes writes, "The most striking feature to me was the closeness of the service [of Rastafari] to Revivalism. In the middle of the proceedings stood a table covered with a white tablecloth. On it were open Bibles, a glass of water and a vase containing a single branch of the leaf of life. This plant, along with ganja, is believed by the Rastafari to be sacred because it was discovered on the grave of Solomon" ("Some Notes on African Survivals," 26).

CHAPTER 14

1. In the censuses of 1943, 1960, and 1970, Rastafarians are unclassified, and in the 1982 census they remain an undifferentiated number among the 629,130 noncommitted and 125,091 "other" respondents (1982 Population Census "Final Count" [Kingston: Statistical Institute of Jamaica], 2–4). See also Diane J. Austin-Bros, "Pentecostals and Rastafarians: Cultural, Political, and Gender Relations of Two Religious Movements," *Social and Economic Studies* 36, no. 4 (1987): 1–39.

2. "The Coronation of an Ethiopian Messiah," *New York Times* (November 3, 1930). See also Robert Hill, "Leonard P. Howell and Millenarian Visions in Early Rastafari," *Jamaica Journal* 16, no. 1 (February 1983): 33.

3. Newsreels and tabloids prominently featured Selassie's coronation in several issues, showing him in golden robes (Helene Lee, *The First Rasta, Leonard Howell and the Rise of Rastafarianism,* trans. Lily Davis [Chicago: Chicago Review Press, 1999]), 58.

4. Leonard E. Barrett, *The Rastafari: A Study of Messianic Cultism* (Rio Piedras, Puerto Rico: Institute of Caribbean Studies, University of Puerto Rico, 1968), 82; Lee, *The First Rasta,* 20–21; Clinton Hutton and Nathaniel Samuel Murrell, "Rastas' Psychology of Blackness, Resistance, and Somebodiness," in *Chanting Down Babylon: The Rastafari Reader,* ed. Nathaniel Samuel Murrell, William David Spencer, and Adrian Anthony McFarlane (Philadelphia: Temple University Press, 1998), 45, 67.

5. Jack A. Johnson-Hill, *I-Sight, The World of Rastafari: An Interpretive Sociological Account of Rastafarian Ethics* (Evanston, Ill.: American Theological Library Association and Scarecrow Press, 1995), 14–15; Hill, "Leonard P. Howell," 25–27.

6. Rupert Lewis states that by 1926 "there were fifty-two branches in Cuba; forty-seven in Panama; thirty in Trinidad; twenty-three in Costa Rica; Jamaica seven, Honduras eight, British Guyana seven," and many other countries with fewer than six (Rupert Lewis, *Marcus Garvey, Anti-Colonial Champion* (Trenton, N.J.: Africa World Press, 1992), 99. Barbara Makeda Lee's "eleven million" members is a huge exaggeration (Barbara Makeda Lee, *Rastafari: The New Creation* [Red Hills, Kingston: Jamaica Media Productions, 1981], 8).

7. E. D. Cronon, *Black Moses—The Story of Marcus Garvey and the Universal Negro Improvement Association* (Madison: University of Wisconsin Press, 1955), 13–16; Judith Stein, "The Ideology and Practice of Garveyism," in *Garvey: His Work and Impact,* ed. Rupert Lewis and Patrick Ryan (Mona, Jamaica: Institute of Social and Economic Research and Department of Extra-Mural Studies, University of the West Indies, 1988), 203.

8. Lewis, *Marcus Garvey,* 51; Barry Chevannes, *Rastafari and Other African-Caribbean Worldviews* (New Brunswick, N.J.: Rutgers University Press, 1995), 9–10.

9. Rupert Lewis, "Marcus Garvey and the Early Rastafarians: Continuity and Discontinuity," in *Chanting Down Babylon,* 146, 148; Robert Hill, *Marcus Garvey and the Universal Negro Improvement Association Papers, Vol. 7 November 1927–August 1940* (Berkeley and Los Angeles: University of California Press, 1990), 440–441; Cronon, *Black Moses,*

16–20; Lee, *The First Rasta*, 29–30. Garvey withdrew his endorsement of the emperor after learning of the suffering of the Ethiopian people under Selassie's administration.

10. Lee, *The First Rasta*, 21, 51, 56–57; Horton and Murrell, "Rastas' Psychology of Blackness," 44–45; Lewis, "Marcus Garvey and the Early Rastafarians," 149; Obiagele Lake, *Rastafari Women, Subordination in the Midst of Liberation Theology* (Durham, N.C.: Carolina Academic Press, 1998), 33–34.

11. Lee, *The First Rasta*, 21; Lake, *Rastafari Women*, 34. Hibbert lived a full life, dying on September 18, 1986, at the age of ninety-three (Frank Jan van Dijk, *Jahmaica: Rastafari and Jamaican Society 1930–90* [Utrecht, The Netherlands: ISOR and the Netherlands Foundation for the Advancement of Tropical Research, 1993], 192).

12. Garveyites saw Howell as a con artist and thought he was an Obeah-man because of his pharmacopeia (Lee, *The First Rasta*, 32–33; Barry Chevannes, *Rastafari: Roots and Ideology* [N.Y.: Syracuse University Press, 1994], 121). Thanks to Helene Lee's groundbreaking biography, much is known now about the shadowy history and mysterious character of Leonard Howell. He was only fourteen in 1912 and was in Panama in 1914; yet he claims he assisted Garvey in establishing a branch of the UNIA in Kingston in 1914.

13. *Daily Gleaner* (November 23, 1940); Barrett, *The Rastafarians*, 82, 85–86; Chevannes, *Rastafari and Other Worldviews*, 11; Ennis Barrington Edmonds, *Rastafari: From Outcast to Culture Bearers* (New York: Oxford University Press, 2003), 36; Lake, *Rastafari Women*, 34; Ivor Morrish, *Obeah, Christ, and Rastaman: Jamaica and Its Religions* (Cambridge, U.K.: James Clarke), 69. Helene Lee states that Howell's mystical tone and interest in the Bible had greater mesmeric power in Jamaica than it did in Harlem and that he was not concerned that others would regard him as a charlatan (Lee, *The First Rasta*, 19, 47).

14. Hutton and Murrell, "Rastas Psychology of Blackness," 38; Hill, "Leonard P. Howell," 32–33. Howell saw this as a fulfillment of his prophecy, which added to his belief that he himself was a religious prophet (Hill, "Leonard P. Howell," 5, 33, 36).

15. The Ethiopian World Federation, founded in New York in 1937 and in Michigan and Jamaica in 1938 to organize Africans of the diaspora in support of the resistance, became an avenue for Rastafari preaching, but when the Rastafari message became militant, the federation distanced itself from the group.

16. Barrett, *The Rastafarians*, 85–89; Lee, *The First Rasta*, 2, 4–5; Edmonds, *Rastafari*, 39; Morrish, *Obeah, Christ and Rastaman*, 70–71. This self-sustaining Rastafarian community sold surplus produce to some Jamaican institutions (Chevannes, *Rastafari: Roots and Ideology*, 121–24).

17. Ajai Mansingh and Laxmi Mansingh state, "It must have been in recognition of his Hindu heritage that Howell named himself Ganganguru Maharaj (Lord of the Universe) in 1940." Ajai Mansingh and Laxmi Mansingh, "Hindu Influences on Rastafarianism," in *Caribbean Quarterly Monograph: Rastafari*, ed. Rex Nettleford (Kingston, Jamaica: Caribbean Quarterly, University of the West Indies, 1985), 111; Lake, *Rastafari Women*, 60.

18. Edmonds, *Rastafari*, 39; Makeda Lee, *Rastafari*, 18; Hill, "Leonard P. Howell," 36; Chevannes, *Rastafari: Roots and Ideology*," 122; Sheila Kitzinger, "The Rastafarian Brethren of Jamaica," in *Peoples and Cultures*, ed. Michael M. Horowitz (New York: Natural History Press, 1971), 580; William David Spencer, "The First Chant: Leonard Howell's *The Promised Key*," in *Chanting Down Babylon*, 361–362.

19. Makeda Lee, *Rastafari*, 19; Lake, *Rastafari Women*, 35; Barrett, *The Rastafarians*, 86–87.

20. Katrin Norris, *Jamaica: The Search for an Identity* (London: Institute of Race Relations, Oxford University Press, 1962), 98–99; Barry Chevannes, "Rastafari and the Exorcism of Racism and Classism," in *Chanting Down Babylon*, 60–62.

21. Randal L. Hepner, "The House That Rasta Built: Church-Building and Fundamentalism among New York Rastafarians," in *Gatherings in Diaspora: Religious Communities and the New Immigration*, ed. R. Stephen Warner and Judith G. Wittner (Philadelphia: Temple University Press, 1998), 198, 200; Edmonds, *Rastafari*, 59; Barry Chevannes, "Era of Dreadlocks" (Boston: Unpublished paper given at The American Academy of Religion, November 1999), 15; Theodore Malloch, "Rastafarianism: A Radical Caribbean Movement/Religion," *Center Journal* 3, no. 4 (Fall 1985): 74.

22. Lake, *Rastafari Women*, 44–45; Barry Chevannes, "Repairer of the Breach: Reverend Claudius Henry and Jamaican Society," in *Ethnicity in the Americas*, ed. Frances Henry (The Hague: Mouton, 1976), 263–269; Morrish, *Obeah, Christ and Rastaman*, 72–73. Ready to use were 3,800 detonators, a shotgun, a revolver, several sticks of dynamite, a large quantity of machetes sharpened on both sides, and other weapons (Chevannes, *Rastafari: Roots and Ideology*, 116–117; Lee, *Rastafari*, 20).

23. Murrell, Spencer, and McFarlane, *Chanting Down Babylon*, 8; Chevannes, "Rastafari and the Exorcism Racism," 62–63; Leonard E. Barrett, *Soul-Force: African Heritage in Afro-American Religion* (Gardon City, N.Y.: Anchor Books, 1974), 166, 169; Chevannes, *Rastafari and Other Worldviews*, 13; Lewis, "Marcus Garvey and the Early Rastafarians," 152; Roger Steffens, "Bob Marley: Rasta Warrior," in *Chanting Down Babylon*, 256; Morrish, *Obeah, Christ and Rastaman*, 75–76.

24. Morrish, *Obeah, Christ and Rastaman*, 77–80. Veteran activist and orator Ras Sam Brown ran for the Rasta heartland (a west Kingston seat) on the Black Man's Party ticket.

25. Joseph Hepner, "Chanting Down Babylon in the Belly of the Beast: The Rastafarian Movement in the Metropolitan United States," in *Chanting Down Babylon*, 201–204. Also Ernest Cashmore, *Rastaman: The Rastafarian Movement in England* (London: George Allen and Unwin, 1979/1983), 173–74.

26. Richard C. Slater, "Shooting Dreads on Sight: Violence, Persecution, Millennialism, and Dominica's Dread Act," in *Millennialism, Persecution, and Violence, Historical Cases*, ed. Catherine Wessinger (Syracuse, N.Y.: Syracuse University Press, 2000), 104.

27. Joseph Owens, *Dread: The Rastafarians of Jamaica* (Kingston, Jamaica: Sangster's Book Store, 1976), passim; Michael N. Jagessar, "JPIC and Rastafarians," *One World* 2 (February 1991): 15–16; Claudia Rogers, "What Is Rasta?" *Caribbean Review* 7, no. 1 (January–March 1978): 8–10; Nathaniel Samuel Murrell, "The Rastafari Phenomenon," in *Chanting Down Babylon*, 5–6; Edmonds, *Rastafari*, 72; Carol Yawney, "Lions of Babylon: The Rastafarians of Jamaica as a Visionary Movement" (Montreal, Canada: PhD Dissertation, McGill University, 1978), 258–260.

28. Chevannes, *Rastafari and Other Worldviews*, 28; Rex Nettleford, "Discourse on Rastafarian Reality," in *Chanting Down Babylon*, 315, 318.

29. Dianne M. Stewart, *Three Eyes for the Journey: African Dimensions of the Jamaican Religious Experience* (New York: Oxford University Press, 2005), 24–26, 131–133.

30. Abuna Yesehaq, *Ethiopian Tewahedo Church* (Nashville, Tenn.: James C. Winston Publishing, 1989/1997), 225.

31. Clinton Chisholm, "The Rasta-Selassie Ethiopian Connections," in *Murrell, Chanting Down Babylon*, 173–74.

32. His Imperial Majesty, Haile Selassie I, "Building an Enduring Tower," in *World Congress on Evangelism, vol. 1, Berlin 1966*, ed. Carl F. H. Henry and S. Mooneyham (Minneapolis, Minn.: World Wide Publications, 1967), 19–21.

33. Selassie became Emperor through the legacy of his father, Makonnen, who, with his cousin Menelik II, was assigned by Emperor Yohannes to defeat Muslim leader Abdulah Bim Adul Berk and bring the city of Harar under Christian control. When Menelik II became emperor, the two men decisively defeated Italian invaders at the Battle of Adwa in 1896 (Chisholm, "Rasta-Selassie Ethiopian Connection," 166–167, 173–175).

34. An Ethiopian myth claims that "the Queen was received by Azarias, the son of Zadok, the high priest, and by a large company of priest and noblemen. They wore robes embroidered in gold and belts of gold about their loins, around their necks chains of gold and golden crowns upon their heads" (Yesehaq, *Ethiopian Tewahedo Church*, 6, 14).

35. Yesehaq, *Ethiopian Tewahedo Church*, 19; also 6, 5–8, 15; Sylvia Pankhurst, *Ethiopia: A Cultural History* (Essex, U.K.: Lalibela House, 1955), 19. The *Kebra Nagast* is a document compiled in the early fourteenth century C.E. and designed to prove both that Ethiopian kings descended from the biblical Solomon and that the Hebrew Ark of the Covenant was transferred to Ethiopia by Menelik I.

36. Hutton and Murrell, "Rastas' Psychology of Blackness," 38–39, 40–41; Edmonds, *Rastafari*, 34; Jah Bones, *One Love: Rastafari History, Doctrine, and Livity* (London: Voice of Rastafari, 1985). The Greek translation of the Hebrew Bible replaced the words *Kush* and *Kushites* with *Ethiopia*, which came to represent all black peoples of Africa.

37. Jack A. Johnson-Hill, "Rastafari as a Resource for Social Ethics in South Africa," *Journal for the Study of Religion* 9, no. 1 (March 1996): 3, 9, 17.

38. Barrett, *The Rastafarians*, 228; van Dijk, *Jahmaica*, 189, 211; Morrish, *Obeah, Christ and Rastaman*, 72.

39. Chevannes, *Rastafari and Other Worldviews*, 30–31. These distressed outcasts of society have a different view of history and community from that of the ruling class.

40. The Rastafarian ideology "combines resistance against oppression with an underlying love for the freedom and emancipation of Africa and African peoples" (Horace Campbell, *Rasta and Resistance: From Marcus Garvey to Walter Rodney* [Trenton, N.J.: Africa World Press, 1987], 19; Chevannes, "The Exorcism of Racism and Classicism," 67).

41. John Paul Homiak, "The 'Ancient of Days' Seated Black: Eldership, Oral Tradition and Ritual in Rastafari Culture" (Waltham, Mass.: PhD Dissertation, Brandeis University, 1985), 510; Edmonds, *Rastafari*, 42–49; Ennis Barrington Edmonds, "Dread 'I' In-a-Babylon: Ideological Resistance and Cultural Revitalization," in *Chanting Down Babylon*, 24–26.

42. Dennis Forsythe, *Rastafari: For the Healing of the Nation* (Kingston, Jamaica: Zaika Publications, 1983), 96. Some Rastas include all of Christianity in the damnable metaphor of Babylon.

43. Maureen Rowe, "Gender and Family Relations in Rastafari," in *Chanting Down Babylon*, 74. Note that Marley's names are given in reverse order in pop culture.

44. Frank Jan van Dijk, "The Twelve Tribes of Israel: Rasta and the Middle Class," *New West Indian Guide* 62, nos. 1–2 (1988): 1–26; Hepner, "The House That Rasta Built," 202; Barrett, *The Rastafarians*, 1977.

45. J. Richard Middleton, "Identity and Subversion in Babylon: Strategies for 'Resisting Against the System' in the Music of Bob Marley and the Wailers," in *Religion, Culture and Tradition in the Caribbean*, ed. Hemchand Gossai and Nathaniel Samuel Murrell (New York: St. Martin's Press, 2000), 186–88.

46. Alex Constantine, "Chanting Down Babylon: The CIA and The Death of Bob Marley," in *High Times, Global Harvest Report*, no. 318 (New York: Trans-corporation, February 2002), 46–50.

47. Ibid., 176.

48. Imani J. Tafari-Ama, "Rastawoman as Rebel: Case Studies in Jamaica," in *Chanting Down Babylon*, 90-91.

49. Lake, *Rastafari Women*, 4; Rowe, "Gender and Family," 74. A promiscuous Marley bragged in an interview that he wanted all of the queens for himself (re-aired on National Public Radio with Ziggy Marley, February, 2006).

50. Chevannes, *Rastafari and Other Worldviews*, 25; Warren d'Azevedo, "Gola Womanhood and the Limits of Masculine Omnipotence," in *Religion in Africa: Experience and Expression*, ed. Thomas D. Blakely, Walter E. A. van Beek and Dennis L. Thompson (Portsmouth, N.H.: Heinemann, 1994), 343–362; Simon Ottenberg, "Male and Female Secret Societies among the Bafodea Limba of Northern Sierra Leone," in *Religion in Africa*, 363–387.

51. Maureen Rowe, "The Women in Rastafari," in *Caribbean Quarterly Monograph*, 13–21; Tafari-Ama," Rastawoman as Rebel," 89–105; Lake, *Rastafari Women*, passim; Lauretta Collins, "Daughters of Jah: The Impact of Rastafarian Womanhood in the Caribbean, the United States, Britain, and Canada," in *Religion, Culture and Tradition in the Caribbean*, 227–255.

52. Rowe, "Gender and Family Relations in Rastafari," 72-88; Lake, *Rastafari Women*, passim; Lauretta Collins, "Daughters of Jah: The Impact of Rastafarian Womanhood in the Caribbean, the United States, Britain, and Canada," in *Religion, Culture and Tradition*, ed. Hemchand Gossai and Nathaniel Murrell (New York: St. Martin's Press, 2000), 227–255; Tafari-Ama, "Rastawoman as Rebel," 90–97.

53. Makeda Lee, *Rastafari*, 25. See also Chevannes, *Rastafari and Other Worldviews*, 83; Chevannes, *Rastafari: Roots and Ideology*, 110.

54. These are comparable to the Twelve Tribes of Goodlands, Barbados; Bobo Shanti Tabernacle in Warf Trace, Trinidad; and House of Nyabinghi in Dominica. These houses are classified as "churchical" and "statical." Churchical Rastas practice Judeo-Christian forms of rituals, engage in theological discourse, and promote African culture. Statical houses are politically inclined and committed to working for social change.

55. Eldership is inspirational rather than structural as understood in organized religions (Barrett, *The Rastafarians*, 1997); see Margaret Fernandez Olmos and Lizabeth Paravisini-Gebert, *Creole Religions* (New York: New York University Press, 2003), 167. At a meeting I attended in 1998, a leader brought greetings and reported on his representation of Barbados at a Caribbean Rasta meeting in Jamaica.

56. See Chevannes, *Rastafari and Other Worldviews*, 98–101; Tafari-Ama, "Rastawoman as Rebel," 106. The Bobo Shanti Tabernacle at Warf Trace, St. Joseph, Trinidad, close to where I lived from 1980 to 1983, also adopted this practice. Pious Bobos offer prayers to Jah while entering and exiting gates of the commune; they pray facing Africa, at 6:00 A.M. and noon, to the accompaniment of rhythmic drumming.

57. Chevannes, *Rastafari and Other Worldviews*, 16; Chevannes, *Rastafari: Roots and Ideology*, 158, 172–174, 177–178; Lee, *The First Rasta*, 285; Tafari-Ama, "Rastawoman as Rebel," 92, also endnotes: 106.

58. van Dijk, *Jahmaica*, 325; Chevannes, *Rastafari: Roots and Ideology*, 179; "Rastafari Centralization Organization," *Dreadful Lion* 2, no. 1 (Spring 2000), 8.

59. Frederico Philos, "Nya-Binghi and Selassie," *Jamaica Times* (December 7, 1935); Chevannes, *Rastafari: Roots and Ideology*, 43; K. W. Post, "The Bible as Ideology: Ethiopianism in Jamaica, 1930–38," in *African Perspectives*, ed. C. H. Allen and R. N. Johnson (Cambridge: Cambridge University Press, 1970); Lee, *The First Rasta*, 91.

60. The report held that the secret order included Nambi Azikwe of Nigeria, Jomo Kenyatta of Kenya, Marcus Garvey, and Haile Selassie. For obvious reasons, Rastas

support Philos's claim and delight in exaggerating the strength and influence of the secret order.

61. Verena Reckford, "Rastafarian Music: An Introductory Study," *Jamaica Journal* 11, nos. 1–2 (1977): 9; Homiak, "'Ancient of Days,'" 361; Edmonds, *Rastafari*, 70.

62. Jah Ahkell, *Rasta: Emperor Haile Selassie I and the Rastafarians* (Chicago: Frontline Distribution, 1999), 10–11. Published in Barrett, *The Rastafarians*, 126.

63. Barrett, *The Rastafarians*, 231; van Dijk, "The Twelve Tribes of Israel," 1–2, 10.

64. Barrett, *The Rastafarians*, 228–229. As Chevannes points out, not all middle-class Rasta identify as Twelve Tribes, and there was no large-scale movement among the Jamaican middle-class to become Rastafarian (Chevannes, "Rastafari and the Exorcism of Racism," 67).

65. These trademarks appear on Rastas' art work, accessories, business places, clothing, vehicles, foods, homes, publications, and places of worship or "issembly" (Edmonds, *Rastafari*, 56).

66. Simpson said dreadlocks were not a common feature of the movement when he did research in Jamaica in the early 1950s (George Eaton Simpson, "Personal Reflections on Rastafari," in *Chanting Down Babylon*, 218).

67. Mansingh and Mansingh, "Hindu Influences on Rastafarianism," 109. Campbell, *Rasta and Resistance*, 96–97; M. G. Smith, Roy Augier and Rex Nettleford, "Report on the Rastafari Movement in Kingston, Jamaica" (Kingston, Jamaica: Institute of Social and Economic Research, University of the West Indies Extra Mural Studies, 1960), 9; Ahkell, *Rasta*, 25.

68. In Africa, traditional religious practitioners, especially healers, fold their hair in locks representing the dreadlocks worn by warriors before 600 C.E. or in pre-Islamic times. In the eastern Caribbean, dreadlocks became public in the early 1970s among middle- and lower-class Rastas and disaffected youths.

69. Adrian Anthony McFarlane, "Epistemological Significance of I-an-I," in *Chanting Down Babylon*, 115. See also Dennis Forsythe, "West Indian Culture through the Prism of Rastafarianism," in *Caribbean Quarterly Monograph*, 73; Edmonds, *Rastafari*, 56–58; Austin-Bros, "Pentecostals and Rastafarians," 20.

70. Chevannes, *Rastafari: Roots and Ideology*, 145; Chevannes, *Rastafari and Other Worldviews*, 98–101. Of course, Rastas with shorter hair often sew it into an unnatural hair-like wig to give the locks a thick, rough, woolen appearance.

71. Carole D. Yawney, "Strictly Ital: Rastafari Livity and Holistic Health" (Hertfordshire, Canada: Unpublished paper prepared for the ninth annual meeting of the Society for Caribbean Studies, July 2–4, 1985), 1–3; Leonard Barrett, *The Sun and the Drum: African Roots in Jamaican Folk Tradition* (London: Heinemann, 1976), 68–71.

72. Kenneth Bilby, "Holy Herb: Notes on the Background of Cannabis in Jamaica," in *Caribbean Quarterly Monograph*, 82–83, 84–85; Neil J. Savishinsky, "African Dimensions of the Jamaican Rastafarian Movement," in *Chanting Down Babylon*, 131.

73. Yawney, "Strictly Ital," 3; Chevannes says Rastas' making "a brew made by steeping the green matter in white rum and leaving the mixture buried in the earth for nine days, is thought to make an excellent tonic. Similar techniques are used with other herbs, barks, and roots" (*Rastafari: Roots and Ideology*, 31).

74. Simpson, "Personal Reflections on Rastafari," 218.

75. Chevannes, *Rastafari: Roots and Ideology*, 157. See also Yawney, "Strictly Ital," 3; Barry Chevannes, "Background to Drug Use in Jamaica, a Working Paper of the Institute for Social and Economic Research, University of the West Indies" (Mona, Jamaica: 1988), 7; Edmonds, *Rastafari*, 74, 156; Bilby, "The Holy Herb," 87; *Kebra Nagast*, 61.

76. Chevannes, *Rastafari: Roots and Ideology*, 164–165; Savishinsky, "African Dimensions," 129.

77. Savishinsky, "African Dimensions," 127.

78. The women sang and danced but did not lead songs or chants. In the Barbados camp, every time a sistren began humming a chant as if to lead it, a brethren took it over or stepped up the tempo and volume on a different tune and drowned out her voice.

79. Edmonds, *Rastafari*, 74–76. See also Homiak, "'Ancient of Days,'" 512.

80. Lake, *Rastafari Women*, 66–67; Ryszard Kapuscinski, *The Emperor* (New York: Harcourt-Brace-Jovanovich, 1983), 12, 15; Leonard Mosley, *Haile Selassie: The Conquering Lion* (Englewood Cliffs, N.J.: Prentice-Hall, 1964).

CONCLUSION

1. J. Lorand Matory, *Black Atlantic Religion, Tradition, Transnationalism, and Matriarchy in the Afro-Brazilian Candomble* (Princeton, N.J.: Princeton University Press, 2005), 1.

2. Patrick Bellegarde-Smith, ed., *Fragments of Bone: Neo-African Religions in a New World* (Chicago: University of Illinois Press, 2005), 124–142.

3. Anthony B. Pinn, *Varieties of African American Religious Experience* (Minneapolis, Minn.: Fortress Press, 1998).

Glossary

Abipa: An Alaafin, or king, of the Oyo

Abomey: A town in Benin, formerly the capital of the ancient kingdom of Dahomey

Abrigacaco: A Candomble dance ritual/style

Abuna Fox's Church of Haile Selassie: Rastafarian mansion (church) in Jamaica

Afonso: An orisha in Trinidad

Aganju: The orisha of volcanos and deserts in Yoruba mythology

Agaou: Vodou lwa

Agwe: A Vodou lwa who rules marine life and is patron of fishermen and sailors

Ahijados: Members of a Santeria ile or temple, called godchildren

Aiye/amoraiye: Yoruba earth with its animal life; also, people who perform witchcraft

Ajaka: An Oyo king

Ajeppo: Magic that enables someone to vomit ingested poison

Ajera/ogun awon agba, ataja, ajeppo, awure, iferan, awijare: Different types of African magic that can heal, render poison harmless, cause illness, or protect against evil

Ajiaco: A mix of cultures as rich and varied ingredients in a soup

Ajogun: African supernatural powers who sit on God's left side

Akete: A Jamaican drum used both in Rastafari and Kumina

Akom: A creole term that some scholars use to trace the origin of Kumina

Akposso: An ethnic group living in the Plateau region of southern Togo

Akwamu: A state set up by the Akan people in Ghana

Akwamufie: A city in Ghana

Allada/Alladah: A town in Benin from which the word *Arada* comes

Alreelay/Elreelay: One of the orishas in Trinidad and Cuba

Alufa: One of the orishas

Amala: A West African meal

Anaforuana: Secret signs used by the Abakua society to make a sport sacred

Anagogogoo/Nesufoowea/Tegetege: Ethnic groups associated with Vodou in Benin

Angana-Nzambi: The name for God in Kongo

Angola Cycle: The period in the slave trade when most victims were taken from Angola

Anokye: An Ashanti priest, statesman, and lawgiver

Apele: Sacred palm nuts used in Santeria pharmacopeia

Apoti: A sacred Santeria stool

Ara Arun: A term used in the Yoruba for the earth??

Arada: The place in Benin where the Vodou lwa called Rada originated

Arawak: Amerindians encountered by the Spanish on the larger West Indian islands

Archipelago: A chain or cluster of islands

Asaman/Asamanfo: Akan ancestors

Asase Yaa: The earth goddess of fertility in Ashanti mythology

Ashe: A spiritual force of the orisha in Santeria

Asiento: An initiation in Santeria; also, the right to trade in slavery in Spanish America

Asogwe: A character of the Haitian lwas

Ason: The rattle as symbol of authority; used by the priests in Vodou ceremonies

Asuman/asaman: Personalized spirits (asaman are ancestral spirits)

Ataja: Magic that helps sales

Atibon Legba: One of the characters of the lwa Legba in Vodou

Atuot: An ethnic group from the Sudan

Awijare: Magic that enables one to win a case

Aworos/Babalawos: Professional priests connected mainly to the orisha cultus

Awure: Magic that effects good luck

Axe de Opo Afonja: A Candomble temple

Axis mundi: A ubiquitous symbol that crosses human cultures, referring to a point of connection between sky and earth where the four compass directions meet

Axogun: A person in Candomble who slaughters the sacrificial animal

Ayida Wedo: A character of the lwas in Vodou

Ayizan: A character of the lwas in Vodou

Azaka: A family of Loa in Haitian mythology

Baba olorisha: Male Santeria priests

Babalawo/Babaloricha/babalosha/Babaluaiye/Babalu-Aye/Bablorixa: Male and female Santeria priests

Babylon society: The Rastafarian term for oppressive society

Bafonda Limba/Gola/Sande Bundu/Wara Wara: Ethnic groups in northern Sierra Leone

Bahia: A large city in Brazil that was the biggest slave depot in the world

Bakas/bakos: An evil spiritual force or work performed by priests of a negative nature

Bakongo: A language and a people in the Kongo

Balm-yard: The term used by Rastafarians for the practice of making herbal medicines

Bambuti Pygmy: A large tribal group in Africa

Bands messenger: A spiritual role in the Poco and Zion religions in Jamaica

Bantu: A linguistic group of people throughout central Africa

Baptist-Kuminist: People in Jamaica who are in the Baptist tradition but who practice Kumina

Baron Ravage: A Vodou lwa that represents the anger of the Haitian people

Baron Samedi/Bawon Lakwa/Bawon Samdi/Bawon Simityé: Feared Petro lwa characters or impersonation in Vodou

Barracon: A character among the Vodou lwa

Bataa: A special type of drum that provides the rhythms in some Santeria ceremonies

Batammaliba/Gar-speaking peoples: Linguistic groups in Togo and Benin

Batuques/Autabaque: African religious practices used by priests in Brazil

Bedwardism: Beliefs of the prophet Alexander Bedward of Jamaica (late 1800s)

Bembes tambors/ fiestas de Santos: The most popular Santeria feast, which often follows an initiation ceremony

Big Massa: A Jamaican term for slave master

Bilongos: Magical healing power or force in Santeria pharmacopeia

Bois-Caiman: A port city in Haiti

Bokomo: A system of divination that allows individuals to know their decreed destiny

Bokor: A spirit and magical acts regarded as harmful in Haitian mythology

Bona fide Macumba: A genuine African religious practice in Macumba in Brazil

Bondye: The supreme high god in Vodou who governs and orders the universe

Bongo/Bongoman/Bungo: A religious leader in the Jamaican Kumina and Myal

Bonko enchemiya/empego/tambor de orden: A type of drum in Palo Monte

Bori: A primary initiation ritual in Candomble

Bosal: A novice initiate in Vodou

Boule zen: A death ritual associated with Vodou (translates as "burning of the jar")

Brujo: A folk magician in Afro-Caribbean religion

Burru: An African musical genre that gave birth to reggae

Cabildos/Cofradias/Irmandades: Catholic Brotherhoods in Colonial Cuba, Puerto Rico, and Brazil

Cabinda: A province in Angola

Caboclo/Pretos Velhos/Caboclo Velho: Creole religious traditions in Brazil

Cachaca: Rum brewed by native tribes in Brazil

Cafiotos: An initiate in Macumba

Calabar: A place and an ethnic group in Cameroon

Calalue/ Calaloo: A Caribbean vegetable dish

Camarinha: A room or chamber in a Candomble terreiro or temple

Cannabis: Another name for ganja, said to be of East Indian origin

Capuchin: Catholic missionaries from Spain and Portugal

Caquis: A witch doctor of Native people

Carabalis: A Cuban group, associated with the Abakwa, which came out of Kongo and the Yoruba

Cariacariapemba: An African religious practice in Brazil

Casa de santo: A spiritual house in Santeria

Case kanari: A Haitian death ritual or practice

Catholic Irmandades: Fraternities or brotherhoods in Colonial Brazil

Catimbo: An African religious group in Brazil

Catimozeiros: Practitioners of Catimbo

Ceiba pentandra: A tree used in Afro-Caribbean pharmacopeia

Cemarons: A pejorative Spanish term for runaway slaves

Centros: The center of the religious activity in Santeria

Chac-chacs: Rattles used as a musical instrument in the Caribbean

Challis/Chillum pipe: The ritual pipe smoked by Rastas

Chapelle: A part of a spiritual house in Trinidad Orisha

Chief de section: A rural chief in President Boya's Haiti (1820s), who collected taxes and fees

Chimbundu/Chumundu: A town and a people in Zambia

Chretiens-vivants: Living humans in Vodou who are said to forget their ancestral spirits

Ciboney: Pre-Colombian natives of Greater Antilles

City of Zion: A euphemistic holy city in the Afro-Jamaican Zion religion

Code Noir: The Black Code regulating slave life in colonial Haiti

Cofa de orunla/ mono de orunla: Symbolic elements conferred on female and male initiates in Santeria

Collares: Santeria's sacred emblems of the orisha, given to initiates

Communotheism: A term used to define the relationship of divinities in African traditional religions

Conjunto Folklorico: The folklorized African religions in the Cuba

Consulata: The act of doing spiritual consultation in Candomble

Coptic Theocratic Temple: A Rastafarian religious group in Jamaica

Corpus Christi: An event in the Catholic Church year dealing with the death of Christ

Corvée: Unpaid labor or volunteers in Afro-Caribbean religion

Cotillion: A French-Caribbean dance

Count Ossi's Mystic Revelations: A musical band that influenced Reggae music

Creole/Criollo-religio: The Caribbeanizing of African religion or culture

Criollos: Caribbean-Spanish-born slaves

Cronyism: Showing favors to political supporters

Cuanaldo: A Santeria priest who is conferred the babalawo's sacrificial knife

Da/Danbira: An African ethnic group

Dambada Hwedo/ Dambala: A personification of a Vodou lwa

Dawtas: A Jamaican term for women in Rastafari

Dechoukaj: Political upheaval in Haiti, especially under Duvalier

Dedee Bazile: A Haitian girl who was folklorized for her bravery

Deka: A spiritual endowment received by initiates in Candomble

Denkyiras: A West African tribal group from the Denka people

Despojos: A Santeria herbal bath

Dessounen: A Haitian ritual associated with death and burial to separate the spirit from the body

Deus obsconditus: A hidden or absent god

Dhomey Kongo: One of the Vodou nations

Dilogun (dilloggun): The Santeria practice to determine an initiate's new name and destiny

Dinka: A large tribal group in West Africa

Djouba: One of the Vodou nations

Duppy: A ghost that is believed to walk at night

East African Galla: An African pharmacopeia

Ebbos: An ethnic group in West Africa

Ebge Orisha Ile Wa: A Trinidad and Tobago Orisha spiritual community or church

Ebo: A sacrificial offering (and feast) in Santeria dealing with purification

Ebomin: A senior initiate in Candomble

Eclecticism: A pulling together from different cultural traditions

Edo Olokun: An ethnic group in Benin

Efik/Efor/Efut: Cuban ethnic groups from the Niger Delta and Central Nigeria

Egungun: A festival that honors the ancestors in Yorubaland

Ejagham/Ekoi/Ekpe: Ethnic groups from Calabar (in Cameroon) living in Cuba

Eka-Abassi: The mother-deity of the Ibibio people

Ekuenon: A type of drum used by people performing animal sacrifice in Palo Monte

El dia de la coronacion: The coronation or crowning of the deities in Santeria

Eledaa/Elefon/Elemii: Orishas in Santeria

Elegba/Elegbara/Eleggua/Eshu/Esu: A Vodou lwa
Elekes: A beaded necklace received after a Santeria initiation
Ellegua: A Santeria orisha
Elofa (Aba Lofa): A patron of the chief Orisha/Shango leader in Trinidad and Tobago
Eloogun: Medicine men in the Yoruba religion
Emanjie: One of the spirits in the Orisha religion
Embandas/Cabones/Umbandas: Titles of priests in Macumba
Encomiendas: The precursor to the Caribbean plantation in Spanish America
Engenho Velho: One of the first Candomble houses in Brazil
Enkrikamo: A drum used in Palo Monte to summon spirits of the dead
Entombment: A burial rite in Afro-Caribbean religion
Envizib, sint/les misté: "Invisible" or lwa spirits in Vodou
Erinle: A divinity in the Orisha religion
Espiritismo /Kardecismo: A creole religion in Brazil and Puerto Rico
Ewe-Fon-Dahomey: Large ethnic groups of peoples in West Africa
Ewes: Substances used in Santeria pharmacopeia
Exu: A spirit lwa in Vodou
Ezili Danto/Ezili Freda/je-Rouge/je-wouj/Lasyrenn/Ezili Kawoulo (African):
The lwa of womanhood and motherhood, sensuality, and eroticism in Vodou

Falashas: Ethiopian Jews, some of whom were lifted to Israel in the 1980s
Fanti-Ashanti: A large ethnic group in Ghana
Fiestas de Santos: A Santeria feast
Filhas/filhos: Spiritual sons and daughters of a Candomble house
Firmas: Magical symbols in Palo Monte
French Kardecism: A spiritualist movement that began in France
Fu-fu: A West African dish made out of ground vegetables
Fulas/Fulbe: Muslim ethnic groups in West Africa
Fundamentos: The basic initiation rite in Santeria
Funde/fundeh: A Rastafarian drum

Ga/Gar: A people group in West Africa
Gantois: A spiritual house in Brazilian Candomble
Gbo: Magical charms
Gede: One of the Vodou nations and a lwa
Ginal: A Jamaican con artist
Ginen: A Vodou nation, an abode of the spirits, and a mythological symbol of Africa
Giras: A dance in Umbanda
Glossolalia: Speaking in a foreign language under spirit possession
Gong/Gangunguru Maragh: Names that Rastafari founder Leonard Howell gave himself
Grand Mét/Grand Pére Eternal: Names for God the Creator in Vodou
Guerreros: Spiritual guards in the Santeria religion, received through initiation
Gumbay: An Afro-creole tradition of Kongo origin associated with Abakua in Cuba and Jonkonnu/Jonkunu (John canoe) in Jamaica
Guyanese Hindu Kali Mai Pujah: A creole religious practice in Guyana
Gwo bon-anj: The big spirit, which is a shadow-corps or double of the material body in Vodou

Hausa: A large ethnic Muslim group in West Africa
Haussement: A Vodou initiatory ritual or a Vodou ritual leading to the priesthood

Hijo de Ellegua/hijo de orisha: Spiritual children of a Santeria orisha
Holy Piby: An esoteric booklet published by Leonard Howell, a founder of Rastafari

Ia agan: A woman allowed to be in physical contact with the engungun that perform at annual festivals
Ialorixas: A female priest in Candomble
I-an-I consciousness: Rastafarian self-definition and philosophy
Iao/ Iyawoa: An initiate in Santeria
Ibibio: An ethnic group from Nigeria
Ifa: A deity and cosmological system of divination in the Yoruba religion
Ifa-Orunmila: The orisha divinity of wisdom in Santeria
Iferan: Magic that makes everyone love one another
Igbo: A West African ethnic group
Ijo: Intermediary slave traders between Europeans and Africans
Ile igbodu: A sacred room in which initiation rituals are performed in a Santeria temple
Ile Iya Omin Axe Iyamasse: A Candomble temple named after its founder
Ile-Ife: A historic and legendary city in Nigeria
Ingenios: Large mills supporting the sugar revolution in colonial Cuba
Inquices: Kongo ancestral spirits elevated to the level of divinity
Iroko: An African hardwood
Ital: Rastas' term for organic foods uncorrupted by preservatives
Italero: One who is skilled in the reading of the cowrie shell divination, named after their founders
Iwana: A brass staff or stick of the deity Ogun
Iya Base, Iya Deta, Iya Kala, Iya Kekere, Iya mero, Iya moro: Early women founders of Candomble temples in Brazil
Iya moro/Iya base/Iya kekere: Little mothers and assistants in the Candomble terreiro
Iyalorisha/iyalosha: Ranks of female priests in the Yoruba religion
Iyalorixa/Iyalorixas: Female priests in Brazilian Candomble
Iyanifa: A type of babalawo priest in Santeria

Jagavi/Jhandi: A Rastafarian designation for a Jamaican Hindu holy man
Jah Rastafari: The Rastafarian deity Haile Selassie I
Jah-Jah People: Followers of Rastafari
Jao/jok: Spiritual power of discernment sought by an initiate in African traditional religions
Jogo de buzios: The act of tossing the cowrie shells in Candomble
Jonkunnu: A Caribbean cultural dance and festival of West Central African origin, common in Jamaica and the Bahamas
Joukoujou: The traditional symbolic pole representing the tree of good and evil in Vodou
Juju: A magical property dealing with good luck
Jurema: A ritual dealing with an inebriating drink made from bark in Brazil

Kanuba: Spirit
Kanzo: A Vodou initiation rite of a fiery ordeal given as a symbol of purification and endurance
Ke-belo/libatas: Villages in African Kongo
Kebra Nagast: An Ethiopian epic cherished by followers of Rastafari
Ketu: A nation and ethnic group in West Central Africa
Kikongo: The Bantu language and people in Central and southern Africa

Kimpa Vita (Dona Beatrice): The Kongo prophetess executed on heresy charges for reviving African traditional religious health practices

Kindoki: An evil spirit

Kitomi/itomi: A region and a spiritual leader in Kongo

Konesans: The Vodou concept of knowledge needed for understanding the spiritual cosmos

Kongo Cycle: The period during the slave trade when most victims were taken from Kongo

Kongo Zando/Kongo-Savann: A Vodou lwa originating from the Congo Basin or Angola, reputed to protect devotees from harm

Koromantyns: A West African tribal group

Kouche: A Vodou initiatory rite or ceremony

Kramanti: An African language and an ethnic group

Kroomen: Experienced fishermen in West Africa

Kung: A nomadic ethnic group in the Kalahari Desert

La Caridad del Cobre/La Virgin de la Caridad del Cobre: The patroness of Cuba

La place: A ritual assistant in Vodou

La regla conga: The Palo Monte religion in Cuba

La regla de Ifa: The religion of Santeria

Lakou: A spiritual house and community in Vodou

Lasiren: A Vodou lwa

Latifundi: A large sugar plantation in colonial Cuba

Lav tet: A ritual cleansing of the head in Vodou

Lavagem do Bonfim: Washing on the church of Bonfim

Legba-katarula/Legba-signangon/Legba-zinchan: Personalities of the same Vodou lwa

Legba/Sagbata: A Vodou lwa or divinities of the Fon-Ewe people

Lemba: The great medicine of markets and government

Les misté/lemisté, leml, lemarasa: The spirits, the head, and the sacred twins in Vodou

Limpeza: A bath discharge from Candomble animal sacrifice that relieves negative energy

Linea de santo: Santeria spiritual houses

Linhas: Spiritual ethnic lines in Brazilian Macumba

Lobi: An ethnic group from Burkina Faso

Loko: An ethnic group from Sierra Leone

Lougawou/Lugbawoo: Vodou stereotypic mythology dealing with ghost and zombies

Lukobi lu bakulu/nkulu: Distinguished Kongo ancestors, spiritualized

Lwa kreyol: Spiritual entities in Vodou working as emendations of God, or Bondye

Macoutes: Sacks or bags that Vodou characters carry

Madarikan: Magic that protects people from their enemies

Madrinos/padrinos: Male and female sponsors of a Santeria temple

Maer Salvatoris: A Santeria orisha

Maes de santo: A female priest in Afro-Brazilian religions

Mait Calfour: A Vodou character

Mait Gran Bois: The master of the wood

Manbo: A Vodou female priest

Manje lwa: Food for the Vodou deity or spirit

Manjé-lémo: A Vodou deity

Mano de orunla: One of the leading Orisha deities
Marassas: Sacred twins
Maroon: Runaway slaves who banded together
Massa God: A Jamaican term for slave master
Mau-Mau: A tribal group in Kenya
Mbanza Kongo: A region and a city in Kongo
Mediunidade: A spiritual medium in Umbanda
Mèt tèt: A Vodou ceremonial container representing one's guardian lwa of the head
Mfumu mpu: A chief or clan head whose relics would ultimately find their way into those of the ancestors in Kongo
Mina Jeje: One of the ports of the slave trade
Mondon: One of the Vodou nations
Mongba/iya: A male or female leader of Orisha in Trinidad and Tobago
Moyubbar: A litany of invocation in a Santeria ceremony
Mpungu: Ancestral spirits lodged in Palo Monte vessels
Mumpoko: A Kongo pharmacopeia used in the rituals of healing and blessing

Naciones/Nanchons: Ethnic "nations," mimicking their African tribes, in Afro-Caribbean religions
Nago: One of the Vodou nations
Nanigos: Abakua dancers
Naniguismo: A religious custom in Palo Monte for which followers were persecuted
Nativist Baptist: A locally born Baptist religion in Jamaica
Nazambi-Kalunga (Calunga): An African name for God in Kongo and Palo Monte
Ndebele/Shona: Ethnic groups from Zimbabwe
Nganga: A Kongo spiritual leader of a private disposition
Nkisi: A natural object or charms in the Kongo religion
Nkita: An ancient medicine of lineage fragments
Nkulu: One who lived an honest life and followed the customs of the forefathers
Nkuyu: Family ancestors of the Kongo
Noirist: An indigenous Haitian movement supported by Haitian President Estime, among others
Nuba/Nubia: An ethnic group from the Sudan and lower Egypt
Nuer: A large tribal group in West Africa

Obatala/Oddua/Oddudua/Oduduwa: Leading divinities in Yoruba Orisha
Obayifo: A divinity and spiritualist in African Yoruba
Obi: The reading of four coconut rinds in Santeria divination
Obi O Komfo/ooni, obas: A title, a king, and a chief of the Yoruba people
Obosom: A name for God among the Akan
Obumo: The Ibibio people's deity, who is the son of Eka-Abassi
Ochosi: A name for an orisha in Camdomble Brazil
Odu: An oracle in Santeria for fortune telling and divining the spirits' will
Odun Egungun: The Akan annual festival dedicated to the return of patrilineal ancestors
Odus: Color patterns used in Santeria divinatory science
Odwira: The Akan's national festival in praise of the ancestors and the Blackened Stool
Ogou: The aggressive Petro lwa of war and of weapons of iron and steel
Ogou Balanjo/Ogou Batala/Ogou Desalin/Ogou Yansan/Ogou-badagri/Ogou-ferraille: Characters of Vodou lwa or spirits

Ogoué: A Vodou lwa
Ogun awon agba: Magic that neutralizes the effect of a witch
Ogun Onire/Ogun-Kangun-Dangun: A Vodou lwa or spirit
Okomfo Anokye: A Ghanaian title
Olodumare/Olofi/Olorun: The leading name for God among the Yoruba
Olorie ebi: A priest of the Yoruba family clan
Olorisha: Professional priests connected mainly to the orisha cultus
Olosha: A Santeria priest
Oluwos: Santeria priests coronated during their asiento ceremony to the priesthood
Omela: An Orisha divinity in Trinidad and Tobago
Omiero: An herbal washing ritual in a Santeria ceremony
Omokolobas: A Santeria priest associated with the spirit Olofi
Omolu/Obaluaye or Shopona/Ooni of Ifa: The spiritual head of the worldwide Yoruba religion in Nigeria
Onyankopon (Nyankupon): God in the Akan religion
Ooni/Ohni: A spiritual figurehead in African Yoruba (Ohni is a head of the Yoruba state)
Opele, Opon Ifa, ikin ifa: Methods used in Santeria divination, as well as a chain
Oriate: Santeria officiant or master of ceremony
Orisa-Oko: One of the orishas of the Yoruba people in Nigeria
Orun: The Yoruba word for heaven(s)
Otanes: Sacred stones in Santeria rituals
Ounfo/hunfo: A Vodou temple or sacred place
'Oungan/hungan: A male priest in Vodou
Ovabo: An ethnic group from South Africa

Pa Neezers: A creole name for Obeah-man in Trinidad and Tobago
Pai de santo: A male leader of a Santeria spiritual house
Palais: A roughly made sacred place in the Orisha temple in Trinidad and Tobago
Palero/Mayombero: A practitioner in Palo Monte
Patakis: Yoruba legends and farfetched stories
Patrisib: A kinship system in sociology
Pe: A Vodou altar
Peristil: A partly enclosed sanctuary where Vodou rituals are performed
Perogun: An uncovered structure enclosing emblems of Orisha in Trinidad and Tobago
Peros: Religious mediums in Palo Monte
Petit bon anj: Meaning "small good spirit," the Vodou idea of an aspect of the spiritual self
Petwo (petro): One of the Vodou nations and a group of lwa
Pfemba: An ethnic group from Kongo
Pilon/apoti: A sacred place or throne in a Santeria temple
Planete: A rite of initiation in Palo Monte
Polards: A term used for Palo Monte
Poploi: A Maroon leader and Vodou priests with imposing stature, also called a zamba
Pot tèts: Ceremonial jars in the Vodou rite of investiture
Prenda/Nganga: Spiritual leaders or magicians in Kongo and Palo Monte
Pretsavann: A person who represents a Catholic church in a Vodou ceremony
Prise de yeux: A Vodou ritual for obtaining spiritual insight or knowledge

Proto-metan/Proto-mitan: A sacred pole in the Vodou lakou and the symbolic nexus between the human and the spirit world

Quimbanda/Quimbanderios: A healing specialist or sorcerer in Palo Monte and Macumba

Rada: A class of Vodou spirits from Allada (Dahomey), creolized to Arada/Rada in Haiti
Registro: Membership in Santeria
Religionsgeschichte: The history of religions; the study of religious phenomena
Rogacion dela cabeza: A prayer for the clearing of the head in Santeria
Rosicrucian: An international secret mystical society
Rwa Wango: In Vodou, a Kongo lwa reputed to provide devotees with protection from harm

Sacudimento: A leaf whipping bath
Sagbata: One of the twelve divine twins in the Orisha religion
Samba/Encentodos: Brazilian music and dance
Sasabonsam: A mystical, evil spiritual ghost of African origin
Savalou: A city in Benin
Séance: Communication with the spirits, or spiritual science
Senhores: A Brazilian man
Seremoni: A Brazilian ceremony
Servitor: A male servant or general devotee of a religion
Seseribo: Feathered drums
Shango/Chango: The Sky Father in Yoruba mythology
Shay-Shay: An African-derived broom in Trinidad and Tobago Orisha
Shopona (Shakpana): Divinities in Trinidad Orisha
Shouter Baptists: An Africanized form of Christianity in the Caribbean
Simbi: Kongo spirits in Vodou, represented by one of three cosmic serpents
Sint: "Saint" in Vodou, sometimes used for "spirit"
Sudanic: A generic term for the African languages spoken in the Sahel belt
Sufferahs: A Jamaican term for the poor and oppressed peoples
Sui generis: After its unique kind; in its own right
Suman: Amulets, talismans, or charms
Sunsum: The spirit of a father that protects a child in West African mythology; also, a symbol of purity and spirituality
Syncretism: The attempt to reconcile disparate or contradictory beliefs, often while melding practices of various schools of thought

Tablero of Ifa: The master of divination
Taino: Pre-Colombian inhabitants of the larger Caribbean islands
Tambor de Mina: A creole integration of Catholicism, Kardecist-Spiritualism, and Amerindian religious practices in Brazil
Techiman Bono: A town and a people in Ghana
Teke: An ethnic group in Kongo
Terreiro: A space for worship in Candomble or in a spiritual house
Tertium quids: A "third kind"
Ti bon-anj: The individual consciousness of a person
Ti-Jean Danto/Dantor: A lwa persona of Ezili Danto, associated with trickery

Tonton Macoutes (Makout): A henchmen-type police organization used by President Francois Duvalier to terrorize Haitians

Toots and the Maytals: A musical group that preceded the reggae bands of Jamaica

Torgbi-nyigbla: An African deity

Trench Town: A depressed neighborhood in greater Kingston, Jamaica

Twi: One of the three dialects of the Akan language

Umbanda: An Afro-Brazilian religion that blends African religions with spiritism

Upons: Diviner-consultants

Uwolowu: A deity of the Akposso

Veve/Vévés: A sacred symbolic drawing for attracting Vodou lwa

Via negative: A means of coming to know God and what God is through negation

Vititi Mensu/mpuka mensu: A small mirror that puts the palero in contact with the world of spirits

Wangas/gardes/paketas: Objects or charms that channel spiritual forces to protect Vodou devotees from harm

Wangol: One of the Vodou nations

Warika Hills communes: A Rastafarian camp

White Umbanda: Kardecist Spiritism in Brazil

Winti: An Afro-Guyanese and Surinamese traditional religious tradition

Xevioso: The god of thunder in Dahomey mythology

Yemaja (Iemaja, Yemaya, Yemoja, Yemowo): An orisha in Yoruba mythology

Yorubaland: A large region in Nigeria, home of the Yoruba people

Youth Black Faith: A Rastafari reform group of younger converts who focus on the symbolism of dreadlocks

Zambi/Zambiapungo: Bantu divinities

Zelandor: A father or overseer of the saints

Zoobiblion: An iconographic engraving in Candomble

Zulu: An ethnic group from South Africa

Zumbi: A Brazilian spiritual tribal leader

Selected Bibliography

Works are divided by section: Parts I–V.

PART I: AFRICAN CONNECTIONS

Abimbola, 'Wande. "Ifa: A West African Cosmological System." In *Religion in Africa: Experience and Expression*. Ed. Thomas D. Blakely, Walter E. A. van Beek, and Dennis L. Thompson, 101–116. Portsmouth, N.H.: Heinemann, 1994.

Ahye, Molly. "Orisha Tradition and Culture: A Report on the Second World Conference in Bahia." *Sunday Guardian* (October 30, 1983): 8, 21.

Awolalu, Joseph Omosale. "Sin and Its Removal in African Traditional Religion." *Journal of the American Academy of Religion* 44, no. 2 (1976): 275–287.

——. *Yoruba Beliefs and Sacrificial Rites*. London: Longman Group Publishers, 1979.

Barnes, Sandra T. "The Many Faces of Ogun: Introduction to the First Edition." In *Africa's Ogun, Old World and New*. Ed. Sandra T. Barnes, 1–26. 2nd exp. ed. Bloomington: Indiana University Press, 1997.

——. *Ogun: An Old God for a New Age*. Philadelphia: Institute for the Study of Human Issues, 1980.

Barnes, Sandra T., and Paula Girshick Ben-Amos. "Ogun, the Empire Builder." In *Africa's Ogun: Old World and New*. Ed. Sandra T. Barnes, 39–64. 2nd. exp. ed. Bloomington: Indiana University Press, 1997.

Bascomb, William R. *Ifa Divination: Communication Between Gods and Men of West Africa*. Bloomington: Indiana University Press, 1969.

——. "The Yoruba in Cuba." *Nigeria Journal* 37 (1951): 14–20.

——. *The Yoruba of South Western Nigeria*. New York: Holt, Rinehart and Winston, 1969.

Bastide, Roger. *African Civilization in the New World*. Trans. Peter Green. New York: Harper and Row, 1972.

Ben-Amos, Paula Girshick. "The Promise of Greatness: Women and Power in an Edo Spirit Possession Cult." In *Religion in Africa: Experience and Expression*. Ed. Thomas D. Blakely, Walter E. A. van Beek, and Dennis L. Thompson, 118–134. Portsmouth, N.H.: Heinemann, 1994.

Berns, Marla. "Agbaye: Yoruba Art in Context." In *UCLA Museum of Cultural History Pamphlet Series*. Vol. 1, no. 4, 1–15. University of Southern California Press, 1979.

Blakely, Thomas D., Walter E. A. van Beek, and Dennis L. Thompson, eds. *Religion in Africa: Experience and Expression*. Portsmouth, N.H.: Heinemann, 1994.

Bockie, Simon. *Death and the Invisible Powers: The World of Kongo Belief*. Bloomington: Indiana University Press, 1993.

Bolle, Kees W. "Animism and Animatism." In *Encyclopedia of Religion*. Vol. 1. Ed. Mircea Eliade, 296–303. New York: Simon and Schuster/Macmillan, 1995.

Booth, Newell S., Jr., ed. *African Religions: A Symposium*. New York: NOK Publishers, 1977.

Buah, F. K. *A History of West Africa from AD 1000*. New York: Macmillan, 1986.

Burt, Ben. *The Yoruba and Their Gods, Museum of Mankind Discovering Other Cultures*. London: British Museum Publication, 1977.

Collins, Robert O. *Western African History*. Vol. 1 of *African History: Text and Readings*. New York: Markus Wiener Publishers, 1990.

Craham, Margaret, and Franklin Knight, eds. *Africa and the Caribbean: The Legacy of a Link*. Baltimore, Md.: Johns Hopkins University Press, 1979.

Curry, Mary C. *Making the Gods in New York*. New York: Garland Publishing, 1997.

d'Azevedo, Warren L. "Gola Womanhood and the Limits of Masculine Omnipotence." In *Religions in Africa: Experience and Expression*. Ed. Thomas D. Blakely, Walter E. A. van Beek, and Dennis L. Thompson, 343–362. Portsmouth, N.H.: Heinemann, 1994.

Drewal, Margaret Thompson. *Yoruba Ritual: Performers, Play, Agency*. Bloomington: Indiana University Press, 1992.

Eltis, David. *The Rise of African Slavery in the Americas*. New York: Cambridge University Press, 2000.

———. "The Volume and Structure of the Transatlantic Slave Trade: A Reassessment." *William and Mary Quarterly* 58, no. 1 (January 2001): 1–27.

Fisher, Robert B. *West African Religious Traditions: Focus on the Akan of Ghana*. Maryknoll, N.Y.: Orbis Press, 1998.

Gilbert, Michelle. "Akan Religions." In *Encyclopedia of Religion*. Vol. 1. Ed. Mircea Eliade, 165–168. New York: Simon and Schuster/Macmillan, 1995.

———. "Fon and Ewe Religion." In *Encyclopedia of Religion*. Vol. 5. Ed. Mircea Eliade, 386–387. New York: Simon and Schuster/Macmillan, 1995.

Grottanelli, Vinigi. "African Religions: History of Study." In *Encyclopedia of Religion*. Vol. 1. Ed. Mircea Eliade, 89–96. New York: Simon and Schuster/Macmillan, 1995.

Hackett, Rosalind. *Religion and Women*. New York: State University of New York Press, 1994.

Hart, K. "Annual Review of Anthropology of West Africa." *Annual Review of Anthropology* 4, 1985.

Hayford, Casely J. "Indigenous Institutions of Ghana." In *African Intellectual Heritage: A Book of Sources*. Ed. Molefi K. Asante and Abu S. Abarry, 185–188. Philadelphia: Temple University Press, 1996.

Hilton, Anne. *The Kingdom of Kongo*. Oxford: Clarendon Press, 1985.

Horton, Hal. "Yoruba Religion and Myth: Post-imperial and Post-colonial Literature in English," Brown University, 1998. Available at wwwstg.brown.edu/projects.

Idowu, Bolaji. *African Traditional Religion: A Definition*. London: SCM Press, 1973.

Janzen, John M. "Kongo Religion." In *Encyclopedia of Religion*. Vol. 7. Ed. Mircea Eliade, 362–365. New York: Simon and Schuster/Macmillan, 1995.

Kenyatta, Jomo. *Facing Mount Kenya*. New York: Vintage Books, 1965.

———. "Religion and Ancestral Veneration." In *African Intellectual Heritage: A Book of Sources*. Ed. Molefi K. Asante and Abu S. Abarry, 88–89. Philadelphia: Temple University Press, 1996.

King, Noel Q. *African Cosmo: An Introduction to Religion in Africa*. Belmont, Calif.: Wadsworth Publishing, 1986.

Lawson, E. Thomas. *Religions of Africa: Traditions in Transformation*. Prospect Heights, Ill.: Waveland Press, 1985.

Lightfoot-Klein, Hanny. *Prisoners of Ritual: An Odyssey into Female Genital Circumcision in Africa*. Binghamton, N.Y.: Haworth Press, 1989.

MacGaffey, Wyatt. *Religion and Society in Central Africa: The BaKongo of Lower Zaire*. Chicago: University of Chicago Press, 1986.

Mason, John. *Ebo Eje: Blood Sacrifice*. Brooklyn, N.Y.: Yoruba Theological Archministry, 1981.

Matory, J. Lorand. *Black Atlantic Religion: Tradition, Transnationalism, and Matriarchy in the Afro-Brazilian Candomble*. Princeton, N.J.: Princeton University Press, 2005.

Matthews, Donald. *Honoring the Ancestors: An African Cultural Interpretation of Black Religion and Literature*. New York: Oxford University Press, 1998.

Mbiti, John S. *African Religions and Philosophy*. 2nd ed. Garden City, N.Y.: Doubleday, 1970.

———. *Concepts of God in Africa*. New York: Praeger, 1970.

———. "Flowers in the Garden, the Role of Women in African Traditional Religion." In *African Traditional Religions in Contemporary Society*. Ed. Jacob Olupona, 59–72. St. Paul, Minn.: Paragon House, 1991.

———. *Introduction to African Religion*. 2nd ed. Portsmouth, N.H.: Heinemann, 1991.

———. *The Prayers of African Religion*. Maryknoll, N.Y.: Orbis Press, 1976.

McClelland, E. M. *The Cult of Ifa Among the Yoruba*. Vol. 1 of *Folk Practice and Art*. London: Ethnographic, 1982.

Mercier, Paul. "The Fon of Dahomey." In *Africa Worlds*. Ed. Daryll Forde, 210–234. London: Oxford University Press, 1954.

Metu, Emefie Ikenga. *God and Man in African Religion: A Case Study of the Igbo of Nigeria*. London: Chapman, 1981.

Oduyoye, Mercy Amber. "The African Experience of God through the Eyes of an Akan Woman." *Cross Currents* 47, no. 4 (1997–1998): 493–504.

Olupona, Jacob K. "The Study of Yoruba Religious Tradition in Historical Perspective." *Numen* 40 (1993): 240–271.

———, ed. *African Traditional Religions in Contemporary Society*. St. Paul, Minn.: Paragon House, 1991.

Olupona, Jacob K., and Sulayman S. Nyang. *Religious Plurality in Africa: Essays in Honor of John S. Mbiti*. New York: Mouton De Gruyter, 1993.

Omoyajowo, Joseph Akinyee. "The Role of Women in African Traditional Religion and among the Yoruba." In *African Traditional Religions in Contemporary Society*. Ed. Jacob K. Olupona, 73–80. St. Paul, Minn.: Paragon House, 1991.

Ottenberg, Simon. "Male and Female Secret Societies among the Bafodea Limba of Northern Sierra Leone." In *Religion in Africa: Experience and Expression*. Ed. Thomas D. Blakely, Walter E. A. van Beek, and Dennis L. Thompson, 363–387. Porthsmouth, N.H.: Heinemann, 1994.

Peek, Philip M. *African Divination Systems: Ways of Knowing*. Bloomington: Indiana University Press, 1991.

Peel, J.D.Y. *Religious Encounter and the Making of the Yoruba*. Bloomington: Indiana University Press, 2000.

Pemberton III, John. "The Dreadful God and the Divine King." In *Africa's Ogun: Old World and New.* Ed. Sandra T. Barnes, 105–146. 2nd. exp. ed. Bloomington: Indiana University Press, 1997.

———."Yoruba Religion." In *Encyclopedia of Religion.* Vol. 15. Ed. Mircea Eliade, 535–538. New York: Simon and Schuster/Macmillan, 1995.

Quarcoopome, T.N.O. *West African Traditional Religion.* Ibadan, Nigeria: African University Press, 1987.

Ray, Benjamin C. "African Religions: An Overview." In *Encyclopedia of Religion.* Vol.1. Ed. Mircea Eliade, 60–69. New York: Simon and Schuster/Macmillan, 1995.

———. *African Religions, Symbols, Ritual, and Community.* 2nd ed. Upper Saddle River, N.J.: Prentice Hall, 2000.

Romberg, Rosemary. *Circumcision: The Painful Dilemma.* South Hadley, Mass.: Bergin and Garvey Publishers, 1985.

Salamone, Frank A. "Akan Religion." In *African Intellectual Heritage: A Book of Sources.* Ed. Molefi K. Asante and Abu S. Abarry, 107–108. Philadelphia: Temple University Press, 1996.

———. "A Yoruba Healer as Syncretic Specialist: Herbalism, Rosicrucianism, and the Babalawo." In *Reinventing Religions: Syncretism and Transformation in Africa and the Americas.* Ed. Sidney M. Green and Andre Droogers, 43–53. New York: Rowman and Littlefield Publishers, 2001.

Some, Patrice Malidoma. *Of Water and of the Spirit: Ritual Magic and Initiation in the Life of an African Shaman.* New York: Putman, 1994.

Thornton, John K. *The Kingdom of Kongo: Civil War and Transition 1641–1718.* Madison: University of Wisconsin Press, 1983.

———. "Religious and Ceremonial Life in the Kongo and Mbundu Areas, 1500–1700." In *Central Africans and Cultural Transformations in the American Diaspora.* Ed. Linda Heywood, 71–90. Cambridge: Cambridge University Press, 2002.

Tufuo, J. W., and C. E. Donkor. 1989. *The Ashantis of Ghana: People with a Soul.* Accra, Ghana: Anowuo Educational Publications, 1989.

Walker, Alice. *Warrior Marks: Female Genital Mutilation and the Sexual Blending of Women.* New York: Harcourt Brace, 1993.

Zuesse, Evans M. 1995. "African Religions: Mythic Themes." In *Encyclopedia of Religion.* Vol. 1. Ed. Mircea Eliade, 70–82. New York: Simon and Schuster/Macmillan, 1995.

PART II: VODOU

Bartkowiski, John P. "Claims-Making and Typifications of Voodoo as Deviant Religion: Hex, Lies, and Videotape." *Journal for the Scientific Study of Religion* 37, no. 4 (1998): 559–580.

———. "Systematic Remembering, Systematic Forgetting: Ogou in Haiti." In *Africa's Ogun: Old World and New.* Ed. Sandra T. Barnes, 65–89. Bloomington: Indiana University Press, 1997.

Brown, Karen McCarthy. *Mama Lola: A Vodou Priestess in Brooklyn.* Berkeley: University of California Press, 1991.

———. "Mama Lola and the Ezilis: Themes of Mothering and Loving in Haitian Vodou." In *Unspoken Words: Women's Religious Lives.* Ed. Nancy A. Falk and Rita M. Gross, 235–245. Belmont, Calif.: Wadsworth Publishing, 1989.

———. "Voodoo." In *Encyclopedia of Religion.* Vol. 15. Ed. Mircea Eliade, 296–301. New York: Simon and Schuster/Macmillan, 1995.

Daniel, Yvonne. *Dancing Wisdom: Embodied Knowledge in Haitian Vodou, Cuban Yoruba, and Bahian Candomble*. Chicago: University of Illinois Press, 2005.

Daren, Maya. *Divine Horsemen: The Living Gods of Haiti*. New York: McPherson, 1953.

Davis, Wade. *The Serpent and the Rainbow*. New York: Simon and Schuster, 1985.

Dayan, Joan. *Haiti, History, and the Gods*. Los Angeles: University of California Press, 1995.

———. "Vodoun, or the Voices of the Gods." In *Sacred Possessions: Vodou, Santeria, Obeah, and the Caribbean*. Ed. Margarite Fernandez Olmos and Lizabeth Paravisini-Gebert, 13–36. New Brunswick, N.J.: Rutgers University Press, 1999.

Desmangles, Leslie A. *Faces of the Gods: Vodou and Roman Catholicism in Haiti*. Chapel Hill: University of North Carolina, 1992

Fatunmbi, Awo Shopew Falokun. "The Concept of Male and Female Polarity in Ifa Divination and Ritual." *Journal of Caribbean Studies* 9, nos. 1–2 (Winter/Spring, 1993): 67–85.

Ferere, Gerard A. "Haitian Vodou: Its True Face." *Caribbean Quarterly* 24, nos. 3–4 (1980): 37–48.

Fick, Carolyn E. *The Making of Haiti: The Saint Domingue Revolution from Below*. Knoxville: University of Tennessee Press, 1990.

Genovese, Eugene D. *From Rebellion to Revolution: Afro-American Slave Revolts in the Making of the New World*. New York: Random House, Vintage Books, rep. ed., 1981.

Glassman, Sallie Ann. *Vodou Visions: An Encounter with Divine Mystery*. New York: Villard, 2000.

Hurbon, Laennec. *Vodou: Search for the Spirit*. New York: Harry N. Abrams, 1995.

Hurston, Zora Neal. *Tell My Horse: Vodou and Life in Haiti and Jamaica*. New York: Harper and Row, 1990.

James, C.L.R. *The Black Jacobins: Toussaint L'Overture and the San Domingo Revolution*. 2nd ed. New York: Random House, 1989.

La Guerre, Michael S. *Voodoo and Politics in Haiti*. New York: St. Martin's Press, 1989.

Martinie, Louis and Sallie Ann Glassman. *The New Orleans Voodoo Tarot*. Rochester, Vt.: Destiny Books, 1989.

Metraux, Alfred. *Voodoo in Haiti*. Trans. Hugo Charteris. New York: Shocken Books, 1972.

Mintz, Sidney and Michael-Rolph Trouillot. "The Social History of Haitian Vodou." In *Sacred Arts of Haitian Vodou*. Ed. Donald J. Cosentino, 135–149. Los Angeles: University of California at Los Angeles Museum of Cultural History, 1995.

Mulira, Jessie Gaston. "The Case of Vodoo in New Orleans." In *Africanism in American Culture*. Ed. Joseph Holloway, 34–68. Bloomington: Indiana University Press, 1990.

Pierre, Roland. "Caribbean Religion: The Voodoo Case." *Sociological Analysis* 38, no. 1 (1977): 25–36.

Pinn, Anthony B. *Varieties of African American Religious Experience*. Minneapolis, Minn.: Fortress Press, 1998.

Rigaud, Milo. *Secrets of Voodoo*. Trans. from the 1953 French ed. Robert B. Cross. San Francisco: City Lights Books, 1985.

Rodman, Selden. *Haiti: The Black Republic*. New York: Devin-Adair, 1961.

Rodman, Selden, and Carol Clever. *Spirits of the Night: The Voudun Gods of Haiti*. Dallas, Tex.: Spring Publications, 1992.

Seabrook, William B. *The Magic Island*. New York: Harcourt Brace, 1929.

Wilcken, Lois. *The Drums of Vodou: Lois Wilcken Featuring Frisner Augustin*. Tempe, Ariz.: White Cliffs Media, 1992.

Williams, Joseph J. *Voodoos and Obeahs: Phases of West Indian Witchcraft*. New York: Dial Press, 1932.

PART III: SANTERIA AND PALO MONTE

Barnet, Miguel. *Afro-Cuban Religions*. Trans. from Spanish Christine Renita Ayorinde. Princeton, N.J.: Markus Wiener Publishers, 2001.

———. "La Regla de Ocha: The Religious System of Santeria." In *Sacred Possessions: Vodou, Santeria, Obeah, and the Caribbean*. Ed. Margaret Fernandez Olmos and Lizabeth Paravisini-Gebert, 79–100. New Brunswick, N.J.: Rutgers University Press, 1999.

Bascomb, William. "The African Heritage and Its Religious Manifestations." In *Background to Revolution, the Development of Modern Cuba*. Ed. Robert Freedman Smith, 112–117. New York: Alfred A. Knopf, 1966.

———. *Shango in the New World*. Austin: University of Texas, African and Afro-American Research Institute, 1972.

———. "Two Forms of Afro-Cuban Divination." In *Acculturation in the Americas: Proceedings and Selected Papers of the XXIXth International Congress of Americanists*. Ed. Sol Tax. Chicago: University of Chicago Press, 1969.

Bettleheim, Judith. "Palo Monte Mayombe and Its Influences on Cuban Contemporary Art." *African Arts* 34, no. 2 (Summer 2001): 1–31. Available at EBSCOhost.com.

Bilby, Kenneth. 2006. "Review of Fuentes Guerra, Jesus and Armin Schweler, *legua y ritos del Palo Monte Mayombe: Dioses cubanos y sus fuentes africanas*." *Journal of the Royal Anthropological Institute* (N.S.) 12: 957–1003. Available at EBSCOhost.com.

Brandon, George. "Sacrificial Practices in Santeria, an African-Cuban Religion in the United States." In *Africanism in American Culture*. Ed. Joseph E. Holloway, 119–147. Bloomington: Indiana University Press, 1990.

———. *Santeria from Africa to the New World: The Dead Sell Memories*. Bloomington: Indiana University Press, 1997.

Cabrera, Lydia. *Reglas de Congo, Polo Monte, Mayombe*. Miami, Fla.: Peninsula Printing, 1979.

———. "Religious Syncretism in Cuba." *Journal of Caribbean Studies* 10, nos. 1–2 (Winter/Spring 1994): 81–95.

Castellanos, Isabel. "From Ulkumi to Lucumi: A Historical Overview of Religious Acculturation in Cuba." In *Santeria Aesthetics in Contemporary Latin American Art*. Ed. Arturo Lindsay, 39–50. Washington, D.C.: Smithsonian Institution Press, 1996.

Clark, Mary Ann. "No Hay Ningun Santo Aqui! (There Are No Saints Here!) Symbolic Language within Santeria." *Journal of the American Academy of Religion [JAAR]* 69, no. 1 (2001): 21–41.

———. *Where Men Are Wives and Mothers Rule: Santeria Ritual Practices and Their Gender Implications*. Gainesville: University of Florida Press, 2005.

Curtis, James R. "Santeria: Persistence and Change in an Afro-Cuban Cult Religion." In *Objects of Special Devotion: Fetishism in Popular Culture*. Ed. Ray B. Brown. Bowling Green, Ohio: Popular Press. 1982.

De la Torre, Miguel. *La Lucha for Cuba, Religion and Politics on the Streets of Miami*. Berkeley: University of California Press, 2003.

———. "Oshun: (N) Either the Mother of all Cubans (n)or the Bleached Virgin." *JAAR* 69, no. 4 (December 2001): 837–861.

———. *Santeria: The Beliefs and Rituals of a Growing Religion in America*. Grand Rapids, Mich.: W. B. Eerdmans Publishing, 2004.

Flores, Maria Margarita Castro. "Religions of African Origin in Cuba: A Gender Perspective." In *Nation Dance, Religion, Identity, and Cultural Difference in the Caribbean*. Ed. Patrick Taylor, 54–62. Bloomington: Indiana University Press, 2001.

Flores, Yasmur M. "'Fit for a Queen': Analysis of the Consecration Outfit in the Cult of Yemaya." *Folklore Forum* 23, no. 1 (1990): 47–78.

Fluerant, Gedes. "The Ethnomusicology of Yanvalou: A Case Study of the Rada Rite of Haiti." PhD diss., Tufts University, 1987.

Gonzalez-Wippler, Migene. *Santeria: African Magic in Latin America*. Bronx, N.Y.: Original Publications, 1987.

———. *Santeria: The Religion*. St. Paul, Minn.: Llewellyn Publications, 1998.

———. *The Santeria Experience*. Bronx, N.Y.: Original Publications, 1982.

Hagedorn, Catherine J. *Divine Utterances: The Performance of Afro-Cuban Santeria*. Washington, D.C.: Smithsonian Institution Press, 2001.

Mason, Michael Atwood. "I Bow My Head to the Ground: The Creation of Bodily Experience in Cuban American Santeria." *Journal of American Folklore* 107 (Winter 1994): 18–32.

Matibag, Eugenio. "Ifa and Interpretation: An Afro-Caribbean Literary Practice." In *Sacred Possessions: Vodou, Santeria, Obeah, and the Caribbean*. Ed. Margarite Fernandez Olmos and Lizabeth Paravisini-Gebert, 151–170. New Brunswick, N.J.: Rutgers University Press, 1999.

Morales, Beatrix. "Afro-Cuban Religious Transformation: A Contemporary Study of Lucumi Religion and the Tradition of Spirit Belief." PhD diss., City University of New York, 1990.

Murphy, Joseph. *Santeria: African Spirits in America*. Boston: Beacon Press, 1993.

———. *Santeria: An African Religion in America*. Boston: Beacon Press, 1988.

———. *Working the Spirit: Ceremonies of the African Diaspora*. Boston: Beacon Press, 1994.

Newbold, Puckett. *Folk Beliefs of the Southern Negro*. New York: Negro University Press, 1926/1968.

Nodal, Roberto. "Concept of Ebbo (Sacrifice) as a Healing Mechanism in Santeria." *Journal of Caribbean Studies* 9, nos. 1–2 (Winter 1992/Spring 1993): 113–124.

Nosquers, Gerardo. "Eleggua at the (Post?)Modern Crossroads, the Presence of Africa in the Visual Art of Cuba." In *Santeria Aesthetics in Contemporary Latin American Art*. Ed. Arturo Lindsay: 225–258. Washington, D.C.: Smithsonian Institution Press, 1996.

Ocasio, Rafael. "Babalu Aye Santeria and Contemporary Cuban Literature." *Journal of Caribbean Studies* 9, nos. 1–2 (Spring 1993): 20–35.

Olmos, Margarite Fernandez, and Lizabeth Paravisini-Gebert. *Creole Religions of the Caribbean: An Introduction from Vodou and Santeria to Obeah and Espiritismo*. New York: New York University Press, 2003.

———, eds. *Sacred Possessions: Vodou, Santeria, Obeah, and the Caribbean*. New Brunswick, N.J.: Rutgers University Press, 1999.

Vega, Marta Morena. "From the Alters of My Soul: The Living Traditions of Santeria." In *New Religious Movements A Documentary Reader*. Ed. Dereck Daschke and W. Michael Ashcraft, 183–202. New York: New York University Press, 2005.

Velez, Maria Teresa. *Drumming for the Gods: The Life and Times of Felipe Garcia Villamil, Santero, Palero, and Abakua*. Philadelphia: Temple University Press, 2000.

Viera, Ricardo A., and Randall Morris. "Juan Boza: Travails of an Artist-Priest, 1941–1991." In *Santeria Aesthetics in Contemporary Latin American Art*. Ed. Arturo Lindsay, 171–187. Washington D.C.: Smithsonian Institution Press, 1996.

Wexler, Anna. "I Am Going to See Where My Ogun Is." In *Sacred Possessions: Vodou, Santeria, Obeah, and the Caribbean*. Ed. Margarite Fernandez Olmos and Lizabeth Paravisini-Gebert, 59–78. New Brunswick, N.J.: Rutgers University Press, 1999.

PART IV: CREOLE RELIGIONS OF THE SOUTHERN CARIBBEAN

Afolabi, Niyi. "Axe: Invocation of Candomble and Afro-Brazilian Gods in Brazilian Cultural Production." In *Fragments of Bone: Neo-African Religions in the New World*. Ed. Patrick Bellegarde-Smith. Chicago: University of Illinois Press, 2005.

Ahye, Molly. "Orisha Tradition and Culture: A Report on the Second World Conference in Bahia." *Sunday Guardian* (October 30, 1983): 8, 21, 30.

Aiyejina, Funso, and Rawle Gibbons. "Orisa (Orisha) Tradition in Trinidad." *Caribbean Quarterly* 45, no. 4 (December 1999): 35–50.

Barrett, Leonard. "African Religions in the Americas: The Islands in Between." In *African Religions: A Symposium*. Ed. Newell S. Booth Jr., 183–215. New York: NOK Publishers, 1977.

Bastide, Roger. *African Civilizations in the New World*. Trans. Peter Green. New York: Harper and Rowe, 1972.

———. *Les Religions Africanes au Bresil*. Paris: Presseus Universitaires de France, 1960.

———. *The African Religions of Brazil: Towards a Sociology of the Interpretation of Civilizations*. Trans. Helene Sebba. Baltimore, Md.: Johns Hopkins University Press, 1978.

Bell, Hesketh. *Obeah: Witchcraft in the West Indies*. London: Low, Marston, Searle and Rivington, 1889.

Bilby, Kenneth, Michael Largey, and Peter Manuel. *Caribbean Currents: Caribbean Music from Rumba to Reggae*. Philadelphia: Temple University Press, 1995.

Brereton, Bridget. *A History of Modern Trinidad 1783–1962*. London: Heinemann, 1981.

Brown, Diana DeG. *Umbanda, Religion and Politics in Urban Brazil*. New York: Columbia University Press, 1994.

Burdick, John. "Brazil's Black Consciousness Movement." *Report on the Americas: The Black Americans, 1492–1992* 25, no. 4 (1992): 23–27.

Carr, Andrew T. "A Rada Community in Trinidad." *Caribbean Quarterly* 3 (Spring 1953): 35–54.

Case, Frederick Ivor. "The Intersemiotics of Obeah and Kali Mai in Guyana." In *Nation Dance, Religion, Identity, and Cultural Difference in the Caribbean*. Ed. Patrick Taylor, 40–53. Bloomington: Indiana University Press, 2001.

Curtin, Philip D. *The Atlantic Slave Trades: A Census*. Madison: University of Wisconsin Press, 1969.

de Cosmo, Jan. "Reggae and Rastafari in Salvador, Bahia: The Caribbean Connection in Brazil." In *Religion, Culture and Tradition in the Caribbean*. Ed. Hemchand Gossai and Nathaniel Samuel Murrell: 37-64. New York: St. Martin's Press, 2000.

De Verteuil, L. A. *Trinidad: Its Geography, Natural Resources, Present Condition and Prospects*. London: Ward Lock, 1858.

Drewal, Margaret Thompson. "Dancing for Ogun in Yorubaland and Brazil." In *Africa's Ogun: Old World and New*. Ed. Sandra Barnes, 199–234. 2nd. exp. ed. Bloomington: Indiana University Press, 1997.

Eastman, Rudolph. "An Indigenous African Theology." *Trinidad Express* (*Emancipation Day Pull-Out*) (August 1, 1988): 27–30.

Elder, Jacob D. *African Survivals in Trinidad and Tobago*. London: Karia Press, 1988.

———. "The Yoruba Ancestor Cult in Gasparillo." *Caribbean Quarterly* 16, no. 3 (September, 1970): 6–18.

FAMA, Chief. *Fundamentals of the Yoruba Religion (Orisha Worship)* San Bernadino, Calif.: Orunmila Communications, 1993.

Ferreira Da Silva, Denise. "Out of Africa? Umbanda and the 'Ordering' of the Modern Brazilian Space." In *Fragments of Bone: Neo-African Religions in a New World*. Ed. Patrick Bellegarde-Smith. Urbana: University of Illinois Press, 2005.

Ferretti. Mundicarmo Maria Rocha. "The Presence of Non-African Spirits in an Afro-Brazilian Religion: A Case of Afro-Amerindian Syncretism?" In *Reinventing Religions: Syncretism and Transformation in Africa and the Americas*. Ed. Sidney M. Greenfield and Andre Droogers, 99–111. New York: Rowan and Littlefield Publishers, 2001.

Ferretti, Sergio F. "Religious Syncretism in an Afro-Brazilian Cult House." In *Reinventing Religions: Syncretism and Transformation in Africa and the Americas*. Ed. Sidney M. Greenfield and Andre Droogers, 87–98. New York: Rowan and Littlefield Publishers, 2001.

Frye, Karla Y. E. "An Article of Faith": Obeah and Hybrid Identities in Elizabeth Nunez-Harrell's When Rock Dance." In *Sacred Possessions: Vodou, Santeria, Obeah, and the Caribbean*. Ed. Margarite Fernandez Olmos and Lizabeth Paravisini-Gebert, 195–215. New Brunswick, N.J.: Rutgers University Press, 1999.

Glazier, Stephen D. "African Cults and Christian Churches in Trinidad: The Spiritual Baptist Case." *Journal of Religious Thought* 39 (Fall/Winter 1982–1983): 17–25.

———. "Heterodoxy and Heteropraxy in the Spiritual Baptist Faith." *Journal of Interdenominational Theological Center* 8 (Fall 1980): 89–101.

Greenfield, Sidney M. "The Reinterpretation of Africa: Convergence and Syncretism in Brazilian Candomble." In *Reinventing Religions: Syncretism and Transformation in Africa and the Americas*, 113–129. New York: Rowman and Littlefield Publishers, 2001.

Guerra, F. "Medica Folklore in Spanish America." In *American Folk Medicine*. Ed. W. D. Hand, 169–175. Los Angeles: University of California Press, 1976.

Harding, Rachel E. *A Refuge in Thunder: Candomble and Alternative Spaces of Blackness*. Bloomington: Indiana University Press, 2000.

Hart, Richard. *Slaves Who Abolished Slavery*. Kingston, Jamaica: Institute of Social and Economic Research, 1985.

Hedrick, Basil C., and Janette E. Stephens. *It's a Natural Fact: Obeah in the Bahamas*. Greeley: Museum of Anthropology, University of Northern Colorado, 1977.

Henry, Frances. "Religion and Ideology in Trinidad: The Resurgence of the Shango Religion." *Caribbean Quarterly* 29, nos. 3-4 (1983): 63–69.

———. "Social Stratification in an Afro-American Cult." *Anthropological Quarterly* 38, no. 2 (April 1965): 72–79.

Herskovits, Melville J. "African Gods and Catholic Saints in New World Religious Beliefs." *American Anthropologist* 29 (1939): 635–644

———. *New World Negroes*. Bloomington, Ind.: Minerva Press, Frank and Wagnalls, 1969.

———. "The Southernmost Outpost of the New World Africanism." *American Anthropologist* 45, no. 4 (1943): 495–510.

Herskovits, Melville J., and Francis Herskovits. "Negroes of Brazil." *Yale Review* 32, no. 2 (1942): 263–279.

Higman, B. W. "African and Creole Slave Family Patterns in Trinidad." In *Africa and the Caribbean: The Legacy of a Link*. Ed. Margaret Crahan and Franklin Knight, 41–64. Baltimore, Md.: Johns Hopkins University Press, 1979.

Hoetink. H. *Caribbean Race Relations: A Study of Two Variants*. Trans. Eva M. Hooykaas. New York: Oxford University Press, 1971.

Hood, Robert E. *Must God Remain Greek? Afro Cultures and God-Talk*. Minneapolis, Minn.: Fortress Press, 1990.

Houk, James T. "Patterns of Spirit Possession in Two Afro-American Religious Groups in Trinidad: The Spiritual Baptist and the Shango Cult." Master's thesis, Louisiana State University, 1986.

———. *Spirit, Blood, and Drums: The Orisha Religion in Trinidad*. Philadelphia: Temple University Press, 1995.

Johnson, Christopher Paul. *Secrets, Gossip, and Gods: The Transformation of Brazilian Candomble*. New York: Oxford University Press, 2002.

Laguerre, Michael. *Afro-Caribbean Folk Medicine*. South Hadley, Mass.: Bergin and Garvey Publishers, 1987.

Landers, Jane. *Black Society in Spanish Florida*. Chicago: University of Illinois Press, 1999.

Lerch, Patricia Barker. "An Explanation for the Predominance of Women in the Umbanda Cults of Porto Alegre, Brazil." *Urban Anthropology* 11, no. 2 (1984): 237–261.

———. "Spirit Mediums in Umbanda Evangelizada of Porto Alegre, Brazil: Dimensions of Power and Authority." In *A World of Women*. Ed. Erika Bourguignon, 129–145. New York: Praeger Specialist Studies, 1980.

Lewis, Gordon R. *Main Currents in Caribbean Thought: The Historical Evolution of Caribbean Society in Its Ideological Aspects, 1492–1900*. Baltimore, Md.: Johns Hopkins University Press, 1983.

Maggie, Yvonne. "Afro-Brazilian Cults." In *Encyclopedia of Religion*. Vol. 1. Ed. Mircea Eliade, 102–105. New York: Simon and Schuster/Macmillan, 1995.

———. "Afro-Brazilian Religions." *HarperCollins Dictionary of Religion*. Ed. Jonathan Z. Smith and William Scott Green, 28–31. San Francisco: HarperSanFrancisco, 1995.

Mischel, Frances. "African 'Powers' in Trinidad: The Shango Cult." *Anthropological Quarterly* 30, no. 2 (April 1957): 45–59.

———. "Faith Healing and Medical Practice in the Southern Caribbean." *Southern Journal of Anthropology* 3 (1960): 407–417.

Motta, Roberto Mauro Cortez. "Ethnicity, Purity, the Market and Syncretism in Afro-Brazilian Cults." In *Reinventing Religions: Syncretism and Transformation in Africa and the Americas*. Ed. Sidney M. Greenfield and Andrea Droogers, 71–85. New York: Rowan and Littlefield Publishers, 2001.

———. "Meat and Feast: The Xango Religion of Recife Brazil." PhD diss., Columbia University, 1988.

Omari, Mikelle Smith. "Candomble: A Socio-Political Examination of African Religion and Art in Brazil." In *Religion in Africa: Experience and Expression*. Ed. Thomas D. Blakely, Walter E. A. van Beek, and Dennis L. Thompson, 135–159. Portsmouth, N.H.: Heinemann, 1994.

———. "Cultural Confluence in Candomble Nago: A Socio-Historical Study of Art and Aesthetics in an Afro-Brazillian Religion." PhD diss., Department of Art History, University of Michigan, 1984.

———. *From the Inside to the Outside: The Art and Ritual of Bahian Candomble*. Los Angeles: Museum of Cultural History, University of California at Los Angeles, 1984.

Ortiz, Renato. "Ogun and the Umbanda Religion." In *Africa's Ogun: Old World and New*. Ed. Sandra T. Barnes, 90–102. 2nd. exp. ed. Bloomington: Indiana University Press, 1997.

Pierson, Donald. *Negroes in Brazil: A Study of Race Contact at Bahia*. Chicago: University of Chicago Press, 1942.

Ramchand, Kenneth. "Obeah and the Supernatural in West Indian Literature." *Jamaica Journal* 3, no. 2 (1963): 52–60.

Ramos, Arthur. *The Negro in Brazil*. Washington, D.C.: Associated Publishers, 1939.

Ribeiro, Rene. *Cultos Afro-Brasileiros de Recife: Um Estudo de Adjustmento Social*. Recife: Boletim do Insituto Joaquim Nabuco de Pesquisa Social, 1952.

Richardson, Alan. "Romantic Vodou: Obeah and British Culture, 1797–1804." In *Sacred Possession: Vodou, Santeria, Obeah, and the Caribbean*. Ed. Margarite Fernandez Olmos and Lizabeth Paravisini-Gebert, 171–194. New Brunswick, N.J.: Rutgers University Press, 1999.

Rodrigues, Nina. *O Animismo Fetichista dos Negros Bahianos*. Rio de Janeiro: Civilizacao Brasileira, 1935.

Savory, Elaine. "'Another Poor Devil of a Human Being' . . . Jean Rhys and the Novel as Obeah." In *Sacred Possessions: Vodou, Santeria, Obeah, and the Caribbean*. Ed. Margarite Fernandez Olmos and Lizabeth Paravisini-Gebert, 216–230. New Brunswick, N.J.: Rutgers University Press, 1999.

Simpson, George Eaton. *Black Religions in the New World*. New York: Colombia University Press, 1978.

———. "Caribbean Religions: Afro-Caribbean Religions." In *Encyclopedia of Religion*. Vol. 3. Ed. Mircea Eliade, 90–98. New York: Simon and Schuster/Macmillan, 1995.

———. *Religious Cults of the Caribbean: Trinidad, Jamaica, and Haiti*. Caribbean Monograph Series, 15. Rio Piedras: Institute of Caribbean Studies, University of Puerto Rico, 1970/1980.

———. "The Shango Cult in Nigeria and Trinidad." *American Anthropologist* 64, no. 6 (December 1962): 204–219.

———. *The Shango Cult in Trinidad*. Caribbean Monograph Series, 2. Rio Pedras, Institute of Caribbean Studies, University of Puerto Rico, 1965.

———. *Yoruba Religion and Medicine in Ibadan*. Ibadan, Nigeria: Ibadan University Press, 1980.

Springer, Pearl Eintou. "Orisha and the Spiritual Baptist Religion in Trinidad and Tobago." Unpublished paper presented at the Ecumenical Conference of the Caribbean Conference of Churches. Surinam: Port-of-Spain Public Library, 1994.

———. "The Orisha Religion and National Council of Orisha Elders of Trinidad and Tobago." Unpublished report of Iyalorisa Melvina Rodney, Head of Egbe Orisha Ile Wa, 1–6. Port-of-Spain Public Library, 1994.

Sturm, Fred Gillette. "Afro-Brazilian Cults." In *African Religions: A Symposium*. Ed. Newell S. Booth, 217–239. New York: NOK Publishers, 1977.

Tindall, David. "Drums and Colors." In *Caribbean Beat* (2000). Available at www.caribbean.com.

Todd, Tammy. "Call of the Drums: Afro-Caribbean Religions." *Alternative Religions* 29 (November 2000): 1–16.

Trotman, David V. "The Yoruba and Orisha Worship in Trinidad and British Guiana: 1838–1870." *African Studies Review* 19, no. 2 (1976): 2–16.

Verger, Pierre. *Bahia and the West African Trade: 1549–1851*. Ibadan, Nigeria: Ibadan University Press, 1964.

———. "Bori, Premier Ceremonie d'Initiation au Coute des Orishas Nago a Bahia au Brasil." *Revista do Museu Paulista*. Sao Paulo: n.p., 1955.

Voeks, Robert A. *Sacred Leaves of Candomble: African Magic, Medicine, and Religion in Brazil*. Austin: University of Texas Press, 1977.

Warner-Lewis, Maureen. "Some Yoruba Descendants in Trinidad." *African Studies Association of the West Indies Bulletin* 3 (December 1970): 40–49.

———. *Yoruba Religion: From Mother Tongue to Memory*. Trinidad and Tobago: Press University of the West Indies, 1997.

———. "Yoruba Religion in Trinidad-Transfer and Reinterpretation." *Caribbean Quarterly* 24, nos. 3–4 (1978): 18–46.

Williams, Joseph J. *Voodoos and Obeahs: Phrases of West Indian Witchcraft*. New York: Dial Publication, 1932.

PART V: JAMAICA'S CREOLE RELIGIONS

Aborampah, Osei-Mensah. "Out of the Same Bowl: Religious Beliefs and Practices in Aman Communities in Ghana and Jamaica." In *Fragments of Bone: Neo-African Religions in the New World*. Ed. Patrick Bellegarde-Smith, 124–142. Chicago: University of Illinois, 2005.

Ahkell, Jah. *Rasta: Emperor Haile Selassie I and the Rastafarians*. Chicago: Fortune Distribution and Research Associates School Times, 1999.

Alleyne, Mervyn. *Roots of Jamaican Culture*. London: Pluto Press, 1988.

Ashani, Stafford. "Rasta Now." *Lifestyle* 18 (November/December 1991): 6–11.

Atiba, Alemu I Johnson. *The Rastafari Ible*. Chicago: Fortune Distribution and Research Associates School Times, 1994.

Austin-Bros, Diane J. "Pentecostals and Rastafarians: Cultural, Political and Gender Relations of Two Religious Movements." *Social and Economic Studies* 36, no. 4: 1–39

Aylmer, Kevin J. "Towering Babble and Glimpses of Zion: Recent Depiction of Rastafari in Cinema." In *Chanting Down Babylon: The Rastafari Reader*. Ed. Nathaniel Samuel Murrell, William David Spencer, and Adrian Anthony McFarlane, 284–310. Philadelphia: Temple University Press, 1998.

Babatunji, Ayotunde Amtac. *Prophet on Reggae Mountain: Meditations of Ras Shabaka Maasai, Prophet of Jah Rastafari*. Rochester, N.Y.: Garvey-Tubman-Nzinga, 1994.

Bakan, Abigail B. *Ideology and Class Conflict in Jamaica: The Politics of Rebellion*. Buffalo, N.Y.: McGill-Queen's University, 1990.

Bankston, Carl L. "Rastafarianism." *The African American Encyclopedia*. Vol. 8. Ed. Michael W. Williams and Kibibi V. Mack, 2111–2116. New York: Marshall Cavandish, 2001.

Barrett, Leonard E. "African Roots in Jamaican Indigenous Religion." *Journal of Religious Thought* 35 (1978): 7–26.

———. *The Rastafarians: Sounds of Cultural Dissonance*. Rev. ed. with a new Afterword. Boston: Beacon Press, 1988/1997.

———. *The Rastafarians: A Study of Messianic Cultism in Jamaica*. Rio Piedras: Institute of Caribbean Studies, University of Puerto Rico, 1969.

———. *Soul Force: African Heritage in Afro-American Religion*. Garden City, N.Y.: Anchor Books, 1974.

———. *The Sun and the Drum: African Roots in Jamaican Folk Tradition*. London: Heinemann, 1976.

Bender, Wolfgang. "Liberation from Babylon: Rata Painters in Jamaica." In *Missile and Capsule*. Ed. Jurgen Martini, 129–135. Bremen, Germany: Druckerei der Universitaet Bremen, 1983.

Besson, Jean. "Religion as Resistance in Jamaican Peasant Life: The Baptist Church, Revival Worldview and Rastafari Movement." In *Rastafari and Other African-Caribbean Worldviews*. Ed. Barry Chevannes. New Brunswick, N.J.: Rutgers University Press, .1988, 56

Bilby, Kenneth. "Holy Herb: Notes on the Background of Cannabis in Jamaica." In *Rastafari: Caribbean Quarterly Monograph*. Ed. Rex Nettleford, 82–95. Kingston, Jamaica: University of the West Indies, 1985.

Bilby, Kenneth, and Fu-Kiau Bunseki. "Kumina: A Kongo-Based Tradition in the New World." *Brussels: Les Cahiers du Cedaf* 8 (1983): 1–114..

Bilbey, Kenneth, and Elliot Leib. "Kumina, the Howellite Church and the Emergence of Rastafarian Traditional Music in Jamaica." *Jamaica Journal* 19, no. 3 (1986): 22–28.

Birhan, Iyata Farika. *Jah is I Shepherd*. San Jose, Calif.: Rastas/Roots/Redemption/ Representation Unlimited, 1981.

Bisnauth. Dale. *A History of Religions in the Caribbean*. Kingston, Jamaica: Kingston Publishers, 1989.

Bones, Jah. *One Love: Rastafari History, Doctrine, and Livity*. London: Voice of Rastafari, 1985.

Boot, Adrian. *Bob Marley: Soul Rebel, Natural Mystic*. New York: St. Martin's Press, 1982.

———. *Jamaica: Babylon on a Thin Wire*. London: Thames and Hudson, 1976.

Bowden, W. Errol. "Rastafarianism and the New Society." *Savacou* 5 (1975): 41–50.

Boyne, Ian. "Jamaica: Breaking Barriers between Churches and Rastafarians." *One World* 86 (May 1983): 33–34.

Brathwaite, Edward Kumau. "Kunina, the Spirit of African Survival in Jamaica." *Jamaica Journal* 42 (1978): 44–63.

Breiner, Lawrence A. "The English Bible in Jamaican Rastafarianism." *Journal of Religious Thought* 42, no. 2 (Fall/Winter 1982): 30–43.

Bryan, Maurice. *Roots, Resistance, and Redemption: The Rise of Rastafari*. Africanstory Publisher, 1997.

Bush, Barbara. *Slave Women in Caribbean Society 1650–1838*. Bloomington: Indiana University Press, 1990.

Callam, Neville. "Invitation to Docility: Defusing the Rastafarian Challenge." *Caribbean Journal of Religious Studies* 3 (1980): 28–48.

Campbell, Horace. *Rasta and Resistance: From Marcus Garvey to Walter Rodney*. Trenton, N.J.: Africa World Press, 1987.

———. "Rastafari: A Culture of Resistance." *Race and Class* 22, no. 1 (1980): 1–22.

———. "The Rastafarians in the Eastern Caribbean." *Caribbean Quarterly* 26 (1980): 42–61.

Casmore, Ernest. *Rastaman: The Rastafarian Movement in England*. London: George Allen and Unwin, 1979.

———. "The Rastaman Cometh." *New Society* 41, no. 777 (1977): 382–384.

Chevannes, Barry. "Healing the Nation: Rastafari Exorcism of the Ideology of Racism in Jamaica." *Caribbean Quarterly* 36, nos. 1–2 (1990): 59–84.

———. "The Literature of Rastafari." *Social and Economic Studies* 26 (1977): 239–262.

———. *Rastafari: Roots and Ideology*. Syracuse, N.Y.: Syracuse University Press, 1994.

———. "Rastafari: Towards a New Approach." *New West Indian Guide* 64, no. 3 (1990): 127–148.

———. "Rastafari and Exorcism of Racism and Classism." In *Chanting Down Babylon: The Rastafari Reader*. Ed. Nathaniel Samuel Murrell, William David Spencer, and Adrian Anthony McFarlane, 55–71. Philadelphia: Temple University Press, 1998.

———. "The Rastafari of Jamaica." In *When Prophets Die: The Postcharismatic Fate of New Religious Movements*. Ed. Timothy Miller, 135–148. Albany: State University of New York Press, 1994.

———. "Rastafarianism and the Class Struggle: The Search for a Methodology." In *Methodology and Change: Problems of Applied Social Science Research Techniques in the Commonwealth Caribbean*. Ed. L. Lindsay, 244–251. Mona, Jamaica: Institute of Social and Economic Research, University of the West Indies, 1978.

————. "Repairer of the Breach: Reverend Claudius Henry and Jamaican Society." In *Ethnicity in the Americas*. Ed. Frances Henry, 264–290. The Hague: Mouton, 1976.

————. "Revival and Black Struggle." *Savacou* 5 (June 1971): 27–39.

————. "Revivalism: A Disappearing Religion." *Caribbean Quarterly* 24, nos. 3–4 (1978): 1–17.

————. *Social Origin of the Rastafari Movement*. Mona, Jamaica: Institute of Social and Economic Research, University of the West Indies, 1978.

————. "Some Notes on African Religious Survivals in the Caribbean." *Caribbean Journal of Religious Studies* 5, no. 2 (1983): 18–28.

————, ed. *Rastafari and Other African-Caribbean Worldviews*. New Brunswick, N.J.: Rutgers University Press, 1998.

Chisholm, Clinton. "The Rasta-Selassie Ethiopian Connections." In *Chanting Down Babylon: The Rastafari Reader*. Ed. Nathaniel Samuel Murrell, William David Spencer, and Adrian Anthony McFarlane, 166–177. Philadelphia: Temple University Press, 1998.

Clark, Peter. *Black Paradise: The Rastafarian Movement*. San Bernardino, Calif.: Borgo Press, 1994.

Collins, Lauretta. "Daughters of Jan: The Impact of Rastafarian Womanhood in the Caribbean, the United States, Britain, and Canada." In *Religion, Culture and Tradition in the Caribbean*. Ed. Hemchand Gossai and Nathaniel Samuel Murrell, 227–255. New York: St. Martin's Press, 2000.

Constantine, Alex. 2002. "Chanting Down Babylon: The CIA and the Death of Bob Marley." *High Times, Global Harvest Report* no. 318 (2002): 45–50.

Cooper, Carolyn. "Chanting Down Babylon: Bob Marley's Song as Literary Text." *Jamaica Journal* 19, no. 4 (Winter 1987): 2–8.

Cronon, E. D. *Black Moses—The Story of Marcus Garvey and the Universal Negro Improvement Association*. Madison: University of Wisconsin Press, 1955.

Curtain, Phillip D. *Two Jamaicas: The Role of Ideas in a Tropical Colony, 1830–1865*. Westport, Conn.: Greenwood Press, 1955.

De Cosmo, Janet L. "Reggae and Rastafari in Salvador, de Bahia: The Caribbean Connection in Brazil." In *Religion Culture and Tradition in the Caribbean*. Ed. Hemchand Gossai and Nathaniel Samuel Murrell, 37–64. New York: St. Martin's Press, 2000.

Edmonds, Ennis Barrington. "Dread I In-a-Babylon, Ideological Resistance and Cultural Revitalization." In *Chanting Down Babylon: The Rastafari Reader*. Ed. Nathaniel Samuel Murrell, William David Spencer, and Adrian Anthony McFarlane, 23–35. Philadelphia: Temple University Press, 1998.

————. *Rastafari: From Outcast to Cultural Bearers*. New York: Oxford University Press, 2003.

————. "The Structure and Ethos of Rastafari." In *Chanting Down Babylon: The Rastafari Reader*. Ed. Nathaniel Samuel Murrell, William David Spencer, and Adrian Anthony McFarlane, 349–360. Philadelphia: Temple University Press, 1998.

Edwards, Bryan. "African Religions in Colonial Jamaica." In *Afro-American Religious History: A Documentary*. Ed. Milton C. Sernett, 19–23. Durham, N.C.: Duke University Press, 1985. [Adapted from *An Abridgement of Mr. Edward's Civil and Commercial History of the British Colonies in the Indies in Two Volumes*. Vol. 11. London: J. Parsons and J. Bell, 1974.]

Elkins, W. F. *Street Preachers, Faith Healers and Herb Doctors in Jamaica, 1890–1925*. New York: Revisionist Press, 1977.

Emerick, A. J. *Jamaican Myalism*. Woodstock, N.Y.: n. p., 1916.

Forsythe, Dennis. *Rastafari: For the Healing of the Nation.* New York: One Drop Books, 1995 reprint of the 1983 ed.

———. "West Indian Culture through the Prism of Rastafarianism." In *Rastafari: Caribbean Quarterly Monograph.* Ed. Rex Nettleford, 62–85. Kingston, Jamaica: University of the West Indies, 1985.

Gardner, William James. *A History of Jamaica from Its Discovery by Christopher Columbus to the Year 1872.* London: T. Fisher Unwin 1873/1909.

Garrick, Neville. *A Rasta's Pilgrimage: Ethiopian Faces and Places.* San Francisco: Pomegranate, 1998.

Gossai, Hemchand, and Nathaniel Samuel Murrell, eds. *Religion, Culture and Tradition in the Caribbean.* New York: St. Martin's Press, 2000.

Guano, Emanuela. "Revival Zion: An Afro-Christian Religion in Jamaica." *Anthropos* 89, nos. 4–6 (1994): 517–528.

Hamilton, Grace. "The History of Jamaican Revival Religion." Unpublished paper. Kingston, Jamaica: African-Caribbean Institute of Jamaica, 1959.

Hepner, Randal L. "Chanting Down Babylon in the Belly of the Beast: The Rastafarian Movement in the Metropolitan United States." In *Chanting Down Babylon: The Rastafari Reader.* Ed. Nathaniel Samuel Murrell, William David Spencer, and Adrian Anthony McFarlane, 199–216. Philadelphia: Temple University Press, 1998.

———. "The House That Rasta Built: Church-Building and Fundamentalism among New York Rastafarians." In *Gatherings in Diaspora: Religious Communities and the New Immigration.* Ed. R. Stephen Warner and Judith G. Wittner, 197–234. Philadelphia: Temple University Press, 1998.

Hill, Robert. "Dread History: Leonard P. Howell and Millenarian Visions in Early Rastafarian Religions in Jamaica." *Epoche* (1981): 1–15.

———. "From Marcus to Marley." *Reggae and African Beat* (August 1985): 15–19.

———. "Leonard P. Howell and Millenarian Visions in Early Rastafari." *Jamaica Journal* 16, no. 1 (1983): 24–42.

———. *Marcus Garvey and the Universal Negro Improvement Association Papers. Vol. 7. November 1927–August 1940.* Berkeley: University of California Press, 1990.

Hoenisch, Michael. "Symbolic Politics: Perceptions of the Early Rastafari Movement." *Massachusetts Review* 29 (1988): 432–449.

Hogg, Donald. "The Convince Cult in Jamaica." *Yale Publication in Anthropology No. 58, Papers in Caribbean Anthropology.* Comp. Sidney W. Mintz, 3–24. New Haven, Conn.: Department of Anthropology, Yale University, 1960.

———. "Jamaican Religions: A Study in Variations." Unpublished PhD diss. in Anthropology, Yale University, 1964.

Homiak, John Paul. "The 'Ancient of Days' Seated Black: Eldership, Oral Tradition and Ritual in Rastafari Culture." Unpublished PhD diss., Brandeis University, 1985.

Hutton, Clinton, and Nathaniel Samuel Murrell. "Rastas' Psychology of Blackness, Resistance, and Somebodiness." In *Chanting Down Babylon: The Rastafari Reader.* Ed. Nathaniel Samuel Murrell, William David Spencer, and Adrian Anthony McFarlane, 36–54. Philadelphia: Temple University Press, 1998.

Jagessar, Michael N. "JPIC and Rastafarians." *One World* (February 1991): 15–17.

Jean Von Dijk, Frank. *Jahmaica: Rastafari and Jamaican Society 1930–90.* Utrecht: ISOR and the Netherlands Foundation for the Advancement of Tropical Research, 1993.

———. "Twelve Tribes of Israel: Rasta and the Middle Class." *New West Indian Guide* 62, nos. 1–2 (1988): 1–26.

Johnson-Hill, Jack A. *I-Sight, the World of Rastafari: An Interpretive Sociological Account of Rastafarian Ethics*. Metuchen, N.J.: American Theological Library Association and Scarecrow Press, 1995.

——. "Rastafari as a Resource for Social Ethics in South Africa." *Journal for the Study of Religion* 9, no. 1 (March 1996): 1–18.

Kapuscinski, Ryszard. *The Emperor*. New York: Harcourt-Brace-Jovanovich, 1983.

Kitzinger, Sheila. "Protest and Mysticism: The Ras Tafari Cult of Jamaica." *Journal for the Scientific Study of Religion* 8 (1969): 240–262.

——. "The Rastafarian Brethren of Jamaica." In *Peoples and Cultures*. Ed. Michael M. Horowitz, 580–586. New York: Natural History Press, 1971.

Laguerre, Michael. *Afro-Caribbean Folk Medicine*. South Hadley, Mass.: Bergin and Garvey Publishers, 1987.

Lake, Obiagele. *Rastafari Women: Subordination in the Midst of Liberation Theology*. Durham, N.C.: Carolina Academic Press, 1988.

Lee, Barbara Makeda. *Rastafari: The New Creation*. London: Jamaica Media Productions, 1982.

Lee, Helene. *The First Rasta: Leonard Howell and the Rise of Rastafarianism*. Trans. Lily Davis. Chicago: Chicago Review Press, 1999.

Lewis, Rupert, and Patrick Bryan. *Marcus Garvey: Anti-Colonial Champion*. Trenton, N.J.: Africa World Press, 1992.

——. "Marcus Garvey and the Early Rastafarians: Continuity and Discontinuity." In *Chanting Down Babylon: The Rastafari Reader*. Ed. Nathaniel Samuel Murrell, William David Spencer, and Adrian Anthony McFarlane, 145–158 Philadelphia: Temple University Press, 1998.

——, eds. *Garvey: His Work and Impact*. Mona, Jamaica: Institute of Social and Economic Research, Extra Mural Studies University of the West Indies, 1988.

Lewis, William. *Soul Rebels: The Rastafari*. Prospect Heights, Ill.: Waveland Press, 1993.

Long, Edward. *The History of Jamaica*. London: F. Cass, 1774/1970.

——. *The Report of the Lords of the Committee of the Council Appointed for the Consideration of All Matters Relating to Trade and Foreign Plantation*. London: n.p., 1789.

Luntta, Karl. *Jamaica Handbook*. Chico, Calif.: Moon Publications, 1991.

Malloch, Theodore. "Rastafarianism: Radical Caribbean Movement and Religion." *Center Journal* no. 4 (Fall 1985): 67–87.

Mansingh, Ajai, and Laxmi Mansingh. "Hindu Influences on Rastafarianism." In *Rastafari: Caribbean Quarterly Monograph*. Ed. Rex Nettleford, 96–115. Kingston, Jamaica: University of the West Indies, 1985.

Manuel, Peter, Kenneth Bilby, and Michael Largey. *Caribbean Currents: Caribbean Music from Rumba to Reggae*. Philadelphia: Temple University Press, 1995.

Mason, John. 1985. *Black Gods: Orisa Studies in the New World*. Brooklyn, N.Y.: Yoruba Theological Archministry, 1985.

Mastalia, Francesco, and Alfonse Pagano. *Dreads*. New York: Workman Publishing, 1999.

McPherson, E.S.P. *Rastafari and Politics, Sixty Years of a Developing Cultural Ideology: A Sociology of Development Perspective*. Clarendon, Jamaica: Black International Iyahbinghi Press, 1991.

Middleton, Richard. "Identity and Subversion in Babylon: Strategies for 'Resisting against the System' in the Music of Bob Marley and the Wailers." In *Religion, Culture and Tradition in the Caribbean*. Ed. Hemchand Gossai and Nathaniel Samuel Murrell, 181–205. New York: St. Martin's Press, 2000.

Miller, Marian. "The Rastafarian in Jamaican Political Culture: The Marginalization of a Change Agent." *Western Journal of Black Studies* 17 (1993): 112–117.

Moore, Joseph G. "Religion of Jamaican Negroes: A Study of Afro-Jamaican Acculturation." PhD diss., Northwestern University, 1953.

Morrish, Ivor. *Obeah, Christ and Rastaman: Jamaica and Its Religions*. Cambridge, U.K.:
James Clarke, 1982.

Mosley, Leonard. *Haile Selassie: The Conquering Lion*. Englewood Cliffs, N.J.: Prentice-
Hall, 1964.

Murrell, Nathaniel Samuel, William David Spencer, and Adrian Anthony McFarlane.
"Holy Piby: Blackman's Bible and Garveyite Ethiopianist Epic with Commentary." In
Religion, Culture and Tradition in the Caribbean. Ed. Hemchand Gossai and Na-
thaniel Samuel Murrell, 271–306. New York: St. Martin's Press, 2000.

———, eds. *Chanting Down Babylon: The Rastafari Reader*. Philadelphia: Temple University Press, 1998.

Nettleford, Rex. M. *Caribbean Cultural Identity: The Case of Jamaica*. Kingston: Institute
of Jamaica, 1978.

———. "Discourse on Rastafarian Reality." In *Chanting Down Babylon: The Rastafari
Reader*. Ed. Nathaniel Samuel Murrell, William David Spencer, and Adrian Anthony
McFarlane, 311–325. Philadelphia: Temple University Press, 1998.

———. *Identity, Race and Protest in Jamaica*. New York: William Morrow, 1972.

Norris, Katrin. *Jamaica: The Search for an Identity,* London: Oxford University Press, 1962.

Owens, Joseph. *Dread: The Rastafarians of Jamaica*. Kingston, Jamaica: Sangster's Book
Store, 1976/1993.

Patterson, Orlando. *Slavery and Social Death: A Comparative Study*. Cambridge, Mass.:
Harvard University Press, 1982.

———. *The Sociology of Slavery: An Analysis of the Origins, Development and Structure of Negro Slave Society in Jamaica*. Teaneck, N.J.: Fairleigh Dickinson University Press, 1975.

Phillippo, James M. *Jamaica: Its Past and Present State*. Westport, Conn.: Negro University
Press, 1843/1969.

Pierson, Roscoe M. "Alexander Bedward and the Jamaican Native Baptist Free Church."
In *Black Apostles: Afro-American Clergy Confront the Twentieth Century*. Ed. Randall
K. Burkett, 1–10. Boston: G. K. Hall, 1978.

Pigou, Elizabeth. "A Note on Afro-Jamaican Beliefs and Rituals." *Jamaica Journal* 20, no. 2
(1987): 23–27.

Plummer, John. *Movement of Jah People*. Birmingham, U.K.: Gang Press, 1978.

Pollard, Velma. *Dread Talk: The Language of the Rastafari*. Kingston, Jamaica: Canoe Press,
1994.

———. "Dread Talk—The Speech of the Rastafarian in Jamaica." *Caribbean Quarterly*
26, no. 4 (1980): 32–41.

Post, Ken W. "The Bible as Ideology: Ethiopianism in Jamaica, 1930–38." In *African Perspectives*. Ed. Christopher H. Allen and R. W. Johnson, 185–207. Cambridge: Cambridge University Press, 1970.

Price, Richard, ed. *Rebel Slave Communities in the Americas*. 2nd ed. Baltimore, Md.:
Johns Hopkins University Press, 1979.

Raboteau, Albert J. *Slave Religion: The 'Invisible Institution' in the Antebellum South*.
Oxford: Oxford University Press, 1978.

"Rastafarianism." *Directory of African American Religious Bodies: A Compendium by the
Howard University School of Divinity*. Ed. Wardell J. Payne, 133–136. Washington
D.C. Howard University Press, 1991

Rattley, Jessie Mansfield. "Rastafari." *The African American Encyclopedia*. Ed. Michael
W. Williams and Kibibi Voloria Mark, 211–216. 2nd ed. New York: Marshall Caven-
dish, 2001.

Record, Verena. "Rastafarian Music: An Introductory Study." *Jamaica Journal* 11, nos. 1–2 (1977): 3–13.

———. "Reggae, Rastafarianism and Cultural Identity." *Jamaica Journal* 15, no. 46 (1982): 70–80.

Robotham, Don. "Development of Black Ethnicity in Jamaica." In *Garvey: His Work and Impact*. Ed. Rupert Lewis and Patrick Bryan, 23–38. Mona, Jamaica: Institute of Social and Economic Research, Extra Mural Studies University of the West Indies, 1988.

Rogers, Claudia. "What Is Rasta?" *Caribbean Review* 7, no. 1 (Spring 1978): 8–10.

Rowe, Maureen. "The Woman in Rastafari." In *Rastafari: Caribbean Quarterly Monograph*. Ed. Rex Nettleford, 13–21. Mona, Jamaica: University of the West Indies, 1985.

Salter, Richard. "Shooting Dreads on Sight: Violence, Persecution, and Millennialism, and Dominica's Dread Act." In *Millennialism, Persecution, and Violence, Historical Cases*. Ed. Catherine Wessinger, 101–118. Syracuse, N.Y.: Syracuse University Press, 2000.

Savishinsky, Neil J. "African Dimensions of the Rastafarian Movement." In *Chanting Down Babylon: The Rastafari Reader*. Ed. Nathaniel Samuel Murrell, William David Spencer, and Adrian Anthony McFarlane, 125–144. Philadelphia: Temple University Press, 1998.

———. "Transnational Popular Culture and the Global Spread of the Jamaican Rastafarian Movement." *New West Indian Guide* 68, nos. 3–4 (1994): 260–281

Schuler, Monica. *'Alas, Alas, Kongo': A Social History of Indentured African Immigration into Jamaica, 1842–1865*. Baltimore, Md.: Johns Hopkins University Press, 1980.

———. "Myalism and the African Religious Tradition in Jamaica." In *Africa and the Caribbean: The Legacy of a Link*. Ed. Margaret E. Crahan and Franklin W. Knight, 65–79. Baltimore, Md.: Johns Hopkins University Press, 1979.

Seaga, Edward. "Revival Cults in Jamaica: Notes toward a Sociology of Religion." In *Jamaican Journal* 3, no. 2 (June 1969): 1–13.

Selassie I, Haile. "Building an Enduring Tower." In *World Congress on Evangelism. Vol. 1. Berlin*. Ed. Carl F. H. Henry and S. Mooneyham, 18–22. Minneapolis, Minn.: World Wide Publications, 1966.

Semaj, Leahcim (Michael James). "Inside Rasta: The Future of a Religious Movement." *Caribbean Review* 14, no. 1 (1986): 8–11, 37–38.

Simpson, George Eaton. "Jamaican Revival Cults." *Social and Economic Studies* 5, no. 4 (1956): 321–442.

———. "The Nine Night Ceremony in Jamaica." *Journal of American Folklore* 70, no. 278 (1957): 329–336.

———. "The Rastafari Movement in Jamaica: A Study of Race and Class Conflict." *Social Forces* 34, no. 2 (1955): 167–170.

———. "Religion and Justice: Some Reflections on the Rastafari Movement." *Phylon* 46, no. 4 (1885): 283–291.

———. *Religious Cults of the Caribbean*. Rio Piedras: Institute of Caribbean Studies, University of Puerto Rico, 1970.

———. Some Reflections on the Rastafari Movement in Jamaica West Kingston in the Early 1950s. *Jamaica Journal* 25, no. 2 (1994): 3–11.

Smith, M. G., Roy Augier, and Rex Nettleford. *Report on the Rastafari Movement in Kingston, Jamaica*. Kingston, Jamaica: Institute of Social and Economic Research, University of the West Indies Extra Mural Studies, 1960.

Spencer, William David. "The First Chant: Leonard Howell's the Promised Key, with Commentary by William David Spencer." In *Chanting Down Babylon: The Rastafari*

Reader. Ed. Nathaniel Samuel Murrell, William David Spencer, and Adrian Anthony McFarlane, 361–389. Philadelphia: Temple University Press, 1998.

Steadman, Captain J. G. "Guerrilla Warfare: A European Soldier's View." In *Maroon Societies: Rebel Slave Communities in the Americas.* Ed. Richard Price. Garden City, N.Y.: Anchor Press, 1973.

Stewart, Dianne M. *Three Eyes for the Journey: African Dimensions of the Jamaican Religious Experience.* New York: Oxford University Press, 2005.

Tafair-Ama, Imani Jabulani. "Rasta Woman as Rebel." In *Chanting Down Babylon: The Rastafari Reader.* Ed. Nathaniel Samuel Murrell, William David Spencer, and Adrian Anthony McFarlane, 89–106. Philadelphia: Temple University Press, 1998.

———. "The Rastafari-Successors of Marcus Garvey." *Rastafari: Caribbean Quarterly Monograph.* Ed. Rex Nettleford, 1–12. Kingston, Jamaica: University of the West Indies, 1985.

Talmon, W. Bruce. *Bob Marley: Spirit Dancer.* Text by Roger Steffens and Foreword by Timothy White. New York: W. W. Norton, 1994.

Tanna, Laura. "African Retention: Yoruba and Kikango Songs in Jamaica." *Jamaica Journal* 16, no. 3 (August 1983): 47–52.

Taylor, Patrick. "Rastafari, the Other, and Exodus Politics: EATUP." *Journal of Religious Studies* 17 (1991): 95–108.

Turner, Terisa E. "Rastafari and the New Society: Caribbean and East African Feminist Roots of a Popular Movement to Reclaim the Earthly Commons." In *Arise Ye Mighty People! Gender: Class and Race in Popular Struggles.* Ed. Teresa E. Turner and B. J. Ferguson, 9–55. Trenton, N.J.: Africa World Press, 1994.

van Dijk, Frank Jan. "Chanting Down Babylon Outernational: The Rise of Rastafari in Europe, the Caribbean, and the Pacific." In *Chanting Down Babylon: The Rastafari Reader.* Ed. Nathaniel Samuel Murrell, William David Spencer, and Adrian Anthony McFarlane, 178–198. Philadelphia: Temple University Press, 1998.

———. *Jahmaica Rastafari and Jamaican Society 1930–1990.* Utrecht, the Netherlands: ISOR, 1993.

———. "Twelve Tribes of Israel: Rasta and the Middle Class." *New West Indian Guide* 62, nos. 1–2 (1988): 1–26.

Waddell, Hope Masterson. *Twenty-Nine Years in the West Indies and Central Africa.* London: Frank Cass, 1863.

Warner-Lewis, Maureen. "African Communities in Rastafarian Beliefs." *Caribbean Quarterly* 39, nos. 3–4 (1993): 108–123.

———. *The Nkuyu: Spirit Messenger of the Kumina.* Mona, Jamaica: Savacou Publications, 1977.

———. "The Origins of Revival: A Creole Religion in Jamaica." In *Culture and Christianity.* Ed. George Saunders, 91–116. Westport, Conn: Greenwood Press, 1988.

Waters, Anita M. "African Continuities in the Rastafarian Belief System." *Caribbean Quarterly* 39, nos. 3–4 (1993): 108–123.

———. "The Ancestral Factor in Jamaica's African Religions." In *African Creative Expressions of the Divine.* Ed. Kortright Davis and Elias Farajale Jones, 63–80. Washington, D.C.: Howard University School of Divinity, 1991.

———. *Race, Class, and Political Symbols: Rastafari and Reggae in Jamaican Politics.* New Brunswick, N.J.: Transaction Publishers, 1989.

Wedenoja, William. "The Origins of Revival, a Creole Religion in Jamaica." In *Culture and Christianity: The Dialectics of Transformation.* Ed. George Saunders, 91–116. Westport, Conn.: Greenwood Press, 1988.

White, Timothy. *Catch a Fire: The Life of Bob Marley.* New York: Henry Holt, 1994.

Yawney, Carol. D. "Lions of Babylon: The Rastafarians of Jamaica as a Visionary Movement." Unpublished PhD diss., McGill University, 1978.

———. "Moving with the Daughters of Rastafari: From Myth to Reality." In *Arise Ye Mighty People! Gender, Class, and Race in Popular Struggles*. Ed. Terisa E. Turner and Bryan J. Ferguson, 65–73. Trenton, N.J.: Africa World Press, 1994.

———. "Rasta Mek a Trod: Symbolic Ambiguity in a Globalizing Religion." In *Arise Ye Mighty People! Gender, Class and Race in Popular Struggles*. Ed. Terisa E. Turner and Bryan J. Ferguson, 75–83. Trenton, N.J.: Africa World Press, 1994.

———. "Remnants of All Nations: Rastafarian Attitudes toward Ethnicity and Nationality." In *Ethnicity in the Americas*. Ed. Frances Henry, 231–262. The Hague: Mouton, 1976.

———. "Strictly Ital: Rastafari Livity and Holistic Health." Unpublished paper for the ninth annual meeting of the Society for Caribbean Studies, Hertfordshire, Canada, 1985.

Yesehaq, Abuna. *The Ethiopian Tewahedo Church*. Nashville, Tenn.: James C. Winston Publishing, 1989/1997.

Zip, Werner. *Black Rebels: African-Caribbean Freedom Fighters in Jamaica*. Trans. from German Shelley L. Frisch. Princeton, N.J.: Markus Wiener Publishers, 1999.

Index

Nathaniel Samuel Murrell is Associate Professor of Philosophy and Religion at the University of North Carolina Wilmington and the coeditor of *Chanting Down Babylon: The Rastafari Reader* (Temple).